eBook and Digital Course Materials for

Directions for accessing your
e-Book and Digital Course Materials

*Introduction
to Corrections*

Joycelyn M. Pollock

**This code can be used only
once and cannot be shared!**

Carefully scratch off the silver coating to
see your personal redemption code.

If the code has been scratched off when
you receive it, the code may not be valid.
Once the code has been scratched off,
this access card cannot be returned to
the publisher. You may buy access at
learninglink.oup.com/access/pollock1e.

The code on this card is valid for 2
years from the date of first purchase.
Complete terms and conditions are
available at **learninglink.oup.com.**

Access length: 6 months from redemption
of the code.

VIA  **learning link**

Visit **learninglink.oup.com/access/pollock1e**

Select the edition you are using and
the student resources for that edition.

Click the link to upgrade your access
to the student resources.

Follow the on-screen instructions.

Enter your personal
redemption code when prompted.

VIA YOUR SCHOOL'S LEARNING
MANAGEMENT SYSTEM

Log in to your instructor's course.

When you click a link to a protected resource,
you will be prompted to register for access.

Follow the on-screen instructions.

Enter your personal
redemption code when prompted.

For assistance with code redemption or registration,
please contact customer support at
learninglink.support@oup.com.

OXFORD
UNIVERSITY PRESS

INTRODUCTION TO
CORRECTIONS

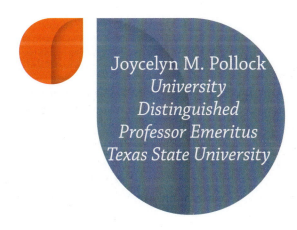

Joycelyn M. Pollock
*University
Distinguished
Professor Emeritus
Texas State University*

New York   Oxford
Oxford University Press

Oxford University Press is a department of the University of Oxford.
It furthers the University's objective of excellence in research, scholarship,
and education by publishing worldwide. Oxford is a registered trade mark of
Oxford University Press in the UK and certain other countries.

Published in the United States of America by Oxford University Press
198 Madison Avenue, New York, NY 10016, United States of America.

For titles covered by Section 112 of the US Higher Education
Opportunity Act, please visit www.oup.com/us/he for the latest
information about pricing and alternate formats.

Library of Congress Cataloging-in-Publication Data
Names: Pollock, Joycelyn M., 1956- author.
Title: Introduction to corrections / Joycelyn M. Pollock, Texas State University.
Description: New York, NY : Oxford University Press, [2023] | Includes
    bibliographical references and index.
Identifiers: LCCN 2021046980 (print) | LCCN 2021046981 (ebook) | ISBN
    9780190642297 (paperback) | ISBN 9780197618943 | ISBN 9780197618950
    (epub) | ISBN 9780190642358
Subjects: LCSH: Corrections—United States. | Imprisonment—United States.
Classification: LCC HV9471 .P647 2023 (print) | LCC HV9471 (ebook) | DDC
    365/.973—dc23
LC record available at https://lccn.loc.gov/2021046980
LC ebook record available at https://lccn.loc.gov/2021046981

9 8 7 6 5 4 3 2 1
Printed by Quad Graphics, Inc., Mexico

Contents

Preface   viii

Chapter 1
Corrections and The Challenge of Mass Incarceration   3

Introduction: The Scope Of Corrections 4

FOCUS ON THE OFFENDER : The Cycle of Crime 6

Mass Incarceration 6
Disparate Rates Across the Country 8
Explaining Mass Incarceration 10
Changing Criminal and Sentencing Laws 11
Racial Disparities Contribute to Mass Incarceration 13
The "Right" Level of Imprisonment 13

Decarceration: The End Of Mass Imprisonment? 15
A Growing Chorus for Decarceration 16
States Lead the Way 18

FOCUS ON A STATE : California's Realignment and Proposition 47 20

Looking Ahead: How To Analyze Correctional Challenges 22

Summary 24
Key Terms 4
Projects 24

Chapter 2
Crimes and Criminology   29

Measuring Crime 30
Three Crime Measures 30

Decades of Declining Crimes 35
What Caused Crime Rates to Fall? 35

Crime Correlates 37

Criminology and Corrections 40
The Classical and Positivist Schools of Criminology 40

FOCUS ON HISTORY : Positivism at Bedford Hills 42
Biological Theories of Crime 41
Psychological Theories of Crime 43
The Chicago School of Criminology 44

Cultural Deviance Theory 45
Economic Opportunity and Strain Theories 46
Social Control Theories 47
Labeling Theory 49
Summary of Crime Theories and Correctional Policies 49

Are There Different Types of Criminals? 49

FOCUS ON THE OFFENDER : Drugs and Economic Strain 52

Summary 52
Key Terms 30
Projects 53

Chapter 3
Sentencing 57

The Purpose of Sentencing 58

The History of Sentencing 59
Post-Revolutionary War Punishments 60
Capital Punishment 61

Sentencing Statutes 64

FOCUS ON A STATE: Texas Penal Code:
Sentencing Statute 65

Indeterminate and Determinate
Sentencing 67

Sentencing Patterns 69
Drug Sentencing 70

FOCUS ON THE OFFENDER: A Life Ruined 73
Clemency/Commutations 73

Sentencing Disparity 74
Geographic Disparity 74
Gender Disparity 76
Racial and Ethnic Disparity 77

Changes in Sentencing 79
Explanations for Sentencing Shifts 80

Summary 81
Key Terms 58
Projects 82

Chapter 4
Jails and Pretrial Diversion 87

Forms of Preconviction Release 88
Citation or Booking 88
Pretrial Release 89
Bail 90
Release on Recognizance 91
Rediscovering Pretrial Release 91

FOCUS ON THE OFFENDER: A Juvenile in
Jail 93

Pretrial Diversion Programs 94

Jails in the United States: Then and
Now 95

A FOCUS ON HISTORY: Early Jail 97
Unconvicted Inmates 99
The Conditions of Jail 102
Jail Staff 105

The Poverty Penalty 105
Fines and Restitution 106
Fees 107
Failure to Pay 108

Summary 110
Key Terms 88
Projects 110

Chapter 5
Probation and Community Corrections 115

Probation and Probationers 116

The History of Probation 118

Probation Supervision 118
The Pre-Sentence Investigation 118
Conditions of Probation 120
The Casework Model 122

FOCUS ON THE OFFENDER: A Slap on the
Wrist? 123

Interstate Compact 125

Recidivism and Revocation 125

Probation Officers 128
Typologies of Supervision 128
Burnout 129

Changes in Probation
Supervision 130
Intensive Supervision Probation 130

Electronic Monitoring 131

Day Reporting Centers 132

Special Offender Caseloads 132

Hawaii's Opportunity Probation with
Enforcement (HOPE) Model 132

Recent Innovations in Probation 133

Kiosk Reporting 133

*Risk/Needs/Responsivity Model of
Correctional Intervention and Cognitive
Based Therapy 134*

**Improving Community
Corrections 135**

FOCUS ON THE STATE **: New York 136**

Summary 137

Key Terms 116

Projects 138

Chapter 6

State and Federal Prisons 143

Prisons in the United States 144

FOCUS ON THE OFFENDER **: Camp Fluffy 145**

History of Prisons 146

The Philadelphia (Pennsylvania) and Auburn
(New York) Models of Prisons 146

From Reformatories to the "Big House" 149

The Rehabilitative Era 151

The Penal Harm Era 152

The Supermax 153

Private Prisons 155

The Debate Surrounding Prison
Privatization 156

Correctional Officers 159

Cross-Sex Supervision 159

Minority Correctional Officers 161

Turnover and Job Satisfaction 161

The Correctional Officer Subculture 163

FOCUS ON HISTORY **: The Infamous
Zimbardo (or Stanford) Prison
Experiment 165**

Types of Power Exerted by Correctional
Officers 166

Correctional Management and
Organizational Justice 167

Summary 168

Key Terms 144

Projects 169

Chapter 7

Prisoners and Special Populations 179

Profile of Prisoners 180

Demographics 180

Crimes that Prisoners Commit 182

Pre-Prison Lives: Education and Income 183

Medical Needs 184

Drug Dependency and Addiction 185

Family and Childhood Abuse 186

**Management Challenges of Special
Prison Populations 187**

The Elderly in Prison 187

Vulnerabilities of Elderly Prisoners 189

*Financial Implications of Elderly
Prisoners 189*

FOCUS ON A STATE **: Connecticut 191**

The Mentally Ill 191

Suicide and Self-Harming Behavior 195

Mental Health Treatment 197

FOCUS ON THE OFFENDER **: The Long Arm of
the Law 199**

The Intellectually Disabled 200

LGBTQ Inmates 200

Summary 202

Key Terms 180

Projects 203

Chapter 8
Prisoner Subculture 211

Prison Subculture 212
Importation and Deprivation Theories 212
FOCUS ON HISTORY : Early Prison Research 213
Prisoner Typologies and the Inmate Code 214
Prison Argot 215
Prison Gangs 216

Prison Violence 217
Prevalence of Violence 218
Correlates of Violence 221
Prison Sexual Violence 222
Prevalence of Sexual Violence 224
Characteristics of Male Perpetrators and Victims 225
Riots and Collective Violence 226
Reducing Prison Violence 227

Adjusting to Prison Life 228
FOCUS ON THE OFFENDER : George Luca: Changed and Change Agent 229

Summary 230
Key Terms 212
Projects 230

Chapter 9
Prisoner Rights 237

Prisoner Rights 238
Religion 240
Speech and Association 242
Unreasonable Search and Seizure 243
Cruel and Unusual Punishment 244
FOCUS ON THE OFFENDER : Trying to Survive 246
Due Process 247

Rights During Community Supervision 252
Probation 252
Parole 253

Collateral Consequences 254
FOCUS ON A STATE : Florida 256

Summary 257
Key Terms 238
Projects 257

Chapter 10
Female Prisoners 261

Women in Prison 262
The History of Women's Prisons 262
The Reformatory and Custodial Models 263
Contemporary Institutions 263

Gendered Pathways 264
Prior Victimization 265
Drug Dependency 266
Family Dysfunction and Intimate Partner Abuse 266
Mental Health 268
Medical Needs 269

Female Prisoner Subculture 271
Violence 271
Sexual Relationships and Sexual Victimization 274

Meeting the Specific Needs of Women 276
Gender-Responsive Programming 278
FOCUS ON THE OFFENDER : A Life Well-Lived 280
Parenting Programs 281

FOCUS ON A STATE **: New York's Bedford
   Hills Nursery Program 283**

   Drug Treatment 283

Reentry 284

Summary 285

   Key Terms 262

   Projects 286

Chapter 11

Rehabilitative Programming 295

The Mission of Corrections 296

   The Rehabilitative Era 297

Prison Programs 298

   Recreation Programs 298

   Religious Programs 299

FOCUS ON A STATE **: Washington's Prison Pet
   Program 300**

   Education 301

   Vocational Training 302

   Prison Labor 303

   Drug and Alcohol Treatment 306

   Therapeutic Communities 307

Prediction and Assessment 308

   Four Generations of Prediction/
   Assessment 309

**Level of Service Inventory-Revised
   (LSI-R) and Risk/Need/
   Responsivity (R/N/R) 310**

   Evaluating CBT Programs 313

   Criticisms of Risk/Need/Responsivity and
   Cognitive Behavioral Therapy 314

Evaluating Prison Programs 315

   Methodological Issues 315

   Program Evaluations 317

FOCUS ON THE OFFENDER **: Predicting
   Risk 320**

Summary 321

   Key Terms 296

   Projects 321

Chapter 12

Parole and Looking Toward the Future 327

Reentry 328

   Challenges 328

Parole 331

   History 331

   The Decision to Parole 332

   Pardons and Commutations 334

   Issues in Parole Supervision 335

      *Relationships Between Parolees and Parole
         Officers 336*

      Liability of Parole Officers 337

Halfway Houses 338

**Recidivism and Successful
   Offenders 339**

   Recidivism Factors 341

FOCUS ON A STATE **: OHIO 342**

   Reducing Recidivism 343

FOCUS ON THE OFFENDER **: Martin Pang:
   Was Justice Served? 344**

**Future Directions in
   Corrections 344**

   Trends and Challenges 344

   International Solutions 346

   International Human Rights and Prisoners 347

   Principles for a Humane and Effective
   Corrections System 352

Summary 353

   Key Terms 328

   Projects 354

Glossary   358

Credits   364

Index   365

PREFACE

There are many textbooks for introductory corrections courses, so why create another? In this text, we meet the needs of curriculums across the country with standard and expected content, but also introduce new approaches and utilize sources that may be less often seen in traditional academic texts. There is a focus on offenders as well as individual state programs. There are current numbers (or as current as possible given publication realities), as well as directions for how students can find information about their own state. There is also a stronger emphasis on why we do what we do in corrections through an extended discussion of criminological theory. International voices are considered via the United Nations "Mandela Rules" for corrections. Finally, we make a concerted effort to integrate information about minorities and women throughout the chapters.

There are helpful ancillaries, including embedded quizzes in the web version of the book and an instructor's guide that includes a test bank, power points, and chapter outlines. Each chapter includes activities that the instructor can assign to help the student become more familiar with their own state's corrections system as well as learn how to use the data sources available, such as the Bureau of Justice Statistics.

The author wishes to thank the editorial and production staff at Oxford for their insight and expertise, especially Sonya Venugopal, editorial assistant, and Ashli MacKenzie, senior production editor. Without Steve Helba's patience and commitment to the book, it would not exist. We also need to thank the reviewers: Amy Grau, Breanne Pleggenkuhle, Chernoh M. Wurie, Frank E. Jones, John J. Shook, John Weigel, Lisa Leduc, Llyod Klein, and Samantha Carlo. Finally, as always, I thank my husband, Eric Lund, for everything he does.

INTRODUCTION TO
CORRECTIONS

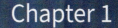

Chapter 1

Corrections and The Challenge of Mass Incarceration

LEARNING OBJECTIVES

1. Recognize the scope of sentencing options under the umbrella of corrections.

2. Examine the number of people under correctional supervision in the United States.

3. Describe how the United States compares to other countries in its pattern of incarceration.

4. Discuss the ways states have attempted to reduce their prison populations.

5. Summarize California's Proposition 47 and Realignment initiative.

CHAPTER OUTLINE

- **Introduction: The Scope of Corrections** 4

- **Mass Incarceration** 6

- **Decarceration: The End of Mass Imprisonment?** 15

- **Looking Ahead: How to Analyze Correctional Challenges** 22

- **SUMMARY** 24

There are about 1.5 million people incarcerated in state and federal prisons.

KEY TERMS

Corrections	Incapacitation	Retribution
Correlates	Incarceration rate	Revocation
Decarceration	Justice Reinvestment	Specific deterrence
General deterrence	Initiative (JRI)	Three-strikes law
Good time	Realignment	"Truth in sentencing"
Habitual felon laws	Recidivism	laws
Imprisonment rate	Rehabilitation	

 # Introduction: The Scope of Corrections

The field of corrections covers everything that happens to a person after he or she has been found guilty of a crime, and even before. **Corrections** encompasses pretrial release programs, pretrial diversion programs, pretrial detainment, jail, probation, prison, halfway houses, parole, and rehabilitative programming, including drug treatment. These experiences are often presented as a chronological timeline in the criminal justice process beginning with arrest, as displayed in Figure 1.1, but the reality is that many people cycle through the system, going backward and forward, because of new and/or multiple charges, non-payment of fees or fines, and revocations of pretrial diversion, probation or parole. Individuals may be in prison but still owe fines and court costs; others may have several probation sentences for different crimes running concurrently; and parolees may pick up a new charge and receive probation for it. Different states have different laws regarding pretrial detention and sentencing options. For instance, some jurisdictions do not have discretionary parole; and, some jurisdictions may not have pretrial release programs other than bail available for arrestees. Across the 50 states, the criminal justice process varies widely. Figure 1.1 may not accurately reflect what happens in a particular jurisdiction; however, it is generally representative of the major components of corrections.

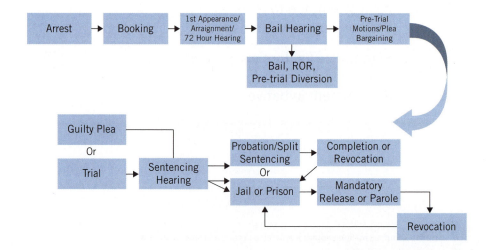

FIGURE 1.1 The criminal justice process.

It is important to know two major facts regarding corrections in the United States:

1. We incarcerate more people per capita than any comparable country; and,
2. **Recidivism** (defined as rearrest, reconviction, or return to prison) is remarkably high.

The numbers of individuals under all forms of correctional supervision are staggering. The most recent figures (year-end 2019) indicate that there are about 6.3 million persons under adult correctional supervision, down from 6.4 million in 2019. The total number has decreased for over ten consecutive years and is now the lowest it has been for 20 years.[1] Roughly 2.0 million are in a confinement facility which is about 35,700 less than 2019 and 211,000 less than in 2009. Of this 2019 total, 1.4 million were in state or federal prison, and 734,500 were in jail.[2] There are about 11 million individual bookings into jail each year. Most arrestees stay a short time until bail or pretrial release can be arranged. There are approximately 1,719 state prisons, 102 federal prisons, 942 correctional institutions for juveniles, 3,283 local jails, and 79 other types of confinement facilities, including reservation jails, military prisons, immigration detention facilities, civil commitment centers, and prisons in the U.S. territories (e.g., Guam, Puerto Rico).[3] Most individuals under correctional supervision are in the community (4,399,000), either under probation supervision (3,540,000) or on parole (878,000).[4]

Millions of people are incarcerated or under some other form of correctional supervision. Offenders range from sociopathic killers to drunk drivers. Crimes range from minor property crimes to murder. Drug offenders comprise roughly a third of all state prisoners. As described in the Focus on the Offender box, these individuals may have addiction or abuse problems.

Corrections refers to the custody, supervision, counseling, and/or treatment of all the many types of offenders that are under correctional supervision. Correctional professionals include probation and parole officers, pretrial investigators, hearing examiners, correctional officers, sheriff's deputies, correctional

A large percentage of the correctional population are addicted to or abuse drugs.

THE CYCLE OF CRIME

Drug addiction and abuse is one of the most intractable problems of our society, and its impact on the corrections system is substantial. When parents abuse drugs, children are affected. When drug usage becomes an intergenerational pattern, involvement in the criminal justice system is inevitably also part of the family dynamic. Roughly a third of individuals in prison are there for public order offenses, which include drug crimes, and a large portion of the increase in the prison population has been due to the increased severity of sentencing for drug offenders. Rob Sullivan's life is not dissimilar to many other offenders. When he was six years old, Rob Sullivan had a gun pointed at his head by two men who were after his father's drug stash. His father beat his mother, and both were sometimes too drunk or too high on drugs to even unlock the door for him when he came home from school. His father spent time in prison. His mother and a cousin died of drug overdoses. Rob was routinely truant and in detention throughout school and did not graduate. He took his first drink of beer at 12, and by 19, he was an alcoholic; eventually he began using heroin. He spent most of his adult years cycling in and out of drug rehabilitation programs and jail or prison. On his most recent release, he lived with his youngest daughter and her mother. For a time, he worked, and things went well, but then his drinking and drug use led to angry outbursts; he explained that the anger came, and he just couldn't control it. He lashed out at his daughter, calling her names and scaring her with his violence. He checked himself in to a rehabilitation facility, but was not comfortable fully participating in the therapy that required he talk about his childhood. He left before completing the program and ended up back in prison.

Questions for Discussion

What sentence do you think possession of heroin deserves?
Should it make a difference if a person grew up with drug-abusing parents?

What do you think are the effects of experiencing extreme childhood violence?

Source: A. Burch, "Linking Childhood Trauma to Prison's Revolving Door," New York Times, October 16, 2017, A10.

nurses, counselors and psychiatrists, and other treatment and custody professionals. Corrections is a huge industry that has grown exponentially in the last 40 years. Estimates vary, but corrections costs $80 billion or more every year.[5] Mass incarceration is recognized as a problem by those who believe that at least some of the 2.3 million people incarcerated in a confinement facility should not be there. Whether the U.S. incarcerates too many people is an empirical, legal, and moral issue.

In this chapter, we will examine the scope of corrections and the challenge of mass incarceration. We will see that the massive increase in the number of individuals incarcerated began in the 1980s. The incarceration rate has now plateaued, and some states have managed to reduce the number of people in prison; in other states, the numbers continue to increase.

Mass Incarceration

The United States has 5 percent of the world's population and 25 percent of its prisoners, incarcerating offenders at a rate that is much higher than comparable countries (see Figure 1.2). While there may be some inaccuracies in how prison

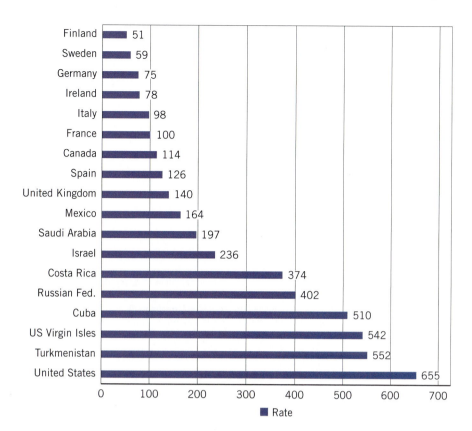

FIGURE 1.2 Imprisonment rates of selected countries. Author created from R. Walmsley, "World Prison Population List, 12th Edition" (Institute for Criminal Policy Research, 2018), https://www.prisonstudies.org/sites/default/files/resources/downloads/wppl_12.pdf

populations are counted and how these rates are constructed, there is no argument that the United States uses prisons and jails at a rate that is four, five, or even eight times greater than that of countries such as the United Kingdom and Germany. Scandinavian countries generally have the lowest rates, while small island countries post high rates (possibly because many people arrested and convicted are tourists and, thus, not counted into population bases). Other countries known as having repressive governments also have high rates of imprisonment; surprisingly, the United States has higher rates than some of these countries.

Imprisonment rates standardize by population, allowing us to compare two periods of time or two locales with different population bases. The rate reads as follows: for every 100,000 people, X are in state or federal prison. An imprisonment rate is influenced by three factors:

a) the number of people who are sent to prison,
b) the length of their sentence, and
c) the number of people who are sent to prison on parole or probation violations.

If more people are sent to prison, if their sentences are longer, or if more people are sent back to prison for parole or probation violations, then the incarceration rate will increase.

This imprisonment pattern is relatively recent (see Figure 1.3). From the 1800s until the 1970s, the rate of incarceration was relatively stable at around 100 per 100,000 people. Even at the beginning of the 1980s, the national rate was only 138. By 1990, however, that rate had roughly doubled to 297 per 100,000 people. The 1980s marked the beginning of the era of mass

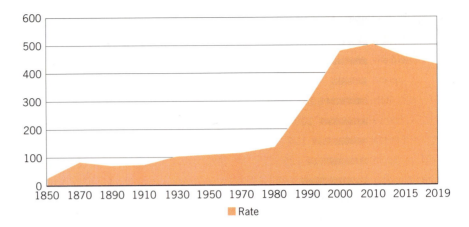

FIGURE 1.3 The rate of imprisonment. Author created from M. Cahalan, *Historical Corrections Statistics in the United States, 1850–1984* (Rockville, MD: Westat Inc., 1987); *Sourcebook of Criminal Justice Statistics* (Washington, DC: USDOJ, BJS, 1997); "State and Federal Prisoners" (Washington, DC: USDOJ, BJS, 1998); P. Harrison and J. Karberg, "Prison and Jail Inmates at Midyear 2002" (Washington, DC: USDOJ, BJS, 2003); H. West, W. Sabol, and S. Greenman, *Prisoners in 2009* (Washington, DC: USDOJ, BJS, 2010); E. Carson and E. Anderson, *Prisoners in 2015* (Washington, DC: USDOJ, BJS, 2016); E. Carson, *Prisoners in 2019* (Washington, DC: USDOJ, BJS, 2020), 1.

incarceration. Many note that the rise in imprisonment was simultaneous with the "war on drugs," but the factors that combined to create the increase go beyond drug interdiction and punishment. The peak of the years represented in Figure 1.3 was 2010, when 500 per 100,000 people were imprisoned, five times the rate in the 1980s. In the last several years, the pattern of yearly increases has finally reversed and, in 2019, the rate had fallen to 419.[6]

Different sources present different numbers as the imprisonment rate. This is because different factors may be counted. For example, there is a difference between the imprisonment rate (which counts those in state and federal prisons only) and the **incarceration rate** (which also includes jail populations, so the *incarceration* rate is always higher than the *imprisonment* rate). There is also a difference in the rate depending on whether one divides the number of people incarcerated by the total population or only by the population of adults over 18. The second rate would be higher because one is dividing by a smaller base. It is important for any longitudinal comparison to utilize the same type of rate consistently over time.

For the purposes of our discussion of the issue of mass incarceration, our challenges are as follows:

1) to determine why the United States utilizes incarceration as a punishment to a degree unlike any comparable Western, industrialized country;

2) to evaluate what the "right" level of imprisonment might be using legal, moral, and practical criteria; and,

3) to determine whether the incarceration rate will continue to fall and what factors have led to what some now call "decarceration."

Disparate Rates Across the Country

Using a national rate of incarceration masks the great variability that occurs between the states. Utilizing data from the Bureau of Justice Statistics, Figure 1.4 shows the most recent rates for each state. Many southern states have higher

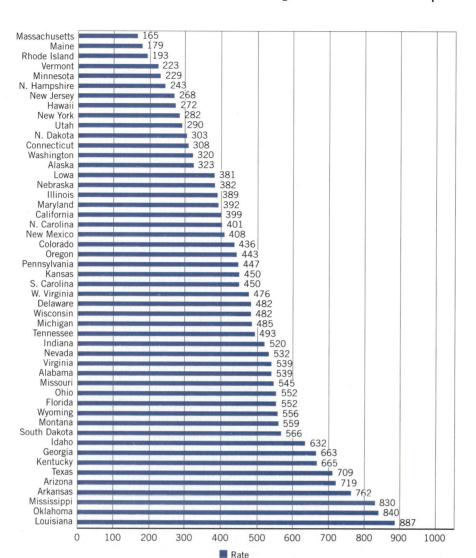

FIGURE 1.4 Incarceration rates. Author created from E. Carson, *Prisoners in 2019* (Washington, DC: USDOJ, BJS, 2020).

rates of imprisonment than northern or western states (for example, Louisiana's rate is more than seven times that of Massachusetts). Recently, some states have dramatically decreased their rates, while other states' rates continue to climb. For instance, Alabama's rate was 790 per 100,000 in 2015 but dropped to 539 per 100,000 in 2019.[7] It is important to be aware that there are some counting issues that make comparing states' rates somewhat problematic. For instance, a few states (Delaware, Hawaii, Rhode Island, and Vermont) combine their jail and prison populations, while other states (Massachusetts and Texas) have local correctional facilities for offenders serving three or fewer years. Some states do not submit yearly numbers to the Bureau of Justice Statistics, and a few states have changed their reporting practices, making comparisons to prior years difficult.

It is instructive to compare the pattern of state imprisonment rates, but some argue that simply knowing how many residents are incarcerated is not as helpful as knowing the total correctional population. Some states use probation more than others, so while their imprisonment rate might be relatively low, the total number under correctional supervision is high compared to other states.

Another argument is that knowing how many residents are imprisoned per 100,000 people is not helpful because what we really want to compare across states is how many *offenders* are imprisoned. Perhaps states with higher incarceration rates have higher crime rates. The Pew Charitable Trust research organization has computed the "punishment rate," which uses sentencing data to tell us the likelihood of certain types of offenders going to prison; however, only eight crimes (aggravated assault, forcible rape, murder, robbery, arson, burglary, larceny-theft, and motor vehicle theft) were utilized. The "punishment rate" for some states was different than their "imprisonment rate": Connecticut, New Jersey, New York, Pennsylvania, South Dakota, Vermont, Virginia, West Virginia, Wisconsin, and Wyoming each had higher ranked punishment rates than imprisonment rates, meaning that these states were more likely to send offenders to prison, but their imprisonment rate was lower because of lower crime rates compared to other states. Alaska, Arkansas, Georgia, South Carolina, Tennessee, Nevada, and New Mexico had lower ranked punishment rates than imprisonment rates.[8] Because the punishment rate does not include drug offenses, it does not tell us how the states deal with that category of offender.

Explaining Mass Incarceration

One initially might assume that the rise in incarceration was due to rising crime rates, but that is only partially true. From 1960 to 1980, violent crime increased 270 percent.[9] Increased prison populations and the rapid building of prisons across the country, especially in the 1980s, were one response to this increase in crime. However, the increased availability of prison spaces is not the only reason, or perhaps even the most influential factor, in the four-decade rise of imprisonment as a correctional alternative. Between the 1970s and 2010, imprisonment rates rose consistently and dramatically, yet in that same period, crime rose, then fell; property crime continued to fall, while violent crime rose and then fell again. What researchers have concluded is that mass incarceration was partially in response to crime, but also a result of increased punitiveness by criminal justice actors, especially prosecutors. Evidence indicates that criminals who would not have gone to prison for their crimes in past decades were now being sent to prison due to changes in

- criminal laws (redefining some acts as more serious);
- sentencing laws (making sentences mandatory or attaching much longer time periods to certain crimes);
- charging patterns of prosecutors (who began to charge with the most serious charges available, seeking long sentences); and
- more punitive sentencing by judges.

What led to these changes? Political history is subjective, but two factors stand out, in addition to rising crime rates: first, the rising social unrest and public demonstrations of the 1960s were equated in the public's mind with crime. Discomfort with social upheaval led to a desire for order, represented by politicians advocating harsher sentencing. Second, the so-called "southern strategy" of Republicans was to utilize President Johnson's civil rights support to shift southern Democrats, who were not in favor of civil rights initiatives such as affirmative action, to vote for Republican politicians, partly by using crime as a coded word for racial problems.[10]

In the 1970s, there was a major decline in industry-related jobs in northern cities because of international competition and technology (e.g., the auto and steel industries). High school dropouts or those with a high school diploma who were making a decent living and could raise families on their factory or semi-skilled labor jobs up until this time were laid off with no hope their jobs would reappear. The dramatic decline of these jobs decimated northern cities. These changes, combined with the migration of southern Blacks to these cities in the 1950s and 1960s, led to rising crime and a growing portion of the population that was un- or under-employed, disaffected, and increasingly pessimistic about their future.

President Johnson is well known for his "war on poverty," which targeted the "root causes" of poverty and crime, including lack of education, lack of employment opportunities, and lack of stable housing. However, by the 1980s, the war on poverty was deemed a failure and the idea that the poor were poor because they didn't try hard enough was a more politically robust position. Congruent with that idea was that criminals deserved harsher punishment and only longer prison sentences would deter crime. A not-insignificant element to the political message was that the crime problem was a race problem.

Further, drug crimes became more heavily policed in the 1970s and 1980s, and more severely punished. It is reported that more than half of the growth in the prison population during the 1980s was driven by the increased likelihood of incarceration given an arrest. In 1980, the incarceration rate for drug crimes was 15 per 100,000 people; however, in 2010, the rate had increased to 143 per 100,000. Between 1980 and 2010, prison commitments for drug offenses rose 350 percent (from 2 to 9 per 100 arrests). Drug offense convictions grew to make up about one-fifth of all state prison inmates and nearly two-thirds of all federal inmates by 1997. Moreover, this category of criminal sentencing shows the clearest disparity among all crimes between Black and white offenders. While sources show drug use, and even drug selling, are similar across racial and ethnic groups, Black offenders are disproportionally arrested for drug offenses.[11]

Thus, researchers conclude that mass incarceration developed because offenders were more likely to be sentenced to prison for any given offense and because prison sentences were, on average, much longer. The first factor was more influential in the 1980s, and the second factor was more powerful in the 1990s. Since 2010, negligible increases and even decreases in imprisonment has been the pattern.[12]

Changing Criminal and Sentencing Laws

Most crimes are state crimes, dealt with by state justice systems. Historically, very few federal crimes existed, e.g., smuggling, tax evasion, and white collar that involved interstate commerce. The "tough-on-crime" political platform emerged in the 1960s and led to a plethora of new federal crimes. The federal government became more involved in the criminal justice systems of states beginning in 1965, when Congress passed the Law Enforcement Assistance Act (LEAA). This legislation created federal grants and programs aimed at law enforcement, court administration, and prison operations. For instance, LEAA funds provided scholarships to police officers to get college degrees.

In the subsequent decades, federal legislation has affected not only federal corrections, but state corrections as well. In 1984, the Comprehensive Crime Control Act abolished federal parole, created the U.S. Sentencing Commission, enabled federal preventive detention, created civil asset forfeiture, and instituted mandatory sentencing guidelines restricting the discretion of federal judges. Sentences for drug offenses in particular were increased, with some mandatory minimums added. In 1986, the Anti-Drug Abuse Act was passed.[13] This legislation imposed 29 new mandatory minimum sentences in the federal system. One

President Clinton signed the Violent Crime Control Act in 1994.

was the mandatory sentence of five years in prison for five grams of crack, the same sentence that was given for 500 grams of powder cocaine. After years of vociferous criticism by advocacy groups, this infamous 1:100 ratio was changed to 1:18 by the Fair Sentencing Act of 2010 during the Obama administration. In 1988, the Anti-Drug Abuse Act was passed, creating a federal death penalty for participation in "continuing criminal enterprises" or any drug-related felony related to the killing of another.[14] The bill also created a "drug czar" position to coordinate the "anti-drug" policy of the White House.

In 1994, President Clinton signed the Violent Crime Control and Law Enforcement Act, which created 16 more federal death penalty crimes and overhauled the federal appeals process, making it harder for defendants to appeal capital cases. The bill also created a federal three-strikes provision, prohibited drug offenders from living in public housing, and made almost $10 billion available for states to build prisons if they enacted **"truth in sentencing" laws**. These laws require states to have more determinate sentencing by reducing the discretion of paroling authorities and limiting the amount of good time an inmate can receive (time taken off a prison sentence due to good behavior). The Act also supported community policing and drug courts as alternatives to jail. For a state to obtain federal funds to help with prison construction, the state needed to show that it had 1) increased the percentage of convicted violent offenders sentenced to prison, 2) increased the average prison time that was served by convicted violent offenders, and 3) increased the percentage of the sentence served in prison by violent offenders.[15]

In response to federal pressure, states passed tough new laws. The federal government withheld federal highway monies to pressure states to enact harsher penalties for drug offenses, and, as a result, Oregon recriminalized small amounts of marijuana in 1986, followed by Alaska in 1990.[16] Sentencing laws like the 1973 Rockefeller drug laws in New York dramatically increased the length of sentences for drug crimes and were used as a model for other states. Nonviolent and non-serious crimes, such as shoplifting or writing a bad check, became felonies. In the 1990s, Congress and more than one-half of the states enacted **habitual felon laws**, also known as "three strikes" laws, that mandated minimum sentences of 25 years or longer for repeat offenders. One report indicated that between 1993 and 2009 the average prison stay increased by 33 percent. Property criminals' sentences increased 18 percent, drug offenders' sentences increased 25 percent, violent offenders' sentences increased 39 percent, and, most dramatically, public order offenders (which include those convicted of DUI and alcohol-related offenses) increased 62 percent.[17] Another element that contributed to higher prison populations was (and continues to be) increased returns to prison for probation and parole violators.[18]

There were also changes in prosecution patterns. Research shows that district attorneys became much more likely to bring felony charges and seek long sentences in the 1990s. The probability that any arrest would result in felony charges roughly doubled between 1994 and 2008, with corresponding increases in prison sentences. This research finding discounts the impact of the war on drugs or racially discriminatory sentencing policies on mass incarceration, pointing to overall prosecutorial aggressiveness and extremely long sentences for violent crimes as the major drivers of the imprisonment rate.[19]

Racial Disparities Contribute to Mass Incarceration

Mass incarceration has impacted Blacks more heavily than whites. In 2010, the incarceration rate for all Blacks was about 1,400 per 100,000, while the rate for all whites was 245. More recently, these disparities have been reduced somewhat. In 2019, the rate for all Blacks was 1,019 and the rate for all whites was 214. For Black *men* under age 40 who had dropped out of high school, the incarceration rate is estimated to be more than 25 times higher than the national average.[20] While some sentencing studies show that sentencing differences are almost completely explained by crime history and severity of crime factors, other research shows that Blacks experience cumulative disadvantage in the system, leading to the dramatic disparity in incarceration rates. Blacks are less likely to be bailed or released on any form of pretrial diversion, they are more likely to utilize public defenders, they receive more severe plea offers, they are more likely to plead guilty, and they are less likely to receive probation.

Hispanics have also been disproportionately affected by the changes in sentencing patterns. From 1972 to 1990, the Hispanic incarceration rate was two to three times higher than the rate for non-Hispanic whites. Through the 1990s, the Hispanic incarceration rate remained roughly flat at around 1,800 per 100,000 people aged 18 to 64. Since 2000, the incarceration rate for Hispanics has fallen and, in 2019, it was 757.[21]

The "Right" Level of Imprisonment

What is the right level of punishment for a burglar? A rapist? A murderer? A National Academy of Sciences report showed that less than 10 percent of those arrested for sexual assault in 1981 were sentenced to prison, for an average of only 3.4 years behind bars, but, in 2010, 30 percent of those arrested for sexual assault were sent to prison for an average of 6.6 years. Prior to 1980, only 40 percent of individuals arrested for murder were sentenced to prison for an average term of 5 years, but, in 2010, 92 percent of convicted murderers were imprisoned for an average of 17 years.[22] Did rapists and murderers receive sentences that were too short in the 1980s? Are they too long now? The right amount of punishment for a drug offender, murderer, rapist, or any other type of criminal is difficult to assess.

The purposes of corrections are said to be retribution, deterrence, incapacitation, and rehabilitation. **Retribution** is punishment for the sake of punishment, proportional to the severity of the offense (i.e., an eye for an eye). Studies indicate that most people agree on the relative seriousness of most crimes; for instance, that murder is more serious than burglary.[23] However, there is little consensus in the amount of punishment any given crime should receive. Further, holding constant the crime's severity, should different criminals receive different punishments? For example, should a 40-year-old three-time offender receive a more severe sentence for burglary than a 16-year-old who has not committed an offense before? Our sentencing systems attempt to reduce disparity while, at the same time, consider exceptional differences between offenders. We will describe sentencing patterns in Chapter 3.

Deterrence is the second purpose of sentencing and corrections. It can be divided into **specific deterrence** (what is done to an offender to stop him or her from committing further crime) and **general deterrence** (what is done to an offender to stop others from committing crime). There is a voluminous amount of literature on deterrence, yet whether correctional alternatives do much to deter people from criminal choices has not been proven with any great success. Even though there has been a dramatic drop in crime since the mid-1990s, research shows that incarceration was not the most significant factor in declining crime rates. One study concluded that up to 25 percent of the decrease in index crime rates in the 1990s was explained by higher incarceration rates.[24] However, a later study found that although higher incarceration accounted for anywhere from 0 to 12 percent of the decline in property crime in the 1990s, since then, higher incarceration rates have had no effect on crime—and might even contribute to crime. Including all years from 1980 up to 2015, only 6 percent of the decrease in property crime rates and 0 percent of the decrease in violent crime rates were explained by higher incarceration rates according to this study.[25]

The third purpose of corrections is **incapacitation,** which refers to preventing an individual from committing crime presently (not in the future, which is the goal of deterrence). The concepts of incapacitation and incarceration often overlap because incarceration is the most obvious and frequently used form of incapacitation; however, they are not synonymous. Offenders incarcerated in prisons or jails can still commit crime (and do) against their fellow inmates and correctional officers. Some prisoners even continue to commit crimes against outside victims through, for instance, phone scams or gang activities. Incarceration is one type of incapacitation, but there are others. For example, placing someone in a residential drug treatment program is a form of incapacitation. Chemical castration is also a form of incapacitation. Ideally, a person is incapacitated until he or she is no longer a threat, a decision that involves prediction. Prediction of future crime and/or dangerousness is notoriously difficult. We will explore this literature in more detail in Chapter 6.

The fourth purpose of corrections is **rehabilitation,** which refers to changing offenders' attitudes and behavior regarding criminal choices. The goal is for an offender to choose not to commit crime even when they are not under observation. Rehabilitation, in the correctional sense, may address underlying causes of crime. For instance, drug treatment is considered a rehabilitative program because many crimes are drug related. Mental illness is also an underlying cause of crime that is addressed in rehabilitative programs. We will explore rehabilitative programming in Chapter 11.

Considering the multiple purposes of corrections and the multitude of different types of offenders, it is not surprising that we do not have a consensus on what is a fair sentence for any given crime or offender. One report offered the following guidelines to ensure sentencing is just and fair:

1. Proportionality: Criminal offenses should be sentenced in proportion to their seriousness.
2. Parsimony: The period of confinement should be sufficient but not greater than necessary to achieve the goals of sentencing policy.
3. Citizenship: The conditions and consequences of imprisonment should not be so severe or lasting as to violate one's fundamental status as a member of society.
4. Social justice: Prisons should be instruments of justice, and, as such, their collective effect should be to promote and not undermine society's aspirations for a fair distribution of rights, resources, and opportunities.[26]

Another source suggests the following elements to be used to determine the appropriate level of sentencing for any crime:

- Seriousness
- Victim impact
- Intent (versus recklessness or negligence)
- Recidivism (the likelihood of reoffending).[27]

Using these criteria, researchers analyzed the current prison population of the United States and determined that an estimated 39 percent were incarcerated with little benefit to public safety. They argued that if these individuals (576,000) were released, it would result in cost savings of nearly $20 billion per year, and almost $200 billion over 10 years—enough to employ 270,000 new police officers, 360,000 probation officers, or 327,000 school teachers. They also concluded that about 25 percent (66,000) of the current prison population could benefit from other sentencing alternatives because they were not receiving the programs necessary to address their issues (mostly drug addiction). Finally, about 14 percent (212,000) of the prison population has served a sufficiently long punishment for what they did.[28] While one may disagree with the conclusion of this group of researchers, there is an argument to be made that some types of offenders can be diverted to sentencing alternatives and do not deserve to be and/or do not need to be in prison for public safety.

Decarceration: The End of Mass Imprisonment?

Figure 1.3 showed that the imprisonment rate at year-end 2019 was 415 prisoners per 100,000 U.S. residents of all ages, following several years of decline.[29] The graphic may illustrate **decarceration**, which refers to a sentencing shift that reduces the use of imprisonment as a punishment. It is possible that the dramatic increases that characterized the 1980s and 1990s have ended as states attempt to reduce their prison populations through a variety of sentencing strategies, reentry programs, and policy changes.

A Growing Chorus for Decarceration

A variety of efforts are underway to reduce the U.S. prison population. Prior to the 2016 presidential election, there was a growing coalition of liberal, conservative, and libertarian individuals and organizations that advocated changing sentencing practices and policies to reduce the number of people incarcerated. Liberal think tanks like the Sentencing Project, the Prison Policy Initiative, the Brennan Center, and others, have illustrated the disproportional use of imprisonment by the United States as compared to comparable countries. Conservative groups, such as Right on Crime, have advocated for change; other conservatives have supported indigent defense and other attempts to reduce prison populations.[30] For instance, the Heritage Foundation, a conservative research organization, has cautiously supported re-evaluating harsh sentencing practices.[31] A nationally representative group of law enforcement leaders published a "Statement of Principles" that argues that the dependence on incarceration for low-level, nonviolent offenders is wrong and offers a list of approaches to address the problem: increasing alternatives to arrest and prosecution, restoring balance to criminal laws, reforming mandatory minimums, and strengthening community–law enforcement ties.[32]

One research study exploring the growing support for decarceration developed a database of editorials, news stories, and legislation from 2008 to 2014 that coded the arguments used in favor of such reforms, which included the following:

- reigning in criminal justice spending;
- enhancing public safety;
- ameliorating racial injustice;
- ensuring that punishments are just and/or proportionate;
- minimizing the collateral consequences of incarceration;
- protecting human rights;
- reducing prison overcrowding;
- forgiveness or redemption;
- incarceration as an inappropriate response to mental illness and/or addiction; and
- the need to overhaul specific aspects of the criminal justice system that are dysfunctional or have been mismanaged.

The arguments against reform were coded into the following categories:

- public safety/hampers law enforcement;
- too lenient/fails to hold offenders accountable;
- too costly and/or will not achieve projected cost savings; and
- too limited in scope to be progressive.

Findings showed that commentary and legislation favored reform over maintaining or adding to punitive policies by a ratio of 3 to 1. The most commonly mentioned theme in support of reform was cost.[33]

Federal reform efforts have included the Sentencing Reform and Corrections Act of 2015, which addressed federal criminal sentencing. In the federal criminal justice system, the Federal Bureau of Prisons grew almost 800 percent between

1980 and 2013, from fewer than 25,000 inmates to more than 215,000. The number of federal correctional facilities increased from 43 to 119, and spending increased from $970 million to $6.7 billion.[34] The most dominant factor in the increase was extremely long sentences for drug offenders, even those peripherally involved, through the application of conspiracy laws. The sentencing reform bill would have, among other things:

- ensured that nonviolent, low-level offenders didn't get lengthy prison sentences intended for drug kingpins;
- retroactively applied the Fair Sentencing Act (reducing the sentences of those sentenced under the 100 to 1 ratio for crack cocaine);
- reduced the number of mandatory minimum sentences attached to specific crimes;
- expanded judicial discretion in sentencing, allowing inmates to shorten their time behind bars by participating in educational, vocational or other programs; and
- banned federal solitary confinement for juvenile offenders in most circumstances.

Although the bill was close to being voted on in 2016, it was blocked and never reached the floor for a vote.

In 2014, the United States Sentencing Commission changed its guidelines for sentencing drug convictions and made the changes retroactive. Prisoners must go before a judge to have their cases reviewed for a sentence reduction based on the new guidelines. While some have been denied, about 40,000 federal prisoners became eligible to have their drug sentences reduced by an average of two years, and 6,000 were released initially after the reduction took effect.[35]

Another federal initiative was a clemency program instituted by President Obama for certain nonviolent drug offenders. Before leaving office, he commuted the sentences of 1,715 offenders, most of whom had been sentenced for

The Federal Bureau of Prisons grew almost 800 percent between 1980 and 2013, largely because of long prison sentences for drug offenders.

drug offenses under the mandatory minimum sentencing laws described earlier.[36] Policy shifts also occurred under the Obama administration, with federal prosecutors instructed to not charge low-level, nonviolent drug offenders with offenses that carry severe mandatory sentences.[37]

President Trump did not continue the commutation program for federal drug offenders, despite thousands of applications backlogged for review. The policy guidance to prosecutors was reversed by former Attorney General Sessions, who issued instructions that federal prosecutors were to charge at the highest level possible for all crimes. Attorney General Barr continued the harsh prosecutorial policy.[38] President Biden's platform includes promises to reduce prison populations and racial inequities in the criminal justice system. It is too soon to say how these promises may be implemented. The federal government can certainly influence states' sentencing policies, but the majority of prisoners are state prisoners and, thus, the plateauing of the national prisoner population has been because of states making concerted efforts to decarcerate.

States Lead the Way

In the past decade, states have used a variety of methods to successfully reduce their prison populations, including expanding diversion programs like drug and mental health courts, reducing mandatory sentencing for drug offenses, instituting early release from supervision for low-level offenders on probation, developing intermediate sanctions for probation violators other than prison, and reclassifying certain felonies as misdemeanors. For instance, New Jersey and California reduced their prison populations by about 25 percent between 2006 and 2012. These reductions occurred without a rise in reported crimes; in fact, in several states, crime rates continued to decline even as the prison population was decreasing.[39] New York reduced the number sent to prison by 18 percent, largely through sentencing changes in New York City that reduced the number of drug offenders going to prison.[40] Legislation in Oregon, Mississippi, Georgia, South Carolina, Delaware, and Colorado reduced penalties for low-level crimes, diverting many from a prison sentence. In March of 2014, Mississippi passed a sentencing reform bill that lowered penalties for simple drug possession, raised the felony threshold for property crimes from $500 to $1,000, and required probation for most property crimes under $1,000, barring exceptional circumstances.[41]

Alabama, Nebraska, and Utah adopted wide-ranging reform packages in 2015. Utah reduced sentencing guidelines for a broad range of offenses, converted all simple drug possession crimes from felonies to misdemeanors, re-instituted good-time credits for inmates (so they could collect points to reduce their prison sentences), and decriminalized more than 200 misdemeanors, meaning they became citation-only offenses and violators could no longer be taken to jail. Utah's legislation was projected to avert most of the state's projected prison growth over the next 20 years.[42]

A study by the Vera Institute of Justice concluded that 46 states in 2014 and 2015 enacted at least 201 bills, executive orders, and ballot initiatives to reform at least one aspect of their sentencing and corrections systems. These included laws that created programs that diverted offenders from prosecution if they successfully completed a set of conditions, problem-solving courts (e.g., mental health, veteran, or drug courts), and laws that empowered arresting officers to divert certain defendants into treatment (e.g., those with mental illness who committed nonviolent, non-serious crimes). Reforms intended to reduce prison populations included the following:

- changing sentencing laws to categorize certain offenses as eligible for community-based sentences;

- redefining or reclassifying crimes or repealing mandatory penalties;

- reinstituting good time, which shortens sentences for inmates who earn credits;

- improving or instituting prediction tools to better classify those receiving parole or early release as well as employ intermediate sanctions;

- increased programming and treatment options in community corrections;

- facilitating family visitation;

- improving employment prospects by limiting bars on professional licenses and providing certificates of rehabilitation and employability;

- waiving fines and fees that often create economic obstacles to reintegration; and

- making it easier to expunge prior convictions.[43]

In 2016, 17 states enacted a range of reforms that addressed many of these categories. For instance, Florida passed Senate Bill 228, which eliminated mandatory minimum sentences for aggravated assault and other crimes. Oklahoma reclassified some offenses from felonies to misdemeanors, which lowered sentences attached to them.[44]

These efforts have resulted in significant reductions. In 2018, seven states had reduced their prison population by over 30 percent from their peak imprisonment levels: New Jersey, Alaska, Connecticut, New York, Alabama, Rhode Island, and Vermont. While 44 states and the federal system had reduced their prison populations from peak levels, six states had increased the number of people they send to prison (Wyoming, Nebraska, Iowa, Wisconsin, Kansas, and Oregon).[45] Each year there are minor shifts, with some states going up and some going down; the general trend has been a slow decline overall.

States have undertaken such changes independently or with the help of organizations and the federal government. For instance, the **Justice Reinvestment Initiative (JRI),** begun in 2006, is a joint undertaking by the Pew Center for the States, the Council for State Governments (CSG), and the Urban Institute, with partial funding from the Bureau of Justice Assistance, U.S. Department of Justice.[46] The initiative has been defined as a data-driven approach to improving safety, reducing corrections-related spending, and reinvesting money saved into strategies that ultimately reduce crime and recidivism.[47] With the help of JRI, more than 30 state and local jurisdictions have worked with advisors to analyze the drivers of their correctional populations and develop evidence-based solutions that will reduce correctional costs without jeopardizing public safety. Local solutions differ, but usually involve passing enabling legislation to change sentencing laws and increase alternative sentencing.[48] For example, according to a summary report, Justice Reinvestment efforts in Texas resulted in $1.5 billion in construction savings and $340 million in annual averted operations costs.[49] The various types of legislative initiatives and programs under the umbrella of Justice Reinvestment include victim advocacy and helping jurisdictions adopt prediction and classification tools. Millions of dollars have been spent on model programs, evaluations, and technical assistance.[50] Some states reduced their prison populations dramatically without any JRI involvement. California's decrease came about largely because of Justice Realignment. The Focus box offers a more detailed examination of California's sentencing changes.

CALIFORNIA'S REALIGNMENT AND PROPOSITION 47

For many years, California was tied with Texas for the largest state prison population. From its record high of 172,298 prisoners in 2006, the state dropped its prison population to 122,687 in 2019. In 2011, the Supreme Court decided *Brown v. Plata*, 563 U.S. 493. Inmates had challenged the conditions in California prisons, alleging they were unconstitutional because of a lack of adequate medical care, safety, and sanitation. The sheer size of the population made it impossible to run the prisons in a manner that met constitutional guidelines. The Supreme Court agreed that California's prisons violated the prisoners' constitutional rights and held that the state must either budget new money and build new prisons or reduce the population to 137.5 percent of design capacity by June 2013 (which equated to about 40,000 inmates).

To reduce the state prison population, California passed the Public Safety Realignment Act (**Realignment**) under Assembly Bill (AB) 109 in October 2011. This policy redirected people convicted of non-serious, nonviolent, and non-sexual offenses ("non-non-non offenses") from state to county supervision to serve their sentences in jails or on county probation rather than sending them to state prison. Realignment also shortened mandatory parole supervision from one year to six months and required that people who were revoked spend only six months in a county jail (rather than return to prison).

California had abolished discretionary parole decades ago, but all prison releasees had a mandatory supervision period after prison. The rate of **revocation** and return to prison was extremely high. Before Realignment, three-year rearrest rates had held at about 75 percent of those paroled. In comparison, the national recidivism rate (measured by arrest) was about 50 percent or less. After Realignment, the percentage of prison releases returned to prison within one year dropped 25 percentage points. Researchers found only a 1.0 percent increase in the felony reconviction rate and a 0.2 percent increase in the misdemeanor reconviction rate.

Studies that examined whether Realignment led to increased crime rates use a methodology that a) forecasts what might have happened if offenders had continued to be imprisoned by modeling from past years, or b) compares counties within California

with those that had sent many offenders to state prisons (and now can't) and those that never did, or c) constructs a model using comparable states' crime rates. One study, for instance, found that in the period affected by Realignment, California's crime rates declined by 9 percent and violent crime declined by 10 percent. Simply looking at crime rate declines does not say much because California might have had even greater declines if offenders had remained in prison; thus, researchers undertake extremely sophisticated modeling analyses to try and determine what happened. Some studies found that Realignment resulted in an increase in motor vehicle theft. One study found a small, non-significant increase in violent crime during the first study period (2010) but a decrease in 2013 and 2014. Similarly, there was a small, non-significant increase in property crime that disappeared in later years. Even motor vehicle theft, which earlier studies found had increased under Realignment, did not show any increase from what projections indicated might have happened without Realignment in later years. Other researchers have agreed with these findings.

Some counties, handling many offenders who had gone to state prisons in the past, adopted a greater enforcement emphasis, while other counties adopted a treatment emphasis. Enforcement-oriented counties spent upwards of four times as many Realignment funds on law enforcement and jails than on rehabilitative programs for offenders. These counties also dramatically increased their use of jail, so that individuals who might have been sent to prison are now incarcerated in county jails. Other counties did not increase their use of jail after Realignment, which means offenders must have received some type of community supervision. Enforcement-oriented counties showed higher recidivism figures as compared to counties that emphasized non-custodial alternatives. Rearrest rates are 1.9 percent higher in enforcement-based counties compared to pre-Realignment in that county, but 2.3 times lower in reentry-based counties compared to pre-Realignment.

One study, examining county sentencing differences, grouped counties into five distinct trajectories that were apparent before Realignment. These differences were influenced by poverty rates,

rates of minorities, racial/ethnic heterogeneity, and "penal punitiveness" (conservative attitudes). The study found that a conservative punitiveness factor predicted less decarceration after Realignment. Poverty, income inequality, the percentage of Blacks in the population, urbanization, and the percentage of Republican voters were strongly associated with high prison use. Alternatively, the percentage of Latinos in the population and the percentage registered to vote were strongly associated with lower prison use. Crime was not a significant predictor of prison use.

In 2014, California passed Proposition 47 with 58 percent of California voters. The law "de-felonized" a range of crimes to misdemeanors—including possession of small amounts of cocaine, heroin, and methamphetamine; and writing a bad check, receiving stolen property, and theft when the value of the property is under $950 in any of those crimes. There was also a provision that made the law retroactive—thereby making over 5,000 California jail and prison inmates immediately eligible for release. By 2015, after the law went into effect, the prison population was reduced by 3 percent and the jail population by 11 percent. Researchers using sophisticated statistical methods to determine what crime rates would have been without Prop 47 have found that the effect has been small or nonexistent.

Some researchers have concluded that it is impossible to attribute any crime increase or decrease to California's sentencing changes because of dramatic differences between California counties. While the overall state rate of crime declined between 2010 and 2016, this average masks double-digit increases in some cities and some counties, and equally large decreases in others. Researchers, employing a synthetic control group design to approximate California's crime rates had Prop 47 not been enacted, found that Prop 47 had no effect on homicide, rape, aggravated assault, robbery, or burglary. Larceny and motor vehicle theft seemed to have increased moderately after Prop 47, but the increases were small enough that researchers could not conclude that Prop 47 was responsible. Thus, it appears that the measures taken in California to reduce the prison population have not led to a significant decline in public safety.

A bill that would have changed Prop 47 to increase the number of offenders who would be eligible for prison rather than a community sanc-

tion was defeated in the November 2020 election, with about 60 percent of voters clearly expressing their desire to continue the experiment in decarceration. California and a few other states are somewhat like laboratories for examining whether decarceration leads to rising crime rates. The link between incarceration and crime is a very difficult issue to research because so many factors are involved. Continued research in California and other states that have dramatically reduced their prison population will help other states in their sentencing reform efforts.

Sources: J. Sundt, E. Salisbury, and M. Harmon, "Is Downsizing Prisons Dangerous? The Effect of California's Realignment Act on Public Safety," *Criminology and Public Policy* 15, 2 (2016): 315–41; M. Bird and R. Gratten, "Realignment and Recidivism," *Annals of the American Association of Policy Sciences*, 664 (2016): 176–95, 183–87; M. Males, *Realignment and Crime in 2014: California's Violent Crime in Decline* (San Francisco, CA: Center on Juvenile and Criminal Justice, 2015), 4, http://www.cjcj.org/uploads/cjcj/documents/realignment_and_crime_in_2014_californias_violent_crime_in_decline.pdf; M. Lofstrom and S. Raphael, "Prison Downsizing and Public Safety Evidence from California," *Criminology & Public Policy* 15, 2(2016): 349–65; A. Verma, "A Turning Point in Mass Incarceration? Local Imprisonment Trajectories and Decarceration Under California's Realignment," *Annals of the American Academy of Political and Social Sciences*, 664, 1(2016): 108–35. DOI: 10.1177/0002716215614311; B. Egelko, "State Crime Mostly Down as Lockup Population Dwindles, Study Says," SFGate.com, September 27, 2016. Accessed November 25, 2018, http://www.sfgate.com/crime/article/State-crime-mostly-down-as-lockup-population-9305631.php; M. Males, "Most California Jurisdictions Show Declines in Property Crime During Criminal Justice Reform Era, 2010–2016" (San Francisco, CA: Center on Juvenile and Criminal Justice). Accessed November 25, 2018, http://www.cjcj.org/news/11799; B. Bartos and C. Kubrin, "Can We Downsize Our Prisons and Jails Without Compromising Public Safety? Findings from California's Prop 47," *Criminology & Public Policy* 17, 3 (2018): 693–715; R. Weisberg, "The Wild West of Sentencing Reform: Lessons from California," *Crime & Justice* 48, no. 1 (2019): 35–77, DOI: 10.1086/701714

Looking Ahead: How to Analyze Correctional Challenges

In this first chapter, we have introduced the field of corrections by examining the very current issue of mass incarceration and the beginning of decarceration efforts. Whether imprisonment rates will continue to decline and whether decarceration will lead to rising crime are important questions in corrections today, but there are many others. Throughout the book, we will focus on similarly complex issues that are difficult to research, but research must take place to inform policy. A short synopsis of the chapters ahead will illustrate some of the issues that will be discussed.

Chapter 2: Crimes and Criminology. It is important to be aware of crime patterns to understand what is happening in corrections. Many people think crime rates are increasing, but, generally, crime has been declining for about 30 years. We will look at longitudinal patterns of crime along with some methodological problems in how we "count" crime. We will also examine whether increased imprisonment caused declining crime rates. Criminological theories provide explanations of why people commit crimes, and we will examine whether such theories seem to fit what we know about crime **correlates** (factors that are statistically associated with crime). Criminological theories must be addressed in a corrections textbook because what we do to criminal offenders in the name of corrections should have some relationship to why we think they committed crime in the first place.

Chapter 3: Sentencing. Sentencing alternatives will be described, with a brief discussion of historical punishments. Drug sentencing will be explored in depth, as this category of crime has exhibited the most dramatic pattern of change. The question of whether race and ethnicity affect sentencing will be examined. We will also present and discuss research on deterrence, revisiting this purpose of corrections. Capital punishment is the ultimate punishment and not a correctional alternative; however, we will provide a summary of the legal challenges and Supreme Court holdings regarding the use of capital punishment in this chapter.

Chapter 4: Jails and Pretrial Diversion. An offender's experience in the corrections system begins with the process of bail, release-on-recognizance, and/or pretrial release. These steps and pretrial diversion programs will be described, and we will then turn our attention to jails. Jails and prisons are different in terms of their population, funding, management, location, and architecture. While many people use the terms interchangeably, there are important differences between the two institutions. This chapter will also include a discussion of how the costs associated with correctional alternatives are differentially experienced by the poor. There is a troubling trend for correctional authorities to impose fines, fees, and costs on offenders who, because they are poor, cannot pay and end up in jail as a result. This has been called the "criminalization of poverty" because poor people cannot get out of correctional supervision, while those with financial resources can.

Chapter 5: Probation and Community Corrections. Probationers are the largest group of those under some form of correctional supervision. In this chapter, probationers will be compared to prisoners and parolees. Historically, probation was offered as one of the first alternatives to a jail or prison sentence. The history and philosophy of probation illustrate how it has been seen as a second chance for some offenders. Unfortunately, recidivism is high and probationers often face revocation. The legal rights of probationers during supervision and revocation will be discussed, as well as the factors that have been associated with recidivism.

Chapter 6: State and Federal Prisons. This chapter introduces prisons to the reader. A brief history of prisons in the United States is offered, and then current issues are discussed, including the supermax prison model and private prisons. Correctional officers (COs) are an important component of the prison experience, and various issues will be discussed, including job satisfaction and the CO subculture.

Chapter 7: Prisoners and Special Populations. This chapter presents prisoner demographics in order to more fully understand their needs and challenges. All prisoners are not alike, and certain groups pose difficult managerial issues. The elderly, for instance, are a growing population, and these prisoners require expanded medical services and architectural accommodations. The mentally ill are a particularly problematic group in prisons that pose difficult managerial and programmatic challenges.

Chapter 8: Prisoner Subculture. Elements of the prisoner subculture will be examined, including violence, gang dominance, and drug markets in prison. Adaptation to the prisoner subculture is known as prisonization, and research shows that some individuals navigate the prison world more adeptly than others.

Chapter 9: Prisoners' Rights. All prisoners have basic rights that, while not exactly the same as those of free people, stem from state and federal constitutions. Prisoners' rights and how courts resolve conflicts between the rights of prisoners versus prison officials will be discussed in this chapter.

Chapter 10: Female Prisoners. Female offenders are different from male offenders in obvious and not-so-obvious ways. "Gender-responsive programming" has become a buzz-word in corrections and refers to programs and policies that consider girls' and women's somewhat different pathways into crime, as well as their unique needs. Issues of victimization and parenting especially must be recognized and addressed, whether the female offender is under community supervision, in prison, or released on parole. This chapter addresses those concerns.

Chapter 11: Rehabilitative Programming. The "rehabilitation era" of the 1970s and early 1980s will be described, along with the subsequent shift to "justice-based" models. The voluminous work that has evaluated correctional programming will be summarized, along with more general research on factors related to recidivism. How do we measure success? Is it the complete abstinence from drugs (for a drug offender) or desistance from crime? Is success when someone is released and commits no crime, or when they commit less serious crime? Is it a failure if the person can't find a job, but does not commit new crimes? What we know about successful programs will be reviewed, including specific research on prediction of risk and whether such instruments are successful in predicting who may benefit from treatment programs.

Chapter 12: Reentry, Parole, and Looking Toward the Future. Almost all prisoners eventually return to society, either under mandatory release or parole. In this chapter, we will look at the models of parole and how some states have improved recidivism rates. The challenges of halfway houses and other community housing alternatives will be examined. The chapter will also explore what we can learn from individuals who have experienced some form of correctional supervision and have gone on to lead law-abiding, productive lives. Finally, a brief review of the major facts of the corrections system will be offered, as well as a look at current issues, such as racial disparity in sentencing, the so-called "criminalization of poverty," the increasing numbers of releasees without marketable skills, and the problem of drug addiction.

Summary

- The United States incarcerates 2.1 million people in prisons, jails, and other confinement facilities. The U.S. comprises 5 percent of the world's population but imprisons 25 percent of its prisoners.

- Mass incarceration began in the 1980s. Before then, prison rates were remarkably stable.

- The dramatic increase in imprisonment rates has been attributed to a rise in crime, political responses to social upheaval, and the involvement of the federal government in criminal justice issues at the state level.

- At 655 per 100,000 people, the rate of incarceration in the U.S. far exceeds the rate of any

comparable country; for example, the United Kingdom's rate is just 140.

- There is great variability in the imprisonment rate across states; Louisiana has the highest imprisonment rate, while Massachusetts has the lowest.

- Decarceration has begun, with states instituting a variety of reform measures to reduce their prison populations. Some states have seen their prison populations drop by 25 percent or more.

- California was forced to reduce its prison population because of *Brown v. Plata*. Realignment has shifted the responsibility for most nonviolent, non-serious offenders to the counties.

PROJECTS

1. Find your state's penal code and determine the sentence range for a burglary, a rape, and a possession of cocaine charge (assume one gram). (You will have choices regarding elements of the crime that make it less or more serious, e.g., use of a weapon). Then choose four other states and compare sentencing. Are they the same, very different, or only slightly different?

2. Go to the Bureau of Justice Statistics (https://bjs.gov/) and browse the corrections section to see what informational resources are available. Look at *Prisoners in 2019* (or the most current report available) to see the total number of prisoners in your state. Has this number increased or decreased in the last year?

NOTES

1. T. Minton, L. Beatty and Z. Zeng, *Correctional Populations in the United States, 2019-Statistical Tables* (Washington, DC: Bureau of Justice Statistics, USDOJ, 2021), 1. L. Maruschak and T. Minton, *Correctional Populations in the U.S., 2017–2018* (Washington, DC: Bureau of Justice Statistics, USDOJ, 2020), 1.

2. Ibid., p. 13

3. P. Wagner and B. Rabuy, "Mass Incarceration: The Whole Pie" (Northampton, MA: Prison Policy Initiative, 2016), accessed November 23, 2018, https://www.prisonpolicy. org/reports/pie2016.html; B. Rabuy and P. Wagner, "Correctional Control: Incarceration and Supervision by State" (Northampton, MA: Prison Policy Initiative, 2016),

accessed November 23, 2018, https://www.prisonpolicy.org/reports/50statepie.html.

4. L. Maruschak and T. Minton, *Correctional Populations in the U.S., 2017–2018* (Washington, DC: Bureau of Justice Statistics, USDOJ, 2020), 2

5. M. McLaughlin, C. Pettus-Davis, D. Brown, C. Veeh, and T. Renn, "The Economic Burden of Incarceration in the U.S." (St. Louis, MO: Institute for Advancing Justice Research and Innovation, 2016), accessed November 23, 2018, https://nicic.gov/economic-burden-incarceration-us-2016.

6. E. Banks, *Prisoners in 2019* (Washington, DC: Bureau of Justice Statistics, USDOJ, 2020).

7. E. Carson, *Prisoners in 2019* (Washington, DC: Bureau of Justice Statistics, USDOJ, 2020).

8. "Punishment Rate Measures Prison Use Relative to Crime" (Washington, DC: Pew Charitable Trusts, 2016), accessed November 23, 2018, http://www.pewtrusts.org/en/research-and-analysis/issue-briefs/2016/03/the-punishment-rate.

9. J. Austin and L. Eisen, "How Many Americans are Unnecessarily Incarcerated?" (New York: Brennan Center, 2016), 4, accessed November 23, 2018, https://www.brennancenter.org/sites/default/files/publications/Unnecessarily_Incarcerated_0.pdf.

10. J. Travis, B. Western, and S. Redburn (Eds), *The Growth of Incarceration in the United States: Exploring Causes and Consequences* (Washington, DC: National Academy of Sciences, 2014), 50, 52, accessed November 23, 2018, http://nap.edu/18613.

11. National Institute on Drug Abuse, "Drug Use Among Racial and Ethnic Minorities" (Washington, DC: U.S. Dept. of Health and Human Services, 2003), accessed November 23, 2018, https://archives.drugabuse.gov/sites/default/files/minorities03_1.pdf.

12. J. Travis, B. Western, and S. Redburn (Eds), *The Growth of Incarceration in the United States: Exploring Causes and Consequences*, (Washington DC: National Academy of Sciences, 2014), 52, accessed November 23, 2018, http://nap.edu/18613. ; E. Carson, *Prisoners in 2019* (Washington, DC: Bureau of Justice Statistics, USDOJ, 2020).

13. Public Law 99–570.

14. Public Law 100–690.

15. J. Travis, B. Western, and S. Redburn (Eds). *The Growth of Incarceration in the United States: Exploring Causes and Consequences* (Washington DC: National Academy of Sciences, 2014), 70, accessed November 23, 2018, http://nap.edu/18613.

16. J. Inciardi, *The War on Drugs, Part III* (Boston: Allyn and Bacon, 2002).

17. J. Austin and L. Eisen, *How Many Americans are Unnecessarily Incarcerated?* (New York: Brennan Center, 2016): 4, accessed November 23, 2018, https://www.brennancenter.org/sites/default/files/publications/Unnecessarily_Incarcerated_0.pdf.4.

18. J. Travis, B. Western, and S. Redburn (Eds). *The Growth of Incarceration in the United States: Exploring Causes and Consequences* (Washington DC: National Academy of Sciences, 2014), accessed November 23, 2018, http://nap.edu/18613. (.

19. J. Pfaff, *Locked In: The True Causes of Mass Incarceration and How to Achieve Real Reform* (New York: Basic Books, 2017).

20. E. Carson, *Prisoners in 2019* (Washington, DC: Bureau of Justice Statistics, USDOJ, 2020), 9; J. Travis, B. Western, and S. Redburn (eds.), *The Growth of Incarceration in the United States: Exploring Causes and Consequences* (Washington DC: National Academy of Sciences, 2014), 66, accessed November 23, 2018, http://nap.edu/18613.

21. E. Carson, *Prisoners in 2019* (Washington, DC: Bureau of Justice Statistics, USDOJ, 2020), 9.

22. J. Travis, B. Western, and S. Redburn (Eds), *The Growth of Incarceration in the United States: Exploring Causes and Consequences* (Washington DC: National Academy of Sciences, 2014), 51, accessed November 23, 2018, http://nap.edu/18613.

23. T. Miethe, "Types of Consensus in Public Evaluations of Crime: An Illustration of Strategies for Measuring 'Consensus,'" *Journal of Criminal Law and Criminology* 75, 2 (1984): 459–73.

24. W. Spelman, "The Limited Importance of Prison Expansion," in *The Crime Drop in America*, edited by A. Blumstein and J. Wallman (Cambridge, England: Cambridge University Press, 2000).

25. O. Roeder, L. Eisen, and J. Bowling, *What Caused the Crime Decline?* (New York: Brennan Center for Justice, 2017).

26. J. Travis, B. Western, and S. Redburn (Eds), *The Growth of Incarceration in the United States: Exploring Causes and Consequences* (Washington DC: National Academy of Sciences, 2014), 23, accessed

November 23, 2018, http://nap.edu/18613..

27. J. Austin and L. Eisen, *How Many Americans are Unnecessarily Incarcerated?* (New York: Brennan Center, 2016).

28. J. Austin and L. Eisen, *How Many Americans are Unnecessarily Incarcerated?* (New York: Brennan Center, 2016).

29. E. Carson. *Prisoners in 2019*, (Washington, DC: Bureau of Justice Statistics, USDOJ, 2020), 1..

30. E. Eckhom, "A.C.L.U. in $50 Million Push to Reduce Jail Sentences," *New York Times*, November 7, 2014, A14.

31. P. Jonsson, "Early Release for 6,000 Federal Prisoners: A Risk to Public Safety?" *Christian Science Monitor*, October 7, 2015, accessed November 23, 2018, http://www.csmonitor.com/USA/Justice/2015/1007/Early-release-for-6-000-federal-prisoners-A-risk-to-public-safety.

32. Law Enforcement Leaders, "Statement of Principles, 2015," accessed November 23, 2018, lawenforceldrs.wpengine.com/wp-content/uploads/2015/10/Statement_of_Principles.pdf.

33. K. Beckett, A. Reosti, and E. Knaphus, "The End of an Era? Understanding the Contradictions of Criminal Justice Reform," *Annals of the American Academy of Political and Social Sciences*, 664, 1 (2016): 238–59, DOI: 10.1177/0002716215598973.

34. A. Gelb, "Sentencing Bill: Another Step Toward Federal Prison Reform," *The Crime Report*, October 7, 2015, accessed November 25, 2018, http://www.thecrimereport.org/

viewpoints/2015-10-sentencing-bill-another-step-toward-federal-prison-r.

35. P. Jonsson, "Early Release for 6,000 Federal Prisoners: A Risk to Public Safety?" *Christian Science Monitor*, October 7, 2015, accessed November 25, 2018, http://www.csmonitor.com/USA/Justice/2015/1007/Early-release-for-6-000-federal-prisoners-A-risk-to-public-safety; S. Horwitz, "Justice Department Set to Free 6,000 Prisoners, Largest One-time Release," *Washington Post*, October 6, 2018, accessed November 25, 2018, https://www.washingtonpost.com/world/national-security/justice-department-about-to-free-6000-prisoners-largest-one-time-release/2015/10/06/961f4c9a-6ba2-11e5-aa5b-f78a98956699_story.html.

36. "In Final Act as President, Obama Commutes 330 Drug Sentences," Foxnews.com, January 19, 2017, accessed November 25, 2018, http://www.foxnews.com/politics/2017/01/19/in-final-act-as-president-obama-commutes-330-drug-sentences.html.

37. S. Horwitz, "Justice Department Set to Free 6,000 Prisoners, Largest One-time Release," *Washington Post*, October 6, 2018.

38. L. Bever, "Prosecutors Are Pushing Back Against Sessions Order to Pursue Most Severe Penalties," *Washington Post*, May 19, 2017, accessed November 25, 2018, https://www.washingtonpost.com/news/post-nation/wp/2017/05/19/prosecutors-are-pushing-back-against-sessions-order-to-pursue-most-severe-penalties/?utm_term=.d0389a648794.

39. "Most States Cut Imprisonment and Crime" (Infographic), Pew Charitable Trusts, accessed November 25, 2018, http://www.pewtrusts.org/en/multimedia/data-visualizations/2014/imprisonment-and-crime; M. Mauer and N. Ghandnoosh, "Can We Reduce the Prison Population by 25%?" *The Crime Report*, August 5, 2014, accessed November 25, 2018, https://thecrimereport.org/2014/08/05/2014-08-can-we-reduce-the-prison-population-by-25/.

40. J. Austin and M. Jacobsen, *How New York City Reduced Mass Incarceration: A Model for Change* (New York City: Vera Institute of Justice, 2012).

41. J. Domanick, "The Message of California's Prop 47," *The Crime Report*, November 7, 2014, accessed November 25, 2018, https://thecrimereport.org/2014/11/07/2014-11-the-message-of-californias-prop-47/.

42. A. Gelb, "Sentencing Bill: Another Step Toward Federal Prison Reform" *The Crime Report*, October 7, 2015..

43. *Justice In Review: New Trends in State Sentencing and Corrections 2014–2015* (New York: Vera Institute of Justice, 2016), http://www.vera.org/pubs/state-sentencing-and-corrections-trends-2014–2015.

44. *State Advances in Criminal Justice Reform, 2016* (Washington, DC: The Sentencing Project, 2016).

45. N. Ghandnoosh, "U.S. Prison Decline: Insufficient to Undo Mass Incarceration," The Sentencing Project, accessed February 25, 2021, https://www.sentencingproject.org/publications/u-s-prison-

decline-insufficient-undo-mass-incarceration/.

46. To read about the Justice Reinvestment Initiative, go to https://www.bja.gov/programs/justicereinvestment/index.html.

47. See, for instance, https://www.vera.org/projects/justice-reinvestment-initiative.

48. H. Schoenfeld, "A Research Agenda on Reform: Penal Policy and Politics Across the States," *Annals of the American Academy of Political and Social Sciences*, 664, 1(2016): 155–74. DOI: 10.1177/0002716215601850.

49. *Lessons from the States: Reducing Recidivism and Curbing Corrections Costs Through Justice Reinvestment* (Washington, DC: Council of State Governments Justice Center, 2013), 2.

50. *Lessons from the States: Reducing Recidivism and Curbing Corrections Costs Through Justice Reinvestment* (Washington, DC: Council of State Governments Justice Center, 2013).

Chapter 2

Crimes and Criminology

LEARNING OBJECTIVES

1. Describe the various measures of crime used to understand the patterns of crime in our society.

2. Compare and contrast the various explanations for the crime decline.

3. Discuss whether crime has increased or decreased and what are the most frequent types of arrests.

4. Identify the strongest crime correlates.

5. Connect the major crime theories with correctional policies and programs.

CHAPTER OUTLINE

- Measuring Crime 30

- Decades of Declining Crimes 35

- Crime Correlates 37

- Criminology and Corrections 40

- Are There Different Types of Criminals? 49

- SUMMARY 52

The journey through the corrections system begins with an arrestee being booked into jail.

KEY TERMS

Anomie
Chicago school of criminology
Classical school of criminology
CompStat
Crime correlate
Criminology
Cultural deviance theory
Dark figure of crime
Deterrence theory
Differential association theory

Differential opportunity
  theory
General strain theory
General theory of crime
Hedonistic calculus
Labeling theory
Longitudinal research
Maturation effect
National Crime Victimization
  Survey (NCVS)

Positivist school of
  criminology
Rational choice theory
Social control theory
Social disorganization theory
Social support theory
Strain-opportunity theory
Symbolic interactionism
Uniform Crime Reports (UCR)

Measuring Crime

Before discussing corrections, it is important to spend some time examining crime causation. After all, how can we develop correctional alternatives without truly understanding crime patterns? First, we will examine the major sources of crime statistics and how crime is measured in each source. In this chapter, we will look at how crime rates have declined substantially from their highs in the 1980s. We are also interested in crime correlates, more specifically, who is likely to be arrested for crimes. It is also important to consider individuals' patterns of crime commission. For instance, there is research that indicates certain individuals begin to commit crimes early, they commit many crimes chronically and consistently throughout their life, and they do not desist or age out of crime in the same way as others. Other offenders commit crimes more sporadically and infrequently. What the corrections system does with offenders should have some relationship with why it is thought they commit crimes, and so we will also review criminological theories and their policy implications.

Three Crime Measures

Society's ability to measure crime is not perfect. Three major measures of crime are used: 1) crime reports made to the police, 2) arrests by police, and 3) victim surveys. All of these have issues in terms of how they are measured. The **Uniform Crime Reports (UCR)**, available through the Federal Bureau of Investigation, is an annual collection of local crime reports and arrest data. The reports began in 1929, and now about 98 percent of police agencies cooperate by sending their crime reports and arrest numbers directly or to a state agency that collects the data and delivers them to the FBI. The Uniform Crime Reports present the number of crime reports for jurisdictions by rates per 100,000 people, which allows for a better comparison across jurisdictions, although the FBI cautions against this because different variables affect crime reports, including police departments' recording practices, urban density, victim reporting practices, and so on. The UCR provides the total number of reported crimes for the following eight index crimes:

- murder and non-negligent manslaughter
- forcible rape

- robbery
- aggravated assault
- burglary
- larceny-theft
- motor vehicle theft
- arson.

The first four crimes are aggregated into a violent crime index, and the last four crimes are aggregated into a property crime index. Figure 2.1 illustrates the crime report rates for violent crime and property crime since 1960. Note that violent crime reports to police peaked in the early 1990s and then began to decline, while property crime peaked earlier and declined throughout the 1990s and 2000s.

One of the most-often cited criticisms of the UCR is that it represents only reported crimes. Crime that is unreported is referred to as the **dark figure of crime**, which varies by the type of crime. For instance, less than half of violent crime victimizations and a little over a third of property crime victimizations are reported to police. Another potential problem is that some police departments may downgrade citizens' reports of crimes in official reports. For example, the New York City Police Department Quality Assurance Division, an academic study, and news investigations exposed patterns of downgrading crimes and discouraging citizens from reporting, evidently because midlevel managers felt great pressure to report crime decreases in some precincts.[1] Similar scandals in other cities have been reported, and it is unknown whether or to what extent the pattern is systemic or pervasive enough to affect crime rates.

The FBI also presents arrest data. Arrest data is helpful as a measure of crime, but there are problems with using it. The first issue is that the FBI reports arrests for only 21 crime categories, which do not cover all types of crimes. Local sources have more comprehensive arrest data, but it is impossible to compare jurisdictions because of different crime definitions. The only national source of arrest data comes from the FBI.

Even if the FBI covered all crime categories, arrests are not a perfect measure of crime. They are influenced not only by the number of actual crimes committed, but also by police officers' actions. For instance, some crimes are harder to solve, thus arrest numbers for these crimes are lower than crime reports for such crime categories. Some crime categories such as prostitution are especially sensitive to enforcement priorities of police agencies with arrests rising and falling, but not necessarily because of a change in the number of people engaged in prostitution.

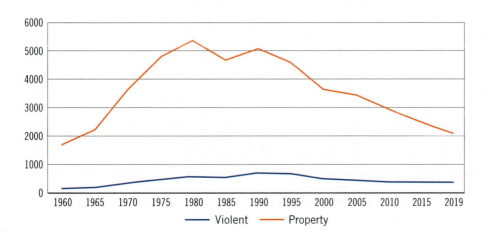

FIGURE 2.1   Reported crimes, 1960–2019. Author created from UCR Data Online analysis tool, https://www.bjs.gov/ucrdata/Search/Crime/Crime.cfm

TABLE 2.1 20 Year Arrest Trends (Number of Arrests per 100,000)

ARREST	1996	2006	2016
Murder and non-negligent manslaughter	7.6	4.5	3.7
Forcible rape	12.8	8.2	7.3
Robbery	64.1	43.2	29.8
Aggravated assault	204.1	151.1	119
Burglary	139.1	102.5	64.3
Larceny-theft	577.3	370	326.5
Motor vehicle theft	69.5	46.5	26.7
Arson	7.2	5.5	3
Other assaults	512.3	439.7	334.2
Forgery and counterfeiting	46.5	36.7	17.5
Fraud	171.0	91.2	39.7
Embezzlement	6.0	6.8	4.9
Stolen property	58.5	41.6	29.1
Vandalism	123.3	101.7	60.7
Weapons	84.9	68.1	48.5
Prostitution	42.7	27.6	11.9
Sex offenses	37.2	29.2	15.8
Drug abuse violations	594.3	636.8	486.4
Gambling	8.9	4.2	1.1
Offenses/family	54.7	42.5	27.3
Driving under the influence	533.9	479.3	313.6
Liquor laws	258.6	216	72.4
Drunkenness	275.3	189	116.9
Disorderly conduct	330.1	239.5	114.5
Vagrancy	11.4	12.5	7.7
All other offenses	1,457.3	1,346.6	1,005.5
Curfew/loitering	75.0	52.8	10.6
Violent crime	288.6	207	159.7
Property crime	793.2	524	420.6

Source: FBI, "Crime in the United States," 1996 (Table 30), 2006 (Table 33), 2016 (Table 19).

Except for some crime categories, arrest rates have declined over the same period as crimes reported to police have declined, which increases confidence in the notion that what we have experienced in the last 30 years is a real and substantial decline in criminal activity.

Looking at Table 2.1, one can see that arrests for homicide are almost half what they were in the mid-1990s and robbery arrests are less than half, as are several other crime categories. This may mean that police are less effective in arresting people for crimes, but it also means that there are fewer crimes being committed (because we see similar declines in reports to police). Drug crimes and embezzlement are the only crime categories that showed an increase in arrests between 1996 and 2006. All other crime categories had declining arrests.

Another way to utilize arrest rates is to see what people are most likely to be arrested for, since, to some extent, this represents the correctional population as well. Figure 2.2 shows the prevalence of drug arrests as a portion of the total number of arrests. Except for an "other" category, drug arrests account for the largest number of arrests. This does not necessarily mean that all arrests result in that person ending up in the corrections system, nor does it mean that all those arrested for drug

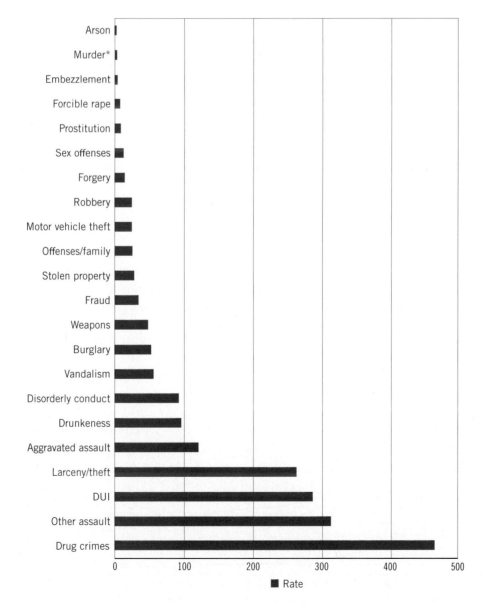

FIGURE 2.2 Selected 2019 arrests (rate per 100,000). Author created from FBI, "Crime in the United States, 2019, Table 30," https://ucr.fbi.gov/crime-in-the-u.s/2019/crime-in-the-u.s.-2019/topic-pages/persons-arrested.

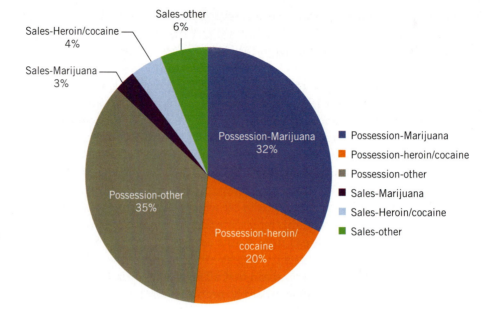

FIGURE 2.3 Percentages of drug arrests. Author created from FBI, "Crime in the United States, 2019," https://ucr.fbi.gov/crime-in-the-u.s/2019/crime-in-the-u.s.-2019/topic-pages/persons-arrested.

crimes have drug addiction or abuse issues. However, it does illustrate the prevalence of drugs in our criminal justice and corrections systems. Figure 2.3 breaks down drug arrests to possession and sales, and by the type of drug. Possession of marijuana accounts for 42 percent of the total number of drug violation arrests.

Another source of crime statistics comes from victimization surveys. The Bureau of Justice Statistics presents findings from the **National Crime Victimization Survey (NCVS)**, a random sample of households selected and surveyed to find out whether they have been victimized and the extent of their damages and/or injuries. The NCVS excludes homicide, arson, commercial crimes, crimes against children under age 12, and victimless crimes such as drug crimes, gambling, or prostitution. In general, the UCR gives us a broad picture of crime patterns (as reported to police), while the NCVS gives us more information about the characteristics of victimizations in certain selected crime categories and reporting trends by victims. The NCVS is subject to all the potential problems of sampling (e.g., lack of representativeness) and survey weaknesses; for instance, respondents may forget they have been a victim of a crime, they may misunderstand the question, or they may not tell the truth for some reason. Despite these issues, however, the NCVS showed declines (see Figure 2.4) over roughly the same period during which the UCR and arrest data reported declines; therefore, we can be confident that there was an actual crime decline.

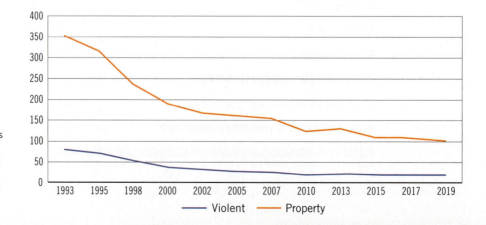

FIGURE 2.4 Victimization rates 1993–2016. Author created from "Violent victimization rates, and property victimization rates," Bureau of Justice Statistics data analysis tool, https://www.bjs.gov/index.cfm?ty=nvat.

Decades of Declining Crimes

Reports to police, arrests, and victimization surveys have all shown dramatic declines over the past 30 years. Figure 2.5 shows that despite all crime measures showing dramatic declines, over half of respondents in national polls persist in thinking that crime is worse.

Public opinion may be influenced by media coverage of individual crimes or spikes in crimes in some cities. Baltimore's and Chicago's spikes in violent crime in 2016 were well publicized, but a 2017 analysis of large cities' crime rates by the Brennan Center indicates that violent crime increased in about half of the cities but decreased in the other half, for an overall national decline of .06 percent between 2016 and 2017.[2] In 2017, murder rate decreases in Detroit (down 25.6 percent), Houston (down 20.5 percent), and New York (down 19.1 percent) were balanced by increases in Charlotte (up 108 percent), Portland (70 percent), and Columbus (40 percent). More recently, there is still variation across cities, with some showing increases and others showing decreases in violent crime.[3] In 2021, it was reported that homicide and aggravated assault spiked in a larger number of cities. This dramatic increase in violent crime was not matched by property crime and has been explained by the stress of the pandemic. It remains to be seen whether these increases will continue or whether it was a momentary reaction to extraordinary events.[4] It is apparent that crime is a local phenomenon and that the factors that affect crime rates vary across cities. It is also apparent that public concern about crime is not closely connected to actual crime rates, with the public only vaguely aware of the historically low crime rates of today. Since public support for correctional alternatives may be related to their fear of crime, it is unfortunate that the mainstream media has not provided information that helps to put crime rates in perspective.

What Caused Crime Rates to Fall?

It seems logical to assume that imprisoning more people led to reduced crime. As described in Chapter 1, there have been numerous studies to determine whether the massive increase in the use of imprisonment led to the decline of crime; the consensus seems to be that there was a moderate influence on crime rates during the early years of the increase in the 1990s, but as the numbers of those sentenced to prison continued to climb, there was a decreasing effect on crime.

As imprisonment rates began their climb, serious and chronic offenders were more likely to be incarcerated rather than given probation or a suspended sentence, and for longer periods of time, which led to a significant impact on crime.

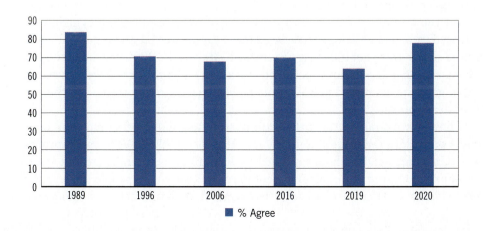

FIGURE 2.5 Percent agreement that "Crime is higher than a year ago." Author created from Gallup Poll, http://news.gallup.com/poll/1603/crime.aspx.

However, as incarceration was used more and more frequently for less and less serious and/or chronic offenders, the net impact on crime was reduced.[5] It seems to be the case that for the last decade or so, a state's incarceration pattern has had minimal effect on crime rates. Some states, such as California, Michigan, New Jersey, New York, and Texas, have reduced their prison populations while crime has continued to fall, while other states' incarceration rates have risen with no impact on crime. In short, there doesn't seem to be much relationship between a state's incarceration rate and its crime rate.[6]

If not because of incarceration, why has crime fallen so dramatically from the early 1990s? Various reasons have been explored. The following factors have been identified as potentially affecting the crime decline in addition to or instead of the greater use of incarceration:

- aging birth cohort of baby boomers;
- stabilization of drug markets;
- community policing;
- "zero tolerance" policing;
- home health care and pre- and postnatal health services;
- violence prevention programs in schools;
- reduction of exposure to lead-based paint; and
- increased numbers of abortions in the late 1970s and 1980s (the idea here is that unwanted children are more likely to become criminals, and with the rise of abortions, there are fewer of them).

A study by the Brennan Center for Justice examined these proposed explanations for the crime drop and concluded that several factors, including others not mentioned previously, affected the crime drop during the 1990s, and that some, but not all, of the explanatory factors for the 1990s continued to affect the declining crime rates of the 2000s. For instance, researchers concluded that in the 1990s, the following factors each affected about 5 to 10 percent of the crime drop: increased incarceration, increased numbers of police, and decreased alcohol consumption. Other factors accounted for between 5 to 7 percent of the crime drop: growth in income, decreased unemployment, and an aging population. The researchers concluded that the following factors could not be proven as influential at all in the crime decline: right-to-carry laws, use of the death penalty, decreased crack use, decreased lead in gasoline, or legalization of abortion. In the 2000s, decreased alcohol consumption, growth in income, and the introduction of **CompStat** were estimated to affect the crime decline by about 5 to 15 percent each. CompStat was the accountability program begun by the NYPD that provided up-to-date crime figures by division; commanders were required to explain if the numbers in their districts went up. Decreased unemployment and increased incarceration might have accounted for between 1 and 3 percent each. Factors shown to be not affecting the crime decline in the 2000s included the following: an aging population, decreased crack use, right-to-carry laws, decreased lead in gasoline, increased police numbers, legalization of abortion, and the use of the death penalty.[7]

One study examined the possible impact of neighborhood groups and nonprofits on children who grew up in the late 1990s and 2000s. Various nonprofits in criminogenic neighborhoods cleaned parks, built playgrounds, created afterschool programs and began employment programs for young people, such as the Pennsylvania Horticultural Society that converted abandoned lots into green spaces and the Concerned Citizens of South Central Los Angeles that created a senior center. The number of these organizations increased in the 1990s, corresponding with the decline of crime. The analysis indicated that for every 10 additional organizations in a city with 100,000 residents, there was an estimated 9 percent drop in the murder rate and a 6 percent drop in violent crime.[8]

Crime Correlates

It is important to understand that crime is not randomly distributed across the population. It is much higher in urban areas than suburban or rural; and, even in cities, there are certain neighborhoods that have higher crime rates than other areas. The chance of victimization is much higher for certain groups of people, as is the chance of being a criminal.

A **crime correlate** is a measurable factor that has a statistical relationship with measures of crime. We tend to use arrest rates as the measure of crime when we look at crime correlates because other measures of crime (reports to police, or victimization surveys) may not have much information about the offender. For instance, if you are burglarized, you probably wouldn't be able to describe the burglar. If you were a victim of auto theft, it is unlikely you would know whether the thief was a man or woman or how old he or she was. Arrest statistics, while representing only some portion of crime, give us information about the offender population. Some correlates are characteristics of the offender (sex, age, race), while others are elements of the crime (location, time, urbanity).

The most obvious correlate of crime is sex. Men are more likely to be arrested than women for all but a few crime categories: 72 percent of the persons arrested in the nation during 2019 were males. They accounted for 79 percent of persons arrested for violent crime and 62 percent of persons arrested for property crime in 2019.[9] Table 2.2 demonstrates that only forgery and embezzlement show similar arrest numbers between men and women. The numbers also indicate that while both men's and women's arrests declined, men's arrest numbers declined more dramatically, which has resulted in the gender differential being reduced but not eliminated for most crimes.

The other major correlate of arrests is age. The so-called **maturation effect** describes the precipitous drop in arrests in people over 35. This might be affected by incarceration rates (criminals are more likely to be in prison by these ages and not subject to arrest), but evidence indicates that, generally, most offenders slow down or completely stop committing crimes in later decades of life. Figure 2.6 shows that about 36 percent of all arrests are of 19- to 29-year-olds.

The other major correlate of crime is race/ethnicity. In Figure 2.7, we see that Blacks represent about 27 percent of all criminal arrests except for violent crimes in which they represent closer to 37 percent. This is disproportional to their representation in the population (which is about 13 percent). The percentage of arrests of Hispanics, which range from 17 percent for property crime to about 25 percent for violent crime, is more like their percentage of the population (about 18 percent).[10]

Thus, those arrested for crimes are more likely to be young men, and mostly white men, although young Black men are disproportionately arrested based on their percentage of the total population, especially for violent crimes. This population describes the correctional population (those in prisons and jails, and on community supervision) as well, although, as we will see in upcoming chapters, the correctional population is even more likely to be male, a bit older than the arrest population, and even more likely to be a member of a minority group.

TABLE 2.2	Arrest Trends by Sex, Adults Only, 1999, 2019

| | MALE | | FEMALE | |
	TOTAL		TOTAL	
Offense charged (% Arrests Female)	1999	2019	1999	2019
Murder and non-negligent manslaughter	8,622	5,461	1,105 (11)	771 (12)
Forcible rape	18,521	13,909	238 (1)	465 (3)
Robbery	66,214	38,294	7,405 (10)	7,321 (16)
Aggravated assault	255,331	175,704	62,720 (20)	53,496 (24)
Burglary	167,661	81,600	24,909 (13)	21,690 (21)
Larceny-theft	512,227	304,860	281,974 (36)	229,976 (43)
Motor vehicle theft	79,660	37,001	14,675 (16)	11,328 (23)
Arson	9,251	4,279	1,560 (14)	1,187 (22)
Violent crime[2]	348,688	233,368	71,468 (17)	62,053 (21)
Property crime[2]	768,799	427,740	323,118 (30)	264,181 (38)
Other assaults	654,386	433,813	190,342 (23)	182,270 (29)
Forgery and counterfeiting	43,033	19,022	26,820 (38)	9,656 (33)
Fraud	127,521	45,167	98,413 (44)	25,958 (36)
Embezzlement	5,690	4,534	5,518 (49)	4,619 (50)
Stolen property; buying, receiving, possessing	67,831	44,099	12,595 (16)	12,858 (22)
Vandalism	154,155	85,838	27,888 (15)	25,686 (23)

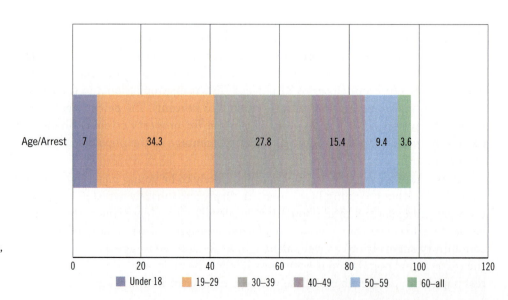

FIGURE 2.6 Arrest/percentage by age. Author created from FBI, "Crime in the United States, 2019, Table 38," https://ucr.fbi.gov/crime-in-the-u.s/2019/crime-in-the-u.s.-2019/tables/table-38.

	MALE		FEMALE	
	TOTAL		**TOTAL**	
Weapons; carrying, possessing, etc.	104,953	82,521	8,927 (8)	8,919 (10)
Prostitution and commercialized vice	25,078	4,985	38,849 (61)	8,511 (63)
Sex offenses (except forcible rape and prostitution)	55,857	23,930	4,263 (7)	1,754 (7)
Drug abuse violations	829,460	690,794	177,542 (18)	236,910 (25)
Gambling	6,151	1,067	872 (12)	447 (29)
Offenses against the family and children	72,365	35,586	20,484 (22)	15,371 (30)
Driving under the influence	782,745	403,075	148,490 (16)	143,138 (26)
Liquor laws	333,530	68,341	94,343 (22)	30,114 (30)
Drunkenness	381,806	146,173	55,347 (13)	40,125 (21)
Disorderly conduct	324,691	131,591	96,971 (23)	54,751 (30)
Vagrancy	16,498	11,578	3,715 (18)	3,422 (23)
All other offenses (except traffic)	1,918,033	1,434,312	498,511 (21)	532,633 (27)
Suspicion	3,888	224	1019 (21)	105 (32)
Curfew and loitering law violations	79,433	7,147	34,787 (31)	3,634 (34)

[1] *Violent crimes are offenses of murder and non-negligent manslaughter, forcible rape, robbery, and aggravated assault. Property crimes are offenses of burglary, larceny-theft, motor vehicle theft, and arson.*

Source: FBI, "Crime in the United States, 1999," Table 42, accessed February 1, 2021, https://ucr.fbi.gov/crime-in-the-u.s/1999/99sec4.pdf; "Crime in the United States, 2019," Table 42, accessed February 1, 2021, https://ucr.fbi.gov/crime-in-the-u.s/2019/crime-in-the-u.s.-2019/topic-pages/tables/table-42.

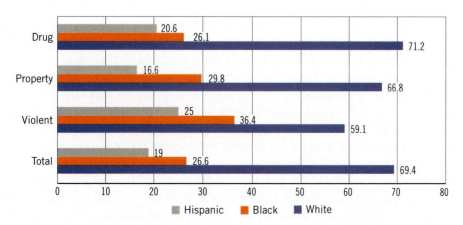

FIGURE 2.7 Arrest/percentage by race. Author created from FBI, "Crime in the United States, 2019, Table 43," https://ucr.fbi.gov/crime-in-the-u.s/2019/crime-in-the-u.s.-2019/tables/table-43.

Criminology and Corrections

What happens to offenders once they are caught and sentenced should have some relationship to why it is believed criminals commit crime in the first place. **Criminology** is the study of criminals; criminological theories propose why individuals choose to commit crime, and why crimes occur in certain areas. We will explore the major criminological theories in the sections below as well as the implications each has for corrections.

The Classical and Positivist Schools of Criminology

Generally, our entire system of punishment is based on the **classical school of criminology** from the 1700s. Philosophers Cesare Beccaria (1738–1794) and Jeremy Bentham (1748–1832) assumed that men were rational and operated with free will. Therefore, laws promising punishment for offenses should deter criminal choices. Bentham's **hedonistic calculus** proposed that the justice system set punishment as slightly more punitive than the perceived profit (or pleasure) of the crime contemplated.[11] Punishment that was swift, certain, and proportional to the perceived benefit of the crime was believed to be more effective. At the time, women were under the legal authority of their fathers and husbands, and any crimes committed by them were the responsibility of their male guardians. Bentham and Beccaria did not mention female offenders in their writing because, in this period, women were perceived as being child-like in their thinking and not as rational as men.

Modern theories that follow the classical school of criminology include **rational choice theory** and **deterrence theory**. Rational choice theories often focus on elements of the crime targets (opportunity) rather than characteristics of the individual criminal. It is presumed that individuals rationally choose criminal action because immediate rewards have a greater influence on decision making than uncertain future punishments; further, certain targets are selected due to logical reasons; for example, a house without a dog is more likely to be burglarized than one with a dog, a convenience store is more likely to be robbed if one cannot see in the window, and so on. Rational choice theories do not explain why certain individuals make criminal choices and others don't; in fact, an underlying premise is that anyone might commit a crime if he or she thought that it could be committed with benefit and no risk of punishment. Theorists have expanded the supposed calculation of potential criminals to include perceived risk of shame or guilt because studies have shown that this factor is highly associated with the inclination to commit crimes. However, this seems to go beyond the origins of rational choice theory because it depends on some type of relationship or non-rational factor (why else would one feel guilt or shame?).[12] Because some research has found that moral belief is more influential than measures of rational choice theory, such as fear of being caught, the idea that the decision to commit crime is made solely on the basis of reward and punishment is questionable.[13]

The correctional implications of the classical school and rational choice theories are not so much what happens to offenders once sentenced, but, rather, how to deter individuals from choosing to commit crime in the first place. One solution is to make targets less appealing; this is called target hardening. For instance, businesses can reduce the risk of being the target of burglaries or robberies by having well-lit parking lots and installing security cameras. Neighborhoods that increase lighting and reduce the number of abandoned buildings make it less likely that offenders will feel comfortable committing crimes there. Furthermore, in a world where so much activity is conducted online, we must know how to protect our online identities and reduce our risk of being a victim of crime by creating strong passwords and monitoring our various online accounts. Rational choice theory would also support publicizing punishments so that those tempted to commit crime will know what might happen to them if they are caught. More generally, the whole system of punishment is based on deterrence, which is consistent with rational choice theory. The idea is that if people fear punishment, they will be deterred from committing future crimes. However, the large percentage of individuals who commit new crimes after release from imprisonment or while on probation seems to call into question how effective deterrence is as a means of crime prevention.

Cesare Lombroso was a famous Italian criminologist and physician, and founder of the Positivist School of Criminology.

A very different approach from the classical school's rational choice approach is one that sees criminals as fundamentally different from law-abiding people. In the 1800s, the **positivist school of criminology** emerged. Cesare Lombroso (1825–1909), an Italian doctor-researcher, is referred to as the "Grandfather of Criminology." Seeking to understand why some people were criminals, he was strongly influenced by Darwinian theory, which had gained acceptance during this time.[14] Lombroso espoused the theory that there were "born criminals" with genetic defects that indicated they were less evolved than non-criminals. Lombroso also believed that there were other types of criminals, such as opportunistic offenders and those whose crimes were influenced by passion. The born criminal group was the smallest according to Lombroso. The important difference between the classical and positivist schools was that positivists saw criminals as different from law-abiding people. See the Focus on History box for a historical description of how positivist criminology influenced corrections.

Biological Theories of Crime

The positivist school of criminology is the historical antecedent of any theory that sees offenders as fundamentally different from law-abiding citizens. For instance, biological theories of crime are much more sophisticated than Lombroso's "born criminal" idea, but the concept remains that there are physical differences between individuals that may increase the risk of criminality. Some of the elements explored include differences in levels of neurotransmitters in the brain, specifically dopamine and serotonin, which lead to behavioral effects. Other factors that may affect criminal decision making include testosterone (associated with aggression), oxytocin (associated with trust), and monoamine oxidase (associated with sensation seeking and impulsivity). Research continues to explore whether these neural hormones may create a greater predisposition toward personality traits that influence behavioral choices leading to delinquency and criminality.[15]

As we have previously discussed, one of the most obvious patterns of crime is the fact that men commit more crime than women, especially violent crime. In Chapter 3, we will discuss the gender disparity of criminal sentencing, referring to the vastly disproportionate numbers of men in the correctional system as compared to women, and evidence of whether gender bias leads to women receiving lenient sentencing. While differential sentencing may explain part of the gender disparity in correctional populations, there is clearly a different behavioral pattern between men and women in their inclination to make criminal choices.

FOCUS ON

HISTORY

POSITIVISM AT BEDFORD HILLS

One of the earliest prisons for women was Bedford Hills in New York, which began as a reformatory in 1901. Interestingly, it was also a place of early research on female offenders by female researchers, a highly unusual occurrence in the early 1900s. The first Superintendent of Bedford Hills was Katharine Davis, who was the first woman to earn a Ph.D. in political science from the University of Chicago. She began to conduct psychological testing of the female inmates in order to determine which inmates were amenable to correctional treatment. She also established the Laboratory of Social Hygiene, a research center within the prison, and hired Jean Weidensall, another Ph.D. from the University of Chicago, to direct it.

The researchers compared female inmates to working-class women using tests of intelligence, skill, mechanical ability, memory, pain, and fatigue. They were also compared in terms of height, weight, hearing, visual acuity, emotional stability, and other measures. The research showed female offenders, on average, to be inferior to the law-abiding women in almost every measure. This research was heavily influenced by Darwinian notions and Lombroso's idea that criminals were biologically different from the law-abiding. Weidensall published her findings in a book entitled *The Mentality of Criminal Women*, published in 1916. Historians note that eugenics motivated such research, with the goal being to determine which inmates were mentally or morally defective and prevent them from having children. It is also true, however, that the research on female offenders showed that many came from extremely dysfunctional backgrounds characterized by poverty, homelessness, alcoholism, early pregnancy from incest and rape, and other life events that are common even today among female offender populations. Bedford Hills' additional focus on environmental factors of crime causation led to advocacy for education and to vocational training for positions other than domestic service for female inmates.

Discussion Questions:

1. If criminality was inherited, what correctional alternatives would be effective?

2. What correctional alternatives follow from the finding that lack of education and economic opportunity leads to crime?

Sources:

E. Fitzpatrick, *Endless Crusade: Women Social Scientists and Progressive Reform*, (Boston, MA: Oxford University Press, 1994).

E. Freedman, *Their Sisters' Keepers: Women's Prison Reforms in America, 1830–1930* (Ann Arbor, MI: University of Michigan Press, 1974).

T. McCarthy, *New York City's Suffragist Commissioner: Correction's Katherine Bement-Davis* (New York, NY: New York City Department of Correction, 1997). Accessed December 10, 2018, www.correctionhistory.org/html/chronicl/pdf/kbd01.pdf.

N. Rafter, *Partial Justice: State Prisons and Their Inmates, 1800–1935* (Boston, MA: Northeastern University Press, 1985).

J. Weidensall, *The Mentality of Criminal Women* (Baltimore: Warwick & York, 1916).

Brain chemical differences between men and women have been suggested as at least partially explaining this gender differential. Men have more testosterone, they are more likely to suffer from learning disabilities, they are more impulsive, and they have a different biological ability to feel the effects of oxytocin, the so-called moral molecule that seemingly affects an individual's ability to trust and feel a part of a group.[16] Researchers who argue that these physical differences between men and women increase the likelihood of men making criminal choices explain that learning social norms utilizes the same processes as learning to read; therefore, learning disabilities may impact prosocial decision making. Impulsivity is a personality trait that has long been associated with criminal behavior. Trust in others and group belongingness are associated with oxytocin and are related to prosocial behaviors such as greater generosity and altruism, characteristics that would impede decisions to commit crime.

Biological theorists also agree that socialization and postnatal influences dramatically affect the potential for criminality. For instance, attentive parenting, specifically interaction and communication with a child, may positively affect the development of neural functioning. Research shows that female infants and girls receive more cuddling and other forms of contact than their male siblings and peers. It is not clear why caregivers treat males and females differently, but the behavioral differences between the sexes would seem to arise through *both* biological and child-rearing differences.[17] Another way that the environment and biology interact is that constant stress (from neglect or abuse) eventually "shuts down" the body's normal responses to stress, and the autonomic nervous system becomes nonreactive to fear and anxiety; this occurs with both boys and girls, but there may also be sex differences in reactivity. The possible effect might be hypo-reactivity (not responding) to mild stressors but hyper-reactivity (overreacting) to severe stressors.[18]

Psychological Theories of Crime

Psychological theories of crime causation might also be placed under the positivist tradition since they also assume that offenders and law-abiding people are different in some way. The field of psychology has identified what are known as the "Big Five" personality traits, with related traits. The "Big Five" are

1. openness (to experiences);
2. conscientiousness (e.g., dutifulness and dependability);
3. extraversion (e.g., sociability and stimulation seeking);
4. agreeableness (including compassion and cooperativeness); and
5. neuroticism (e.g., anxiousness and emotional instability).

Of these, extraversion, impulsivity, aggressiveness, sensation seeking, and others have been associated with delinquency/criminality. Traits that have been directly correlated with delinquency and criminal behavior are aggression, impulsiveness, risk taking, dishonesty, and emotional negativity.[19] It should be noted that these psychological traits are influenced by the biological factors discussed earlier. For instance, lower serotonin levels are associated with negative emotionality and impulsivity.[20] Two traits identified as strongly associated with criminality are stimulation seeking and low self-control. Both may be implicated by biological elements.[21]

The terms *psychopathy* and *sociopathy* are used less frequently today, and the diagnosis of "antisocial personality disorder" has largely replaced the older terms; however, these diagnoses have been associated with criminality. One diagnostic tool known as Hare's Psychopathy Checklist, for instance, includes such descriptors as superficial charm, grandiose sense of self-worth, pathological lying, conning/manipulativeness, lack of remorse or guilt, parasitic life style, poor behavioral controls, early behavior problems, impulsivity, juvenile delinquency, and so on. A person with these traits would have no conscience and be unable to form sincere, affectionate bonds with others. Whether such characteristics are due to innate biological traits or dysfunctional upbringing has not been resolved. It is also not inevitable that such an individual would necessarily be a criminal or that all offenders have antisocial personality disorder. However, we can be confident that we are more likely to find these individuals in the ranks of a prison population rather than in the Boy Scouts.

Current psychological theorists identify characteristics of the immediate environment and individual characteristics to explain crime choices. They focus specifically on the traits of low self-control/impulsivity, stimulus seeking, and negative emotionality (a feeling that one has been mistreated).[22] They point to the attitudes, values, beliefs, and rationalizations held by a person with regard to antisocial behavior, social support for antisocial behavior (perceived support from others), a history of having engaged in antisocial behavior, self-management and problem-solving skills, and other stable personality characteristics conducive to antisocial conduct. Then they relate these to a behavioral explanation of criminality where rewards and costs of crime are mediated by these individual differences.

A long line of psychological research has identified differences between female and male offenders, finding that female offenders are more likely to come from extremely dysfunctional backgrounds. Since there seems to be more cultural support for delinquency/criminality for boys and men, this finding makes sense, in that a dysfunctional upbringing may overcome cultural influences working against females' decisions to commit crime.[23]

The focus of the positivist approach is on the criminal self, as opposed to societal factors that may be criminogenic. The correctional policy implication of Lombroso's idea of "born criminals" would have been merely incapacitation, since there was no expectation that the offender could behave in any other way. In later eras, however, a positivist approach would be consistent with anything done to reform or change an offender that focuses on individual reasons for criminal choices, for example addiction, personality traits, or learning disabilities.

The Chicago School of Criminology

While the classical school focused on legal systems and how they can deter rational people from choosing crime, and the positivist school focused on individual differences between the offender and the law-abiding, the **Chicago School of criminology**, emerging from early sociologists at the University of Chicago, focused on societal influences on crime. In the 1930s, University of Chicago sociologists observed that crime occurred more often in "interstitial zones" of the city. These were mixed zones of residential, commercial, and industrial activity characterized by low home ownership, property damage, graffiti, high rates of alcoholism, domestic violence, and mental health problems.

Community gardens are examples of how to improve social efficacy. Crime flourishes in socially disorganized communities.

The social support and social disorganization theories that emerged in the late 1980s and 1990s closely resemble the early Chicago School in their observations and presumptions that certain areas of cities are criminogenic. **Social support theories** predict that strong families and other social organizations (such as school and neighborhood associations) provide support and informal social control to individuals, thus reducing crime/delinquency. **Social disorganization theories** predict that the lack of informal social controls is often associated with higher racial income inequality, poverty, and low occupational status. Social disorganization is measured by such factors as low socioeconomic status, residential mobility, racial heterogeneity, family disruption, weak or nonexistent local social organizations, weak local friendship networks, low organizational participation, and unsupervised teenage groups. The result is higher rates of delinquency and crime.[24] The idea is that individual differences do not cause crime so much as the misfortune of being born into a criminogenic community.

Cultural Deviance Theory

The Chicago School diverged into two lines of explanation for crime causation. The first noted that there was a different culture in some areas of the city whereby crime was not stigmatized; this was known as **cultural deviance theory**. In the 1930s and 1940s, Chicago criminologists Clifford Shaw and Henry D. McKay believed that a criminal culture was transmitted in the interstitial zone.[25] Individuals are socialized within a deviant subculture in the same manner as socialization occurs within a dominant culture. In a deviant subculture, criminality is acceptable according to the cultural deviance theory. Edwin Sutherland, one of the most influential American criminologists, first introduced the theory of **differential association** in 1939, describing it as the mechanism by which culture was transmitted; basically, those who grew up learning that criminal behavior was appropriate would be criminal, and those who grew up with the notion that law-abiding behavior was appropriate would be law-abiding.[26] Criminals learned not only the "how-to" of crime, but also the rationalizations and belief systems that supported the idea that crime was acceptable. Frequency, duration, priority, and intensity of associations affected the likelihood of delinquency. In other words, one's family and friends were more influential than outsiders such as school officials in determining whether a youth grew up to be criminal.[27]

A later version of differential association theory added social learning concepts such as modeling (we learn by patterning our behavior after those we look up to) and reinforcement (we adopt values and behaviors that are rewarded), but the basic idea remained that the strength of criminal values and behavior depended on the frequency and intensity of criminal associations. This theory explains the gender differential (the fact that women are much less likely to be arrested for crimes) through the idea that girls and women are more likely to absorb messages that indicate criminal behavior is not appropriate for them.[28] The most recent formulations of the differential association/learning theory include structural elements (e.g., age, gender, community, poverty) that mediate social learning variables (e.g., differential reinforcement, peer associations, opportunities, and individual factors).[29] Some research has indicated that social learning variables are more powerful influences on criminal decision making than structural factors, such as poverty.[30]

The correctional implications of cultural deviance theory and differential association theory would be to increase the number and intensity of prosocial messages and relationships so that young people would absorb the messages of law-abidingness rather than delinquency/criminality. Any type of gang intervention, Big Brother/Big Sister program, "midnight basketball" programs, or mentoring programs are based on the idea that prosocial role models will transmit cultural messages that counteract criminogenic influences. Learning theory tells us, however, that frequency and intensity of messaging makes a difference; thus, if family members and close peers are criminal, it is difficult to counteract that influence through any type of program with limited contact. Ironically, what we often do to criminal offenders is to lock them up with other offenders, which would seem to be in direct conflict with what social learning theory tells us to do. In fact, prisons have been called "schools of crime" because offenders learn criminal values and rationalizations from each other.

Economic Opportunity and Strain Theories

The second major theory to emerge from the Chicago School proposed that lack of economic opportunities led to crime. Thomas Merton (1910–2003) was an American sociologist who is known for his theories on the sociology of science, mass communication, and the structure of society. In the late 1930s, he developed a theory known as anomie theory, strain theory, or opportunity theory. We will refer to it as **strain-opportunity theory**. It explains how some youths, especially in the interstitial zones of cities, are blocked from using legitimate means, such as employment, education, family connections, or talent, to achieve financial and social success. This leads to strain and normlessness (**anomie**) and some type of adaptation: conformity, ritualism, retreatism, rebellion, or innovation.[31] *Conformity* refers to those youth who accept societal goals and "go through the motions" by trying to achieve success through education and/or hard work. *Ritualism* also refers to those who "go through the motions" expected of them, but without truly internalizing or caring about the goals of society. On the other hand, youths reacting to strain and normlessness may adapt by way of *retreatism*, rejecting goals and means, perhaps through drug abuse or retreating from society entirely, and *rebellion*, violently rejecting societal goals and means. The fifth form of adaptation, according to Merton, is *innovation*, which refers to accepting societal definitions of success but using innovative and/or illegitimate means to achieve success. His quintessential example was the American gangster who achieved financial success, and sometimes societal acceptance, through crime.

In the 1950s, criminologist Albert Cohen (1918–2014), merged cultural deviance theory and strain theory into a class-based theory of delinquency.[32] According to Cohen, boys who felt blocked from economic opportunities banded together into lower-class gangs to protect their self-respect and engaged in antisocial activity that affirmed their toughness and masculinity with a subcultural value system that rejected societal definitions that would label them as failures. In this theory, gangs and a lower-class culture that values instant gratification over delayed gratification are the result of blocked economic opportunities.

In the 1960s, American sociologists Richard Cloward (1926–2001) and Lloyd Ohlin (1918–2008) developed **differential opportunity theory**.[33] The theory describes how some boys have access to legitimate economic opportunities and group together (e.g., Boys Club), some have access to illegitimate opportunities (e.g., organized crime or gang activity) and group together, and some are blocked from both avenues: this latter group of boys also band together and engage in more uncontrolled criminal activity.

The theory supported the notion that legitimate economic opportunities would prevent crime, and Cloward and Ohlin became advisors in President Johnson's "war on poverty" program efforts in the 1960s. In Merton's theory and Cloward and Ohlin's differential opportunity theory, any form of job training or employment program should reduce criminal choices. This is still the foundation for many correctional programs, including education, vocational training, and job placement programs, in prison or in the community.

Robert Agnew developed **general strain theory** in the 1980s, reformulating Merton's original strain theory to include other sources of strain in addition to the lack of economic opportunities.[34] According to general strain theory, strain occurs whenever (a) individuals fail to achieve positively valued goals, (b) there is a removal of something that is positively valued (e.g., through divorce or death), or (c) there are negative/noxious experiences (e.g., victimization, child abuse). These strains create a negative affective state of anger or frustration that leads to the pressure for corrective action. If coping skills or resources are available, the affective state does not result in delinquency/crime, but if they are not available, delinquency/crime results. In later developments of the theory, Agnew has said that strain is more likely to result in delinquency when the events creating the strain are perceived as unjust; the severity/magnitude, duration, recentness, and centrality of the strain is also important. He also has incorporated low self-control (strain from erratic parental discipline) and high self-control (strain due to parental expectations) into his theory, spurring some to criticize that the theory includes so many factors that it is difficult to use it to predict criminality or to develop crime prevention programs or correctional policy. Researchers do find correlations between measures of strain and measures of delinquency/criminality, although social-control and social-learning variables are significant too.

The correctional implications of general strain theory are more complicated than the original strain theory since there are so many factors identified; however, the general idea is that if individuals can either reduce their strains or improve their coping abilities, they are less likely to make criminal choices. We will examine cognitive behavioral programs later on in Chapter 11. These programs help offenders identify situational cues and thinking patterns that lead to criminal choices. Offenders learn how to make better choices when faced with obstacles, and these programs are consistent with general strain theory.

The theories that identify economic obstacles as the reason for criminal choices don't explain the gender differential in crime commission very well because both men and women experience blocked economic opportunities. Research indicates the levels of strain experienced by males and females do not fully explain the gender differential in crime rates.[35] These theories do predict that crime is more likely to occur in economically depressed neighborhoods, and official arrest figures support this prediction. However, one might argue that the only reason formal arrest figures include disproportionate numbers of poor people is that the crimes of rich people are more difficult to investigate and punish. In other words, it may be that the major difference between a poor criminal and a criminal who is not poor is the type of crime chosen (e.g., robbery versus fraud or Ponzi schemes).

Social Control Theories

In the late 1960s, criminologist Travis Hirschi (1935–2017) produced one of the most well-known theories of delinquency by focusing on why people did *not* commit crime instead of why people did.[36] His theory, **social control theory** (or what has been called bond theory or social bond theory), stated that most of us are controlled by our bonds to society through attachment, commitment, involvement, and belief. However, the delinquent or criminal is not controlled by these bonds—they have weak attachments to others (e.g., parents); they have no commitment to future success; they are less involved in such activities as school, work, athletics, and church; and they do not have a strong belief system that accepts the basic goals, rules, and laws of society. Research has found that delinquents score lower on these measures; however, research also showed that low bonds coupled with an association with delinquent peers are more likely to lead

Strong social bonds (attachment), such as the bond between a parent and child, are believed to be associated with conformity and negatively correlated with delinquency.

to delinquency than either factor separately. Control theory does seem to be supported by what we know about crime correlates: female adolescents generally have stronger levels of attachment to adult figures and peers than male adolescents and, as individuals age and are more likely to acquire attachments such as spouses and children, they are less likely to commit crimes.[37]

Abandoning his social control theory, Hirschi, along with criminologist Michael Gottfredson, proposed in the **general theory of crime** that individuals are raised to have either higher or lower levels of self-control, and those with low self-control are more likely to commit all types of crimes.[38] They reject the idea that there are different types of criminals, arguing that all criminals are generalists who commit a wide variety of crimes. They described low self-control types as those who lacked diligence; were adventuresome, active, and physical; and could not delay gratification. They would also be more likely to drive fast, smoke, gamble, have illegitimate children, and abuse drugs and alcohol. Low self-control types tended to be self-centered, indifferent, or insensitive to the suffering and needs of others.[39] Many studies have identified an association between these activities and criminal activity, and between other measures of low self-control and crime; however, there is also strong criticism that the theory does not explain white collar crime, organized crime, or the crime differential between men and women.[40] The researchers specifically rejected biological causation, pointing to ineffective parenting as the cause of low self-control.

The correctional implication of social control theory is to increase bonds with others. Youth programs, sports, youth groups at church, parenting programs or family stabilization programs, and other efforts to increase and improve social bonds are consistent with this theory. Increasing the beliefs of youth that they have a future through stay-in-school programs, scholarships, and tutoring programs are also consistent with this theory. For adult offender populations, social control theory would support enhanced visitation programs and support programs for achieving stable employment and family reunification because any bonds to society reduce the likelihood of re-offending.

The correctional implications of the general theory of crime, which points solely to low self-control, is to develop self-control in offenders through some program in which they can gradually develop good habits. Preventing children from growing up with low self-control by investing in parenting programs to teach people appropriate discipline and child-rearing practices would be consistent with this crime theory. The child protective system might also be considered as congruent with these theories if one assumes that a child is better off in the care of the state than their own parent(s).

Labeling Theory

The idea that our interactions with others shape our perceptions of self and our behaviors is known as **symbolic interactionism**, upon which labeling theory relies. According to **labeling theory**, everyone commits primary deviance (small offenses early in life), but only some get labeled and stigmatized; the deviant commits secondary deviance in reaction to this labeling and stigmatization after the deviant label is incorporated into their identity.[41] The implication for correctional policy is somewhat problematic with this theory in that it postulates that it is best not to stigmatize primary deviance, based on the assumption that the individual will then not advance to secondary deviance. Zero tolerance and delinquency programs are very inconsistent with this theory because they isolate and identify those who commit minor acts of deviance. Reducing the use of institutional corrections for juveniles, pretrial diversion, and other programs that reduce contact with the criminal justice system would be consistent with this theory.

Summary of Crime Theories and Correctional Policies

Crime policies and correctional interventions are based explicitly or implicitly on one or more of the theories we have discussed. Table 2.3 offers a list of the crime theories described previously alongside the correctional policies that would be supported by such theories.

Crime theories seem to be developed to explain "street" crime, such as robbery, burglary, drug crimes, and theft, rather than what might be called "suite" crimes, such as embezzlement, stock market swindles, consumer frauds, political crimes, and toxic waste dumping.[42] Because of this focus, most of what is done in the name of crime prevention and corrections is oriented toward the first type of offender.

Are There Different Types of Criminals?

Most theories of crime do not specify a specific type of criminal, and a few, such as the general theory of crime, explicitly say the theory explains all crime, and all criminals' choices. Others have found evidence that there are differences in patterns of criminality over the lifespan and between offenders. **Longitudinal research** follows cohorts (a group of people with something in common, e.g., born in a certain year) over many years to identify how life events affect the individual. Life-course or integrated theories have emerged from this research; these show that there are, indeed, different types of offenders, at least in the pattern of their offending. Because longitudinal research is very expensive (some studies follow the cohort for decades and collect data every few years), there are not many of these studies. The studies that have been done oversample urban youth, males, and those in high-crime neighborhoods.

The findings from various longitudinal studies identify certain variables that do seem to predict a higher risk of criminal activity (at least as measured by official arrests). In childhood, these include having many siblings, poverty, a one-parent household, poor supervision, harsh and erratic parenting, criminal parents, school problems, and delinquent friends. In adulthood, these include

| TABLE 2.3 | Crime Theories, Causations, and Correctional Policies |

THEORY	CRIME CAUSATION	CORRECTIONAL POLICY
Classical school of criminology	Rational choice based on perceived risk versus benefit	Deterrence by threatened punishment
Rational choice theory	Rational choice based on perceived risk versus benefit	Deterrence by "target hardening"
Positivist school of criminology	Characteristic of criminal causes them to commit crime	Depends on difference identified as criminogenic
Born criminal theory	Genetic	Incapacitation
Biological theories of crime	Genetic or not, various biological differences predispose some to criminal choice	Address the biological difference through intervention (either pharmacological or learning)
Psychological theories of crime; sociopathy/psychopathy	Biology/childhood experiences	Therapy
Chicago school of criminology	Neighborhood culture	Urban renewal programs
Social disorganization/social support theories	Lack of positive interactions, disintegrating social control	Poverty programs, community policing
Cultural deviance theory	Deviant culture is transmitted	Anti-gang programs
Differential association theory	Transmission of pro-deviant messages through interactions with others	Youth programs, such as Big Brother/Big Sister, Boy and Girl Scouts
Strain-opportunity and differential opportunity theories	Lack of legitimate opportunities leads to criminal choices	Job programs, education, vocational training
General strain theory	Inability to cope with negative events; anger and frustration leads to delinquency/crime	Therapy to improve coping skills
Social control theory (also known as bond or social bond theory)	Lack of social bonds (involvement, attachment, belief, commitment) leads to delinquency	Sports, after-school programs, any youth programs, family strengthening
General theory of crime	Low self-control because of poor parenting	Parenting programs, correctional programs to improve self-control
Labeling theory	Stigmatization of primary deviance leads to secondary deviance	Limit official recognition and stigma related to punishment

a lack of bonds (job, marriage, school). Characteristics of those who were more likely to be offenders included difficult temperament, hyperactivity/impulsiveness, risk taking, overt or covert conduct problems, overt or covert aggressiveness, withdrawal, poor peer relationships, academic problems, association with deviant peers, difficulty mastering tasks, and trouble negotiating conflict. Some longitudinal researchers identified biological factors (e.g., difficult temperament due to neurophysiology) as interacting with environmental factors (e.g., poor parenting) to increase the risk of delinquency/offending.[43] Some research indicates about 10 percent of all children can be identified as "difficult" in infancy, with characteristics such as intense reactions to stimuli, a generally negative mood, slowness in adapting to change, and irregularities in sleep, hunger, and other bodily functions. These children are more likely to develop conduct disorder issues with tantrums and problematic behaviors. If the child is born into an environment of poor parenting with erratic discipline, the risk of delinquency is high.[44]

Another finding of longitudinal studies was that many of the participants moved out of delinquency as they got married and/or became employed or joined the military; however, if there was a divorce or period of unemployment, criminality was more likely to begin again. Thus, the well-established maturation effect, referring to the fact that most criminals reduce their criminality after age 35, has been more directly tied to jobs, marriages, and children. Several studies identified a small number of offenders who began their crimes early and became chronic offenders who did not reduce their criminal activities as they got older to the same extent as others. For most offenders, delinquency reached its highest level in the late teens and early 20s and then dropped off; however, this other smaller group persisted in their criminality. The idea that there are certain offender groups who persist in offending throughout the life course and are "career criminals" is not without critics. Opposing groups of criminologists have disagreed as to the existence of a career criminal group, partly because of the policy implication that these individuals, once identified, should be selectively incarcerated, and, possibly, may be incapable of change.[45] Whether this smaller group could be identified with any certainty is also problematic.[46]

In all delinquent groups, males outnumber females, but this is especially so in the early onset, chronic group of offenders.[47] Gender-specific pathways research, emerging in the late 1980s and 1990s, was somewhat similar to longitudinal research in that these researchers identified sex-specific life events that pushed some girls/women into delinquency/crime. Specifically, this research focuses on the greater likelihood of girls to be subject to childhood victimization that leads to running away, high-risk sexual activity, early pregnancy and single motherhood, drug use, and crime.[48]

Integrated theories look at a wide range of factors, including biological and environmental. These theories are also life-phase-specific. Latent traits (biological predispositions/traits, such as low cognitive functioning) and primary caregivers influence the likelihood of crime, especially in poor surroundings. During school-age years, these latent traits can lead to delinquency through failure, rejection, and labeling; delinquent peers then become important in reinforcing and increasing delinquent behaviors. As the individual matures, bonds such as a job and marriage can reduce or eliminate criminal choices, but the absence of these bonds can lead to a second spurt of criminality in one's thirties. Other researchers have identified predisposing factors (low family socioeconomic status, family size, family disruption, residential mobility, parents' deviance, household crowding, being foreign born, mother's employment), and individual factors (difficult temperament, persistent tantrums, early conduct disorder), which interact with social control processes (family, lack of supervision, threatening/erratic harsh discipline, parental rejection, school, weak attachment, poor performance, delinquent influence, peer delinquent attachment, sibling delinquent attachment), leading to delinquency, which, in turn, damages social bonds and reduces the likelihood of employment and strong family ties.[49]

In the Focus on the Offender box, what theory seems to best explain the criminality of the individual described? What correctional option might be best suited to deter and/or rehabilitate the offender?

FOCUS ON THE OFFENDER

DRUGS AND ECONOMIC STRAIN

While we know drug abuse and addiction are related to crimes other than drug possession and sales, not all drug dealers become involved in crime because they are addicted. A news story explained how one man saw drugs as a way out of economic stress. Donel Clark grew up in a southeast Dallas neighborhood. He was known as a "square" who didn't do drugs or drink alcohol, went to church regularly, and worked. A few years after high school, he was married and working two jobs. He and his wife had a son and bought a house. He was also supporting his wife's child from a previous relationship and his child from a prior girlfriend. Clark was then fired from one job; the second job disappeared too because the owner sold the liquor store where Clark worked. Needing to pay his bills, Clark asked a former high-school classmate and known drug dealer for a job. The drug dealer tried to dissuade him, but Clark persisted. He began to package drugs and supervised those who cooked crack cocaine, making $1,000 a week. About a year and a half later, he was arrested. At trial, he was convicted of conspiracy with intent to distribute 50 kilos of cocaine, using the phone to commit a felony, and manufacturing cocaine near a school because one member of the conspiracy lived within 1,000 feet of one. At 29 years old, Clark was sentenced to 35 years in prison.

Questions for Discussion

1. Which theory of crime best explains Mr. Clark's decision to become involved in crime?

2. What would be the best crime prevention approach to deter individuals like Mr. Clark from becoming involved in crime?

Source: S. Horwitz, "Slow Steps to Freedom," Washington Post, October 6, 2015, http://www.washingtonpost.com/sf/national/2015/10/07/out-of-federal-prison-slow-steps-to-freedom/?tid=a_inl&utm_term=.bdbb7ea7c6f1.

Summary

- Three measures of crime are the Uniform Crime Reports (reports to police collected and presented by the FBI), arrest numbers (also provided to and collected by the FBI), and victimization surveys. The third measure of crime comes from the National Crime Victimization Survey and is available on the Bureau of Justice Statistics website.

- All measures of crime have recorded major declines since about the mid-1990s; property crime began falling even earlier.

- Researchers estimate that incarceration affected crime declines by only about 10 percent. Increased police numbers, community policing, and decreased use of alcohol in the population at large were also influential. Other explanations have been offered, but there is little evidence that these have had any appreciable influence. These include aging baby boomers, stabilization of drug markets, "zero tolerance" policing, reduction of exposure to lead-based paint, and increased numbers of abortions beginning in the late 1970s.

- The most frequent arrests are for drug violations and, of those, marijuana possession is the most frequent drug violation. There are many more property crimes than violent crimes.

- Young men are responsible for most crimes, except for forgery/fraud and embezzlement, where arrests are about evenly divided between men and women.

- Whites account for over 70 percent of all arrests. Blacks are disproportionately arrested, especially for violent crimes, compared to their percentage of the population; however, arrests of Hispanics are roughly proportional to their percentage of the population. We must always keep in mind that the number of arrests, as a measure of crime, is problematic because it also measures the decisions of formal actors (police) in decisions to arrest.

- Crime theories explain crime as based on rational choice (the classical school of criminology and rational choice theory) or on individual differences (the positivist school of criminology, biological theories, psychological theories, general theory of crime, and general strain theory).

- Sociological theories of crime look at elements of society as criminogenic (the Chicago School of criminology, social disorganization and social support theories, cultural deviance theory, and strain theory).

- Some theories point to both individual differences and societal factors (e.g., social bond theory, learning theory, and differential association theory).

- Each type of theory supports some type of correctional response; for instance, rational choice theory supports deterrence policies such as longer terms of prison for more serious crimes; social bond theory promotes after-school and athletic programs; and strain theory dictates that crime can be prevented by increasing economic opportunities, and so on.

PROJECTS

1. Go to the website for the Bureau of Justice Statistics data analysis tool (https://www.bjs.gov/index.cfm?ty=nvat). Go to the tab called "Custom Tables" and create a table of victimization rates for the last five years for violent or property victimization using at least two variables.

2. Browse the news for the last week or so, find a story about a criminal, and determine which, if any, of the theories presented in this chapter explain why the person made criminal choices.

NOTES

1. A. Baker, "19 Bronx Officers Distorted Crime Data, Police Say," *New York Times*, July 18, 2015, A17; J. Eterno, A. Verma, and E. Silverman, "Police Manipulations of Crime Reporting: Insiders' Revelations," *Justice Quarterly*, 33, 5 (2016): 811–35.; R. Parascandola, "NYPD Report Supports Claims by Adrian Schoolcraft, Cop Whistleblower," *New York Daily News*, March 7, 2012, accessed December 10, 2018, https://www.nydailynews.com/news/nypd-report-supports-claims-adrian-schoolcraft-whistleblower-article-1.1035037.

2. J. Gramlich, "Voters' Perceptions of Crime Continue to Conflict with Reality," Pew Research Center, November 16, 2016, accessed December 10, 2018, http://www.pewresearch.org/fact-tank/2016/11/16/voters-perceptions-of-crime-continue-to-conflict-with-reality/; A. Grawert and J. Cullen, *Crime in 2017: A Preliminary Analysis* (New York City, NY: Brennan Center for Justice, September 6, 2017), accessed December 10, 2018, https://www.brennancenter.org/publication/crime-2017-preliminary-analysis.

3. A. Grawert and J. Cullen, *Crime in 2017: A Preliminary Analysis* (New York City, NY: Brennan Center for Justice, September 6, 2017).

4. A. Cipriano, "An Unprecedented Crime Spike Reported for 2020," The Crime Report, February 1, 2021, accessed February 12, 2021, https://thecrimereport.org/2021/02/01/unprecedented-violent-crime-spike-reported-for-2020/.

5. See O. Roeder, L. Eisen, and J. Bowling, "What Caused the Crime Decline?" (New York City, NY: Brennan Center for Justice, 2015), accessed December 10, 2018, https://www.brennancenter.org/publication/what-caused-crime-decline.

6. O. Roeder, L. Eisen, and J. Bowling, "What Caused the Crime Decline?" (New York City, NY: Brennan Center for Justice, 2015); Bureau of Justice Statistics, Corrections Statistics Analysis Tool—Prisoners), http://www.bjs.gov/index.cfm?ty=nps.

7. O. Roeder, L. Eisen, and J. Bowling, "What Caused the Crime Decline?" (New York City, NY: Brennan Center for Justice, 2015).

8. P. Sharkey, G. Torrats-Espinosa, and D. Takyar, "Community and the Crime

Decline: The Causal Effect of Local Nonprofits on Violent Crime" American Sociological Review, 82, 6 (2017). Also, see E. Badger, "The Unsung Role That Ordinary Citizens Played in the Great Crime Decline," *New York Times*. November 9, 2017, accessed December 10, 2018, https://www.nytimes.com/2017/11/09/upshot/the-unsung-role-that-ordinary-citizens-played-in-the-great-crime-decline.html?ref=collection%2Fsectioncollection%2Fus&action=click&contentCollection=us&region=stream&module=stream_unit&version=latest&contentPlacement=5&pgtype=sectionfront&_r=0.

9. FBI, *Crime in the United States, 2019*, Table 33.

10. United States Census, 2016, https://www.census.gov/quickfacts/fact/table/US/PST045217.

11. J. Bentham, "The Rationale of Punishment," in *Ethical Choice: A Case Study Approach*, edited by R. Beck and J. Orr (New York, NY: Free Press, 1843/1970), 326–40.

12. H. Grasmick, and R. Bursik, "Conscience, Significant Others, and Rational Choice: Extending the Deterrence Model," *Law and Society Review* 24 (1990): 837–62; H. Grasmick, R. Bursik, and K. Kinsey, "Shame and Embarrassment as Deterrents to Non-compliance with the Law: The Case of an Anti-littering Campaign," *Environment and Behavior* 23, 2(1991): 233–51; S. Tibbetts, "Differences Between Women and Men Regarding Decisions to Commit Test Cheating," *Research in Higher Education* 40, 3 (1999): 323–42.

13. A. Piquero and S. Tibbetts, "Specifying the Direct and Indirect Effects of Low Self-control and Situational Factors in Offenders' Decision Making: Toward a More Complete Model of Rational Offending," *Justice Quarterly*, 13 (1996): 481–510.

14. C. Lombroso and W. Ferrero, *The Criminal Man* (New York: Appleton, 1975/1972).

15. For a review of biological theories, see J. Wright, K. Beaver, M. DeLisi, M. Vaughn, D. Boisvert, and J. Vaske, "Lombroso's Legacy: The Miseducation of Criminologists," *Journal of Criminal Justice Education*, 19, 3 (2008): 325–38. Other sources include: J. Barnes, K. Beaver, and B. Boutwell, "Examining the Genetic Underpinnings to Moffitt's Developmental Taxonomy: A Behavioral Genetic Analysis," *Criminology* 49 (2011): 923–54; K. Beaver, "Genetic Influences on Being Processed through the Criminal Justice System: Results from a Sample of Adoptees," *Biological Psychiatry* 69 (2011): 282–87; P. Zak, *The Moral Molecule* (New York: Dutton, 2012).

16. T. Moffitt, A. Caspi, M. Rutter, and P. Silva, *Sex Differences in Antisocial Behavior: Conduct Disorder, Delinquency, and Violence in the Dunedin Longitudinal Study* (Cambridge, UK: Cambridge University Press, 2001); A. Walsh, "Genetic and Cytogenetic Intersex Anomalies: Can They Help us to Understand Gender Differences in Deviant Behavior?" *International Journal of Offender Therapy and Comparative Criminology* 39 (1995): 151–66; J. Eysenck and G. Gudjonsson, *The Causes and Cures of Criminality* (New York: Plenum., 1989), 140.

17. E. Maccoby, "Social Groupings in Childhood: Their Relationship to Prosocial and Antisocial Behavior in Boys and Girls," in *Development of Antisocial and Prosocial Behavior: Theories, Research and Issues*, edited by D. Olweus, J. Block, and M. Radke-Yarrow (Orlando, FL: Academic Press, 1985), 263–85).

18. A. Walsh, *Intellectual Imbalance, Love Deprivation and Violent Delinquency: A Biosocial Perspective* (Springfield, IL: Charles C. Thomas, 1991), 80.

19. D. Andrews, and J. Bonta, *The Psychology of Criminal Conduct* (Cincinnati, OH: Anderson Publishing Company, 2010); A. Caspi, T. Moffitt, P. Silva, M. Stouthamer-Loeber, R. Krueger, and P. Schmutte. "Are Some People Crime-prone? Replications of the Personality–Crime Relationship Across Countries, Genders, Races, and Methods," *Criminology* 32 (1994): 163–95.

20. A. Raine, *The Psychopathology of Crime: Criminal Behavior as a Clinical Disorder* (San Diego, CA: Academic Press, 1993), 93.

21. D. Andrews and J. Bonta, *The Psychology of Criminal Conduct* (Cincinnati, OH: Anderson Publishing Company, 2010).

22. D. Andrews and J. Bonta, *The Psychology of Criminal Conduct* (Cincinnati, OH: Anderson Publishing Company, 2010).

23. For a review, see J. Pollock, *Women's Crimes, Criminology and Corrections* (Long Grove, IL: Waveland Press, 2014).

24. R. Sampson and W. Groves, "Community Structure and Crime: Testing Social-Disorganization Theory," *American Journal of Sociology* 94 (1989): 774–802; J. Byrne and R. Sampson (eds.), *The Social Ecology of Crime* (New York, NY: Springer-Verlag, 1986).

25. C. Shaw and H. McKay, *Juvenile Delinquency and Urban Areas* (Chicago, IL: University of Chicago Press, 1934/1972).

26. E. Sutherland and D. Cressey, *Principles of Criminology Revised* (Dix Hills, NY: General Hall, 1960/1992).

27. E. Sutherland and D. Cressey, *Principles of Criminology Revised* (Dix Hills, NY: General Hall, 1960/1992).

28. R. Burgess and R. Akers, "A Differential Association-Reinforcement Theory of Criminal Behavior," *Social Problems* 14 (1966): 128–47.

29. R. Akers, *Social Learning and Social Structure: A General Theory of Crime and Deviance* (Boston: Northeastern University Press, 2009).

30. G. Lee, R. Akers, and M. Borg, "Social Learning and Structural Factors in Adolescent Substance Use," *Western Criminology Review* 5, 1(2004): 17–34.

31. R. Merton, "Social Structure and Anomie," *American Sociological Review* 3, 6 (1938): 672–82.

32. A. Cohen, *Delinquency in Boys: The Culture of the Gang* (New York, NY: Free Press, 1955).

33. R. Cloward and L. Ohlin, *Delinquency and Opportunity* (New York, NY: Free Press, 1960).

34. R. Agnew, "A Revised Strain Theory of Delinquency," *Social Forces*, 64 (1985): 151–67; R. Agnew, *Pressured into Crime: An Overview of General Strain Theory* (Boston: Oxford University Press, 2005).

35. For a review, see J. Pollock, *Women's Crimes, Criminology and Corrections* (Long Grove, IL: Waveland Press, 2014).

36. T. Hirschi, *Causes of Delinquency* (Berkeley, CA: University of California Press, 1969).

37. J. Pollock, *Women's Crimes, Criminology and Corrections* (Long Grove, IL: Waveland Press, 2014).

38. M. Gottfredson and T. Hirschi, *A General Theory of Crime* (Stanford, CA: Stanford University Press, 1990).

39. M. Gottfredson and T. Hirschi, *A General Theory of Crime* (Stanford, CA: Stanford University Press, 1990).

40. See review in Pollock, *Women's Crimes, Criminology and Corrections* (Long Grove, IL: Waveland Press, 2014).

41. E. Lemert, *Social Pathology; A Systematic Approach to the Theory of Sociopathic Behavior* (New York: McGraw-Hill, 1951), 76.

42. For a discussion of political elements in crime control, see J. Hagan, *Who Are the Criminals? The Politics of Crime Policy* (Princeton, NJ: Princeton University Press, 2010).

43. T. Moffitt, "Life-course-persistent and Adolescence-limited Antisocial Behavior: A 10-Year Research Review and a Research Agenda," in *Causes of Conduct Disorder and Juvenile Delinquency*, edited by B.A. Lahey, T.E. Moffitt, and A. Caspi (New York: Guilford, 2003).

44. D. Andrews and J. Bonta, *The Psychology of Criminal Conduct* (Cincinnati, OH: Anderson Publishing Company, 2010).

45. J. Hagan, *Who Are the Criminals? The Politics of Crime Policy* (Princeton, NJ: Princeton University Press, 2010), 111.

46. J. Hagan, *Who Are the Criminals? The Politics of Crime Policy* (Princeton, NJ: Princeton University Press, 2010), 122.

47. Selected sources include: D. Farrington and D. West, "Criminal, Penal and Life Histories of Chronic Offenders: Risk and Protective Factors and Early Identification," *Criminal Behavior and Mental Health* 3(1993): 492–523; B. Kelley, R. Loeber, K. Keenan, and M. DeLamatre, *Developmental Pathways in Boys' Disruptive and Delinquent Behavior* (OJJDP Bulletin. Washington, DC: U.S. Dept. of Justice); D. Denno, *Biology and Violence: From Birth to Adulthood* (New York: Cambridge University Press, 1990); T. Moffitt, "Adolescence-limited and Life-course Persistent Antisocial Behavior: A Developmental Taxonomy," *Psychological Review* 100(1993): 674–701.

48. For review, see Pollock, *Women's Crimes, Criminology and Corrections* (Long Grove, IL: Waveland Press, 2014).

49. J. Laub, and R. Sampson, *Shared Beginnings, Divergent Lives: Delinquent Boys to Age 70* (Cambridge, MA: Harvard University Press, 2003).

Chapter 3

Sentencing

LEARNING OBJECTIVES

1. Identify the purposes and types of punishments utilized both historically and today.

2. Explain general and specific deterrence and whether research supports the effectiveness of punishment.

3. Discuss how sentencing for drug offenders has impacted state and federal prison populations.

4. Determine, from research, whether sentencing disparities exist by sex, race, and ethnicity.

5. Describe the recent sentencing reforms that have reduced or slowed the rate of incarceration.

CHAPTER OUTLINE

- The Purposes of Sentencing 58

- History of Sentencing 59

- Sentencing Statutes 64

- Sentencing Patterns 69

- Sentencing Disparity 74

- Changes in Sentencing 79

- SUMMARY 81

Judges and juries sentence offenders within the parameters of state or federal sentencing statutes.

KEY TERMS

Benefit of clergy
Chivalry hypothesis
Common Law
Comprehensive Crime
　　Control Act
Corporal punishment
Correctional supervision rate
Determinate sentencing
Fair Sentencing Act of 2010

Gaols
General deterrence
Good time
Harrison Act of 1914
Indeterminate sentencing
Mandatory minimum laws
Parole
Plea bargaining
Sentencing disparity

Sentencing Guidelines
Sentencing Reform Act
　　of 1984
Specific deterrence
Three-strikes laws/sentencing
　　(habitual offender laws)
Truth-in-sentencing laws
Violent Crime Control Law
　　Enforcement Act

The Purpose of Sentencing

The purposes of sentencing include retribution (punishment), reform and/or rehabilitation, and deterrence. Historically, retribution and deterrence were the only purposes of punishment. There are two kinds of deterrence: **general deterrence** is what is done to one person so that others do not commit crimes; **specific deterrence** is what is done to one person so that he or she does not commit future crimes. Punishments used to be public in order for others to see the pain (and perhaps death) of offenders and deter them from following the same path. Despite our assumptions regarding general deterrence, evidence indicates there is no correlation between states' crime rates and imprisonment rates. We would assume that states that were more likely to incarcerate offenders should have lower crime rates; however, some states have both declining crime and imprisonment rates, some states have increasing rates of both, and some states show that crime is going up and imprisonment is going down, or vice versa. For instance, New Jersey saw a 37 percent decrease in prison admissions between 2000 and 2015 and a 30 percent decrease in crime rates during the same period. Among the 10 states with the largest decreases in crime rates between 2000 and 2015, five also reduced incarceration rates. Between 2007 and 2019, 34 states reduced both their rate of incarceration and their crime rates.[1] If the use of punishment were effective as a specific deterrent, we would see offenders with extremely low recidivism rates after punishment. Unfortunately, studies show high recidivism rates, ranging from 30 to 70 percent. This range is wide because various researchers study different lengths of time after release, define recidivism differently, and study different populations, among other factors. How would we explain why prison may not act as a deterrent to would-be criminal offenders? Any deterrent effect of prison is arguably countermanded by its negative effects, such as delaying adult development and stunting personal responsibility, post-punishment restrictions on employment and education, and anti-social norms and criminal associations. There are pragmatic issues related to housing and employment difficulties for ex-prisoners that also contribute to the likelihood of recidivating.

The History of Sentencing

In this chapter, the full range of sentencing alternatives will be described, along with a brief discussion of historical punishments. Corporal punishment and/or fines were the most common punishments up until the nineteenth century at which time, the use of jails, prisons, and reformatories as punishment became more common. In the twentieth century, probation became widely used; however, incarceration (either in prison or jail) has been the most frequent sentence handed down in felony courts for the last several decades.

Historically, **corporal punishment** was used to punish and deter offenders. Corporal punishment, which might take the form of whipping, branding, or other injury and pain inflicted on a person, was done in public so that the rest of the community could watch and, presumably, be deterred from committing similar crimes. When the American colonies were established, punishments for criminal offenders were carried over from English **Common Law**. Because most communities were small, deterrence was a powerful force and the threat of corporal punishment and stigmatization was enough to deter most people from crime. The legal system punished a greater range of behaviors in colonial times— blasphemy, gossip, not going to church, illicit sex, and even practical jokes could result in formal punishments. **Gaols** (jails) were used primarily either to hold people until some type of corporal punishment could be carried out or to detain those who could not pay fines. Some of the common types of punishments used during the colonial period included the following:

- *Stocks*: A wooden device with foot holes where a seated person's ankles were locked in with his or her legs straight out. The stocks would be in the town square so that passersby could jeer and scold the miscreant.

Historical punishments included the pillory.

- *Pillory*: The pillory had holes for a person's head and hands, and the offender stood rather than sat. The citizenry might throw rotten fruit or rocks at the confined person, sometimes resulting in their accidental death. These offenders might have been convicted of treason, sedition, arson, blasphemy, witchcraft, perjury, wife beating, cheating, forgery, coin clipping, slandering, fortune-telling, or drunkenness.

- *Whipping Post*: Whipping was a common punishment, and the whipping post was usually in front of the courthouse or towns square to allow an audience to be present during the punishment. Sometimes the offender was tied to the back of a cart and paraded through town, being whipped along the way.

- *Ducking Stool:* The ducking stool consisted of a wooden chair mounted on a long arm. Individuals were tied into the chair and dunked into a body of water (most early communities were by rivers or the sea). Offenders might have been convicted of being a "common scold," slanderer, brawler, unruly pauper, or "brewer of bad beer." Quarreling married couples would be tied back-to-back and dunked.

- *Brank or "Gossip's Bridle":* This was a heavy iron cage that fit over one's head, with a spike that would spear the tongue of the unfortunate offender. This punishment was used for slanderers, nags, and gossips.

- *Branding:* Some offenders were branded; for instance, a burglar might be branded with a B on his hand for the first offense, on the other hand for his second, and on his forehead if he burglarized on a Sunday. SL was the brand for seditious libel and would be inflicted on the offender's cheek. Other brands denoted other crimes; for instance, M (manslaughter), T (thief), R (rogue or vagabond), and F (forgery).

- *Fines:* The law typically specified the size of the fine for each crime, and the fine would increase for the second offense. Generally, those of financial means might receive a fine as punishment, while poor people would be subjected to corporal punishment.

- *Binding Out/Indentureship:* If the offender was a child, he or she might be "bound out" to a family or craftsman for labor (essentially a type of apprenticeship), but adults could also be indentured for a set number of years in lieu of a fine. Indentureship was forced, unpaid labor. If the offender was already an indentured servant (whose fare for passage from England was paid for by a period of indentureship), additional years were added. Free people could also be indentured as punishment. Women, for instance, might be indentured if they had an illegitimate child or were found to have engaged in illicit sex.

- *Gallows:* Violent and chronic offenders were either banished or sent to the gallows.

Many felonies were punishable by death, although individuals could escape a death sentence by claiming a fictional "**benefit of clergy**." This claim was supposed to be used by clergymen who would escape secular punishment because they would be punished by the church; however, the test as to whether someone belonged to the clergy was simply to read a psalm. Often, people simply memorized a psalm and claimed the benefit whether they were clergymen or not.[2]

Post-Revolutionary War Punishments

In the late 1700s, older forms of punishment, which depended on public humiliation, became less effective. As cities grew, communities became less cohesive, and populations were mobile; thus, new forms of social control were necessary. The congregate care facility was created to control and provide services to different problematic groups.[3] Orphanages were used to house orphaned or abandoned youngsters; hospitals were created to house the sick and infirm; and mental institutions were opened to take care of those who were unable to function in society. Workhouses or poorhouses (called "almshouses" in England) were used to control and house indigents who had no work or means of making a living. Houses of correction were created to "correct" poor vagrants by teaching them a trade to change their life of idleness to one of productive work.[4]

The workhouse, house of correction, and gaol housed a similar and overlapping population; specifically, the poor who might also be minor criminals. Communities controlled vagrants by forcing them to go to workhouses. Workhouses were run with a rigorous system of discipline in place, and at times, inmates were sent there against their will. Alternatively, a poor vagrant who might have committed minor crimes to survive would be sent to either a house of correction or a gaol. In many cases, there was not much difference between these institutions. Houses of correction were modeled after Bridewell Palace in London, established in 1556, which was used to house minor offenders. Later, any house of correction came to be known as a "bridewell." Inmates were petty offenders, but also might be lepers, disobedient children, orphans, or the mentally ill. Houses of correction were established in Massachusetts in 1632, Pennsylvania in 1682, and New York in 1736, among other locations, while gaols also existed to house individuals before trial and punishment. Individuals were also detained in gaols until they or their families paid outstanding debts.[5] In 1790, the Pennsylvania legislature passed a new criminal code that abolished the death penalty for all crimes except murder and imposed imprisonment instead of corporal punishment for many crimes. However, it would be many years before all states abolished corporal punishment.[6]

Probation as a form of punishment began in the mid-1800s, although not all states had enabling statutes until 1956. Originally probation officers were volunteers or police officers, but over time evolved to paid professionals. This history of probation will be discussed more fully in Chapter 5.[7]

Today, offenders may be sentenced to pay a fine, or be sentenced to jail, prison, or probation. It is entirely possible that an offender is sentenced to some combination of these punishments, i.e., a fine, a suspended sentence of prison, and several years on supervised probation; or, a short term of jail followed by supervised release on probation (split-sentence). Diversion is also possible; we will discuss this further in Chapter 4.

Capital Punishment

The most controversial sentence imposed is the death penalty. The philosophical rationale for the death penalty is purely retributive. Researchers agree that there is little or no evidence that capital punishment is effective as a general deterrent.[8] Public support for the death penalty has increased and decreased over the years. Support for the death penalty in the U.S. was low throughout the 1960s, dipping in 1966 to its lowest level of support (42 percent) recorded by the Gallup poll.[9] In 2016, the Gallup poll reported that 60 percent of Americans favored capital punishment for murderers, and the Pew Research Center's survey reported that 56 percent of respondents favored capital punishment.[10]

As Figure 3.1 shows, the number of executions has declined substantially from a high of 98 executions in the year 1999 to 21 in 2018. In 2020, the federal government executed 10 people. This was unusual because there had only

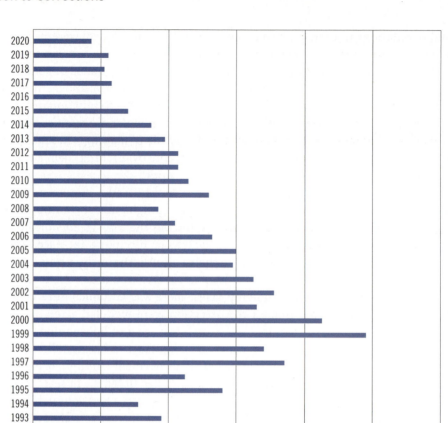

FIGURE 3.1 Number of executions. Author created from information at Death Penalty Information Center, 2018, https://deathpenaltyinfo.org/documents/FactSheet.pdf.

been three federal executions since 1988. Currently, 30 states still have the death penalty as a possible sentence. While Nebraska reinstituted its death penalty in 2016, the trend has been for states to pass laws eliminating the death penalty, substituting life without parole as an alternative sentence. Figure 3.2 shows the most recent information regarding states' sentencing laws regarding the death penalty. In early 2021, Virginia's legislature voted to ban the death penalty.

There is a long history of legal challenges to capital punishment that argue that the death penalty is cruel and unusual punishment in violation of the Eighth Amendment. Clearly, there was capital punishment at the time of the writing of the Bill of Rights; however, legal advocates have argued that what is considered cruel and unusual is different today and now includes the death penalty. Legal challenges to the death penalty have included the way the sentence is determined, who is eligible, and the way executions are carried out. Challenges

Death Penalty States

States with the Death Penalty (28)

Alabama, Arizona, Arkansas, California, Florida, Georgia, Idaho, Indiana, Kansas, Kentucky, Louisiana, Mississippi, Missouri, Montana, Nebraska, Nevada, North Carolina, Ohio, Oklahoma, Oregon, Pennsylvania, South Carolina, South Dakota, Tennessee, Texas, Utah, Virginia, Wyoming

States without the Death Penalty/Year Abolished (22)

Alaska (1957), Colorado (2020), Connecticut (2012), Delaware (2016), Hawaii (1957), Illinois (2011), Iowa (1965), Maine (1887), Maryland (2013), Massachusetts (1984), Michigan (1846), Minnesota (1911), New Hampshire (2019), New Jersey (2007), New Mexico (2009), New York (2007), North Dakota (1973), Rhode Island (1984), Vermont (1964), Washington (2018), West Virginia (1965), Wisconsin (1853) ALSO: District of Columbia (1981)

States with Gubernatorial Moratoria (3)

Colorado (2013), Oregon (2011), Pennsylvania (2015)
Notes Omitted.

FIGURE 3.2 Death penalty states. Author created from information at Death Penalty Information Center, 2020, https://deathpenaltyinfo.org/states-and-without-death-penalty.

arguing that the death penalty is cruel and unusual because it is rarely applied, that it is administered capriciously, and/or that it is administered in a discriminatory manner have not been successful.[11]

In *Furman v. Georgia*, 408 U.S. 238 (1972), the Supreme Court held that the procedure used for capital punishment sentencing in Georgia (and in Texas, in an attached, companion case) was arbitrary and capricious because there was no guidance on who should get the death penalty, thus violating the Eighth Amendment's prohibition against cruel and unusual punishment. The majority did not rule that executions were, by their nature, unconstitutional; they ruled, rather, that only the sentencing procedures used in Georgia at the time were unconstitutional, violating the Constitution. In response, states changed their sentencing statutes to include more due process in capital cases. One change that was resisted was removing discretion entirely. The Supreme Court ruled in *Woodson v. North Carolina*, 428 U.S. 280 (1976) that states could not make capital punishment mandatory for certain crimes. In *Gregg v. Georgia*, 428 U.S. 153 (1976), the Supreme Court approved the changes Georgia had made to its capital punishment procedures, which included a separate sentencing hearing after a guilty verdict, requiring at least one aggravating circumstance beyond a reasonable doubt, and automatic appeals. Executions, which had been suspended across the country since *Furman*, resumed.

In other legal challenges to the death penalty, the Supreme Court has ruled that

- a statistical analysis showing a pattern of racial disparities was not enough to prove intentional discrimination in a specific case (*McCleskey v. Kemp*, 481 U.S. 279, 1987),
- death is a disproportional sentence for rape (*Coker v. Georgia*, 433 U.S. 584, 1977), even rape of a child (*Kennedy v. Louisiana*, 554 U.S. 407, 2008),

- capital punishment for felony murder is not a violation of the Eighth Amendment when the perpetrator was a major participant in the felony and showed a reckless indifference to human life even if the offender did not kill or intend to kill the victim (*Tison v. Arizona*, 481 U.S. 137, 1987),

- it is cruel and unusual to execute those who committed their crimes at or below the age of 16 (*Stanford v. Kentucky*, 492 U.S. 361,1989), then extended that ruling to those who committed the crime before the age of 18 (*Roper v. Simmons*, 543 U.S. 551, 2005),

- it is cruel and unusual to execute those who are mentally handicapped (*Atkins v. Virginia*, 536 U.S. 304, 2002), and subsequent cases determined what level of handicap was necessary to serve as a bar to capital punishment and the means to test levels of intelligence (*Hall v. Florida*, 572 U.S. 701, 2014; *Moore v. Texas*, 581 U.S. ___, 2017),

- it is cruel and unusual to execute someone who is mentally ill if their mental illness makes them unable to understand what they did or what they did was wrong; they also cannot be executed if they do not understand what is happening to them or why (*Ford v. Wainwright*, 477 U.S. 399, 1986),

- the 6th amendment right to a jury trial required that a jury and not a judge make findings on aggravating circumstances to justify the imposition of a death sentence (*Ring v. Arizona*, 536 U.S. 584, 2002), and that

- it is not cruel and unusual for states to use lethal drug combinations to execute offenders (*Baze v. Rees*, 553 U.S. 35, 2008; *Glossip et al. v. Gross et al.*, 135 S. Ct. 2726, 2015).

It seems unlikely that the Supreme Court will rule that capital punishment is a violation of the Eighth Amendment anytime soon. However, it is possible that states may continue to reduce its use due to the high cost of appeals and the growing concern over wrongful convictions. According to the Death Penalty Information Center, since 1973, more than 160 people have been released from death row with evidence of their innocence.

Sentencing Statutes

All states and the federal system have sentencing statutes that create the legal authority to punish individuals, describe the punishments, and assign the punishment for each crime (or provide a range or possible sentences for each crime). Judges cannot sentence anyone to a punishment outside these statutory limits. These statutes are unique to each state and, although there are similarities, the types of punishments may vary from state to state. Even who sentences an offender varies by state: in some states, a jury decides upon the sentence after being given statutory guidelines; in other states, a jury only convicts or acquits an offender, and a judge determines the sentence within the statutory authority; in yet others, state legislatures have set punishments by determinate sentencing statutes, meaning that the judge has little or no discretion.

Most sentences are determined through **plea bargaining**, during which a prosecutor offers both a charge and a recommended sentence in return for a guilty plea. A judge almost always goes along with the agreed-upon sentence, and, if he or she does not, an offender has the right to withdraw the plea of guilty. Prosecutors may opt to utilize **habitual felon laws**, or **three-strikes laws**, which increase the potential punishment for the offender; under such laws, a life

TEXAS STATE PENAL CODE SENTENCING STATUTE

Texas, like many states, has an indeterminate sentencing structure, but it also has mandatory minimums. In the accompanying sentencing paragraphs from the Texas Penal Code, note that for first degree felonies, the offender must be sentenced to **"**any term of not more than 99 years or less than 5 years." That is a fairly broad range of indeterminacy. However, note also that in Section 12.35, Texas has created a hybrid category of crimes called "state jail felonies" that call for a sentence in a state jail "for any term of not more than two years or less than 180 days."

SUBCHAPTER C. ORDINARY FELONY PUNISHMENTS

Sec. 12.31. CAPITAL FELONY. (a) An individual adjudged guilty of a capital felony in a case in which the state seeks the death penalty shall be punished by imprisonment in the Texas Department of Criminal Justice for life without parole or by death. An individual adjudged guilty of a capital felony in a case in which the state does not seek the death penalty shall be punished by imprisonment in the Texas Department of Criminal Justice for:

(1) life, if the individual committed the offense when younger than 18 years of age; or
(2) life without parole, if the individual committed the offense when 18 years of age or older.

(b) In a capital felony trial in which the state seeks the death penalty, prospective jurors shall be informed that a sentence of life imprisonment without parole or death is mandatory on conviction of a capital felony. In a capital felony trial in which the state does not seek the death penalty, prospective jurors shall be informed that the state is not seeking the death penalty and that:

(1) a sentence of life imprisonment is mandatory on conviction of the capital felony, if the individual committed the offense when younger than 18 years of age; or
(2) a sentence of life imprisonment without parole is mandatory on conviction of the capital felony, if the individual committed the offense when 18 years of age or older.

[legislative history deleted]

Sec. 12.32. FIRST DEGREE FELONY PUNISHMENT. (a) An individual adjudged guilty of a felony of the first degree shall be punished by imprisonment in the Texas Department of Criminal Justice for life or for any term of not more than 99 years or less than 5 years.

(b) In addition to imprisonment, an individual adjudged guilty of a felony of the first degree may be punished by a fine not to exceed $10,000.

[legislative history deleted]

Sec. 12.33. SECOND DEGREE FELONY PUNISHMENT. (a) An individual adjudged guilty of a felony of the second degree shall be punished by imprisonment in the Texas Department of Criminal Justice for any term of not more than 20 years or less than 2 years.

(b) In addition to imprisonment, an individual adjudged guilty of a felony of the second degree may be punished by a fine not to exceed $10,000.

[legislative history deleted]

Sec. 12.34. THIRD DEGREE FELONY PUNISHMENT. (a) An individual adjudged guilty of a felony of the third degree shall be punished by imprisonment in the Texas Department of Criminal Justice for any term of not more than 10 years or less than 2 years.

(b) In addition to imprisonment, an individual adjudged guilty of a felony of the third degree may be punished by a fine not to exceed $10,000.

[legislative history deleted]

Sec. 12.35. STATE JAIL FELONY PUNISHMENT. (a) Except as provided by Subsection (c), an individual adjudged guilty of a state jail felony shall be punished by confinement in a state jail for any term of not more than two years or less than 180 days.

(b) In addition to confinement, an individual adjudged guilty of a state jail felony may be punished by a fine not to exceed $10,000.

(c) An individual adjudged guilty of a state jail felony shall be punished for a third degree felony if it is shown on the trial of the offense that:

(1) a deadly weapon as defined by Section 1.07 was used or exhibited during the commission of the offense or during immediate flight following the commission of the offense, and that the individual used or exhibited the deadly weapon or was a party to the offense and knew that a deadly weapon would be used or exhibited; or

(2) the individual has previously been finally convicted of any felony:

(A) under Section 20A.03 or 21.02 or listed in Article 42A.054(a), Code of Criminal Procedure; or

(B) for which the judgment contains an affirmative finding under Article 42A.054(c) or (d), Code of Criminal Procedure.

[*legislative history deleted*]

This punishments section is not complete, however. For instance, there are also a few mandatory sentences in the Texas Penal Code. For instance, driving while intoxicated can result in a mandatory jail sentence for a second offense as the following excerpt the Texas Penal Code illustrates:

Sec. 49.09. ENHANCED OFFENSES AND PENAL-TIES. (a) Except as provided by Subsection (b), an offense under Section 49.04, 49.05, 49.06, or 49.065 is a Class A misdemeanor, with a minimum term of confinement of 30 days, if it is shown on the trial of the offense that the person has previously been convicted one time of an offense relating to the operating of a motor vehicle while intoxicated, an offense of operating an aircraft while intoxicated, an offense of operating a watercraft while intoxicated, or an offense of operating or assembling an amusement ride while intoxicated.

(b) An offense under Section 49.04, 49.05, 49.06, or 49.065 is a felony of the third degree if it is shown on the trial of the offense that the person has previously been convicted:

(1) one time of an offense under Section 49.08 or an offense under the laws of another state if the offense contains elements that are substantially similar to the elements of an offense under Section 49.08; or

(2) two times of any other offense relating to the operating of a motor vehicle while intoxicated, operating an aircraft while intoxicated, operating a watercraft while intoxicated, or operating or assembling an amusement ride while intoxicated.

(b-1) An offense under Section 49.07 is:

(1) a felony of the second degree if it is shown on the trial of the offense that the person caused serious bodily injury to a firefighter or emergency medical services personnel while in the actual discharge of an official duty; or

(2) a felony of the first degree if it is shown on the trial of the offense that the person caused serious bodily injury to a peace officer or judge while the officer or judge was in the actual discharge of an official duty.

(b-2) An offense under Section 49.08 is a felony of the first degree if it is shown on the trial of the offense that the person caused the death of a person described by Subsection (b-1).

(b-3) For the purposes of Subsection (b-1):

(1) "Emergency medical services personnel" has the meaning assigned by Section 773.003, Health and Safety Code.

(2) "Firefighter" means:

(A) an individual employed by this state or by a political or legal subdivision of this state who is subject to certification by the Texas Commission on Fire Protection; or

(B) a member of an organized volunteer firefighting unit that:

(i) renders fire-fighting services without remuneration; and

(ii) conducts a minimum of two drills each month, each at least two hours long.

(b-4) An offense under Section 49.07 is a felony of the second degree if it is shown on the trial of the offense that the person caused serious bodily injury to another in the nature of a traumatic brain injury that results in a persistent vegetative state.

Source: Texas State Legislature. Title 3. Punishments, Chapter 12. Punishments. Title 10. Offenses Against Public Health, Safety, and Morals. Chapter 49. Intoxication and Alcoholic Beverage Offenses. Texas State Penal Code.. Retrieved from http://www.statutes.legis. state.tx.us/docs/PE/htm/PE.12.htm

sentence is possible for habitual felons. Three-strikes laws must be created by statute, and states' versions vary, especially in the types of felonies that make an offender eligible for a three-strikes sentence. State sentencing statutes also vary in terms of which crimes are eligible for a probation sentence, although all states allow probation as a possible sentence for at least some offenders.

Indeterminate and Determinate Sentencing

One of the most important distinctions between state sentencing statutes is whether the state has an indeterminate or determinate sentencing system. Basically, **indeterminate sentencing** does not specify the exact number of years in prison to be served, meaning an offender is sentenced to a range of possible years in prison (e.g., 5–15 years), whereas **determinate sentencing** is when a presumptive sentence specifying an exact number of years is provided by the sentencing statute for any crime (e.g., 5 years). This simple definition doesn't precisely capture actual sentencing systems, however, because even in determinate sentencing structures, there is usually a small sentencing range with the use of mitigating or aggravating factors to determine the exact punishment.

Indeterminate sentencing structures became prevalent by the 1970s. The seeds of indeterminacy were first set during the 1870 Prison Congress, in which correctional professionals of the time established principles that promoted the idea that offenders should be able to earn their way to freedom based on good behavior. Graduated liberties were promoted and put into place by penologist Zebulon Brockway when he was appointed the head of the Elmira Reformatory in New York in 1876. This new type of institution was different from the penitentiary in that the goal was to reform young offenders through strict discipline and education. The Elmira Reformatory provided a type of early parole for well-behaved inmates. Gradually, other states began their own form of graduated, supervised release that shortened prison sentences. By 1942, all states had a **parole** system, which can be defined as early release from prison to some type of community supervision based on good behavior. Some states continued to use volunteer parole officers until the 1950s.[12]

Good time refers to time taken off the end of a prison sentence, usually for good behavior, but some states also require program participation or other conditions before good time is awarded. Good time can potentially reduce a prison sentence by as much as half or more. Some states set good time rates by as much as 2 to 1: for every day in prison with no disciplinary infractions, a sentence would be reduced by two days, meaning that many inmates would serve only a third of their sentence.

By the 1970s, because of indeterminate sentencing, the possibility of parole, and reductions in the length of prison sentences due to good time, prisoners often had no idea as to when they might be released. The most extreme example of this uncertainty during this decade was in California, where every inmate was sentenced to a prison term of zero to life and the release decision was made not by the sentencing judge but by the parole authorities.

The broad swath of indeterminate sentencing that characterized corrections in the 1960s and 1970s had a short lifespan, however, because dissatisfaction and campaigns to return to more definite sentencing grew in volume and strength throughout the 1970s. Both conservatives and liberals criticized indeterminate sentencing. Conservatives believed that offenders were being released too early and that the public should know the length of an offender's sentence at the time of sentencing. Liberals believed that due process was violated when a non-judicial body, such as a paroling authority, determined the length of a sentence rather than a judge or jury. In fact, there didn't seem to be much science applied or clarity expressed in when offenders were released, since paroling boards were often political appointees who had no special skills or background in corrections, much less in risk prediction. California eliminated its indeterminate sentencing structure and abolished discretionary parole in 1976, replacing it with a determinate sentencing structure.[13]

One of the problems of indeterminate sentencing was that there was little consistency between offenders in the length of prison time served. **Sentencing disparity** refers to when similar offenders who commit similar crimes receive different punishments, with some offenders receiving sentences toward the shorter end of a range and other offenders serving much longer terms. A lack of procedural fairness, transparency, and predictability, as well as allegations of racial bias, led to states abandoning indeterminacy and discretionary parole. By the mid-1980s, many states had reverted to forms of determinate sentencing. Statutory changes that brought back various forms of determinate sentencing included the following:

1. *Presumptive sentencing structures/sentencing guidelines.* **Sentencing guidelines** present a "presumptive" sentence for judges to administer, based on the seriousness of the offense and the criminal history of the offender. For instance, the federal sentencing guidelines were created from the Sentencing Reform Act of 1984 and implemented in 1987. The Federal Guidelines Sentencing Commission has developed a manual that details how to use the sentencing table. Offense level is determined by the charge, the use of a weapon, and, if relevant, the amount of drugs involved. The criminal history score is based on criminal record. The offender's cooperation with the government can be used as a factor to reduce the sentence indicated by the guidelines. In the federal system, the guidelines identify a lower and upper limit for any recommended prison term, each with no more than a 25 percent difference between the lower and upper limits.

2. *Mandatory minimum laws.* **Mandatory minimum laws** require minimum prison terms for people convicted of specified crimes. By 1983, 49 of the 50 states had adopted such laws for certain offenses.[14] Mandatory minimum sentences are generally used for drug offenses, murder, aggravated rape, felonies involving firearms, and felonies committed by people who have previous felony convictions. Note that a state can have an indeterminate sentencing structure, with most crimes receiving a sentence range, e.g., 5–15 years, but also have mandatory minimum sentences attached to some specific crimes.

3. Three-strikes sentencing laws. **Three-strikes laws** create the possibility of long sentences upon a conviction for a second or third felony. California's three-strikes law, which has received the most media attention, was passed in 1994 in response to the case of Polly Klaas, a twelve-year old girl who was kidnapped from her home and murdered by a chronic violent offender who had already served a prison term for kidnapping. California's original three-strikes provision created a 25-year-to-life sentence for a third felony. The law also included a "two-strikes" provision, which could double the sentence attached to a felony if the offender had been convicted of one before and if the prosecutor pursued the two-strikes option. In 2012, Proposition 36, a voter-initiated ballot, passed and subsequently changed California's three-strikes law. Now, only certain violent felonies are eligible for the application of three-strikes laws. A provision also allowed those in prison with life sentences under the original three-strikes provision to petition to have their sentences revised.

4. *Truth-in-sentencing laws.* **Truth-in-sentencing laws** required that people sentenced to imprisonment serve at least 85 percent of their nominal sentences and not be released early on parole or due to good-time sentence reductions.

5. *Life without possibility of parole laws.* These laws have been passed often in conjunction with the abolition of capital punishment. The idea is that voters would agree to abolish the death penalty if there was a certainty that the offender would remain behind bars.

Sentencing Patterns

Recall from Chapter 1 that from 1925 to the 1980s, the rate of incarceration was stable. The imprisonment rate began its dramatic climb in the 1980s, eventually identifying the United States as one of the world's most notorious nations for incarcerating its residents. An imprisonment rate is affected by three factors:

a) the likelihood of convicted offenders receiving a prison sentence rather than a community supervision sentence (e.g., probation),

b) the length of the sentence, and

c) the likelihood that probationers or parolees are revoked and sent to prison.

For all offenders convicted of felonies, well over a third are sentenced to prison as seen in Figure 3.3. The percentage hasn't seemed to dramatically increase over the years for which data is available, although there seems to be more variability in the number of people sentenced to jail or probation. Another way to examine sentencing information, however, is to look at one type of crime category. Doing that, researchers have found that for many convicted offenders, a prison sentence was more likely beginning in the 1980s. The reason that the percentage of all felons receiving a prison sentence (as compared to either jail or probation) did not go up was that there were larger numbers of less serious felonies in the total group (who were more likely to get a jail or probation sentence).[15]

In the federal system, imprisonment overtook probation as the most frequently given sentence—probably because more drug laws were passed with more severe sentences attached. Beginning in 1980, as the federal offender population shifted from mostly white-collar criminals to drug offenders, the use of probation declined and the use of prison increased.[16]

As for the second factor affecting incarceration rates, the *average* length of prison sentences did not seem to increase from the 1980s through the 1990s. However, looking more closely at individual crimes, researchers have found that a robbery prison term was 20 percent longer and a rape prison term was 75 percent longer. In fact, most offenses netted a longer prison term. Looking only at the average length for *all* crimes was misleading because there were many more offenders sentenced for less serious crimes as years went by, bringing down the average sentence length. When we look at average length changes over time within crime categories, both violent and property offenders experienced an increase in average sentence lengths.[17]

In a sentencing study conducted in conjunction with the Vera Institute of Justice, it was found that crime rates, the proportion of Blacks in the population, and the ideologies favored by a state's citizens were the most influential factors affecting imprisonment rates. Having a presumptive sentencing guideline system lowered a state's imprisonment rate by 72 per 100,000. Other variables, although less influential, included the percentage of the population aged 18–34 years and the poverty level. On the other hand, determinate sentencing, mandatory sentencing policies, and truth-in-sentencing legislation did not seem to have much effect on prison admission rates, contrary to what many believe.[18]

Drug Sentencing

There is no doubt that the war on drugs and the concomitant arrests and sentencing of drug offenders has contributed to rising imprisonment rates. One estimate suggests that about 45 percent of the increase observed in the period of the 1980s and 1990s was due to drug offenders.[19] Consider that about 7 percent of court commitments to prison were for drug offenses in 1980, but by 1992, close to 31 percent of prison commitments were for drug offenses.[20] Figure 3.3 shows the breakdown of prison admissions by type of crime. Percentage of total figures must be interpreted carefully, since percentages of crime types are influenced by other crime categories. In general, however, we see that drug offenders represent about a third of the admissions to prison, but that percentage seems to be trending down. Unfortunately, the Bureau of Justice Statistics does not present this data every year, so no illustration is available for what has happened in more recent years.

A greater percentage of federal prison admissions than state prison admissions are for drug offenses because federal offenders are typically drug or white-collar criminals. One study of federal drug offenders revealed that of offenders incarcerated in federal prisons for drug offenses, three-fourths were determined to have no serious history of violence, only 14 percent were leaders in the drug business, and 78 percent were sentenced under mandatory minimums. Those sentenced under mandatory minimum sentences were serving an average of 11 years compared to others, whose sentences averaged 6 years.[21]

Do the increased arrests and prison admissions for drug arrests and trafficking indicate more drug use? It doesn't seem so. Various sources that track drug use indicate that drug use has gone up and down sporadically, but usage patterns don't seem to parallel arrest or sentencing data in any way.[22]

Drug use was not always considered a criminal offense. A wide variety of patent medicines, containing derivatives of morphine, cocaine, and/or alcohol, were marketed in the early 1900s, with no oversight or control by the government. That changed with the **Harrison Act of 1914**, which required documentation of prescriptions and taxation of drugs, and eventually led to the regulation and/or prohibition of all drugs. In the 1930s, federal attention focused on marijuana. Congress passed the Marijuana Tax Act of 1937, which placed marijuana on the same list as heroin and cocaine and defined it as a controlled substance.[23] Federal

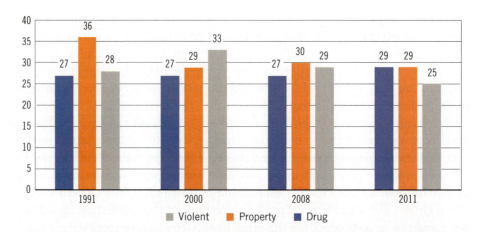

FIGURE 3.3   Prison admissions by type of crime. Author created from H. West and W. Sabol, *Prisoners in 2009* (Washington, DC: USDOJ, BJS, 2010), Table 10; E. Carson and D. Golinelli, D, *Prisoners in 2012. Trends in Admissions and Releases, 1991–2012*, Table 4 (Washington, DC: USDOJ, BJS, 2014).

penalties for possession of marijuana ranged from 2 to 20 years, depending on whether it was a first, second, or third offense, and the quantity possessed. Then, in the 1960s, public views shifted to support treatment rather than punishment. Almost every state reduced criminal penalties for marijuana between 1969 and 1972; by 1973, simple possession was only a misdemeanor in all but eight states. Some states decriminalized small amounts completely.[24]

Presidents Gerald Ford and Jimmy Carter promoted both enforcement and treatment almost equally; however, President Ronald Reagan took an aggressive stance on drugs, beginning the modern "War on Drugs." As mentioned in Chapter 1, the **Comprehensive Crime Control Act** was passed in 1984; it included the Sentencing Reform Act, which abolished federal parole and created a Sentencing Commission that, in turn, created the Sentencing Guidelines for federal crimes. Under the **Sentencing Reform Act of 1984**, all federal prisoners had to serve 85 percent of their sentences before becoming eligible for release, with a maximum of 15 percent set aside as a reward for good behavior.[25]

By 1986, drugs, especially crack cocaine, dominated the news. Stories about cocaine overdoses, drug gang violence, and the problem of babies born addicted to crack were prevalent. Congress passed the Anti-Drug Abuse Act of 1986, imposing 29 new mandatory minimum sentences. The Anti-Drug Abuse Act of 1988, signed by President George H.W. Bush when he took office in 1989, created a federal death penalty for participation in "continuing criminal enterprises" or any drug-related felony that related to the killing of another. President Bill Clinton signed the **Violent Crime Control Law Enforcement Act** in 1994, which, among other provisions, directed the Sentencing Commission to eliminate parole for those who sold drugs near schools. New federal laws also prohibited drug offenders from living in public housing, forcing families to choose between eviction and providing a place to stay for relatives who had been released.[26]

The average length of time served by federal inmates more than doubled from 1988 to 2012, rising from 17.9 to 37.5 months. For drug offenders, roughly half of the federal prison population, time served increased from less than two years to nearly five years as the average sentence. From 1988 to 2012, the

President Ronald Reagan took an aggressive stance on drugs, including signing the Comprehensive Crime Control Act in 1984 that created the Federal Sentencing Guidelines.

President Barack Obama signed the Fair Sentencing Act of 2010.

number of annual federal prison admissions almost tripled, increasing from 19,232 to 61,712 in 2011; it has dropped slightly since then. The overall federal prison population increased 336 percent from 1988 to 2012. Researchers note that drug offenders are the single greatest contributor to this increase.[27]

More recently, public opinion and legislative response seems to be changing back to a less punitive approach to drug use. In the early 2000s, some states eliminated mandatory minimum sentences for drug offenses, instituted drug courts to divert first-time drug offenders from prison, and used other means to reduce the numbers of drug offenders who cycled in and out of prison without treatment.[28] By 2020, 10 states and Washington, DC, had decriminalized small amounts of marijuana for personal use, and only six states had not legalized and regulated medical use of marijuana.[29] The recent opiate crisis seems to be presented in the media more as a public health issue than a crime issue, indicating, perhaps, that attitudes toward addiction and drug use have shifted from a purely punitive response.

At the federal level, President Barack Obama signed the **Fair Sentencing Act of 2010**, changing the ratio of the sentence length for crack cocaine compared to powder cocaine from 100 to 1 down to 18 to 1. By that time, the Supreme Court had already made sentencing guidelines less restrictive for federal judges in a series of holdings. In 2004, in *Blakely v. Washington*, 542 U.S. 296, the Court invalidated the mandatory use of Washington State sentencing guidelines because elements not introduced and proven in court were used, such as the number of prior offenses or use of a weapon. In *United States v. Booker*, 543 U.S. 220 (2005) and *United States v. Fanfan*, 542 U.S. 296 (2004), the Supreme Court extended this reasoning to federal sentencing guidelines. In *Booker*, the Supreme Court ruled that the guidelines violated due process because the factors used in them had not been proven in court; thus, they could only be advisory rather than mandatory. The Supreme Court ruled in *Gall v. United States*, 552 U.S. 38 (2007) that if an offender was sentenced to a term outside the presumptive guidelines by a federal district judge, that sentence should not be presumed unreasonable, nor did a judge need extraordinary circumstances to do so. This decision strengthened the authority of district court judges to depart from the sentencing guidelines.

FOCUS ON THE

OFFENDER   **A LIFE RUINED**

Those incarcerated for drug use are not all addicted, but in many cases, addiction to illegal substances begins the path toward drug dealing and other crime. For instance, Mark Weller was 28 years old when he pleaded guilty in federal court to two counts of distributing methamphetamine. His mother, in her letter to the court for his sentencing, explained that she was an alcoholic who was also manic depressive and schizophrenic. Mark's childhood included being beaten by his mother, as well as seeing her drunk and trying to kill herself. As a four-year-old, he visited her in a mental hospital. He often lived in a house with no electricity. He had started using marijuana at age 12, drinking whiskey at 14, using cocaine at 16, and then turned to methamphetamine.

Even with such early drug use, he graduated from high school, married, and had a daughter. He worked for six years at a slaughterhouse, earning $18 an hour. Then, when his wife moved with their daughter out-of-state to be with a man she met on the internet, Weller started drinking heavily and lost his job. In his description of this time of his life, he said he also lost his morals and self-control. He sold everything he had for meth, spending as much as

$200 each day on the drug. Then he started selling it. He had 223 grams of methamphetamine when he was arrested, and was charged with a federal offense because he had sold the drugs across state lines. Several others were willing to testify that he had dealt 2.5 kilograms in exchange for avoiding their own mandatory minimum drug sentences. This amount was necessary for a mandatory minimum of 10 years, even for a first offense with no criminal history. Weller's maximum sentence was life without parole.

In this case, as in many others, individuals make bad decisions because of drug use. Drug use and addiction may be caused by childhood trauma and/or mental illness. It is possible that people may self-medicate with illegal drugs because they have not sought or cannot obtain professional assistance from legitimate healthcare outlets. The federal system of sentencing rewards those who cooperate and attaches extremely long sentences for those who deal drugs. It is possible that changes to federal mandatory minimum laws being discussed by Congress may provide some relief to this man and others like him.

Questions for Discussion

1. Is life without parole a just sentence for a drug dealer?

2. Why didn't the possibility of a life without parole sentence deter this man from selling drugs? What might have?

Source: E. Saslow, "Against His Better Judgment," The Washington Post, June 6, 2015, http://www.washingtonpost.com/sf/national/2015/06/06/against-his-better-judgment/?utm_term=.64849d88e462.

Clemency/Commutations

In a major effort to ameliorate the most draconian drug sentencing at the federal level, President Obama issued over 1,000 clemency/commutation orders, most of which were for drug offenders sentenced under mandatory minimum sentences or under federal sentencing guidelines in place when the sentence for crack cocaine was 100 times harsher than that for powder cocaine. The Department of Justice set up a system to evaluate applications from federal inmates, primarily drug offenders who had been sentenced under mandatory minimums. Eventually, private attorneys had to be called in to handle the great numbers. The Clemency Project 2014 utilized volunteer attorneys who evaluated the applications. Inmates had to have served at least 10 years, have no significant criminal history, and have no connection to gangs, cartels, or organized crime. They must have demonstrated good conduct in prison. If they would likely have received a substantially lower sentence if convicted of the same offense after sentencing reforms, then they would be eligible for clemency. By the end of his term, President Obama had given 1,715 commutations, more than the past 12 presidents combined. He also granted 212 pardons.[30] Some reports indicated that 33,000 (roughly 15 percent of the entire federal prison population) applied for clemency.[31] Approximately 7,881 commutation petitions remained pending with a recommendation from the Justice Department as of January 19, 2017; however, President Trump did not continue the program and those applications were rendered moot.[32] It is unclear at this point whether President Biden will reconstitute the program or consider the previous applications.

Another avenue of federal sentencing reform led to even more federal drug inmates being released. In 2015, the U.S. Sentencing Commission changed the federal sentencing guidelines to reduce the sentences attached to some drug crimes. The reform was also made retroactive, meaning that more than 40,000 incarcerated drug offenders were eligible for an average two-year reduction if a judge, in each case, found that they were not a public safety risk.[33]

While there is growing consensus that many nonviolent drug offenders have received unnecessarily long sentences, dramatically reducing the number of drug offenders sent to prison would not bring down the national prison population very much, however, because drug offenders comprise about 50 percent of the federal prison population, but only 16 percent of the state prison population.[34] Drug offenders comprise about a third of prison admissions, but serve shorter sentences; therefore, they make up a small percentage when looking at the total prisoner population in any given year. Violent offenders receive much longer sentences, and so they "stack up" and comprise a much bigger percentage of the prison population than drug offenders. Cutting drug offenders' sentences in half would reduce the national prison population by only about 7 percent, according to one study.[35]

Sentencing Disparity

Recall that sentencing disparity refers to when similar offenders, committing similar crimes, receive dissimilar punishment. One of the major reasons for the push for determinate sentencing and sentencing guidelines was to reduce the disparity that was said to exist between judges, between locales, and between groups of offenders—for example, racial/ethnic or gender disparity.

Geographic Disparity

Recall from Chapter 1 that states have widely disparate rates of incarceration. For every 100,000 adult residents, Louisiana incarcerates 1,019 compared to Maine, which incarcerates only 163.[36] What accounts for the fact that Louisiana incarcerates approximately six times more of its population than does Maine? There are many explanations, but much of the difference lies simply in the inclination to punish with a prison sentence as opposed to some other form of punishment.

Most state comparisons present imprisonment rates which show the number of residents incarcerated per 100,000 people in that state. Another important statistic to be aware of is a state's **correctional supervision rate**. This rate includes all those under *any* form of correctional supervision, including those on probation or parole. It may be the case that states that have high rates of

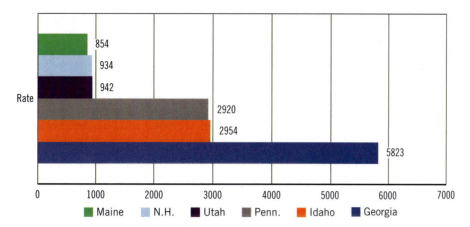

FIGURE 3.4 Highest and lowest state correctional supervision rates per 100,000, 2016. Author created from B. Rabuy and P. Wagner, "Correctional Control: Incarceration and supervision by state, June 1, 2016," Prison Policy Initiative, http://www.prisonpolicy.org/reports/50statepie.html

correctional supervision are not those states that are ranked highest in their use of prison. For instance, Georgia has the highest rate of correctional supervision at 5,823 per 100,000 adult residents, largely because of its high probation rate. At 4,565 per 100,000 adult residents, Georgia puts far more of its residents under probation supervision than any other state, although its imprisonment rate (the number of people sent to prison) is only 521 per 100,000 adults, which is much lower than many states.[37] On the low end, Maine's correctional supervision rate is only 854 (see Figure 3.4), and it also has a low incarceration rate.

Even within a state, there is wide variability in patterns of sentencing between counties. Some counties are more likely to incarcerate sentenced offenders rather than use community correctional alternatives and to hand down longer sentences. For example, one report indicated that Dearborn County in Indiana sent more people to prison per capita than nearly any other county in the United States. An offender who sold 6.8 grams of heroin would probably be sentenced to five years or less in other counties and states, but in Dearborn County, such an offender received a 35-year prison sentence.[38] Counties that are rural, conservative, and have a majority white population are more likely to hand down long prison sentences. Dense population centers with large percentages of minorities have more moderate sentencing practices. Due to campaigns from 2006 to 2014 to reduce the number of people sent to prison, annual prison admissions dropped in urban counties; for instance, by 36 percent in Indianapolis, 37 percent in Brooklyn, 69 percent in Los Angeles County, and 93 percent in San Francisco. However, prison admission rates in counties with fewer than 100,000 people have risen. People in small counties are about 50 percent more likely to go to prison than people from urban counties. This disparity is starting to reduce the percentage of minorities in prison because they are more likely to live in urban counties. Whereas the number of Black prison admissions fell by about 25 percent from 2006 to 2013, and the number of Hispanic admissions declined by 30 percent, new white admissions dropped by only 8 percent.[39]

Rural counties continue to use prison as punishment disproportionately, even in states that have been successful at changing laws and reducing the use of incarceration statewide. Cities and suburban areas are more likely to have drug courts, treatment options, diversion programs, and other resources, while rural counties are more likely to respond to drug offenders with prison sentences. This disparity between counties means that an offender's sentence is highly influenced by where he or she was convicted, perhaps even more than other sentencing variables like criminal history.

Gender Disparity

Sentencing disparity between male and female offenders has been noted for many decades, with research going back to the 1950s studying what has been called the **chivalry hypothesis**. This theory suggests that women are less likely to be arrested, charged, or convicted, and, if convicted, they are sentenced less harshly than men for similar crimes. This occurs not because of factors that justify such disparity, but because the system is "chivalrous," treating female offenders more gently.[40] The difficulty, however, is in controlling for all factors that affect sentencing. Prior record, seriousness of crime, victim injury, offender culpability, motivation, and other factors may affect sentencing, and gender may affect these factors.

Any study should, ideally, start at the point of the arrest decision and include the decision to charge, pretrial decisions such as bail or release on recognizance (ROR), and conviction, as well as sentencing. Each decision point affects what comes after it. Typically, studies are done only at the point of sentencing, which ignores any potential disparity in each of the preceding decision points. These methodological issues are also present in any discussion of racial/ethnic sentencing disparity.

Some research has shown that even when matching type of crime, for example embezzlement, there are many differences between male and female offenders and their criminal activity.[41] Many earlier studies have found that women receive less severe sentencing and are less likely to be in custody before trial; however, findings are mixed as to whether women are less likely to be convicted and less likely to be sent to prison if convicted. While these studies generally control for race, offense, and prior record, many have not controlled for level of participation, the types of crimes in prior arrests, the level of participation in current crime, the level of injury or loss in the current crime, and other influential factors, such as mental health.[42] Studies show that women are different than men on many variables including prior felony convictions (women have fewer), severity of past crimes (crimes committed by women tend to be less serious), single versus multiple offenses (women generally face single counts of a crime), use of a gun (women are much less likely to commit a weapon-related crime), victimization of a stranger (women are more likely to victimize family or acquaintances rather than strangers), being represented by a public versus private attorney (women are more likely to be represented by a private attorney), and pretrial release (women are more likely to be released prior to conviction).[43] The factors of race and ethnicity also seem to interact with sex: for example, young Black men receive the most punitive sentencing, and older white women receive the lightest sentences.[44]

The sentencing reforms that implemented sentencing guidelines seemed to increase sentence lengths for women more than men, perhaps because the mitigating factors that had reduced women's sentences (e.g., being the primary caretaker of young children) were no longer considered. Women receive severe sentences for drug crimes because they have no information to barter with to reduce their sentence.[45] Recent studies continue to find that women's sentencing seems to be more lenient than men's, even with sentencing guidelines in place; however, studies still do not control for all variables (such as participation level, type of criminal history, and other factors).[46] Other studies have found that men and women are sentenced equally under guidelines.[47]

There are some studies showing that sentencing disparity between men and women increased as federal judges have regained their discretion to sentence outside of guidelines. One study of federal sentencing between 2011 and 2016 found that female offenders of all races received shorter sentences than white male offenders. This difference increased as federal judges gained more discretion in sentencing after sentencing guidelines were ruled to be only advisory. White female offenders received sentences that were 24.1 percent shorter than those of white male offenders; Black female offenders received sentences that were 27.1 percent shorter than those of white male offenders; and Hispanic females received sentences that were not statistically different from those for white male offenders.[48]

Racial and Ethnic Disparity

Between 1980 and 1999, the imprisonment rate for Blacks (both men and women) increased from 551 to 1,789, compared to whites' rate increase (85 to 217) and Hispanics' rate increase (163 to 719).[49] When Hispanics are separated from the counts of white prisoners, the disparity is even more dramatic. In 2019, the imprisonment rate of Blacks was 1,446 compared to the rate of 263 for whites. The imprisonment rate for Hispanics was 757.[50]

What accounts for this disparity? Researchers have identified three possible, non-exclusive explanations. It may be because Black offenders are more likely to be involved in crimes that deserve harsher punishments. The second explanation is that discretionary decisions by local criminal justice officials during arrest, charging, conviction, and sentencing systematically and cumulatively produce disparity. The third explanation is that sentencing policies, especially mandatory minimums and sentencing guidelines, differentially impact Blacks and Hispanics.[51]

Disparity may occur at each point of the criminal justice system. In one review, 15 of 24 studies found no effect of race on charging decisions, although the remaining nine studies did.[52] One plea bargaining study found that Black offenders were less likely than white offenders to receive charge reduction offers from prosecutors, and both Black and Hispanic offenders were more likely than whites to receive a plea offer that included a prison term. The plea offer differences were largely explained by legal factors such as evidence and arrest history, but even after controlling for these factors, some unexplained differences remained.[53] One meta-analysis found that a slight majority of studies showed racial bias in sentencing.[54] Researchers have found that prosecutors were almost twice as likely to seek mandatory sentences against Hispanic defendants than white defendants.[55] Other research showed that Black defendants were more likely to be charged with and receive third-strike sentences than white defendants, particularly for offenses known as "wobblers," which can be prosecuted either as a felony or a misdemeanor.[56]

In one study that utilized both federal and state sentencing data, researchers first noted that studies conducted to date have usually found young Black, and, to a lesser extent, Hispanic, male defendants to be sentenced more severely than other defendants. Longer sentences occurred partially because prosecutors were more likely to apply mandatory minimums to minorities and less likely to agree to charge reductions. These researchers, in their study, found that when controlling for other variables such as prior history, the disparity between Black males' sentencing as compared to white males' (whether the offender would receive prison rather than probation), was reduced by 78 percent, and the Hispanic males' sentencing disparity was reduced by 73 percent. This means that factors other than race cannot explain all the sentencing disparity between Blacks and whites. Disparity in sentence *length* (how long prison sentences were for similar crimes) was reduced by 98 percent and 97 percent respectively, which makes sense because the federal system and state system (Pennsylvania) utilized in this research incorporated sentencing guidelines. Researchers found that U.S. citizenship and pre-sentence detention were highly influential in the sentence length decision for Hispanics. The researchers concluded that a great deal of disproportionality is mediated by sentencing policy structures—presumptive sentence recommendations and mandatory minimums. They also found a significant amount of between-court racial and ethnic disparity in the target state, even with sentencing guidelines in place. The conclusion was that guidelines reduced, but did not eliminate, racial and ethnic sentencing disparity because judges used their ability to make guideline departures in sentencing.[57]

Generally, researchers have agreed that there is an observed racial and ethnic disparity in sentencing, but it is largely through indirect effects. For instance, those who are detained prior to trial (versus being released before trial on bail or recognizance) are more likely to receive prison sentences, and Blacks are more likely than whites to experience pretrial detainment. Interaction effects exist with race, sex, and age affecting bond amounts, pretrial detention, and type of sentence, and with young, Black males receiving cumulative disadvantage across these decisions. Prior criminal history and type of attorney representation (private or public) also affect sentencing, and, in these two areas, Blacks are differentially impacted in the sentencing decision. Thus, a history of imprisonment, a higher bail amount (meaning that the offender probably would not make bail and gain release), and the absence of a hired attorney were all disadvantages, with Blacks experiencing these disadvantages differentially.[58]

Past research has shown that Blacks and Hispanics receive longer sentences in the federal system even after controlling for other sentencing variables such as criminal history.[59] The sentencing of Native American offenders also seems to be disproportionally severe as compared to whites.[60] Researchers have found that, in the federal system, young Hispanic male defendants have the highest odds of incarceration and young Black male defendants receive the longest sentences.[61] In comparing federal sentences from 2005 (when federal sentence guidelines were mandatory) to 2012 (after the Supreme Court eliminated the mandatory nature of the guidelines), studies found a 4 percent increase in disparity after federal judges gained greater discretion in their sentencing powers. Researchers also found that some federal circuits tend to have more lenient sentencing patterns for both Black and white offenders, while other circuits sentence more harshly; for instance, the Second Circuit sentence is an average of 0.46 standard deviation units below the national average, but the Fifth Circuit averages are above the national average. Also, while federal judges sentenced everyone more leniently on average once guidelines were no longer mandatory, it appeared that whites benefitted more from this change than did Blacks, increasing the disparity between these two groups. There was less disparity for very serious crimes. This study also found that females receive sentences that are less harsh than those of their male counterparts, and that Black and white female offenders receive similar sentences.[62]

One study found that between 2011 and 2016, Black male offenders received sentences that are on average 19.1 percent longer than similarly situated white male offenders. Black male offenders were 21.2 percent less likely than white male offenders to receive a downward departure from sentencing guidelines for mitigating factors. Black violent male offenders received a sentence that was 20 percent longer than similar white offenders. The difference in sentence length between Black and white male offenders had substantially decreased, largely due to resentencing of offenders who were sentenced under mandatory minimums for crack cocaine, a crime category largely dominated by Black offenders. Other than this crime category, disparity in sentencing between Black and white offenders remained relatively unchanged, with an average difference of 34 months. This study found no significant disparity between the sentencing of white and Hispanic offenders.[63]

More recently, Black imprisonment rates are decreasing, and racial disparity in sentencing has been declining. According to one source, between 2000 and 2015 the imprisonment rate of Black men dropped by more than 24 percent. At the same time, the white male rate increased slightly. From 2000 to 2015, the Black female imprisonment rate dropped by nearly 50 percent, but the white female rate increased by 53 percent. The racial disparity between Black and white women's incarceration has declined from a ratio of 6:1 down to 2:1. Another source reported that from 2000 to 2016, racial and ethnic disparities declined across prison, jail, probation, and parole populations in the U.S. The black-white state imprisonment disparity fell from 8.3-to-1 to 5.1-to-1, and the Hispanic-white parole disparity fell from 3.6-to-1 to 1.4-to-1. Among women, the black-white disparity in imprisonment fell from 6-to-1 to 2-to-1, a sharper decrease than the decline among men. The largest decrease in disparity occurred in sentencing for drug offenses. In 2000, black people were imprisoned for drug crimes at 15 times the rate of whites; by 2016, that ratio was just under 5-to-1. Explanations include shifts in the war on drugs that target drugs more likely to be used by whites (such as methamphetamine and opioids), and more active criminal justice reform efforts in cities where minorities are more likely to live without corresponding reforms in rural areas more likely to be populated by whites.[64]

Changes in Sentencing

The annual incarceration rate increases that occurred throughout the last several decades seem to be over. In the last several years, incarceration rates have declined or at least plateaued. Declining incarceration rates are caused by reduced crime, but also by changes in sentencing statutes. Across the country, states have been reforming their sentencing systems to reduce the problems of mass incarceration. Some of the sentencing reforms that have occurred in various states include the following:

- reducing or eliminating mandatory minimums;
- reforming good time/increase parole eligibility;
- revising juvenile life-without-parole;
- reclassifying some felonies to misdemeanors, reducing possible sentence;
- increasing the number of crimes eligible for probation;
- modifying three-strikes law;
- increasing diversion programs/deferred adjudication;
- abolishing death penalty;
- revising probation and parole revocation to reduce number of returns to prison; and
- expanding problem-solving courts (e.g., drug courts, veterans' courts).[65]

In some states, several types of sentencing reform were combined in a single legislative act. For instance, Alaska Senate Bill 91, signed into law in 2016, was written to limit prison growth and reduce recidivism by expanding incarceration alternatives, including

- reducing jail terms for misdemeanor offenses;
- reclassifying drug possession as a misdemeanor offense;
- reducing presumptive sentencing ranges for certain felony-level offenses;
- expanding eligibility for discretionary parole;
- streamlining parole releases for persons sentenced for a first-time nonviolent offense; and
- capping prison stays for technical violations of probation and parole conditions.[66]

In other states, the changes occurred in a more piecemeal fashion. Recall from Chapter 1 that California passed a series of laws that significantly impacted criminal sentencing and the number of offenders in prison from 2010 to 2016, spurring some to refer to this period as the "reform era" in criminal sentencing.[67] In 2011, Senate Bill 1449 reduced the penalties for possession of marijuana. Also, in 2011, Assembly Bill 109 (Public Safety Realignment) was passed. In 2012, voters passed Proposition 36, which narrowed California's three-strikes law to apply only to serious and violent felons. In 2014, California passed Proposition 47, which "de-felonized" a range of crimes down to misdemeanors. In 2016, Proposition 57 reduced the practice of prosecuting juveniles as adults and extended earlier parole opportunities to adults sentenced to prison for nonviolent offenses.[68]

As noted in Chapter 1, trying to determine whether these sentencing changes have impacted crime rates is difficult. Research on California's Realignment is mixed. Researchers identified increases in crime after the changes, but only in some counties and cities. There doesn't seem to be a statewide pattern of increase that can be attributed to sentencing changes.[69]

Between 1996 and 2014, New York reduced its jail and state prison incarceration rates by 55 percent, while the combined incarceration rate in the remainder of the United States rose by 12 percent. Crime rates also fell: from 1996 to 2014, New York City's crime rate declined by 58 percent, while index crime nationally declined by 42 percent. Felony drug arrests in New York City dropped from 45,978 in 1998 to 15,507 in 2015, due partially to the Drug Treatment Alternative to Prison (DTAP) program. The DTAP program was evaluated by Columbia University's Center on Addiction and Substance Abuse, which found that those offenders diverted to treatment were 36 percent less likely to be reconvicted than a matched comparison group. One study showed that between 1996 and 2014, felony drug sentences declined by 72 percent. This dramatic reduction in drug-offending prisoners was due to diversion, incentivized release programs, and sentencing reform, with no crime increases attributed to reduced numbers in prison.[70]

Explanations for Sentencing Shifts

The pervasiveness and depth of these sentencing changes led to a real impact on the U.S. prison population, creating a downward trend. Generally, sentencing reforms must have bipartisan support to be successfully passed into law. Politicians have become somewhat more supportive of sentencing reform and reducing prison populations, probably because there is increasing public support for such change. A 2019 Gallup poll showed that 66 percent of Americans favor legalization of marijuana and even greater numbers support treatment for drug abusers.[71] Polls show that close to 70 percent prefer that offenders with drug problems take part in a mandatory intensive treatment program over serving a prison sentence, and 83 percent support diverting lower-level offenders from prison.[72] Between 60 and 70 percent of respondents agree that federal prisons in the U.S. house too many nonviolent criminals, and 70 percent agree that the criminal justice system should rehabilitate criminals. Respondents also favor removing barriers that prevented ex-prisoners from finding jobs and dropping mandatory minimum sentences for nonviolent offenders.[73]

There are organized advocacy groups pushing for sentencing reform. Families Against Mandatory Minimums is one grassroots organization that advocates at both the state and federal level for rollbacks in the use of mandatory minimum sentencing. In December 2018, Congress finally passed a sweeping criminal justice reform bill that reduced the mandatory minimums this group has advocated against. Louisianans for Prison Alternatives, a project of the Southern Poverty Law Center, is another advocacy group promoting sentencing reform to reduce Louisiana's high imprisonment rate. Other states have similar advocacy groups.[74] Ultimately, our correctional population is formed by politics and public opinion as well as offenders' decisions to commit crime.

Summary

- Historically, corporal and public punishment were used to punish and deter offenders. The use of jails and prisons as punishment became more common, and brutal corporal punishments were abandoned in the late 1700s and 1800s.

- The most common sentences today are a fine, jail, prison, probation, or some combination of these. Although deterrence is one stated purpose of corrections, research indicates that correctional sentencing is ineffective in accomplishing either specific or general deterrence.

- All states and the federal system have sentencing statutes that create the legal authority and describe the available punishment for each crime. Most sentences are determined through plea bargaining.

- States have either an indeterminate or determinate sentencing system.

- Dissatisfaction with indeterminate sentencing systems led to many states passing sentencing reforms that made sentencing more determinate.

- Other reforms included sentencing guidelines, mandatory minimums, truth-in-sentencing laws, three-strikes legislation, the abolishment of discretionary parole, and good time.

- Average sentence lengths from the 1980s to today haven't changed much, but less serious offenders are more likely to receive prison sentences. Within crime categories, offenders are more likely to receive a prison sentence and receive a longer prison sentence than in years past.

- Sentencing disparity refers to when similar offenders, committing similar crimes, receive dissimilar punishment. States have widely disparate rates of incarceration. The correctional supervision rate includes probation and other forms of supervision, and like incarceration rates, states have very different correctional rates.

- There is apparent sex and racial and ethnic disparity in sentencing, but it is difficult to control for all factors that affect sentencing. Prior record, seriousness of crime, victim injury, offender culpability, motivation, and other factors may affect sentencing. Findings are mixed as to whether there is still gender disparity operating in state and federal sentencing.

- Since 2011, sentencing reforms across the country have included reducing the types of crimes that are punished by a prison sentence (as opposed to jail or probation), reducing the use of

mandatory minimums, increasing the use of problem-solving courts, and increasing pretrial release options and diversion, in addition to a range of other changes that may reduce the number of people in prison. Some states have been very successful in reducing their use of prison, even closing prisons that are not needed.

PROJECTS

1. Investigate your state to determine if there have been sentencing reform bills either passed or proposed. Which legislators and groups supported the sentencing reform? Which groups opposed the legislative change? For what reasons?

2. Conduct research using the Bureau of Justice Statistics to determine if prison populations in your state have increased, decreased, or remained relatively stable over the last five years.

NOTES

1. "Policy Brief: Fewer Prisoners, Less Crime" (Washington, DC: The Sentencing Project, 2014); D. Stemen, *The Prison Paradox: More Incarceration Will Not Make Us Safer* (New York City: Vera Institute of Justice, 2018); *Between 2007 and 2017, 34 States Reduced Crime and Incarceration in Tandem* (New York City, NY: Brennan Center, 2019), retrieved February 5, 2021 from https://www.brennancenter.org/our-work/analysis-opinion/between-2007-and-2017-34-states-reduced-crime-and-incarceration-tandem.

2. J. Cox, "Colonial Crimes and Punishments," Colonial Williamsburg website, n.d., accessed December 20, 2018, from http://history.org/Foundation/journal/spring03/branks.cfm.

3. D. Rothman, *The Discovery of the Asylum: Social Order and Disorder in the New Republic* (Boston: Little, Brown, 1971/1990).

4. D. Rothman, *The Discovery of the Asylum: Social Order and Disorder in the New Republic*.

5. N. Johnston, "Evolving Function: Early Use of Imprisonment as Punishment," *The Prison Journal* 89, 1 (2009): 105–45.

6. H.E. Barnes, "The Historical Origin of the Prison System in America," in *Police, Prison and Punishment: Major Historical Interpretations*, edited by K. Hall (New York, NY: Garland Press).

7. L. Friedman, *Crime and Punishment in American History* (New York: Basic Books, 1993).

8. D. Nagin and J. Pepper, *Deterrence and the Death Penalty* (Washington, DC: National Research Council, 2012).

9. GALLUP Poll, accessed December 20, 2018, http://www.gallup.com/poll/1606/death-penalty.aspx.

10. "American Support for Death Penalty Declining,"

Pew Research Center, 2015, accessed December 20, 2018, www.people-press.org/2015/04/16/less-support-for-death-penalty-especially-among-democrats.

11. R. Warden and D. Lennard, "Death in America under Color of Law: Our Long, Inglorious Experience with Capital Punishment," *Northwestern Journal of Law and Social Policy* 13, 4 (2018): 194–306.

12. J. Petersilia, "Meeting the Challenges of Prisoner Reentry," in *What Works and Why: Effective Approaches to Reentry*, edited by the American Correctional Association (Lanham, MD: American Correctional Association, 2005).

13. Paula A. Johnson, Comment, Senate Bill 42—The End of the Indeterminate Sentence, 17 Santa Clara L. Rev. 133 (1977), accessed December 20,

2018, http://digitalcommons.law.scu.edu/lawreview/vol17/iss1/4.

14. S. Shane-Dubow, A. Brown, and E. Olsen, *Sentencing Reform in the United States* (Washington, DC: U.S. Dept. of Justice, National Institute of Justice, 1985).

15. B. Western, *Punishment and Inequality in America* (New York: Russell Sage Foundation, 2006).

16. "More Prison, Less Probation for Federal Offenders," The Pew Charitable Trusts, 2016, http://www.pewtrusts.org/en/research-and-analysis/fact-sheets/2016/01/more-prison-less-probation-for-federal-offenders.

17. S. Raphael and M. Stoll, *Do Prisons Make Us Safer? The Benefits and Costs of the Prison Boom* (New York City: Russell Sage Foundation, 2008); B. Western, *Punishment and Inequality in America* (note 15).

18. J. Sorenson and D. Stemen, "The Effect of State Sentencing Policies on Incarceration Rates," *Crime and Delinquency* 48, 3 (2002): 456–75.

19. B. Western, *Punishment and Inequality in America* (note 15), 45.

20. D. Gilliard and A. Beck, *Prisoners in 1993* (Washington, DC: USDOJ, BJS,1994), 7.

21. *Who Gets Time for Federal Drug Offenses? Data Trends and Opportunities for Reform* (Washington, DC: Urban Justice Institute, Charles Colson Task Force, 2015).

22. "Drug Use Trends: October 2002," Office of National Drug Control Policy, accessed December 20, 2018, http://www.whitehousedrugpolicy.gov/publications/factsht/druguse/index.html; "Drug Facts," National Institute on Drug Abuse, accessed December 20, 2018, https://www.drugabuse.gov/publications/.drugfacts/nationwide-trends.

23. J. Inciardi, *The War on Drugs* (Boston: Allyn & Bacon, 2002).

24. D. Cole, *No Equal Justice: Race and Class in the American Criminal Justice System* (New York: The Free Press, 1999).

25. C. Parenti, *Lockdown America: Police and Prisons in the Age of Crisis* (New York: New Left Books, 1999).

26. J. Inciardi, *The War on Drugs* (note 23).

27. *Prison Time Surges for Federal Inmates* (New York: Pew Charitable Trusts, 2015).

28. J. Greene and V. Schiraldi, *Cutting Correctly: New State Policies for Times of Austerity* (Washington, DC: Justice Policy Institute, 2002).

29. "Marijuana Legalization Status, 2020," Cannabis Marketing Agency, accessed June 10, 2020, https://www.marijuanaseo.com/marijuana-legal-states/.

30. S. Horwitz, "Obama Grants Final 330 Commutations to Nonviolent Drug Offenders," *Washington Post*, January 19, 2017, accessed December 20, 2018, https://www.washingtonpost.com/world/national-security/obama-grants-final-330-commutations-to-nonviolent-drug-offenders/2017/01/19/41506468-de5d-11e6-918c-99ede3c8cafa_story.html?utm_term=.0ace09448f50.

31. S. Horwitz, "Struggling to Fix a 'Broken' System: For Many Drug Offenders, Their Only Hope is President Obama's Clemency Power. And His Time is Running Out," *Washington Post*, December 5, 2015, accessed December 20, 2018, http://www.washingtonpost.com/sf/national/2015/12/05/holderobama/.

32. *The Clemency Initiative*, USDOJ website, accessed August 22, 2021, https://www.justice.gov/archives/pardon/obama-administration-clemency-initiative.

33. S. Horwitz, "Struggling to Fix a 'Broken' System: For Many Drug Offenders, Their Only Hope is President Obama's Clemency Power. And His Time is Running Out" (note 31).

34. E. Carson and E. Anderson, *Prisoners in 2015* (Washington, DC: USDOJ, Bureau of Justice Statistics, 2016), Tables 9, 10.

35. C. Ingraham, "Drug Offenders Make Up Nearly One-Third of Prison Admissions, New Analysis Shows," *Washington Post*, November 27, 2015, accessed December 20, 2018, https://www.washingtonpost.com/news/wonk/.wp/2015/11/27/heres-why-ending-the-drug-war-will-have-a-bigger-impact-on-prisons-than-you-might-think/.

36. E. Carson and E. Anderson, *Prisoners in 2015* (note 34), Table 6.

37. B. Rabuy and P. Wagner, *Correctional Control: Incarceration and Supervision by State, June 1, 2016*, Prison Policy Initiative, accessed December 20, 2018, http://www.prisonpolicy.org/reports/50statepie.html.

38. J. Keller and A. Pearce, "This Small Indiana County Sends More People to Prison than San Francisco and Durham, N.C., Combined. Why?" *New York Times*, September 2, 2016.

39. J. Keller and A. Pearce, "This Small Indiana County Sends More People to Prison than San

Francisco and Durham, N.C., Combined. Why?" (note 38).

40. J. Pollock, *Women's Crimes, Criminology and Corrections* (Prospect Heights, IL: Waveland, 2014).

41. K. Daly, "Gender and Punishment Disparity," in *Inequality, Crime, and Social Control*, edited by G.S. Bridges and G. Beretta (Boulder, CO: Westview Press, 1994), 117–33.

42. I. Nagel and J. Hagan, "Gender and Crime: Offense Patterns and Criminal Court Sanctions," in *Crime and Justice: An Annual Review of Research*, Vol. 14, edited by M. Tonry and N. Morris (Chicago: University of Chicago Press, 1983), 91–144; K. Daly and R. Bordt, "Sex Effects and Sentencing: An Analysis of the Statistical Literature," *Justice Quarterly* 12 (1995): 141–68; for review, see J. Pollock, *Women's Crimes, Criminology and Corrections* (note 40).

43. C. Spohn and J. Spears, "Gender and Case Processing Decisions: A Comparison of Case Outcomes for Male and Female Defendants Charged with Violent Felonies," *Women and Criminal Justice* 8, 3(1997): 29–50.

44. C. Visher, "Gender, Police Arrest Decision, and Notions of Chivalry," *Criminology* 21 (1983): 5–28; B. Crew, "Sex Differences in Criminal Sentencing: Chivalry or Patriarchy?" *Justice Quarterly* 8 (1991): 60–78.

45. K. Daly and R. Bordt, "Sex Effects and Sentencing: An Analysis of the Statistical Literature" (note 42); M. Raeder, "Gender and Sentencing: Single Moms, Battered Women and Other Sex-Based Anomalies in the Gendered World of Federal Sentencing Guidelines,"

Pepperdine Law Review 20, 3(1993): 905–90; B. Blackwell, D. Holleran and M. Finn, "The Impact of the Pennsylvania Sentencing Guidelines on Sex Differences in Sentencing," *Journal of Contemporary Criminal Justice* 24(2008): 399–418.

46. S. Van Slyke and W. Bales, "Gender Dynamics in the Sentencing of White-Collar Offenders," *Criminal Justice Studies*, 26, 2 (2013): 168–96; J. Doerner, "Gender Disparities in Sentencing Departures: An Examination of U.S. Federal Courts," *Women & Criminal Justice* 22 (2012): 176–205.

47. B. Koons-Witt, "The Effect of Gender on the Decision to Incarcerate Before and After the Introduction of Sentencing Guidelines," *Criminology* 40 (2002): 297–328.

48. *Demographic Differences in Sentencing: An Update to the 2012 Booker Report* (Washington, DC: U.S. Sentencing Commission, 2017).

49. J. Austin, M. Bruce, L. Carroll, P. McCaul, and S. Richards, *The Use of Incarceration in the U.S.*, National Policy White Paper: American Society of Criminology, accessed December 20, 2018, https://www.ssc.wisc.edu/~oliver/RACIAL/Reports/ascincarcerationdraft.pdf.

50. E. Carson. *Prisoners in 2019*, Washington, DC: USDOJ, Bureau of Justice Statistics, 2016, 10.

51. J. Ulmer, N. Painter-Davis, and L. Tinik, "Disproportional Imprisonment of Black and Hispanic Males: Sentencing Discretion, Processing Outcomes, and Policy Structures," *Justice Quarterly*, 44 (2014): 642–81.

52. M. Free, "Race and Presentencing Decisions in the United States: A Summary and Critique of the Research," *Criminal Justice Review*, 27 (2002): 203–32.

53. B.L. Kutateladze, N.R. Andiloro, and B.D. Johnson, "Opening Pandora's Box: How Does Defendant Race Influence Plea Bargaining?" *Justice Quarterly*, 33 (2016): 398–426, DOI: 10.1080/07418825.2014.915340.

54. B. Kutateladze, B. Lynn, and E. Liang, "Do Race and Ethnicity Matter in Prosecution?" Vera Institute of Justice, 2012, accessed 29 October 29, 2013, http://www.vera.org/pubs/do-race-and-ethnicity-matter-prosecution-review-empirical-studies.

55. J.T. Ulmer, M.C. Kurlycheck, and J.H. Kramer, "Prosecutorial Discretion and the Imposition of Mandatory Minimum Sentences," *Journal of Research in Crime and Delinquency*, 44 (2015): 427–58.

56. E.Y. Chen, "The Liberation Hypothesis and Racial and Ethnic Disparities in the Application of California's Three Strikes Law," *Journal of Ethnicity in Criminal Justice*, 6 (2008): 83–102.

57. J. Ulmer, N. Painter-Davis, and L. Tinik, "Disproportional Imprisonment of Black and Hispanic Males: Sentencing Discretion, Processing Outcomes, and Policy Structures" (note 55).

58. C. Spohn, "Evolution of Sentencing Research," *Criminology and Public Policy* 14, 2 (2015): 225–43; J. Wooldredge, J. Frank, N. Goulette, and L. Travis, "Is the Impact of Cumulative Disadvantage on Sentencing Greater for Black Defendants?"

Criminology and Public Policy 14, 2 (2015): 187–223.

59. J. Doerner and S. Demuth, "The Independent and Joint Effects of Race/ethnicity, Gender and Age on Sentencing Outcomes in U.S. Federal Courts," *Justice Quarterly* 27, 1 (2010): 1–26; A. Anderson and C. Spohn, "Lawlessness in the Federal Sentencing Process: A Test for Uniformity and Consistency in Sentence Outcomes," *Justice Quarterly*, 27, 3 (2010): 360–93.

60. T. Franklin, "Sentencing Native Americans in U.S. Federal Courts: An Examination of Disparity," *Justice Quarterly* 30, 2 (2013): 310–39.

61. J. Doerner and S. Demuth, "The Independent and Joint Effects of Race/ethnicity, Gender and Age on Sentencing Outcomes in U.S. Federal Courts," *Justice Quarterly* 27, 1: 1–26.

62. W. Rhodes, R., Kling, J. Luallen, and C. Dyous, *Federal Sentencing Disparity: 2005–2012* (Cambridge, MA: BJS Working Paper, ABT Associates, 2015), 41.

63. *Demographic Differences in Sentencing: An Update to the 2012 Booker Report* (Washington, DC: U.S. Sentencing Commission, 2017).

64. E. Hager, *A Mass Incarceration Mystery. Why are Black Imprisonment Rates Going Down? Four Theories*, The Marshall Project, 2017, accessed December 20, 2018, https://www.themarshallproject.org/2017/12/15/a-mass-incarceration-mystery. W. Sabol, J. Thaddeus, L. Johnson and A. Caccavale. *Trends in Correctional Control by Race and Sex*. Washington, DC: Council on Criminal Justice, December 2019.

65. N. Porter, *The State of Sentencing, 2012: Developments in Policy and Practice* (Washington, DC: The Sentencing Project, 2015).

66. *State Advances in Criminal Justice Reform, 2016* (Washington, DC: The Sentencing Project, 2017),.

67. M. Males, *Most California Jurisdictions Show Declines in Property Crime During Justice Reform Era, 2010–2016*, Center on Juvenile and Criminal Justice, October 2017, accessed December 20, 2018, http://www.cjcj.org/uploads/cjcj/documents/most_california_jurisdictions_show_declines_in_property_crime_during_justice_reform_era.pdf.

68. J. Domanick, "The Message of California's Prop 47," *Los Angeles Times*, November 7, 2014; C. Chang, M. Gerber, and B. Poston, "Unintended Consequences of Prop. 47 Pose Challenge for Criminal Justice System," *Los Angeles Times*, November 6, 2015; M. Males, "Most California Jurisdictions Show Declines in Property Crime During Justice Reform Era, 2010–2016," (note 67).

69. M. Males, *Most California Jurisdictions Show Declines in Property Crime During Justice Reform Era, 2010–2016* (note 67); J. Sundt, E. Salisbury, and M. Harmon, "Is Downsizing Prisons Dangerous? The Effect of California's Realignment Act on Public Safety," *Criminology & Public Policy* 15, 2 (2016): 315–41.

70. J. Greene and V. Schiraldi, "Better by Half: The New York City Story of WinningLarge-Scale Decarceration while Increasing Public Safety," *Federal Sentencing Reporter*, 29, 1 (2017): 22–38.

71. Gallup Poll, October 2019, accessed June 10, 2019. https://news.gallup.com/poll/267698/support-legal-marijuana-steady-past-year.aspx.

72. *Prison Count 2010: State Population Declines for the First Time in 38 Years* (Washington DC: Pew Center on the States, 2011), 6.

73. T. Gest, "Public Strongly Favors Prison Reform, Surveys Find," *The Crime Report*, February 18, 2016.

74. L. Laird, "States Featuring Bipartisan Support Rally for Criminal Justice Reform," *ABA Law Journal*, December 2017, accessed December 20, 2018, http://www.abajournal.com/magazine/article/criminal_justice_reform_louisiana_alaska/P1.

Chapter 4

Jails and Pretrial Diversion

LEARNING OBJECTIVES

1. Summarize the processes of bail, release on recognizance, and pretrial release.

2. Describe pretrial diversion programs.

3. Differentiate between the various populations in jail.

4. Characterize the differences between jails and prisons in terms of funding, management, location, and architecture.

5. Discuss how poverty impacts criminal justice processing.

OUTLINE

- Forms of Preconviction Release 88

- Pretrial Diversion Programs 94

- Jails in the United States: Then and Now 95

- The Poverty Penalty 105

- SUMMARY 110

The Metropolitan Correctional Center is the federal jail where accused sex trafficker Jeffrey Epstein committed suicide on August 10, 2019.

KEY TERMS

Appearance bond
Bail
Bond
Booking
Citation
Civil Rights of
    Institutionalized Persons
    Act (CRIPA)
Day fines

Deferred adjudication
Fee system
Gaol
Indigency
Legal financial obligations
    (LFOs)
Partially secured bond
Pluralistic ignorance
Poverty penalty

Pretrial diversion programs
    (deferred adjudication)
Preventive detention hearing
Release on recognizance (ROR)
Restitution
Secured bond
Surety bond
Unsecured bond
Walnut Street Jail

Forms of Preconviction Release

Corrections encompasses everything that happens to an offender after a finding of guilt, but to fully understand the system and what happens to people once they are arrested, we must also discuss various forms of pre-verdict custody and diversion. Over 90 percent of guilty verdicts derive from plea bargaining, not trial. This means that the sentence has been agreed upon, in most cases, by the offender and prosecutor, with the judge issuing the plea-bargained sentence. Before the verdict is accepted, and sentence imposed, the arrested person may be in jail or in the community on some type of bail, bond, or pretrial release. Pretrial *diversion* programs, if offered in a particular jurisdiction, are different from pretrial *release*, because diversion programs offer an offender a way to avoid a criminal conviction entirely. We will discuss these possibilities in this chapter as well as the jail experience.

Citation or Booking

When you receive a traffic citation, a ticket is given "in lieu of arrest." That means that a traffic offense could result in a full custodial arrest (depending on the state law), but most of the time, you receive a **citation** (or ticket) that requires your presence in front of a magistrate at some predetermined date to argue the charge (or you can simply admit guilt and pay a fine for the offense). In many states, this same citation option in lieu of arrest is also available for minor offenses other than traffic violations; for example, minor misdemeanors. If the person who receives a citation does not appear before a magistrate and does not pay, there will be a warrant issued and an additional charge of failure to appear. Generally, these minor offenses do not carry a jail sentence as a potential punishment, only court fees, and a fine or some form of community supervision. If the person does not pay the fine, there will be late charges assessed. Eventually, failure to pay can result in a contempt citation, which could result in a jail sentence. Of course, each state has slightly different penal codes and sentencing structures, so the description offered here may not accurately represent what occurs in your particular jurisdiction.

A custodial arrest occurs when police officers have probable cause that a person has committed a crime or there has been an arrest warrant issued by

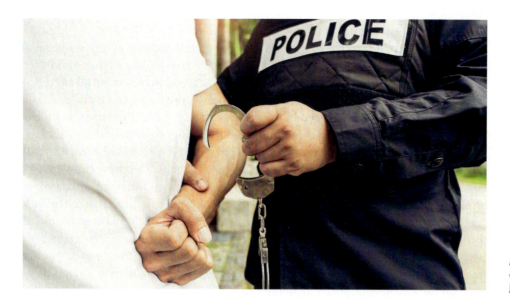

An arrest begins the individual's experience with the criminal justice system.

a magistrate after probable cause has been established. Once arrested, the individual is brought to jail to be booked. **Booking** involves fingerprinting, surrender of personal property, and sometimes changing into jail uniforms. Alternatively, the individual may remain in a holding cell until a bail hearing and then be released after paying some type of bond. **Bail** refers to the amount of money the magistrate has determined is sufficient to ensure an individual's appearance at further court hearings. **Bond** is the amount of money an individual is required to pay in lieu of the total amount along with a promise for the rest, either to a bail bonds office or, in some jurisdictions, the court itself. The Supreme Court has insisted that an arrestee must see a magistrate within 48 hours of being arrested.[1] At this first appearance or bond hearing, the magistrate confirms that there is probable cause the suspect committed the alleged crime. The magistrate may set a bail amount and determine whether the individual is indigent. **Indigency** is defined by the jurisdiction, but, generally, it means that the person does not have financial means to hire an attorney. If indigency is determined, a public defender or court-appointed attorney will be provided for the defendant if the potential sentence is incarceration in a jail or prison. If the crime is so minor that only a fine could be assessed, then the Supreme Court has held that the right to counsel provided in the Sixth Amendment does not require the state to provide an attorney; the right to an attorney exists only when the defendant faces a possible punishment of incarceration.[2]

Pretrial Release

It is possible for years to go by between an arrest and a final conviction or exoneration. While some people spend only a few hours in jail after an arrest before being released on bail or some type of pretrial release, others may spend months in jail before a resolution of their charges. Bail is a way for individuals to be released from jail prior to the resolution of their charges; however, because many people cannot afford bail, other forms of release also exist, such as release on recognizance and various pretrial release programs. Generally, there is no attempt at corrections before a determination of guilt; however, some pretrial release programs do mandate drug treatment, education, or other requirements that begin a rehabilitative process even before a finding of guilt.

BAIL

The purpose of bail is solely to ensure that the suspect appears at any subsequent court appearance; therefore, the more serious the charge, the higher bail is set, based on the assumption that if the suspect is facing a longer potential sentence, then more money is needed to deter him or her from fleeing the jurisdiction. If the offender is perceived to pose a great risk to the public, there may be no bail set. The Supreme Court has held that, under the Eighth Amendment, there is no constitutional right to bail, only the right not to be assessed *excessive* bail. Therefore, a **preventive detention hearing** may be held. The prosecutor may be able to show that even though the defendant is presumed innocent until proven guilty, there is a high probability that the defendant poses a great risk to the public if released.[3] In these cases, no bail is granted, and the defendant stays in jail. Generally, jurisdictions base bail amounts on the seriousness of the crime, not the ability of the offender to pay. A $1 million bail amount may not be enough to keep a very rich person from fleeing the country, and $200 may as well be $1 million for an indigent person. Therefore, our jails are filled with people arrested for petty crimes such as aggressive panhandling, public camping, public intoxication, and other public order crimes. The potential punishment is not especially severe, but bail amounts are typically higher than these people can afford; therefore, they spend weeks and months in jail before their case is resolved. Often, when their case is finally heard, the judge either dismisses the charge or, in the case of a guilty finding, sentences the offender to the time he or she has already spent in jail awaiting adjudication and credits the offender with that time, ensuring an immediate release.

The Eighth Amendment states that excessive bail is prohibited; however, this has been interpreted as determining whether the bail amount is disproportional to that given for similar crimes, not by evaluating the individual's financial resources.[4] In most jurisdictions, bail is usually obtained through the services of a bail bonds office. If bail is set at $5,000, for instance, the suspect must pay the bonds person a nonrefundable fee (e.g., 10 percent). The bail bonds agency guarantees to the court that the suspect will appear. If the person does not appear, the bond is forfeited, and the bonds office must pay the court the full amount of bail. The bond company has a strong incentive to find the person and get them to court (hence the use of bounty hunters).

Some jurisdictions eliminate the need for a bail bonds company by having the court itself take on the fee and the risk of forfeiture. The defendant must still pay a nonrefundable fee of 10 percent or more, except in those very few jurisdictions that offer a no-fee, or low administrative fee, bond option. Looking more closely at one jurisdiction, New York City's average bail amount on felony cases is $5,000, and misdemeanor cases is $1,000. However, more than 7,000 people are detained on any given day because they cannot afford their bail.[5] About half of arrestees are released within seven days or less, but the other half spend a longer amount of time; 10 percent of the jail population remains detained for at least six months or longer, awaiting resolution of their criminal cases. In only about 10 percent of felony cases and 13 percent of non-felony cases does the charged person immediately make bail. In about 45 percent of felony and 43 percent of misdemeanor cases, the charged person is never released prior to case disposition.[6]

New York law offers different forms of release. There are distinctions in terms of who must pay the bail amount, and in how much of the total amount must be paid. Related to who pays, a **surety bond** requires that someone other than the defendant pledge a bond amount, and an **appearance bond** requires the defendant to be the sole person paying the bond. As for how much must be paid, there are secured, partially secured, and unsecured bonds. A **secured bond** requires the cash amount or secured collateral deposited to the court, a **partially secured bond** requires 10 percent of the bond (or less), and an **unsecured bond** requires nothing other than the promise to appear and liability for the full amount upon failure to appear.[7] Judges typically only assign surety bonds that require the person to put up the full amount in cash or collateral. The reason other alternatives are not used seems to be a lack of training or understanding on the part of judges, defense attorneys, and prosecutors about the existence of or procedures required for these alternative forms of release. Ironically, bail is often set under $2,000, but that amount makes it financially unfeasible for a bail bonds office to bother with the case and, since the individuals involved usually don't even have that much, they stay in jail.[8]

RELEASE ON RECOGNIZANCE

As far back as the 1960s, there was concern regarding the number of people who spent time in jail before a resolution of their case simply because they could not afford bail. In 1961, the Vera Institute of Justice evaluated the Manhattan Bail Project, a program in New York City that utilized risk assessment to determine if individuals could be released without a money bond to ensure their appearance.[9] The Bail Project interviewed defendants and recommended **release on recognizance (ROR)**, meaning the defendant is released solely on their promise to return without having to produce any money for a bond if there is a low risk of flight based on employment history, local community ties, and past criminal record. The evaluation showed that 98 percent of individuals released returned to court and were 250 percent more likely to be acquitted at the end of their cases than those who remained in jail. These results spurred other jurisdictions to create pretrial release programs that allowed low-risk individuals to be released without paying anything.

Pretrial services divisions in probation departments or attached directly to the court assess the risk that a person will not return for court if released. Low-risk individuals are those who have the indices of reliability and stability; for instance, if they have a steady job, stable housing, and relatives in the area, they are considered likely to appear in court. The recommendation may lead to a judge's decision to release on recognizance or whatever the prerelease program is called in that jurisdiction. Some jurisdictions attach additional methods of monitoring during the release period, such as release under house arrest and/or electronic monitoring.

REDISCOVERING PRETRIAL RELEASE

Even though early release options were created and researched in the 1960s, they essentially disappeared in many jurisdictions, or were used sparingly. A different issue is when they are available but used only if the defendant can afford to pay a supervision fee (which we will discuss later in the chapter). Partly because of the decline in pretrial release opportunities, the number of individuals detained in jail prior to resolution of their cases has expanded dramatically since the 1990s. Across the country, fully two-thirds of the jail population have not been convicted and are awaiting trial or the resolution of their case. While a few of these individuals have been determined to be too dangerous to be released, most remain in jail because they can't afford bail. In fact, almost all of the increase in the jail population over the last 15 years is due to pretrial detainees, not an increase in the number of offenders convicted who receive a jail sentence. While in earlier decades there were roughly equal numbers of convicted and non-convicted in jail, the number of pretrial detainees relative to convicted inmates began to increase in the late 1990s.

In recent years, the problem of individuals in jail solely because of their inability to make bail has become the focus of media investigations, advocacy groups, and reform efforts.[10] Some jurisdictions have aggressively addressed the issue of pretrial detainees by increasing the use of pretrial release options rather than bail. For instance, in Washington, DC, only about eight percent of those arrested are jailed before resolution of their case; 92 percent are released prior to trial or final verdict. Release is determined by a prediction of flight, not ability to pay. Reports indicate that 90 percent of defendants appear for trial and are not rearrested before their cases are resolved.[11] New Jersey has also implemented the use of risk assessment to determine whether a person should be detained or not and eliminated the use of cash bail, and the state reduced its pretrial detainees by 15 percent in the first six months of use.[12] Kentucky also adopted a risk-assessment tool and shifted to a nonfinancial pretrial release program. Its pretrial release rate increased from 68 to 70 percent, and its court appearance rate rose from 89 to 91 percent, and arrests for new criminal activity while on pretrial release dropped by 15 percent. Colorado also uses a risk-assessment tool rather than an offense-based bail schedule and has a 95 percent court appearance rate and a 91 percent public safety rate.[13]

A study in New York City examined the use of unsecured or partially secured bonds and tracked cases over a twelve-month period. Although researchers did not utilize the standard scientific methodology of evaluations, the results supported bail alternatives. The court appearance rate was 88 percent, which is similar to the appearance rate of those released on secured bonds. Overall, the citywide average rate of failure to appear is 11 percent in felony cases and 14 percent in non-felony cases. About 8 percent of those released on unsecured or partially secured bonds were rearrested for new felonies during the pretrial release period. Importantly, most cases were resolved with a disposition that was less serious than the initial charge, with one-third ending in outright dismissal and another 19 percent ending in a noncriminal disposition. These individuals would have served months in jail before these dispositions.[14]

Lawsuits allege that due process and equal protection are violated when poor defendants facing minor charges end up spending time in jail simply because they cannot afford the nonrefundable fee to a bail bondsman[15] In a case against Harris County, Texas (Houston), a federal judge forced officials to release misdemeanor defendants who couldn't afford bail within 24 hours of their arrest, finding that the county discriminated against poor people, who were held in jail only because they could not pay their bond, while those with similar risk were released because they could pay. After the county appealed, the Fifth Circuit largely upheld the lower court's findings, and the county eventually settled the lawsuit by setting up procedures whereby most misdemeanants will be released on personal bonds.[16] This lawsuit, and others like it, allege that minor offenders arrested on invalid licenses, public intoxication, or public camping charges spend days in jail before seeing a magistrate who often then dismisses the charges. These minor offenders fill up jail cells simply because they cannot pay bail. In 2016, the Department of Justice filed an amicus brief in a similar case, arguing that fixed bail schedules without regard to ability to pay "unlawfully discriminate based on indigence." The John D. and Catherine T. MacArthur Foundation has allocated grant money to jurisdictions who promise to reduce their jail populations by 18 to 30 percent using pretrial risk assessment,

FOCUS ON THE

OFFENDER — A JUVENILE IN JAIL

In 2010, 16-year-old Kalief Browder was arrested for second-degree robbery. He and a friend were arrested when a man identified them to police officers as the teens who had stolen his backpack and hit him in the face two weeks earlier. His friend was released pending resolution of the case, but Browder was remanded with a bail of $3,000 because he was already on probation for an earlier case where he pled guilty to stealing and crashing a delivery truck. Because his family could not pay the $3,000, he was sent to New York City's Rikers Island. When the prosecutor received an indictment from the Grand Jury for aggravated assault, the possibility of bail was removed.

Browder was appointed a public defender, but his case was one of thousands in the Bronx courts. Every time the case came up for trial and the prosecutor asked for a week's continuance, the delay would turn into six weeks. The Sixth Amendment includes the promise of a speedy trial, but if the prosecutor says the state is ready for trial, scheduling delays are not counted. After two years had elapsed and Browder's case had not been resolved, a judge offered to let him go with time served if he would plead guilty to two misdemeanors, but he refused because he said he wasn't guilty and wanted his trial. Finally, in 2013, after three years and appearing in court over 37 times without any resolution, Browder was told by the judge that the prosecutor's office was not able to proceed to trial because their witness/victim had moved away, and he was released.

While in Rikers Island, Browder had been confined in a unit with 600 other boys 16–18 years old. The jail is notorious for its high level of violence perpetrated by both inmates and correctional officers. Gangs rule the housing units, and Browder was involved in several fights. He alleged was beaten by correctional officers and had spent the equivalent of two years in solitary confinement. He attempted suicide at least six times while incarcerated.

Once released, he passed the GED on his first attempt and tried to move on with his life, but he suffered flashbacks, depression, and paranoia. While at Rikers, his friends had completed high school, graduated, and begun college or jobs. In contrast, Browder now lived at home and couldn't seem to get past the violence and fear he had experienced in jail. He was uncomfortable around people and spent a lot of time in his room pacing. He attempted suicide six months after his release. With help, he began anti-anxiety and anti-psychotic medication and re-enrolled in community college. His case received a good deal of media attention and he worked with an attorney on a lawsuit against the city for his long incarceration. However, in June 2015, he committed suicide. The district attorney's office expressed regret that the case had been so long delayed but argued no one there was at fault—it was just the system.

Questions for Discussion

1. Why didn't Browder simply plead guilty so that he could be released from jail?

2. How would you address the problem of individuals spending long periods of time in jail before their case is resolved?

Sources: D. Ford, "Man Jailed as Teen Without Conviction Commits Suicide," CNN.com, June 8, 2015, accessed December 26, 2018, www.cnn.com/2015/06/07/us/kalief-browder-dead/; J. Gonnerman, "Kalief Browder, 1993–2015," The New Yorker, June 7, 2015, accessed December 26, 2018, www.newyorker.com/news/news-desk/kalief-browder-1993-2015; J. Gonnerman "Before the Law," The New Yorker, October 6, 2013, accessed December 26, 2018, www.newyorker.com/magazine/2014/10/06/before-the-law.

expanded electronic monitoring, and reminders to courts to try to release more defendants without bail.[17]

Holding poor defendants in jail who are charged with relatively minor crimes and are not flight risks is not only a basic fairness issue, there is also evidence that indicates it affects the outcome of their cases. There is a positive correlation between pretrial custody and harsher sentencing decisions. If ultimately convicted or they plead guilty, defendants who have been on some form of pretrial release receive less severe sentences than those who have been in jail, possibly because they have been able to maintain a job, pay restitution, enter a treatment program, and/or show the court their potential for reformation.[18] There is even evidence that pretrial custody affects convictions. The New York City Criminal Justice Agency published a report in 2012 that showed that, based on ten years' worth of criminal statistics, in non-felony cases, only half of defendants who were not detained were eventually convicted, but 92 percent of detained defendants were convicted. Even controlling for other factors, pretrial detention was the single greatest predictor of conviction.[19] Arguably, the high conviction rate is because those jailed eventually plead guilty just to resolve their case. There also seems to be an association between pretrial custody and recidivism. In several studies, there was a positive correlation found between pretrial detention and subsequent criminal activity after the current sentence had been served.[20]

Efforts to curb pretrial detention, however, are opposed by the bail-bond industry, which lobbies strongly against pretrial release options and contributes heavily to elections of prosecutors, sheriffs, and judges. The argument against forms of release that increase the number of defendants in the community prior to final disposition is that they pose a greater threat to public safety. However, there is no evidence that public safety is protected when only those with financial means are released.[21] Another argument against release made by prosecutors is that it provides less incentive for defendants to plea bargain. Those waiting in jail for their case to be resolved often endure months of confinement simply because of court delays. The Focus on the Offender box describes a tragic case of a teenager detained in Rikers Island for years before his case was dismissed. There is a strong pressure to plead guilty simply to get out of jail, even if it means a conviction will be on their record. If a defendant is released prior to case disposition, there is less incentive to resolve the case, and the prosecutor has less bargaining power. Civil rights advocates argue that is a good thing; prosecutors argue that it needlessly delays resolution of cases when the defendant is guilty.

Pretrial Diversion Programs

There is a distinction between the pretrial *release* programs that we have been discussing thus far and pretrial *diversion* programs. Pretrial *release* includes any of the means described above that allow a person charged with a crime to live in the community until their case has been resolved. Pretrial *diversion* is an opportunity for an arrested person to completely avoid a criminal conviction.

Pretrial diversion programs give the defendant the chance to avert a conviction by staying out of trouble for some predetermined time, usually nine to twelve months. Some jurisdictions may call this option **deferred adjudication** or deferred adjudication in contemplation of dismissal, meaning that any final court action is deferred, and, if the defendant is successful, the original charges are dismissed. Individuals are selected for these programs based on a risk assessment of future crimes, utilizing such factors as prior criminal history, employment history, educational status, and other criteria. Individuals agree to a contract whereby, in addition to avoiding any further arrests, they must pay court fees, restitution, and, possibly, supervision fees. Participants may have to show gainful employment, and there may be other conditions attached. The probation office generally supervises this group of people along with a regular probation caseload and monitors completion. If all goes well, an appearance is made before the judge, the original charge is dismissed, and the individual can honestly say they have not had a criminal conviction.

All too often, however, things don't go well, and the individual gets arrested again, or does not pay court fees and fines. In these cases, the person is brought back to face the original judge. In many jurisdictions, one of the requirements to enter the program is to offer a provisional guilty plea so that, if there is a failure on deferred adjudication, the court does not need to go through any fact-finding of guilt on the original charge. Sentencing is then imposed on the original charge, although it may be part of a broader plea agreement if there have been additional charges.

Pretrial diversion has the potential to divert nonviolent, low-risk individuals away from the criminal justice system. This is good for them and good for society because the costs associated with confinement are eliminated. An important element of pretrial diversion is prediction. It is important to be able to offer diversion only to those individuals who will not abuse the privilege. Another issue is making conditions reasonable enough that most individuals can achieve success. One of the problems with diversion programs has been that the offender is required to pay high supervision fees they cannot afford, and failure is inevitable. We will discuss this issue more thoroughly in the last section of this chapter.

A national symposium on pretrial diversion and release made the following conclusions based on a review of research:

- Only five percent of arrestees end up in prison, but almost 50 percent of arrestees are jailed pending outcome of their case;
- Research shows pretrial detention of low- and moderate-risk defendants increases the likelihood of committing crime;
- Most jurisdictions do not use risk assessment; instead, a bail schedule assigns bail amounts based on the offense charged; and,
- The average pretrial jail bed costs about $60 a day but goes as high as $200 a day in some jurisdictions.

At the same symposium, the following recommendations were presented:

- Jurisdictions should use citations rather than jail when possible;
- Bond schedules based on offense should be eliminated and risk prediction instruments should be used;
- Early prosecutorial screening should be conducted to dismiss weak cases before the accused is jailed;
- Appointment of defense counsel should occur at the first hearing to advocate for pretrial release;
- Training and support should exist for court personnel making pretrial release recommendations; and
- A pretrial services agency should exist in every jurisdiction to conduct a risk assessment on all defendants and provide supervision of defendants released by the court.[22]

Jails in the United States: Then and Now

American jails (historically called **gaols**) are an older form of incarceration than penitentiaries, and have existed since colonial times. People were held in gaols before and during their trials and before being punished; in some cases, they were held for debt. Being punished by incarceration itself was not common until the development of the penitentiary. The earliest penitentiaries in the United States did not emerge until the late 1770s.

Colonial jails housed everyone together—men, women, and children, as well as the sick and healthy—in large common rooms. If typhus, known as jail fever, or any contagious illness took hold, it was devastating to the jail population. Sometimes there were barred windows to the street where the detainees begged passersby for food or coins. Jails were run by the **fee system**, which meant that the jailer may have received a nominal amount of money from the city or county to provide mere sustenance, but most of his income came from the inmates themselves. Inmates who were lucky enough to have the financial resources to pay the jailer could pay for a private room, more and better food, and coal for a fire. Some even had their servants stay with them while they were incarcerated. Those who could not pay were given the bare minimum to survive, and sometimes not even that.

The horrific conditions of gaols were critiqued by early reformers, such as the English philanthropist and sheriff John Howard (1726-1790) who, in 1777, wrote a treatise on the squalid and dangerous conditions of gaols and prisons in England.[23] He advocated more enlightened treatment of prisoners, promoting the philosophy and practices of the Hospice of San Michele in Rome, which housed young male offenders under a strict regimen of work and penance, and the Maison de Force at Ghent, Belgium, where four sections separately housed male offenders, beggars, women, and unemployed laborers and abandoned children.[24]

Philadelphia's original **Walnut Street Jail**, built in 1773, adhered to the architecture of the time; it included large rooms where all prisoners were housed together. Quaker reformers were appalled at the debauchery and inhumane conditions they found in Walnut Street and other jails. In response, the group formed the Philadelphia Society for Alleviating the Miseries of Public Prisons (now called the Pennsylvania Prison Society) with the goal of improving the conditions under which prisoners were held (see the Focus on History box). Some of their reforms were adopted when an addition to the jail was built in 1790. Women and men were separated, children were kept separate from adults, and the sick were isolated so they did not infect the healthy. This new building had small individual cells instead of large common rooms. Inmates were supposed to contemplate their sins in silence. The new institution became the first penitentiary in the United States, and the change in name reflected the new goals of religious penitence and redemption.[25]

Unfortunately, overcrowding and corruption occurred within a few years. By 1817, it was not uncommon to have 30 to 40 men in one sleeping room in the Walnut Street Jail, and observers noted that alcohol, riots, and escapes were common. Eventually, the reforms that had begun at the Walnut Street Jail were carried over to the Eastern State Penitentiary on the outskirts of Philadelphia, which was started in 1822 but took many years to fully complete.[26] The history of the Eastern State Penitentiary and other early prisons will be discussed in Chapter 7.

Today, there is a vast difference in the types of jails that exist across the country. The largest jail is Los Angeles County's, which houses about 14,000 inmates. Harris County (Houston), Texas, and Cook County (Chicago), Illinois, both have close to or over 10,000 inmates. Some of the smallest jails have a daily population of around 25, or even less. Jails that house less than 100 inmates comprise 57 percent of all jails (but only hold about 10 percent of all jail inmates).

HISTORY

EARLY JAILS

In 1787, the Philadelphia Society for Alleviating the Miseries of Public Prisons was formed. The founders included religious leaders, doctors, lawyers, and businessmen, including Benjamin Franklin. A committee of the members visited the Walnut Street Jail regularly, checking on the conditions of confinement and examining the influence of the confinement upon the morals of the prisoners. The members who were physicians provided medical advice. The Society was committed to reforming the Walnut Street Jail and all early jails. These men observed the horrific conditions. In the following quote, a description illustrates their observation of what needed to change.

> In one common herd were kept by day and night prisoners of all ages, colors and sexes. There was no separation of the most flagrant felon from the prisoner held on suspicion for some trifling misdemeanor. There was no separation of the fraudulent swindler from the unfortunate, and often estimable debtor. This assembly of the most vicious of both sexes resulted in unspeakable conditions. There was little furniture and no bedding. Unless supplied by their friends, the inmates lay on the floor. A small loaf of bread was allowed each day to each prisoner, and nought else was obtainable unless the prisoner had money. Intoxicating drinks were supplied to all who could pay for them, and it was a common custom to strip newcomers of most of their garments in order to pawn the clothing for drink. The keeper readily connived at all these purchases in as much as he charged a liberal commission for attending to their vicious demands. Parents were allowed to have their children with them in jail, and these youthful culprits were exposed to all the corrupting influences of association with confirmed and reckless villains. There was no employment of any sort. Innocent persons detained as witnesses were thrown in with the most abandoned felons. The keeper had power to retain prisoners till certain fees were paid so that often persons were kept in this unwholesome lazarette for months or years after their legal term had expired.

The Society advocated for separation of men from women, the young from the old, and hardened criminals from minor offenders. They also advocated for individual separation, believing that housing criminals together only created "schools for crime." In 1790, they were successful in getting legislation supporting separation and banning alcohol. In 1794, legislation mandated single cells, but keepers could not comply because of overcrowding. Also in 1794, the jail fee was abolished in favor of a set salary for the keeper, reducing the incentives for corruption. Corporal punishments such as the pillory, branding with hot irons, and the whipping post were abolished. Many of the ideas of the Society were implemented in 1829 when the Eastern Penitentiary was built, but their greatest influence, perhaps, was in alleviating the conditions of those offenders who were incarcerated in the early jail. The Society changed its name to the Pennsylvania Prison Society in the mid-1800s and began publishing the *Journal of Prison Discipline and Philanthropy*, which is still published today as *The Prison Journal*. While jails in Philadelphia improved in some ways, descriptions of other jails throughout the 1800s were similarly shocking. In 1878, for instance, at the Fifth Annual National Conference of Charities and Correction, one report described the common practice of housing all prisoners together:

> But the almost universal practice is still to allow the prisoners, old, young, experienced and first offenders, boys, debauched and debauching villains, to spend a large part of each day in mutual instructions in crime. Abundant time is thus afforded for rehearsing vile and demoralizing stories of personal adventures; and, strangest of all, in planning schemes of jail-breaking and escapes, often including the maiming or murdering of the very officers by whose leniency, indifference, or ignorance, this school of crime is permitted.

Advocates insisted that the contagion effect of prisoners associating with each other would lead to more crime; the ideal jail was one where they had no contact. Ohio's Board of State Charities published a plan for county jails in 1868:

> The distinguishing feature of this jail plan is the central corridor, between the line of cells. The rear doors of the cells, all opening into this central corridor, are solid, with no opening except a small bull's-eye, covered with a

shield, movable only by the keeper, from the outside, to enable him to observe safely, or secretly when necessary, the action of the prisoners within. All the movements of the prisoners are through these solid doors, and along this central corridor; thus avoiding entirely the sight or observance of one prisoner by another, and enabling each prisoner to remain unknown to all his fellow-prisoners, if he desires it. This arrangement carries the front of the cells well out to the outer walls of the prison; and these fronts should be constructed largely of open lattice-work, and

facing each cell a window in the outer wall should be formed. This secures, if proper ventilation is adopted, abundance of light, sun, and good air, which are the first requisites of healthful confinement. With this arrangement, of course, all the constantly improving appliances for safety and convenience may be incorporated.

This general plan was implemented in the early penitentiary, but few jails followed the model, although, eventually, holding all inmates together in a large hall was abandoned in favor of separate cells.

Sources: *C. Henderson. Papers, [Box 2, Folder 10], Special Collections Research Center, University of Chicago Library, accessed December 26, 2018, at https://socialwelfare. library.vcu.edu/corrections/pennsylvania-prison-society/; J. Hansan, "Proceedings of the Fifth Annual Conference of Charities and Correction Held in Cincinnati, Ohio in May 1878." In Corrections: Part II—Background and Jails (2012), accessed December 25, 2018, at https://socialwelfare.library.vcu.edu/corrections/corrections-part-ii-background-and-jails-1878/.*

In 2018, the average daily population of the nation's jails was 738,400 and in 2019, it was 734,500, down from 776,600 in 2008. There are about 10.6 million separate admissions to jails in any given year.[27] Between 1983 and 2013, annual admissions to jails increased from 6 million to 11.7 million, while the average daily number of jail inmates rose from 224,000 to 731,000.[28] See Table 4.1 for a breakdown of how the U.S. jail population has changed from 2000 to 2018.

Most jails are managed by county sheriffs, and their budgets come from their respective counties; however, there are a few jurisdictions that combine state and county prisoners in one facility (e.g., Rhode Island), and some areas have created regional jails with several counties coming together to fund the facilities. There are about 3,000 jails across the country. Jails are different from prisons in terms of structures, resources, procedures, operations, equipment, and staffing.[29]

Jails are usually located within the county seat (to be close to criminal courts), and they typically consist of one building. In many counties, the jail may not even have a separate building and, instead, comprises several floors of a government building. There is usually no outdoor exercise area except the roof, and very few programs are offered because it is expected that those in the jail will be there for a short period of time. Unlike most prisons, which are single-sex facilities, most jails have both male and female inmates. Given that jails are closer to the towns or cities where individuals are arrested, inmates receive more visits than prison inmates because prisons may be hundreds of miles away from an offender's family. Visitation in jail often occurs through glass as opposed to contact visits without glass. There is a lot of inmate movement to manage in a jail because individuals are constantly being booked and then bailed out, and many must be taken to court for first and subsequent court appearances. Additionally, many individuals may be frequently entering and exiting the jail under some form of weekend reporting, work release, or treatment programs.

TABLE 4.1					

U.S. Jail Population, 2000–2018

YEAR	NUMBER IN LOCAL JAILS	RATE	% FEMALE	% WHITE/ BLACK/ HISPANIC	% UNCONVICTED
2000	621,149	226	11.4%	42/41/15	56%
2005	747,529	252	12.7%	44/39/15	62%
2010	748,700	xx	12.2%	44/38/16	61%
2015	693,300*	230	14.2%	48/35/14	63%
2018	738,400	226	15.6%	50/33/15	66%

*Does not match year-end figure, but BJS calculated race/ethnicity/sex figures from this total.

Source: T. Minton and Z. Zeng, Jail Inmates in 2015 (Washington, DC: Bureau of Justice Statistics, OJPDOJ, 2016); A. Lurigio, "Jails in the United States," The Prison Journal, 96, no. 1 (2016): 3–9. Z. Zeng, Jail Inmates in 2018 (Washington, DC: Bureau of Justice Statistics, OJPDOJ, 2020).

Unconvicted Inmates

A major difference between prisons and jails is that jails house people who have not been convicted and are presumed innocent. As noted earlier, the number of pretrial detainees (those who are not convicted offenders) has risen in relation to the convicted and now comprises about two-thirds of the jail population in the United States (see Figure 4.1). Before the late 1990s, the proportion of unconvicted to convicted was about equal.

One might think that individuals who are awaiting a finding of guilt or innocence would be treated differently and given more liberties than those who have been found guilty of a crime and are being punished by a jail sentence. Unconvicted detainees argue that their rights of due process and equal protection under the Fourteenth Amendment require that they be treated more similarly to the unconvicted who are out on bail than convicted jail inmates who are being punished for their crimes. In 1979, the Supreme Court, in *Bell v. Wolfish* disagreed with this argument and decided that the administrative need to run a safe

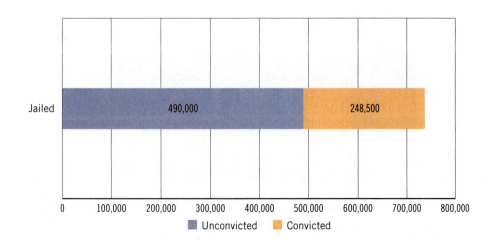

FIGURE 4.1 Number of unconvicted vs. convicted jail inmates. Created by author from Z. Zeng, "Jail Inmates in 2018" (Washington, DC: Bureau of Justice Statistics, OJPDOJ, 2020).

and secure facility was more important than the rights of the unconvicted to be treated as closely to those on bail as possible (i.e., with more privileges than the convicted in jail).[30] Thus, jails generally have no different procedures for detainees and convicted prisoners in terms of visitors, programming, searches, and so on.

In *Florence v. County of Burlington*, a man was arrested after a traffic stop when it was found he had an outstanding warrant for an unpaid fine.[31] He was strip searched and held for more than five days before it was confirmed that he had already paid the fine and the warrant was in error. He sued, arguing that individuals who are arrested for minor offenses, such as unpaid fines, with no reasonable suspicion that they may be bringing in contraband should not be subject to the humiliation of a strip search. Supporting legal arguments noted that strip searches of unconvicted detainees were forbidden in ten states and were forbidden in international human rights treaties, but in other states, anyone might be strip searched—even those arrested for violating the city's leash law or having a loud muffler. In one case, a nun was strip searched after a trespass arrest for a nonviolent protest. The opposing argument is that even those with nonviolent arrests might bring in contraband to the jail. The Supreme Court sided with the government's position and held that it was not a violation of due process or any other constitutional right to be strip searched regardless of the reason for the arrest because of the jail officials' interests in preventing the entry of contraband.[32]

In jail, there is a wide range of individuals who may be innocent or guilty of crimes, ranging from minor public order to serious offenses. Figure 4.2 shows the types of crimes committed by those who are serving jail sentences. Generally, those convicted of a felony who receive a sentence longer than a year are sentenced to a state prison, while those convicted of a misdemeanor or minor felony and sentenced to less than a year of imprisonment remain in jail. Public order offenses (e.g., public drunkenness, public disorder, gambling, and prostitution) are the largest category of offenders. Others may be arrested simply for having unpaid traffic tickets. Two-thirds of jail inmates are detainees waiting for a resolution of their case; the other one-third have been convicted of a misdemeanor and will serve their sentence in jail, or have been convicted of a felony and are waiting for transfer to a state prison.

In prison, everyone is convicted, everyone has committed a felony, and everyone's background (e.g., mental illness and criminal history) is known and documented in their file, which arrives with them at the prison. In jail, when someone is admitted, very often nothing is known about them. If they are

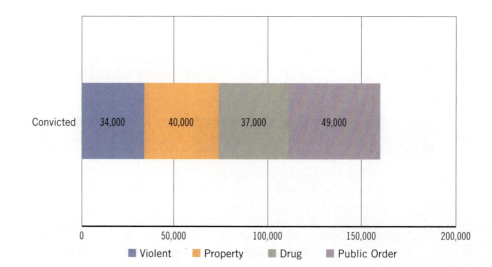

FIGURE 4.2 Crimes committed by convicted individuals. Created by author from W. Sawyer and P. Wagner, "Mass Incarceration: The Whole Pie, 2020," Prison Policy Initiative, https://www.prisonpolicy.org/reports/pie2017.html.

impaired, they may be in a drunken stupor or they may be suffering from hypo-glycemia; they may be actively psychotic or under the influence of an unknown substance; they may be a seriously violent offender or simply have an unpaid traf-fic ticket. The constant movement in and out of a jail, with the level of unknowns regarding those who are booked into the jail, poses a logistical and management challenge. Jail officials do their best to protect inmates from each other and themselves and do so partly by restricting movement much more than is the gen-eral pattern in prisons.

In addition to detainees awaiting resolution of their case and those serving a jail sentence, jail inmates may include probation, parole, and bail-bond violators; juvenile detainees; mentally ill people (pending transfer to mental institutions); military violators (pending transfer to military facilities); contempt violators; material witnesses; those awaiting extradition; and state prisoners awaiting transfer. In a few jurisdictions, jails may house those who have been convicted of lower-level felonies. For instance, Texas has state jails, which are run by the state department of corrections and house state jail felons who have sentences of up to three years.

Juveniles arrested for a crime may be taken to a jail for adults if there is no secure detention facility for juveniles in that jurisdiction. In past decades, there were more juveniles in jails, but the number has been declining. In 2000, there were about 6,100 juveniles age 17 or younger who were held as adults and 1,500 held as juveniles. In 2018, only 2,700 juveniles were held as adults and 700 held as juveniles.[33]

The racial and ethnic profile of the jail population is roughly similar to that of the national prison population. As Figure 4.3 shows, the percentage of jail in-mates who are identified as Black/African American has been declining, while the percentage of jailed inmates identified as white has increased. There is no clear answer as to why this is occurring, although some have speculated it is because of the reduction of arrests for marijuana possession charges and other petty crimes that may be disproportionately directed to minority populations.

The percentage of jail inmates who are women has increased from about 11 percent in 2000 to over 15 percent in 2018 (see Table 4.1). The daily population of women in U.S. jails in 2000 was about 71,000, but in 2018 that number had increased to 115,500. In comparison, the number of men was 550,200 in 2000 and 623,400 in 2018.[34] Although the number of women in jail is still small com-pared to the number of men, it is troubling that the rate of increase for women is so much higher. It is not clear why this increase is occurring, but it is possible

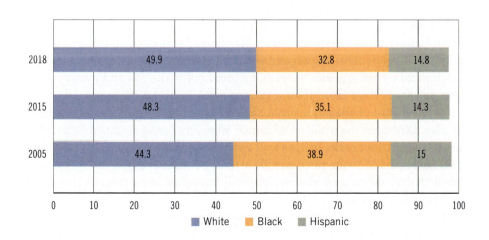

FIGURE 4.3 Percentage of jail inmates by race/ethnicity. Created by author from T. Minton and Z. Zeng, "Jail Inmates in 2015" (Washington, DC: Bureau of Justice Statistics, OJPDOJ, 2016), Table 4.

that the reduced use of pretrial release options over the last 30 years has led to a higher percentage of women in jail who may have been more likely to receive pretrial release options in earlier decades.

As mentioned above, the jail population is an especially difficult population to manage because of drug and alcohol dependence, mental illness, and other challenges. Reports indicate that about 70 percent of jail inmates used drugs regularly before incarceration, and about half had used in the month prior to their arrest.[35] This means that jail inmates may be suffering from withdrawal symptoms, sometimes to an extent that poses serious health risks. Mental health issues are also present. A national survey that received responses from 39 states found that about 10 percent of jail inmates could be considered as having a serious mental health issue. This figure is consistent with years of data concerning the level of mental health problems in jail populations. Jail staff have estimated that 11 percent or more of their time is spent dealing with the mentally ill.[36] The jail has been described as holding the permanent underclass of society—the so-called rabble who are the addicted, the mentally ill, and the homeless, as well as those who are perennially caught up in the criminal justice system and revolve in and out of the jail.[37]

The Conditions of Jail

The American Jail Association and the American Correctional Association have created jail standards that cover everything from sanitation to staffing to programming. Table 4.2 details core jail standards, but very few jails meet these standards because jails are a low priority for counties, especially in times of fiscal austerity. Jails are often overcrowded, housing many more inmates than the rated capacity. There is some attempt to separate the violent from potential victims, but because there is constant movement in a jail population, this is difficult to do.

Jails are often the target of lawsuits because of alleged unconstitutional conditions. Healthcare, or more accurately, the lack of it, is frequently the subject of such lawsuits. According to a November 2015 investigation by the *Houston Chronicle*, 75 people had died in the Harris County Jail since the Justice Department began an investigation in 2009. The report stated that 19 people died from medical issues that were "either treatable or preventable, or in which delays in care, or staff misconduct, could have played a role."[38] The *Huffington Post*, in its investigation of jail deaths, estimated that about 1,000 people die in jails every year, and stated that official records undercount jail deaths.[39] In 2020, the COVID-19 pandemic posed an incredible challenge to jail and prison administrators. It is virtually impossible to social distance in crowded dormitories. Some jails closed entirely and transferred jail inmates to neighboring counties.

Jail deaths are often suicides, such as the 2015 death of a 28-year-old Black woman named Sandra Bland in Texas. Bland had been stopped for failing to signal but arrested because she argued with the police officer about putting out her cigarette and refusing to exit her car. She could not make bail and was found dead in her cell three days later of an apparent suicide. Bland's case gained national notoriety because of allegations that she was arrested because she was Black. The case also illustrates the problem of minor offenders being detained in jail simply because they cannot make bail, as well as the danger of jail suicide. While Bland's intake forms did indicate prior suicide attempts, she answered "no" to questions related to depression and whether she had thoughts of suicide, so she was not placed on suicide watch.

The legal arguments used by jail inmates to assert their rights include the **Civil Rights of Institutionalized Persons Act (CRIPA)**, passed in 1980, which

Sandra Bland's suicide in a Texas jail after a traffic stop led to numerous protests.

was created to protect the elderly, disabled, and mentally ill in institutions. CRIPA protection extends to the jail population. The Department of Justice may sue a county jail if there is evidence that conditions are dangerous to the safety of someone protected under CRIPA, although these lawsuits can stretch on for decades.

Even those who are not in the protected groups identified in CRIPA have legal recourse if they feel that jail conditions are egregious. However, only jail inmates who have been found guilty and are serving a sentence can allege that horrible jail conditions violate the Eighth Amendment. Pretrial detainees who have not been convicted are not technically being punished; therefore, the Supreme Court has held that they cannot allege cruel and unusual punishment.[40] They can, however, use the due process clause of the Fourteenth Amendment to argue that they are being deprived of constitutional rights without due process of law. These types of jail lawsuits also frequently target the lack of healthcare, as well as alleged abuse by jail guards, sanitation issues, lack of programming, lack of visitation, and other deprivations.

Generally, larger jails appear to have more problems, but that may be just because they attract more press coverage. For instance, the New York State Commission of Corrections announced that New York City's plan to close Rikers Island within 10 years was not soon enough due to conditions at Rikers that endangered both staff and inmates. In 2016 and 2017, commission inspectors found there was a pattern of violating the constitutional rights of inmates at Rikers. They found numerous health and safety violations, including incidents of prisoners left unsupervised, improper population counts, inadequate inspections, documentation of firearms used at the facility, and unsanitary conditions in jail cells and food service areas. In some instances, inmates died because of lack of medical care. In 2020, the *New York Times* reported that violence in Rikers was at "an all-time high" despite a federal monitor and promise by the city to reduce violence. The city still has plans to close the jail by 2026.[41]

Because jails are not supposed to house inmates for a long period of time, there are few, if any, rehabilitative programs. Even though jails are housed within communities, few volunteer programs exist in many jails because of security

| TABLE 4.2 | Core Jail Standards |

I. SAFETY
Sanitation, handling of vermin, disposal of hazardous waste, cleaning and maintenance protocols, water quality, size of cells, size of dayrooms, lighting, ventilation, smoking controls, vehicle safety and inmate transfer protocols, emergency preparedness and evacuation plans, fire safety, furnishings and supplies meeting standards of non-flammable and non-toxic, emergency power and communication

II. SECURITY
Control of facility through communications, posting of COs, personal contact; maintain secure perimeter, female staff member for female inmate, no inmate control over other inmates, control of inmate movement, sufficient staffing, inmate management system, use of counts, facility design, legal and medical review of admissions, admissions procedures (e.g. search, criminal history check), inmate orientation, classification system, prohibition of youthful offenders in general population, segregation availability and conditions, healthcare, use-of-force policies and procedures, use of restraint devices policies and procedures, weapons control procedures, procedures for searches, tool and key control

III. ORDER
Inmate rules and discipline, dietary provisions, food service management, bedding and other provisions, including hygiene products, access to health care and health screens, pregnancy plans, communicable diseases, dental care, mental health care and suicide prevention, detoxification procedures, pharmaceutical control, health care staff qualifications, notification policies, confidentiality/HIPPA, sexual assault prevention and investigation, sexual conduct of staff

V. PROGRAM AND ACTIVITY
Programs and services, programs to preserve family and community ties, visitation, mail, telephone, release plans, access to exercise and recreation including outdoor, access to library services, working conditions, religious programs, access to religious programs, canteen

VI. JUSTICE
Access to courts, counsel and legal materials, needs of foreign nationals, protection from abuse, freedom of personal grooming, indigence, grievance procedures, fair treatment and lack of discrimination, needs of disabled inmates, due process in discipline procedures,

VII. ADMINISTRATION AND MANAGEMENT
Selection, retention and promotion of staff, training and staff development, written policies and procedures, financial audits, control of inmate records, fair treatment of staff, maintenance of facility and equipment

Source: Core Jail Standards, 2010, American Correctional Association, http://correction.org/core-jail-standards/.

issues. Many jail inmates spend a great deal of time being idle, playing cards, or watching television. Some inmates have trustee status and do the cooking and cleaning, and some jails have work-release programs for low-risk inmates that allow participants to exit the jail for daily work assignments. However, there are seldom outside work opportunities.

Despite agreement that a substantial percentage of those in jail need mental health services, in one survey just over a third of the jails surveyed offered psychiatric care, and only 42 percent offered stabilizing drugs for those who needed them. Fewer than 25 percent of the jails said they offered any support for the mentally ill who were discharged into the community. About 60 percent of the jails reported offering two hours or less of annual training for staff in how to deal with the mentally ill.[42] In 2014, the Mentally Ill Offender Treatment and Crime Reduction Act funded 254 grants in 46 states for planning, implementation, and expansion of initiatives to help identify, classify, and provide services to the mentally ill in local jails. A few programs collected evaluation data and showed improvement in indices of mental health and fewer subsequent arrests and/or fewer jail days. Many programs, however, were phased out after federal money was gone.[43] Advocacy groups propose that diverting the mentally ill from jail, if possible, and providing treatment alternatives would prevent further offenses and arrests. Unfortunately, it is often the case that the offender's mental illness is not considered during the criminal justice process and/or that the offender is released without any services provided, which results in a revolving door of arrests and releases until he or she does something so serious that the consequences become more severe.

Jail Staff

In 2018, there were 174,500 individuals designated as jail correctional officers. About 75 percent were men.[44] Most often jails are staffed with sheriff's deputies, although in some jurisdictions there is a separate job designation for jail officer. Sometimes, sheriffs use the jail assignment as punishment or as a probation assignment for new deputies. Even though there is a different skill set required for jail officers than for street deputies, there is often a lack of specific training. If the position is a separate job designation, the jail officer's entry salary is less than that of a sheriff's deputy. Jail managers face problems with maintaining high levels of professionalism among jail staff because of low salaries, turnover, and recruitment difficulties.

One study of jail officers found that they were fairly punitive in their orientation toward jail inmates and expressed a need to keep social distance from them. However, there was some evidence of **pluralistic ignorance**, a term used to refer to the situation whereby a majority of correctional officers privately have pro-inmate views (regarding rehabilitation and the ability for inmates to change), but incorrectly assume that the majority do not believe in those concepts because a minority of verbal correctional officers have expressed opposite views.[45] Only 44 percent of officers in the sample agreed with the statement "rehabilitation programs are a waste of time and money"; however, 68 percent of the officers believed that their colleagues agreed with this statement. The researchers concluded that jail officers perceived their fellow officers to be less accepting of counseling roles and more punitive than they were. The implication of this finding is that correctional officers could be helpful in rehabilitation efforts if allowed to do so, and if they recognized that others supported them.[46]

 # The Poverty Penalty

In the 1770s, those who owed money to others or the state were often detained in gaols until they or their families paid their debts. While detained, they might incur further debt to the jailer because the fee system required that they pay for their room and board in jail. Imprisoning individuals because they owed other people money was eventually prohibited in the United States. In the early 1800s, Kentucky became the first state to abolish its jail for debtors, followed by other states that either passed legislation prohibiting imprisonment for debt or, in court challenges, found that such imprisonment violated state constitutional rights. In 1933, legislation was passed at the federal level that prohibited imprisonment for debt.[47] The only debt one can still be imprisoned for is debt to the government.

Throughout this chapter we have seen how economic resources can influence the experience of those who end up in the criminal justice system. For those who can afford to pay, pretrial release is likely if one pays either a bail bonds office or the court a secured or semi-secured bond. Those with financial resources can pay a private attorney, who can help secure bail, negotiate a plea agreement, and, if necessary, prepare for trial. Paying a fine may end criminal justice involvement. Poor defendants cannot pay their fines and are ensnared in a cycle of late fees, and, ultimately, jail for nonpayment. They can't pay supervision fees, so they are not eligible for pretrial diversion programs that require such payment. Probation and/or electronic monitoring are welcome alternatives to prison, but, again, defendants must be able to pay the monthly fee for these programs and are in violation of their probation if they do not pay. In the United States today, 10 million people hold criminal debt from fines and fees totaling over $50 billion.[48] It is estimated that, in 2010, half of arrests and up to one-quarter of incarcerations in Ohio alone were for nonpayment of fines and court costs. A Brennan Center study of several counties in different states showed that most counties spent 41 cents on collection efforts for every $1.00 they collected and one county spent over $1.17 for every $1.00 collected.[49]

Fines and Restitution

Some argue that the continual increase in fees, fines, and court costs in the last 30 years has created a two-tiered justice system where those who have financial resources are more likely to pay their way out of involvement with the criminal justice system, and those who cannot are trapped in a cycle of nonpayment, additional charges for late fees, contempt and, often, incarceration because of nonpayment.[50] Fines are supposed to be a deterrent. If the risk of punishment when committing a crime is too great, arguably, the individual will choose not to do it. An example of this type of correctional rationale are those public service advertisements that warn people a DUI will cost $10,000. The problem with this calculus, however, is that fines do not generally consider individual circumstance. A $10,000 fine for one person might as well be $1 million, and, for another, it might be a minor inconvenience. If a corporation is fined for some criminal or civil violation, the fine may be considered the cost of doing business.

Generally, fines are set by the offense; less serious offenses receive smaller fines and more serious offenses garner higher fines. However, in Europe and in some jurisdictions in the United States, **day fines** are used; these consider an offender's income, and the fine is calculated at a specific number of days' pay. This system balances the financial strain felt by those with and without high incomes. However, if the offender has no income at all, day fines cannot be used.

In 1971, in *Tate v. Short*, the Supreme Court rejected the standard practice at the time of equating days in jail with fines.[51] Texas law at that time permitted incarceration at a rate of $5 per day to pay off fines, so someone who could not afford to pay a $500 fine could serve 100 days in jail instead. The United States Supreme Court found that this use of incarceration violated the Equal Protection Clause of the Constitution because the poor were treated differently than those who could afford to pay the fine; in addition, it did not further any penal objective of the state. This decision, however, did not resolve the problem of how the poor should pay their fines.

Fines are usually assessed along with a probation sentence so that the probation officer can monitor payment. In fact, many jurisdictions have what is called pay-only probation, where courts impose probation solely because the defendant is unable to pay fines or court costs immediately after sentencing. Defendants who can pay exit the system, but those who cannot are sentenced to probation solely to monitor repayment, and, often, must pay supervision fees along with the original fine and court costs. These offenders typically have committed traffic violations and other minor offenses that do not generally deserve a sentence of imprisonment.

Fines are also increasingly being assessed against those who are sentenced to prison. This means that, upon release, the individual may have a large fine to pay or their parole may be revoked. Fines are imposed in 42 percent of cases heard in courts of general jurisdiction (misdemeanors and felony charges), and courts of limited jurisdiction (city and county violations and misdemeanors) assess fines in 86 percent of cases. About 38 percent of felony cases involve fines, even if the person is also sentenced to prison. Judges generally do not consider the financial situation of the defendant.[52]

Most people's conceptions of the criminal justice system involve serious felony offenses and trial. However, most offenses are misdemeanors, and trials are rare. Misdemeanors comprise 80 percent of court dockets—around 10 million separate cases a year compared to about 3 to 4 million felonies. Offenses such as drunk driving, public intoxication, marijuana possession, and simple assault take up a huge amount of criminal justice resources (including police, courts, and corrections). Misdemeanor offenders are very likely to receive a fine regardless of their ability to pay, and this financial obligation often begins a long involvement with the criminal justice system because of nonpayment.

Another type of payment imposed on criminals is **restitution**, compensation made by an offender meant to alleviate a victim's injury or losses. Judges may impose restitution as a part of sentencing instead of or in addition to fines. All states have enabling legislation for judges to utilize restitution. A study found that state courts imposed restitution in 18 percent of felony cases.[53] The recipients of restitution are often governmental agencies; for example, someone who commits welfare fraud must pay restitution to the state. In many cases, the defendant is required to pay restitution to the victim's insurance company. A defendant's failure to make restitution payments can also result in revocation of probation.

Fees

The proliferation of court fees and other types of fees assessed against criminal defendants has become a major issue and one that has led to concern over the so-called **poverty penalty**. By some accounts, nearly a quarter of the jail population is there simply because of nonpayment, and the numbers may be significantly higher in some jurisdictions.[54]

The main categories of **legal financial obligations (LFOs)** are fines, restitution charges, and fees. LFOs have escalated dramatically over the last 40 years. The percentage of federal inmates with LFOs grew from 25 percent in 1991 to 66 percent in 2004. Only 4 percent of state prisoners in 1986 had also received a fine; by 2004, that figure was seven times higher (28 percent).[55] While no current national figures of the percentage of prisoners who also were assessed fines and fees are available, a 2017 report on LFOs reported that fines and fees have proliferated dramatically in many states. For instance, Texas has 15 categories of court costs that are "always assessed" and an additional 18 discretionary LFOs that include fees for being committed to or released from jail. In Washington state, a convicted offender is subjected to 24 fines and fees.[56] The range of fees assessed against suspects, defendants, and the convicted is unprecedented. Fees vary by jurisdiction, but there may be fees for arrest, issuance of warrants, booking, fingerprinting, lab testing, pretrial detention, jury, application for a public defender, bail, deferred prosecution agreement, pretrial abatement, pretrial supervision fees, and rental of monitoring devices.

Despite Supreme Court cases that establish a constitutional right to an attorney regardless of ability to pay, there are fees for public defenders in 43 states, ranging from $25 to $100. Many of these fees are nonrefundable even if the defendant is found not guilty. Across the country, more than 80 percent of all defendants qualify for public defenders, indicating that most defendants do not have the financial ability to meet these obligations.[57]

At least 43 states allow charges for room and board in jails and/or prisons, and 35 states permit charges for medical care. Ironically, these daily fees are like the fees jailers charged in the 1700s and 1800s. Jail inmates may be charged $20–$60 a day regardless of whether they are serving time or being held before adjudication. Ironically, even if they are acquitted or the charges are dropped, they still must pay the jail fee in some jurisdictions. If they can't pay, the debt follows them after release. In jails and prisons, excessive telephone rates far above the prevailing market generate millions of dollars annually and have been the subject of lawsuits because the rates are imposed disparately upon the poor families of offenders.

Those who have money can buy comfort in pay-to-stay jails. For example, defendants in Los Angeles can pay up to $175 a day to be housed in suburban jails rather than the Los Angeles County jail, where they can enjoy iPods, flat-screen televisions, computer access, private cells, and work-release programs. At least 26 small cities around Los Angeles offer to take prisoners as long as they can pay the daily fee. Some of these jails even accept offenders from out of state.[58]

About 44 states charge for probation and/or electronic monitoring, with monthly charges ranging from $180 to $360 per month, although they can be much higher.[59] In some states and counties, private companies are contracted to provide probation supervision. Probation that is administered by for-profit companies has become attractive to jurisdictions because the companies undertake the supervision of probationers for free, obtaining money from the probationers themselves. In over a dozen states and 1,000 courts, private probation companies charge probationers enrollment fees and supervision fees. Private probation officers have been accused of threatening incarceration for nonpayment and not informing offenders of their right to counsel. There are concerns that many probationers have successfully completed other terms of their probation and have not committed new crimes but are continued on probation solely because of nonpayment of fees.[60]

It appears that the proliferation of fees has more to do with revenue generation than penal objectives. A report on the Ferguson Police Department by the Department of Justice in 2015 concluded that police ticketing practices and the assessment of late fees by the municipal courts in Ferguson, Missouri, were largely designed to extract revenue from low-income residents through the imposition of fines and fees for petty crimes and traffic offenses rather than serving any corrective or penal objective.[61] Financial pressures in local governments have shifted many of the costs of the criminal justice system to offenders, which, to a great extent, only prolongs the involvement of many in the system because of nonpayment.

Failure to Pay

In *Argersinger v. Hamlin*, the Supreme Court held that the Sixth Amendment requires an attorney be provided if a defendant is indigent but only if he or she is facing a potential punishment of any form of imprisonment.[62] In *Scott v. Illinois*, the Supreme Court declined to extend the Sixth Amendment right to counsel to cases in which the defendant faced only a possible fine.[63] But what happens when the offender cannot or will not pay the fine? Generally, confinement then becomes a possibility under a criminal contempt charge. Offenders who are assessed a fine along with probation may end up in prison or jail after revocation when they do not pay their fines, court fees, or supervision fees. In 2019, the Supreme Court finally incorporated the Eighth Amendment protection against excessive fines to individuals against state actions in a case that involved the state of Indiana seeking to seize a defendant's $42,000 Land Rover as punishment for a crime that had a statutory maximum fine of $10,000.[64] This case decision may not be applicable to excessive fees assessed for jail stays and probation supervision because, arguably, these are different from criminal fines and are not assessed for punishment.

The Supreme Court has held that it is unconstitutional to incarcerate solely because of nonpayment of fines or fees. In 1970, in *Williams v. Illinois*, the Supreme Court held that the Equal Protection clause of the Fourteenth Amendment prohibited extending the incarceration of an individual who was unable to pay his criminal justice debt beyond the maximum statutory term for that crime.[65] In 1983, in *Bearden v. Georgia*, the Supreme Court determined that the sentencing court should assess the offender's ability to pay before revoking probation for failure to pay fines or restitution.[66] If the person can pay but willfully refuses to do so, then revocation is warranted; however, if the person's economic situation is such that they cannot pay their fines and fees because they don't have enough income to support themselves or their family, then there can be no revocation, and the probation officer must rework the payment schedule to make it feasible to pay.

Even though it is unconstitutional to revoke probation solely because of an inability to pay, probationers may not know this, and it appears many are not provided with attorneys to protect their rights. In *Alabama v. Shelton*, the Supreme Court held that felony or misdemeanant probationers who could be subject to incarceration under the terms of their probation have the right to counsel regardless of their ability to pay; however, low-level courts often fail to appoint counsel or assess indigency in motion-to-revoke proceedings.[67] Lower courts, especially, have been known to ignore Supreme Court holdings on the right of indigents to counsel, either failing to hold indigency hearings or deciding that the person is not indigent despite clearly meeting statutory definitions of indigency.[68] For instance, in one case, a Georgia pharmacist became addicted to drugs and lost his family, home, and job. He ended up on probation for public drunkenness and theft when he stole a can of beer from a convenience store. He was required to wear an electronic monitor to detect alcohol use. The monitor cost $12 a day, along with a $50 set-up fee and a $39 monthly fee to a private probation company. He also needed to install a landline phone for the system to work. In total, his probation sentence cost more than $400 a month. He couldn't pay, so he was sent to jail for 12 months, but ultimately won his release when an attorney helped him challenge his fees.[69]

Most of the states with the highest prison populations impose the largest range of fees, and high revocation rates for parole and probation contribute to higher prison and jail populations. One study in Ohio found that potentially thousands of offenders were jailed simply for nonpayment, and many probationers had their probations revoked for nonpayment. In 2014, the Ohio Supreme Court created an informational pamphlet for judges that clearly set out the restrictions on the use of incarceration for nonpayment. The Ohio Supreme Court distinguished court fees as civil debt that was not subject to confinement for nonpayment. Other states have followed this practice of distinguishing fines and fees, with all court and supervision fees designated as civil debt, thus removing the threat of confinement as a consequence of nonpayment.[70] The criminal justice system has evolved in such a way that fines and court costs fund a substantial portion of the system. Recently, changes have been underway. For instance, San Francisco has eliminated booking, probation, and electronic monitoring fees. In March 2019, the Missouri Supreme Court ruled that courts cannot jail people when they cannot pay incarceration fees. Nevada has passed a law eliminating juvenile fines and fees; and, New Hampshire has repealed its law that allowed jail fees.[71] In 2017, New Orleans dramatically reduced the use of money bail for people arrested for municipal offenses, and the city began to replace revenue lost by the Criminal District Court as it reduced money bail and conviction fees.[72] It will be difficult to moderate the dependence on fines and fees, even though it will be necessary in order to reduce the number of people who cannot escape their involvement with the system solely because of nonpayment.

Summary

- The array of pretrial release options developed in the late 1970s and 1980s seem to have fallen out of favor; today, the largest percentage of jail inmates are there because they are poor and cannot afford bail.
- There are about 10 million separate admissions to jails every year.
- Jails house the innocent and the guilty, and serious offenders as well as very minor offenders. Individuals come into jail with mental health issues, addictions, and physical health problems.

- Jail staff are usually sheriff's deputies with very little specialized training on how to deal with jail inmates.
- The poverty penalty refers to the burgeoning number of fines and fees assessed against offenders, to the extent that many cannot extricate themselves from the criminal justice system because of what they owe, not because they are continuing to commit crime. Others continue their involvement with the criminal justice system in a revolving door of jail visits, fine assessments, and failure to pay.

PROJECTS

1. Go to the Pretrial Justice Institute webpage (http://www.pretrial.org/) and research whether any progress has been made on the recommendations presented in this chapter.

2. Explore any online information that is available about your local jail. How big is it? What programs are available for jail inmates? What pretrial release or diversion options are available?

NOTES

1. *County of Riverside v. McLaughlin*, 500 U.S. 44 (1991).

2. *Argersinger v. Hamlin*, 407 U.S. 25 (1972).

3. *United States v. Salerno*, 481 U.S. 739 (1987).

4. *Stack v. Boyle*, 342 U.S. 1 (1951).

5. I. Rahman, *Against the Odds: Experimenting with Alternative Forms of Bail in New York City's Criminal Courts* (New York City: Vera Institute of Justice, 2017).

6. I. Rahman, *Against the Odds: Experimenting with Alternative Forms of Bail in New York City's Criminal Courts* (New York City: Vera Institute of Justice, 2017), 17.

7. I. Rahman, *Against the Odds: Experimenting with Alternative Forms of Bail in New York City's Criminal Courts* (New York City: Vera Institute of Justice, 2017), 8.

8. N. Pinto, "The Bail Trap," *New York Times*, August 16, 2015: MM38.

9. C. Ares, "The Manhattan Bail Project: Preliminary Report," *New York University Law Review*, 38 (1963): 1–27.

10. See, for instance, "U.S. Gets 'Abysmal' Grade on Pretrial Justice," *The Crime Report*, November, 1, 2017, accessed December, 26, 2018, https://thecrimereport.org/2017/11/01/u-s-gets-abysmal-grade-on-pretrial-justice/.

11. E. Luna (Ed.), *Reforming Criminal Justice: Introduction and Criminalization, Vol. 1* (Phoenix, AZ: Arizona State University, 2017), 91

12. "U.S. Gets 'Abysmal' Grade on Pretrial Justice," *The Crime Report* November, 1, 2017, accessed December, 26, 2018, https://thecrimereport.org/2017/11/01/u-s-gets-abysmal-grade-on-pretrial-justice/.

13. E. Luna, *Reforming Criminal Justice: Introduction and Criminalization (Vol. 1)* (Phoenix, AZ: Arizona State University, 2017), 91.

14. I. Rahman, *Against the Odds: Experimenting with Alternative Forms of Bail in New York City's Criminal Courts* (New York City: Vera Institute of Justice, 2017), 20.

15. R. Reilly, "Mark Zuckerberg and Priscilla Chan Are Funding the Fight to End Money Bail," *Huffington Post*, October 10, 2017, accessed December, 26, 2018, https://www.huffingtonpost.com/entry/chan-zuckerberg-bail-industry-criminal-justice-reform_us_59dcda8de4b0b34afa5c78c5.

16. *O'Donnell v. Harris County*, 227 F.Supp.3d 706 (S.D. Tx, Dec. 16, 2016); *O'Donnell v. Harris County*, No. 18-20466 (5th Cir. 2018).

17. R. Reilly, "Mark Zuckerberg and Priscilla Chan Are Funding the Fight to End Money Bail," *Huffington Post*, October 10, 2017.

18. P. Heaton, S. Mayson, and M. Stevenson, "The Downstream Consequences of Misdemeanor Pretrial Detention," *Stanford Law Review*, 69 (2017): 711.

19. N. Pinto, "The Bail Trap" *New York Times*, August 16, 2015: MM38.

20. O. Roeder et al., *What Caused the Crime Decline?* (New York City, NY: Brennan Ctr. for Justice, 2015), available at https://www.brennancenter.org/publication/what-caused-crime-decline, 22; C. Spohn and D. Holleran, "The Effect of Imprisonment on Recidivism Rates of Felony Offenders: A Focus on Drug Offenders," *Criminology* 40 (2002): 327–47; C. Lowenkemp et al., *The Hidden Costs of Pretrial Detention* (New York: The Arnold Foundation, 2013), accessed December 26, 2018, http://www.arnold-foundation.org/wpcontent/uploads/2014/02/LJAF_Report_hidden-costs_FNL.pdf. https://www.arnold-foundation.org/wp-content/uploads/2014/02/LJAF_Report_hidden-costs_FNL.pdf.

21. R. Reilly, "Mark Zuckerberg and Priscilla Chan are Funding the Fight to End Money Bail," *Huffington Post*, October 10, 2017.

22. *Implementing the Recommendations of the National Symposium on Pretrial Justice: The 2013 Progress Report* (Gaithersburg, MD: Pretrial Justice Institute, 2014).

23. J. Howard, *The State of the Prisons in England and Wales* (London: William Eyres, 1777).

24. N. Johnston, "Evolving Function: Early Use of Imprisonment as Punishment,"

25. *The Prison Journal* 89, 1 (2009): 105–45.

25. D. Garland, *Punishment and Modern Society: A Study in Social Theory* (Chicago: University of Chicago Press, 1990); A. Hirsch, *The Rise of the Penitentiary: Prisons and Punishment in Early America* (New Haven, CT: Yale University Press, 1992).

26. N. Johnston, "Evolving Function: Early Use of Imprisonment as Punishment" *The Prison Journal* 89, 1 (2009): 105–45.

27. Z. Zeng, *Jail Inmates in 2018* (Washington, DC: Bureau of Justice Statistics, OJDOJ, 2020). T. Minton, L. Beatty and Z. Zeng. *Correctional Populations in the United States, 2019 – Statistical Tables* (Washington, DC: Bureau of Justice Statistics, OJDOJ, 2021).

28. R. Subramanian, *Incarceration's Front Door: The Misuse of Jails in America* (New York: Vera Institute of Justice, 2015), 15, accessed December 26, 2018, http://www.vera.org/sites/default/files/resources/downloads/incarcerations-front-door-report.pdf.

29. A. Lurigio, "Jails in the United States," *The Prison Journal*, 96, 1 (2016): 3–9.

30. *Bell v. Wolfish*, 441 U.S. 520 (1979).

31. *Florence v. Board of Chosen Freeholders*, 566 U.S. (2012).

32. A. Liptak, "Supreme Court Ruling Allows Strip-Searches for Any Arrest," *New York Times*, April 2, 2012, accessed December 26, 2018, at https://www.nytimes.com/2012/04/03/us/justices-approve-strip-searches-for-any-offense.html.

33. Z. Zeng, *Jail Inmates in 2018* (Washington, DC: Bureau of Justice Statistics, OJDOJ, 2020).

34. Z. Zeng, *Jail Inmates in 2018* (Washington, DC: Bureau of

Justice Statistics, OJDOJ, 2020).

35. "Percent of Jail Inmates Reporting Drug Use," Table 6.21, University of Albany, http://www.albany.edu/sourcebook/pdf/t621.pdf; P. Harrison and A. Beck, *Prison and Jail Inmates at Midyear 2004* (Washington, DC: Bureau of Justice Statistics, 2005).

36. S. Kleiner, "National Survey Shows Jails Ill-equipped to Handle Surge of Mentally Ill Inmates," *Richmond Times-Dispatch*, July 14, 2016, accessed December 26, 2018, http://www.richmond.com/news/virginia/article_86ba02dd-1551-5100-90d9-78ea69404c2b.html.

37. J. Irwin, *The Jail: Managing the Underclass in American Society* (Los Angeles, CA: University of California Press, 1985).

38. A. Santo, "When an Old Law Makes It Hard to Fix a Troubled Jail," *The Marshall Project Newsletter*, September 13, 2016, accessed December 26, 2018, https://www.themarshallproject.org/2016/09/13/when-an-old-law-makes-it-hard-to-fix-a-troubled-jail.

39. R. Reilly, "Ten Jails. More Than 40 Deaths. What Happened in One Year?" *Huffington Post*, December 26, 2016, http://www.huffingtonpost.com/entry/jail-deaths-statistics_us_58518e13e4b0ee009eb4f1a9?etd7d44defh6j8xgvi&utm_medium=email&utm_campaign=The%20Morning%20Email%20121616&utm_content=The%20Morning%20Email%20121616+CID_c4d94ec0eb9d9238f8882e58d44b9d70&utm_source=Email%20marketing%20software&utm_term=Dana%20Liebelson%20and%20Ryan%20Reilly%20HuffPost&.

40. *Bell v. Wolfish*, 441 U.S. 520 (1979).

41. G. Blain, "Plan to Close Rikers in 10 Years is Inadequate: Commission Report," *New York Daily News*, February 14, 2018, accessed December 26, 2018, https://www.msn.com/en-us/news/us/plan-to-close-rikers-in-10-years-is-inadequate-commission-report/ar-BBJ8LkG; B. Weiser, "Violence at Rikers at an 'All-Time High' Despite City's Promise to Curb It," *New York Times*, August 6, 2020.

42. S. Kleiner, "National Survey Shows Jails Ill-equipped to Handle Surge of Mentally Ill Inmates*Richmond Times-Dispatch*, July 14, 2016.

43. H. Steadman, J. Morrissey, and T. Parker, "When Political Will is Not Enough: Jails, Communities, and Persons with Mental Health Disorders," *The Prison Journal*, 96,1 (2016): 10–26.

44. Z. Zeng, *Jail Inmates in 2018* (Washington, DC: Bureau of Justice Statistics, OJDOJ, 2020).

45. J. Klofas and H. Toch, "The Guard Subculture Myth," *Journal of Research in Crime & Delinquency*, 19 (1982): 238–54.

46. C. Cook and J. Lane, "Professional Orientation and Pluralistic Ignorance Among Jail Correctional Officers," *International Journal of Offender Therapy and Comparative Criminology* 58,6 (2014): 735–57.

47. S. Fraser, "Another Day Older and Deeper in Debt," *Raritan*, 33, 2 (2013): 67–78.

48. B. Colgan, "Fines, Fees, and Forfeitures," in *Reforming Criminal Justice: Punishment, Incarceration, and Release* (Vol. 4), edited by E. Luna (Phoenix, AZ: Arizona State Univ, 2017), 205–35.

49. K. Beckett and A. Harris, "On Cash and Conviction: Monetary Sanctions as Misguided Policy," *Criminology and Public Policy*, 10

(2011): 509–24. M. Menendez, M. Crowley, L. Eisen, and N. Atchison. *Costs of Criminal Justice Fees and Fines: A Fiscal Analysis of Three States and Ten Counties* (New York, NY: Brennan Center, 2019).

50. D. Evans, *The Debt Penalty— Exposing the Financial Barriers to Offender Reintegration* (New York, NY: Research and Evaluation Center, John Jay College of Criminal Justice, 2014); A. Bannon, M. Nagrecha, and R. Diller, *Criminal Justice Debt: A Barrier to Reentry* (Washington, DC: Brennan Center, 2010), http://www.brennancenter.org/sites/default/files/legacy/Fees%20and%20Fines%20FINAL.pdf.

51. *Tate v. Short*, 401 U.S. 395 (1971).

52. B. Ruback, "The Abolition of Fines and Fees: Not Proven and Not Compelling," *Criminology and Public Policy*, 10 (2011): 569–83.

53. S. Rosenmerkel, M. Durose, and D. Farole, *Felony Sentences in State Courts, 2006* (Washington, DC: Bureau of Justice Statistics, USDOJ, 2009).

54. B. Colgan, "Fines, Fees, and Forfeitures" in *Reforming Criminal Justice: Punishment, Incarceration, and Release* (Vol. 4), edited by E. Luna (Phoenix, AZ: Arizona State Univ, 2017), 205–35.

55. K. Beckett and A. Harris, "On Cash and Conviction: Monetary Sanctions as Misguided Policy"*Criminology and Public Policy*, 10 (2011): 509–24.

56. K. Martin, S. Smith, and W. Still, "Shackled to Debt: Criminal Justice Financial Obligations and the Barriers to Re-Entry They Create," *New Thinking in Community Corrections Bulletin* (Washington, DC: U.S. Department of Justice,

National Institute of Justice, 2017), NCJ 249976.

57. R. Subramanian, *Incarceration's Front Door: The Misuse of Jails in America* (New York: Vera Institute of Justice, 2015).

58. A. Santo, V. Kim, and A. Flagg, "Upgrade Your Jail Cell—For a Price," *Los Angeles Times*, March 9, 2017, accessed December 26, 2018, http://www.latimes.com/projects/la-me-pay-to-stay-jails/.

59. J. Shapiro, "As Court Fees Rise, the Poor Are Paying the Price," NPR, May 19, 2014, accessed December 26, 2018, http://www.npr.org/2014/05/19/312158516/increasing-court-fees-punish-thepoor; also see I. Zaluska, "Paying to Stay in Jail: Hidden Fees Turn Inmates into Debtors," *The Crime Report*, September 17, 2019, accessed January 7, 2020https://thecrimereport.org/2019/09/17/paying-to-stay-in-jail-hidden-fees-turn-inmates-into-debtors/.

60. H. Rappleye and L. Seville, "The Town that Turned Poverty into a Prison Sentence," *The Nation*, March 14 2014, accessed December 26, 2018, http://www.thenation.com/article/178845/town-turnedpoverty-prison-sentence; "The Outskirts of Hope: How Ohio's Debtors' Prisons are Ruining Lives and Costing Communities" (American Civil Liberties Union of Ohio, 2013), accessed December 26, 2018, http://www.acluohio.org/wp-content/uploads/2013/04/TheOutskirtsOfHope2013_04.pdf.

61. *Investigation of the Ferguson Police Department* (Washington, DC: United States Department of Justice Civil Rights Division, 2015), accessed December 26, 2018, https://www.justice.gov/sites/default/files/opa/press-releases/attachments/2015/03/04/ferguson_police_department_report.pdf.

62. *Argersinger v. Hamlin*, 407 U.S. 25 (1972).

63. *Scott v. Illinois*, 440 U.S. 367, 373–374 (1979).

64. *Timbs v. Indiana*, 139 S. Ct. 682 (2019).

65. *Williams v. Illinois*, 399 U.S. 235 (1970).

66. *Bearden v. Georgia*, 461 U.S. 660, 671–673 (1983).

67. *Alabama v. Shelton*, 535 U.S. 654 (2002).

68. S. Dewan and A. Lehren, "After a Crime, the Price of a Second Chance," *New York Times*, December 12, 2016, accessed December 26, 2018, https://www.nytimes.com/2016/12/12/us/crime-criminal-justice-reform-diversion.html?_r=0.

69. J. Shapiro, "Measures Aimed at Keeping People Out of Jail Punish the Poor," NPR, May 24, 2014, accessed December 26, 2018, https://www.npr.org/2014/05/24/314866421/measures-aimed-at-keeping-people-out-of-jail-punish-the-poor.

70. "Modern-Day Debtors' Prisons: The Ways Court-Imposed Debts Punish People for Being Poor," American Civil Liberties Union of Washington and Columbia Legal Services, 2014, accessed December 26, 2018, https://aclu-wa.org/sites/default/files/attachments/Modern%20Day%20Debtor's%20Prison%20Final%20(3).pdf.

71. I. Zaluska, "Paying to Stay in Jail: Hidden Fees Turn Inmates into Debtors," *The Crime Report*, September 17, 2019, accessed 7/1/2020 from https://thecrimereport.org/2019/09/17/paying-to-stay-in-jail-hidden-fees-turn-inmates-into-debtors/.

72. "Paid in Full: A Plan to End Money Injustice in New Orleans," Vera Institute, June 2019, https://www.vera.org/downloads/publications/paid-in-full-report.pdf.

Chapter 5

Probation and Community Corrections

CHAPTER OBJECTIVES

1. Differentiate between the probation population and the prisoner and parole populations.

2. Outline the history of probation.

3. Discuss the conditions of probation and the issues involved in supervision, including the various supervision approaches by probation officers.

4. Describe the process of revocation and the legal rights of probationers during supervision and revocation.

5. Identify the factors associated with recidivism.

6. Compare recent innovations in community corrections to the correctional practices developed in the 1970s.

CHAPTER OUTLINE

- Probation and Probationers 116

- The History of Probation 118

- Probation Supervision 118

- Recidivism and Revocation 125

- Probation Officers 128

- Changes in Probation Supervision 130

- Improving Community Corrections 135

- SUMMARY 137

Probation supervision instead of incarceration is a possible sentence for adult and juvenile offenders

KEY TERMS

Burnout
Casework model
Cognitive behavioral therapy (CBT)
Conditions
Deferred sentencing
Effective Practices in Community Supervision (EPICS)
Intensive supervision probation

Intermediate sanctions
Interstate Compact for Adult Offender Supervision (ICAOS)
Net-widening
Parole
Pre-sentence investigation
Pre-sentence report (PSR)
Probation
Probation subsidies
Recidivism

Restitution
Revocation
Risk/Needs/Responsivity (R/N/R) model
Scarlet letter conditions
Split sentencing (shock probation)
Suspended sentencing
Technical violations

Probation and Probationers

The term probation derives from the Latin verb *probare*, meaning to prove or test. **Probation** is a court-ordered period of correctional supervision in the community as a punishment for a crime. In some jurisdictions, probation can be combined with a period of confinement; in this sentencing scenario, an offender spends a short period of time in prison or jail followed by period of community supervision. This is called **split sentencing** or **shock probation**. A sentence of probation is often combined with a fine, court fees, and, in many states, probation supervision fees and/or fees for drug or alcohol testing or electronic monitoring. Many people confuse parole and probation, but the terms refer to different stages in the corrections process. **Parole** is an early release from a prison sentence and the decision to grant parole is made by a paroling authority, whereas probation is a sentence handed down by the sentencing judge (or jury) along with (typically) a suspended prison sentence. If a person commits a new crime or violates the conditions (rules) of probation, then the probation can be revoked, and the offender is subjected to the prison sentence that had been suspended. Some sentencing statutes restrict the possibility of probation to only certain types of offenses; some crimes can be punished by prison or probation; and others (generally more serious felonies or violent offenses) are not eligible for probation at all. If a sentencing statute allows for probation or prison, it is up to the judge or jury, or, more often, part of the plea bargain between the prosecutor and defendant, as to whether a probation sentence will be given instead of prison.

In 2019, there were about 6.3 million people under some form of correctional supervision (about 1 in every 40 adults). The largest group of offenders under any form of correctional supervision are probationers (see Figure 5.1). In 2018 and 2019, there were about 3.5 million probationers.[1]

The number of individuals on probation has been decreasing, while the parole population has increased slightly. This may mark the beginning of a consistent decline in the total prisoner population as state and federal prisoners are released on parole in greater numbers than in years past. It is too soon to tell if the trend will continue. In Table 5.1 we see that the rate of probation per 100,000 people is more than four times as high as the rate of parole.

The Bureau of Justice Statistics reports that in 2006 (the last year for which data is available), only about 27 percent of felony offenders who were convicted received probation, and 69 percent received either a sentence of prison or jail. For those who received probation, the average sentence was about three years.[2] Even though probation departments receive less than 10 percent of state and local government expenditures, they deal with almost 60 percent of all offenders.[3]

The number of people on probation varies tremendously from state to state, as does the rate per population. For instance, in 2018, Texas had 474,600 probationers and parolees (for a community supervision rate of 1,640 per 100,000), but Utah only had 16,600 on probation and parole (and a community supervision rate of 520 per 100,000).[4] Of course, the two states' populations are quite different, but rates help to see the patterns of use by standardizing per 100,000 people. For instance, while the state of New Hampshire has a probation supervision rate of 355 (per 100,000), Georgia had a rate almost 16 times higher at 5,166 (per 100,000). The average rate for the United States was 1,389 per 100,000 in 2018.[5] According to the Bureau of Justice Statistics, in 2015,

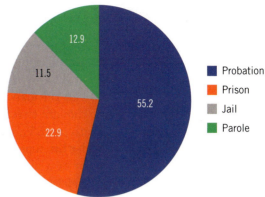

FIGURE 5.1   Percentage under correctional supervision by type. Percentages do not equal 100% because some offenders may have dual correctional status and are counted twice. Created by author from L. Maruschak and T. Minton, "Correctional Populations in the United States, 2017-2018" (Washington, DC: Bureau of Justice Statistics, OJPDOJ, 2016).

- about 25 percent of probationers were women;
- about 55 percent of probationers were white, 30 percent were Black, and 13 percent were Hispanic;
- about 62 percent were on probation for felony sentences (and the rest for misdemeanors); and
- about 26 percent were drug offenders, 25 percent were property offenders, 22 percent were violent offenders, 14 percent were public order offenders, with 12 percent recorded as "other."[6]

TABLE 5.1	**Probation and Parole Populations**				
YEAR	**PROBATION**	**PAROLE**	**TOTAL**	**PROBATION RATE/100,000**	**PAROLE RATE/100,000**
2000	3,839,400	725,500	4,564,900	1,818 (1 in 55)	344
2005	4,162,300	784,400	4,946,600	1,864 (1 in 54)	351
2010	4,059,900	840,700	4,888,500	1,714 (1 in 58)	355
2015	3,789,800	870,500	4,650,900	1,522 (1 in 66)	350

Note: Total population includes those who have dual status, e.g., on probation and parole concurrently.

Sources: D. Kaeble and T. Bonczar, Probation and Parole in the United States, 2015 (Washington, DC: Bureau of Justice Statistics, OJPDOJ, 2016), Tables 2 and 3.

The History of Probation

Probation began as a second chance for nonviolent offenders. In 1841, John Augustus, a Boston bootmaker and strong believer in the temperance movement, intervened in the case of a drunk who was being sent to jail. He posted bail for the man and asked the judge to defer sentencing for three weeks because he thought that he could help the man get his life in order. From 1841 until his death in 1859, he aided in the release of more than 1,800 adults and children under his supervision. He chose first-time offenders, helped them find employment or a place to live, and reported their progress to the court. Most of the offenders released into his custody were charged with violations of vice or temperance laws.[7] Up until 1878, when Massachusetts hired its first probation officer, volunteers undertook the supervision of those released on probation. Other states then followed. In 1901, New York passed a statute authorizing probation for adults, and volunteers or police officers supervised probationers. Early probation officers were usually retired sheriffs and policemen who worked directly for judges. In 1925, the federal government created an enabling statute for federal probation. In 1931, there were only 62 federal probation officers, but by 1956, all states had enabling legislation that allowed for probation sentences to be handed out by judges.[8]

Today, there are about 2,000 separate probation agencies across the United States.[9] Probation departments can be purely county or state agencies, but most often they operate as a combined model. A state executive agency provides hiring and procedural standards and budgetary subsidies, but probation is administered by counties. Probation officers are county employees who write progress and violation reports that are submitted to sentencing judges. Centralized systems provide consistency in terms of employees and procedures.[10] In a few states, probation and parole caseloads are combined and supervised under one agency.

Probation Supervision

Probation officers have two major roles: making sentence recommendations and supervision. These duties are sometimes divided by offices or assignment, or, alternatively, each probation officer is required to do both. Supervision is the primary duty, however. Individuals on probation are under a restricted form of liberty and do not have the same rights as the rest of us. In order to stay out of jail or prison and serve their sentences in the community, probationers are supervised by probation officers, who ensure that probationers comply with the terms of probation set by the sentencing judge.

The Pre-Sentence Investigation

In some states, probation officers are responsible for conducting **pre-sentence investigations** and writing pre-sentencing reports. These reports provide relevant information about the offense and the offender to be used for sentencing. In larger jurisdictions, there is a separate division within probation departments for pre-sentencing, or, in some jurisdictions, there is a separate pretrial services division that evaluates individuals for pretrial release and writes the pre-sentence report.

The pre-sentence investigation concludes with a sentencing recommendation to the court. Information in a **pre-sentence report (PSR)** may include: risk (typically through a scoring instrument), personal circumstances (such as work, family, and education), what sentencing or programmatic options are available, and ultimately, a sentencing recommendation. States may require a pre-sentence investigation in felony cases, but very few require one in misdemeanor cases.[11]

A legal issue that occurs with PSRs is confidentiality. In 1949, the Supreme Court held that information in the PSR could not be kept from the offender if he or she had been sentenced to death. Due process required that the offender be able to know the information in the report to contest it as inaccurate or misleading.[12] So far, however, theSupreme Court has refused to extend this reasoning to any sentence other than death; thus, whether the report is available to the defense is based on the law and procedural rules of the jurisdiction. Many jurisdictions share at least some of the report with the offender or his/her attorney. The Federal Rules of Criminal Procedure, for instance, require that the PSR be made available to the defendant unless it might disrupt rehabilitation, when the information was obtained with a promise of confidentiality, or when harm may result to any person because of the disclosure. New York State passed CPL (Criminal Procedural Law) 390.50(2)(a), which provides in relevant part: "...the pre-sentence report or memorandum shall be made available by the court for examination and for copying by the defendant's attorney, the defendant himself, if he has no attorney..." giving defendants the legal right to see the PSR so that if there are errors in it, they can be corrected.

Before the 1980s, PSRs were rehabilitation focused, in the sense that they provided information about the defendant's background, including educational history, drug use, vocational aptitude, and so on. A recommendation was made as to how amenable the offender was to rehabilitative programming; in addition, programs such as drug treatment might be identified in the report. As the entire system of corrections shifted focus in the 1980s to emphasize determinate sentencing and retribution rather than rehabilitation, the PSR became more of a description of risk rather than amenability to rehabilitation. In many cases today, the PSR utilizes or is primarily an objective risk instrument that is scored by the probation officer. These instruments, whether developed in-state or purchased by proprietary companies, predict whether a defendant is low risk, medium risk, or high risk for recidivism. We will discuss the instruments and some issues that have been raised with using objective instruments for risk prediction and sentencing decisions in Chapter 6.

Probation officers have quasi-judicial immunity for their sentencing recommendations, meaning that, like judges, they are not legally liable for any harm that comes if an offender commits a new crime after being released based on the probation officer's recommendation. Also, the defendant cannot sue the probation officer (or court service officer) who prepares the pre-sentence report for mistakes or false information.

Probation officers can be sued, however, for their supervision-related activities. Causes of action may exist under state tort laws, state laws related to actions by public officials, and under Section 1983 of the Civil Rights Code for alleged violations of constitutional rights of the probationer. If the probation agency is a state agency, the state cannot be sued, but the individual probation officer can be (although the state may indemnify the officer); conversely, if the probation agency is local (funded with county money), then the probation officer and the agency may be sued because the local entity does not have the sovereign immunity of the state.[13] Section 1983 lawsuits occur when there is an allegation that the probation officer, acting under color of law and within the scope of his or her duties, violates any constitutional right of the probationer. For instance, if the officer subjects the probationer to an illegal search or a detention without due process of law, or otherwise abuses the authority of the office, there may be cause for a legal claim. To be successful, the plaintiff must prove the constitutional violation and that a reasonable probation officer would have known it was a violation.

Ordinarily, decisions of the probation officer regarding recommendations for release or conditions of probation fall under a probation officer's quasi-judicial decision making and are protected by quasi-judicial immunity. However, there have been some cases where third parties successfully sued probation officers or probation departments for wrongful death or other causes of action when a probationer has injured or killed a victim. Two possibilities of such suits are when there is a special relationship between the probation officer and victim (e.g., if the probationer is on probation for domestic violence and there is a court order that the victim be notified of any change in supervision) or if the officer's gross negligence in supervision resulted in the death or injury of someone at the hands of the probationer; for instance, if the probation officer did not notify the court that the probationer had been released from a residential facility, such as a drug treatment facility or a halfway house. These cases are rare, however, because the standard of negligence is high.[14]

Conditions of Probation

After pre-sentencing recommendations are made, a judge (or jury) determines whether the offender will receive probation or a prison sentence. In some jurisdictions, the offender may receive split sentencing or shock probation. Only the judge sets the conditions of probation, although conditions may be recommended in the pre-sentence report. **Conditions** are the rules of probation as well as required activities the probationer must complete. The following general conditions apply to everyone:

- Obey all laws.
- Pay all fines and fees.
- Do not possess firearms.
- Do not associate with known criminals.
- Maintain employment.
- Notify probation officer of address changes.

Probationers may also have specific conditions that apply to them because of the nature of their crimes or their respective backgrounds. Examples include drug offenders being required to attend drug treatment, DWI offenders being required to attend Alcoholics Anonymous, and young offenders being required to complete educational requirements, such as obtaining a GED. Other conditions may be assessed based on the unique circumstances and background of a particular offender; for instance, a doctor convicted of Medicare fraud might be required to perform community service in a free health clinic, or an entertainer might be required to give a charity performance as community service for some crime he or she committed. In other cases, the type of crime spurs the unique condition: for instance, those convicted of vehicular manslaughter have been required to go to high schools and talk about the devastating consequence of choosing to drink and drive. It has been reported that probationers have, on average, about 15 conditions to comply with while on probation.[15]

Scarlet Letter conditions are conditions designed to humiliate the offender or warn others to keep away from him or her. For instance, a sex offender may be required to post signs in their front yard warning people of their sex offender status, DWI felons may be required to put bumper stickers on their cars identifying themselves as drunk drivers, and so on. If the condition is reasonably related to the goal of rehabilitation and is not considered to be cruel and unusual punishment, the judge has wide discretion in assigning general or specific conditions to each probationer. Sometimes, a judge goes too far, such as when an appellate court in Florida agreed with an offender that his probation condition, which involved wearing a diaper in a treatment program, was not suitably related to a rehabilitative objective.[16] However, several courts have upheld the requirement of DWI or DUI felons to complete community service hours wearing signs that identify them to passersby as drunk drivers.[17] In other cases, judges have been overruled when they require compulsory contraception.[18] Most often, probationers do not challenge conditions because the alternative to saying no to them is a prison sentence.

As we discussed in Chapter 4, **restitution** is an order by the court that requires the offender to compensate the victim for injury or loss suffered as a result of the crime. Every state has enabling legislation, and many states mandate restitution as a condition of probation unless there are compelling reasons not to do so. Victim-centered restitution includes the victim in the determination of the amount to be compensated. The offender either pays the victim directly or through the court, but there is a direct link between the offender and his or her victim. In other forms of restitution programs, victims are not involved, and the money is paid to a state victim compensation or restitution fund. This form of restitution is more like a criminal fine. Restitution orders have been found to be more commonly imposed on female offenders, property offenders, those with no prior record, and white offenders. Studies indicate that restitution orders are difficult to enforce. One study indicated that only about a third of the total restitution ordered in a Chicago court was ever paid over a three-year period. Enforcement practices such as registered letters or telephone solicitations threatening adverse action raised the percentage of compliance substantially, as did declaring amnesty days, where accrued interest would be deducted from the amount owed.[19]

Community service as a sanction of probation can be a meaningful and life-changing experience for the offender. In some jurisdictions, offenders perform needed services for the elderly, poor, or children. Offenders may be required to assist in food kitchens, help winterize houses, clear parks, or otherwise contribute to the community or to the specific class of victim harmed by their crime. Some critics object to this, arguing that it is not a good idea to place offenders among vulnerable populations where they can interact with potential victims. However, community service is more often manual labor for the county or municipality, such as road crews assigned to pick up litter or wash police cars, because such settings do not create undue risk or liability.

As discussed in Chapter 4, offenders are often charged supervision fees when performing community service. This may prevent the poor from being eligible for community service at all. Even if there is no supervision charge attached, requiring hundreds of hours of community service is a burden to those who make minimum wage and require 40 hours or more of work a week just to pay their bills. Finding the time to do community service, especially when the times are designated by the program, also makes completion difficult. Disabled offenders are at a disadvantage if the only community service available is in the form of physical labor; therefore, some offenders may receive a jail or prison sentence instead of

Community service is often manual labor for the county or municipality, such as road crews assigned to pick up litter.

community service, simply because of their inability rather than their unwillingness to participate.

The Casework Model

Probation follows the **casework model**, meaning the professional (the probation officer) interacts with each client (the probationer) individually, serving as the primary, and sometimes only, service provider. Typically, the probation officer meets with the offender and monitors whether he or she is meeting the conditions of their probation, such as repayment of fines, and asks about any arrests or contacts with law enforcement. Discussions may also cover employment and/or drug treatment options. Probation officers make referrals to various types of programs and sometimes assist the probationer in securing aid, such as disability payments.

Most probationers are required to come into the office at least once a month to see their probation officer and fill out a report, and the probation officer makes at least one field contact, where the officer meets the offender in his or her own home or workplace as an additional monitoring check of how the probationer is doing. Offenders may also be required to submit to drug testing. Probation officers also make collateral contacts with family members, neighbors, and employers, to gather more information about the probationer. The probation officer writes periodic progress reports to the sentencing judge detailing the probationer's success in completing the conditions of probation. If a probationer is not compliant, the probation officer may have to write a violation report informing the judge of a new arrest or violations of the rules. Probation is considered a minor punishment, but conditions can make the sentence quite onerous. In the Focus on the Offender box, one controversial probation sentence is described.

OFFENDER   A SLAP ON THE WRIST?

In 2015, Stanford University student and champion swimmer Brock Turner was discovered on top of an unconscious woman behind a dumpster. He was chased and held for police by two passersby. The half-naked woman explained that she had been at a fraternity party but did not remember going outside or the assault. She woke up in the hospital and learned of the night's details from media reports. At Turner's trial, he insisted the two "hooked up" and that she had consented. The jury found him guilty of assault with intent to commit rape of an intoxicated woman, sexually penetrating an intoxicated person with a foreign object, and sexually penetrating an unconscious person with a foreign object.

Turner faced a maximum of ten years in prison, and the prosecutor asked for six years. The probation department, in their pre-sentence report, recommended probation and a jail sentence. Letters describing his character from former teachers, friends, and relatives described him as having a good character, respectful, and someone who wouldn't harm anyone. In his letter to the judge, Turner explained his actions by the fact that he was inexperienced in drinking and made mistakes because of his intoxication; however, court records show that his social media accounts indicated he had used drugs and alcohol in high school and when he arrived at college. The judge, citing Turner's age, his lack of a criminal record, and the low risk that he would be a danger to others in the future, agreed with the PSR recommendation and gave him probation and a six-month jail

sentence. He also was required to register as a sex offender. Stanford banned Turner from campus and he was banned for life by USA Swimming.

There was a groundswell of opposition to the sentence and a recall effort against the judge. The rape victim published a letter explaining how the assault impacted her and pointed out how Turner's statements were self-pitying and ignored how the assault had devastated her. Similar criticism was leveled at the letter Turner's father sent to the judge before sentencing, which focused on the negative impact of the events on his son. Turner served three months in jail and was released for good behavior. After release, he returned to his home in Ohio, where he is serving his probation sentence. As part of his probation, Turner must submit to polygraph tests. Additional requirements include notifying law enforcement of changes in address, employment, education schedule, vehicles, telephone numbers, and volunteer work. He must provide his passwords for emails and internet accounts. He is not allowed to use or possess alcohol or drugs. Turner's picture, conviction information, and address are publicly available in the state's sex offender registry. Anyone living within 1,250 feet of Turner's address will be notified with a postcard. He will not be allowed to live within 1,000 feet of schools or playgrounds. He must participate in a sex offender management program consisting of group counseling using cognitive behavioral treatment for at least one year.

Questions for Discussion

1. Was this a fair punishment for Turner? Why or why not?
2. Probation is often considered a slap on the wrist, but sometimes comes with a multitude of conditions, such as in this case. Is probation too lenient a sentence for violent or sex crimes?

Source: S. Webber, "Brock Turner's Stanford Rape Case: Everything You Need to Know," US Magazine, June 7, 2016, accessed December 27, 2018, https://www.usmagazine.com/celebrity-news/news/brock-turners-stanford-rape-case-everything-you-need-to-know-w209237/; E. Grinberg and C. Shoichet, "Brock Turner Released from Jail After Serving 3 Months for Sexual Assault," CNN Online, September 2, 2016, accessed December 27, 2018, https://www.cnn.com/2016/09/02/us/brock-turner-release-jail/index.html; T. Kaplan, "Stanford Sex Offender's Court File Shows He Lied About Drug Use," The Mercury News, June 7, 2016, accessed December 27, 2018, https://www.mercurynews.com/2016/06/07/stanford-sex-offender-brock-turners-court-file-shows-he-lied-about-drug-use/.

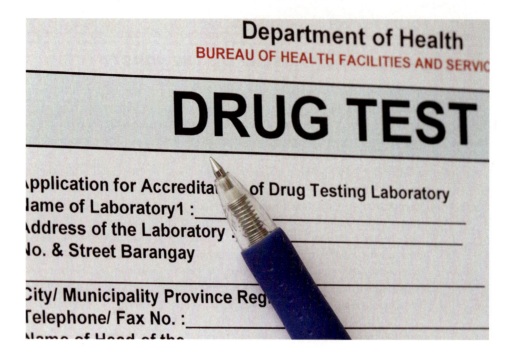

Random, mandatory drug tests are a frequent condition of probation.

Generally, as part of the probation order, probationers have given the probation officer the right to search their person or home without a search warrant. While the Fourth Amendment protects against unreasonable searches or seizures by governmental actors, generally defined as requiring probable cause, probationers (and parolees) have diminished liberty interests. Courts have upheld the right of the probation officer to search without a warrant even though the search also intrudes upon the privacy of other people living in the house.[20] The reasoning is that the probationer is under a restricted liberty status and the special need to protect the public justifies the lack of a warrant requirement. The Supreme Court found in *Griffin v. Wisconsin* that it was acceptable for the state to replace the probable cause for a search requirement with a reasonable grounds standard as the test for justifying the search. This is not a reasonable suspicion standard, and, in fact, may be met by the state's regulation requiring all probationers to submit to such searches as part of the conditions of probation.[21]

In *United States v. Knights* in 2001, the Supreme Court upheld a conviction of conspiracy to commit arson, among other related crimes, against a California man who had challenged a search of his home, which resulted in the finding of explosives, while he was on probation for drug possession.[22] The search was done by his probation officer and law enforcement officers because he was suspected of damaging government property. The probationer's challenge made a distinction between searches to ensure conditions are met on the current probation sentence versus law enforcement investigatory searches regarding new crimes, but the Supreme Court declined to make that type of search distinction when done by probation officers. Probationers in California were required to submit to searches with or without warrants or even reasonable cause by any probation officer or law enforcement officer. The Supreme Court stated that the legitimate interests of the State in preventing further crime by convicted probationers greatly outweighed the privacy interests of the probationer because of his/her diminished liberty status.

As with all Supreme Court decisions regarding federal constitutional rights, a state may recognize greater rights through the state constitution. States may limit the scope of the searches, require some standard of proof, or require the police officer to conduct the search with a probation or parole officer.[23] One legal review indicated that 13 states allowed warrantless searches by police officers, although some of these states required reasonable suspicion. North Carolina allows warrantless searches of the person or vehicle, but not the residence. Louisiana only permits police to search convicted sex offenders, with reasonable suspicion. Alaska, Florida, Indiana, Massachusetts, Michigan, Mississippi, Montana, New Hampshire, New York, and Oregon require police officers to be with probation or parole officers who conduct the search. About half of the states do not have enabling statutes or caselaw that allow warrantless searches by police officers, but these states do require the probationer or parolee to give permission for any search by a probation or parole officer as a condition of probation.[24]

Interstate Compact

You might be wondering how probationers can move to another state if they are under probation. In some cases, they cannot because the sentencing judge will not allow it. However, years ago, it became clear that states needed to develop some type of agreement to supervise offenders who needed to move from one state to another for employment or family reasons. The Interstate Compact was created in September 1937. All states participate, and each state has an interstate compact office that accepts case transfers from other states. For instance, Brock Turner, the subject of Focus on the Offender, was sentenced in California, but his probation supervision was transferred to Ohio. The offender must abide by the general conditions in both states. Even if there was no probation supervision fee in the sentencing state, the offender may be required to pay one in the receiving state. Generally, the sending state sets the amount of time the offender is supervised, but the receiving state sets the level of supervision. Today, the **Interstate Compact for Adult Offender Supervision (ICAOS)** is the national body that coordinates interstate agreements. Some states may not allow certain types of offenders (e.g., sex offenders). On the other hand, some will not accept misdemeanants for supervision (evidently seeing those minor offenders as not worth the resources expended). There is no payment from the sending state to the receiving state; the idea is that as people move in and out of states, participating states will receive and send probationers in roughly equal proportions.

Recidivism and Revocation

If the probationer does not pay restitution for several months, tests positive for drugs, associates with felons, or violates or does not complete other conditions, the probation officer may work with the offender to resolve the issue or file a violation report. **Technical violations** are violations of rules/conditions of probation, but not criminal behavior. New crimes, of course, might also spur a violation report. Violation reports are sent to the sentencing judge. The prosecutor's office may file a motion to revoke probation (MRP), or a judge may issue a summons and a revocation hearing is held. The judge decides whether to continue probation, continue probation but with modified conditions (e.g., imposing curfew, treatment, intermediate sanction, etc.), or to revoke probation and send the person to jail or prison. In some states, the time spent on probation may not be counted at all toward the completion of the sentence, or the judge will have the discretion to consider time served or not.

The act of an offender reoffending is referred to as **recidivism**. There are different ways to measure recidivism, and any of the following definitions, or combination of them, may be used: rearrest, reconviction, or **revocation**. The percent of probationers who recidivate varies depending on the definition used. If recidivism is defined as rearrest or revocation (including technical violations), this results in the highest recidivism figures. Probationers may be arrested, but then have charges dropped, and technical violations are easy to commit, especially if the probation term is for many years. However, if recidivism is defined only as reconviction on a new crime, then recidivism rates are much lower. It is very difficult, unfortunately, to discover the true percentage of probationers who commit new crimes. On the one hand, even if there is probable cause, prosecutors may not charge the probationer with the new crime if their existing probation is going to be revoked and they are heading to prison anyway. On the other hand, it is misleading to think that high recidivism figures refer to new crimes if recidivism is measured in a way that also counts technical violations.

The Supreme Court has ruled that the Fifth Amendment rights established for criminal suspects do not apply in the same way to probationers. For instance, probation officers do not have to give Miranda warnings before asking offenders questions about criminal activities unless the offender is already in custody.[25] Relatedly, the question of whether probationers can be punished for refusing to answer incriminating questions has arisen. In a few cases, probationers convicted of sexual offenses have refused to answer questions about their sexual history because it would expose them to new criminal charges. Whether they can then have their probation revoked because of a refusal to answer has been decided in different ways by different jurisdictions.[26]

Although no defendant has the right to probation, once given, it is considered a protected liberty interest and there must be some due process before probation is taken away. In earlier decades, courts used **deferred sentencing**, meaning that when probation was given, the possible prison sentence that the offender would face upon violation was not established. In *Mempa v. Rhay*, in 1967, the Supreme Court ruled that in cases of deferred sentencing, the revocation hearing became a type of sentencing hearing, and, because it was more like a sentencing hearing, the probationer had a Sixth Amendment right to an attorney because it was considered a critical stage of the processing.[27]

After that case, states began to use **suspended sentencing**, in which the judge decides upon and issues a prison sentence, but then suspends it, pending successful completion of probation. If probation is revoked, the suspended sentence is imposed. In this instance, there is nothing to decide regarding the length of the sentence and the revocation hearing is more like an administrative hearing, not a sentencing hearing. This means that there is no Sixth Amendment right to counsel, but due process still applies. The right to an attorney in these cases is conditional and is required when there would be a threat to due process if denied. Under due process rights, the probationer must receive

- the notice of alleged violations of probation and evidence,
- an opportunity to appear and to present evidence and witnesses,
- the right to confront adverse witnesses,
- a neutral decision maker,
- a written report, and
- a *conditional* right to counsel when there is a question of guilt or innocence or the individual is not likely to understand the proceedings.[28]

In 1986, 74 percent of probationers successfully completed their term. In 1992, 67 percent were successful, but by 1998, only 50 percent successfully completed probation; in 2008, about 48 percent of probationers were successfully discharged.[29] In the latest report available, a little over half of probationers were successfully discharged. Figure 5.2 shows the percentage of probationers who were sent to prison in 2015, as well as other discharge information. The "other" category includes those discharged to another jurisdiction on detainers (legal documents where one jurisdiction requests another jurisdiction to hold an offender for extradition to face charges or punishment in the requesting jurisdiction), as well as those listed as either "other" or "other unsatisfactory." There is also a large number in a category reported as "unknown or not reported."

The number of special/punitive conditions has increased. Increased conditions of probation may result in a higher rate of failure in completing a probation sentence because it is hard to abide by numerous and/or stringent rules for years—for example, never entering a bar or never leaving the county.[30] The number of people on probation who were revoked and sent to jail (or prison) increased by 50 percent from 1990 to 2004.[31] Studies show that probationers are most likely to fail within the first three months of probation. In one study, it was found that most failed because of technical violations, not new crimes. Probationers were likely to fail because of the following:

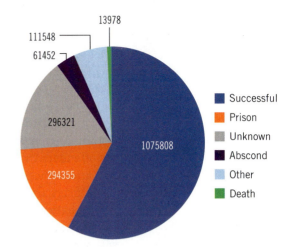

FIGURE 5.2 Probation discharges. Created by author from D. Kaeble and M. Alper, "Probation and Parole in the United States, 2017-2018" (Washington, DC: Bureau of Justice Statistics, 2020, Appendix), Table 3.

- failed drug tests;
- failure to attend or successfully complete programming; or
- failure to perform community service.[32]

The following factors have been associated with revocation of probation:

- burglary and property crimes;
- prior record;
- unemployment;
- status of being single;
- younger age;
- drug use; and
- lack of program participation.[33]

A meta-analysis of several studies of recidivism found the following factors were associated with failure on probation:

- sex (males have higher revocation rates);
- age (older offenders are more likely to be arrested for serious felonies, but younger offenders are more likely to fail overall);
- race (findings are mixed, but some show minorities have higher revocation rates);
- education (higher levels are associated with success);
- marital status (most studies find marriage is related to success);
- employment (being employed was associated with success on probation); and
- prior criminal history (especially property offenders).[34]

Probation Officers

Almost all states require probation officers to have a college degree, and salary ranges from $30,000 to $67,000, depending on location.[35] The professional organization for probation officers is the American Probation and Parole Association (http://www.appa-net.org/eweb/about). In some jurisdictions, there are different probation officers for misdemeanor versus felony probationers. Many jurisdictions have created specialized caseloads so that probation officers supervise only sex offenders, or only veterans. There is often special training provided for these probation officers. In a few jurisdictions where probation is a state agency, probation officers also supervise parolees in mixed caseloads.

Probation officers report various sources of stress in their jobs. One study found that the most important stressor identified by officers was inadequate salary and the least mentioned stress factor was insufficient training, although those who felt they had adequate training did show lower levels of stress than those who felt their training was insufficient.[36]

In support of adequate training, one meta-analysis found, based on 10 studies, that when offenders were supervised by officers who received training in core correctional practices, there was a significant reduction in recidivism as compared with those offenders supervised by probation officers without such training. Five dimensions of effective core correctional practice that should appear in training curricula were 1) effective use of authority, 2) prosocial modeling, 3) effective problem-solving strategies, 4) the use of community resources, and 5) interpersonal relationship factors. The relationship between a probation officer and client has been found to be influential in whether the offender recidivates. Research shows that the higher the quality of the relationship, the greater the reduction in recidivism. The most effective relationship seems to be one where the client describes the probation officer as "firm but fair." Providing training for probation officers in how to maximize their ability to influence the probationers on their caseload seems to have measurable effects on recidivism.[37]

Typologies of Supervision

As in any profession, even though probation officers have the same duties, officers approach those duties in somewhat different ways. Researchers have developed typologies of probation (and parole) officers that capture these differences. The different approaches taken may be because of individual differences among officers or office policies. The two most extreme roles are the enforcer and the counselor types, emphasizing how some officers view their role primarily as enforcing the rules and others see their role as helping the offender stay out of trouble. In one study, it was found that those who adopted a law enforcement approach to the job issued technical violation reports for 42.5 percent of their caseload, while those who had adopted more of a social work role issued technical violation reports for only 5.4 percent of their caseload.[38] It is probably true that the emphasis on determinate sentencing that occurred in the 1980s has influenced more probation officers to embrace the enforcer role today, even though probation is still considered as being more on the counseling end of the spectrum than parole.

In one typology, the following types of probation officer are described:

- *Service officer*: This officer is focused on the offender's needs and develops a casework relationship with the offender and may make allowances when violations occur if the offender shows progress.

- *Surveillance officer*: This officer is more likely to go by the book and file violation reports upon any instance of noncompliance. The goal of these officers is to enforce the rules and get the offender off the streets quickly upon a violation.
- *Broker officer*: This officer sees the job as providing the means to change and is likely to provide referrals to community resources, appropriate agencies, and service providers. Such officers balance surveillance and service.
- *Burned-out officer*: This officer is merely showing up to get a paycheck. These officers are not invested in the success of probationers and do the minimum possible to keep their job.[39]

In a survey of 40 probation officers across 18 states, researchers found that probation officers supervised probationers by enforcing conditions, limiting criminogenic opportunities, and encouraging productive hobbies and activities. Probation officers were concerned if the probationer had too much unstructured time. They explained they would refuse to allow probationers to engage in certain activities or hang out in certain places. They would not give permission for the probationer to live in crime-ridden areas and limited their association with criminal friends. Probation officers encouraged prosocial activities such as going to school and enlisted family members to help motivate offenders to change their lives.[40]

Burnout

Burnout has been described as when workers are not invested in their job and are simply going through the motions without any effort. Various researchers have identified three distinct elements of burnout: emotional exhaustion, a perception that they have not accomplished personal and professional goals, and depersonalization (feeling detached about what one is doing). It can result in workers providing inferior services to clients in the helping professions, including corrections. There is not much research on burnout on probation officers specifically, and studies are typically done with small samples in only one state or even one region within a state. Therefore, study findings should be treated with caution. An early study from 1985 found that burnout was associated with two primary factors: an absence of social support by supervisors and seniority.[41] Another study from 2013 found that probation officers who dealt with offenders who committed violent or sexual offenses against children, offenders who threatened or assaulted the officer or his/her family, and offenders who committed suicide were most vulnerable to burnout.[42] In a study that measured the element of emotional exhaustion, researchers found that African American officers reported lower levels, but females and those with more seniority reported higher levels. Also, officers who reported higher levels of work stress, role overload, role conflict, and role ambiguity reported higher levels of burnout.[43]

Another study found that education and age were not significant predictors of burnout. Seniority was found to be associated with the perception of lacking personal accomplishment, but not other elements, such as emotional exhaustion. This study found that those who felt they were in poor health were more likely to indicate the elements of burnout. These researchers found similar findings to the previous study that women were more likely to show burnout in the emotional exhaustion measure, but not the depersonalization or personal accomplishment measures. Perceptions of low salary were also associated with burnout measures, as was a perception of the respondent that one's education and training were inadequate for the demands of the job.[44]

Changes in Probation Supervision

In the 1970s there was a great interest in reducing the prison population, even though prisons held only a small fraction of the number they hold today, and probation and parole were targeted as strategies to reduce the use of prison. Probation was considered a front-end strategy, in terms of reducing the number of people heading to prison, and parole was a back-end strategy, reducing the number of people in prison by using early release. The 1967 President's Commission on Law Enforcement and the Administration of Justice published a final report that encouraged communities to develop community-based corrections. One financial disincentive for communities was that when an offender was sentenced to a state prison, the cost was borne by the state, not the local community; however, if the offender was sentenced to probation, the county was often the primary funder of probation services. An effort was made to ameliorate this financial disincentive by way of **probation subsidies**, meaning the state would reimburse counties for those individuals kept in the community on probation. Minnesota led the way in the use of probation subsidies so much so that their methods became known as the Minnesota model. As years went by, however, this concept seemed to fall out of favor across the country in favor of simply charging probationers supervision fees, relieving both the county and the state from the financial obligation of keeping offenders in the community.

Over the years, probation has seen various innovations and changes in supervision models. The goal typically is to make probation an attractive option to sentencing judges to divert offenders from prison sentences and keep them in the community. Sometimes, what happens, however, is **net-widening**, which occurs when diversion programs designed for those who would have been sentenced to prison are, instead, used for offenders who would have received even less severe punishment. Instead of reducing the number of individuals sent to prison, the proliferation of community-based programs increases the total number of people under some form of correctional supervision. In the following sections, we will discuss the various types of programs in probation. Some of them have become prevalent across the country, and some have not.

Intensive Supervision Probation

By the 1980s, probation had come under extreme criticism as being a mere "slap on the wrist" rather than sufficient punishment, and for its high recidivism rates. One response to the criticism was **intensive supervision probation**. This new approach to probation reduced the size of probation officers' caseloads and required more contact hours per month; for instance, some probation officers were given caseloads of 40 instead of 150 in order to increase their ability to monitor probationers. Arguably, if probationers were watched more closely, they would be less likely to recidivate. Only high-risk offenders were supposed to end up on intensive supervision caseloads, but, because of net-widening, many probationers who might otherwise have been supervised on regular probation caseloads were placed in intensive supervision probation.

Some versions of intensive supervision probation paired two correctional professionals with a probationer. One was the traditional probation officer who acted as a referral agent for programs and other assistance, and the other was a surveillance officer (often an ex–law enforcement officer) who employed various methods of investigation and monitoring to determine if the probationer was committing crimes.

The results of evaluations were mixed with some evaluations showing higher recidivism rates than regular caseloads. Of course, this should have been expected, since these probationers were watched more closely. Generally, the high failure rates were due to technical violations, not necessarily new crimes. Ultimately, evaluators concluded that there was little difference in the outcomes between intensive supervision probation and regular probation.[45]

Electronic Monitoring

Electronic monitoring (EM) emerged in the mid-1980s as a supplement to traditional probation or parole supervision. Evidently, a New Mexico judge inspired by a Spider-Man comic strip thought of the idea, guiding an engineer to design the device. One of the first electronic monitoring programs in the country was implemented in Palm Beach, Florida. Programs now exist in virtually all U.S. states, as well as several other countries.[46]

Electronic monitoring utilizes an electronic device strapped to the ankle or wrist of the offender. The individual is required to have a land-line telephone that is linked to the device, and an alarm sounds when the offender is too far away from the telephone. The program is set up so that the offender can travel from home to work and back again without the alarm being triggered, but otherwise highly restricts the person's movements. Some versions of EM employ a global positioning system (GPS) to track the offender's movements throughout the day.

Evaluations of EM report mixed findings. Some evaluations show no difference in recidivism between those on some form of EM and those on regular probation caseloads.[47] Other studies have found that EM, combined with treatment elements, reduced recidivism for moderate-risk offenders but not lower-risk offenders.[48] However, some studies have found that EM programs result in slightly higher recidivism.[49] Recidivism rates in EM programs have been reported as low as 8 percent and as high as 70 percent.[50] Because acceptance into an EM program is discretionary, it is possible that some of the programs that have lower recidivism rates deny entry to all but the lowest-risk offenders, ensuring better success rates. The factors associated with failure on EM programs are like those that predict failure on probation in general, including gender (male), age (younger), unemployment, criminal history, marital status (single), and type of crime committed (drug or property).[51]

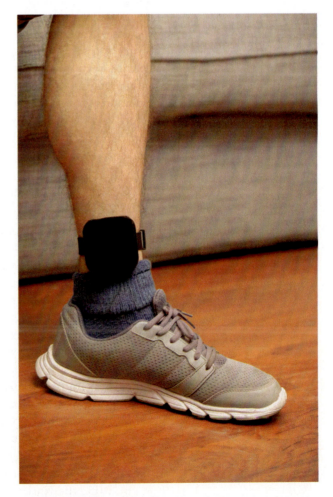

Even with the cost of the device and supervision costs, EM programs offer significant savings over incarceration, but not over regular probation.[52] One study compared the costs of electronic monitoring at about $20 a day compared to incarceration at about $50 a day.[53] Since regular probation is about $10 a day, the extra cost of GPS monitoring may be justified if the alternative is a prison sentence, but not if the alternative would be regular supervision in a diversion program or a regular probation sentence.[54]

As we discussed in Chapter 4, the monthly fees associated with electronic monitoring are increasingly charged to the offender. Costs for offenders may run as high as $500–$1000 per month. Nonpayment is considered a violation and can mean revocation if EM is a condition of probation or pretrial release.[55]

Electronic monitoring (EM) emerged in the mid-1980s as a supplement to traditional probation or parole supervision.

EM programs are often run by private for-profit companies. The GEO Group, for instance, has EM programs in every state.[56] Critics argue that the entry of private entities into community correctional supervision has not improved supervision or reduced recidivism, but has introduced a profit motive to keep clients under supervision. The pervasive presence of private community supervision in pretrial, probation, and parole supervision through halfway houses requires a closer look at their effectiveness compared to public options.[57]

Day Reporting Centers

Probationers or pretrial releasees may be required to check in to day reporting centers as a condition of their supervision. These centers offer both supervision and usually an array of job counseling and placement, educational, and social services. Centers may be publicly or privately operated and provide services to probationers and/or pretrial diversion clients. In a survey of 54 day reporting centers, one researcher found that centers reported an average failure rate of about 50 percent; however, the range across all of the centers surveyed was from 14 percent to 86 percent. Failure included rule violations as well as new arrests.[58]

Special Offender Caseloads

In the 1990s and early 2000s, some probation departments began creating special caseloads so probation officers with additional expertise could supervise, for instance, sex offenders, drug offenders, or domestic violence perpetrators. These special caseloads might have added requirements for probationers such as attendance at group therapy sessions. Also gaining acceptance in these decades was the use of **intermediate sanctions**, meaning that when probationers violate the terms of their probation in a way that poses no great risk to public safety, it is deemed better overall for the judge to impose a community-based punishment rather than revoke probation and send the probationer to prison. Thus, after a violation, a probationer may be required to have a curfew, spend weekends in jail, return to a residential drug treatment facility, or perform additional community service hours. This avoids the use of prison, unless the probationer continues to violate the terms or commits new crimes.

Hawaii's Opportunity Probation with Enforcement (HOPE) Model

In 2004, Hawaii's Opportunity Probation with Enforcement (HOPE) was created. The program involved rapid responses to violations and frequent warning hearings with judges when probationers were in danger of having violation reports written. Also required were random, frequent, and unannounced drug tests. Under HOPE, judges used short jail sentences as punishment for violations instead of probation revocation and prison. Drug treatment and mental health counseling was provided for probationers who needed such services. An early evaluation of the program showed that HOPE probationers spent about the same number of days in jail as a control group but in shorter and more frequent time periods. The most encouraging findings, however, were that the recidivism rate for program participants was half that of other probationers in the one-year period of the study (7 percent compared to 15 percent), and that the percentage of HOPE participants who tested positive for drugs was less than one-third of other probationers (13 percent compared to 46 percent). Participants were half as likely to be rearrested (21 percent compared to 47 percent).[59]

In 2011, the National Institute of Justice funded an evaluation to examine the long-term effects of the program. The original 2007 cohort was used to collect and analyze data for a 76-month follow-up period. Results showed that HOPE probationers had slightly fewer new charges on average, and also had fewer violations on average (6.3 versus 7.1). HOPE probationers also experienced fewer returns to prison on average than regular probationers (13 percent versus 32 percent) among those who served conventional probation only.

The positive evaluations of HOPE led to replications of the supervision model in other jurisdictions. The HOPE demonstration field experiment (DFE) evaluated replications of the HOPE program in four jurisdictions: Clackamas County, Oregon; Tarrant County, Texas; Saline County, Arkansas; and Essex County, Massachusetts. With data from all sites combined, the results showed no statistical difference between HOPE and conventional probation in the average number of arrests (738 versus 758), but did find a slight reduction in property arrests (15 percent versus 20 percent) and drug arrests (12 percent versus 15 percent). HOPE probationers also were found to have more probation revocations (26 percent versus 22 percent). Researchers found that the four jurisdictions were different in the effects of HOPE on probationers, suggesting that the implementation might not have been similar in all four sites.[60] Researchers noted differences in the cultures of the probation offices, legal restrictions on revocation, differences in judicial inclinations to revoke, and other elements that could have contributed to differences in revocation rates. In fact, the difference in revocation rates between the sites was quite striking: 13 percent in Oregon, 21 percent in Massachusetts, 23 percent in Arkansas, and 38 percent in Texas.[61] Later studies failed to find positive effects of the HOPE model even when it was implemented effectively. The findings illustrate the difficulties of identifying and implementing successful programs.[62]

Recent Innovations in Probation

The programs discussed above are no longer innovations in that many have been in existence for decades and incorporated into probation services. They all have been designed to increase the effectiveness of probation supervision. Almost all operate on a purely deterrent rationale—that is, if probationers are watched more closely, they will be less likely to recidivate. Higher recidivism rates among program participants than among those on regular probation might have been expected since under special caseloads, intensive supervision, and electronic monitoring, probation officers are more likely to become aware of misconduct. More recent innovations in probation also focus on better ways of monitoring, but program sponsors don't presume that the intensiveness of the supervision will reduce recidivism.

KIOSK REPORTING

Kiosks, used as early as the 1990s in a few jurisdictions, are designed to streamline the reporting process for probationers. Reporting kiosks, located in probation offices, courthouses, or police departments, are like ATMs. Probationers can complete required check-ins with the supervising probation agency using biometric information (e.g., handprint or fingerprint scan) for identification. The probationer answers questions that would be asked by a probation officer, including questions regarding housing and employment status, on the kiosk keypad. The kiosks are also generally the place where probationers deposit their monthly fees and fine amounts via a secure drop box. The probationer gets a receipt that indicates he or she has completed the required monthly check-in.

Low-risk offenders have minimal interaction with the criminal justice system when using kiosks. Research has found that low-risk offenders can be monitored at lower levels of intensity without increasing prevalence, frequency, and seriousness of new offenses or decreasing the average time to a new arrest.[63] In fact, it has been found that exposing low-risk groups to correctional interventions increases the rate of recidivism for them, while correctional interventions can decrease the recidivism of high-risk groups.[64] There is speculation that some type of peer contagion may be at work when low-risk offenders show worse outcomes after exposure to criminal justice programs such as probation. Kiosk reporting may reduce peer contagion and exposure to criminal associates.[65] Evaluations of kiosks have shown small decreases in recidivism; for example, a 3 percent decrease from the average recidivism rate in New York City and 8 percent in Maryland. Since recidivism rates do not seem to increase with this less intensive form of supervision, the use of kiosks presents a cost savings to probation agencies.

Kiosk use frees up probation officers to concentrate on higher-risk offenders and provides more flexibility to the probationer since the locations are accessible over a larger time span than probation officers would be available for face-to-face meetings. The New York City Department of Probation implemented kiosk reporting with all low-risk probationers and reduced their probationer-to-probation-officer ratio from a range of about 100–150:1 to 65:1 for higher-risk (or special offender) caseloads. A recent nationwide survey of kiosk use found that more than 75,000 probationers were assigned to kiosk reporting in 21 jurisdictions with a reporting kiosk program. The most common reasons agencies decided against adopting kiosk reporting included costs, lack of research, and concern over net-widening.[66]

RISK/NEEDS/RESPONSIVITY MODEL OF CORRECTIONAL INTERVENTION AND COGNITIVE BASED THERAPY

Under the **Risk/Needs/Responsivity (R/N/R) model** of corrections, an offender is assessed using a risk assessment tool called the Level of Service Inventory–Revised, or LSI–R, that scores the offender on a list of factors that have been statistically associated with reoffending. (This risk instrument, and others like it, will be discussed in Chapter 6.) The risk assessment incorporates not only static factors that do not change over time (such as age at first arrest), but also dynamic factors (such as number of criminal friends) that can change over time. The R/N/R model has become ubiquitous in the correctional field and is incorporated into many current innovations. The main points of the R/N/R approach are as followed:

- Risk is determined by static and dynamic factors.
- Dynamic factors (or needs) that are criminogenic should be the focus of correctional intervention.
- Dynamic risks can change based on intervention; thus, needs should be periodically re-evaluated.
- Correctional interventions should be targeted to high-risk offenders, and low-risk offenders should have minimal contact with the system.
- Programs that follow the R/N/R model are more effective than those that do not.[67]

Cognitive behavioral therapy (CBT) programs are consistent with R/N/R principles because they focus on thinking and behavioral patterns that lead to criminality. CBT helps offenders change maladapted and antisocial thought patterns by teaching them to observe and manage such thoughts. CBT helps offenders recognize distortions in their thinking, for example, "everyone commits crimes," or "I must hit someone who disrespects me."

Effective Practices in Community Supervision (EPICS) is a correctional program begun around 2005 by professors at the University of Cincinnati. EPICS is a cognitive behavioral program designed to be administered by probation or parole officers to help offenders practice self-control. EPICS programs have probation officers lead the probationer in a series of homework exercises that help the offender see how patterns of behavior and thinking lead to criminal decisions; for instance, offenders are asked about their friendships and whether these increase the chances of committing another crime. Other topics include discussing the costs and benefits of a criminal lifestyle. The program is highly structured so that the probation officer does not have much discretion in how or when to assign the exercises designed as part of the program. Probation officers are trained in the interaction steps, and they are monitored to make sure they are implementing EPICS correctly. Some probation officers don't like this structure, preferring the more traditional model where what happens in probation officer–probationer meetings is purely at the discretion of the probation officer. Offenders, especially older adults, may also be unenthusiastic about completing the assignments, which include worksheets and flash cards.

An Ohio evaluation of an EPICS program found that the program led to lower rates of rearrest and re-incarceration, particularly among clients who had been assessed as high risk for reoffending, but only when it was implemented correctly with fidelity to the original protocols (meaning it was implemented in the way the developers intended). When it wasn't, the program resulted in worse recidivism than a control group. A meta-analysis of 10 evaluations of EPICS and similar community supervision models found that the average recidivism rate for offenders was about 13 percent lower when officers received training in an EPICS-like model than the rate for a control group.[68]

A different cognitive behavioral program in Philadelphia called "Choosing to Think, Thinking to Choose" was administered to high-risk probationers in a 12-week session of one two-hour class each week. The evaluation of this program found that it was difficult to administer because of participants' lifestyles and likelihood of absences. Participants committed fewer crimes than a control group in a one-year follow-up. Researchers noted that crime commission patterns were similar to the control group's crimes for the first two months, but then the pattern diverged: study participants committed fewer crimes and were less and less likely to commit crimes as the weeks progressed. Unfortunately, only 35 percent of participants completed the full 12-week course.[69]

Improving Community Corrections

If recidivism rates could be reduced, probation services could be a more viable alternative to incarceration. One group of professionals presented a set of principles for probation:

1. Treat everyone with dignity and respect. Assume their ability to change. Provide clear and predictable incentives and graduated and calibrated punishments.

2. Realign incentives so that cost considerations for communities do not favor using prison (offenders sent to prison are paid for by the state; if they remain in the community, it is the county who usually pays). Provide subsidies for community placements of offenders. Another warped incentive is the dependence on fines because communities have no incentive to reduce crime or recidivism when they depend on fines for their budget.

3. Impose the least restrictive sanctions necessary and minimize the collateral consequences associated with criminal processing (long-term job prospects, health, children's experience of having a parent incarcerated, loss of civil rights such as voting).

4. Strengthen communities, including access to housing, social services, and employment.

5. Reduce institutional bias and promote fair and equal access to the justice system.

6. Use evaluation to invest in programs and practices that work.[70]

FOCUS ON THE

STATE   NEW YORK

New York State is one of the states that has drastically reduced the number of prisoners in state prisons (31 percent decrease between 1999 and 2017). The state has closed 13 prisons and more than 6,000 prison beds, saving the state $160 million annually through reducing mandatory minimums, increasing the possibility of parole, and using sanctions other than prison as punishment. In addition to reductions in the prison population, the state has also seen decreases in the jail and probation populations. The population of locally operated jails throughout New York State declined by 2.8 percent between 2016 and 2017. The decline has been more dramatic in New York City than elsewhere in the state, with a decline of almost 4 times that of the statewide average. Interestingly, only parole violators, among all other groups in jails, have increased, and the percentage increase is highest in New York City. It appears that these violators are more likely to be committing technical violations than new crimes.

Reports also show that the number on probation, at least in New York City, has also declined.

Between 1996 and 2014, probation sentences for felony arrests in New York City declined by 60 percent. Instead, conditional discharges, fines, and other alternatives were used more often. This has not seemed to spur a decline in public safety; in fact, over the same period, the city's violent crime rate declined by 57 percent. The effort to reduce the number of people on probation was aided by using kiosk reporting, increasing early discharges, a reduction in rearrests (from 52 percent to 47 percent), and a new law that allowed for less than a five-year probation sentence. There was also a 45 percent decrease in the number of revocations between 2009 and 2014. Unlike the prison closures, however, the decline in numbers has not saved the taxpayers money. The per capita spending on probationers increased three-fold because of added services, but it is still much less expensive than prison. Advocates of the New York City model argue that the use of prison and probation can be reduced with no increase in crime.

Questions for Discussion

1. Why do you think the number of revocations went down so dramatically between 2009 and 2014?

2. Would New York City's experience be replicated in other smaller towns? Why or why not?

Source: M. Jacobson, V. Schiraldi, R. Daly, and E. Hotez, "Less is More: How Reducing Probation Populations Can Improve Outcomes" (note 9); V. Schiraldi and J. Arzu, "Less is More in New York: An Examination of the Impact of State Parole Violations on Prison and Jail Populations," New York City: Columbia University Justice Lab, January 29, 2018, accessed December 28, 2018, http://justicelab.iserp.columbia.edu/img/Less_is_More_in_ New_York_Report_FINAL.pdf.

Another group of correctional professionals were convened to evaluate the future of probation and parole. This group advocated reducing the number of people supervised by corrections and supported efforts to

- reserve community correction supervision only for those who need it;
- reduce the terms of corrections to what is necessary to accomplish sentencing goals;
- reduce supervision conditions to those necessary to achieve the objectives of supervision;
- incentivize progress by granting early discharges;
- eliminate or significantly curtail supervision fees; and
- use savings from reducing caseloads to provide community-based services.[71]

There is a growing number of people who argue that probation is used excessively and that probationers receive unrealistically long sentences and are revoked for rule violations rather than new crimes.[72] Future changes we may see include improving the risk prediction instruments, continuing to evaluate programs like HOPE to determine best practices for reducing recidivism, and developing ways to shorten probation terms and make supervision fees less onerous for probationers. Improving probation for probationers does not need to reduce public safety, as we can see in New York (see Focus on the State) and other jurisdictions.

Summary

- Most people under correctional supervision are on probation (over 56 percent), but probation does not receive a commensurate share of the correctional budget.
- Probation can be purely a county agency or a state agency, but is most often a combined model.
- Probation and parole are often confused; probation is a sentence given by a judge, while parole is an early release from prison decided by a paroling authority.
- The origins of probation, beginning with John Augustus, included the goal of reforming the offender through providing services to address the issues that caused criminal behavior.
- Individuals on probation are under a restricted form of liberty and do not have the same rights as the rest of us. Probation officers can search these individuals' person or home, and they are not given Miranda warnings when questioned by a probation officer (unless they are already in police custody).
- If a probation officer files a violation report, there may be a revocation hearing; in these cases, the probationer deserves some due process. The right to an attorney is contingent on state law or a determination that the probationer needs someone to help defend against the allegations.
- Over half of probationers complete their sentence successfully, but the rate of recidivism is at 40 percent; in some jurisdictions, it is much higher.
- Innovations in probation have included various means of improving surveillance, such as the use of electronic monitoring and smaller caseloads. More recently, programs such as HOPE and EPIC have been created to attempt to provide more structured rehabilitative assistance to the probationer.

PROJECTS

1. Find out how many people are on probation in your community and whether probation is a state agency, a county agency, or a mixed model.

2. Ask several of your friends what their perception of probation is. Do they think it is a "slap on the wrist" or a viable correctional sanction? How long should the average probation term be according to your small sample?

NOTES

1. L. Maruschak and T. Minton, *Correctional Populations in the United States, 2017–2018* (Washington, DC: Bureau of Justice Statistics, OJPDOJ, 2020). T. Minton, L. Beatty, and Z. Zeng, Correctional Populations in the United States, 2019-Statistical Tables (Washington, DC: Bureau of Justice Statistics, OJPDOJ, 2021).

2. S. Rosenmerkel, M. Durose, and D. Farole, *Felony Sentences in State Courts, 2006—Statistical Tables* (Washington, DC: Bureau of Justice Statistics, 2009), 2.

3. L. Glaze, T. Bonczar, and F. Zhang, *Probation and Parole in the United States, 2009* (Washington, DC: Bureau of Justice Statistics, 2010). Washington, DC: Bureau of Justice Statistics.

4. L. Maruschak and T. Minton, *Correctional Populations in the United States, 2017–2018* (Washington, DC: Bureau of Justice Statistics, OJPDOJ, 2020), 12.

5. D. Kaeble and M. Alper, *Probation and Parole in the United States, 2017–2018* (Washington, DC: Bureau of Justice Statistics, 2020), Appendix, Table 2.

6. D. Kaeble and M. Alper, *Probation and Parole in the United States, 2017–2018* (Washington, DC: Bureau of Justice Statistics, 2020), Table 4.

7. L. Friedman, *Crime and Punishment in American History* (New York: Basic Books, 1993), 18.

8. L. Friedman, *Crime and Punishment in American History* (New York: Basic Books, 1993), 18.

9. M. Jacobson, V. Schiraldi, R. Daly, and E. Hotez, *Less is More: How Reducing Probation Populations Can Improve Outcomes* (Boston, MA: Harvard Kennedy School. Program in Criminal Justice Policy and Management, 2017).

10. J. Petersilia, *Reforming Probation and Parole* (Lanham, MD: American Correctional Association, 2002), 38.

11. J. Petersilia, *Reforming Probation and Parole* (Lanham, MD: American Correctional Association, 2002), 25; S. Walker, *Popular Justice: A History of American Criminal Justice*, 2d Ed. (New York: Oxford University Press, 2002), 25.

12. *Williams v. New York*, 337 U.S. 241 (1949).

13. *Monell v. Department of Social Services*, 436 U.S. 658 (1978).

14. P. Lyons and T. Jermstad, *Civil liabilities and Other Legal Issues for Probation/Parole Officers and Supervisors* (Washington, DC: National Institute of Corrections, 2013), file:///C:/Users/joypo/Desktop/New%20 corrections%20text/ legalliability.pdf.

15. M. Jacobson, V. Schiraldi, R. Daly, and E. Hotez, *Less is More: How Reducing Probation Populations Can Improve Outcomes* (Boston, MA: Harvard Kennedy School. Program in Criminal Justice Policy and Management, 2017).

16. *Bienz v. State*, 434 So. 2d 913 (Fla. Dist. Ct. App. 1977).

17. *Blanton et al. v. City of North Las Vegas*, 489 U.S. 538 1989.

18. J. Ginzberg, "Compulsory Contraception as a Condition of Probation: The Use and Abuse of Norplant," *Brookings Law Review* 58 (1992): 979–1001.

19. R. Ruback, G. Ruth, J. Shaffer, "Assessing the Impact of Statutory Change: A Statewide Multi-level Analysis of Restitution Orders in Pennsylvania," *Crime and Delinquency* 51, 3 (2005): 334–59. A. Lurigio and A. Davis, "Does a Threatening Letter Increase Compliance with Restitution Orders?" *Crime and Delinquency* 36,4 (1984): 537–48.

20. *Griffin v. Wisconsin*, 483 U.S. 868, 1987.

21. *Griffin v. Wisconsin*, 483 U.S. 868, 1987.

22. *United States v. Knights*, 534 U.S. 112 (2001).

23. P. Lyons and T. Jermstad, *Civil liabilities and Other Legal Issues for Probation/Parole Officers and Supervisors* (Washington, DC: National Institute of Corrections, 2013).

24. A. Matz, J. Turner, and C. Hemmens, "Where and When Police Officers Can Conduct Warrantless Searches of Probationers/Parolees: A Legal Review," *Perspectives* (Winter, 2015), accessed December 27, 2018, http://www.appa-net. org/Perspectives/Perspectives_ V39_N1_P42.pdf.

25. *Minnesota v. Murphy*, 465 U.S. 420, 1984.

26. *United States v. Chapman*, U.S. App LEXIS 12301, 2000; P. Lyons and T. Jermstad, *Civil liabilities and Other Legal Issues for Probation/Parole Officers and Supervisors* (Washington, DC: National Institute of Corrections, 2013).

27. *Mempa v. Rhay*, 389 U.S. 128, 1967.

28. *Gagnon v. Scarpelli*, 411 U.S. 778, 1973.

29. T. Bonczar and L. Glaze, *Probation and Parole in the United States, 1998* (Washington, DC: Bureau of Justice Statistics, 1999), 6.; L. Glaze, T. Bonczar, and F. Zhang, *Probation and Parole in the United States, 2009* (Washington, DC: Bureau of Justice Statistics, 2010).

30. J. Petersilia, *Reforming Probation and Parole* (Lanham, MD: American Correctional Association, 2002), 31.

31. P. Burke, A. Gelb, and J. Horowitz, *When Offenders Break the Rules: Smart Responses to Parole and Probation Violations* (Public Safety Policy Brief No. 3) (Washington, DC: The Pew Center on the States, 2007), accessed December 27, 2018, https://www.pewtrusts.org/ en/research-and-analysis/ reports/2007/11/16/public-safety-policy-brief-when-offenders-break-the-rules.

32. M. Gray, M. Fields, and S. Maxwell, "Examining Probation Violations: Who,

What, and When," *Crime and Delinquency* 47, 4 (2001): 537–57.

33. J. Petersilia, *Reforming Probation and Parole* (Lanham, MD: American Correctional Association, 2002), 58.

34. M. Gray, M. Fields, and S. Maxwell, "Examining Probation Violations: Who, What, and When" *Crime and Delinquency* 47, 4 (2001): 537–57.

35. "Payscale," retrieved February 20, 2018, from https://www. payscale.com/research/US/ Job=Probation_Officer/Salary.

36. W. Pitts, "Educational Competency as an Indicator of Occupational Stress for Probation and Parole Officers," *American Journal of Criminal Justice*, 32(2007): 57–73.

37. N. Chadwick, A. Dewolf, and R. Serin, "Effectively Training Community Supervision Officers: A Meta-Analytic Review of the Impact on Offender Outcomes," *Criminal Justice and Behavior* 42, 10 (2015): 977–89.

38. F. Taxman, "No Illusions: Offender and Organizational Change in Maryland's Proactive Community Supervision Efforts," *Criminology and Public Policy* 7, 2 (2008): 278–89.

39. C. Klockars, "A Theory of Probation Supervision," *Journal of Criminal Law and Criminology and Police Science*, 63, 4 (1972): 550–57.

40. J. Miller, K. Copeland, and M. Sullivan, "Keeping Them Off the Corner: How Probation Officers Steer Offenders Away from Crime Opportunities," *The Prison Journal*, 95, 2 (2015): 178–98.

41. J. Whitehead, and C. Lindquist, "Job Stress and Burnout Among Probation/parole Officers: Perceptions and Causal Factors," *International*

Journal of Offender Therapy and Comparative Criminology, 29 (1985): 109–19; J. Whitehead and C. Lindquist, "Correctional Officer Job Burnout: A Path Model," *Journal of Research in Crime & Delinquency*, 23 (1986): 23–42.

42. K. Lewis, L. Lewis, and T. Garby, "Surviving the Trenches: The Personal Impact of the Job on Probation Officers," *American Journal of Criminal Justice*, 38 (2013): 67–84.

43. M. Gayman and M. Bradley, "Organizational Climate, Work Stress, and Depressive Symptoms Among Probation and Parole Officers," *Criminal Justice Studies*, 26 (2013): 326–46.

44. G. Rhineberger-Dunn, K. Mack, K. Baker, "Comparing Demographic Factors, Background Characteristics, and Workplace Perceptions as Predictors of Burnout Among Community Corrections Officers," *Criminal Justice and Behavior*, 44, 2 (2017): 205–25.

45. F. Taxman, "No Illusions: Offender and Organizational Change in Maryland's Proactive Community Supervision Efforts*Criminology and Public Policy* 7, 2 (2008): 278–89, 279.

46. J. Bonta, S. Wallace-Capretta and J. Rooney, "Can Electronic Monitoring Make a Difference? An Evaluation of Three Canadian Programs," *Crime and Delinquency* 46, 1 (2000): 61–75; R. Gable, "From B.F. Skinner to Spiderman to Martha Stewart: The Past, Present, and Future of Electronic Monitoring of Offenders," *Journal of Offender Rehabilitation* 46, 3 (2008): 101–18.

47. J. Bonta, S. Wallace-Capretta, and J. Rooney, "Can Electronic Monitoring Make a Difference? An Evaluation of Three Canadian Programs" *Crime and Delinquency* 46, 1

(2000): 61–75; M. Renzema and E. Mayo-Wilson, "Can Electronic Monitoring Reduce Crime for Moderate to High-Risk Offenders?" *Journal of Experimental Criminology* 1 (2005): 1–23.

48. J. Bonta, S. Wallace-Capretta, and J. Rooney, "Can Electronic Monitoring Make a Difference? An Evaluation of Three Canadian Programs" *Crime and Delinquency* 46,1 (2000): 61–75.

49. P. Gendreau, C. Goggin, F. Cullen, and D. Andrews, "The Effects of Community Sanctions and Incarceration on Recidivism," *Forum* 12, 2 (2000): 10–13.

50. A. Gibbs and D. King, "The Electronic Ball and Chain? The Operation and Impact of Home Detention with Electronic Monitoring in New Zealand," *Australian and New Zealand Journal of Criminology* 36 (2003): 1–17.

51. J. Lilly, R. Ball, G. Curry, and J. McMullen, "Electronic Monitoring of the Drunk Driver: A Seven-Year Study of the Home Confinement Alternative," *Crime and Delinquency* 39 (1993): 462–84.

52. J. Lilly, R. Ball, G. Curry, and J. McMullen, "Electronic Monitoring of the Drunk Driver: A Seven-Year Study of the Home Confinement Alternative" *Crime and Delinquency* 39 (1993): 462–84.

53. R. Stutzman, "Ankle Monitors Show a Higher Rate of Success," *Orlando Sentinel*, December 29, 2002, B1; R. Stutzman, "State Takes Eyes off Inmates," *Orlando Sentinel*, December 29, 2002, B2.

54. A. Gibbs and D. King, "The Electronic Ball and Chain? The Operation and Impact of Home Detention with Electronic Monitoring in New Zealand" *Australian and New*

Zealand Journal of Criminology 36 (2003): 1–17.; J. Bonta, S. Wallace-Capretta, and J. Rooney, "Can Electronic Monitoring Make a Difference? An Evaluation of Three Canadian Programs" *Crime and Delinquency* 46,1 (2000): 61–75; P. Gendreau, C. Goggin, F. Cullen, and D. Andrews, "The Effects of Community Sanctions and Incarceration on Recidivism" *Forum* 12, 2 (2000): 10–13; M. Renzema and E. Mayo-Wilson, "Can Electronic Monitoring Reduce Crime for Moderate to High-Risk Offenders?" *Journal of Experimental Criminology* 1 (2005): 1–23.

55. I. Zaluska, "Paying to Stay in Jail: Hidden Fees Turn Inmates into Debtors," *The Crime Report*, September 17, 2019. Accessed July 1,2020 from https://thecrimereport.org/2019/09/17/paying-to-stay-in-jail-hidden-fees-turn-inmates-into-debtors/.

56. J. Byrne, K. Kras, L. Marmolejo, "International Perspectives on the Privatization of Corrections," *Criminology & Public Policy* 18 (2019): 477–503.

57. E. Latessa and L. Lovins, "Privatization of Community Corrections," *Criminology & Public Policy* 18 (2019): 323–41.

58. D. Parent, J. Byrne, V. Tsarfaty, L. Valade, and L. Esselman, *Day Reporting Centers: Issues and Practices in Criminal Justice, Vol. 1* (Washington, DC: National Institute of Justice, 1995); R. Jones and J. Lacey, *Evaluation of a Day Reporting Center for Repeat DWI Offenders* (Washington, DC: National Highway Traffic Safety Administration, 1999); D. Parent, "Day Reporting Centers: An Evolving Intermediate Sanction," *Federal Probation* 60, 4 (1996): 51–4.

59. P. Bulman, *In Brief: Hawaii HOPE* (Washington, DC: USDOJ, NIJ J. 266 (2010), accessed December 27, 2018, http://www.ojp.usdoj.gov/nij/journals/266/hope.htm.

60. P. Lattimore, D. MacKenzie, G. Zajac, D. Dawes, El Arsenault, and S. Tueller, "Outcome Findings from the HOPE Demonstration Field Experiment: Is Swift, Certain, and Fair an Effective Supervision Strategy?" *Criminology & Public Policy* 15, 4 (2016): 1103–41.

61. P. Lattimore, D. MacKenzie, G. Zajac, D. Dawes, El Arsenault, and S. Tueller, "Outcome Findings from the HOPE Demonstration Field Experiment: Is Swift, Certain, and Fair an Effective Supervision Strategy?" *Criminology & Public Policy* 15, 4 (2016): 1103–41, 1122.

62. E. Martin, *A Hopeful Approach — Understanding the Implications of the HOPE Program.* NIJ Webpage Programs for Drug Involved Offenders, October 2017, accessed December 27, 2018, https://nij.gov/topics/corrections/community/drug-offenders/Pages/hawaii-hope-demonstration-field-experiment.aspx; G. Zajac, D. Dawes, and E. Arsenault, "The Implementation of the Honest Opportunity Probation with Enforcement Demonstration Field Experiment: Experiences from the Field," *Journal of Crime and Justice*, 44 (2021): 1, 103–18.

63. G. Barnes, L. Ahlman, C. Gill, L. Sherman, E. Kurtz, and R. Malvestuto, "Low-Intensity Community Supervision for Low-Risk Offenders: A Randomized, Controlled Trial," *Journal of Experimental Criminology*, 6 (2010): 159–89.

64. C. Lowenkamp, E. Latessa, and A. Holsinger, "The Risk

Principle in Action: What Have We Learned From 13,676 Offenders and 97 Correctional Programs?" *Crime & Delinquency*, 52 (2006): 77–93; J. Miller and C. Maloney, "Practitioner Compliance with Risk/Needs Assessment Tools: A Theoretical and Empirical Assessment," *Criminal Justice and Behavior*, 40 (2013): 716–36.

65. E. Ahlin, C. Hagan, M. Harmon, and S. Crosse, "Kiosk Reporting Among Probationers in the United States," *The Prison Journal*, 96, 5 (2016): 688–708.

66. J. Wilson, J. Austin, and W. Naro, "Implementing Automated Kiosk Reporting for Low-risk Probationers: Does it Work?" (Executive Exchange, Bryan, TX: National Association of Probation Executives, 2008); J. Wilson, W. Naro, and J. Austin, *Innovations in Probation: Assessing New York City's Automated Reporting*

System (Washington, DC: The JFA Institute, 2007).

67. D. Andrews, J. Bonta, and J. Wormith, "The Risk-Need-Responsivity (RNR) Model: Does Adding the Good Lives Model Contribute to Effective Crime Prevention?" *Criminal Justice and Behavior*, 38 (2011): 735–55.

68. J. Wogan, "The Changing Relationship Between Ex-Criminals and Their Parole Officers," *Governing*. October 2015, accessed December 27, 2018, http://www.governing.com/topics/public-justice-safety/gov-probation-parole-states-community-supervision.html.

69. G. Barnes, J. Hyatt, and L. Sherman, "An Implementation and Experimental Evaluation of Cognitive-Behavioral Therapy for High-Risk Probationers," *Criminal Justice and Behavior*, 44, 4 (2017): 611–30.

70. B. Broderick and S. Raphael, *Building Trust and Legitimacy Within Community Corrections* (Washington, DC: US Dept. of Justice, NIJ, 2016), NCJ 249946.

71. "Statement on the Future of Community Corrections," Harvard / Kennedy School Program in Criminal Justice Policy and Management, 2017, available at www.hks.harvard.edu/sites/default/files/centers/wiener/programs/pcj/files/statement_on_the_future_of_community_corrections_final.pdf.

72. *Too Big to Succeed: The Impact of the Growth of Community Corrections and What Should Be Done About It*, Columbia University Justice Lab, January 29, 2018, accessed December 27, 2018, athttp://justicelab.iserp.columbia.edu/img/Too_Big_to_Succeed_Report_FINAL.pdf.

Chapter 6

State and Federal Prisons

LEARNING OBJECTIVES

1. Compare and contrast the similarities and differences between the Philadelphia and Auburn prison models.

2. Describe the criticisms of the supermax prison.

3. Summarize the arguments for and against private prisons.

4. Identify the factors associated with job satisfaction and organizational commitment of correctional officers.

5. Outline the elements of the correctional officer subculture.

CHAPTER OUTLINE

- Prisons in the United States 144

- History of Prisons 146

- Private Prisons 155

- Correctional Officers 159

- SUMMARY 168

There are more than 1,800 prisons in the United States.

KEY TERMS

Ashurst-Sumners Act
"Big house" prisons
"Code of silence"
Congregate care system
    (Auburn system)
Hawes-Cooper Act
Houses of correction
Hulks
Leased labor system

Lockstep
Martinson Report
Organizational commitment
Organizational justice
Penal harm era
Plantation prisons
Pluralistic ignorance
Reciprocity
Reformatory

Rehabilitative era
Separate system (Philadelphia
    or Pennsylvania system)
Silent system
Structured conflict
Supermax prison
Tokenism
Warehouse prisons

Prisons in the United States

There were 1,821 prisons in the United States in 2005 (the last year the federal government published a census report on them).[1] About five percent of them are private, and the rest are either state or federal institutions. Prisons have different custody levels, ranging from minimum to maximum security. Minimum-security institutions house inmates who are not considered escape or security risks. They have chain-link fences instead of walls, and inmate movement is less restricted inside the facility. Inmates may have work assignments that take them out of the facility. Urban work release facilities, for instance, may allow inmates to check out of prison to go to work in the community and then check back in after work. Forestry camps are used in several states where eligible inmates undergo training by the state forestry service to fight wildfires alongside state firefighters. Minimum- and medium-security institutions hold offenders that are not considered security risks, such as the infamous prisoner described in the Focus on the Offender box.

Medium-security institutions have fences and perimeter security. Inmates are more controlled than in the minimum-security camps, although there is usually quite a lot of inmate movement. Groups or individuals walk to education, rehabilitative programs, and work assignments. A yard where inmates can exercise and socialize is usually open during the day and evening hours. In contrast, maximum-security institutions usually have high walls, razor wire, and guard towers. Inmates' movements are strictly controlled. Maximum-security prisons sometimes have a minimum-security camp or housing unit on the same grounds, sometimes outside the walls of the maximum-security prison. These inmates may be used to provide maintenance services such as groundskeepers. Sometimes a facility will be identified as both maximum and medium security. In this case, the classification level of individual inmates will dictate where they are housed, what programs they are eligible for and the level of movement they are allowed in the facility.

A few maximum-security prisons are considered "supermax" prisons, the most secure facilities in the world, where inmates spend 23 hours a day in their cells with no access to programs and extremely limited exercise and visitation. Medium-security institutions bear some characteristics of both minimum and maximum, and are protected by both chain-link fencing and razor wire. Some smaller states do not have medium-security prisons at all, but states with many

FOCUS ON THE
OFFENDER CAMP FLUFFY

Former investment advisor Bernie Madoff was responsible for one of the biggest Ponzi schemes in history. He is said to be responsible for $20 billion in cash losses and $65 billion in paper losses of investors who gave him money to invest, which he used to pay earlier investors. Although he got away with it for about 16 years, his scheme came crashing down, along with the stock market, in 2008. He pled guilty in 2009 and was serving a 150-year sentence at a medium-security federal correctional complex in Butner, North Carolina, known as Camp Fluffy before his death from kidney failure in 2021. The prison holds 758 inmates who are classified as vulnerable if put into the general population of larger maximum-security prisons. There are pedophiles, terrorists, white-collar criminals, drug lords, and individuals who cooperated with authorities in prosecutions of others.

The prison resembles a campus. There are no bars, no perimeter wall (only a fence), and the grounds are nicely landscaped. There is a gym, a library, pool tables, a chapel, a volleyball court, a bocce-ball court, and even an Indian sweat lodge. Madoff had a picture window in his cell. He exercised by walking around the track. His job was to sweep the mess hall. Inmates are quick to point out that it is still a prison, and inmates are told when to eat, sleep, and work, although there is little to do that could be considered meaningful work. Their movement is limited. They must request medical care. Every evening, inmates stand in the "pill line" to receive medications, such as for blood pressure and cholesterol.

Inmates can spend up to $290 in the commissary to buy their own food, clothing, radios, and other goods. Inmates are allowed three pairs of standard-issue khakis. Madoff reportedly paid another inmate eight dollars a month to clean and press them. Even in this low-security prison, there are cliques (or "cars"), social groups of inmates who protect each other.

Given Madoff's significant financial crimes and the irreparable harm caused to his victims and his family, some people argued his punishment wasn't severe enough. In 2010, one of Madoff's sons committed suicide because of the scandal, and his other son died of cancer in 2014. His wife and grandchildren never visited him. He died in prison surrounded by strangers rather than his family.

Questions for Discussion

1. Should inmates who pose no physical danger to society, and can be housed in minimum- or medium-security facilities like Camp Fluffy, be punished in some other way than prison?

2. Medium- and minimum-security prisons sometimes have recreational facilities to keep inmates occupied; is that a good thing or not?

Sources: B. Ross, R. Schwartz, "Bernie Madoff 'Doing Fine' in Prison Despite Heart Issues, Few Visitors," ABC News, February 2, 2016, https://abcnews.go.com/US/bernie-madoff-fine-prison-heart-issues-visitors/story?id=36552841.

S. Fishman, "Bernie Madoff, Free at Last: In Prison He Doesn't Have to Hide His Lack of Conscience. In Fact, He's a Hero for It," New York Magazine, June 6, 2010, http://nymag.com/news/crimelaw/66468/.

prisons designate some as medium security for inmates who have had no prison infractions. They have more programming than maximum-security prisons, but do not allow inmates out into the community. Although the stereotypical image of prisons is inmates living in barred single or double cells, most prisoners today are housed in dormitories.

The Federal Bureau of Prisons (BOP) manages about 100 facilities from low-security camps to penitentiaries, in addition to running immigration detention facilities. Immigration detention facilities bear many of the same characteristics as prisons in that movement is tightly controlled and there is perimeter security, although some facilities house children and/or families. Some states, like California and Texas, have dozens of correctional facilities, while smaller states have only a few.

Before discussing today's prisons, we will look back at the history of prisons in the United States, and then go on to cover some important current issues, including the use of "supermax" prisons, which, in some ways, are like the very earliest prisons. We will also discuss the role of correctional officers and issues related to the job.

History of Prisons

Historically, offenders were usually punished with corporal punishment, fines, banishment, or death. However, imprisonment was also used as a punishment, even in ancient times. In England and Europe, some of the earliest places of confinement were owned by churches for wayward clerics.[2] Bridewell Palace was given to London by Edward III and opened as a place of confinement in 1556; in Amsterdam, Holland, two **houses of correction** were set up in the late 1500s. These places were not exactly prisons in our sense of the term—they housed minor offenders, in addition to orphans, the poor, disobedient children, and the mentally ill. From 1776 until about 1850, England even used old navy ships called **hulks** to house offenders. Houses of correction, modeled after these early institutions in Europe, later appeared in the American colonies as well.

The work of British philanthropist John Howard (1726–1790), an early prison reformer, helped to shape the structure of prisons in the United States. After being elected High Sheriff of Bedfordshire, he toured many gaols and prisons in Britain and Europe; appalled by what he saw, he published the first of four editions of *The State of the Prisons* in 1777. He criticized the brutality, debauchery, and poor sanitation that were present in many places of confinement but spoke with admiration of the Hospice of San Michele in Rome and Maison de Force at Ghent, Austrian Flanders (later Belgium). These places of confinement utilized individual cells, separated men from women and children, and employed constructive work programs for inmates. These institutions served as models for the development of the Philadelphia model of prison architecture in the United States, and Howard's writings were instrumental in the development of the first American penitentiary with single cells and the philosophy of penitence.

The Philadelphia (Pennsylvania) and Auburn (New York) Models of Prisons

As discussed in Chapter 3, imprisonment as punishment was not widely utilized in the United States until the late eighteenth century. In the colonial era, offenders were usually dealt with in the community through some form of public humiliation. As cities grew, places of confinement included houses of correction, which housed an assortment of poor and/or criminal inmates, and gaols, which housed individuals until trial or corporal punishment was carried out.

Philadelphia's Walnut Street Jail is often noted as the first penitentiary. Even though it was a jail (see Chapter 4), it was also the first location in which the philosophy of the penitentiary was developed and implemented. When it was built in 1773, large rooms housed all prisoners. Quaker reformers, very much influenced by John Howard, were instrumental in the opening of a new section of the

Walnut Street Jail in 1790, which was specifically called a prison.[3] A block of 16 cells was built with the idea of housing inmates in solitary confinement, following the European practice John Howard had championed. Prison reformers advocated for such concepts as classification and reformation through penitence. Women and men were separated, children were kept separate from adults, and the sick were isolated so they did not infect the healthy.[4]

Subsequently, over the years the facility became extremely overcrowded, with 30 or 40 inmates to a room. Escapes, drunkenness, and riots were common. In 1829, Eastern State Penitentiary was opened on the outskirts of Philadelphia, although it was not completed until 1836. The architecture was designed to follow a silent, solitary system, with individual cells and exercise yards. Clergymen, politicians, and educators all believed that the penitentiary was the perfect place to instill the characteristics of sobriety, regularity, and piety, and it was thought that this could be achieved by physically separating inmates and encouraging silent reflection. Outside influences were kept to a minimum and silence was maintained to reduce contamination from other inmates. The only influence permitted was the Bible and a religious guide to aid in finding salvation. In addition to quiet contemplation, prisoners were expected to work on producing goods that could be made in their cells, not for profit, but rather to induce a work ethic. After a due period of "penitence," the individual was expected to emerge as a new person.[5] As such, this practice became known as the **separate system**, or Philadelphia or Pennsylvania model. The penitentiary became a showpiece, and visitors included Charles Dickens, Presidents Andrew Jackson and John Quincy Adams, the Marquis de Lafayette, and Edward, Prince of Wales, later to be Edward VIII of Great Britain.

Meanwhile, in 1816 the New York legislature approved funds to build Auburn Prison, and it was completed in 1823.[6] This facility adopted some of the principles of the Pennsylvania model, such as maintaining silence among prisoners, having an ordered schedule, and an emphasis on penitence, but rejected the practice of total isolation because it was found to cause mental deterioration in inmates. The biggest difference was that at Auburn Prison, inmates worked,

Eastern State Penitentiary.

ate, and exercised together in lockstep, although they slept in 550 solitary cells at night. Cells were much smaller than those at Eastern State Penitentiary because inmates were not in them during the day. The prison provided opportunities to exploit prisoner labor, so industrial manufacturing replaced the individual handcrafts that inmates worked at in Philadelphia. Ultimately, this prison structure became known as the **congregate care system**, or Auburn system. Proponents of the Auburn system agreed with the Philadelphia model in that communication between prisoners or the outside world was not seen as helpful in their reformation; thus, harsh punishments were implemented to deter talking. Prisoners were to work, eat, and move about the prison in complete silence—this unnatural situation was referred to as the **silent system**. During a visit to the United States from 1831 to 1832, French philosopher Alexis de Tocqueville and French magistrate and prison reformer Gustave de Beaumont investigated American prisons and published their observations. The following quote describes the silent system in their words:

> Everything passes in the most profound silence, and nothing is heard in the whole prison but the steps of those who march, or sounds proceeding from the workshops ... the silence within these vast walls ... is that of death. We felt as if we traversed catacombs; there were a thousand living beings, and yet it was a desert solitude.[7]

One of the hallmarks of the silent system was called **lockstep** where inmates were moved from place to place by having them place their hand on the opposite shoulder of the man in front of them. In this way, large numbers shuffled along, and any disturbance was easy to detect by guards. It was eventually abolished in the first several decades of the twentieth century as treatment of prisoners evolved.[8]

During the early 1800s, the relative merits of the Philadelphia (Pennsylvania) and Auburn (New York) models became the subject of enthusiastic public interest, with editorials, debates, and public speeches comparing the two systems. Prisons were believed to be transformational in reforming bad people to good, and, indeed, saving society from the increasing degradations observed with the new age. In the following quote, the Reverend James Finley, a minister and active prison proponent, expressed his optimism:

> Could we all be put on prison fare, for the space of two or three generations, the world would ultimately be the better for it. Indeed, should society change places with the prisoners, so far as habits are concerned, taking to itself the regularity, and temperance, and sobriety of a good prison, then the grandiose goals of peace, right, and Christianity would be furthered.[9]

The historian David Rothman described the shared vision of the two penitentiaries as the trinity of separation, obedience, and order. Rothman noted how the penitentiary was like other congregate care facilities emerging in this period, created to control and provide services to larger numbers of people. Orphanages were used to house orphaned or abandoned youngsters; hospitals were created to house the sick and infirm; and mental institutions were opened to take care of those who were unable to function. These new institutions joined workhouses or poorhouses and houses of correction as the size of cities grew. Local communities, which had up until this time absorbed the poor, sick, itinerant, mentally ill, and others, could no longer do so, forcing the need for a more formalized, institutionalized response.[10]

From Reformatories to the "Big House"

In 1870, correctional reformers came together in the National Prison Congress to renew the debate about the best prison model and other correctional practices. The principles endorsed at the 1870 Prison Congress (and reaffirmed 100 years later at the 1970 Prison Congress) included the following:

- Corrections must demonstrate integrity, respect, dignity, and fairness.
- Sanctions imposed by the court shall be commensurate with the seriousness of the offense.
- Offenders shall have the opportunity to engage in productive work, and participate in programs and other activities that will enhance self-worth, community integration, and economic status.[11]

At the 1870 Prison Congress, a new model for imprisonment was born—the **reformatory**. The reformatory was aimed at youthful offenders who were believed to be most amenable to change. In 1876, Zebulon Brockway, an active participant in the Prison Congress, implemented the idea of classification, in which the inmates earned privileges of liberty, education, and training, at the Elmira Reformatory in Elmira, New York. Young offenders, who could benefit from a strict regimen of disciplined living and education, were targeted for the new reformatory. Discipline was harsh. Brockway believed in earning liberties, but he was known for inflicting harsh punishments as well. Along with the idea of the reformatory came the concept of **graduated release**, what we know today as parole. In this way, inmates could be rewarded for good behavior, and the possibility of release encouraged them to behave.[12]

As new prisons were built, they followed the Auburn model. These prisons were cheaper to build because they did not require the larger cells and exercise yards of the separate system, and the state could recoup some of the costs of imprisonment by having prisoners work at some type of industry. While the penitentiary and reformatory became the models for prison architecture in the north, the southern states followed a different course. Because so much of the south's economy depended on agriculture, the prison farm emerged. Originally, northern prisons were built in rural areas with thousands of acres available for crops, but prison industry became the more important economic contribution by the early 1900s. Northern states either produced goods for sale or leased the institution and/or prisoner labor to private industry. In the south, the factory prison model did not develop as quickly. Prisoners were much more likely to work in fields than in prison factories. Historians have described the so-called **"plantation prisons"** of the south as essentially replacing slavery. It has been reported that up to 75 percent of inmates were Black, and they were forced to work in the fields, either for the prison itself or leased out to plantation owners.[13] The contracts between landowners and states whereby landowners fed, clothed, and housed prisoners in return for their labor came to be known as the **leased labor system**. In some cases, conditions were horrific, with landowners literally working the prisoners to death. In fact, the average lifespan of a prisoner during this time was no more than six or seven years. Periodic exposés of the terrible conditions in which these prisoners lived spurred some oversight and change, but the system continued in some states well into the 1940s.[14]

There were a few women incarcerated in early penitentiaries. Separate institutions for women did not exist until the late 1800s, so women were confined in attics or basements, left unsupervised, and subjected to sexual abuse.[15] Reformatories for young men focused on education, militaristic drills, and strict discipline.

The lease labor system was a hallmark of the "plantation prisons" of the South, c. 1884-1991.

Reformatories for women were some of the first separate places of confinement built specifically for women and sought to recreate home-like environments.[16]

The grand vision of early proponents of prisons and reformatories was that they could become a place for reformation and enlightenment. Before and even after the Civil War, penitentiary models (i.e., the separate system versus congregate care) were a topic of public debate; reformers believed that prisons could solve all the ills of society because of the perfect order that could be created behind prison walls. However, by the turn of the century, prisons were largely forgotten. During the early to mid-1900s, prisoners worked at often-meaningless labor, such as piling rocks. There was no purpose, and no institutional mission, other than incapacitation and punishment.

Prison historian Robert Johnson called the prisons of the early twentieth century **"big house" prisons**. In these prisons, there were no programs, little education, and little expectation that the men and women inside were capable of change. It was "a world populated by people seemingly more dead than alive, shuffling where they once marched, heading nowhere slowly."[17] Virtually no public attention was directed to prisons throughout the time period encompassing both World Wars. Typically, prison wardens were expected to keep prisons out of the newspapers. If they managed to do that, they were considered successful.

"Big house" prisons were not large, certainly not by today's standards; few housed more than 500 inmates. These were typically older offenders with long criminal histories. There was a large gulf between guards and inmates that neither side breached. Each group knew their place, and both sides valued predictability and order. In American sociologist and criminologist Gresham Sykes' classic study *The Society of Captives*, he described the prison society at Trenton State Prison in the 1950s as a world where the strong preyed upon the weak. A few prisoners were able to obtain a range of goods, including alcohol and sex, by barter or with money from the outside. Prisoners were expected to "do their own time" and ignore the victimization of their fellow inmates.

In the decades preceding the 1950s, prisoners did see some improvements in conditions, spurred by greater professionalism in corrections as well as some early prisoner rights lawsuits. The leased labor system, with its inhumane practices of starvation and slave labor, was eventually abolished throughout the South.[18] The practice of sending children, sometimes as young as nine years old, to prisons for adults gradually changed as states began building reformatories and juvenile detention facilities. Corporal punishment was slowly abolished. Even though the lash continued to be used well into the 1960s, other forms of punishment were abolished, such as the "yoke" (a piece of wood with holes for the neck and wrists that the inmate was locked into) and shower bath (inmates were bound and doused with cold water).[19] Furthermore, by 1930, many states had some form of conditional release for good behavior or commutation of sentence.

The Rehabilitative Era

In the 1950s, a rash of prison riots brought prisons to the front pages of newspapers and to the attention of politicians who felt the need to advocate for reform. It was also during this time that the disciplines of sociology, psychology, and psychiatry began to influence prison operations. Prison sociologists began developing rudimentary prison classification systems that differentiated prisoners' risk of violence toward other inmates or guards. Prisons also began to offer prisoners more privileges, such as yard access and recreational activities, more liberal mail and visitation policies, and occasional movies or concerts. The more important development, however, was the implementation of educational, vocational, and therapeutic programs.

Such changes ushered in the **rehabilitative era** of corrections, which began in the 1960s and ended in the late 1970s. During this period, in varying degrees across the country, prison programs were initiated, educational opportunities expanded, and prerelease programs were developed. Inmates were released through a variety of work- and educational-release programs. Eligible inmates were transferred to halfway houses or minimum-security facilities so that they could take college classes or work during the day and return to the facility at night. There was minimal security, but inmates were considered escapees if they did not return when they were supposed to. In addition to basic and advanced education, prisoners might have had the opportunity to partake in group therapy, transactional analysis, or behavior modification; even transcendental meditation and yoga were offered in some prisons. Prisons were renamed and became *correctional institutions*, once again with the goal of reform rather than just punishment or deterrence. Women's correctional institutions also followed the mission of reform. Some women's prisons experimented with having apartment-like minimum-security buildings, where female inmates could go out to work in the community, returning to the prison-based apartment at night.[20]

The strength of the rehabilitative mission varied across the country. Southern prisons never adopted wholescale the idea of rehabilitation and continued to exhibit characteristics of big houses and plantation prisons. In some prisons, brutal discipline practices continued well into the 1970s. Texas prisons utilized "building tenders," who were fellow inmates tasked with controlling the inmate population by whatever means necessary. Inmates were forced to work in the fields and, according to one prison warden, if they didn't work hard enough or if they committed other types of infractions, they could be punished by being made to stand on a rail—a two-by-four placed on its side. If they fell off, the punishment would begin again. Other inmates would have their hands hand-cuffed above their heads and be left to hang there all day.[21] These types of punishments existed well into the 1970s in some prisons.

However, in other states, inmates started their prison terms in classification centers, where they took a multitude of educational, aptitude, and interest tests and underwent medical examinations. These tests were then used to determine what prison they would be sent to and the appropriate mix of educational, vocational, and treatment programs to which they would be assigned. Inmates had access to GED classes, college programs, and many other opportunities to better themselves, such as group therapy and therapeutic communities.

Despite these reforms, there were a spate of prison riots across the country in the 1970s.[22] The Attica riot, which occurred at the Attica Correctional Facility in western New York in 1971, is the most infamous. Tensions had mounted over prisoners' demands for better living conditions and programs, and came to a boil after the killing of inmate George Jackson in California; this led to an uprising during which over 1,000 prisoners took guards and prison employees hostage, effectively taking control of the prison. Negotiations lasted for four days until New York state police regained control after a bloody assault. One guard was killed by inmates during the initial takeover, three inmates were killed during the four days of inmate control, and the rest (9 guards and 29 inmates) were killed by state police in the retaking of the prison; dozens more were injured. Such riots took place in a time not only of rehabilitative reform, but also of political upheaval. Many prisoners were politicized, having taken part in Vietnam War protests, civil rights demonstrations, or other public protest movements.

A blow to the rehabilitative trend was the **Martinson Report** of 1974.[23] Paid for and then suppressed by New York State, the report was written by Robert Martinson, a sociologist at the City College of New York, and his colleagues Douglas Lipton and Judith Wilks. It was a meta-analysis and evaluation of over 200 prison and correctional programs across the country. According to the first articles published from this study, no correctional program was successful in reducing recidivism. The findings were more complicated, and Martinson attempted in later articles to modify his original harsh stance, but the damage had been done. Politicians began to campaign on "tough on crime" platforms. Academics offered philosophical justification for retribution.[24] Prisoner advocates also argued against the rehabilitation ethic, believing that individualized programs ignored societal factors such as poverty, and indeterminate sentencing was a violation of due process and equal sentencing. The unusual alliance between conservatives who wanted more punishment and less treatment and liberals who wanted more transparency and clarity in sentencing and release decisions created the political environment whereby indeterminate sentencing was discarded in some states and treatment eventually ceased to be the primary goal of the penitentiary. By the early 1980s, the rehabilitative era had ended.[25]

The Penal Harm Era

In the 1980s, the rehabilitative era gave way to what has been referred to as the **penal harm era**.[26] Prisons shifted from correctional institutions to **warehouse prisons**. Even though states may have still called them correctional systems, some argue that the mission and function of prisons changed to one of simply incapacitation—or worse. Increasing numbers of prisoners and the disenchantment with the concept of rehabilitation led to what has been described as simply warehousing or replacing rehabilitation with penal harm, either intentionally or by neglect.. Rehabilitative programs were cut, and prison administrators struggled to find beds for increasing prisoner populations.[27] Even women's prisons changed. Women were told they were going to be treated like inmates rather than women, and the unique characteristics of women's prisons, such as more generous visitation and clothing allowances, were systematically eliminated.[28]

The Supermax

Before the creation of the modern supermax prison, institutions like the federal penitentiaries at Alcatraz Island in California and McNeil Island in Washington state were built to house prisoners deemed the worst of the worst—those whose violent tendencies or organized crime connections made it impossible to house them in lower-security prisons. The Federal Bureau of Prisons closed Alcatraz in the 1960s, but in the 1980s and 1990s, states began to build their own Alcatraz-type prisons, called **supermax prisons**, institutions designed to provide the highest level of security and that place strict limitations on inmate contact. Most supermax prisons confine inmates to their cells for 23 or even 24 hours a day and offer no programming. The original impetus for such facilities was to isolate gang leaders and inmates who were chronically violent toward other inmates and officers. By 2008, 44 states had opened supermax prisons.[29]

It should be noted that there is no unanimous agreement on the definition of what makes a prison a supermax, and this lack of consistency has led to confusion and difficulty when researching the facilities.[30] As criticisms of supermax prisons have increased in the last several years, states have redefined some prisons as maximum security instead of supermax, although the prisons still have inmates that are kept in their cells 23 hours a day with no programming. Given the practice of renaming facilities, there is no general agreement on even the number of such facilities, much less their relative need or worth. These prisons are even more expensive to build and run than a regular prison. In Ohio, for example, an inmate in supermax confinement costs nearly $60,000 per year, compared to $40,000 per year in a regular maximum-security prison.[31]

Recent estimates suggest that 25,000 inmates are in some form of supermax; this number also includes inmates in administrative or punitive segregation in regular prisons.[32] For the purposes of this discussion, we will refer only to those facilities that are separate institutions. States vary in whether they have a separate supermax institution, and in how many of their inmates are sent there if there is one. In some states, less than one percent of the prisoner population is housed in a supermax (e.g., Pennsylvania), but in other states more than 10 percent of the total state prisoner population is housed in a supermax (e.g., Mississippi).[33] States also vary in the level of due process administered before an inmate is sent to a supermax. In some states, due process hearings determine whether an inmate is dangerous enough to require supermax housing. In

Alcatraz Prison.

other states, placement is a classification decision; for example, a suspected gang member may go directly to the supermax upon entry into the corrections system. Few states that have a supermax prison have any type of transitional program whereby supermax prisoners are eased back into the general prison population before release into the community.[34]

There are several criticisms directed at supermax prisons. One is that in some states, inmates are sent to such facilities not because of a prediction of extreme violence, but rather because they are being punished for demanding rights or for being troublemakers.[35] In a study of a Florida supermax, researchers found that inmates were about four times as likely to have committed violence in prison as non-supermax inmates, but they were about seven times more likely than non-supermax prisoners to have exhibited "defiant behavior." They also found that in the Florida correctional system, supermax inmates have an average of four stays in the supermax, with an average stay of about 13 months, but about a third of the inmates spent up to a third of their entire prison stay in the supermax.[36]

The supermax prison is different from traditional solitary confinement in terms of the length of time prisoners live in the conditions of total isolation.[37] As such, critics argue that the supermax prison is psychologically harmful.[38] Estimates suggest that 80,000 men and women are in solitary confinement in the United States, confined to their cells for 23 hours a day. Most of these inmates are in supermax or maximum-security institutions.[39] Psychologists assert that this type of social isolation and sensory deprivation can have traumatic effects on the brain.[40] One research study found that more than 4,000 prisoners with serious mental illness were being held in solitary confinement.[41] Several experts have argued that the isolation inmates are subjected to in the supermax prison can exacerbate mental health issues and cause symptoms even in those who were mentally ill before imprisonment. Symptoms noted include massive free-floating anxiety, hyper-responsiveness to external stimuli, perceptual distortions and hallucinations, a feeling of unreality, difficulty with concentration and memory, acute confusion, emergence of primitive aggressive fantasies, persecutory ideation, motor excitement, and/or violent destructive or self-mutilation. Also noted have been appetite disruptions, panic, rage, lethargy, paranoia, and loss of control. Another symptom is paradoxically increased social withdrawal so that the inmate becomes unable to interact with others.[42] The National Academy of Sciences, the National Commission on Correctional Health Care (NCCHC), and the American Psychological Association have all condemned the indiscriminate use of solitary confinement and stated that evidence shows deleterious effects on those subjected to solitary confinement for all but the shortest periods.[43]

The supermax also does damage to guards as well as prisoners. There exists an "ecology of cruelty" in the supermax whereby guards are socialized to be even more punitive and harsh toward prisoners than in regular prisons.[44] This leads to extreme behavior on the part of inmates, which then spurs more harsh reaction from the guards. In these escalating cycles, abnormal levels of violence and inhumanity become normal—as uniquely a product of the environment of the supermax. Arguably, if guards go into a prison with the expectation that the prisoners within are the worst of the worst, and treat them that way, they may create the very behavior they expected.[45]

Supermax prisons concern prisoners' rights' groups. Some critics believe that the supermax violates the 1994 *UN Convention Against Torture and Other Cruel, Inhuman or Degrading Treatment or Punishment*. Advocates for prisoners have filed lawsuits alleging that the supermax violates the Eighth Amendment prohibition against cruel and unusual punishment, while others argue that prisoners deserve due process before being transferred to a supermax. Generally, courts have not found the conditions of the supermax prison to constitute cruel and unusual punishment, except for the mentally ill. However, the supermax was considered so extreme and so different from a regular prison that there had to be some due process for inmates before being transferred there.[46]

One of the most notorious supermax prisons is Pelican Bay State Prison, located in California. Built in 1989 in a remote region of northern California, it has been the target of lawsuits, journalistic investigations, and American Civil Liberties Union action. In *Madrid v. Gomez* (1995), a federal court ruled that there was an insufficient number of medical and mental health professionals, excessive force had been used, and policies regarding the use of force were inadequate.[47] Pelican Bay, like most supermax prisons, confines inmates in their cells 23 or 24 hours a day. That alone is enough to generate concern, since cell confinement has been found to be detrimental to mental and physical health.[48]

Despite such criticism, a few studies have found supermax prisons to have favorable effects: in one study, supermax prisoners said they had benefitted from the experience in that they had time to think and control themselves and not be influenced by negative peers.[49] Another study found that there was reduced violence against officers in those states that used supermax facilities (although no reduction in intra-inmate violence occurred).[50]

Some studies suggest that supermax prisoners, once released, have higher recidivism rates than other inmates, but some studies suggest the difference is not statistically significant; in other studies, the difference has been found to be very small.[51] Generally, researchers have determined that there is little evidence the supermax is necessary to reduce violence in prison systems; there is also some evidence that supermax prisoners, if released directly into the community, have higher recidivism rates than inmates from the general prison population.[52]

Private Prisons

Private-sector involvement in prisons is nothing new. There has been privatization since the advent of prisons in the United States. In the 1800s, some states contracted with private firms to create and manage the first prison in the state.[53] The leased labor system, which was especially pervasive in the South, involved inmates being leased to private landowners for their labor. There were also lease labor arrangements in the industrial prisons of the north where factory owners would pay the state for prisoner labor.

In the early days of prisons, some states saw prisons as revenue generators, either by partnering with private industry to produce goods or leasing inmate labor. Opposition from labor groups toward private companies utilizing inmate labor eventually led to federal legislation. In 1929, the **Hawes-Cooper Act** allowed states to bar prison-made goods from being transported across state lines to compete with private businesses and in 1935, the **Ashurst-Sumners Act** made it a federal offense to take prison-made goods across state lines. This legislation, in effect, destroyed private–public partnerships in the prison management industry until the 1980s.

In the 1980s, as states were experiencing massive increases in prison populations without having the prison beds to accommodate the new prisoners, several private companies emerged that offered to build prisons for states and/or manage prisons for a per diem prisoner cost. The capacity of private prisons has grown from almost 4,000 in 1999 to over 100,000 today. In 2019, around 115,954 federal and state prisoners were housed in private prisons. Private prisons held 7 percent of state prisoners and 16 percent of federal prisoners.[54] Five states housed more than 20 percent of their prison population in privately operated facilities at year-end 2019: Montana (47%), New Mexico (36%), Tennessee (29%), Oklahoma (25%), and Hawaii (24%).[55] However, 23 states had no private prisons at all in 2018.[56]

The two largest private prison companies are CoreCivic (formerly Corrections Corporation of America, or CCA) and the GEO Group, Inc. (formerly Wackenhut). Both companies' stocks trade on the New York Stock Exchange, and both build and manage prisons in foreign countries as well as the United States. The GEO Group also runs mental health facilities and addiction treatment centers. It owns or manages about 140 prisons, immigration detention centers, and other facilities nationwide and derives nearly half of its revenue from federal contracts.[57] In addition to the big two, there are over a dozen smaller companies across the nation that compete for private prison bids put out by the states.

It should also be noted that state-run prisons may contract out services, such as healthcare, drug treatment, food services, education, or other services essential to the maintenance and operation of the prison. Thus, even a public prison may have privatized services. Corrections is a huge industry. In one study, 3,100 separate vendors were identified that provided a range of services, such as case management, food service, health care, transportation, video visitation, and other operations, taking in more than half of the $80 billion spent on incarceration annually.[58]

The studies discussed below compare state prisons to private facilities that represent the build/operate model of privatization, meaning that the private company builds the facility and is responsible for operating it in return for per diem costs per inmate paid by the state. Generally, there is a conditional clause in such contracts that requires the state to send inmates to meet a guaranteed level of occupancy.[59]

The Debate Surrounding Prison Privatization

As private companies have become more involved in the U.S. correctional system, questions have been raised regarding the propriety of private prisons:

- Should the government (whether county, state, or federal) delegate its responsibility to incarcerate?
- Do these private institutions cost less, as promised?
- Even if they cost less than public facilities, is it at the expense of quality, either in security or service?
- Does the profit motive encourage more imprisonment?
- Does the private sector respond more quickly with more flexibly to changing needs?
- Does the private sector have the legal authority to ensure security?
- Who is liable—the state or the private vendor or both—for issues of violation of rights of prisoners or victimization if there is an escape?
- Is the private sector better or less able to control corruption?[60]

Proponents of privatization argue that the private sector can build prisons faster and more cheaply than state agencies or the federal government. It may be true that private prisons can be built faster because private corporations are not bound by restrictions placed on government. For instance, a state would most likely have to go to voters to pass a bond to build new prisons; however, a state can contract with a private provider without voter approval. Unlike private corporations, state and local governments are bound by a myriad of bidding and siting restrictions, but private companies have more freedom to build where they want to. Proponents also argue that private facilities can lower operational costs, and that they can provide a better quality of service to inmates. Personnel costs are the largest single portion of correctional costs and private prisons generally pay lower wages than the state or federal correctional systems. This difference is the main reason why private prisons can offer lower per diem rates. The strongest argument for privatization has always been a projected cost savings. Libertarian and conservative groups that seek to reduce government spending favor privatization, believing that private enterprise is inherently more efficient than government agencies.

Groups that favor privatization have shown substantial cost savings.[61] For instance, Segal and Moore reported that private prisons resulted in a cost savings of up to 17 percent.[62] However, other research utilizing the same data found that there were too many differences between the institutions to fairly compare costs.[63] Other research that has carefully controlled for various factors and indirect costs have found no evidence of a cost savings.[64] Some studies have found that private prisons may show a cost savings; however, there are more operational problems in private prisons than state prisons (e.g., escapes, staff assaults, lack of programs) that are not factored into such analyses.[65] Most evaluations have found little difference in costs between private and public facilities in strict comparisons.[66] It is difficult to compare studies, however, because the measurement of costs varies and there is no consensus in what should be counted. The conclusion of a recent review of the research was that there was no clear evidence supporting the notion that either private or publicly run correctional institutions were more effective or provided cost savings to taxpayers.[67]

There have only been a few studies that have compared private and public prisons on rates of recidivism. For the most part, no differences have been found.[68] In one recent review of evaluations, authors identified only two studies that showed private prison releasees had lower recidivism rates. In the other studies available, findings indicate either no difference or that private prison releasees showed higher recidivism rates.[69] The most favorable conclusion one can reach after a survey of available evaluations is that private prisons may be comparable to state institutions, but the cost savings are largely because of reduced salaries for correctional personnel.[70]

Critics argue that legislators should have to seek public approval before committing a state to multiyear, multimillion-dollar contracts with private vendors. Instead of voters agreeing to take on the debt of new prison construction, legislators can simply approve a contract that commits a state to pay a certain per diem rate for a certain number of prisoners for a given number of years. As a part of these contracts, the private vendor may agree to build a prison in exchange for a contract to run it for a certain number of years, after which the state is obligated to purchase the facility for a pre-determined amount. Although the money involved can be as much in the long run as a prison construction project, voters do not need to be consulted.[71] Unions oppose privatization largely because private prisons pay much less than state prisons; therefore, it is not surprising that southern states with historically weak union presence utilize private prisons more than any other region.

From an ethical perspective, opponents of privatization argue that there is something philosophically wrong with making a profit from incarcerating human beings. The major argument against privatization is that government should not delegate what should be a uniquely state function—that is, confining individuals and holding them against their will.[72] Legal questions of authority and liability exist. The Supreme Court has made it clear that delegating imprisonment to private actors is not unconstitutional if there is state oversight; however, prisoners may not have the same protections as those in state-run prisons. In *Minneci v. Pollard* (2012), the Supreme Court decided that prisoners in a private prison could not utilize federal courts to allege constitutional violations since prison employees were private employees.[73] As private employees, prison workers are not protected by qualified immunity as are state employees, therefore prisoners may utilize state tort remedies.[74] This does create an equal protection issue between prisoners housed in private prisons compared to prisoners in state or federally run prisons. Some states have equalized the protections for state versus private guards and inmates through legislation.[75] Another legal issue is that private prisons seem to be exempt from open records laws. Under the Freedom of Information Act (FOIA), members of the public can request documents from federal prisons and immigration detention facilities—but private prisons are exempt from FOIA requests under both federal and state laws.

To oversee private institutions, states use monitoring practices, which enforce contractual obligations such as mandating the number of programs offered and periodically inspecting the doctor-to-inmate ratio. Opponents, however, argue that monitoring is nonexistent or lax and point to a string of scandals, including escapes, abusive conduct by officers, and poor management practices that contribute to high rates of violence.[76]

Furthermore, there seems to be little doubt that the fortunes of private prison companies and politics are intertwined. Private prison corporations contribute to political campaigns and parties that support their objectives.[77] GEO Group and CoreCivic have given nearly $9 million over the past 15 years to state candidates and parties.[78] Company representatives also lobby legislators regarding sentencing policies that result in more people spending longer periods of time in prison. From 2003 to 2010, CoreCivic registered 179 lobbyists in 32 states, and the GEO Group registered 63 in 16 states.[79] In the 2016 election cycle, GEO, through its employee-financed political action committee (PAC), gave federal candidates, PACs, and parties about $732,000—more than four times as much as in the previous presidential cycle, with 87 percent going to Republicans.[80]

In 2016, a scathing Inspector General Report analyzed data from the Federal Bureau of Prisons (BOP) and found that private prisons housing federal prisoners reported higher incidences than BOP prisons in almost all operating areas, including (1) contraband, (2) reports of incidents, (3) lockdowns, (4) inmate discipline, (5) telephone monitoring, (6) selected grievances, (7) urinalysis drug testing, and (8) sexual misconduct.[81] After that report, former Attorney General Sally Yates reported that the Bureau of Prisons would phase out the use of private prisons. The stock price of both the GEO Group and CoreCivic plunged.[82] Shortly after the 2016 election, however, newly appointed Attorney General Jeff Sessions rescinded the Yates decision and announced major new contracts with private providers. GEO's stock tripled within one year.[83] Shortly after the 2020 election, President Biden signed an executive order sharply curtailing the use of private prisons for federal prisoners. It was reported that GEO and CoreCivic could lose as much as a quarter of their revenue, about $1 billion a year between them. Both companies' stocks have fallen more than 80 percent since the end of Donald Trump's presidency.[84]

Correctional Officers

The discussion thus far has described the history of prisons and some of the characteristics of prisons across the country. Now we will turn to some of the personnel who work within these facilities. There are many occupations within a prison, but one of the most essential positions is that of the correctional officer. The relationship between inmates and officers is characterized by **structured conflict**, represented by their respective uniforms. In other words, inmates and officers respond to each other primarily based on the uniforms they each wear, and both are conditioned to expect conflict.[85] Stereotypes of correctional officers (COs) as sadistic and brutal are reinforced by movies and books written by inmates, but the reality is that some COs go out of their way to help inmates cope with imprisonment, and many others simply want to do their job and get home safely. Prisons vary tremendously in how inmates and officers interact. Minimum-security work camps and treatment facilities have less antagonistic relationships between officers and inmates, while maximum-security institutions often seethe with a high level of tension and frequent altercations between inmates and staff.[86]

There are approximately 431,600 COs working across the country, which is lower than in previous years. There is a projected decline in the number of CO jobs available because states are making efforts to reduce prison populations. Qualifications for correctional officers are usually merely good health and a high-school diploma or a GED. According to the *Occupational Outlook Handbook*, the average annual salary for a correctional officer is about $42,820 ($20.59 per hour), although some states pay less.[87] In some states, officers can substantially increase their salary through overtime; in California, for instance, many officers can double their salary.[88]

An estimated 445,000 employees were working in state and federal correctional facilities at year-end 2005; this included administrators, correctional officers, clerical/maintenance, educational, professional/technical, and other categories of personnel. (Unfortunately, the information we have about prisons comes from a national census of correctional facilities, but there have not been more recent updates.) There were twice as many male employees as female employees and three times as many in those jobs that require direct contact with inmates. In 2005, in federal facilities, 87 percent of correctional officers were men and 13 percent were women. In private prisons, 52 percent of correctional officers were men and 48 percent were women. In state operated facilities, about 74 percent of correctional officers were men and 26 percent were women.[89]

Cross-Sex Supervision

Historically, it was mostly men who worked in corrections and supervised the mostly male inmate population. In the seventeenth and eighteenth centuries, female prisoners were housed together with men in jails and guarded by men. These women were raped and sexually exploited, and sold themselves for food and other goods. With the development of the Walnut Street Jail and penitentiaries, women were separated from male inmates but still guarded by men, and sexual exploitation continued. Various scandals and exposés of prostitution rings led to women's reform groups pressuring legislatures to build separate institutions for women in the late 1800s and early 1900s. Women's prisons hired women to be matrons to reduce sexual exploitation, but also to serve as good, upstanding role models who represented "feminine virtue" for the female inmates.

This pattern continued until the mid-1970s, when female officers challenged hiring patterns that barred them from working in prisons for men. Female officers had a very constricted career path in corrections when they were allowed only in institutions for women—few could get promoted, and they often had to move great distances to the only facility in the state for women. In *Dothard v. Rawlinson* (1977), Diane Rawlinson challenged Alabama's refusal to let her work in a men's prison.[90] The Supreme Court decided that the prison's high levels of violence (it was already under a federal monitor) created a legitimate reason for the state's refusal to allow women to work in the prison for men, but explained that most prisons were not as violent as those in Alabama at the time. Many states accepted the fact that female COs would have to be allowed to work in men's prisons and, throughout the 1980s, small numbers of female COs began working in prisons for men.

Due to their small numbers, women experienced some features of **tokenism**. Tokenism refers to the phenomenon of individuals being scrutinized more closely and, to some degree, viewed with bias and stereotyping, when they are members of a disproportionately small group; for example, women in traditionally male-only occupations or minorities in primarily white communities. Management and male officers feared that women would not be able to handle aggressive inmates, would be subject to harassment and assault, and would be co-opted by inmates. However, evaluations of female officers have found that they perform their duties as well as men. By most objective indicators, there are few differences between male and female officers.[91]

Another objection to female officers in prisons for men was the fact that inmates would lose a certain amount of privacy by having opposite-sex guards watching them shower and perform other private bodily functions. In most court cases, there was little sympathy for this challenge, at least when presented by male inmates arguing against the entry of female officers.[92] On the other hand, courts were more sympathetic to female prisoners who argued against the entry of male corrections officers. For the most part, resistance to women working in prisons for men has dissipated.

The effect of the entry of women officers into prisons for men was that male officers were no longer barred from working in prisons for women. In the early 1980s, small numbers of male officers were employed in prisons for women, but they were restricted to public places. However, throughout the late 1980s and 1990s, male officers were routinely assigned to all posts inside prisons for women, including sleeping and shower areas.

The presence of female correctional officers in prisons for men and male correctional officers in prisons for women creates the potential for sexual relationships and/or exploitation, although there is also the possibility of same-sex sexual relationships and exploitation. Some researchers have estimated that as much as 19 to 45 percent of all sexual interactions in prison involve officers.[93]

As the number of female correctional officers in prisons for men increased, instances of sexual relationships between female officers and inmates also increased.[94] In one national survey of sexual victimization, sexual activity with staff was reported by 2.9 percent of male inmates and 2.1 percent of female inmates, with only half of such encounters being reported as consensual. About 69 percent of male victims reported a female staff member as perpetrator, and 72 percent of women reported a male staff member as perpetrator. Male inmates were twice as likely as female inmates to report that no pressure or force was used (64 percent versus 30 percent). Men were also less likely to report injury (9 percent versus 19 percent), and they were less likely to report the sexual activity to authorities (21 percent versus 35 percent).[95] Reports of male correctional officers and staff using their position to exploit female inmates are sadly not new, and these reports increased as the number of male correctional officers in prisons for women increased in the 1990s and 2000s.

Today, it is a crime in all states to have a sexual relationship with an inmate because of the difficulty of proving non-consent. Arguably, an inmate is in an unequal position relative to any staff member, such that they are unable to give free and voluntary consent. However, prison staff members who engage in sexual misconduct are generally not prosecuted. The most common punishment is being fired, followed by a forced resignation. Cross-sex supervision, while here to stay, is also a management issue that creates problems for officers and inmates alike.

Minority Correctional Officers

In rural prisons in the 1970s, prisoners were disproportionately Black and correctional officers were usually white. In the 1980s, there was a concerted effort to hire minority and female officers to work in prisons for men. The first minority officers were subjected to racial slurs from their white colleagues and other forms of discrimination. Initially, white officers mistrusted minority officers, believing them to be sympathetic to inmates. It has been reported that Black officers felt completely unprotected by white colleagues and depended on inmates to keep them safe from other inmates.[96]

Some research indicates that neither race nor ethnicity is related to job satisfaction, although minority officers report more feelings of effectiveness in working with inmates.[97] In a study from 1997 of 2,979 correctional officers, using the Prison Social Climate Survey, it was found that race and sex did influence the officers' perception of their work environment, with minority and female officers reporting more stress.[98] Another early study found that there was a wide gap between Black and white officers in their perceptions of the available opportunities for advancement for minority officers. The white officers perceived greater advancement opportunities for minority officers than did minority officers themselves. This finding has been recurrent in more recent studies, with minority women expressing the least confidence in equitable treatment and opportunities for advancement.[99]

Turnover and Job Satisfaction

Like many industries, prisons must also deal with the issue of turnover. Each year there is about 15 to 25 percent turnover among correctional officers.[100] Reasons include low pay, the nature of the job, long hours, stress, and a poor fit between person and job. Studies indicate that over two-thirds of correctional officers wished they were in a different job, and their satisfaction level was lower than that of most other occupations measured.[101] Job stress can lead to burnout, which results in decreased work performance, increased absenteeism, turnover, and other negative behaviors.[102] Findings are mixed as to whether female COs experience the same or more stress than male COs, whether younger versus older COs experience elements of burnout (such as emotional depersonalization), or whether COs experience burnout to a greater degree than non-custody staff.[103]

Correctional officers experience high levels of medical and social problems related to stress, such as heart disease, obesity, smoking, alcoholism, and divorce. Two of the major reasons for disability leave are stress-related alcoholism and cardiac problems, and correctional officer suicides might be as great a problem as law enforcement suicides.[104] Unfortunately, there is little research in this area, and national figures are difficult to come by. One report noted that there were 96 confirmed or suspected suicides among current and retired members of the correctional officer union in California between 1999 and 2015, and that the annual rate of suicide among correctional officers was as much as four times that of the general population in at least one year.[105]

One survey of Michigan correctional staff reported that they experienced a range of negative health outcomes as compared to the general public. Researchers reported that, using a screening instrument, correctional staff experienced generalized anxiety at a rate 16 times the national average, and nearly 10 times the rates for military. About 1 in 4 custody employees working at male facilities met criteria for a major depressive disorder. About 41 percent of custody staff working at male facilities met criteria for PTSD. The rates of PTSD were nearly 7 times higher than the national average in the general population and four times higher than the rate for first responders. The rate of alcohol abuse was 2.7 times higher than the national average and twice as high as the rate for first responders. Approximately 9 percent (about 1 in 11) of all correctional employees reported scores indicative of suicidal ideation on a valid screening instrument. These outcomes were correlated with "work health" measures (demoralization, exhaustion, and job dissatisfaction). As traumatic exposure increased, work health worsened among respondents. Work health measures also affected physical, mental and family health. The elements that contributed to work health scores included the amount of voluntary and mandatory overtime, traumatic exposure, length of time working in corrections, and the type of facility. Those who worked in facilities for male inmates showed the most negative health effects. Other reports also indicate that unpredictable shift work, fear of being injured, lack of support or trust in supervisory staff, and inadequate training contributes to correctional officer stress.[106]

Healthy coping skills to address the stress that develops when working in a prison are not typically taught in corrections. The problem is exacerbated because prisons are often located in rural areas where mental health professionals are scarce and there are likely to be guns and other weapons available at home. Programs designed to address these issues typically teach COs to recognize when they are experiencing stress, to use exercise and develop hobbies to reduce stress, and learn to communicate more openly and honestly with family members.[107] There is an emerging understanding of how some correctional officers suffer from post-traumatic stress disorder (PTSD) due to being exposed to violence; COs may be assaulted, witness extreme acts of violence, or even be taken hostage. This exposure results in hypervigilance, anger issues, trouble sleeping, and other negative symptoms.[108]

Stress is caused by the pervasive sense of potential danger in the prison, the lack of predictability, feeling trapped in the job, low salaries, inadequate training, an absence of standardized policies, procedures, and rules, lack of communication with management, and little participation in decision making. What is clear, however, is that management can alleviate or exacerbate many of these elements. Research indicates that role conflict (conflicting orders), role overload (unreasonable expectations), and role ambiguity (lack of a clear mission) lead to job stress and reduced job satisfaction.[109] Other research indicates that lack of input in decision making, supervision, feedback, and instrumental communication were greater predictors of stress than individual attributes.[110] The lack of control over rules and procedures, shift work, and a feeling of lack of support create the negative feelings officers have for prison management.[111]

Correctional officers who express greater job satisfaction are also more likely to support rehabilitation and to show reduced absenteeism and better performance.[112] It could be that those with greater job satisfaction perceive a greater role in rehabilitation or vice versa.[113] Research on COs' support for rehabilitation shows that it seems to be highest when the individual enters corrections (which makes sense if the correctional academy training promotes support for the rehabilitative mission) and then declines.[114] However, support increases again in later phases of a CO's career, indicating perhaps a commitment to the mission and goals of corrections as he or she becomes invested in corrections as a profession.[115] Research on what factors are associated with COs' support for rehabilitation has resulted in mixed findings, but generally, younger officers, officers from larger cities, African American and Hispanic officers, correctional administrators, and female correctional officers seem to be more positively oriented toward rehabilitative treatment programs, for example, education and drug treatment. One study found that those who entered the field of corrections in the 1970s when rehabilitation was emphasized expressed stronger support for treatment than did those who entered corrections in the 1980s.[116] Another study found that the correctional officers' perception of risk of assault by inmates was negatively associated with support for treatment and social distance from inmates. Not surprisingly, COs who feel unsafe in a prison environment are less likely to show support for the rehabilitative mission.[117] Correctional officer stress was also negatively associated with support for rehabilitative treatment programs.[118] Other studies show that support for treatment programs among correctional staff can become more positive after a training experience.[119] Perceptions that training has been adequate are also related to greater job satisfaction and less stress.[120] It is also theorized that correctional officers have more negative views of inmates and rehabilitation when they feel that the prison is understaffed and there are not enough resources for safety or rehabilitation.[121]

The Correctional Officer Subculture

As with inmates, which we will discuss in Chapter 8, there is a correctional officer subculture. The changes in the nature of incarceration that occurred in the 1970s during the rehabilitative era were met with resistance because rehabilitative programs and the prisoner rights identified in some court cases, such as *Wolff v. McDonnell* (1974), which required some level of due process before inmates were sent to punitive segregation, were perceived to increase the risk of physical harm to officers.[122] In the decades since, support for prisoners' rights and the expectation that prisoners should have at least some program opportunities have been embedded in the mission and values of corrections departments; however, opposing views still persist. For example, some aspects of the subcultural norms and values of COs are at odds with the formal culture expressed by prison administrators and public documents. Earlier researchers described the following as the norms and values of the correctional officer subculture:

- Always go to the aid of an officer in distress.
- Never make a fellow officer look bad in front of inmates.
- Always support an officer in a dispute with an inmate.
- Always support another officer's sanctions against an inmate.
- Show concern for fellow officers.
- Don't lug drugs.
- Don't be a "white hat" (sympathetic to inmates).[123]

These norms promote safety and a unified front, but they also encourage a curtain of secrecy that protects officers who violate the rules or break laws in their treatment of inmates. Later researchers identified the following as important principles:

- Always go to the aid of an officer in real or perceived physical danger.
- Do not get too friendly with inmates.
- Do not abuse your authority with inmates.
- Keep your cool.
- Back your fellow officers in decisions and actions.
- Do not stab a coworker in the back.
- Do not admit to mistakes.
- Carry your own weight.
- Defer to the experience and wisdom of veteran officers.
- Mind your own business.[124]

One of the most challenging issues in prison management is the subcultural practice of protecting other officers, the so-called **"code of silence."** Officers experience extreme difficulty in the workplace when they testify against each other or in any way break the code. Even though only a small number of officers may be engaged in illegal or unethical practices, they are protected by the large silent majority, who are afraid to come forward because of the powerful subcultural prohibitions against exposing fellow officers. One officer described why it is difficult to "blow the whistle" on peer officers:

> If an incident went down, there was no one to cover my back. That's a very important lesson to learn. You need your back covered and my back wasn't covered there at all. And at one point I was in fear of being set up by guards. I was put in dangerous situations purposely.[125]

The "code of silence" and correctional officer unions create a force that is resistant to some attempted innovations in prison management and programming when such changes are seen as tipping the balance of power between inmates and officers.[126]

Part of the belief system of the correctional officer subculture is that all inmates are scum, that they are dishonest, lazy, and manipulative.[127] Even though individual COs may not believe this to be true of all inmates, they incorrectly assume that most officers feel this way; this is called **pluralistic ignorance**. Officers are mistaken in their assumptions because there are a sizable number of officers who do not agree with the subcultural beliefs regarding inmates.[128] However, officers who do express positive views of inmates are quickly rebuked and made to question their beliefs by discussing the inmate's crimes or reciting the negative behaviors of other inmates.

As with many subcultural elements, these belief systems are in place as a cultural protection: COs who are too friendly or sympathetic to inmates are not to be trusted. They may put other COs at risk. As early as the 1950s, prison researcher Gresham Sykes discussed the concept of **reciprocity**, referring to the reliance on inmates some new officers develop as they learn their job.[129] He described how some officers slowly and insidiously become dependent on inmates to help them with their tasks and to get things done. The officer may find himself allowing special favors and rewards to the inmates who help him, putting him at risk of discipline or even losing his job. Officers who trade favors with inmates, in effect, give up a certain amount of their power to the inmates.[130] Over time, the power balance shifts between officer and inmate because the officer knows the inmate could report him for numerous rule violations. Although officers are trained to avoid this type of manipulation, the process is so slow and deceptive that many officers still get trapped in some type of reciprocal relationship with one or more inmates.

The risk that COs will be manipulated by inmates probably lies at the heart of why there is such a strong CO subcultural prohibition against being an "inmate lover." However, the danger of the subcultural indoctrination that all inmates are bad people is that it opens the door to brutality. In the famous Stanford prison experiment, young male college students were randomly assigned the role of guards or inmates. After six days, the experiment was abandoned because of the transformation of the students into brutal, sadistic "guards" who took pleasure in cruelty, illustrating the potential of the truism that power corrupts. About one-third of the guards became "tyrannical in their arbitrary use of power."[131] Although many argue that the experiment was quite different from real prison

FOCUS ON

HISTORY

THE INFAMOUS ZIMBARDO (OR STANFORD) PRISON EXPERIMENT

In 1971, on the grounds of Stanford University, Dr. Phillip Zimbardo conducted an infamous experiment. He was interested in how individuals would respond when given power over others. In his experiment, college men were arbitrarily assigned to be correctional officers or inmates. In the basement of a college building a mock prison was set up which included "the hole"—a closet used to punish "inmates." The changes in both inmates and guards, even though they were all role-playing, were so profound that the experiment was canceled after six days. Zimbardo reported that about one-third of the correctional officers became brutal and authoritarian, and prisoners became manipulative and exhibited signs of emotional distress and mental breakdown. Because he gave himself the role of prison warden, he found that even he had been corrupted by the experience of being "warden" and his decision making began to be based on that power rather than scientific curiosity or humane caring toward the men who were suffering as "inmates." What was even more shocking than the brutality exhibited by some "guards" was that others, clearly uncomfortable with the gratuitous cruelty, did nothing to stop them. If

college men who knew the experiment was artificial succumbed to the temptation to inflict their will on the powerless, the inescapable conclusion was that the environment itself caused people to act in ways that they would not otherwise.

Later analysis disputed some of the profound findings the experiment is known for, arguing that individuals act in ways expected of them, and that might entail brutality and authoritarianism, but it does not mean that everyone is likely to exhibit those traits when given power over others. However, given the reality of the prison subculture, it still has a great deal of resonance in understanding the relationships between correctional officers and inmates. The experiment continues to serve as a stark reminder that the adage that "power corrupts" has some degree of truth. The experiment also led to much more stringent protections for human subjects who volunteer for medical or social science experiments, especially those connected to universities. Today, the Stanford experiment probably would not be approved by any university's human subject review board.

Sources: P. Zimbardo, "The Prison Game," in Legal Process and Corrections, ed. N. Johnston and L. Savitz, 195–98 (New York: Wiley, 1982).
"Stanford Prison Experiment," accessed October 15, 2019, https://www.prisonexp.org/
M. Konnikova, "The Real Lesson of the Stanford Prison Experiment," The New Yorker, June 12, 2015, accessed October 10, 2019, https://www.newyorker.com/science/maria-konnikova/the-real-lesson-of-the-stanford-prison-experiment.

in that prisons today are governed by a panoply of laws, regulations, policies, and procedures, unfortunately there is continuing evidence that, if conditions are ripe, COs will abuse their power.[132]

It should be noted that COs' distrust of inmates is not without cause. There is some evidence that assaults on correctional officers have increased from earlier decades. Research indicates that many assaults are unplanned and unpredictable.[133] Inmates who assault COs are likely to be young, either Black or white, and have prior incarcerations, be incarcerated for a violent crime, and have a long sentence.[134] Other correlates were related to the prison itself: maximum security (versus other levels), overcrowding, and poor facilities are also associated with increased likelihood of assaults.[135] In one study of over 1,500 COs in 45 different facilities, about 34 percent had been assaulted in some way by an inmate; 31 percent reported that they had been threatened in the past month, with a majority being threatened more than once. Ironically, 88 percent reported that they felt safe during their shift.[136]

Reciprocal violence between inmates and correctional officers is an important challenge in correctional management. In one study of personal liability lawsuits against correctional officers, researchers found that of 44 cases, 31 involved allegations of excessive use of force. The most frequent type of force used was described as retaliatory. Researchers note that this type of misconduct may be collectively tolerated, endorsed, and rewarded by peers as a means to resolve disputes. To enlighten correctional officers about the legal liability for excessive force, more training is recommended. Correctional staff should also have training on multiple supervisory styles (especially those that are attuned to correctional staff–prisoner confrontation), de-escalation techniques, and effective listening.[137]

Types of Power Exerted by Correctional Officers

Correctional officers' power has been categorized into five types:

1. *legitimate* (power is based on the officer's uniform, i.e., he or she must be obeyed because of their role in the organization),
2. *expert* (power is derived from training and skills, i.e., a work crew supervisor who tells inmates how to fix something),
3. *referent* (power is derived from the individual's reputation, i.e., inmates respect a certain officer and will do as he or she asks),
4. *coercive* (power is derived from the implicit or explicit threat of physical force), and
5. *reward* (power comes from promises of certain benefits within the CO's power that are offered, i.e., a phone call or time out of a cell before lights out).[138]

A recent study examined these types of power and their effects on inmates. Researchers surveyed over 5,000 inmates and close to 2,000 COs in two states and 45 different correctional facilities and asked them why inmates obeyed them, with answer choices matching the types of power previously described. They found that the powers used most often were associated with officer demographics, job training, experiences, and several characteristics of the prisons themselves. White male COs relied more on coercive power than women or minority officers, and were less likely to rely on expert, referent, and reward power relative to Black and Latino officers. Women relied more on referent power than male COs did. Experienced officers relied significantly less on coercive power and more on expert and legitimate power. The type of facility also played a role, with both male and female officers working in facilities for women more likely to use referent power and officers working with higher-risk populations more likely to rely on coercive power. Researchers also found that greater use of coercive power reduced inmates' perceptions of officer legitimacy, or fairness and justice. In other words, when COs used coercive power, inmates were less likely to agree that officers were fair, equitable, and doing a good job.[139] Additionally, the more an inmate perceived a CO to have legitimate power, the more likely they were to comply with orders.[140]

Research shows that inmates are willing to accept COs' legitimacy, and that a "good" officer, according to inmates, is one who is consistent, treats inmates with respect, and is ethical. Inmates reacted negatively to officers who were inconsistent in how they enforced the rules, who mistreated inmates either physically or verbally, who were dishonest, who accepted cash for smuggling cellphones or drugs into prison, and who paid inmates to hurt other inmates. COs who were consistent, respectful, and honest were viewed positively by inmates.[141]

There is also research indicating that surprisingly positive interactions between inmates and COs do occur. Given that COs are with inmates daily, they exert a much more consistent and powerful influence than treatment personnel. Some inmates report that COs have helped them by being role models or informally advising them in personal matters.[142] Personal reports of inmates who describe how correctional officers have been an important influence in their lives support the notion that COs can be a positive influence on inmates and play a very important role in rehabilitation.[143]

Correctional Management and Organizational Justice

Organizational culture affects the attitudes and behavior of correctional workers. The correctional officer subculture is separate from, and sometimes antagonistic to, the formal culture comprising the norms, values, and ways of doing things promoted by management.[144] **Organizational commitment** refers to the level of commitment to formal organizational values held by workers. An individual who scores high on organizational commitment would be someone who believes in the mission and values of the organization and goes "above and beyond" to accomplish necessary tasks. The way management treats workers and implements policies and procedures either increases or reduces organizational commitment among workers. Research has shown that correctional workers who feel they are treated fairly and heard by management are more satisfied in their roles and measure higher on organizational commitment to the organization.[145] **Organizational justice** is the perception that an organization is fundamentally fair, but researchers have separated it into distinct sub-themes: voice, fairness, respect, and trustworthiness. These concepts are measured by agreement with statements in an organizational justice survey. Voice refers to the perception that workers feel heard by management. Fairness refers to the perception that decisions are made impartially and not arbitrarily or giving special treatment to some workers. Respect refers to the perception that workers feel they are treated with esteem by supervisors and administrators. Trustworthiness refers to the belief that managers are making decisions for the greater good. These concepts are correlated but distinct, and all make up the larger perception of organizational justice.[146] The presence of organizational justice seems to be associated with greater job satisfaction, lower turnover, and more organizational commitment, which may be associated with workers being more likely to perform in ethical ways.[147] Thus, good leaders who act in ways that increase the perception of organizational justice promote organizational good-citizenship behavior, including ethical behavior.[148]

Until the 1970s, wardens ruled their prisons out of sight of public scrutiny. Today, prison administrators must respond to a multitude of legal, political, social, and economic pressures stemming from courts, officers' unions, the media, ex-prisoner and family groups, and legislators. Various sources maintain that a well-run prison requires well-articulated policies, adequate training, compliance audits, benchmarking (comparing the institution to others), accreditation, identification of corruption, and strategic planning.[149] Thus, correctional leaders must demonstrate their commitment to the organization, provide adequate training and education for correctional staff, create a climate of change, trust staff to take responsibility, listen, share management tasks, institutionalize feedback, and demonstrate integrity.[150] Arguably, staff who don't have a clear sense of what the organization stands for and what is expected of them will have low morale.

It is a sad reality that there are instances where correctional officers and other staff abuse their positions. Trafficking in contraband, theft, sexual relations with inmates, assisting in escape, and brutality are just some of the unethical behaviors that occur.[151] One typology of correctional corruption described 1) abuse of power, which includes illegal use of force, exploitation, and harassment, and 2) using one's authority for personal gain, which includes extortion, smuggling, theft, and accepting kickbacks. Instances of corruption are committed at every level, from officers to the top ranks of correctional administrators.[152] To reduce corruption in corrections, there must be a concerted effort to improve hiring practices (including background checks and psychological testing), institute more rigorous training, employ supervisory devices to reduce temptation and punish wrongdoers, and increase organizational commitment overall.

Summary

- The first prisons in the United States were exemplified by the Philadelphia or Pennsylvania model (also called the separate system), which kept inmates in separate cells 24 hours a day, and the Auburn or New York model (also called the congregate care system), which allowed inmates out of their cells during the day. Eventually, the Auburn system became the model for penitentiaries in the U.S.

- The "big house" era gave way to correctional institutions and the rehabilitative era of the 1960s and 1970s. The focus on rehabilitation was fleeting; the 1980s became known as the era of penal harm and saw the introduction of "warehouse prisons."

- As state and federal prison populations exploded in the 1980s and 1990s, private prisons fulfilled the need for rapidly constructed, lower-cost facilities.

- Privatization has vociferous critics. Opponents argue that research does not support the idea that private prisons are cheaper, that legislators should need public approval before committing states to costly, long-term contracts, that it is wrong to profit from incarcerating people, and that the government should not delegate what should be a state function.

- Correctional officers face a great deal of job-related stress and have developed their own subculture to deal with it. Research on organizational justice demonstrates that administrators who treat COs fairly and with respect, and who make decisions in the best interest of the organization, result in COs who have more job satisfaction and organizational commitment. Correctional officers who treat inmates the same way are more apt to elicit perceptions of legitimacy and compliance.

PROJECTS

1. Review a movie that is set in a prison (any movie within the last 30 years). Are correctional officers portrayed objectively, sympathetically, or stereotypically?

2. Go to your state's correctional system's website and discover how many prisons exist, what security level they are, and where they are located.

NOTES

1. J. Stephen, *Census of State and Federal Correctional Facilities, 2005* (Washington, DC: Bureau of Justice Statistics, USDOJ, 2008).

2. N. Johnston, "Evolving Function: Early Use of Imprisonment as Punishment," *The Prison Journal*, 89, 1(2009):10–34.

3. H. Barnes, "The Historical Origin of the Prison System in America," in *Police, Prison and Punishment: Major Historical Interpretations*, edited by K. Hall (New York, NY: Garland Press, 1987).

4. D. Garland, *Punishment and Modern Society: A Study in Social Theory* (Chicago: University of Chicago Press, 1990).

5. R. Johnson, 1997, "Race, Gender, and the American Prison: Historical Observations," in J. Pollock (ed.), *Prisons: Today and Tomorrow* (Gaithersburg, MD: Aspen Publishing), 26–51.

6. H. Barnes, "The Historical Origin of the Prison System in America" in *Police, Prison and Punishment: Major Historical Interpretations*, edited by K. Hall (New York, NY: Garland Press, 1987).

7. Alexis de Tocqueville and Gustave Auguste de Beaumont describing Auburn Prison in 1831, as cited in D. Rothman, *The Discovery of the Asylum: Social Order and Disorder in the New Republic* (Boston: Little, Brown, 1971): 575.

8. N. Johnston, "Evolving Function: Early Use of Imprisonment as Punishment." *The Prison Journal*, 89, 1 (2009):10–34; C. Crosley, *Unfolding Misconceptions: The Arkansas State Penitentiary, 1836–1986* (Arlington, VA: Liberal Arts Press, 1986); D. Rothman, *The Discovery of the Asylum: Social Order and Disorder in the New Republic* (Boston: Little, Brown, 1971); R. Johnson, *Hard Time* (Belmont, CA: Wadsworth/ITP, 2002).

9. Reverend James B. Finley, quoted in Rothman, 1971: 84–88.

10. D. Rothman, *The Discovery of the Asylum: Social Order and Disorder in the New Republic* (Boston: Little, Brown, 1971/1990).

11. American Correctional Association (1970/revised 2002), accessed January 2, 2004, www.aca.org/pastpresentfuture/principles.asp.

12. S. Walker, *Popular Justice: A History of American Criminal Justice* (New York: Oxford University Press, 1980); L. Sullivan, *The Prison Reform Movement: Forlorn Hope* (Boston: Twayne Publishing, 1990).

13. N. Johnston, "Evolving Function: Early Use of Imprisonment as Punishment." *The Prison Journal*, 89, 1 (2009):10–34; R. Johnson, "Race, Gender, and the American Prison: Historical Observations" in J. Pollock (ed.), *Prisons: Today and Tomorrow* (Gaithersburg, MD: Aspen Publishing), 26–51.

14. R. Johnson, *Hard Time: Understanding and Reforming the Prison* (Belmont, CA: Wadsworth Publishing, 1996/2002), 44; B. Crouch, J. Marquart, *An Appeal to Justice: Litigated Reform of Texas Prisons* (Austin, TX: University of Texas Press, 1989).

15. N.H. Rafter, *Partial Justice: Women, Prisons, and Social Control*, second ed. (Boston: Northeastern University Press, 1990), xxvi.

16. N. Rafter, *Partial Justice: Women, Prisons, and Social Control* (Boston: Northeastern University Press, 1990); E. Freedman, *Their Sisters' Keepers: Women's Prison Reform in America, 1830–1930* (Ann Arbor: University of Michigan Press, 1981).

17. R. Johnson, *Hard Time: Understanding and Reforming the Prison* (Belmont, CA: Wadsworth Publishing, 1996/2002), 42.

18. M. Gottschalk, "The Prison and the Gallows: The Politics of Mass Incarceration in America (Cambridge, NJ: Cambridge University Press, 2006); J. Zimmerman, "The Penal Reform Movement in the South During the Progressive Era, 1890–1917," in K. Hall (ed.) *Police, Prison and Punishment* (New York, NY: Garland Press, 1987), 462–92.

19. J. Zimmerman, "The Penal Reform Movement in the South During the Progressive Era, 1890–1917," in K. Hall (ed.) *Police, Prison and Punishment*

(New York, NY: Garland Press, 1987), 462–92.

20. J. Pollock, *Prisons and Prison Life: Costs and Consequences* (Boston, MA: Oxford University Press, 2012); J. Pollock, *Women's Crimes, Criminology and Corrections* (Prospect Heights, IL: Waveland, 2014).

21. L. Glenn, *Texas Prisons: The Largest Hotel Chain in Texas* (Austin, TX: Eakin Press, 2001).

22. M. Gottschalk, *The Prison and the Gallows: The Politics of Mass Incarceration in America* (Cambridge, NU: Cambridge University Press, 2006), 178.

23. R. Martinson, "What Works? Questions and Answers About Prison Reform," *Public Interest* (Spring 1974): 22–54.

24. A. Von Hirsch, A. *Doing Justice* (New York City: Hill and Wang, 1976).

25. D Garland, *The Culture of Control: Crime and Social Order in Contemporary Society* (Chicago: University of Chicago Press, 2001).

26. T. Clear, *Harm in American Penology: Offenders, Victims, and Their Communities* (Albany, NY: State University of New York Press, 1994).

27. J. Irwin, *The Warehouse Prison: Disposal of the New Dangerous Classes* (Los Angeles: Roxbury Press, 2004).

28. A. Rierden, *The Farm: Life Inside a Women's Prison* (Amherst, MA: University of Massachusetts Press, 1997); J. Pollock, J. *Women's Crimes, Criminology and Corrections* (Long Grove, IL: Waveland, 2014).

29. D. Mears and W. Bales, "Supermax Housing: Placement, Duration, and Time to Reentry," *Journal of Criminal Justice* 38 (2010): 545–54.

30. A. Naday, J. Freilich, and J. Mellow, "The Elusive Data on Supermax Confinement. The Prison Journal 88, 1 (2008): 69–93; D. Mears, "Supermax Prisons: The Policy and the Evidence," *Criminology and Public Policy* 12, 4 (2013): 681–719.

31. H. Butler, B. Steiner, M. Makarios, and L. Travis, "Assessing the Effects of Exposure to Supermax Confinement on Offender Postrelease Behaviors," *The Prison Journal* 97, no. 3 (2017): 275–95.

32. J. Pizarro, K. Zgoba, and S. Haugebrook, "Supermax and Recidivism: An Examination of the Recidivism Covariates Among a Sample of Supermax Ex-Inmates," *The Prison Journal*, 94, 2 (2014): 180–97; D. Mears, "Supermax Prisons: The Policy and the Evidence," *Criminology and Public Policy* 12, 4 (2013): 681–719.

33. J. Pizarro and R. Narag, "Supermax Prisons: What We Know, What We Do Not Know, and Where We Are Going," *The Prison Journal*, 88, 1 (2008): 23–42; J. Pizarro, K. Zgoba, and S. Haugebrook, "Supermax and Recidivism: An Examination of the Recidivism Covariates Among a Sample of Supermax Ex-Inmates," *The Prison Journal*, 94, 2 (2014):180–97.

34. J. Pizarro and R. Narag, "Supermax Prisons: What We Know, What We Do Not Know, and Where We Are Going," *The Prison Journal*, 88, 1 (2008): 23–42.

35. C. Haney, "A Culture of Harm: Taming the Dynamics of Cruelty in Supermax Prisons," *Criminal Justice and Behavior* 35, 8 (2008): 956–84.

36. D. Mears and W. Bales, "Supermax Housing: Placement, Duration, and Time to Reentry," *Journal of Criminal Justice* 38 (201): 545–54.

37. C. Haney, "Mental Health Issues in Long-Term Solitary and 'Supermax' Confinement," *Crime and Delinquency* 49, 1 (2003): 124–56.

38. D. Mears, "Supermax Prisons: The Policy and the Evidence," *Criminology and Public Policy* 12, 4 (2013): 681–719.

39. C. Haney, "Restricting the Use of Solitary Confinement," *Annual Review of Criminology* 1 (2018): 285–310.

40. D. Smith, "Neuroscientists Make a Case against Solitary Confinement," *Scientific American*, November 9, 2018, accessed November 25, 2018, https://www.scientificamerican.com/article/neuroscientists-make-a-case-against-solitary-confinement/.

41. E. Pilkington, "More Than 4,000 Mentally Ill Inmates Held in Solitary in US—Report," *The Guardian*, October 10, 2018, accessed December 28, 2018, https://www.theguardian.com/us-news/2018/oct/10/mental-health-inmates-solitary-confinement-us-prisons.

42. P.S. Smith, "The Effects of Solitary Confinement on Prison Inmates: A Brief History and Review of the Literature," in N. Morris and M. Tonry (eds.), *Crime and Justice: An Annual Review of Research* Vol. 34 (Chicago, IL: University of Chicago Press, 2006), 441–528; C. Haney, C. 2003, "Mental Health Issues in Long-Term Solitary and 'Supermax' Confinement," *Crime and Delinquency* 49, 1 (2003): 124–56; C. Haney, "A Culture of Harm: Taming the Dynamics of Cruelty in Supermax Prisons," *Criminal Justice and Behavior* 35, 8 (2008): 956–84; T. Kupers, *Prison Madness: The Mental Health Crisis Behind Bars and What We Must Do About It* (San Francisco, CA: Jossey-Bass Publishing, 1999; S. Grassian, "Psychiatric Effects of Solitary Confinement, *Washington*

University Journal of Law and Policy 22 (2006): 325-391.

43. C. Haney, "Restricting the Use of Solitary Confinement," *Annual Review of Criminology* 1 (2018): 285–310.

44. C. Haney, "A Culture of Harm: Taming the Dynamics of Cruelty in Supermax Prisons," *Criminal Justice and Behavior* 35, 8 (2008): 956–84.

45. H. Toch, H. "The Future of Supermax Confinement," *The Prison Journal* 81 (2001): 376–88.

46. *Madrid v. Gomez*, 889 F. Supp. 1146 (1995) (California); *Taifa v. Bayhm*, 846 F. Supp. 723 (1994) (Indiana); *Wilkinson v. Austin*, 544 U.S. 74 (2005) (Ohio); *Joslyn v. Armstrong*, No. 3: 01-cv-00198-CFD, slip op. at 1 (D. Conn., October 17, 2001); *Jones'El v. Berge*, 374 F.3d 541 (2004) (Wisconsin).

47. *Madrid v. Gomez*, 889 F. Supp. 1146 (N.D. Cal. 1995).

48. C. Haney, C. 2002, "Infamous Punishment: The Psychological Consequences of Isolation," in L. Alarid and P. Cromwell (eds.), *Correctional Perspectives* (Los Angeles, CA: Roxbury Press, 2002), 101–70; 162.

49. R. King, R. 2005, "The Effects of Supermax Custody," in A. Liebling and S. Maruna, *The Effects of Imprisonments* (Devon, UK: Willan, 2005), 112–154.

50. C. Briggs, J. Sundt, and T. Castellano, "The Effect of Supermaximum Security Prisons on Aggregate Levels of Institutional Violence," *Criminology* 41, 4 (2003): 1341–76; J. Sundt, T. Castellano, and C. Briggs, "The Sociopolitical Context of Prison Violence and its Control: A Case Study of Supermax and its Effect in Illinois," *The Prison Journal* 88 (2008): 94–122.

51. D. Lovall, L.C. Johnson, and K. Cain, "Recidivism of Supermax Prisoners in Washington State," *Crime & Delinquency* 53, 4 (2007): 633–56; D. Mears and W. Bales, "Supermax Incarceration and Recidivism," *Criminology* 47, 4 (2009): 1131–66; D.P. Mears, "Supermax Prisons: The Policy and the Evidence," *Criminology & Public Policy*, 12 (2013): 681–719; H. Butler, B. Steiner, M. Makarios, and L. Travis, L., "Assessing the Effects of Exposure to Supermax Confinement on Offender Postrelease Behaviors," *The Prison Journal* 97, no. 3 (2017): 275–95.

52. D.P. Mears, "Supermax Prisons: The Policy and the Evidence," *Criminology andPublic Policy* 12 (2013): 681–719.

53. A. Schneider, "Public–Private Partnerships in the U.S. Prison System," *American Behavioral Scientist* 43, 1 (1999): 192–208.

54. E. Carson, *Prisoners in 2019* (Washington, DC: Bureau of Justice Statistics, Dept. of Justice, 2020), 26; A. Geiger, "U.S. Private Prison Population Has Declined in Recent Years," Pew Research Center, 2017, http://www.pewresearch.org/fact-tank/2017/04/11/u-s-private-prison-population-has-declined-in-recent-years/.

55. E. Carson, *Prisoners in 2019* (Washington, DC: Bureau of Justice Statistics, Dept. of Justice, 2020), 26.

56. J. Byrne, K. Kras, and L. Marmolejo, " International Perspectives on the Privatization of Corrections," Criminology & Public Policy 18 (2019): 477–503.

57. A. Brittain and D. Harwell, "Private-Prison Giant, Resurgent in Trump Era, Gathers at President's Resort," *Washington Post*, October 25, 2017; "Fact Sheet: Private Prisons in the United States," The Sentencing Project, December 28, 2018, https://www.prisonlegalnews.org/news/publications/sentencing-project-fact-sheet-private-prisons-united-states-2017/.

58. Urban Institute, reported in J. Byrne, K. Kras, and L. Marmolejo, "International Perspectives on the Privatization of Corrections," *Criminology and Public Policy* 18 (2019): 477–503, 483.

59. A. Montes and D. Mears, "Privatized Corrections in the 21st Century: Reframing the Privatization Debate," *Criminology and Public Policy* 18 (2019): 217–39; G. Gaes, "Current Status of Prison Privatization Research on American Prisons and Jails," *Criminology and Public Policy* 18 (2019): 269–293.

60. C. Logan, "The Propriety of Proprietary Prisons," *Federal Probation* 53, 3 (1987): 35–40.

61. C. Bourge, "Sparks Fly Over Private v. Public Prisons," United Press International, 2002. Reprinted by Prison Policy Initiative. Retrieved March 1, 2012 from http://www.prisonpolicy.org/scans/sparksfly.shtml.

62. G.F. Segal and A.T. Moore, "Weighing the Watchmen: Evaluating the Costs and Benefits of Outsourcing Correctional Services. Part II: Reviewing the Literature on Cost and Quality Comparisons," Reason Public Policy Institute Study No. 290 (2002), retrieved from reason.org/ps290.pdf.

63. D. Perrone and T.C. Pratt, "Comparing the Quality of Confinement and Cost-Effectiveness of Public Versus Private Prisons: What We Know, Why We Do Not Know More, and Where to Go from Here," *The Prison Journal* 83, no. 3 (2003): 301–22; G. Gaes, "Current Status of Prison Privatization Research on

American Prisons and Jails," *Criminology and Public Policy* 18 (2019): 269–93.

64. W.D. Bales, L.E. Bedard, S.T. Quinn, D.T. Ensley, and G.P. Holley, "Recidivism of Public and Private State Prison Inmates in Florida," *Criminology and Public Policy*, 4, no. 1 (2005), 57–82.

65. G. Gaes, "Current Status of Prison Privatization Research on American Prisons and Jails," *Criminology and Public Policy* 18 (2019): 269–93; T. Pratt, "Cost–Benefit Analysis and Privatized Corrections," *Criminology and Public Policy* 18 (2019): 447–456; J. Greene, "Bailing Out Private Jails," *American Prospect* 12, no. 16 (2001): 23–7.

66. *Private and Public Prisons—Studies Comparing Operational Costs and/or Quality of Service*, Government Accounting Office (G.A.O.) (Washington DC: U.S. Government Printing Office, 1996); T. Pratt and J. Maahs, "Are Private Prisons More Cost-Effective Than Public Prisons? A Meta-Analysis of Evaluation Research Studies," *Crime and Delinquency* 45, 3 (1999): 358–71.

67. T. Pratt, "Cost–Benefit Analysis and Privatized Corrections," *Criminology and Public Policy* 18 (2019): 447–56; G. Gaes, "Cost, Performance Studies Look at Prison Privatization," *NIJ Journal* 259, (2008). Retrieved August 21, 2021 from https://nij.ojp.gov/topics/articles/cost-performance-studies-look-prison-privatization ; G. Gaes, "Current Status of Prison Privatization Research on American Prisons and Jails," *Criminology and Public Policy* 18 (2019): 269–93.

68. W. Bales, L. Bedard, S. Quinn, D. Ensley, and G. Holley. 2005, "Recidivism of Public and Private State Prison Inmates in Florida," *Criminology and Public Policy* 4, 1: 57–92.

69. J. Byrne, K. Kras, and L. Marmolejo, "International Perspectives on the Privatization of Corrections," *Criminology and Public Policy* 18 (2019): 477–503.

70. C. Bourge, "Sparks Fly Over Private v. Public Prisons," United Press International, 2002. Reprinted by Prison Policy Initiative. Retrieved March 3, from http://www.prisonpolicy.org/scans/sparksfly.shtml.

71. J. Dyer, *The Perpetual Prison Machine* (Boulder, OH: Westview Press, 2000).

72. M. Reisig and T. Pratt, "The Ethics of Correctional Privatization: A Critical Examination of the Delegation of Coercive Authority," *Prison Journal* 80, 2 (2000): 210–22.

73. *Minneci v. Pollard*, 132 S. Ct. 617, 2012.

74. *Richardson v. McKnight*, 521 U.S. 399 (1997); *United States v. Thomas*, 240 F.3d 445 (5th Cir. 2001).

75. L. Eisen, "Privatized Corrections: Questions of Legality," *Criminology and Public Policy* 18 (2019): 419–436.

76. *Gaming the System: How the Political Strategies of Private Prison Companies Promote Ineffective Incarceration Policies* (Washington, DC: Justice Policy Institute, 2011); E. Perez, 2001, "For Profit Prison Firm Wackenhut Tries to Break Shackles to Growth," *Wall Street Journal*, May 9, 2001, retrieved May 15, 2001; J. Greene, "Bailing Out Private Jails," American Prospect 12, 16 (2001): 23–7.

77. *Gaming the System: How the Political Strategies of Private Prison Companies Promote Ineffective Incarceration Policies* (Washington, DC: Justice Policy Institute, 2011), 19.

78. B. Burkhardt, "The Politics of Correctional Privatization in the United States," *Criminology and Public Policy* 18 (2019): 401–18.

79. *Gaming the System: How the Political Strategies of Private Prison Companies Promote Ineffective Incarceration Policies* (Washington, DC: Justice Policy Institute, 2011).

80. A. Brittain and D. Harwell, "Private-Prison Giant, Resurgent in Trump Era, Gathers At President's Resort," *Washington Post*, October 25, 2017.

81. *Review of the Federal Bureau of Prisons' Monitoring of Contract Prisons* (Washington, DC: U.S. Department of Justice, Office of the Inspector General, 2016).

82. E. Kennedy, "CCA Announces Nashville Layoffs Amid Scrutiny of For-Profit Prisons," *Nashville Business Journal*, September 27, 2016.

83. D. Gambacorta, "Dead Bodies and Billions in Tax Dollars," *Philly.com*, August 27, 2017, http://www.philly.com/philly/news/crime/private-prisons-sessions-yates-geo-assault-death.html; A. Brittain and D. Harwell, "Private-Prison Giant, Resurgent in Trump Era, Gathers At President's Resort," *Washington Post*, October 25, 2017.

84. K. Duguid, "Private Prison Revenue Under Pressure from New Biden Rules," Reuters, January 27, 2021, accessed February 10, 2021 from https://www.reuters.com/article/us-usa-companies-biden-prisons/u-s-private-prison-revenue-under-pressure-from-new-biden-rules-iduskbn29w14z.

85. J. Jacobs and L. Kraft, "Integrating the Keepers: A Comparison of Black and White Prison Guards in Illinois," *Social Problems* 25 (1978): 304–18.

86. A. Lin, *Reform in the Making: The Implementation of Social Policy in Prison* (Princeton, NJ: Princeton University Press, 2000).

87. *Occupational Outlook Handbook*, Bureau of Labor, 2017. Retrieved from https://www.bls.gov/ooh/protective-service/correctional-officers.htm.

88. D. Morain, "Overtime Pays Off at Prison," LATimes.com, February 10, 2003.

89. J. Stephens, *Census of State and Federal Correctional Facilities, 2005* (Washington, DC: Bureau of Justice Statistics, Department of Justice, 2005). Unfortunately, this report series seems to have been discontinued by the BJS researchers and there are no more recent reports available.

90. *Dothard v. Rawlinson*, 433 U.S. 321 (1977).

91. R. Lawrence and S. Mahan. 1998, "Women Corrections Officers in Men's Prisons: Acceptance and Perceived Job Performance," *Women and Criminal Justice* 9, 3 (1998): 63–86; R. Freeman, "Management and Administrative Issues," in J. Pollock (ed.), *Prisons: Today and Tomorrow* (Gaithersburg, MD: Aspen Publishing Company, 1997), 270–99; L. Zupan, "The Progress of Women Correctional Officers in All-Male Prisons," in I. Moyer (ed.), *The Changing Roles of Women in the Criminal Justice System* (Prospect Heights, IL: Waveland, 1992), 323–43; L. Zimmer, *Women Guarding Men* (Chicago: University of Chicago Press, 1986); J. Pollock, J. 1995, "Women in Corrections: Custody and the 'Caring Ethic'," in A. Merlo and J. Pollock (eds.), *Women, Law and Social Control* (Needham Heights, MA: Allyn and Bacon, 1995), 97–116.

92. *Johnson v. Phelan*, 69 F.3d 144 (7th Cir. 1995); *Timm v. Gunter*, 917 F.2d 1093 (8th Cir. 1990).

93. C. Struckman-Johnson, L. Rucker, K. Bumby, and S. Donaldson, "Sexual Coercion Reported by Men and Women in Prison," *Journal of Sex Research* 33, 1 (1996): 67–76.

94. J. Marquart, M. Barnhill, M., and K. Balshaw-Biddle, "'Fatal Attraction': An Analysis of Employee Boundary Violations in a Southern Prison System, 1995–1998," *Justice Quarterly* 18, no. 4 (2001): 877–911.

95. A. Beck, P. Harrison, M. Berzofsky, R. Caspar, and C. Krebs, *Sexual Victimization in Prisons and Jails, Reported by Inmates, 2008–2009* (Washington, DC: Bureau of Justice Statistics, U.S. Dept. of Justice, 2010), 24.

96. B. Owen, 1985, "Race and Gender Relations Among Prison Workers," *Crime and Delinquency*, January 31 (1985): 147–59.

97. R. Wright and W. Saylor, "Comparison of Perceptions of the Work Environment Between Minority and Non-Minority Employees of the Federal Prison System," *Journal of Criminal Justice* 20, 1 (1992): 63–71.

98. D. Britton, D., "Perceptions of the Work Environment Among Correctional Officers: Do Race and Sex Matter?" *Criminology* 35, 1 (1997): 85–105.

99. S. Camp, T. Steiger, K. Wright, W. Saylor, and E. Gilman, "Affirmative Action and the 'Level Playing Field': Comparing Perceptions of Own and Minority Job Advancement Opportunities," *Prison Journal* 77, 3 (1997): 313–334; M. Griffin, G. Armstrong, and J. Hepburn, "Correctional Officers' Perceptions of Equitable Treatment in the Masculinized Prison Environment," *Criminal Justice Review* 30, 2 (2005): 189–206.

100. E. Lambert and N. Hogan, "The Importance of Job Satisfaction and Organizational Commitment in Shaping Turnover Intent: A Test of a Causal Model," *Criminal Justice Review* 34 (2009): 96–118.

101. R. Johnson, *Hard Time: Understanding and Reforming the Prison* (Belmont, CA: Wadsworth Publishing, 1996/2002); also, see A.K. Matz, Y. Woo, and B. Kim, B., "A Meta-Analysis of the Correlates of Turnover Intent in Criminal Justice Organizations: Does Agency Type Matter?" *Journal of Criminal Justice*, 42 (2014): 233–43.

102. E.G. Lambert and E. Paoline, "Take This Job and Shove It: Turnover Intent Among Jail Staff," *Journal of Criminal Justice* 38 (2010): 139–48; E. Lambert, N. Hogan, E. Paoline, and A. Clarke, "The Impact of Role Stressors on Job Stress, Job Satisfaction, and Organizational Commitment Among Private Prison Staff," *Security Journal* 18 (2005): 33–50; E. Lambert and N. Hogan, "The Importance of Job Satisfaction and Organizational Commitment in Shaping Turnover Intent: A Test of a Causal Model," *Criminal Justice Review* 34 (2009): 96–118; E. Lambert, N. Hogan, and S. Barton, "Satisfied Correctional Staff: A Review of the Literature on the Antecedents and Consequences of Correctional Staff Job Satisfaction," *Criminal Justice and Behavior* 29 (2001): 115–43; Lambert, E., N. Hogan, and K. Tucker, "Problems at Work: Exploring the Correlates of Role Stress Among Correctional Staff," *The Prison Journal*, 89, 4 (2009): 460–81.

103. G. Gross, S. Larson, G. Urban, and L. Zupan. 1994, "Gender Differences in Occupational Stress Among Correctional Officers," *American Journal of Criminal Justice* 18, 2 (1994): 219–34; K. Dial, R. Downey, and W. Goodlin, "The Job in the Joint: The Impact of Generation and Gender on Work Stress in Prison," *Journal of Criminal Justice* 38 (2010): 609–15; E. Lambert, N. Hogan, I. Altheimer, and J. Wareham, "The Effects of Different Aspects of Supervision Among Female and Male Correctional Staff: A Preliminary Study," *Criminal Justice Review* 35, 4 (2010): 492–513; T.E. Hurst and M.M. Hurst, "Gender Differences in Mediation of Severe Occupational Stress Among Correctional Officers," *American Journal of Criminal Justice* 22 (1997): 121–37; J.R. Carlson, R.H. Anson, and G. Thomas, "Correctional Officer Burnout and Stress: Does Gender Matter?" *The Prison Journal* 83 (2003): 277–88; J.R. Carlson and G. Thomas, "Burnout Among Prison Caseworkers and Corrections Officers," *Journal of Offender Rehabilitation* 43, no. 3 (2006): 19–34; E.G. Lambert, "The Relationship of Organizational Citizenship Behavior With Job Satisfaction, Turnover Intent, Life Satisfaction, and Burnout Among Correctional Staff," *Criminal Justice Studies* 23 (2010): 361–80; E.G. Lambert, N.L. Hogan, K. Cheeseman Dial, S. Jiang, and M.L. Khondaker, "Is the Job Burning Me Out? An Exploratory Test of the Job Characteristics Model on The Emotional Burnout of Prison Staff," *The Prison Journal* 92 (2012): 3–23;**;** R.D. Morgan, R.A. Van Haveren, and C.A. Pearson, "Correctional Officer Burnout: Further Analyses," *Criminal Justice and Behavior* 29 (2002): 144–60.

104. K. Kauffman, *Prison Officers and Their World* (Cambridge, MA: Harvard University Press, 1988); F. Cheek and M. Miller, "The Experience of Stress for Correction Officers: A Double-Bind Theory of Correctional Stress," *Journal of Criminal Justice* 11 (1983): 105–20; H. Williamson, *The Corrections Profession* (Newbury Park, CA: SAGE, 1990); G. Gross, S. Larson, G. Urban, and L. Zupan. 1994, "Gender Differences in Occupational Stress Among Correctional Officers," *American Journal of Criminal Justice* 18, 2 (1994); J. Kamerman, "Correctional Officer Suicide," *The Keepers' Voice* 16, 3 (1995): 7–9.

105. D. Thompson, "California Examines Prison Guards' High Suicide Rate," AP News, January 9, 2018, https://apnews.com/96fdc27aea0c401ea590b1c74162c43a.

106. C. Spinaris and N. Brocato, "Descriptive Study of Michigan Department of Corrections Staff Well-being: Contributing Factors, Outcomes, and Actionable Solutions" (New York City, NY: Vera Institute of Justice, 2019). retrieved August 25, 2021 from http://safealternativestosegregation.vera.org/resource/study-of-michigan-department-of-corrections-staff-well-being/.; Also see *Reimagining Prison* (New York: Vera Institute of Justice, 2018).

107. R. Hudson, "Ending 'Death Culture' for Prison Workers," *The Crime Report*, August 21, 2017, https://thecrimereport.org/2017/08/21/ending-the-death-culture-for-prison-workers/.

108. D. Lisitsina, "'Prison Guards Can Never Be Weak': The Hidden PTSD Crisis in America's Jails," *The Guardian*, May 20, 2015, http://www.theguardian.com/us-news/2015/may/20/corrections-officers-ptsd-american-prisons; C. Spinaris, M. Denhof, and J. Kellaway, "Posttraumatic Stress Disorder in United States Correctional Professionals: Prevalence and Impact on Health and Functioning" (Florence, CO: Desert Waters Correctional Outreach, 2012), retrieved from http://www.correctionsfatigue.com/images/PTSD_Prevalence_in_Corrections_2012.pdf.

109. E. Lambert, N. Hogan, E. Paoline, and A. Clarke, "The Impact of Role Stressors on Job Stress, Job Satisfaction, and Organizational Commitment Among Private Prison Staff," *Security Journal* 18 (2005): 33–50.

110. E. Lambert, N. Hogan, and K. Tucker, "Problems at Work: Exploring the Correlates of Role Stress Among Correctional Staff," *The Prison Journal*, 89, 4 (2009): 460–81.

111. R. Freeman, "Correctional Officers: Understudied and Misunderstood," in J. Pollock (ed.), *Prisons: Today and Tomorrow* (Gaithersburg, MD: Aspen Publishing, 1997): 306–37.

112. F. Cullen, B. Link, J. Cullen, and N. Wolfe, "How Satisfying is Prison Work? A Comparative Occupational Approach," *Journal of Offender Counseling, Services and Rehabilitation* 14 (1989): 89–108; E. Lambert, N. Hogan, and S. Barton, "Satisfied Correctional Staff: A Review of the Literature on the Antecedents and Consequences of Correctional Staff Job Satisfaction,"

Criminal Justice and Behavior 29 (2001): 115–43.

113. J. Hepburn and P. Knepper, "Correctional Officers as Human Service Workers: The Effects of Job Satisfaction," *Justice Quarterly* 10, 2 (1993): 315–37.

114. B.M. Crouch and G.P. Alpert, "Sex and Occupational Socialization Among Prison Guards: A Longitudinal Study," *Criminal Justice and Behavior* 9 (1982): 159–76.

115. R. Tewksbury and E.E. Mustaine, "Correctional Orientations of Prison Staff," *The Prison Journal* 88, no. 2 (2009): 207–33.

116. A. Paboojian and R. Teske, "Pre-Service Correctional Officers: What Do They Think About Treatment?" *Journal of Criminal Justice* 25, 5 (1997): 425–33; F. Cullen, E. Latessa, V. Burton, and L. Lombardo, "The Correctional Orientation of Prison Wardens: Is the Rehabilitative Ideal Supported?" *Criminology* 31, 1 (1993): 69–92; R. Tewksbury and E. Mustaine, "Correctional Orientations of Prison Staff," *The Prison Journal* 28, 2 (2008): 207–33; M.S. Gordon, "Correctional Officer Control Ideology: Implications for UnderstandingA System," *Criminal Justice Studies* 19 (2006): 225–39. For a review of older research studies, see J. Lasswell, "An Assessment of Individual and Organizational Characteristics and their Impact on Correctional Officers' Perceptions of Professionalism and Treatment Orientation) (dissertation, Indiana University of Pennsylvania, 2010).

117. F. Ferdik, "Correctional Officer Risk Perceptions and Professional Orientations," *Criminal Justice and Behavior* 45, no. 2 (2018): 264–85.

118. C. Dowden and C. Tellier, "Predicting Work-Related Stress in Correctional Officers: A Meta-Analysis," *Journal of Criminal Justice* 32, 1 (2004): 31–47.

119. M. Antonio, J. Young, J. and L. Wingeard, "When Actions and Attitude Count Most: Assessing Perceived Level of Responsibility and Support for Inmate Treatment and Rehabilitation Programs Among Correctional Employees," *The Prison Journal*, 89, no. 4 (2009): 363–82; similar results found in M. Talpade, C. Talpade, and E. Marshall-Story, "Impact of Therapeutic Community Training on Knowledge and Attitudes of Correctional Officers," *International Journal of Psychosocial Rehabilitation* 17, no. 1 (2012): 6–17.

120. E. Lambert and E. Paoline, "The Impact of Jail Medical Issues on the Job Stress and Job Satisfaction of Jail Staff: An Exploratory Study," *Punishment and Society: The International Journal of Penology* 7 (2005): 259–75.

121. S. Shannon and J. Page, "Bureaucrats on the Cell Block: Prison Officers' Perceptions of Work Environment and Attitudes toward Prisoners," *Social Service Review* 88, no. 4: 630–57.

122. B. Crouch, *The Keepers: Prison Guards and Contemporary Corrections* (Springfield, IL: Charles C. Thomas, 1980); *Wolff v. McDonnell*, 418 U.S. 539 (1974).

123. K. Kauffman, *Prison Officers and Their World* (Cambridge, MA: Harvard University Press, 1988).

124. M. Farkas, "Normative Code Among Correctional Officers: An Exploration of Components and Functions,"

Journal of Crime and Justice 20, 1 (1997): 23–36.

125. An officer reported in J. Houston, *Correctional Management: Functions, Skills, and Systems* (Chicago: Nelson-Hall Publishers, 1999), 365.

126. B. Crouch, "Guard Work in Transition," in K. Haas and G. Alpert (eds.), *The Dilemmas of Corrections, Third Edition* (Prospect Heights, IL: Waveland Press, 1995), 183–203.

127. J. Riley, "Sensemaking in Prison: Inmate Identity as a Working Understanding," *Justice Quarterly* 17, 2 (2000): 359–76.

128. J. Klofas and H. Toch, "The Guard Subculture Myth," *Journal of Research in Crime and Delinquency* 19, 2 (1982): 238–54.

129. G. Sykes, "The Corruption of Authority and Rehabilitation," *Social Forces* 34 (1956): 257–65.

130. L. Lombardo, *Guards Imprisoned: Correctional Officers at Work*.(Cincinnati, OH: Anderson Press, 1989); B. Crouch, "Guard Work in Transition," in K. Haas and G. Alpert (eds.), *The Dilemmas of Corrections, Third Edition* (Prospect Heights, IL: Waveland Press, 1995), 183–203; S. Stojkovic, "Accounts of Prison Work: Corrections Officers Portrayals of the Work Worlds," *Perspectives on Social Problems* 2 (1990): 211–30.

131. P. Zimbardo, "The Prison Game," in *Legal Process and Corrections*, ed. N. Johnston and L. Savitz, 195–98 (New York: Wiley & Sons, 1982).

132. J. Pollock, *Ethical Dilemmas and Decisions in Criminal Justice*, 7th Ed. (Belmont, CA: Wadsworth/Cengage, 2018).

133. S. Light, "Assaults on Prison Officers: Interactional

Themes," *Justice Quarterly* 8, 2 (1991): 242–61; S. Light, "Assaults on Prison Officers: Interactional Themes," in M. Braswell, R. Montgomery, Jr., L. Lombardo (eds.), *Prison Violence in America* (Cincinnati, OH: Anderson, 1999), 207–23.

134. D. Ross, "Assessment of Prisoner Assaults on Corrections Officers," *Corrections Compendium*, 21, 8 (1996): 6–10.

135. K. Lahm, "Overlooked Form of Prison Violence: Inmate Assaults on Prison Staff: A Multilevel Examination," *The Prison Journal* 89, 2 (2009): 139–50.

136. B. Steiner and J. Wooldredge, "Individual and Environmental Influences on Prison Officer Safety," *Justice Quarterly*, 34 (2017): 2, 324–49.

137. D. Rembert and H. Henderson, "Correctional Officer Excessive Use of Force: Civil Liability Under Section 1983," *The Prison Journal* 94, 2(2014): 198–219.

138. J. Hepburn, "The Exercise of Power in Coercive Organizations: A Study of Prison Guards," *Criminology* 23 (1985): 145–64.

139. J. Wooldredge and B. Steiner, "The Exercise of Power in Prison Organizations and Implications for Legitimacy," *The Journal of Criminal Law and Criminology* 106, no. 1 (2016): 125–65.

140. J. Wooldredge and B. Steiner, "Examining the Sources of Correctional Officer Legitimacy," *The Journal of Criminal Law and Criminology* 105, no. 3 (2016): 679–703.

141. L. Vieraitis, J. Medrano, and A. Shuraydi, A. 2018, "'That's a Damn Good Officer Any

Day of the Week': Inmates' Perceptions of Correctional Officers," *Criminal Justice Studies* 31, no. 2 (2018): 143–59.

142. M. Silberman, *A World of Violence: Corrections in America* (Belmont, CA: Wadsworth, ITP, 1995); M. Vuolo and C. Kruttschnitt, "Prisoners' Adjustment, Correctional Officers, and Context," *Law and Society Review* 42 (2008): 307–35; T. Conover, *Guarding Sing Sing* (New York: Random House, 2000); H. Toch, "Is a 'Correctional Officer' By Any Other Name a 'Screw'?" in R. Ross, *Prison Guard/ Correctional Officer* (Toronto: Butterworth Publishing, 1981), 87–103.

143. R. Johnson, "The Complete Correctional Officer: Human Service and the Human Environment of Prison," *Criminal Justice and Behavior* 8, 3 (1981): 343–73.

144. Z. Meil, B. Iannacchione, M. Stohr, C. Hemmens, M. Hudson, and P. Collins, "Confirmatory Analysis of an Organizational Culture Instrument for Corrections," *The Prison Journal* 97, no. 2 (2017): 247–69.

145. E. Lambert, N. Hogan, and M. Griffin, "The Impact of Distributive and Procedural Justice on Correctional Staff Job Stress, Job Satisfaction, and Organizational Commitment," *Journal of Criminal Justice* 35 (2007): 644–56; E. Lambert, "Justice in Corrections: An Exploratory Study of the Impact of Organizational Justice on Correctional Staff," *Journal of Criminal Justice* 31 (2003): 155–68; K. Wright, W. Saylor, E. Gilman, and S. Camp, "Job Control and Occupational Outcomes Among Prison

Workers," *Justice Quarterly* 14, 3 (1997): 525–46.

146. These are the elements of procedural justice. See T.R. Tyler, *Why People Obey the Law* (Princeton, NJ: Princeton University Press, 2006).

147. M.K. Stohr, C. Hemmens, M. Kifer, and M. Schoeler, "'We Know It, We Just Have to Do It': Perceptions of Ethical Work in Prisons and Jails," *The Prison Journal* 80 (2000), 126–50;

148. T. Baker, J. Gordon, and F. Taxman, "A Hierarchical Analysis of Correctional Officers' Procedural Justice Judgments of Correctional Institutions: Examining The Influence of Transformational Leadership," *Justice Quarterly* 32 (2015): 6, 1037–63; E.G. Lambert, N.L. Hogan, S.B. Barton-Bellessa, and S. Jiang, "Examining the Relationship Between Supervisor and Management Trust and Job Burnout Among Correctional Staff," *Criminal Justice and Behavior*, 39 (2012): 938–57; E. Lambert, N. Hogan and S. Jiang "A Preliminary Examination of The Relationship Between Organizational Structure and Emotional Burnout Among Correctional Staff," *The Howard Journal* 49 (2010): 125–46; E.G. Lambert, N. Hogan, S. Jiang, O. Elechi, B. Benjamin, A. Morris, and P. Dupuy, "The Relationship Among Distributive and Procedural Justice and Correctional Life Satisfaction, Burnout, and Turnover Intent: An Exploratory Study," *Journal of Criminal Justice*, 38 (2010): 7–16.

149. P. Carlson, "Management and Accountability," in P. Carlson and J. Garrett (eds.), *Prison and Jail Administration*

(Gaithersburg, MD: Aspen Publishing Co., 1999), 41–46.

150. K. Wright, *Effective Prison Leadership* (Binghamton, NY: William Neil Publishing, 1994).

151. B. McCarthy, "Keeping an Eye on the Keeper: Prison Corruption and Its Control," in M. Braswell, B. McCarthy, and B. McCarthy (eds.), *Justice, Crime, and Ethics* (Cincinnati: Anderson, 1991), 239–53; S. Souryal, "Corruption of Prison Personnel," in P. Carlson and J. Garrett (eds.) *Prison and Jail Administration: Practice and Theory* (Gaithersburg, MD: Aspen Publishing, 1999), 171–77; J. Pollock, *Ethical Dilemmas and Decisions in Criminal Justice*, 7th Ed. (Belmont, CA: Wadsworth/Cengage, 2018).

152. See J. Pollock, *Ethical Dilemmas and Decisions in Criminal Justice*, 7th Ed. (Belmont, CA: Wadsworth/Cengage, 2018).

Chapter 7

Prisoners and Special Populations

LEARNING OBJECTIVES

1. Describe the demographic profile and other characteristics of prisoners.

2. Outline the issues involved in managing the elderly in prison.

3. Describe the prevalence of mental health problems among prisoners and the management issues they present.

4. Describe the prevalence of prisoners who are cognitively challenged and the management issues they present.

5. Compare the rates and characteristics of prison suicide to suicide in the general U.S. population and discuss prevention efforts that may reduce prison suicides.

CHAPTER OUTLINE

- **Profile of Prisoners 180**

- **Management Challenges of Special Prison Populations 187**

- **SUMMARY 202**

Most prisoners are men. Women make up only about 7.5 percent of the total national prison population.

Profile of Prisoners

As we discussed in Chapter 1, there are about 1.3 million individuals in state and federal prisons. This is an 11 percent decline from 2009, when the prisoner population in the United States peaked.[1]

In this chapter we will look more closely at the people behind bars in the United States, from demographics (sex, racial/ethnic identity, and age) to the types of crimes that prisoners commit. We will also review background characteristics, such as the level of education prisoners typically achieve, the medical needs of the prison population, and the chronic issues of drug dependency and addiction. We will then go on to examine the special management problems that exist with "special populations," which include the elderly, those who have mental health issues, and those with intellectual disabilities.

Demographics

Most prisoners are men. Women made up only 7.5 percent of the total national prison population at year-end 2019.[2] Prisons are disproportionately populated by young minority men. In Figure 7.1, we see that whites represent about 64 percent of the general U.S. population, but only 39 percent of the prison population, while Blacks represent only 16 percent of the general U.S. population but 40 percent of the prison population. Other racial and ethnic groups have less disparity between their representation in the general U.S. population and prison population.

FIGURE 7.1 Percentage of prisoners by race/ethnicity. Created by author from P. Wagner and B. Rabuy, "Mass Incarceration: The Whole Pie, 2017," Prison Policy Initiative, https://www.prisonpolicy.org/reports/pie2017.html.

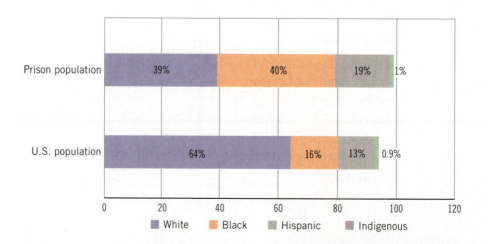

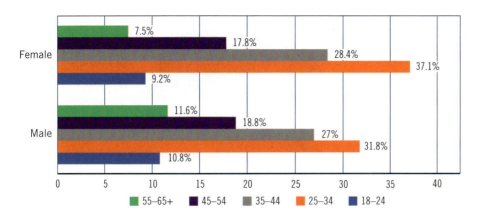

FIGURE 7.2 Age range of prisoners. Created by author from E. Carson, *Prisoners in 2016* (Washington, DC: Bureau of Justice Statistics, USDOJ, January 2018), Table 9.

Between 2009 and 2019, the number of Black prisoners declined by almost 23 percent, from 584,800 at year-end 2009 to 452,800 at year-end 2019. The number of white prisoners decreased almost 14 percent, from 490,000 to 422,800. The number of Hispanic prisoners declined almost 6 percent, from 341,200 to 320,700 in 2019.[3] Estimates of prisoners' racial/ethnic identity are problematic. There is disparity between the Bureau of Justice Statistics' (BJS) National Prisoner Statistics Program (NPS), an administrative database from all state and federal prison systems, and the Survey of Prison Inmates (SPI), a survey where prisoners self-identify their race and ethnicity. For instance, the NPS indicates that 39 percent of male prisoners are white, but the SPI indicates that only 30 percent of male prisoners identify as white. For female prisoners, the NPS indicates 61 percent are white, but the SPI records 47.5 percent. Fewer prisoners identify themselves as white or Black than official records indicate, and more prisoners self-identify as Hispanic, Black, or multiracial than official statistics indicate.[4]

In 2016, states held fewer than 1,000 prisoners age 17 or younger in adult facilities, and the federal prison system held fewer than 50 prisoners age 17 or younger in private contract facilities.[5] As Figure 7.2 shows, for both male and female prisoners, the largest age group in prison are those between 24 and 34, but the average age of prisoners is increasing. This is due to longer sentences, which result in prisoners aging in prison, and the average age of those admitted to prison increasing.

In 1993, male and female prisoners ages 25 to 29 had the highest imprisonment rates; by 2013, the age range had shifted: males and females ages 30 to 34 experienced the highest rate of imprisonment (1,866 per 100,000 males and 163 per 100,000 females). This was true for all racial and ethnic groups: 602 prisoners per 100,000 non-Hispanic whites, 2,893 per 100,000 non-Hispanic Blacks, and 1,155 per 100,000 Hispanics were the imprisonment rates for the age group 30–34; all were the highest rate of incarceration for all age groups.[6]

People admitted to prison are getting older: there were almost 2 million fewer arrests in the United States in 2012 than in 1993, but almost all the decrease was because of fewer arrests for persons aged 39 or younger. Over the same period, arrests of persons aged 40 to 54 increased 44 percent, and arrests of persons aged 55 or older increased 77 percent. The same pattern can be seen in commitments to prison after conviction, with older age groups showing an increase over time and younger age groups showing a decrease. Older offenders have a longer criminal history that can make them eligible for enhanced sentences under three-strikes laws, which contribute to the increased average age of admission and, over time, to the aging of the prisoner population because of the enhanced sentence lengths.[7]

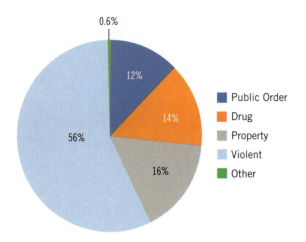

FIGURE 7.3   State prisoners' crimes of conviction. Created by author from E. Carson, *Prisoners in 2019* (Washington, DC: Bureau of Justice Statistics, USDOJ, October 2020), Table 13.

FIGURE 7.4   Total violent crimes by type of crime. Created by author from E. Carson, *Prisoners in 2019* (Washington, DC: Bureau of Justice Statistics, USDOJ, October 2020), Table 13.

Crimes that Prisoners Commit

Most state prisoners (54 percent) have been convicted of violent crimes. Figure 7.3 shows that property, drug, and public order crimes account for roughly equal portions of the remaining prisoner population.

Looking specifically at violent crimes, Figure 7.4 shows that roughly equal percentages of assault, murder, robbery, and rape/sexual assault make up the bulk of the violent crime category, with much smaller percentages of manslaughter and other violent crimes making up the rest. One of the effects of states' attempts to reduce prisoner populations by changing sentencing legislation to reduce sentences for non-violent crimes and increase the use of parole is that those left in prisons are more likely to be chronic or violent offenders.

Comparing male and female state prisoner populations, in Figures 7.5 and 7.6, we see that violent crimes comprise a larger percentage of the male prisoner population than the female prisoner population. Drug and property crimes comprise a higher percentage of the female prisoner population as compared to male prisoners.

Because violent criminals are sentenced to long terms of imprisonment and they are less likely to receive parole, they "stack up" in prison, which is why they comprise

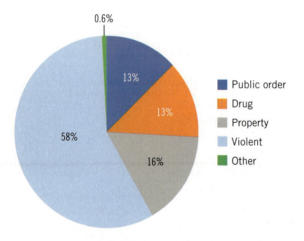

FIGURE 7.5   State male prisoners' crimes of conviction (percentage of total). Created by author from E. Carson, *Prisoners in 2019* (Washington, DC: Bureau of Justice Statistics, USDOJ, October 2020), Table 13.

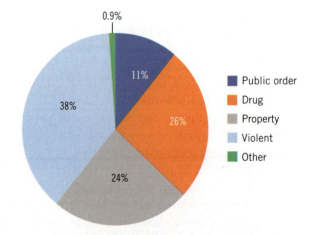

FIGURE 7.6   State female prisoners' crimes of conviction (percentage of total). Created by author from E. Carson, *Prisoners in 2019* (Washington, DC: Bureau of Justice Statistics, USDOJ, October 2020), Table 13.

over 50 percent of the total prison population. The percentage of those *admitted* to prison in any year for violent crimes compared to other crimes is much lower. The Bureau of Justice Statistics shows that in 2006 (the most recent year available), violent offenders accounted for a smaller percentage of convictions than property or drug crimes: 18 percent of all felony commitments in state courts were for violent offenses, 28 percent were for property offenses, and 33 percent were for drug offenses.[8]

Federal prisoners are more likely than state prisoners to be drug offenders. Most violent and property offenses are violations of state, not federal, laws. Drug laws, however, are often prosecuted by federal authorities, even if there is a corresponding state law that has been violated. This skews the crime of conviction for federal prisoners to include more drug and public order (including immigration) offenses as shown in Figure 7.7. It should also be noted that these numbers do not include all those held for immigration violations. According to official sources, 19,000 people are in federal prison for immigration offenses, but there are an additional 17,000 people being held in Immigration and Customs Enforcement (ICE) facilities or private facilities, and 16,000 others are in local jails under contract with ICE for detaining immigration violators.[9]

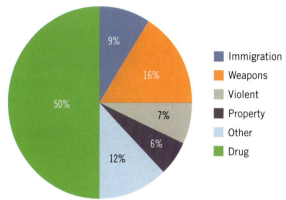

FIGURE 7.7 Federal prisoners' crimes. Created by author from P. Wagner and B. Rabuy, "Mass Incarceration: The Whole Pie, 2017," Prison Policy Initiative, https://www.prisonpolicy.org/reports/pie2017.html.

According to the Bureau of Justice Statistics, the percent of those admitted to prison for parole violations increased during the 1990s and 2000s, but more recently, this number has decreased. These individuals may have committed a new crime, or they may have been returned to prison for violating the rules of parole, such as testing positive for drugs. In 1980, only about 17 percent of new admissions were admitted for parole violations; in 2009, about 35 percent of all prison admissions were parole violators, but in 2016, the percentage decreased to 29 percent.[10]

These profiles of the crimes committed by prisoners should be considered estimates. Sources of information on crimes of conviction record only the most serious offense; therefore, if a person was convicted of multiple offenses, all but the most serious would not be counted. Also, these numbers represent crimes of conviction and almost all convictions result from plea bargaining. Individuals often plead guilty in exchange for being charged with a less serious offense, meaning the crime of conviction may not accurately represent the crime committed.

Pre-Prison Lives: Education and Income

Many inmates are either functionally illiterate, meaning they are unable to read or write, or do not have a high school diploma or its equivalent. Thus, the largest education programs in prison are basic education (literacy) and General Education Development (GED) certification. The median education of an incarcerated person ages 27–42 is 11 years completed, and the education gap between prisoners and the general U.S. population is growing.[11] While the overall educational attainment of Americans has grown since 1980, the number of incarcerated persons with less than a high school diploma grew over this same period.[12]

Related to the topic of education is income. Without a high school degree, job opportunities are limited. About two-thirds of prisoners were working prior to their imprisonment.[13] However, incarcerated people in all gender, race, and ethnic groups earned substantially less income prior to their incarceration than their non-incarcerated counterparts of similar ages. One study discovered that in 2014 U.S. dollars, prisoners in the 27- to 42-year-old age group had a median annual income of $19,185 prior to their incarceration, which is 41 percent less than non-incarcerated people of similar ages. Most prisoners came from the lowest income brackets: 57 percent of prisoners had pre-incarceration incomes of less than $22,000, compared to only 23 percent of non-incarcerated individuals in the same age and income brackets. In contrast, 57 percent of the non-incarcerated group had incomes higher than $37,500, while only 22 percent of prisoners had earned that level of income prior to incarceration.[14]

Medical Needs

Prisoners tend to have more physical infirmities and medical problems than the general U.S. population in all age groups. About 11 percent of both state and federal inmates report some medical problem, such as circulatory, respiratory, kidney/liver conditions, HIV/AIDS, or diabetes. About a quarter report being injured in prison. Poor medical care in prison most likely contributes to poor health outcomes, but part of the reason for higher medical needs among a prison population are their pre-prison lifestyles, which often involved alcohol or drug abuse, poor nutrition, smoking cigarettes, homelessness, and lack of preventive medical care.[15]

Healthcare costs for women are generally higher than healthcare costs for male prisoners. One study showed that the per capita lifetime healthcare expenditure is estimated to be $361,192 for females compared to $268,679 for males in the general U.S. population. This differential exists in prisoner healthcare costs as well.[16] Higher costs for women are due to gynecological and obstetric needs as well as the tendency of women to seek medical care more quickly than men. In a national survey of incarcerated men and women, about 25 percent of women and 20 percent of men reported some type of medical condition, but the percentages reversed when asked about injury, where 29 percent of men and 21 percent of women reported being injured.[17]

Inmates are about twice as likely as the general U.S. population to develop AIDS due to the use of shared needles by drug users and indiscriminate sexual practices.[18] They are also more likely to have Hepatitis C, called the "silent killer" because people can carry the virus asymptomatically for years while infecting others. Hepatitis C can result in liver problems, and some reports estimate

Alcatraz Prison hospital cell.

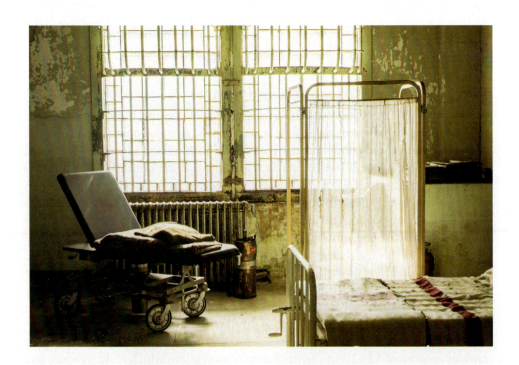

rates of infection among prisoner populations as high as 40 percent, while the general U.S. population's rate of infection is around 2 percent.[19] Any contagious disease is extremely problematic in prison because of crowding and poor sanitation. Outbreaks of tuberculosis, pneumococcal pneumonia, and meningitis have occurred in jails and prisons around the country.

In 2020, the COVID-19 pandemic spread across the country, including in prisons. In fact, the crowding, close contact, and lack of medical resources in prisons exacerbated transmission of the virus. The rate of transmission of COVID in prisons is 4 to 5.5 times the national average, and the mortality rate is two to three times that of the general population. In prisons and jails, the virus spread rapidly. In one Ohio prison, three-quarters of the prisoner population were infected within two months of the first case; 35 died. In an East Texas prison, nearly 6 percent of inmates died. More than 2,200 San Quentin prisoners, along with 298 staff members, got sick, and 28 inmates and one staff person died. Prison dormitories make it impossible to quarantine sick inmates. Inmates are either exposed to others or locked in their cells for days. By December 2020, 1,700 inmates had died and 1 in 5 prisoners in the United States had tested positive for the coronavirus; in some states, more than half of prisoners had been infected. COs are just as exposed as inmates. One response has been to reduce prison and jail populations. California had released 6,000 inmates by November 2020. New Jersey passed legislation that allowed the release of 20 percent of state inmates, primarily people who were within a year of the end of their sentence. Between March and May 2020, prison populations dropped an average of 8 percent, and jail populations decreased about 30 percent; however, jail populations have since increased, as has the infection rate.[20]

There are widespread allegations of medical neglect across the U.S. prison system, including interruption of prescribed medicines, neglect of diagnosed conditions, and nonmedical staff making "gateway" decisions (deciding who is sick enough to see the doctor).[21] California, for example, has spent years under court monitors because of court cases in which the state was held responsible for the deaths of inmates through inadequate or delayed medical care.[22] There are periodic exposés of medical neglect and poor care in prisons. For instance, a federal judge fined the state of Arizona $1 million for deficiencies in prison medical care provided by a for-profit company, including delayed or denied treatment, too few doctors and nurses, and referrals and medication refills that are routinely lost. According to testimony, a 59-year-old inmate died after nurses "repeatedly ignored his desperate pleas for help...even after open weeping lesions on [his body] were swarmed by flies." The for-profit company has faced lawsuits in other states, including Idaho and Alabama, for poor medical care.[23]

Drug Dependency and Addiction

Both jail and prison inmates disproportionately abuse or are dependent upon illegal drugs and alcohol. Studies have indicated that up to 83 percent of arrestees test positive for some type of drug, with marijuana being the most frequently detected.[24] In one study, about 68 percent of jail inmates reported symptoms consistent with alcohol and/or drug use disorders.[25] Less than 10 percent of the general U.S. population of adults are characterized as dependent or abusers; however, some reports indicate that 53 percent of prison inmates meet such criteria. Over 80 percent report prior drug use, and almost 60 percent used drugs in the month leading up to arrest.[26] Another study indicated that 46 percent of federal prisoners in the year prior to their arrest met the *Diagnostic and Statistical Manual of Mental Disorders*, Fifth Edition (DSM-V) criteria for substance dependence or abuse. Using these standard definitions of dependency, it has been reported that 60 percent of women and 53 percent of men in state prison are dependent on or abusing drugs.[27] According to the U.S. Department of Justice and Substance Abuse and Mental Health Services Administration (SAMSA) surveys, 35 percent of parolees and 40 percent of probationers have drug or alcohol dependence or abuse problems.[28]

Drug education and outpatient counseling are the most prevalent forms of treatment in the criminal justice system; however, there are not enough program slots for those who need them.[29] In one study of arrestees, 83 percent tested positive for drugs, but fewer than 25 percent had ever participated in any outpatient drug or alcohol treatment, and less than 30 percent had ever participated in any inpatient treatment.[30] Other studies show that less than 20 percent of offenders have received treatment services during their period of incarceration.[31] We will discuss drug treatment programs more fully in Chapter 11.

On the one hand, some individuals who are convicted of drug crimes (e.g., possession or trafficking) are not drug dependent, and their use or non-use of drugs may not affect future criminality. On the other hand, some individuals who are drug dependent commit crimes other than those related to drugs, for example burglary. It is widely believed that these individuals have a higher recidivism potential if their drug dependency is not addressed. Some studies have found that opiate and cocaine use have a statistical relationship with committing future crimes, while marijuana use does not.[32]

Family and Childhood Abuse

About 47 percent of inmates in state prisons have a parent or other close relative who has been previously incarcerated. Half of all juveniles in custody have a father, mother, or other close relative in jail or prison.[33] Children with a parent in prison are six times more likely to end up in jail themselves. These children are at higher risk for emotional problems, school difficulties, and delinquency.[34]

Prisoners also are more likely than those in the general U.S. population to report they were victims of childhood abuse. About 38 percent of female prisoners and 14 percent of male prisoners said they had been abused before the age of 18. About a quarter of women reported both physical and sexual abuse, while about 12 percent of men reported physical abuse and only 5 percent reported sexual abuse. Those who reported abuse were more likely to have been raised in foster care if their parents or caregivers were heavy users of drugs or alcohol and/or if either parent or caregiver spent time in prison. Furthermore, abuse seems to be linked to violent crime, especially for men. Both men and women who reported having been abused were also more likely to be drug abusers.[35]

In a Bureau of Justice Statistics study of prisoner-parents with children under 18, it was found that Black children were seven and a half times more likely, and Hispanic children two and a half times more likely, to have a parent in prison than white children. Men and women were equally likely to report being the principle financial supporter of their children before incarceration (52 percent of women compared to 54 percent of men). Women were more likely than men to report weekly or more frequent contact with their children while in prison (56 percent compared to 39 percent). Despite almost all states having at least some type of parenting program, only 12 percent of all parents reported having participated during incarceration.[36] Parenting programs in prisons and jails may involve expanded visitation, transportation assistance to facilitate visitation, parenting education classes that cover child development and discipline, and counseling. Parenting programs will be more fully discussed in Chapter 10.

Management Challenges of Special Prison Populations

Managing a prison is replete with unique challenges. As we have discussed, prisoners are sometimes violent individuals who can and do victimize other prisoners and correctional officers. Racial discord among prisoners requires that prison administrators pay close attention to who is housed together to prevent violence. Prison administrators also face staff shortages, overcrowding, and lack of resources to provide services such as healthcare or rehabilitation and educational programs. Even in the best cases, managing a prison population is difficult; however, certain groups have special vulnerabilities and/or troublesome behavior that create additional challenges for management.

Extremely long sentences are creating a growing class of prisoners who face or have served long periods of time. Long-term prisoners differ in several ways from prisoners who face shorter sentences. For example, prisoners who receive exceptionally long or life prison sentences are hard to control because they are not afraid of the consequences of rule breaking (losing good time or parole) as those with shorter terms might be. Long-term prisoners, as they age, incur higher medical costs. Also, some researchers have found a greater likelihood of mental health issues among long-term prisoners, including chronic post-traumatic stress disorder (PTSD), and institutionalized personality traits, such as distrusting others, difficulty engaging in relationships, hampered decision making, social-sensory disorientation, and social and temporal alienation. This is due, in part, to the fact that the longer a person is in prison, the less likely they are to have supportive family contacts, or any contacts at all, outside the prison world.[37] These special populations are typically more vulnerable than the general population of prisoners and are also at a higher risk of committing suicide. The needs of these prisoner populations are difficult to manage, which begs the question, to what extent are prisons obligated to meet these needs under the law?

The Elderly in Prison

As we discussed in Chapter 3, sentencing laws such as mandatory minimum laws and three-strikes sentencing statutes, which increase punishment for offenders who have committed previous felonies, have resulted in exceedingly long and life-without-parole sentences. In 1984, one in every 13 prisoners were serving life sentences; by 2012, one in every nine prisoners were serving a life sentence. As a result, the average age of prisoners is increasing in the United States. Departments of corrections consider ages 50 or 55 the beginning of the elderly category because prisoners typically have such poor health histories that their physical age is about 10 years older than someone in the general U.S. population.[38] Today, prisoners 50 and older represent the fastest-growing population in crowded federal correctional facilities, their ranks having swelled by 25 percent to nearly 31,000 from 2009 to 2013.[39] In fiscal year 2011, there were slightly over 5,000 prisoners age 65 and older (approximately three percent of the federal prisoner population), but the number of prisoners 65 and older tripled by 2019.[40]

State prisons show similar increases in the number of older prisoners. In 2010, there were some 246,000 prisoners ages 50 and older in state and federal prisons combined.[41] The number of state prisoners age 55 or older increased 400 percent, from three percent of the total state prison population in 1993, to 10 percent in 2013 and it was 22 percent in 2019. The increase was due to long sentences with prisoners growing old in prison and an increase in defendants over 55 being sentenced to prison.[42] It is estimated that by 2030, one in three people

Prisoners 50 and older represent the fastest-growing population in crowded federal correctional facilities.

in federal or state prisons will be aged 55 or older—more than triple the proportion in the early 1990s.[43]

Many states have some form of **compassionate release** so that low-risk elderly or sick prisoners can petition to be released from prison. At the end of 2009, 15 states and the District of Columbia had provisions for compassionate, or geriatric, release. Program provisions and restrictions vary. For instance, in Virginia and Wisconsin, people 65 and older must serve at least five years of their sentence, and those aged 60 to 64 must serve at least 10 years before being eligible for release. Other states, such as Connecticut, Missouri, Oregon, Texas, Washington, and Wyoming, have no age restrictions but specify that the individual must suffer from age-related physical or mental debilitation to qualify for compassionate release.[44]

Most elderly prisoners, however, are not released through compassionate release programs, even in those states in which they are available, despite the fact research shows that older inmates have a dramatically lower risk of recidivism than younger inmates. One study found that while 60 percent of 20-year-olds recidivate, only about 30 percent of 60-year-olds and 20 percent of 70-year-olds recidivate.[45] Another study reported that nationwide, 43.3 percent of all released individuals recidivate within three years, while only 7 percent of those aged 50–64 and 4 percent of those over 65 return to prison for new convictions.[46] One study found that four factors contributed to the lack of compassionate release:

- Political considerations and public opinion: politically, there is no interest group that advocates for older inmates, many of whom have committed murder or sex crimes.

- Eligibility requirements: requirements often exclude those convicted of violent crimes, sexual offenses, or who were sentenced to life without parole.

- Application procedures: the process can be cumbersome, applying may prevent being considered for regular parole, and there is little effort to publicize the opportunity.

- Referral and review processes: the process takes a very long time, and reviewers may be inclined to deny release, especially for those convicted of violent crimes.[47]

Some offenders are so old when they are finally released that they require nursing or hospice care, yet some nursing homes will not accept them. Release may hold nothing for them, since family and friends may all be dead, leaving the inmate with nowhere to go. Such inmates have even been known to refuse parole, preferring the familiar world of the prison to the unfamiliar world outside.[48]

VULNERABILITIES OF ELDERLY PRISONERS

Prisons are set up for younger inmates, and, as such, there are a myriad of problems for prisoners who experience some of the physical disabilities of old age. Older prisoners have a more difficult time in prison than their younger cohorts: they have difficulty climbing to a top bunk, they have trouble with stairs, they cannot stand in line for long periods of time, they can't drop to the ground when an alarm goes off or get up quickly afterwards, and they may not hear commands from correctional officers. Elderly prisoners experience failing eyesight, decreased mobility, loss of mental acuity, loneliness, and disorientation. They often suffer from chronic diseases, including diabetes, heart failure, cognitive impairment, and liver disease. Older female prisoners are two times as likely as older male prisoners to report serious health problems such as cardiac, degenerative, and respiratory illnesses.[49]

As a result, states have had to make physical modifications in prisons to accommodate older prisoners and those with physical disabilities, including ramps, grab bars in showers, and wider doorways for wheelchairs. Many prisons have what are essentially assisted-living centers, with full-time nursing staff working alongside correctional officers. Many prisons also have hospice units for dying prisoners.[50]

The combination of physical impairment, chronic medical conditions, fear of release but also fear of dying in prison, and increased vulnerability in prison can result in depression, but not necessarily misconduct. In their later years, long-term prisoners show declining participation in misconduct, but increased risk of victimization.[51] Elderly prisoners are especially vulnerable to victimization because they cannot defend themselves as well as younger inmates. Older inmates are less likely to be involved in violence because of debts or gambling, but they are more likely to be victims of extortion and theft. In one study, it was found that 17 percent of the elderly prisoners in the sample had been threatened in the past year with a weapon, and a quarter had been threatened with being hit. About 10 percent had been hit, punched, or shoved. About 85 percent of the sample reported having had other inmates cut in front of them in line, a seemingly innocuous form of victimization, but one that is often a test to determine if the inmate will fight back. Older inmates reportedly did not fight back against these actions as they would have in their younger years. Since many geriatric prisoners are imprisoned for sex crimes, the dual elements of being a "baby raper" and an elderly inmate set the individual up for severe risk of victimization.[52]

FINANCIAL IMPLICATIONS OF ELDERLY PRISONERS

One of the consequences of the growing number of older prisoners is that healthcare costs are increasing. The Federal Bureau of Prisons saw healthcare expenses for inmates increase 55 percent from 2006 to 2013, when it spent more than $1 billion.[53] The average cost of housing federal inmates nearly doubles for aging prisoners. One estimate suggests that the cost of housing a prisoner in the general population is $27,549 a year, and the cost associated with an older inmate who needs more medical care, including prescription drugs and treatments, such as inhalation treatments for chronic asthma or dialysis for kidney disease, is $58,956.[54] Other estimates put the cost of housing the elderly (including medical costs) at three times that for a non-elderly prisoner.[55]

One debate regarding the management of elderly prisoners is whether there should be **age segregation** in prisons; for example, placing all inmates of a certain age in the same facility or unit. Older inmates have been mainstreamed into the general population because correctional managers commonly believe older inmates have a stabilizing influence on younger inmates and can control their violence. There has been little empirical evidence for this assumption, although it is true that younger inmates are responsible for a disproportional amount of prison misconduct. Another advantage of mainstreaming the elderly is that they have access to more available programming than if they were segregated in one facility.[56]

However, segregating inmates by age has the advantage of reducing risks of victimization and localizing medical costs and requirements for physical accommodations. The **Americans with Disabilities Act of 1990 (ADA)** also applies to federal and state prisoners and requires that prison officials make adaptations to accommodate disabilities, including those that occur with age. Prisoners must have access to all facilities, programs, and services, or reasonable alternatives.[57] These accommodations are not easy to make in some facilities that are old and do not have elevators; thus, placing all elderly inmates together reduces the need for physical changes to be made to all facilities. Facilities or units for the elderly generally require lower levels of security as well. Research indicates that older inmates are easier to supervise because they are less likely to escape, violate prison rules, or receive disciplinary reports.[58]

Researchers and policy experts who study the elderly prisoner population have been warning correctional authorities for years of the increasing costs and management challenges of this population. Some of the recommendations that have been offered include the following:

- Develop and use an assessment/screening tool for correctional officers to identify common geriatric symptoms (e.g., sensory impairment, functional impairment, incontinence, and cognitive impairment) and have this information available for routine use to improve understanding of prisoner needs and abilities.

- Train correctional officers in more depth about aging and the health and safety issues of geriatric prisoners.

- Expand preventive healthcare (especially dental care), which may avoid more serious health problems and lead to substantial savings in healthcare costs.

- Consider early release mechanisms for those who pose a low risk to public safety and whose healthcare needs can be better met in the community through compassionate release and medical parole.[59]

- Improve conditions inside prisons and jails for those aging within them.

- Improve discharge planning and reentry preparation for older people by addressing their housing, medical/health, mental health, post-incarceration, financial, family, and employment needs.[60]

- Shift the response to violence from excessively long sentences to expanding services for victims and survivors of crime.

There are several programs across the country that address the issues of elderly inmates. For instance, in 2017, the Connecticut Department of Corrections created a nursing home that houses older people who have been paroled because of physical or mental illness or disability. The released prisoners receive funds from Medicare and Medicaid Services.[61]

FOCUS ON A

STATE   CONNECTICUT

Like many states, Connecticut has seen a more than 40 percent increase from 2010 to 2016 in the over-60 prisoner population. The state reports that the annual price of healthcare for an inmate increased from $4,814 in fiscal year 2010 to $5,201 in 2015, as more inmates required regular healthcare. Connecticut has responded to the problem of the rising population of sick and elderly inmates by paroling them to a privately owned, 95-bed nursing facility that contracts with the state to take the paroled inmates. Many residents are on "nursing-home-release parole," created by the Connecticut state legislature in 2013. To qualify, the Department of Correction must decide that inmates are "suffering from a terminal condition, disease or syndrome" and "be physically incapable of presenting a danger to society." In December 2017, the facility was the first in the United States to receive notice that they were eligible for federal funds from the Centers for Medicare and Medicaid Services (CMS). This was significant because it presented a new way for the state to finance the care of its aging and ailing inmates who are not public safety risks. Even so, many of these inmates would have had difficulty finding a nursing home that would have accepted them. Medicaid covers half the cost of their care in the private facility but would not cover any of it if the inmates were still incarcerated.

Not all the residents at 60 West are from the Connecticut Department of Correction. Others have been referred from state psychiatric hospitals, and residents suffer from a range of conditions including Alzheimer's disease, dementia, brain injuries, HIV,

cancer, Huntington's disease, and psychiatric conditions such as schizophrenia, depression, personality disorders, and anxiety.

Connecticut's community-based approach to serving the needs of its aging and terminally ill prisoners has influenced other states to work toward doing the same. At least three states—Kentucky, Michigan, and Wisconsin—have explored creating similar facilities. One state representative from Michigan introduced a bill in 2016 that would have permitted medically frail inmates to be cared for in licensed healthcare facilities rather than prisons. However, it did not pass because of funding concerns. Other states are modifying prison housing units to accommodate elderly, ill, and disabled inmates. For instance, Virginia has an assisted-living unit inside a prison to care for infirm and geriatric inmates.

In addition to 60 West, Connecticut also has a prison hospice program in which fellow inmates care for dying prisoners. The program started in 2001 at the MacDougall-Walker Correctional Institution and is now in three prisons in the state, including York Correctional Institution, a women's prison.

Connecticut's efforts to implement criminal justice reform and set an innovative example for the rest of the county have not gone unopposed. The facility has fought lawsuits from neighbors who believe it has lowered property values and violates local zoning regulations. Despite community resistance, though, there have been no reported criminal incidents since the facility opened.

Discussion Questions

1. What should be done with old and/or sick inmates? Should they remain in prison or be released to some type of community supervision?
2. Recently, some correctional systems have been releasing inmates early when they are at

high risk for contracting COVID-19, especially because prisons have been "hot spots" of infection, do you agree with this policy decision? Why or why not?

Source: A. Wisnieski, "'Model' Nursing Home for Paroled Inmates to Get Federal Funds," Connecticut Health Team, April 25, 2017, retrieved February 10, 2019 from http://c-hit. org/2017/04/25/model-nursing-home-for-paroled-inmates-to-get-federal-funds/

The Mentally Ill

Most people who suffer from some form of mental illness are not violent and do not commit crimes; however, those with mental health disorders who do enter the criminal justice system are an especially problematic population.[62] While in the system, they are more likely to have behavioral problems and higher rates of victimization and are more likely to recidivate. The American Psychiatric Association does not use the term mental illness, but, rather, defines a **mental disorder** as "a syndrome characterized by a clinically significant disturbance in an individual's cognition, emotion regulation, or behavior that reflects a dysfunction in the psychological, biological, or developmental processes underlying mental functioning..."[63] A Bureau of Justice Statistics (BJS) report indicated that 56 percent of all state prison inmates had a mental health problem, defined as either a diagnosis or symptoms that met the criteria of a mental disease or disorder, compared to about 11 percent of the public who could be categorized as having a mental health problem. The report indicated that comparative figures in federal prisons were 45 percent and, in jails, 64 percent. In this same report, it was estimated that 15 percent of the prisoner population met the criteria for a psychotic disorder, and 65 percent of prisoners had a diagnosed substance abuse disorder.[64] A BJS report from a 2011-2012 survey stated that about one in seven state and federal prisoners and one in four jail inmates self-reported experiences that met the threshold for **serious psychological distress (SPD)**. Serious psychological distress is defined in this report as a score of 13 or higher on the Kessler 6 (K6) Nonspecific Psychological Distress Scale, a six-question tool developed to screen for serious mental illness among adults age 18 or older. Inmates were asked how often during the 30 days prior to the interview they felt nervous, hopeless, restless or fidgety, so depressed that nothing could cheer them up, that everything was an effort, or worthless. A summary scale of combined responses had a range of 0 to 24. Inmates with a score of 13 or higher were considered to have SPD, inmates with a score of 8 to 12 were considered to have an anxiety disorder (not reported), and inmates with a score of 7 or lower were considered to not have an indicator of a current mental health problem.[65] This compares with one in 19 persons in the general U.S. population.[66] Another source estimated that 15 to 24 percent of prison inmates had a mental health illness that had been or could be diagnosed.[67]

A 2006 Bureau of Justice Statistics (BJS) survey indicated that women, whites, and young inmates were more likely to exhibit mental health problems in jail. About 75 percent of women in jails exhibited mental health problems compared to 63 percent of male inmates. About 71 percent of whites, 63 percent of Blacks, and 51 percent of Hispanics were found to have a mental health problem. Jail inmates with mental health problems are more likely to have been previously incarcerated, used drugs, experienced homelessness, experienced physical or sexual abuse, and/or have parents who abused drugs or alcohol.[68] In another study of more than 20,000 adults booked into five U.S. jails, 14.5 percent of men and 31 percent of women met criteria for a **serious mental illness (SMI)**—prevalence rates at least three times higher than those found in the general U.S. population.[69] These percentages are lower than the BJS prevalence rates because the definition of an SMI is more restrictive, defined as major depressive disorder; depressive disorder not otherwise specified; bipolar disorder I, II, and not otherwise specified; schizophrenia spectrum disorder; schizoaffective disorder; schizophreniform disorder; brief psychotic disorder; delusional disorder; and psychotic disorder not otherwise specified. Larger percentages are reported when self-reports of symptomology and the broader term *mental health disorder* are used; smaller percentages are reported when only formally diagnosed SMIs or stays in mental health institutions are counted.

Most studies indicate that female inmates are more likely to have mental health issues than male inmates, and that female jail and prison inmates have more severe mental health problems than their male counterparts.[70]

The previously mentioned 2006 BJS survey reported that while 55 percent of male prison inmates had a mental health issue, 73 percent of female prison inmates did. About 23 percent of women had been diagnosed by a mental health professional in the last year—three times the rate of male prisoners.[71] The 2011–2012 BJS study indicated that, in prisons, 20 percent of females and 14 percent of males met the threshold for serious psychological distress (SPD). In jails, 32 percent of females and 26 percent of males met the threshold for SPD. Sixty-six percent of female prisoners and 35 percent of male prisoners had been told by a mental health professional that they had a mental health disorder.[72]

It has been reported that twice as many mentally ill are in our nation's prisons and jails as are in mental health facilities, and others put the figure at three times as many. The rate of individuals sent to mental hospitals declined when many of these facilities were closed in the late 1970s after a series of court decisions required more extensive due process and proof that patients were benefitting from the hospital setting.[73] Community-based mental health services were supposed to replace state mental hospitals, but, unfortunately, jails and prisons have become the largest providers of mental health services in the nation. These institutions also have the least trained staff, are the least equipped, and are the most under-resourced of facilities with mentally ill residents. In the 2006 BJS study of the mentally ill in prison, only one in three state prisoners had ever received mental health treatment during the course of their imprisonment.[74]

Inmates may be especially vulnerable to mental health issues because of their pasts. A large percentage of inmates have been exposed to violence, sometimes starting very early in their childhood. It has been estimated that they are three times as likely as the general U.S. population to have experienced traumatic events such as the death of a loved one, homelessness, victimization (sexual, physical, or both), and so on.[75] It is not uncommon at all for inmates to relate experiences in which they have seen people die violently, sometimes loved ones, when they were quite young. It is probable that many individuals who grew up in poverty-stricken, high-crime areas and experienced violence suffer from untreated post-traumatic stress disorder. In the 2006 BJS study of the mentally ill in prison, it was found that state prisoners with mental health problems were more than twice as likely as those without mental health problems to have been sexually or physically abused. They were also more likely to have had family members who abused drugs, alcohol, or both, and to have had a family member incarcerated.[76]

The most common mental health diagnosis for inmates is some form of depressive disorder, as Figure 7.8 shows. Depressive disorders are diagnosed when symptoms last for at least two years, with episodes of major depression along with

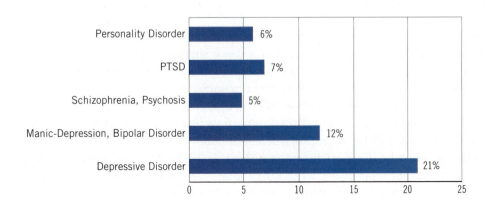

FIGURE 7.8 Diagnosed mental health disorders of people in the criminal justice system (percent diagnosed). Created by author from K. Kim, K. M. Becker-Cohen, and M. Serakos, *The Processing and Treatment of Mentally Ill Persons in the Criminal Justice System.* (Washington, DC: Urban Institute, March 2015), 15.

periods of less severe symptoms. Symptoms include some combination of persistent sadness or anxiety, feelings of hopelessness, pessimism, irritability, guilt, worthlessness, or helplessness, loss of interest or pleasure in hobbies and activities, decreased energy or fatigue, difficulty concentrating, remembering, or making decisions, difficulty sleeping, early-morning awakening, or oversleeping, appetite and/or weight changes, and/or thoughts of death or suicide, or suicide attempts.

The next most commonly diagnosed illness is bipolar disorder, which is diagnosed when a person experiences episodes of extremely low moods that meet the criteria for major depression, but also experiences extreme high—euphoric or irritable—moods called "mania" or a less severe form called "hypomania."[77] Another common diagnosis with this group of people is either antisocial personality disorder and borderline personality disorder or both, although these diagnoses have been criticized as being vague and misused as catch-alls for too many individuals.[78] Similarities between the two diagnoses include disinhibition, hostility, and suicidality. The behavioral indices for either of these disorders include a pervasive pattern of disregard for the rights of others, being manipulative, volatile, disruptive, and aggressive. When an individual exhibits two or more diagnoses—for example, depression and schizophrenia or, more frequently, some form of SMI and drug dependency—this is known as **co-occurring disorders**.[79] As might be expected, co-occurring disorders are very common in prison and jail inmate populations, and treatment staff note that it is difficult to address drug use unless underlying mental health issues are addressed as well.

Those with mental health problems are likely to abuse drugs and exhibit drug dependency. Over 50 percent of state prisoners with mental health problems were found to have abused drugs, and over a third of them had used drugs at the time of their offense. Almost a quarter had used cocaine or crack cocaine in the month before their offense, but marijuana was the more frequently used drug.[80] One study found that approximately 59 percent of state prisoners with mental illness had a co-occurring drug or alcohol problem.[81] Another study found that individuals suffering from schizophrenia were four times more likely to be drug dependent than others; those with bipolar disorder were more than five times as likely to be drug dependent.[82]

There is some indication that the mentally ill use illegal drugs to self-medicate. Closed out of mainstream healthcare due to lack of income or disinclination to pursue professional help, they use drugs to feel better or to suppress auditory or visual hallucinations. This group of offenders may not receive the proper treatment or medications because they are poor, disproportionately persons of color, uninsured, and/or homeless, and thus develop co-occurring substance abuse disorders. They continually cycle through the mental health, substance abuse, and criminal justice systems, and may eventually commit a sufficiently serious crime to receive a long prison sentence.

The prison experience stresses even the most even-tempered and mentally healthy inmate. For those who suffer from mental illness, extreme overcrowding, perceived and/or real danger, lack of emotional support, and other deprivations may trigger deterioration of mental health or even a psychotic breakdown.[83] In prison, the mentally ill are particularly vulnerable to various types of victimization, such as taunting, intimidation, and theft.

The mentally ill are also a difficult group to supervise. Correctional officers may be unable to differentiate between an inmate who is unwilling to follow an order and one who is experiencing a psychotic episode or may be psychologically unable to conform his or her behavior to what is ordered. An inmate with paranoid delusions may suddenly and unpredictably attack a nearby inmate because

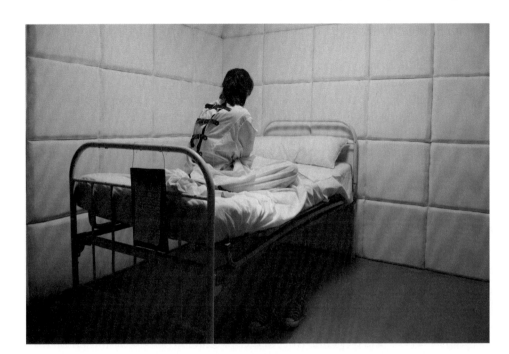

It has been reported that there are twice as many mentally ill individuals in our nation's prisons and jails as there are in mental health facilities

of some delusion. Mentally ill prisoners are more likely than others to be involved in assaultive incidents.[84] They are more likely to be violent offenders (53 percent versus 46 percent of other inmates). Those with diagnosed mental health problems are seven and a half times more likely to get disciplinary reports than other prisoners.[85] One study noted that 80 percent of unusual incident reports in one women's prison involved women who were on mental health caseloads.[86] In another study, almost 58 percent of those with mental health problems had rule violations compared to 43 percent of prisoners without mental health problems, but when looking only at violent infractions in prison, over twice as many were committed by those who were known to have mental health issues.[87]

Inmates with SMIs or some form of mental health issue are more likely to recidivate. About 75 percent have already been in prison or on probation.[88] Inmates with any major psychiatric disorder were found to be almost two and a half times more likely to have four or more repeat incarcerations than inmates with no major psychiatric disorder. Those with bipolar disorder were three and one-third times more likely to be reincarcerated.[89]

SUICIDE AND SELF-HARMING BEHAVIOR

While some may argue that suicide is not a mental illness, one can certainly agree that it is a symptom of mental distress. Rates of suicide in prisons and jails are much higher than in the general U.S. population; the suicide rate in prisons only (excluding jails) is about twice that of the general U.S. population, but it varies from state to state.[90] Recently, the rate of suicide in prisons and jails has increased. In jails, as of 2014, suicides accounted for nearly a third of all deaths, more than any other cause. In state prisons, suicides account for 7 percent of all deaths. There was an 85 percent increase in state and federal prison suicides from 2001 to 2018. In Texas, for instance, there were 50 prison suicides in 2020, the highest number in at least 20 years, even while the number of people in Texas prisons droppd by 20,000.[91] Critics also argue that the national reporting system is inadequate and probably undercount the number of deaths.[92] For men, the rate of suicide is about five to six times higher in prisons and jails than on the outside, and for women, the rate can be as much as 20 times higher.[93] The highest risk of suicide is soon after initial imprisonment, which is why jails have much higher rates of suicides than prisons.[94]

Rates of attempted suicide and self-harm are also high. Self-harming behavior is defined as "the deliberate destruction or alteration of body tissue" without the intent to commit suicide. These behaviors include cutting, scratching, or burning the skin; hitting oneself; pulling one's hair; reopening one's wounds; and breaking one's bones. Severe self-injury includes eye gouging, face mutilation, and amputation of limbs, breasts, and genitals.[95] Research indicates that the incidence of self-harm among male prisoners was 5 to 6 percent, and 20 to 24 percent among female prisoners.[96] Other studies report self-harm rates of between 2 to 4 percent of the general prisoner population and 15 percent of prisoners who have received psychiatric treatment.[97] Those who attempt or commit suicide are much more likely than others to have histories of self-harm. In one study of over 1,000 incidents in one state prison, researchers differentiated incidents where inmates committed acts of self-harm with no indicators that suicide was intended, acts that were clearly suicide attempts, and incidents where it wasn't clear, perhaps even to the inmate, whether suicide was intended but self-harm definitely occurred.[98]

Most suicides occur by hanging, and the second most common method is by cutting or stabbing. A report from the World Health Organization and other research studies indicate that a disproportionate number of suicides and a higher suicide risk occurs with those who are in solitary housing situations.[99]

Those most vulnerable to suicide are prisoners who have been diagnosed with depression, who have poor social and family support, a history of mental illness and/or emotional problems, are withdrawing from substance abuse, and who have a history of prior suicide attempts.[100] Jail inmates who commit suicide are typically pretrial inmates who are male, young (20–25 years old), unmarried, and first-time offenders who have been arrested for minor, usually substance-related, offenses. They are typically intoxicated at the time of their arrest and commit suicide at an early stage of their confinement. In contrast, prison inmates who commit suicide are generally older and have spent years in prison.[101] High-risk prisoners can also include those who are experiencing their first incarceration; those who are young, single, Caucasian, and/or male; those who have a psychiatric diagnosis; and those with a history of alcohol and substance abuse.[102] Reasons for suicide have included conflict (either in prison or with family), depression, despair over long sentences, anxiety about release, being denied parole, being raped, missing loved ones, receiving negative news such as finding out that one has a serious medical condition or that loved ones have divorced or disowned the inmate, and fear of being in prison.[103]

In an older British study, long semi-structured interviews were used along with statistical methods to investigate how those who attempted suicide were different from other inmates. Researchers found that suicide attempters had suffered greater disadvantage, experienced more violence, had more family problems in their histories, and had had more frequent contact with social services and criminal justice agencies. Suicide attempters were found to have poor coping skills, which made the prison experience more difficult, thus increasing the likelihood of attempted escape through suicide.[104]

Rates of suicide had declined because of suicide prevention efforts implemented in jails and prisons, but recently has increased. It has been recommended that all incarceration facilities implement screening procedures and policies that require monitoring, and that services be available for those who are at high or moderate risk for suicide. All staff should be trained in identifying suicide risk and communication skills. In one study, the following factors were identified as assisting in reducing the risk of suicide:

- removal of lethal means;
- consistent 24-hour monitoring;
- reasons for living (programs or connections in prison that give meaning to life);
- social connectedness (e.g., pseudo-families) or supportive staff;
- communication with family in the community;
- participation in support groups;
- education concerning medication use;
- cell placement with social support; and
- use of religious services.[105]

Caring, informed correctional staff who monitor inmates for cues that indicate they are at risk for suicide attempts can reduce the rate of suicide. Alternatively, staff who are overworked and/or uncaring, or, worse, who show hostility to those experiencing stress, can contribute to an increase in the number of suicides.[106]

MENTAL HEALTH TREATMENT

Often, mentally ill inmates are housed with the general population and receive minimal special attention unless they commit an act that attracts the attention of custodial officials. Mental health treatment often consists of stabilizing the inmate using anti-psychotic drugs and then sending the person back into the general population. Some object to the use of psychotropic medications because they can be easily abused, they may be used simply as behavior controls, they may not be accompanied by any professional therapy, and they may be given to an inmate for long periods of time, leading to a range of side effects. One such example is the "Thorazine shuffle," referring to the brand-name drug, whereby an inmate walks with short, shuffling steps, speech becomes slurred, and mental reactions deteriorate.[107] Perhaps the most troubling element of the use of psychotropic medications is that inmates may have their medications stopped abruptly upon release.

The Bureau of Justice Statistics reports that more than half of prisoners (54 percent) and a third of jail inmates (35 percent) who met the threshold for SPD had received mental health treatment since admission to their current facility. Treatments included prescription medication, counseling or therapy, or a combination of the two. About 37 percent of prisoners and 38 percent of jail inmates who had ever been told they had a mental disorder said they were currently receiving treatment for a mental health problem. An estimated 30 percent of each group said they were currently taking prescription medication.[108]

Mental health treatment is difficult at best, but the challenges of providing treatment inside a prison are extreme. Mental health treatment is expensive, and it is especially so in prison. The overall annual per-inmate health cost has been estimated at $4,780, while health costs for inmates with serious mental illness have increased to $12,000 because of the addition of psychiatric and psychological staff and the administration of psychotropic drugs.[109] In addition to costs, it is difficult to provide inmates with effective and comprehensive treatment beyond simply providing medication. In the prison and jail environments, inmates are constantly stressed and anxious and receive little emotional support from peers or authorities. They spend little time doing prosocial activities. They receive little contact from family or friends. The culture of security and skepticism colors relationships with all staff members. Privacy is nonexistent. Clinicians often must interact with clients while correctional officers are in the room. In some units, group therapy is conducted with prisoners in single cages set in a semicircle around the therapist, which is not a setting conducive to building trust or healthy reflection.[110]

Court cases have established inmates' rights to some form of mental health treatment if not doing so constitutes deliberate indifference. This **deliberate indifference standard** comes from the Supreme Court case *Estelle v. Gamble* (1976), which will be discussed in Chapter 9. It refers to a situation where prison staff are aware of a need for treatment to prevent or alleviate pain or injury yet deliberately refuse or neglect to provide such treatment. In *Ruiz v. Estelle* (1980), a federal district judge enumerated the minimal necessary elements for a mental health system in prison:

- a systematic screening procedure;
- treatment that entails more than segregation and supervision;
- treatment that involves a sufficient number of mental health professionals to adequately provide services to all prisoners suffering from serious mental disorders;
- maintenance of adequate and confidential clinical records;
- a program for identifying and treating suicidal inmates; and
- a ban on prescribing potentially dangerous medications without adequate monitoring.[111]

However, almost 40 years later, there is still the need to establish guidelines and enforce standards regarding the treatment of the mentally ill in prisons and jails. For those with co-occurring mental health and addiction issues, integrated service models are necessary which address both problems.[112]

There have been recent attempts to address the needs of veterans who are suffering from PTSD and other mental health issues. Ideally, intervention would occur early enough so that such individuals would be diverted from the corrections system, assuming this would not increase the risk to the public. The sequential intercept model identifies locations in which persons with mental illness can be identified, diverted, treated, and returned to the community. It provides guidelines for states to create programs which identify the mentally ill early in the criminal justice process and provide needed diagnosis and treatment throughout the correctional supervision period and, most importantly, wraparound services upon release. The model rests on two principles: minimize the inappropriate penetration of persons with mental illness into the criminal justice system, and successful treatment should occur in the community.[113]

One of the problems concerning treatment for the mentally ill is the lack of resources and interagency conflict over which agency should fund treatment (state corrections, mental health agencies, or federal agencies such as Medicaid). For an offender in the community, judges may require treatment services be provided to stay out of confinement, but Medicaid officials either can't or won't fund the treatment, which then means the offender may be incarcerated because of a lack of community care alternatives.[114]

Studies show that treatment programs can successfully reduce recidivism when they provide sufficient resources to meet the needs of the mentally ill prisoner population. In several evaluations, it was shown that programs that provided "wraparound" services (meaning a continuation of the same psychotropic drug and counseling services from the prison into the community) to released inmates could reduce recidivism as compared to similarly situated inmates who did not receive such services. These programs typically utilize a multidisciplinary team of professionals (psychiatrists, psychologists, and health social workers); assist the ex-inmate in receiving Medicaid assistance, if necessary, for continuing mental health treatment; and provide assistance in housing and job placement. One of these programs in Washington state used a community-based team including a mental health case manager, psychiatrist, nurse practitioner, registered nurse, substance abuse counselor, community corrections officer, and residential

FOCUS ON THE
OFFENDER

THE LONG ARM OF THE LAW

Meek Mill, born Robert Rihmeek Williams, grew up in difficult circumstances yet began to build a career as a rapper when he was a teenager. In 2007, Mill was arrested for drug possession and carrying a firearm without a license. The court case took two years, and, ultimately, he was found guilty and sentenced to 11 and a half to 23 months in prison, followed by five years of probation. This is an example of a split sentence, where the sentencing judge can continue monitoring the offender because of the probation term; otherwise, supervision would pass to prison and paroling authorities.

Mill was released early for good behavior in 2009 and began his probation sentence. He also began to rebuild his music career, gaining national recognition. Over the years, he had several hearings in front of the judge because of violations, such as traveling out of Pennsylvania without court approval. In 2014 he was jailed for five months. In 2016, he was placed on electronic monitoring for 90 days, was ordered to complete community service, and was barred from traveling. His probation was extended past the original five-year period. That same year, he won the 2016 Billboard Music Award for Top Rap Album. In 2017,

he was arrested for a fight (but the charges were dropped), and for doing dirt-bike stunts. He also tested positive for the painkiller Percocet. The judge revoked his probation in November 2017 and sent him to prison to serve his original sentence of two to four years, even though an assistant district attorney and Mill's probation officer had recommended that he not be incarcerated because he had only technical violations and no new arrests. After widespread media attention, Mill was released on bail in April 2018 while he challenged his original conviction. He has received support from national celebrities and criminal justice professionals who argue that probation should not be held over someone's head for 10 years and that a prison sentence is too severe a sanction for what were, essentially, rule violations, not new crimes. The case also illustrates the national issue of wrongful convictions, since he is challenging his original conviction based on allegations that a police officer committed perjury, which resulted in his wrongful conviction. Mill has now partnered with Amazon Prime for a six-part documentary series about flaws in the criminal justice system.

Questions for Discussion

1. Does Mill represent the demographic profile of prisoners described in this chapter?

2. Do you think prison was an appropriate sentence for him?

Sources: Phelps, M., "The Lesson of Meek Mill: A Probation System 'Set Up to Fail,'" The Crime Report, January 31, 2018, https://thecrimereport.org/2018/01/31/the-enduring-lesson-of-meek-mill-a-probation-system-set-up-to-fail/.

Phillips, K., "Meek Mill Denied Bail Again as Judge Calls Rapper a 'Danger to the Community,'" Washington Post, December 4, 2017, https://www.washingtonpost.com/news/arts-and-entertainment/wp/2017/11/20/how-rapper-meek-mills-actions-in-2007-fueled-racial-politics-in-2017/?utm_term=.3711a09a91ae.

Ryan, R., "Rapper MM Released from Prison," USA Today, May 3, 2018, https://www.usatoday.com/story/life/tv/2018/05/03/meek-mill-amazon-documentary-series-jay-z-prison-release/576142002/.

house manager. These professionals made sure that the mentally ill offenders continued their psychotherapy and medications; had access to housing, drug treatment, and other basic services; and reported as required to their parole officers. The ex-offenders participated in structured programming and had daily contact with team members. The recidivism rate for this group was only 19 percent, which was less than half that of a matched sample of inmates who did not receive such services (42 percent).[115]

The Intellectually Disabled

Another vulnerable prisoner population are prisoners who have intellectual disabilities. The **intellectually disabled** have an IQ of 70 or below and have significant limitations in intellectual functioning (reasoning, learning, and problem solving) and adaptive behavior, which covers a range of everyday social and practical skills.[116] They are characterized as being childlike in their lack of understanding and gullibility. It is estimated that 1 to 2 percent of the general U.S. population is intellectually disabled, and up to 10 percent of prison populations can be defined as having developmental issues (although most studies put the figure at around 4 percent). These individuals are disproportionately low income and minority. They are easily convicted of their crimes and receive longer sentences. At times, justice personnel may not even be aware of the individual's mental status. In prison, they are unlikely to receive special treatment.[117]

The intellectually disabled are often targeted and victimized by inmate predators because they are easily manipulated, so fellow inmates use them to conduct rule violations. Unless such individuals request protective custody, there is little protection offered by correctional authorities. There are no special housing units for the intellectually disabled and it is inappropriate to house them with mentally ill prisoners.

The Americans with Disabilities Act (ADA) requires that accommodations be made for the intellectually disabled if their condition prevents them from benefiting from prison programs. Authorities are obligated to identify, classify, and offer appropriate educational programs for such inmates.

LGBTQ Inmates

A group that is especially vulnerable in prison are those in the LGBTQ community (lesbian, gay, bisexual, transgender, queer). It has been reported that LGB populations go to prison at a rate three times higher than the heterosexual population. Transgender men and women have imprisonment rates that is reportedly as high as four times the general population.[118] Lesbians, gay men, and bisexuals make up about 3.5 percent of the U.S. general population; however, 9.3 percent of male prisoners are sexual minorities, including 5.5 percent gay or bisexual men and 3.8 percent identifying as men who have had sex with men but do not identify as gay or bisexual. Among women in prison, 42.1 percent have been identified in surveys as sexual minorities. This percentage includes 33.3 percent lesbian or bisexual women and 8.8 percent identifying as having had sex with women but not identifying as gay or bisexual. Evidence indicates that sexual minorities (those who self-identify as lesbian, gay, or bisexual or report a same-sex sexual experience before arrival at the facility) are disproportionately incarcerated: the incarceration rate of is 1,882 per 100,000, more than three times that of the general population.[119] In the next chapter, prison sexual violence will be more fully explored and will be discussed as a part of the prisoner subculture; in this chapter we look at sexual minorities as a special population with unique issues and management concerns.

Non-heterosexual inmates are much more likely to be victimized in prison; they have an especially high risk of sexual victimization. In a national inmate survey, 12.2 percent of non-heterosexual people in prison and 8.5 percent of non-heterosexual people in jail reported inmate-on-inmate sexual assaults within the last 12 months, compared with 1.2 percent of straight inmates in both prisons and jails. With respect to staff sexual abuse, 5.4 percent of non-heterosexual people in prison reported victimization, compared with 2.1 percent of straight people in prison. Additionally, the survey shows that non-heterosexual victims are at least twice as likely to be subjected to sexual victimization by prison staff members. There were differences, however, between male and female sexual minorities. Men who self-identified as a sexual minority were more likely than straight men to be sexually victimized by staff and other inmates in both prisons and jails. Sexual minority women reported a greater risk of sexual assault compared to straight women by inmates but not by staff.[120] Prison authorities are supposed to screen for vulnerability to victimization upon entry into the prison, but these rates indicate that not enough is being done to protect sexually vulnerable inmates.

Male and female inmates also engage in consensual sexual acts with a same-sex partner, sometimes without self-identifying as gay, bi, or lesbian.[121] Officials punish consensual inmate sexual behavior in prison; gay and bi inmates are more likely to be scrutinized by correctional officers, leading to disproportional disciplinary infractions. It has been reported that the rate of HIV infection among the U.S. penal population is five times greater than that of the general population. The greatest risk for HIV transmission is consensual sex, yet prisons generally do not address this sexual health need (e.g., by providing education and condoms).[122]

In addition to disproportional victimization and prison discipline, among the identified problems of LGBTQ prisoners are the following:

- the refusal of prison officials to allow any LGBTQ literature;
- being confined to one housing unit comprised of sexual minorities or being placed in isolation for protection;
- restrictions on visitation of same-sex partners or differential restrictions on physical touching;
- parole denials rooted in homophobic attitudes; and
- being removed from coveted jobs within the prison because of sexual orientation.[123]

Equal protection challenges are not usually successful if prison authorities can show any security reasons for treating LGBTQ inmates differently.

Transgender inmates are especially vulnerable because states typically house these offenders according to their birth sex. Thus, for instance, one inmate who transitioned to be a woman at 18 years old has always been housed with men during her 25-year prison term despite her feminine appearance. The 2015 U.S. Transgender Survey found that transgender people were nine times more likely than the general prison population to be sexually assaulted by other inmates; other estimates are even higher.[124] An estimated 40 percent of transgender people in state and federal prisons report a sexual assault in the previous year.[125] In California, transgender women housed with men were 13 times more likely to be sexually assaulted than male prisoners in the same facilities.[126] In one study, researchers interviewed transgender inmates who had been released to ask them about their experience in prison. They relayed stories of constant taunting and harassment by inmates and staff and frequent sexual assaults.[127]

In *Farmer v. Brennan* (1994), the Supreme Court set the current standard governing prison officials' legal obligations toward protecting inmates from assault.[128] The case involved a transgender woman who was repeatedly sexually assaulted and beaten by other prisoners despite asking for protective custody. In that case, the Supreme Court stated that prison officials may be liable for violating the Eighth Amendment constitutional right to not be subject to cruel and unusual punishment when 1) the official showed "deliberate indifference" to the safety of the inmate by disregarding a known substantial risk, and 2) the injury the inmate incurred was severe. In the deliberate indifference standard, the official must know of and disregard an excessive risk to inmate health or safety. When a prisoner belongs to "an identifiable group of prisoners who are frequently singled out for violent attack by other inmates," such as being a sexual minority member, and officials know that the person is a member of such a group and therefore vulnerable, then failure to take adequate steps to protect them from abuse can violate the Constitution. This deliberate indifference standard applies to all inmates, not just transgender victims; however, it is a difficult standard to meet. Prisoners must prove not only that prison officials failed to take steps to stop or prevent abuse, but also that the officials knew that the abuse was likely to happen.[129]

Even if they are not assaulted, transgender inmates may be placed in solitary for their own protection, which can lead to psychological distress of a different kind. Although things are changing and transgender rights are beginning to be recognized, many facilities deny them access to gender-appropriate clothing or grooming items and punish them for attempting to express their gender identity.[130] Searches are especially problematic for transgender inmates when they are housed based on biological sex rather than gender identity. Guidance from the U.S. Department of Justice policies on searching transgender prisoners include providing transgender prisoners with an opportunity to indicate whether they would feel safer being searched by male or female staff, but these guidelines are not routinely followed in prisons.[131] Medical professionals generally agree that treatment for **gender dysphoria** (discomfort or distress due to a mismatch between biological sex and gender identity) is medically necessary; however, many agencies refuse to provide transitioning medical care (hormones and surgery). Federal courts have stated that a facility cannot have a blanket policy that prohibits specific types of treatments; however, they also have not recognized an absolute right to such medical services either.[132]

Summary

- There are about 2.3 million people in state prisons, federal prisons, juvenile correctional facilities, local jails, and other types of confinement facilities in the U.S. About 93 percent are men, and the most common age group is 24 to 34.

- Most prisoners (54 percent) were convicted of violent crimes; however, violent offenders comprise only about 20 percent of prison admissions.

- Prisoners are much less likely to have a high school diploma than the general U.S. population;

they earn 41 percent less; and they are more likely to have chronic health problems and be drug dependent than comparable groups in the general population.

- The number of state prisoners age 55 or older has increased since the early 1990s, and it is expected to continue to increase. Older prisoners have a more difficult time in prison because of age-related infirmities and health issues, which make them vulnerable to victimization.

- Those with mental health problems are more likely to have experienced childhood abuse and dysfunctional families, and are more likely to abuse drugs and exhibit drug dependency. The mentally ill are more likely than others to be involved in assaultive incidents in prison, both as victims and as assaulters; to receive all forms of disciplinary reports; and to recidivate.
- Suicide accounts for at least half of all deaths in prison, but suicides are more likely to occur in jails than in prisons. For men, the rate of suicide is about five to six times higher in prisons and jails than in the general U.S. population, and for women, the rate can be as much as 20 times higher.
- Up to 10 percent of prison populations can be defined as intellectually disabled.
- LGBTQ inmates are up to 10 times as likely to be sexually victimized as straight inmates. They face discriminatory treatment in many different areas.

PROJECTS

1. Go to your state's prison system webpage and determine the following: how many prisons are in your state, where they are located, how many inmates are incarcerated, and any demographic information you can find. Compare the prisoner demographic information to what you've read in this chapter.

2. Develop a set of guidelines as to how a prison should manage prisoners who are diagnosed with mental health disorders.

NOTES

1. T. Minton, L. Beatty and Z. Zeng, *Correctional Populations in the United States, 2019-Statistical Tables* (Washington, DC: Bureau of Justice Statistics, USDOJ, July 2021).

2. E. Carson, *Prisoners in 2019* (Washington, DC: Bureau of Justice Statistics, USDOJ, October 2020), 2.

3. E. Carson, *Prisoners in 2019* (Washington, DC: Bureau of Justice Statistics, USDOJ, October 2020), 9.

4. P. Wagner and B. Rabuy, *Mass Incarceration: The Whole Pie 2017*, Prison Policy Initiative, https://www.prisonpolicy.org/reports/pie2017.html.

5. E. Carson, *Prisoners in 2016* (Washington, DC: Bureau of Justice Statistics, USDOJ, January 2018).

6. E. Carson and W. Sabol, *Aging of the State Prison Population, 1993–2013* (Washington, DC: Bureau of Justice Statistics, USDOJ, 2016).

7. E. Carson and W. Sabol, *Aging of the State Prison Population, 1993–2013* (Washington, DC: Bureau of Justice Statistics, USDOJ, 2016).

8. *Felony Sentences in State Courts, 2006—Statistical Tables* (Washington, DC: USDOJ, Bureau of Justice Statistics, 2011), Table 1.1.

9. P. Wagner and B. Rabuy, *Mass Incarceration: The Whole Pie, 2017*, Prison Policy Initiative, https://www.prisonpolicy.org/reports/pie2017.html.

10. H. West, W. Sabol, and S. Greenman, *Prisoners in 2009* (Washington DC: Bureau of Justice Statistics, USDOJ, 2010), Table 8; E. Carson, *Prisoners in 2016* (Washington, DC: Bureau of Justice Statistics, USDOJ, January 2018), Table 8.

11. B. Rabuy and D. Kopf, *Prisons of Poverty: Uncovering the Pre-Incarceration Incomes of the Imprisoned*, Prison Policy Initiative, July 9, 2015, http://www.prisonpolicy.org/blog/2015/07/09/income_report/.

12. B. Pettit, *Invisible Men: Mass Incarceration and the Myth of Black Progress* (New York: Russell Sage Foundation, 2012), 16.

13. Lin, A., *Reform in the Making: The Implementation of Social Policy in Prison* (Princeton, NJ: Princeton University Press, 2000).

14. B. Rabuy and D. Kopf, *Prisons of Poverty: Uncovering the Pre-Incarceration Incomes of the Imprisoned*, Prison Policy Initiative, July 9, 2015, http://www.prisonpolicy.org/blog/2015/07/09/income_report/.

15. L. Maruschak and A. Beck, *Medical Problems of Inmates, 1997* (Washington DC: Bureau of Justice Statistics, USDOJ, 2001).

16. K. Kim and B. Peterson, *Aging Behind Bars: Trends and*

Implications of Graying Prisoners in the Federal System (New York: Urban Institute, 2014).

17. L. Maruschak and A. Beck, *Medical Problems of Inmates, 1997* (Washington DC: Bureau of Justice Statistics, USDOJ,2001).

18. L. Maruschak, *HIV in Prisons, 2005* (Washington, DC: Bureau of Justice Statistics, U.S. Dept. of Justice, 2007).

19. T. Herivel and P. Wright, *Prison Profiteers: Who Makes Money from Mass Incarceration?* (New York: The New Press, 2007).

20. L. Hawks, S. Woolhandler, and E. McCormick, "COVID-19 in Prisons and Jails in the United States," JAMA Network, August 8, 2020, https://jamanetwork.com/journals/jama/fullarticle/2768249; "A State-by-State Look at Coronavirus in Prisons," Marshall Project, 2020, retrieved November 28, 2020, from https://www.themarshallproject.org/2020/05/01/a-state-by-state-look-at-coronavirus-in-prisons; C. Standifer and F. Sellers, "Prisons and Jails Have Become a 'Public Health Threat' During the Pandemic, Advocates Say," *Washington Post*, November 11, 2020, https://www.washingtonpost.com/national/coronavirus-outbreaks-prisons/2020/11/11/b8c3a90c-d8d6-11ea-930e-d88518c57dcc_story.html.

21. M. Ward, M., "UT Calls for Independent Review of Prison Medical Care," *Austin American Statesman*, October 12, 2002.

22. *Coleman v. Wilson* (E.D. Cal 1995) 912 F. Supp. 1282; *Madrid v. Gomez* 889 F. Supp. 1146, 1206 (N.D. Cal 1995).

23. B. Schwartzapefel, "How Bad is Prison Health Care? Depends on Who's Watching?" The Marshall Project, February 26, 2018, retrieved December 30, 2018, https://www.themarshallproject.org/2018/02/25/how-bad-is-prison-health-care-depends-on-who-s-watching.

24. *ADAM II, 2013 Annual Report* (Washington, DC: Office of National Drug Control Policy, 2014), retrieved June 28, 2016, from https://www.whitehouse.gov/sites/default/files/ondcp/policy-and-research/adam_ii_2013_annual_report.pdf.

25. J. Karberg and D. James, *Substance Dependence, Abuse, and Treatment of Jail Inmates, 2002* (Washington, DC: Bureau of Justice Statistics, 2005).

26. F. Taxman and M. Perdoni, "A Case Study in Gaps in Services for Drug- Involved Offenders," in *Simulation Strategies to Reduce Recidivism: Risk Need Responsivity (RNR) Modeling for the Criminal Justice System* (New York: Springer, 2013), 21–40.

27. C. Mumola and J. Karberg, *Drug Use and Dependence, State and Federal Prisoners, 2004* (Washington, DC: Bureau of Justice Statistics, 2005), Table 6.

28. T. Feucht and J. Gfroerer, *Mental and Substance Use Disorders among Adult Men on Probation or Parole: Some Success against a Persistent Challenge* (Rockville, MD: Substance Abuse and Mental Health Services Administration, Center for Behavioral Health Statistics and Quality, 2011).

29. F. Taxman and M. Perdoni, "A Case Study in Gaps in Services for Drug- Involved Offenders," in *Simulation Strategies to Reduce Recidivism: Risk Need Responsivity (RNR) Modeling for the Criminal Justice System* (New York: Springer, 2013), 21–40.

30. *ADAM II, 2013 Annual Report* (Washington, DC: Office of National Drug Control Policy, 2014), retrieved June 28, 2016 from https://www.whitehouse.gov/sites/default/files/ondcp/policy-and-research/adam_ii_2013_annual_report.pdf.

31. F. Taxman and M. Perdoni, "A Case Study in Gaps in Services for Drug- Involved Offenders," in *Simulation Strategies to Reduce Recidivism: Risk Need Responsivity (RNR) Modeling for the Criminal Justice System* (New York: Springer, 2013), 21–40.

32. F.S. Taxman, A. Pattavina, M.S. Caudy, J. Byrne, and J. Durso, "The Empirical Basis for the RNR Model with an Updated RNR Conceptual Framework," in *Simulation Strategies to Reduce Recidivism: Risk Need Responsivity (RNR) Modeling for the Criminal Justice System*, eds. F. Taxman, A. Pattavina (New York: Springer, 2013), 73–111.

33. F. Butterfield, "Father Steals Best: Crime in an American Family," *New York Times*, retrieved Aug. 15, 2002, from www.nytimes.com/2002/08/21/national/21FAMI.html.

34. L. Glaze and L. Maruschak, *Parents in Prison and Their Minor Children* (Washington, DC: Bureau of Justice Statistics, USDOJ, 2008).

35. C. Harlow, *Selected Findings: Prior Abuse Reported by Inmates and Probationers* (Washington, DC: Bureau of Justice Statistics, USDOJ, 1999).

36. L Glaze and L. Maruschak, *Parents in Prison and Their Minor Children* (Washington, DC: Bureau of Justice Statistics, USDOJ, 2008).

37. L. Kazemian and J. Travis, "Imperative for Inclusion of Long Termers and Lifers in Research and Policy," *Criminology and Public Policy* 14, 2 (2015): 355–95.

38. M. Ollove, "Elderly Inmates Burden State Prisons," *Stateline*, March 17, 2016, retrieved from http://www.pewtrusts.org/en/

research-and-analysis/blogs/stateline/2016/03/17/elderly-inmates-burden-state-prisons.

39. S. Horwitz, "The Painful Price of Aging in Prison," *Washington Post*, May 2, 2015, retrieved February 5, 2019 from http://www.washingtonpost.com/sf/national/2015/05/02/the-painful-price-of-aging-in-prison/?utm_term=.ae3ed0db11db.

40. K. Kim and B. Peterson, *Aging Behind Bars: Trends and Implications of Graying Prisoners in the Federal System* (New York: Urban Institute, 2014).

41. *At America's Expense: The Mass Incarceration of the Elderly* (New York: American Civil Liberties Union), retrieved February 5, 2019 from https://www.aclu.org/report/americas-expense-mass-incarceration-elderly.

42. E. Carson and W. Sabol, *Aging of the State Prison Population, 1993–2013* (Washington, DC: Bureau of Justice Statistics, USDOJ, 2016); E. Carson, *Prisoners in 2019* (Washington, DC: Bureau of Justice Statistics, USDOJ) 15.

43. M. Chen, "Our Prison Population Is Getting Older and Older," *The Nation*, December 11, 2017, retrieved February 5, 2019 from https://www.thenation.com/article/our-prison-population-is-getting-older-and-older/.

44. T. Chiu, *It's About Time Aging Prisoners, Increasing Costs, and Geriatric Release* (New York: Vera Institute of Justice, 2010).

45. K. Kim and B. Peterson, *Aging Behind Bars: Trends and Implications of Graying Prisoners in the Federal System*, (New York: Urban Institute, 2014), 12.

46. *The High Cost of Low Risk: The Crisis of America's Aging Prison Population* (New York: Osborne Association, 2018), 11, retrieved from www.osborneny.org/aging.

47. T. Chiu, *It's About Time Aging Prisoners, Increasing Costs, and Geriatric Release*(New York: Vera Institute of Justice, 2010)..

48. E. Crawley and R. Sparks, "Is There Life After Imprisonment? How Elderly Men Talk about Imprisonment and Release," *Criminology and Criminal Justice*, 6, 1 (2006): 63–82.

49. J. Kerbs and J. Jolley, "A Commentary on Age Segregation for Older Prisoners Philosophical and Pragmatic Considerations for Correctional Systems," *Criminal Justice Review* 34, 1 (2009): 119–39.

50. H. Habes, "Paying for the Graying: How California Can More Effectively Manage Its Growing Elderly Inmate Population," *Southern California Interdisciplinary Law Journal*, 20, 2 (2011): 395–422.

51. L. Kazemian and J. Travis, "Imperative for Inclusion of Long Termers and Lifers in Research and Policy," *Criminology and Public Policy* 14, 2 (2015): 355–95.

52. J. Kerbs and J. Jolley, "Inmate-on-Inmate Victimization Among Older Male Prisoners," *Crime and Delinquency* 53, 2 (2007): 187–218.

53. S. Horwitz, "The Painful Price of Aging in Prison," *Washington Post*, May 2, 2015.

54. S. Horwitz, "The Painful Price of Aging in Prison," *Washington Post*, May 2, 2015.

55. S. Scaggs and W. Bales, "The Growth in the Elderly Inmate Prison Population: The Role of Determinate Punishment Policies," *Justice Research and Policy*, 16, 1 (2015): 99–118; M. McKillop and A. Boucher, "Aging Prison Populations Drive Up State Costs," Stateline.org., February 20, 2018, retrieved February 8, 2019 from https://www.pewtrusts.org/en/research-and-analysis/articles/2018/02/20/aging-prison-populations-drive-up-costs.

56. J. Kerbs and J. Jolley, "A Commentary on Age Segregation for Older Prisoners Philosophical and Pragmatic Considerations for Correctional Systems," *Criminal Justice Review* 34, 1 (2009): 119–39.

57. *Pennsylvania Department of Corrections v. Yeskey*, 524 U.S. 213 (1998).

58. J. Kerbs and J. Jolley, "A Commentary on Age Segregation for Older Prisoners Philosophical and Pragmatic Considerations for Correctional Systems," *Criminal Justice Review* 34, 1 (2009): 119–39.

59. K. Kim and B. Peterson, *Aging Behind Bars: Trends and Implications of Graying Prisoners in the Federal System*(New York: Urban Institute, 2014).

60. *The High Cost of Low Risk: The Crisis of America's Aging Prison Population* (New York: Osborne Association, 2018), retrieved from www.osborneny.org/aging.

61. *The High Cost of Low Risk: The Crisis of America's Aging Prison Population* (New York: Osborne Association, 2018), retrieved from www.osborneny.org/aging.

62. H. Steadman, E. Mulvey, J. Monahan, P. Robbins, P. Appelbaum, T. Grisso, L. Roth, and E. Silver, "Violence by People Discharged from Acute Psychiatric Inpatient Facilities and by Others in the Same Neighborhoods," *Archives of General Psychiatry* 55, 5 (May 1998): 393–401.

63. *Diagnostic and Statistical Manual of Mental Disorders, Fifth Edition* (Arlington, VA: American Psychiatric Association, 2013), http://dsm.psychiatryonline.org/book.aspx?bookid=556.

64. D. James and L. Glaze, *Mental Health Problems of Prison and Jail Inmates* (Washington, DC: Bureau of Justice Statistics, USDOJ, 2006).

65. J. Bronson and M. Berzofsky, *Indicators of Mental Health Problems Reported by Prisoners and Jail Inmates, 2011–12* (Washington, DC: Bureau of Justice Statistics, USDOJ, 2017), 1; also see R. Kessler, J. Green, M. Gruber, N. Sampson, E. Bromet, M. Cuitan, and A. Zaslavsky, "Screening For Serious Mental Illness in the General Population with the K6 Screening Scale: Results from the WHO World Mental Health Survey Initiative," *International Journal of Methods in Psychiatric Research*, 19 (2010): 4–22.

66. J. Bronson and M. Berzofsky, *Indicators of Mental Health Problems Reported by Prisoners and Jail Inmates, 2011–12* (Washington, DC: Bureau of Justice Statistics, USDOJ, 2017), 1.

67. K. Kim, M. Becker-Cohen, and M. Serakos, *The Processing and Treatment of Mentally Ill Persons in the Criminal Justice System*. (Washington DC: Urban Institute, 2015), 1.

68. D. James and L. Glaze, *Mental Health Problems of Prison and Jail Inmates* (Washington, DC: Bureau of Justice Statistics, USDOJ, 2006).

69. H. Steadman, F. Osher, P. Robbins, B. Case, and S. Samuels, "Prevalence of Serious Mental Illness Among Jail Inmates," *Psychiatric Services* 60, 6 (June 2009): 761–65.

70. B. Veysey, K. DeCou, and L. Prescott, "Effective Management of Female Jail Detainees with Histories of Physical and Sexual Abuse," *American Jails* (May/June, 1998): 50–63.

71. D. James and L. Glaze, *Mental Health Problems of Prison and Jail Inmates* (Washington, DC: Bureau of Justice Statistics, USDOJ, 2006).

72. J. Bronson and M. Berzofsky, *Indicators of Mental Health Problems Reported by Prisoners and Jail Inmates, 2011–12* (Washington, DC: Bureau of Justice Statistics, USDOJ, 2017).

73. *Ill-Equipped: U.S. Prisons and Offenders with Mental Illness* (New York: Human Rights Watch, 2003), 4; also available through website: http://www.hrw.org/en/reports/2003/10/21/ill-equipped.

74. D. James and L. Glaze, *Mental Health Problems of Prison and Jail Inmates* (Washington, DC: Bureau of Justice Statistics, USDOJ, 2006), 4.

75. A. Hochstetler, D. Murphy and R. Simons, "Damaged Goods: Exploring Predictors of Distress in Prison Inmates," *Crime & Delinquency* 50, 3 (2004): 436–57.

76. D. James and L. Glaze, *Mental Health Problems of Prison and Jail Inmates* (Washington, DC: Bureau of Justice Statistics, USDOJ, 2006).

77. See https://www.nimh.nih.gov/health/topics/depression/index.shtml.

78. *Ill-Equipped: U.S. Prisons and Offenders with Mental Illness*, (New York: Human Rights Watch, 2003).

79. K. Adams and J. Ferrandino, "Managing Mentally Ill Inmates in Prisons," *Criminal Justice and Behavior*, 35, 8: 913–27.

80. D. James and L. Glaze, *Mental Health Problems of Prison and Jail Inmates*, (Washington, DC: Bureau of Justice Statistics, USDOJ, 2006), 6.

81. P. Ditton, *Mental Health and Treatment of Inmates and Probationers* (Washington, DC: Bureau of Justice Statistics, 1999).

82. D. Regier, M. Farmer, D. Rae, B. Locke, S. Keith, L. Judd, and F. Goodwin, "Co-morbidity of Mental Disorders with Alcohol and Other Drug Abuse," *Journal of the American Medical Association* 264, 19 (1990): 2511–18.

83. T. Kupers, *Prison Madness: The Mental Health Crisis Behind Bars and What We Must Do About It* (San Francisco, CA: Jossey-Bass Publishing, 1999).

84. K. Adams and J. Ferrandino, "Managing Mentally Ill Inmates in Prisons," *Criminal Justice and Behavior*, 35, 8: 913–27, 918.

85. P. Ditton, P., *Mental Health and Treatment of Inmates and Probationers* (Washington, DC: Bureau of Justice Statistics, 1999).

86. *Ill-Equipped: U.S. Prisons and Offenders with Mental Illness*, (New York: Human Rights Watch, 2003), 39.

87. D. James and L. Glaze, *Mental Health Problems of Prison and Jail Inmates* (Washington, DC: Bureau of Justice Statistics, USDOJ, 2006), 10.

88. P. Ditton, *Mental Health and Treatment of Inmates and Probationers* (Washington, DC: Bureau of Justice Statistics, 1999).

89. Reported in K. Kim, K. M. Becker-Cohen, M. Serakos. *The Processing and Treatment of Mentally Ill Persons in the Criminal Justice System* (Washington DC: Urban Institute, 2015)., 18.

90. R. Cramer, H. Wechsler, S. Miller, and E. Yenne, "Suicide Prevention in Correctional Settings: Current Standards and Recommendations for Research, Prevention, and Training," *Journal of Correctional Health Care* 23, 3 (2017): 313–28.

91. K. Blakinger. "Prison Suicides Have Been Rising for Years. Experts Fear the Pandemic Has Made it Worse." The Marshall Project, Aug. 12, 2021, retrieved from https://www.nbcnews.com/news/us-news/prison-suicides-have-been-rising-years-experts-fear-pandemic-has-n1276563.

92. M. Sainato, "Deaths Behind Bars Spur Concerns Across the U.S.," *The Crime Report*, May 28, 2019, retrieved July 31, 2019 from https://thecrimereport.org/2019/05/28/deaths-behind-bars-spur-concerns-across-the-u-s/.

93. "Preventing Suicide in Prison Inmates," www.psychiatryadvisor.com., 2017, https://www.psychiatryadvisor.com/suicide-and-self-harm/preventing-suicide-in-jail-prison-inmates/article/719501/.

94. "Preventing Suicide in Prison Inmates," www.psychiatryadvisor.com., 2017, https://www.psychiatryadvisor.com/suicide-and-self-harm/preventing-suicide-in-jail-prison-inmates/article/719501/.

95. H. Smith, R. Kaminskia, J. Power, and K. Slade, "Self-Harming Behaviors in Prison: A Comparison of Suicidal Processes, Self-Injurious Behaviors, and Mixed Events," *Criminal Justice Studies* 32, no. 3 (2019): 264–86.

96. "Preventing Suicide in Prison Inmates," www.psychiatryadvisor.com., 2017, https://www.psychiatryadvisor.com/suicide-and-self-harm/preventing-suicide-in-jail-prison-inmates/article/719501/.

97. H. Smith, R. Kaminskia, J. Power, and K. Slade, "Self-Harming Behaviors in Prison: A Comparison of Suicidal Processes, Self-Injurious Behaviors, And Mixed Events," *Criminal Justice Studies* 32, no. 3 (2019): 264–86.

98. H. Smith, R. Kaminskia, J. Power, and K. Slade, "Self-Harming Behaviors in Prison: A Comparison of Suicidal Processes, Self-Injurious Behaviors, And Mixed Events," *Criminal Justice Studies* 32, no. 3 (2019): 264–86.

99. "Preventing Suicide in Jails and Prisons, 2007," retrieved June 1, 2018, from http://www.who.int/mental_health/prevention/suicide/resource_jails_prisons.pdf; Also see R. Bonner, "Stressful Segregation Housing and Psychosocial Vulnerability in Prison Suicide Ideators," *Suicide and Life-Threatening Behavior* 36, 2 (2006): 250–54.

100. "Preventing Suicide in Prison Inmates," www.psychiatryadvisor.com., 2017, https://www.psychiatryadvisor.com/suicide-and-self-harm/preventing-suicide-in-jail-prison-inmates/article/719501/.

101. "Preventing Suicide in Jails and Prisons," World Health Organization, retrieved June 1, 2018, from http://www.who.int/mental_health/prevention/suicide/resource_jails_prisons.pdf.

102. R. Cramer, H. Wechsler, S. Miller, and E. Yenne, "Suicide Prevention in Correctional Settings: Current Standards and Recommendations for Research, Prevention, and Training," *Journal of Correctional Health Care* 23, 3 (2017): 313–28.

103. A. Liebling, "Vulnerability and Prison Suicide," *British Journal of Criminology*, 2 (1995): 173–87.

104. A. Liebling, "Vulnerability and Prison Suicide," *British Journal of Criminology*, 2 (1995): 173–87.

105. R. Cramer, H. Wechsler, S. Miller, and E. Yenne, "Suicide Prevention in Correctional Settings: Current Standards and Recommendations for Research, Prevention, and Training," *Journal of Correctional Health Care* 23, 3 (2017): 313–28.

106. R. Cramer, H. Wechsler, S. Miller, and E. Yenne, "Suicide Prevention in Correctional Settings: Current Standards and Recommendations for Research, Prevention, and Training," *Journal of Correctional Health Care* 23, 3 (2017): 313–28.

107. L. Glenn, *Texas Prisons: The Largest Hotel Chain in Texas* (Austin, TX: Eakin Press, 2001), 272.

108. J. Bronson and M. Berzofsky, *Indicators of Mental Health Problems Reported by Prisoners and Jail Inmates, 2011–12* (Washington, DC: Bureau of Justice Statistics, USDOJ, 2017).

109. Studies reported in F. Osher, D. D'Amora, M. Plotkin, N. Jarrett and A. Eggleston, *Adults with Behavioral Health Needs under Correctional Supervision: A Shared Framework for Reducing Recidivism and Promoting Recovery* (New York, NY: Council of State Governments Justice Center, 2012).

110. "There May be no Worse Place for Mentally Ill People to Receive Treatment than Prison," *Boston Globe*, The Spotlight Team, November 25, 2016, retrieved from https://apps.bostonglobe.com/spotlight/the-desperate-and-the-dead/series/prisons/.

111. 503 F. Supp. 1265 (S.D. Tex. 1980)

112. F. Osher, D. D'Amora, M. Plotkin, N. Jarrett and

A. Eggleston, *Adults with Behavioral Health Needs under Correctional Supervision: A Shared Framework for Reducing Recidivism and Promoting Recovery*(New York, NY: Council of State Governments Justice Center, 2012).

113. H. Steadman, J. Morrissey, and T. Parker, T, "When Political Will is Not Enough: Jails, Communities, and Persons with Mental Disorders," *The Prison Journal* 96, 1 (2016): 10–26.

114. H. Steadman, J. Morrissey, and T. Parker, "When Political Will is Not Enough: Jails, Communities, and Persons with Mental Disorders," *The Prison Journal* 96, 1 (2016): 10–26.

115. Reported in K. Kim, K. M. Becker-Cohen, and M. Serakos, *The Processing and Treatment of Mentally Ill Persons in the Criminal Justice System*(Washington DC: Urban Institute, 2015)., 31–32.

116. Definition provided by the American Association on Intellectual and Developmental Disabilities: http://aaidd.org/intellectual-disability/definition/faqs-on-intellectual-disability#.VF7YHfTF-iI.

117. J. Petersilia, "Justice for All? Offenders with Mental Retardation and the California Corrections System," *The Prison Journal*, 77, 4 (1997): 358–80.

118. *Reimagining Prison* (New York: Vera Institute of Justice, 2018).

119. I. Meyer, A. Flores, L. Stemple, A. Romero, B. Wilson, and J. Herman, "Incarceration Rates and Traits of Sexual Minorities in the United States: National Inmate Survey, 2011–2012," *Transgender Health* 107, 2 (2017): 234–40.

120. A. Beck, *Victimization in Prisons and Jails Reported by Inmates, 2011–12* (Washington, DC: Bureau of Justice Statistics, U.S. Dept of Justice), 30–31; Giovanna Shay, "PREA's Elusive Promise: Can DOJ Regulations Protect LGBT Incarcerated People?" *Loyola Journal of Public Interest Law* 15 (2014): 343-56; I. Meyer, A. Flores, L. Stemple, A. Romero, B. Wilson, and J. Herman, "Incarceration Rates and Traits of Sexual Minorities in the United States: National Inmate Survey, 2011–2012," *Transgender Health* 107, no. 2 (2017): 234–40.

121. C. Hensley, *Prison Sex: Policy and Practice* (Boulder, CO, and London: Lynne Rienner Publishers, 2002); C. Hensley, R. Tewksbury, and J. Wright, J., "Exploring the Dynamics of Masturbation and Consensual Same-Sex Activity Within a Male Maximum Security Prison," *The Journal of Men's Studies* 10, no. 1 (2001) 59–71.

122. C. Lea, T. Gideonse, and N. Harawa, "An Examination of Consensual Sex In a Men's Jail," *International Journal of Prisoner Health* 14, 1 (2018): 56–62.

123. M. McNamara, "Better to Be Out in Prison Than Out in Public: LGBTQ Prisoners Receive More Constitutional Protection If They Are Open About Their Sexuality While in Prison," *Law and Sexuality*, 23 (2014): 134–54.

124. K. Sosin, "At San Quentin, LGBTQ Prisoners and Once-Biased Inmates Try To Heal Together," NBC News, May 26, 2019, retrieved Oct. 5, 2019, from https://www.nbcnews.com/feature/nbc-out/san-quentin-lgbtq-prisoners-once-biased-inmates-try-heal-together-n1010026.

125. A.J. Beck, *Sexual Victimization in Prisons and Jails Reported by Inmates, 2011–12: Supplemental Tables: Prevalence of Sexual Victimization Among Transgender Adult Inmates* (Washington, DC: Bureau of Justice Statistics, 2014),; A.J. Beck, M. Berzofsky, R. Caspar, and C. Krebs, *Sexual Victimization in Prisons and Jails Reported by Inmates, 2011–12* (Washington, DC: Bureau of Justice Statistics, 2013).

126. V. Jenness, C.L. Maxson, K.N. Matsuda, and J.M. Sumner, J. M., *Violence in California Correctional Facilities: An Empirical Examination of Sexual Assault* (Irvine, CA: Center for Evidence-Based Corrections, 2009), 3; also see T. Maschi, J. Rees, and E. Klein, "Coming Out" of Prison: An Exploratory Study of LGBT Elders in the Criminal Justice System," *Journal Of Homosexuality* 63, no. 9 (2016): 1277–95.

127. T. Maschi, J. Rees, and E. Klein, "'Coming Out' of Prison: An Exploratory Study of LGBT Elders in the Criminal Justice System," *Journal of Homosexuality* 63, no. 9 (2016): 1277–95.

128. *Farmer v. Brennan*, 511 U.S. 825, 837 (1994).

129. A. Liptak, "Inmate Was Considered 'Property' of Gange, Witness Tells Jury in Prison Rape Lawsuit," *New York Times*, Sept. 25, 2005, A14.

130. "LGBTQ People Behind Bars: A Guide to Understanding the Issues Facing Transgender Prisoners and their Legal Rights," National Center for Transgender Rights.

N.D., retrieved Oct. 10, 2019, from https://transequality.org/sites/default/files/docs/resources/TransgenderPeopleBehind Bars.pdf.

131. Giovanna Shay, "PREA's Elusive Promise: Can DOJ Regulations Protect LGBT Incarcerated People?" *Loyola Journal of Public Interest Law* 15 (2014): 343–56.

132. "LGBTQ People Behind Bars: A Guide to Understanding the Issues Facing Transgender Prisoners and their Legal Rights," National Center for Transgender Rights. N.D., retrieved Oct. 10, 2019, from https://transequality.org/sites/default/files/docs/resources/TransgenderPeople BehindBars.pdf.

Chapter 8

Prisoner Subculture

LEARNING OBJECTIVES

1. Define prisonization and identify the elements of the prison subculture.

2. Compare the two theories of the development of prisoner subcultures: the importation and deprivation theories.

3. Discuss the prevalence of and factors related to violence in prison.

4. Describe the prevalence of and factors related to sexual violence in prison.

5. Describe the various types of adjustment to prison.

CHAPTER OUTLINE

- Prison Subculture **212**
- Prison Violence **217**
- Adjusting to Prison Life **228**
- SUMMARY **230**

When an inmate enters prison, he or she undergoes prisonization, a concept that refers to the socialization and adherence of the prisoner to the prison subculture.

KEY TERMS

Correlate
Deprivation theory
Importation theory
Inmate code
Powder keg theory

Power vacuum theory
Prison argot
Prison Rape Elimination Act
  (PREA)
Prisonization

Relative deprivation/rising
  expectation theory

 # Prison Subculture

In this chapter we will discuss the prisoner subculture and how prisoners adapt to prison life. When an inmate enters prison, he or she undergoes **prisonization**, a concept that refers to the socialization and adherence of the prisoner to the prison subculture. The prisoner subculture is composed of values, rules and norms, prison argot, and inmate typologies. In most prisons, the influence of prison gangs is a strong element of the subculture. We will discuss the prevalence and correlates of prison violence, as well as ways to reduce violence.

Today's prison subculture is similar in some ways to the very earliest descriptions of prison subculture. Accounts from the 1940s through the early 1960s described a prison social order where inmates and guards avoided each other. This is still true today, and inmates who are perceived to be too friendly with correctional officers are distrusted. The inmate hierarchy, as described by early researchers (see Focus on History: Early Prison Research) indicated that "right guys" (organized crime bosses and bank robbers) were at the top of the social hierarchy with child molesters at the bottom. Child molesters are still at the bottom of the prison social order, but gang leaders, major drug dealers, and anyone who has the skills or connections to get goods or services in prison are at the top of the social hierarchy today. In early descriptions of prison subcultures, there was an "honor among thieves" social norm, at least as an ideal, asserting that inmates should not exploit each other. Today, there doesn't seem to be any remnants of this ideal, and the norm is to protect one's own interests and expect nothing from fellow inmates.

Importation and Deprivation Theories

Gresham Sykes, one of the first sociologists to describe the prison world, explained that the culture of a prison was a direct result of the deprivations inmates experienced.[1] This was called **deprivation theory**, and it explained why certain circumstances existed in the prison environment; for example, homosexuality occurred because of the deprivation of the opposite sex; the black market developed because of the deprivation of autonomy and goods and services; and so on. Later research through the 1960s and 1970s tested and expanded on these original ideas. For instance, it was hypothesized and proven that maximum-security institutions have stronger subcultures because these prisons are less permeable and have more deprivations.

Other researchers, however, noted that many of the elements of the prison subculture appeared to be imported from the street, which led to

Although there are scattered historical records of prisons and jails in the late 1800s and early 1900s, the sociological study of prisons began in earnest in the 1930s and 1940s. One early sociological analysis of the social world of prisoners was conducted by Hans Reimer, a graduate of the University of Chicago. For his study, he was voluntarily committed to Kansas State Penitentiary in 1936. Almost all court and prison officials were unaware of the nature or purpose of his prison commitment, so he was treated and lived like all other prisoners. In his description of the prison, he wrote that the prison population was largely controlled by two groups. The "politicians" were inmates who had positions or connections that allowed them to distribute special benefits or privileges. The other group was made up of the "right guys," trustworthy criminal leaders who never abused or took advantage of other inmates and were loyal to the interests of the convicts.

In the 1940s, other descriptions of prisons came from University of Washington professor Norman Hayner and his students. One student, Ellis Ash, spent four months at a Washington reformatory as a researcher. With Hayner as co-author, Ash published a study in 1949, describing the prison as a community with an inherent conflict and hostility between "screws" (guards) and "cons" (prisoners). Their main thesis was that the prison did not prepare prisoners for release because it was not a prosocial community. Another student of Hayner's, Clarence Schrag, worked as a classification officer in a prison while he collected data for his study of the prison social world, which resulted in one of the earliest and best-known typologies, or categorization of prisoners into identifiable types:

- "Con politician"—an articulate inmate who interacted with the administration in a manipulative manner to further his own interests;
- "Outlaw"—a prisoner who used violence to get what he wanted;
- "Square john"—a middle-class offender who was not part of the criminal subculture and not trusted by others;
- "Right guy"—a career criminal who subscribed wholly to a criminal lifestyle and who was either an organized crime member or a bank robber.

Schrag explained that these types of inmates would have different potential for recidivism, with the square john the least likely to recidivate and the right guy the most likely to recidivate. Indeed, later studies found that one's adherence to the prisoner subculture was negatively correlated with success upon release.

In 1954, sociologist Gresham Sykes published *The Society of Captives*, a seminal work in the identification and description of the prisoner subculture. Sykes identified more prisoner roles than did Schrag, although several were similar. In addition to his typology of prisoners, Sykes is known for the idea that the "pains of imprisonment" (the deprivation of sex, freedom, safety, etc.) give rise to elements of the prison subculture. For instance, the deprivation of sex leads to sexual assault, the deprivation of safety leads to the formation of gangs, and so on.

Sources:

D. Clemmer, The Prison Community (Boston: The Christopher Publishing House, 1940).

N. Hayner and E. Ash, "The Prison as a Community," American Sociological Review 5 (1940): 577–83.

D. Mears, E. Stewart, S. Siennick, and R. Simons, "The Code of the Street and Inmate Violence: Investigating the Salience of Imported Belief Systems," Criminology 51 (2013): 695–728.

F. Haynes, "The Sociological Study of the Prison Community," The Journal of Criminal Law and Criminology 39, 4 (1949): 432–40.

H. Reimer, "Socialization in the Prison Community," Proceedings of the 67th Annual Conference of the American Prison Association 1 (1937): 151–55.

C. Schrag, Social Types in a Prison Community, Unpublished M.S. Thesis, University of Washington, 1944; C. Schrag, "A Preliminary Criminal Typology," Sociological Perspectives, 4, 1 (1961): 11–16.

G. Sykes, The Society of Captives (Princeton, NJ: Princeton University Press, 1958).

the **importation theory** of prisoner subculture. Researchers, including former-prisoner-turned-sociologist John Irwin, presented evidence that the prison culture was not purely a creation of deprivation. Rather, many aspects of the culture came from the street.[2] Importation theorists noted, for instance, that the street drug culture beginning in the late 1960s had found its way into prison, both in terms of types of prisoners and in changing values. Drug offenders did not have entrenched criminal identities, nor were they socialized to the criminal underworld on the street; therefore, they showed less adherence to codes of conduct. The entry of different types of offenders also meant that they did not defer to status hierarchies whereby certain inmates were respected because of their crimes or associations. The influx of drug offenders led to increased drug use, and ultimately increased prison violence, which we will discuss later in the chapter.

By the 1990s, researchers came to the common-sense conclusion that both theories helped explain prison subculture. Additionally, the type of prison affects the degree of influence of the subculture with harsher, more isolated prisons having a stronger subculture, and those with more outside contacts and a transitory population having a weaker subculture. Prisoner populations can also influence a prison subculture. Prisons housing chronic offenders with long criminal histories have a different culture than facilities with more first-time offenders. In maximum security prisons with repeat offenders with long sentences, the social distance between inmates and correctional officers is more extreme. Those who are considered "rats" are much more likely to be violently punished, and there is a more organized black market.[3]

Prisoner Typologies and the Inmate Code

As we discussed in the Focus on History, early prison researchers classified inmates by social types. These typologies help make sense of the prison world in terms of who has power and who is more likely to be prosocial or antisocial. The original typologies have not been updated, although modern researchers have added types. For instance, one description separates all prisoners into "convicts," those who adhere to the prisoner subculture, and "inmates," those who do not (e.g., square johns).[4] Another researcher described the types associated with prison gangs: shot-caller (leader), lieutenant (second-in-command), soldiers (gang members), associates (not members but will fight with the gang), and prospects (inmates who are being recruited into the gang).[5]

The **inmate code**, first described by prison researchers in the 1940s, refers to the informal rules by which all inmates lived and included the following:

- Don't snitch.
- Don't exploit other inmates.
- Be cool.
- Do your own time.
- Be tough.
- Never talk to a screw [guard].[6]

A more recent prisoner-author's description of the informal rules of prison illustrates that some elements of the modern inmate code are very similar to the code from decades earlier:

- Don't snitch.
- Don't borrow.
- Don't mess with homosexuals.

- Don't "see," don't "hear," don't "say."
- Don't gossip.
- Watch who you walk with.
- Don't debate PRS (politics, religion, sports).[7]

Recent accounts of prison culture suggest that the inmate code and its rules are, for the most part, designed to keep conflict to a minimum in order to keep correctional authorities from interfering in inmates' lives. Shot-callers (either gang leaders or others who hold informal leadership roles over other prisoners) use the threat of violence to control their own members. Large scale race riots may be avoided when prisoner leaders punish their own members for disrespecting a member from a different racial gang. More generally, there are specific rules unique to each prison regarding interactions, for example, television watching, and prisoners are kept in line to avoid conflict that would involve everyone. One inmate described the code as follows:

> There are so many rules about who goes first in line for meals and who gets the TV first. If you follow all these rules, you end up doing easy time. I was a con which means I follow the code so you have to know the rules and you have to teach the new guys how to be a con and follow the rules.[8]

Accounts of prison life also note that rules against snitching are routinely broken, and gossip and not paying debts are also routine.[9] As in the free world, social norms are sometimes ideals or aspirations of behavior, with actual behavior often not living up to the ideals.[10]

Prison Argot

As with all cultures and subcultures, language is an important and defining aspect, and this holds true for prison subculture. **Prison argot** is the unique language of prisoners. Prison argot is dynamic, and as words find their way into the lexicon of the larger society, prisoners continue to reinvent their own vocabulary. Words such as snitch, hack, con, and others originated in the prison. The importance of a concept is reflected by the number of words used to define it; for instance, the prison snitch, the prison guard, and, especially, drugs have many words to describe them. Use of argot is an indication of familiarity and identification with a subculture. Outsiders don't use the words and sometimes don't even know what they mean.[11] Prison slang terms are used to describe the black market, sex, scams, and types of food.[12] Women in prison use similar terms to the ones men use, but also have some that are unique to their environment, such as these from Texas prisoners: "spit boxing" (arguing), RPGs ("rape prevention goggles," referring to the black-framed, state-issued eyeglasses), and "ho bath" (washing in the sink rather than a shower).[13]

Jimmy Lerner, a white-collar executive who was sentenced to prison for murder, described the prison from the perspective of a "fish," a newly arrived inmate.[14] Once in prison, he became a "lawdog," since he had a college education and could help other inmates interpret court papers. Soon, he adopted the prison slang into his vocabulary, including

- "dawgs" (friends, associates, acquaintances)
- "queens" (homosexual men who dress like women)
- "punks" (the sexually victimized or anyone who is taken advantage of)
- "woods" (from "peckerwoods," a name for whites)

- "toads" (a derogatory name for whites)
- "shot-callers" (prisoners who had some power)
- "wiggers" (whites who associated with Blacks)
- "fishcops" (new COs)
- "yard trick" (one who carried contraband and did menial labor for others)
- "old heads" (older cons who liked to talk about the old days in prison)
- "heartcheck" (a challenge where one must show a willingness to fight)
- "full sleeves" (many tattoos), and
- "kites" (requests to see a counselor or go to sick call, from the phrase "go fly a kite," meaning there was a good chance nothing would happen in response to the request).

Prison Gangs

Prison gangs are part of the social organization of a prison, and gang norms influence the inmate code, albeit in a greater or lesser degree depending on how prevalent gang activity is in a particular prison. Gang culture in prison has become almost synonymous with prisoner subculture, and the norms of street gangs are imported to prison; prison gang norms have reciprocally permeated street culture as well. There is a strong focus on strength and the use of violence to achieve respect, as in the street; however, norms also protect and facilitate business interests by holding racial and other conflict in check. In prison, despite racial and inter-gang hostility, most gangs will sell drugs to gang members from other racial groups.[15]

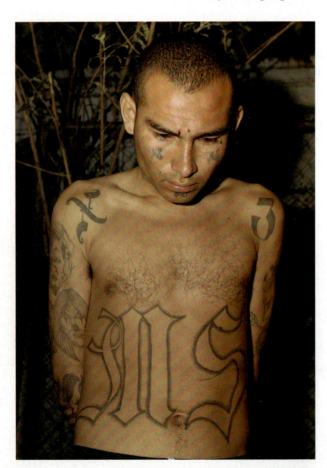

The prisoner subculture is heavily influenced by prison gangs.

Prison gangs originally formed and grew during the Black Power movement and street activism of the 1960s, but quickly dropped their political agendas and took over prison black markets. Lucrative drug markets encouraged the rise of race-based prison gangs who had no compunction against using violence to protect members and their control of drug markets in prison. In California, Texas, and Illinois, gangs such as the Mexican Mafia, the Texas Syndicate, La Nuestra Familia, and the Black Guerrilla Family have taken over prison drug markets and force inmates to join or be victimized by the gang.[16] White prisoners responded to the threat of gang victimization by forming gangs of their own, usually with some neo-Nazi element, such as the Aryan Brotherhood and the Nazi Lowriders. However, white prisoners are still less likely to belong to any gang than minority prisoners.[17]

Today, prison gangs have more to do with making money rather than racial identity. Gangs largely control the black-market economy in prisons and may partner with other gangs if it is good for business. Gangs have members in and outside the prison, and the gang facilitates the entry of drugs, cellphones, and other contraband. In some known instances, gangs "groomed" members who applied for and were hired as correctional officers in order to facilitate drug smuggling into the prison.[18]

Obviously, prison officials view gangs as a serious management challenge. Researchers estimate that about 13 percent of jail populations and 17 percent of state prisoners are gang members but admit that they have little information on prevalence because of the disinclination of prisoners to self-identify as gang members and the secrecy regarding information gathered by gang intelligence officers. Other estimates suggest that gang members constitute anywhere from 0 to nearly 50 percent of the inmate population, depending on the population studied; for instance, gang membership is more prevalent in administrative segregation and supermax populations and less so in lower-custody-level institutions. Yet another estimate puts membership at 19 percent of the state prison population.[19] Prison gang membership is more prevalent in states that have a greater number of street gang members: Illinois, California, Colorado, New Mexico, and Nevada have high per capita figures of gang membership.[20] Prison gangs have been found to be more organized and more racially and ethnically homogenous than street gangs.[21]

Gang membership is associated with higher rates of prison misconduct, and gang members also have higher rates of victimization than non–gang members.[22] Researchers report that gangs are responsible for 43 to 80 percent of prison violence.[23] Prison officials attempt to prevent gang violence by identifying gang members as they enter prison, often isolating gang leaders in administrative segregation or transferring them to supermax prisons, even if they have not yet been guilty of any prison misconduct. Prison officials also sometimes transfer gang members out of state to disrupt communication and dominance. Correctional administrators admit that nothing is completely successful in stopping gang violence or the practice of prison gangs recruiting members.[24] Gang members pose difficult correctional challenges, since research shows that criminal value systems are strong and gang members are more likely to recidivate than non–gang-members.[25]

Prison Violence

The culture of hypermasculinity, a pervasive black market that creates debts and opportunities for extortion and theft, gangs, crowded conditions, boredom and lack of programming, and the importance of reputation and not being perceived as a victim all contribute to the likelihood of violent incidents occurring in prison. Researchers have described how violence is a part of the subculture and can be seen partly as an extension of the "code of the street," which also emphasizes a hypermasculine status hierarchy where honor must be protected by the use of violence.[26]

Prison violence includes the following types of violence:

- intrapersonal (e.g., self-mutilation, suicide attempts);
- interpersonal (sexual, physical, or psychological);
- group (gang activity or loose associations);
- organized (riots or organized attacks on officers); and
- institutional (beatings or other physical or emotional harm inflicted by officers).[27]

Prison violence has been described in terms of following several "scripts" that typically play out in violent incidents. For example, retaliation is a common theme: inmates who feel victimized punish the person who threatened or

Violence is a part of the prisoner subculture.

harmed them in some way; another example is respect, where inmates feel compelled to respond to slights or verbal insults with violence. Research has found that there was significant overlap between victims and offenders in assaults that derived from respect issues; however, there was not much overlap in violence associated with robberies and extortion.[28] In this section, we will discuss the prevalence of violence in prison, correlates of violence, and the different types of violence that are predominant in prison.

Prevalence of Violence

The inmate code and other aspects of the prison subculture were relatively stable until the 1960s. However, the entry of drug offenders, a younger prisoner population, and politicized Blacks changed the prison world.[29] The influx of drug offenders led to increased drug use, which contributed to rising prison violence in several ways:

- some drugs (e.g., PCP) induced violent behavior;
- prison gangs and dealers used violence against drug debtors; and
- dealers used violence or the threat of violence to coerce other inmates and their families to participate in drug smuggling.

Prison researchers during the 1950s barely mentioned Black prisoners. Their relative absence from prison writings changed with the rise of the Civil Rights Movement in the 1960s, the war on drugs, and mass incarceration. The Black Power movement of the 1960s and 1970s resulted in political awareness and opposition, leading to increased conflict, racial strain, and violence with other inmates and prison administrators. The killing of George Jackson, a Black Panther activist, at San Quentin in 1971 during a botched escape attempt became a rallying cry for collective violence by Black prisoners. The 1971 Attica prison riot, one of the most notorious prison riots in history, was said to be partially influenced by George Jackson's killing, along with inmate demands for better conditions. Up until the 1960s, prisons were racially segregated by policy, and prisoners had always self-segregated in the yard and mess halls, but eventually court holdings forced state systems to desegregate.[30] The only research that has directly measured the impact of court-imposed desegregation and violence found that cell integration (requiring Black and white inmates to cell together) did not increase violence.[31] Racial gangs, however, have been associated with retaliatory and instrumental violence by prison administrations and researchers alike. Racial strain and violence continued to increase in the 1980s, fueled in part by the rise of prison gangs.

In the 1980s, the prisoner population explosion and the upheaval of social norms in prison strained resources and exacerbated existing tensions, resulting in predictable conflict. For instance, in Texas, the number of prison homicides increased from 16 during the period 1970–1978 to 52 during 1984–1985; additionally, there were 641 non-fatal stabbings.[32] Officer-on-inmate violence escalated as well during the same time period in Texas prisons. In 1984, 200 disciplinary actions were taken against officers who had used excessive force.[33] Violence also increased in Walpole Prison in Massachusetts, a prison in Rhode Island, and Pennsylvania's Graterford prison.[34] Beginning in the mid-1990s, however, prison violence seemed to follow the downward trend of violent street crime. Analysts proposed that prisons were brought under control by able administrators and good management skills.[35]

More recently, in some states prison violence is increasing. For example, although the prisoner population in South Carolina is decreasing, violence has increased: in 2017, 12 inmates were murdered by other inmates and six killed themselves. These fatalities far exceed previous years; for instance, there were only two deaths in 2009. There were also 250 assaults that required taking inmates to outside hospitals in 2016 and 2017, more than double the number in the previous two years. Attacks on correctional officers have also increased. Reported reasons for the increase in violence are gangs and a shortage of correctional officers.[36]

In North Carolina, a shortage of correctional officers and lax security were cited as contributing factors in the deaths of four workers at Pasquotank Correctional Institution in 2017. Within the facility, a sewing plant that employs inmates operated with poor security measures, allowing inmates to check out and hide hammers, scissors, and other tools that could be used as weapons. In a botched escape attempt, four inmates were charged in the stabbing and beating deaths of two correctional officers, a plant manager, and a maintenance worker. All four of the inmates were in prison for violent crimes, including shooting a state trooper, stabbing a woman, and shooting a coworker to death. According to a federal report, about one-quarter of the officer positions at the prison were vacant at the time of the escape attempt, which led to lax security and poor oversight.[37]

Violent incident reporting is highly subject to reporting discrepancies, and there is no national database to track longitudinal trends.[38] The Bureau of Justice Statistics tracks state and federal prison deaths; the percentage of all deaths in prison by homicide increased from 1.4 percent in 2001 to 2.4 percent in 2014. The percentage of deaths by suicide increased from 5.9 percent in 2001 to 7.1 percent in 2014. Almost all other deaths were from illness (87 percent), with cancer and heart disease accounting for more than half.[39]

Academic studies of prison violence use inmate surveys to estimate prevalence. One study found that 48 percent of respondents reported some type of victimization.[40] Another study of both male and female inmates from 12 prisons in a single state found that more than three-quarters of male inmates and 80 percent of female inmates reported one or two types of victimizations. The most common victimization reported was theft.[41] Theft and extortion are pervasive in most prisons. Theft can lead to assault, and extortion involves the threat of violence to gain goods. One prisoner-author's firsthand account of life in prison asserts that "beat-down crews" use violence or the threat of violence to rob fellow inmates.[42]

Although physical assaults occur less often than theft, they are not rare. In the multi-prison study described previously, about 20 percent of female inmates and 25 percent of male inmates reported being assaulted during their sentence, and a third of men and a quarter of women reported physical victimization within the previous six-month period. Most inmates did not report these victimizations to prison officials.[43] Table 8.1 shows findings from the same study and illustrates that women reported more physical victimization from other inmates than did men when a general question was asked (e.g., have you ever been physically assaulted by another inmate), and only slightly less than men when specific questions were asked (e.g., have you ever been hit; have you ever been stabbed; etc.).

Another study found that 32 percent of a prisoner sample reported being sexually or physically victimized or a victim of property crime in the previous year. About 16 percent of the respondents had been victimized by staff, and 24 percent reported inmate perpetrators.[44] In a different survey of 5,640 inmates from 46 prisons in Ohio and Kentucky, researchers found that 7 percent of respondents had been physically assaulted by another inmate in the previous six months. Prevalence of victimization varied by prison with a range of 1–17 percent of inmates reporting being victimized.[45] The Bureau of Justice Statistics conducted a nationally representative survey of 91,177 inmates housed in 233 state and federal prisons and 358 local jails during 2011–2012, reporting that 13 percent of prison respondents and 17 percent of jail respondents had been involved in a physical altercation with another inmate (or staff member) in the previous year.[46] Thus, reported physical victimization ranges from 1 to 33 percent, with differences probably due to type of methodology, type of prison, and the target period.

| **TABLE 8.1** | **Six-Month Prevalence of Physical Victimization in Statewide Correctional System by Gender (Rate per 1,000)** |

	FEMALE (N = 564)	**MALE (N = 7,221)**
Inmate-on-inmate physical violence	92	75
With weapon	94	141
Using specific examples	185	192
Staff-on-inmate physical violence	51	156
With weapon	23	149
Using specific examples	57	206

Source: N. Wolff, C. Blitz, J. Shi, and J. Siegel, "Physical Violence Inside Prisons: Rates of Victimization," Criminal Justice and Behavior, 34, 5(2007): 588–99.

Correlates of Violence

A **correlate** is a factor that has a significant statistical relationship with another factor. Perpetrator correlates of violence include age (younger), criminal history (longer), race (Black, although results are somewhat mixed), and type of custody classification (higher custody level). For instance, one study found that inmates who were designated close custody (the highest classification level) had twice as many violent incidents as those in an admissions center.[47] Age is the strongest correlate with prison misconduct: violence is much more likely among younger inmates, who are involved as both perpetrators and victims.[48] Criminal history is also positively associated with increased violence.[49] Inmates with shorter sentences are more violence-prone, and those who have been in prison for longer periods of time are less likely to be involved in violence.[50]

There are also correlates of victimization. As noted, younger age is associated with being both a perpetrator and victim of prison violence. Both men and women seem to be similarly vulnerable to violent victimization. One study found that the six-month victimization prevalence rates of men and women for violent victimization were about the same (206/205 per 1,000); however, men were more likely to report having been assaulted by staff members. These victimization rates are 18 times higher than the national rates for the general male population outside of prison and 27 times higher than the general female population outside prison. They are also 10 times higher than the victimization rates reported by the urban poor, which is a more appropriate comparison to a prison population. Other predictors of victimization are number of hours spent attending educational classes (more hours predicts less violence), gang membership, and prior incarceration.[51]

In addition to inmate-specific correlates, certain prison characteristics also seem to be associated with more violence, including higher rates of staff-on-inmate violence.[52] Maximum-security prisons have more violent incidents than medium or minimum security prisons.[53] Institutions that are crowded and have higher numbers of younger prisoners have higher levels of violence.[54] One researcher found that institutions with higher numbers of Black inmates,

Younger inmates are more likely to be both victims and perpetrators.

maximum-security prisons, lower ratios of correctional officers to inmates, and a lack of structured inmate routines experienced higher levels of violent misconduct. However, in contrast to a previously made statement, crowding seemed to have no effect on violence in this study.[55]

One study indicated that although there is a substantial amount of literature on the culture of prison and how it contributes to violence, not much empirical evidence exists to substantiate that claim. In this study, it was found that there was not adequate evidence to link violence to culture, crowding, staff–inmate ratios, experienced versus inexperienced staff, the ratio of Black inmates to white guards, or the number of female guards. These researchers observed that prison security classification did not reduce violence; it only predicted who was likely to be violent, although placing inmates with the highest security classification in medium-security prisons did not increase violence. However, the study did conclude that there was clear evidence that increased levels of programming was associated with reduced rates of prison violence.[56]

A comprehensive study utilized a national sample of 18,185 inmates housed within 326 facilities to explore correlates of violence. About 13 percent of this sample reported being violently victimized (which included being shoved, kicked, stabbed, or hit). Most of the correlates of violence in this study replicated prior research, including the findings that white inmates who were smaller in size had a greater risk of victimization. In addition, inmates who were charged with a violent or sex offense, were previously victimized, were not married, were without a work assignment, misbehaved, did not participate in programs, used alcohol or drugs, or had a depression or personality disorder were more likely to be victimized.

The type of prison also accounted for about 8 percent of the variance in violence rates. Prisons with high proportions of violent offenders, males, inmates from multiracial backgrounds, and inmates with major infractions had increased odds of victimization. However, the sex composition of the prison has significant main and interactive effects predicting victimization. Specifically, being convicted of a drug crime, drug use, military service, major infractions, and diagnosed personality disorders are all variables that differ in their impacts on victimization between men and women. Being housed in a male prison increased the odds of victimization by 45 percent. Drug use increased the risk of victimization to a greater extent for men than it did for women. Military service reduced the risk of victimization for men, but it significantly increased the odds of victimization for women. The risk of victimization was significantly higher for men with personality disorders than for women. This study illustrates the importance of paying attention to how factors interact in how they influence violence in prisons for men and women.[57]

Prison Sexual Violence

One of the most ubiquitous elements of prison life is the threat of sexual assault. The risk is so well known it is used as a threat during plea bargaining or as a joke in popular media. This section focuses on sexual violence in prisons for men. In Chapter 10, sexual violence perpetrated by inmates and correctional staff in women's prisons will be discussed. Victims of sexual assault in prison are traumatized by the experience, often suffering from post-traumatic stress disorder (PTSD) and/or contracting sexually transmitted diseases, such as HIV. This type of prison violence has been chronicled since the early 1900s. Correctional officers have been said to ignore sexual victimization and provide little assistance to potential victims, believing that male victims should be able to defend themselves against it.[58]

In 2003, Congress passed the **Prison Rape Elimination Act (PREA)**. The Act's provisions included making the prevention of prison rape a top priority for state prison systems; developing and maintaining a national standard for the detection, prevention, reduction, and punishment of prison rape; increasing the available data and information on the incidence of prison rape through national surveys of adult and juvenile facilities; standardizing the definitions used for collecting data on the incidence of prison rape; and increasing the efficiency and effectiveness of federal expenditures through grant programs dealing with social and public health issues.[59]

An important element of PREA requires the Office of Justice Programs under the Department of Justice to conduct national surveys of prison rape. The Bureau of Justice Statistics (BJS) is responsible for these surveys of men's and women's prisons, and youth facilities. The BJS defines sexual victimization as including a) nonconsensual sex acts, and b) abusive sexual contacts. Nonconsensual sex acts are defined as unwanted contacts with an inmate or any contacts with staff that involved oral, anal, or vaginal penetration; hand jobs; and other sexual acts. Abusive sexual contacts are defined as unwanted contacts with another inmate or any contacts with staff that involved touching of the inmate's buttocks, thighs, penis, breasts, or vagina in a sexual way.[60]

Generally, the threat of rape and other forms of sexual victimization are more common than nonconsensual sex acts. Sexual assault in men's prisons include strong arm rape (physical force by one or several), extortion rape (the victim is coerced to trade sex for a debt owed), date rape (usually of a homosexual inmate who has had sex with others or the rapist but is unwilling at that time), confidence rape (heterosexuals are "groomed" by a prison wolf [see definition below]), and drug rape (the victim is drugged before sex).[61]

Research on nonconsensual sex in men's prisons confirms that sexual predators use tricks, debt, and threats in addition to physical violence to gain compliance by the victim, and threats or economic inducements are much more common than physical assaults. It is reported that victims may submit to sexual relationships to forestall a rape incident or because they owe the aggressor a debt and do not want to be seriously injured for nonpayment. Aggressors do not consider themselves to be homosexual. While it does not impact one's masculinity to be the aggressor (in fact, in a way, it enhances it), the "catcher" or "receiver" is considered less than a man. Once made into a punk, these men are sometimes bartered, traded, and sold in prison. They are forced to do service labor, including laundry, cleaning, and food preparation.[62] According to one prison observer, "The men tend to treat their catchers much as they habitually did their female companions, so a wide range of relationships, ranging from ruthless exploitation to romantic love, exists."[63] More current descriptions identify "jockers," who, if aggressive, are called "wolves." Non-aggressive "jockers," "daddies," or "teddy bears" typically do not sexually assault their sex partners as do "wolves." Rather, they have consensual sexual relationships with "queens" or closeted gays. These inmates do not self-identify as gay or even bisexual and maintain their heterosexual identity by taking an active role in sex dominating a passive partner. According to researchers, the role of "queen" has been subdivided into "fish" and "closeted gay." Although, in prison argot, the term "fish" has been used to denote new inmates and "fishcop" to mean a new correctional officer, some usage now refers to a male inmate who is openly gay. In the prison argot, inmates "hook up" with another inmate taking on a specific sexual role: the "jocker," "wolf," or "daddy" buys or comes to an agreement with another inmate (the "punk," "fuck-boy," "kid," or "catcher"). These agreements are considered enforceable contracts in which the "kid" provides the "jocker" with sexual gratification, along with any other tasks or chores desired by the "jocker." In exchange, the "jocker" protects the "kid" from any trouble.[64]

PREVALENCE OF SEXUAL VIOLENCE

One of the earliest studies of prison sexual violence in the late 1960s reported that about 3 percent of inmates in the Philadelphia jail system experienced sexual assault in a 26-month period. Estimates of prison rape in past studies have ranged from 1 percent to 28 percent of prisoners having been sexually victimized at some point during their prison sentence. All research showed that estimates of sexual coercion or harassment were higher than physical rape.[65]

In one multi-prison study, in a surprising finding, researchers noted that female inmates were more than four times more likely to report sexual victimization by other prisoners than male prisoners were. The six-month prevalence rates for unwanted sexual acts were 3.2 percent for women and 1.5 percent for men (compared to sexual assault rates for the general population of 0.2 to 0.9 percent). Staff-on-inmate sexual victimization was reported at 1.7 percent for women and 1.9 percent for men. Abusive sexual contacts (touching only) by other inmates were much more likely to be reported than nonconsensual sex acts: 21.2 percent of women and 4.3 percent of men reported unwanted sexual touching.[66]

The Bureau of Justice Statistics has published two reports on sexual victimization from surveys of prisoners, the first of which was from a national survey of selected prisons in 2008–09 (published in 2010). The survey was conducted in 167 state and federal prisons. About 4.4 percent of prisoners reported one or more incidents of sexual victimization. An unexpected finding was that male inmates reported more staff sexual misconduct than female inmates did. Additionally, staff sexual misconduct was more likely to be reported by Blacks and younger inmates. About half of the sexual contacts with staff were "willing," and this was more likely to be the case for male prisoners and female staff members.[67] Prior research had also uncovered that about half of all staff sexual misconduct is between female correctional officers and male inmates.[68] This is not surprising considering that most prisoners (about 93 percent) are male. Inmate–inmate victimization was more likely to be reported by women (whether white or multiracial) with college degrees who had never married. Inmates with a same-sex orientation were significantly more likely to report sexual victimization than heterosexual inmates, both by other inmates (11.2 percent compared to 1.3 percent) and staff perpetrators (6.6 percent compared to 2.5 percent).[69]

One of the findings of both BJS surveys was that the percentage of inmates who reported victimization varied greatly across prisons. Some facilities had rates of inmate–inmate sexual victimization as high as 8.6 percent in men's prisons and 11.9 percent in women's prisons. Sexual misconduct by staff members was also much higher in some facilities: 8.2 percent in one men's prison and 11.5 percent in a women's prison.[70] Prisoners in other institutions reported very low rates of victimization, and in some facilities, prisoners reported no incidents of sexual victimization at all.

The most recent PREA prisoner survey data available is from a survey conducted in 2011 (published in 2014). Inmates were randomly selected for participation from 233 prisons, 358 jails, and 15 special detainment facilities. Only 44 of the prisons housed women (7,141 female prisoners participated), and four of the jails housed women. This survey maintained the Bureau of Justice Statistics definitions for nonconsensual sex acts and abusive sexual contacts, with sexual victimization including both categories.

| TABLE 8.2 | National Estimates of Total Allegations of Sexual Victimization, by Type of Incident, 2007–2011 |

INCIDENT	2011	2010	2009	2008	2007
Total	8,763	8,404	7,855	7,457	7,374
Inmate-on-inmate nonconsensual sexual acts	2,984	2,660	2,147	2,343	2,421
Inmate-on-inmate abusive sexual contacts	1,479	1,360	1,417	1,220	834
Staff sexual misconduct	2,800	2,692	2,650	2,528	2,436
Staff sexual harassment	1,500	1,692	1,517	1,169	1,298

Source: R. Rantala, J. Rexroat, and A. Beck, Sexual Victimization Reported by Adult Correctional Authorities, 2009–11 *(NCJ 243904), (Washington, DC: Bureau of Justice Statistics, 2014), 4.*

The 2008–09 survey results are partially displayed in Table 8.2. It is important to remember that allegations may reflect a greater willingness to report sexual victimization rather than an increase in prevalence. Consistent with prior reports, more women than men in prison reported any type of sexual victimization by other inmates (6.9 percent of women compared to 1.7 percent of men). About equal numbers of women and men in prison reported staff sexual misconduct of any type (2.3 percent of women compared to 2.4 percent of men). About 3.6 percent of female jail inmates reported any type of sexual victimization by other inmates compared to 1.4 percent of males; and 1.4 percent of female jail inmates reported sexual misconduct by guards compared to 1.9 percent of males. Survey results indicated that the most vulnerable inmates were those who reported having mental health issues, those who were committed for sex offenses, and those who were homosexual or bisexual (these results are from the combined pool of male and female prison and jail inmates). Juveniles were not statistically more likely to report victimization than adults. It's important to realize that these national averages mask quite extreme differences in the amount of sexual violence in different facilities. In some institutions, almost 10 percent of inmates reported sexual victimization, while in other institutions, only about 1 percent of inmates reported sexual victimization. Any national average will be somewhat misleading unless it also includes the range across institutions.[71]

One of the most important findings of the study was that sexual assault (rape) was rare, but that more inmates experience other forms of sexual victimization involving unwanted touching and sexual harassment. Also notable was the prevalence of inmate–inmate sexual victimization in women's facilities, even though such victimization was not often physical rape, but rather unwanted touching and sexual harassment. Further, female inmates were more likely to be victimized by each other rather than by a staff member, as was previously thought.

CHARACTERISTICS OF MALE PERPETRATORS AND VICTIMS

In this section, the focus will be on male perpetrators and victims; the problem of sexual violence in women's prisons and jails will be more fully discussed in Chapter 10. Research suggests that certain characteristics are idiosyncratic of perpetrators of sexual assault. One study compared 121 male perpetrators of sexual assault to non-assaulters. They found that sexual aggressors were more likely to have been sexually abused as a child, be serving a life sentence, and have had adult sexual assault convictions and juvenile robbery convictions. A review of the literature on sexual assault revealed that these characteristics were consistent in past studies of sexual assault in prison.[72]

When it comes to characteristics of victims, research indicates that victims in men's prisons tend to be younger prisoners who are physically smaller and weaker than the average inmate. They are more often white, first-time offenders, middle class, and convicted of nonviolent crimes. Other research shows that the most likely victims are prison "fish" (newcomers), inmates with a weak public image, and/or who are physically attractive. Other predictors include being a known homosexual, being convicted of a sexual offense against a child, having had a prior victimization (before age 18), possessing a mental disorder, having higher levels of education, and finally, a perceived high level of gang activity in the facility.[73] Research also indicated that only about a third of male victims reported their rape to authorities.[74] In some circumstances, male victims experience powerlessness that sometimes leads to victimizing someone else. In the following quote, an inmate describes how sexual assault can be contagious in a sense:

> It's fixed where if you're raped, the only way you [can escape further abuse is if] you rape someone else. Yes, I know that's fully screwed, but that's how your head is twisted. After it's over you may be disgusted with yourself, but you realize you're not powerless and that you can deliver as well as receive pain. Then it's up to you to decide whether you enjoy it or not. Most do, I don't.[75]

Riots and Collective Violence

Prison disturbances occur with some regularity. In fact, it is reported that there were over 1,300 prison riots in the twentieth century.[76] Two of the most notorious riots in this country are the Attica (1971) and Santa Fe (1980) riots. As we discussed in Chapter 7, at Attica, rioters took over the prison to force the governor of New York and prison commissioner to concede to a list of demands for better living conditions. After several days of negotiations, state police stormed the prison and regained control, but in the process, 10 guards and 33 inmates were killed, all but one by state police. Abuses occurred after the riot, including making naked prisoners run a gauntlet of officers who beat them with sticks, clubs, and guns. It was years before all court actions against inmates were complete. Despite photographs and eyewitness accounts, no officials were ever convicted of abuse of power. A lawsuit brought by inmates who had been beaten and tortured after the violent retaking of the facility was finally settled almost thirty years later in February 2000, for $8 million to be divided among all the injured inmates who were still alive.[77]

The 1980 Santa Fe riot was a display of horrific violence by inmates against other inmates. Specifically, protective custody inmates were targeted and subjected to various types of torture before being killed, including being set on fire, hung on cell bars and literally filleted, and thrown off tiers. Other killings took place as roving bands of prisoners took advantage of the chaos. Over 200 inmates were severely injured. Guards were beaten, stabbed, and sodomized. There was no agenda, no political consciousness, and no control. The wild killing spree ended in the deaths of 33 inmates.[78]

More recently, in 2017, a corrections officer was killed when inmates took four COs and other inmates hostage in a Delaware prison. The incident lasted 20 hours. Two officers were released by the inmates during the siege and one was rescued when officials stormed the prison. The fourth CO was found dead.[79] In April 2018, seven inmates died at Lee Correctional Institution in South Carolina in what has been called one of the worst prison riots in the last 25 years. Seventeen other prisoners were seriously injured.[80] This was labeled a riot, although the fighting was between inmates, not against the institutional staff. Inmates fought each other for seven hours before SWAT teams and prison officials could retake the prison. The prison housed 1,500 inmates, but only 44 correctional officers were on duty when the riot occurred; prison officials faced criticism that they didn't move sooner to prevent the deaths of inmates. It was the most inmates slain in a single riot in the U.S. since nine prisoners and a guard died in 1993 at the Southern Ohio Correctional Facility.

What causes prisoners to riot? Those who study riots and prison disturbances explain that the months with the most riots and disturbances in descending order of frequency are December, November, August, and July, indicating that Christmas and the holiday season were more powerful triggers than the heat of summer. These same researchers identified a long list of causes and triggering events for riots, including food, racial tension, rules, regulations and policies, mass escape attempts, gangs and other special groups, rumors, security issues, conflict with other inmates, conflict with correctional staff, and alcohol and drug usage.[81] Riot theories include the **powder keg theory**, which presumes that the prison is full of violent individuals and that when incidents accumulate, there is an explosion. Another theory is the **relative deprivation/rising expectation theory** that presumes that when conditions improve, but don't improve fast enough, there is a higher likelihood of a disturbance. Another theory, the **power vacuum theory**, assumes riots take place when there is no strong authority in control.[82]

Other researchers cite five causal factors to riots:

1. new and increased demands on prison administrators from external sources without an increase in resources;
2. internal pressures from correctional staff along with dissension and alienation;
3. internal pressure from prisoners regarding conditions;
4. riotous prisoner ideologies; and
5. internal actions perceived as unjust.[83]

One study found that "oppressive" administrative control that allowed for no input from prisoners was more predictive of collective violence than a lack of administrative control.[84] According to these researchers, if prisoners feel totally oppressed, anger and frustration will result in collective violence, especially when there is also an element of institutional breakdown or disorganization that leads to a lack of essential services and procedures (e.g., food service, recreation, commissary).[85]

Reducing Prison Violence

Recent incidents of prison violence have been attributed to inadequate staffing levels, and it seems obvious that too few correctional officers and poor security can create the opportunity for violence between inmates or toward officers.

Academics have addressed how the elements of the prison contribute to the potential for violence, and recommendations for reducing violence include the following:

- Increasing transparency: Prisons tend to be out of the public's sight and mind.

- Establishing measurable national health and safety standards for prisons in such areas as ratio of prisoners to guards, ratio of prisoners to medical staff, numbers of programs offered, and nutritional goals. Publishing these measures demonstrates to the public how prisons are performing.

- Utilizing evidence-based practices for rehabilitative programming, such as drug treatment or violence reduction: This is achieved by conducting evidence-based reviews of practices using experimental design, the so-called "gold standard" for measuring effectiveness, which calls for random assignment to an experimental group and a control group.

- Measuring the moral performance of prison: While program success and national standards on health and safety can be measured, it is also important to measure the moral atmosphere of a prison, or how prisoners are treated. This can be measured by inmates' views of the moral authority of staff members, which is influenced by their perceptions of procedural justice. Procedural justice consists of being treated with respect and fairness, being allowed a voice, and the perception that authority figures are making decisions for the right reasons.[86]

One prison researcher proposes that the "moral performance" of a prison can contribute to or reduce the potential for violence.[87] The correctional officer culture of cynicism; desensitization to drugs, self-harm, and violence; and machismo (hypermasculinity) all contribute to the level of violence in prison. It was found that how staff felt about inmates affected the atmosphere of the prison and its programming. Quality of life improved for prisoners when staff felt safer, enjoyed their work, trusted senior management, and had satisfaction with their level of responsibility. This, in turn, affected how they treated inmates and led to reduced staff-to-inmate violence and even inmate-to-inmate violence. However, staff had to feel their needs were being met before they felt able or willing to take on the problems of the prisoners.[88]

Adjusting to Prison Life

Prisoners adapt to prison in different ways. Some individuals adapt in reasonably effective ways and tend to cope better the longer they are in prison.[89] For example, some prisoners try to find some semblance of safety in job or program assignments that keep them away from the general population and avoid the mess hall, yard, or any other place where they may get involved in trouble. Some inmates, especially older inmates or those who have spent many years in prison, create a more structured, safe, and orderly life to the degree possible.[90] These inmates stay in their cells during free time, develop only a few relationships with other prisoners, and avoid the black market. One of the main adjustments that older prisoners describe is "letting things go," meaning that they do not respond to perceived slights or insults with immediate violence.[91] Inmates develop these "niches" and limit their interactions to control their exposure to potential

FOCUS ON THE
OFFENDER

GEORGE LUNA: CHANGED AND CHANGE AGENT

George Luna was physically abused by half-brothers as a child and learned to fight in self-defense. He joined a gang and started committing crimes. He cycled in and out of many of California's prisons, eventually serving a total of 35 years. In one earlier release, he had been supporting his family and doing well but began to use drugs again when he found out that his mother had died. He committed 92 felonies in 45 days before being sent back to prison. At San Quentin, he finally committed himself to a prison program called Guiding Rage into Power (GRIP). The program helps male prisoners come to recognize "toxic masculinity" and the reasons why they have been violent. During the classes and discussions, he came to terms with what the curriculum refers to as the "original pain" that is at the root of anger. For him, it was the abuse he experienced as a young child. The program was a turning point, and he decided to seek an education and turn his life around. George Luna goes into prisons now as one of these facilitators instead of as an inmate. After 35 years of being incarcerated, he has changed his life and is now helping others.

As of 2019, he had been out of prison 10 years. It has not been easy for him. Police, community members, and even family could not believe that he had changed. His looks and demeanor intimidate people. His daughter experienced addiction, and he was unable to convince authorities that he could be a good guardian for her children. However, he persists in trying to be positive and do positive things. He travels up to six hours to go into the prisons that he knew all too well from earlier in his life. In the groups, the toxic culture of prison is discussed, and men learn that they can change.

Questions for Discussion

1. What do you think toxic masculinity refers to, especially in prison?

2. Do you think that prison helped or harmed George Luna?

Sources: A. Sterling, "Prisoners Unlearn the Toxic Masculinity That Led to Their Incarceration," HuffPost, July 13, 2019, https://www.huffpost.com/entry/incarcerated-men-gender-roles-recidivism_n_5d378544e4b004b6adb78912.

"I'm Going to Make a Difference," Inside Out (Newsletter), ND, https://insight-out.org/index.php/insights/stories-from-prison/92-stories-i-m-going-to-make-a-difference.

trouble.[92] While some inmates isolate themselves to avoid trouble, others engage heavily in the inmate subculture and align themselves with "partners," "associates," or "homeboys" for the support and security they provide.

Research indicates that different ethnic groups and men and women experience prison differently because of different needs related to activity, privacy, safety, emotional feedback, support, structure, and freedom. Hispanics and women more acutely feel the absence of support and emotional feedback, while freedom resonated more strongly in samples of African American men. Prisoners who cannot adapt often experience breakdowns. For some, prison pushes them into crisis because their needs are not met; for example, their need for safety is so high that the prison experience creates a mental crisis.[93]

Positive adjustment appears related to the ability to find meaning in the prison sentence. According to research, the most positively adjusted inmates see imprisonment as an opportunity to change their lives and focus on self-improvement. These inmates pursue prison programming, become involved in religion, and/or participate in prison volunteer programs that give meaning to their lives and give them positive skills to take with them upon release.[94]

Summary

- Prisons operate according to a particular set of rules and norms outside the realm of regular society, known as prison subculture, which is made up of role types, the inmate code, and prison argot.

- The rate of physical victimization in prison ranges from 1 to 33 percent. Aggressors tend to be younger, with a violent criminal history, and in maximum-security institutions. Increased levels of programming can reduce violence.

- In 2003, Congress passed the Prison Rape Elimination Act (PREA), making the prevention of prison rape a top priority for state prison systems. It also created a national survey of prisons to collect data and information on the incidence of prison rape.

- Sexual assault (rape) in prison is rare, but inmates experience other forms of sexual victimization involving unwanted touching and sexual harassment.

PROJECTS

1. Watch a popular movie or television show about prisons made in the last 20 years and see whether any aspect(s) of the prison subculture described here is represented.

2. Find the latest BJS report on prison sexual violence and confirm whether the facts presented in this chapter are still accurate.

NOTES

1. G. Sykes, *The Society of Captives* (Princeton: Princeton University Press, 1958/1966).

2. J. Irwin and D. Cressey, "Thieves, Convicts, and the Social Inmate Culture," *Social Problems* 10 (1962): 142–55; J. Irwin, *The Felon* (Englewood Cliffs, NJ: Prentice Hall, 1970); C. Schrag, "Leadership Among Prison Inmates," *American Sociological Review* 19 (1961): 37–42.

3. R.N. Akers, N. Hayner, and W. Grunninger, "Prisonization in Five Countries," *Criminology* 14 (1977): 527–54; C. Krebs, "High Risk HIV Transmission Behavior in Prison and the Prisoner Subculture," *The Prison Journal* 82 (2002), 1: 19–49; T. Winfree, G. Newbold, and S. Tubb, "Prisoner Perspectives on Inmate Culture in New Mexico and New Zealand: A Descriptive Case Study," *The Prison Journal* 82 (2002), 2: 213–33.

4. C. Terry, "The Function of Humor for Prison Inmates," *Journal of Contemporary Criminal Justice* 13, 1 (1997): 23–40; R. Trammell, "Values, Rules, and Keeping the Peace: How Men Describe Order and the Inmate Code in California Prisons," *Deviant Behavior* 30, 8 (2009): 746–71.

5. R. Trammell, "Values, Rules, and Keeping the Peace: How Men Describe Order and the Inmate Code in California Prisons," *Deviant Behavior*, 30, 8 (2009): 746–71; D. Skarbek, *The Social Order of the Underworld: How Prison Gangs Govern the American Penal System* (New York: Oxford Univ. Press, 2014); D. Kreager and C. Kruttschnitt, "Inmate Society in the Era of Mass Incarceration," *Annual Review of Criminology* 1 (2018): 261–83.

6. G. Sykes and S. Messinger, "The Inmate Social System," in *Theoretical Studies in the Social Organization of the Prison*, edited by R. Cloward, D. Cressey, G. Grosser, R. McCleery, L. Ohlin, G. Sykes, and S. Messinger (New York: Social Science Research Council, 1960), 5–19.

7. V. Hassine, *Life Without Parole: Living in Prison Today* (Los Angeles: Roxbury Publishing Company; Reprint, New York: Oxford University Press, 1999/2004/2010).

8. R. Trammell, "Values, Rules, and Keeping the Peace: How Men Describe Order and the Inmate Code in California Prisons," *Deviant Behavior* 30, 8 (2009): 746–71, 756.

9. M. Santos, *Profiles from Prison: Adjusting to Life behind Bars* (Westport, CT: Praeger Publishers, 2003); M. Santos, *Inside: Life behind Bars in America* (New York: St. Martin's Press, 2006); K. Carceral, *Prison, Inc.: A Convict Exposes Life Inside a Private Prison* (New York, NY: NYU Press, 2005).

10. M. Santos, *Profiles from Prison: Adjusting to Life behind Bars* (Westport, CT: Praeger Publishers, 2003); M. Santos, *Inside: Life behind Bars in America* (New York: St. Martin's Press, 2006); M. Fleisher, *Beggars and Thieves: Lives of Urban Street Criminals* (Madison: University of Wisconsin Press, 1995).

11. T. Einat and H. Einat, "Inmate Argot as an Expression of Prison Subculture: The Israeli Case," *The Prison Journal* 80, 3 (2000): 309–25.

12. C. Hensley, C.K. Wright, R. Tewksbury, and T. Castle, "The Evolving Nature of Prison Argot and Sexual Hierarchies," *The Prison Journal* 83, 3 (2003): 289–300.

13. C. Johnson, C. Bina, T. Cornelius, B. Holder, T. Kennerer, and L. Larson, *From the Big House to Your House* (Charleston, SC: CreateSpace (an Amazon Affiliate, 2010).

14. J. Lerner, *You've Got Nothing Coming: Notes from a Prison Fish* (New York City: Broadway Books, 2002).

15. G. Hunt, S. Riegel, T. Morales, and, and D. Waldorf, "Change in Prison Culture: Prison Gangs and the Case of the Pepsi Generation," *Social Problems* 40 (1993): 398–409; D. Pyrooz, S. Decker, and M. Fleisher, "From the Street to the Prison, From the Prison to the Street: Understanding and Responding to Prison Gangs," *Journal of Aggression, Conflict and Peace Research* 3 (2011): 12–24.

16. G. Hunt, S. Riegel, T. Morales, and, and D. Waldorf, "Change in Prison Culture: Prison Gangs and the Case of the Pepsi Generation," *Social Problems* 40 (1993): 398–409; C. Parenti, *Lockdown America: Police and Prisons in the Age of Crisis* (New York City: Verso New Left Books, 1999).

17. C. Parenti, *Lockdown America: Police and Prisons in the Age of Crisis* (New York City: Verso New Left Books, 1999); M.E. Pelz, J. Marquart, and C. Terry Pelz, "Right Wing Extremism in Texas Prisons: The Rise and Fall of the Aryan Brotherhood of Texas," *Prison Journal* 71, 2 (1991): 38–49.

18. D. Skarbek, *The Social Order of the Underworld: How Prison Gangs Govern the American Penal System* (New York: Oxford Univ. Press, 2014).

19. M. Griffin, "Prison Gang Policy and Recidivism: Short-Term Management Benefits, Long-Term Consequences," *Criminology and Public Policy* 6, no. 2 (2007): 223–30; J. Winterdyk and R. Ruddell, "Managing Prison Gangs: Results from a Survey of U.S. Prison Systems," *Journal of Criminal Justice* 38 (2010): 730–36.

20. D. Pyrooz, S. Decker, and M. Fleisher, "From the Street to The Prison, from the Prison to the Street: Understanding and Responding to Prison Gangs," *Journal of Aggression, Conflict and Peace Research* 3, 1 (2011): 1–24.

21. M. Mitchell, C. Fahmy, D. Pyrooz, and S. Decker, "Criminal Crews, Codes, and Contexts: Differences and Similarities across the Code of the Street, Convict Code, Street Gangs, and Prison Gangs," *Deviant Behavior* 38 (2017): 1197–1222.

22. S. Decker, C. Melde, and D. Pyrooz, "What Do We Know About Gangs and Gang Members and Where Do We Go from Here?" *Justice Quarterly* 30, 3 (2013): 369–402.

23. M. Mitchell, C. Fahmy, D. Pyrooz, and S. Decker, "Criminal Crews, Codes, and Contexts: Differences and Similarities across the Code of the Street, Convict Code, Street Gangs, and Prison Gangs," *Deviant Behavior* 38 (2017): 1197–1222; J. Winterdyk, and R. Ruddell, "Managing Prison Gangs. Results from a Survey of U.S. Prison Systems," *Journal of Criminal Justice* 38 (2010): 730–36.

24. M. Griffin, D. Pyrooz, and S. Decker, "Surviving and Thriving: The Growth, Influence and Administrative Control of Prison Gangs," in *Crime and Crime Reduction: The Importance of Group Processes*, edited by J. Wood and T. Gannon (New York: Routledge, 2013), 137–56.

25. M. Mitchell, C. Fahmy, D. Pyrooz, and S. Decker, "Criminal Crews, Codes, and Contexts: Differences and Similarities across the Code of the Street, Convict Code, Street Gangs, and Prison Gangs," *Deviant Behavior* 38 (2017): 1197–1222.

26. M.D. Harer and D.J. Steffensmeier, "Race and Prison Violence," *Criminology* 34 (1996): 323.

27. M. Braswell, R. Montgomery, and L. Lombardo, *Prison Violence in America* (Cincinnati, OH: Anderson, 1994).

28. K. Edgar, I. O'Donnell, and C. Martin, *Prison Violence: The Dynamics of Conflict, Fear, And Power* (Cullompton: Willan Publishing, 2003).

29. J. Irwin, *Prisons in Turmoil* (Boston: Little, Brown & Co., 1980); J. Austin and J. Irwin, *It's About Time: America's Imprisonment Binge* (Belmont, CA: Wadsworth, 2001).

30. L. Carroll, *Hacks, Blacks and Cons: Race Relations in a Maximum-Security Prison* (Lexington, MA: Lexington Books, 1974).

31. B. Crouch and J. Marquart, *An Appeal to Justice: Litigated Reform of Texas Prisons* (Austin, TX: University of Texas Press, 1989). C. Trulson and J. Marquart, "The Caged Melting Pot: Toward an Understanding of the Consequences of Desegregation in Prisons," *Law & Society Review* 36, 4 (2002): 743–82.

32. P. Ralph and J. Marquart., "Gang Violence in Texas

Prisons," *The Prison Journal* 71, 2 (1991): 38–49.

33. S. Martin and S. Eckland-Olson, *Texas Prisons: The Walls Came Tumbling Down* (Austin, TX: Texas Monthly Press, 1987).

34. K. Kauffman, *Prison Officers and Their World* (Cambridge, MA: Harvard University Press, 1988); L. Carroll, *Lawful Order: A Case Study of Correctional Crisis and Reform* (New York: Garland Press, 1998); V. Hassine, *Life Without Parole: Living in Prison Today* (Los Angeles: Roxbury Publishing Company, 2nd Edition, 1999/2004).

35. K. Wright, *Effective Prison Leadership* (Binghamton, NY: William Neil Publishing,1994); A. Lin, *Reform in the Making: The Implementation of Social Policy in Prison* (Princeton, NJ: Princeton University Press, 2000); but, see V. Hassine, *Life Without Parole: Living in Prison Today* (Los Angeles: Roxbury Publishing Company, 1999/2004; 2nd Edition, New York: Oxford University Press, 2010); M. Rolland, *Descent into Madness: An Inmate's Experience of the New Mexico State Prison Riot* (Cincinnati, OH: Anderson Publishing, 1997).

36. S. Bailey, "Prison Deaths Pile Up in South Carolina: Does Anybody Care?" *The Crime Report*, March 28, 2018, https://thecrimereport.org/2018/03/28/prison-deaths-pile-up-in-south-carolina-does-anybody-care/.

37. A. Alexander, "Three NC Officials Moved from Jobs after Fatal Prison Attacks and Scathing Federal Report," *Charlotte Observer*, January 31,2018, http://www.charlotteobserver.com/news/local/article197640629.html#storylink=cpyhttp://www.charlotteobserver.com/

news/local/article197640629.html.

38. J. Byrne and J. Hummer, "The Nature and Extent of Prison Violence," in J. Byrne, D. Hummer, and F. Taxman (eds), *The Culture of Prison Violence*,. (Boston, MA: Allyn & Bacon, 2008), 12–27.

39. M. Noonan, *Mortality in State Prisons, 2001–2014—Statistical Tables* (Washington, DC: Bureau of Justice Statistics, USDOJ, December 2016).

40. J. Woolredge, "Inmate Lifestyles and Opportunities for Victimization," *Journal of Research in Crime & Delinquency* 35 (1998): 480–502.

41. N. Wolff, C. Blitz, J. Shi, J. Siegel, and R. Bachman, "Physical Violence Inside Prisons: Rates of Victimization," *Criminal Justice & Behavior* 34, 5 (2007): 588–99; N. Wolff and J. Shi, "Type, Source, and Patterns of Physical Victimization: A Comparison of Male and Female Inmates," *The Prison Journal* 89, 2 (2009): 172–91.

42. K. Carceral, *Prison, Inc.: A Convict Exposes Life Inside a Private Prison* (New York, NY: NYU Press, 2005).

43. N. Wolff, D. Blitz, J. Shi, R. Bachman, and J. Siegel, "Sexual Violence Inside Prisons: Rates of Victimization," *Journal of Urban Health: Bulletin of the New York Academy of Medicine*, 83, 5 (2006): 835–48; N. Wolff, C. Blitz, J. Shi, J. Siegel, and R. Bachman, "Physical Violence Inside Prisons: Rates of Victimization," *Criminal Justice & Behavior* 34, 5 (2007): 588–99. N. Wolff and J. Shi, "Type, Source, and Patterns of Physical Victimization: A Comparison of Male and Female Inmates," *The Prison Journal* 89, 2 (2009): 172–91.

44. D. Perez, A. Gover, K. Tennyson, and S. Santos,

"Individual and Institutional Characteristics Related to Inmate Victimization," *International Journal of Offender Therapy and Comparative Criminology* 54, 3 (2010): 378–94.

45. J. Wooldredge and B. Steiner, "Violent victimization among State Prison Inmates," *Violence and Victims*, 28, 3 (2013): 531–51.

46. A.J. Beck, M. Berzofsky, R. Caspar, C. and Krebs, C. *Sexual Victimization in Prisons and Jails Reported by Inmates, 2011–2012 Update* (Washington, DC: Bureau of Justice Statistics. (2013).

47. J. Sorenson and M. Cunningham. 2010, "Conviction Offense and Prison Violence," *Crime & Delinquency* 56, 1: 103–25.

48. D. Perez, A. Gover, K. Tennyson, and S. Santos. "Individual and Institutional Characteristics Related to Inmate Victimization," *International Journal of Offender Therapy and Comparative Criminology.* 54, 3 (2010): 378–394; K. Lahm, "Inmate-on-Inmate Assault: A Multilevel Examination of Prison Violence," *Criminal Justice and Behavior* 35, 1 (2008): 120–37.

49. K. Lahm, K, "Inmate-on-Inmate Assault: A Multilevel Examination of Prison Violence," *Criminal Justice and Behavior* 35, 1 (2008): 120–37.

50. J. Sorenson and M. Cunningham, "Conviction Offense and Prison Violence," *Crime & Delinquency* 56, 1 (2010): 103–25.

51. N. Wolff, C. Blitz, J. Shi, J. Siegel, and R. Bachman, "Physical Violence Inside Prisons: Rates of Victimization," *Criminal Justice & Behavior* 34, 5 (2007): 588–99.

52. N. Wolff, C. Blitz, J. Shi, J. Siegel, and R. Bachman, "Physical Violence Inside Prisons: Rates of Victimization," *Criminal Justice & Behavior* 34, 5 (2007): 588–99.

53. D. Perez, D., A. Gover, K. Tennyson, and S. Santos, "Individual and Institutional Characteristics Related to Inmate Victimization," *International Journal of Offender Therapy and Comparative Criminology* 54, 3 (2010): 378–94.

54. K. Lahm, "Inmate-on-Inmate Assault: A Multilevel Examination of Prison Violence," *Criminal Justice and Behavior* 35, 1 (2008): 120–37.

55. B. Steiner, "Assessing Static and Dynamic Influences on Inmate Violence Levels," *Crime & Delinquency* 55, 1 (2009): 134–61; B. Steiner and J. Wooldredge, "Rethinking the Link Between Institutional Crowding and Inmate Misconduct," *The Prison Journal* 89, 2 (2009): 205–33; B. Steiner, B. and J. Wooldredge, "Individual and Environmental Effects on Assaults and Nonviolent Rule Breaking by Women in Prison," *Journal of Research in Crime and Delinquency* 46 (2009): 437–67.

56. J. Byrne and D. Hummer, "Examining the Impact of Institutional Culture on Prison Violence and Disorder: An Evidence-Based Review," in J. Byrne, D. Hummer and F. Taxman (eds), *The Culture of Prison Violence* (Boston, MA: Allyn & Bacon, 2008), 40–91.

57. B. Teasdale, L. Daigle, S. Hawk, and J. Daquin., "Violent Victimization in the Prison Context: An Examination of the Gendered Context of Prison," *International Journal of Offender Therapy and Comparative Criminology* 60, 9 (2016): 995–1015.

58. J. Gilligan, J., "How to Increase the Rate of Violence and Why," in T. Gray (ed.), *Exploring Corrections* (Boston: Allyn & Bacon, 2002), 200–14; W. Rideau and R. Wikberg, *Life Sentences: Rage and Survival Behind Bars* (New York City: Times Books, 1992); *No Escape: Male Rape in U.S. Prisons*, Human Rights Watch, 2001, www.hrw.org/reports/2000/usa/. H. Eigenberg, "Correctional Officers' Definitions of Rape in Male Prisons," *Journal of Criminal Justice* 28, 5 (2000): 435–49.

59. "Prison Rape Elimination Act of 2003," Public Law (2003), 108–79.

60. A. Beck and J. Karberg, *Prison and Jail Inmates at Midyear 2000* (Washington DC: Bureau of Justice Statistics, USDOJ, 2001).

61. V. Hassine, *Life Without Parole: Living in Prison Today.* (Los Angeles: Roxbury Publishing Company1999, 2004). Reprint, New York: Oxford University Press, 2010.

62. C. Hensley (ed.), *Prison Sex: Practice and Policy* (Boulder, CO: Lynne Rienner Publishers, 2002); C., Hensley, T. Castle, and R. Tewksbury, "Inmate-to-inmate Sexual Coercion in a Prison for Women," *Journal of Offender Rehabilitation* 37, 2 (2003): 77–87; C., Hensley, C. Struckman-Johnson, and H. Eigenberg, "Introduction: The History of Prison Sex Research," *The Prison Journal* 80, 4 (2000): 360–67; D. Keys, "Instrumental Sexual Scripting: An Examination of Gender-Role Fluidity in the Correctional Institution," *Journal of Contemporary Criminal Justice* 18, 3 (2002): 258–78.

63. S. Donaldson, "A Million Jockers, Punks, and Queens," in D. Sabo, T. Kupers, and W. London (eds), *Prison Masculinities* (Philadelphia, PA: Temple University Press, 2001), 118–26.

64. A. Lara, "Forced Integration of Gay, Bisexual and Transgendered Inmates in California State Prisons: From Protected Minority to Exposed Victims," *Southern California Interdisciplinary Law Journal* 19 (2010): 589–614.

65. C. Hensley (ed.), *Prison Sex: Practice and Policy* (Boulder, CO: Lynne Rienner Publishers, 2002); C. Krebs, "High Risk HIV Transmission Behavior in Prison and the Prisoner Subculture," *The Prison Journal* 82, 1 (2002): 19–49; M. Fleisher and J. Krienert, *The Culture of Prison Sexual Violence* (Washington, DC: National Institute of Justice, U.S. Dept. of Justice, 2006).

66. N. Wolff, C. Blitz, J. Shi, R. Bachman, J. Siegel, "Sexual Violence Inside Prison: Rates of Victimization," *Journal of Urban Health*, 3 (2006): 835–48; also see N. Wolff, J. Shi, R. Bachman, "Measuring Victimization Inside Prison: Questioning the Questions," *Journal of Interpersonal Violence* 23 (2008): 1343–62; N. Wolff, C. Blitz, J. Shi, J. Siegel, and R. Bachman, "Physical Violence Inside Prisons: Rates of Victimization," *Criminal Justice & Behavior* 34, 5 (2007): 588–99.

67. A. Beck, P. Harrison, M. Berzofsky, R. Caspar, and C. Krebs, *Sexual Victimization in Prisons and Jails, Reported by Inmates, 2008–2009* (Washington, DC: Bureau of Justice Statistics, U.S. Dept. of Justice).

68. J. Marquart, M. Barnhill, and K. Balshaw-Biddle, "'Fatal Attraction': An Analysis of Employee Boundary Violations in a Southern Prison System, 1995–98," *Justice Quarterly* 18 4 (2001): 877–911.

69. A. Beck, P. Harrison, M. Berzofsky, R. Caspar, and C. Krebs, *Sexual Victimization in Prisons and Jails, Reported by Inmates, 2008–2009* (Washington, DC: Bureau of Justice Statistics, U.S. Dept. of Justice).

70. A. Beck, P. Harrison, M. Berzofsky, R. Caspar and C. Krebs. *Sexual Victimization in Prisons and Jails, Reported by Inmates, 2008–2009* (Washington, DC: Bureau of Justice Statistics, U.S. Dept. of Justice, 2011).

71. R. Rantala, J. Rexroat, and A. Beck. *Sexual Victimization Reported by Adult Correctional Authorities, 2009–11* (NCJ 243904) (Washington, DC: Bureau of Justice Statistics, 2014).

72. M. Morash, S. Jeong, and N. Zang, "An Exploratory Study of the Characteristics of Men Known to Commit Prisoner-on-Prisoner Sexual Violence," *The Prison Journal* 90, 2 (2010): 161–78.

73. C. Hensley (ed.), *Prison Sex: Practice and Policy* (Boulder, CO: Lynne Rienner Publishers, 2002); C. Struckman-Johnson, L. Rucker, K. Bumby, and S. Donaldson., "Sexual Coercion Reported by Men and Women in Prison," *Journal of Sex Research* 33, 1(1996): 67–76; S. Donaldson, "A Million Jockers, Punks, and Queens," in D. Sabo, T. Kupers, and W. London, *Prison Masculinities* (Philadelphia, PA: Temple University Press, 2001), 118–26.; N. Wolff, C. Blitz, J. Shi, J. Siegel, and R. Bachman, "Physical Violence Inside Prisons: Rates of Victimization," *Criminal Justice & Behavior* 34, 5 (2007): 588–99.

74. C. Struckman-Johnson, L. Rucker, K. Bumby, and S. Donaldson. 1996, "Sexual Coercion Reported by Men and Women in Prison," *Journal of Sex Research* 33, 1: 67–76.

75. An inmate, quoted in J. Mariner, "Body and Soul: The Trauma of Prison Rape," in J. May and K. Pitts (eds.), *Building Violence* (Thousand Oaks, CA: Sage Publishing, 2001), 125–31.

76. R. Montgomery and G. Crews, *A History of Correctional Violence: An Examination of Reported Causes of Riots and Disturbances* (Lanham, MD: ACA, 1998).

77. D. Chen, "Ex-Attica Inmates Recount Shattered Lives and Dreams," *New York Times*, March 1, 2012, 2000, retrieved from www.nytimes.com/yr/mo/day/news/national/regional/ny-attica-case.html.3/1/2012 from http://www.nytimes.com/2000/02/15/nyregion/ex-attica-inmates-recount-shattered-lives-and-dreams.html?pagewanted=all&src=pm.

78. M. Colvin, The Penitentiary in Crisis: From Accommodation to Riot in New Mexico (Albany, NY: SUNY Press, 1992); B. Useem and P. Kimball, *States of Siege: U.S. Prison Riots, 1971–86* (New York: Oxford University Press, 1989); M. Rolland, Descent into Madness: An Inmate's Experience of the New Mexico State Prison Riot (Cincinnati, OH: Anderson Publishing, 1997).

79. "Delaware Prison Riot and Hostage Situation," *Heavy News*, February 2017, https://heavy.com/news/2017/02/smyrna-delaware-vaughn-rebellion-prison-riot-guards-hostage-inmates-demands-photos-video-audio-call-injuries-stabbing/.

80. 9News.com "Seven Inmates Killed in Worst Prison Riots for 25 Years in US," Apr 17, 2018, https://www.9news.com.au/world/2018/04/17/13/20/seven-inmates-killed-in-worst-prison-riots-for-25-years-in-us.

81. R. Montgomery and G. Crews, *A History of Correctional Violence: An Examination of Reported Causes of Riots and Disturbances* (Lanham, MD: ACA, 1998).

82. R. Montgomery and G. Crews, *A History of Correctional Violence: An Examination of Reported Causes of Riots and Disturbances* (Lanham, MD: ACA, 1998).

83. J. Goldstone and B. Useem, "Prison Riots as Microrevolutions: An Extension of State-Centered Theories of Revolution," *American Journal of Sociology*, 104, 4 (1999): 985–81.

84. B. Useem. and M. Reisig, "Collective Action in Prisons," *Criminology* 37 (1999): 735–59.

85. J. Rynne, R. Harding, and R. Wortley, "Market Testing and Prison Riots: How Public-Sector Commercialization Contributed to a Prison Riot," *Criminology and Public Policy* 7, 1 (2008): 117–42.

86. J. Byrne and J. Hummer, "The Nature and Extent of Prison Violence," in J. Byrne, D. Hummer and F. Taxman (eds), *The Culture of Prison Violence* (Boston, MA: Allyn & Bacon. 2008), 12–27.

87. A. Liebling, "Why Prison Staff Culture Matters," in J. Byrne, D. Hummer and F. Taxman (eds), *The Culture of Prison Violence* (Boston, MA: Allyn & Bacon. 2008), 105–23.

88. Ibid, 118.

89. R. Johnson and A. Dobrzanska, "Mature Coping Among Life-Sentenced Inmates: An Exploratory Study of Adjustment Dynamics," *Corrections Compendium* 30 (2005): 8–9.

90. E. Zamble and F. Porporino, *Coping Behavior and Adaption in Prison Inmates* (New York: Springer-Verlag 1988); H. Toch, *Living in Prison: The Ecology of Survival* (New York: Free Press,

1977); H. Toch and K. Adams, *Coping and Maladaptation in Prison* (New Brunswick: Transaction Press. 1989.

91. L. Leban, S. Cardwell, H. Copes, and T. Brezina, "Adapting to Prison Life: A Qualitative Examination of the Coping Process among Incarcerated Offenders," *Justice Quarterly* 33, 6 (2015):1-27. 6

92. R. Johnson, R. *Hard Time: Understanding and Reforming the Prison.* (Belmont, CA: Wadsworth Publishing Co., 1996/2002); B. Owen, *"In the Mix": Struggle and Survival in a Women's Prison.* (Albany, NY: State University of Albany Press, 1998); J. Irwin, *Prisons in Turmoil* (Boston: Little, Brown & Co., 1980).

93. H. Toch, *Men in Crisis: Human Breakdowns in Prison* (Chicago: Aldine, 1975); H. Toch, *Living in Prison: The Ecology of Survival* (New York: Free Press, 1977); H. Toch, *Violent Men* (Cambridge, MA: Schenkman Publishing, 1980); H. Toch, *Mosaic of Despair: Human Breakdowns in Prison* (Washington DC: American Psychological Association, 1982); H. Toch, K. Adams, and D. Grant, *Coping: Maladaptation in Prisons* (New Brunswick, NJ: Transaction Books, 1989); R. Johnson and H. Toch, *The Pains of Imprisonment* (Prospect Heights, IL: Waveland Press, 1982).

94. E. Van Ginneken, "Doing Well or Just Doing Time? A Qualitative Study of Patterns of Psychological Adjustment in Prison," *The Howard Journal* 54, 4 (2015): 352–70; also, see S. Maruna, *Making Good: How Ex-Convicts Reform and Rebuild Their Lives* (Washington, DC.: American Psychological Association, 2001); A. Liebling, "Prison Suicide and Prisoner Coping," *Crime and Justice* 26 (1999): 283–59; A. Liebling, and H. Arnold, *Prisons and their Moral Performance: A Study of Values, Quality and Prison Life* (Oxford: Clarendon Press, 2004); A. Liebling and S. Maruna, "Introduction: The Effects Of Imprisonment Revisited," in A. Liebling and S. Maruna (eds.), *The Effects of Imprisonment* (Cullompton: Willan, 2005).

Chapter 9

Prisoner Rights

LEARNING OBJECTIVES

1. Identify what types of prisoner rights stem from the First, Fourth, Eighth, and Fourteenth Amendments.

2. Explain how a lack of medical care could be an unconstitutional violation of the Eighth Amendment.

3. What rights do prisoners have before being transferred to segregation? Transferred to a more secure prison? Transferred to a prison out of state?

4. Do probationers and parolees have the same rights as free people? Explain.

5. Explain what collateral consequences are and provide some examples.

CHAPTER OUTLINE

- **Prisoner Rights** 238

- **Rights During Community Supervision** 252

- **Collateral Consequences** 254

- **SUMMARY** 257

During the "hands off" era of prisoner rights, it was believed that prisoners had no civil rights; however, the Supreme Court has recognized that prisoners do have a range of rights, for instance, under the 1st, 8th, and 14th Amendments.

KEY TERMS

Activist era
Administrative segregation
Building tenders
Collateral consequences
Deliberate indifference
    standard
Disenfranchisement
Due deference approach

Good time
Hands-off era
Jailhouse lawyer
Prisoner Litigation Reform Act
    (PLRA)
Rational relationship test
Religious Freedom Restoration
    Act (RFRA)

Religious Land Use and
    Institutionalized Persons
    Act (RLUIPA)
Section 1983 suit
Strict scrutiny test
Totality of the circumstances

 # Prisoner Rights

Once an individual has been found guilty and sentenced to prison, many people assume that he or she has (or should have) no rights. Up until the 1960s this was, to some extent, true. Federal and state courts refused to hear prisoners' rights cases or decided such cases in a way that made it clear that prisoners had few, if any, of the rights of free people. This era was called the **hands-off era**, meaning that the federal courts rarely became involved in prisoners' rights cases. In *Ruffin v. Commonwealth* (1871), for example, the Virginia Supreme Court stated that the inmate was a "slave of the state," with only those rights given to him by the state.[1] Even though some court decisions in the late 1800s and early 1900s condemned inhumane treatment, generally, prisoners were not seen as having any rights at all.[2]

During the Warren Court era (1953–1969), named after Chief Justice Earl Warren, the Supreme Court published several opinions that expanded the civil rights of students, the mentally ill, racial minorities, criminal defendants, and prisoners. During this **activist era** of the late 1960s, the Court utilized the Fourteenth Amendment to expand the protections enumerated in the Bill of Rights. In *Wolff v. McDonnell* (1974), the U.S. Supreme Court made it clear that prisoners were not simply slaves of the state in saying: "There is no iron curtain drawn between the Constitution and the prisons of this country."[3] Cases established rights related to religion, speech and association, cruel and unusual punishment, and due process. The activist era was short-lived, however, and after Chief Justice Warren Burger replaced Chief Justice Earl Warren, the Burger Court (1969–86) swung to what has been called the **due deference approach**, meaning that if correctional authorities had any rational reason for denying prisoners' rights, they could do so.

In 1996, Congress passed the **Prisoner Litigation Reform Act (PLRA)**, which was very successful in its intent to dramatically reduce the number of prisoner rights cases heard in federal courts. The new law required prisoners to exhaust all administrative remedies before filing a **Section 1983 suit**, a civil suit alleging that an agent of the state has violated one's constitutional rights, that had been used frequently by inmates against government officials. The source for this type of lawsuit comes from Title 42 U.S.C. Sec. 1983, which strips officials of immunities enjoyed by governmental entities if they violate an individual's constitutional rights. In effect, the suit is against the official in his or her individual capacity. The prisoner must show that there has been a constitutional deprivation or violation by the governmental official acting under color of law. Under Section 1983, the prisoner is entitled to actual and punitive damages and injunctive relief if successful. The passage of PLRA made these lawsuits much more difficult to file and win: inmates had to show physical injury and pay a $120 court filing fee (even for poor inmates), and attorneys' pay had to come out of any judgment won. The law also prohibited federal judges from imposing indefinite consent decrees (the vehicle by which many state prisons were brought into compliance with humane standards) and limited a special master's (court monitor's) pay to $40 an hour. The Supreme Court upheld the constitutionality of the PLRA, and prisoner rights litigation shifted to state courts, using state constitutions as the source of rights because federal courts were perceived to be unsympathetic.[4]

In every case involving prisoners' rights, there is a decision to be made between the alleged right of the prisoner and the state's interest to run a safe, secure, and orderly prison. In most cases, prisoners' rights come from either the federal or state constitutions. For instance, the right to practice one's religion freely comes from the First Amendment; the right to be free from excessive brutality comes from the Eighth Amendment; and so on. In older cases, a **strict scrutiny test** was used to weigh these competing interests. In this test, when an inmate alleges that one of their rights is being violated, the state has to prove an "overriding" state interest, a close relationship between the rule or procedure at issue and the safety or security of the institution, and that no less intrusive means are available to reach the goal of safety and security.

In almost all cases today, the court applies a **rational relationship test** which makes it easier for states to win. When inmates allege a right is being violated by a prison rule or procedure, prison administrators must prove a state interest and "some" relationship between that interest and the rule or procedure in question. More specifically, as described in *Turner v. Safley* (1987), states must prove that 1) there is a "valid, rational connection" between the regulation and a legitimate and neutral governmental interest; 2) prisoners have alternative means of exercising the asserted right; 3) accommodation of the asserted right has a negative impact on prison staff, prisoners, and the allocation of limited prison resources; and 4) the regulation does not represent an "exaggerated response" to prison concerns.[5]

Most often, prisoners look to the Bill of Rights and the Fourteenth Amendment for the source of the right at issue (see Figure 9.1). The protections in the Bill of Rights apply only to individuals against actions of the federal government. However, rights can be "incorporated" into one's rights as a state citizen (against state actors) by case law through an application of the due process clause of the Fourteenth Amendment. In other words, the original First Amendment only protected individuals against the federal government infringing upon First Amendment rights, for example, acts of suppression by federal agents. Only after that right was "incorporated" did it protect against a city or state depriving individuals of their rights of free speech. Of course, courts have recognized that states and the federal government can impose reasonable limits on when and how any right is expressed. In addition to the federal Bill of Rights, prisoners might also have rights recognized under their own state constitution.

Bill of Rights

[1] *Congress shall make no law respecting an establishment of religion, or prohibiting the free exercise thereof; or abridging the freedom of speech, or of the press; or the right of the people peaceably to assemble, and to petition the Government for a redress of grievances.*

[2] *A well-regulated Militia, being necessary to the security of a free State, the right of the people to keep and bear Arms, shall not be infringed.*

[3] *No Soldier shall, in time of peace be quartered in any house, without the consent of the Owner, nor in time of war, but in a manner to be prescribed by law.*

[4] *The right of the people to be secure in their persons, houses, papers, and effects, against unreasonable searches and seizures, shall not be violated, and no Warrants shall issue, but upon probable cause, supported by Oath or affirmation, and particularly describing the place to be searched, and the persons or things to be seized.*

[5] *No person shall be held to answer for a capital, or otherwise infamous crime, unless on a presentment or indictment of a Grand Jury, except in cases arising in the land or naval forces, or in the Militia, when in actual service in time of War or public danger; nor shall any person be subject for the same offence to be twice put in jeopardy of life or limb; nor shall be compelled in any criminal case to be a witness against himself, nor be deprived of life, liberty, or property, without due process of law; nor shall private property be taken for public use, without just compensation.*

[6] *In all criminal prosecutions, the accused shall enjoy the right to a speedy and public trial, by an impartial jury of the State and district wherein the crime shall have been committed, which district shall have been previously ascertained by law, and to be informed of the nature and cause of the accusation; to be confronted with the witnesses against him; to have compulsory process for obtaining witnesses in his favor, and to have the Assistance of Counsel for his defense.*

[7] *In suits at common law, where the value in controversy shall exceed twenty dollars, the right of trial by jury shall be preserved, and no fact tried by a jury, shall be otherwise re-examined in any Court of the United States, than according to the rules of the common law*

[8] *Excessive bail shall not be required, nor excessive fines imposed, nor cruel and unusual punishments inflicted.*

[9] *The enumeration in the Constitution, of certain rights, shall not be construed to deny or disparage others retained by the people.*

[10] *The powers not delegated to the United States by the Constitution, nor prohibited by it to the States, are reserved to the States respectively, or to the people.*

FIGURE 9.1 Bill of Rights, U.S. Constitution.

Source: U.S. Constitution

Religion

The First Amendment states that "Congress shall make no law respecting an establishment of religion, or prohibiting the free exercise thereof. . ." Arguments for restricting religious practices in prison usually involve security concerns and if it is a reasonable argument, the state usually wins. Notwithstanding such arguments, prisoners have had religious liberties recognized when they do not conflict with prison security. Some practices that have been litigated include wearing religious jewelry, for example, a crucifix (Christianity); wearing hair in dreadlocks (Rastafarian); refusing to take a shower in front of others (Islam); demanding the prison allow a sweat lodge to be built (Native American); wearing a head covering (Islam and Judaism); demanding the prison provide a pork-free diet (Islam and Judaism); and demanding the space and time for religious ceremonies (all religions).

Prisoners have a First Amendment right to practice their religion as long as it does not interfere with the safety and security of the prison.

Early cases balancing religious rights against institutional security tended to be brought by Black Muslims who were denied the opportunity to meet for religious purposes, access religious leaders, wear religious emblems, and so on. Prison officials in the 1960s and 1970s believed that the Muslim faith included beliefs that threatened the security of the institution, so Muslims were usually treated differently from those who practiced other faiths. Generally, prisoners won these cases if the state could not prove there was a security risk.[6] In *Cruz v. Beto* (1972), the Supreme Court held that inmates cannot be denied the opportunity to practice an unconventional American religion (in this case, Buddhism) when other inmates are given the chance to pursue conventional faiths.[7] In some cases, courts did accept the state's argument of economics or convenience (e.g., that there were too few inmates practicing the faith to justify special accommodations).[8]

Most cases involve established religions such as Islam, Christianity, or Judaism. However, some prisoners' rights cases dealt with unrecognized and/or newer religions (arguably cults or made-up religions). For instance, several cases beginning in the 1970s concerned a group of inmates who had created the "Church of the New Song" (CONS). They argued that to practice this religion, they had to eat steak and drink cream sherry. Eventually this so-called religion was practiced in several different states.[9] Interestingly, some courts did recognize it as a religion, but prisoners could not convince any court of their need to drink Harvey's Bristol Cream sherry as part of their religious doctrine.[10]

There have been conflicts between federal circuits. Some federal appellate courts held that prison officials could not deny entry to Muslim religious leaders (due to their criminal records); other federal appellate courts held that such prohibitions were justified by security concerns. Most federal appellate courts have held that states do not need to provide a pork-free diet or pork alternative for Muslims, but a few courts said that the state must provide a pork substitute with low-cost protein, such as peanut butter. While some federal appellate courts held that prison officials could not prohibit religious publications or materials, others held that as long as there was some opportunity to practice religion, those materials that might be misconstrued or inflammatory could be denied. In *O'Lone v. Shabazz* (1987), the Supreme Court, using the rational relationship test, determined that prison authorities were justified in not allowing Muslim prisoners on a work detail back into the prison for a religious service and made it clear that so long as prison authorities had a rational reason (usually a security concern) for denying some religious practice, they could do so.[11]

In 1993, Congress passed the **Religious Freedom Restoration Act (RFRA)**.[12] Prisons and jails were not expressly excluded from the protection of the Act; thus, it appeared that the law would drastically limit the state's ability to restrict or prohibit religious practices even in prison. Under the RFRA, if the state restriction constituted a "substantial burden" on one's ability to practice his or her religion, then the government must show that the restriction "is in furtherance of a compelling governmental interest" and that it is the "least restrictive means" of furthering that interest. (In effect, Congress was forcing the courts to use the strict scrutiny test instead of the rational relationship test.) The Supreme Court, in *City of Boerne v. Flores* (1997), declared that Congress did not have the power to pass the RFRA and ruled it unconstitutional, at least as it applied to the states.[13] Then, in 2000, Congress passed the **Religious Land Use and Institutionalized Persons Act (RLUIPA)**. This act reinstated the strict scrutiny test when government actions presented a substantial burden to the practice of religion in cases of land use (zoning) and, surprisingly, extended the protections of religious liberty to prisoners. The RLUIPA was used in *Cutter v. Wilkinson* (2005), when a Wiccan, a Satanist, and a member of a racist Christian cult challenged an Ohio prison's restrictions against their religions.[14] Although the state argued the RLUIPA violated the establishment clause because it led to more favorable policies for those who followed a religion over those prisoners who followed no religion, the Supreme Court disagreed, upheld the RLUIPA, and remanded the case to a lower court to determine if the state met the strict scrutiny test for restricting those religions. *Holt v. Hobbs* (2015), another RLUIPA case, was decided in favor of an inmate who challenged a prison's policy of denying Muslim prisoners the right to grow a short beard to follow religious doctrine. In this case, the Supreme Court ridiculed the prison administrators' argument that short beards posed security concerns since it was much more likely, according to the court, that weapons would be hidden in long hair and clothing rather than in a beard half an inch long.

There have been a few cases challenging prison requirements that prisoners attend Alcoholic Anonymous (AA) meetings because AA refers to a higher power and does have religion as one of its core values. Because the First Amendment protects individuals from state-sponsored religion, some courts have forbidden states to require AA attendance.[15] In other cases, prisoners have challenged special privileges given to prisoners in faith-based prison programs, and some courts have agreed that more favorable treatment violates the establishment clause of the First Amendment.[16]

Speech and Association

The First Amendment also states that "Congress shall make no law . . . abridging the freedom of speech, or of the press . . ." and thus protects free speech. However, as you might expect, prisoners' rights regarding speech are substantially curtailed because of their status. Most prisoners' rights cases involving free speech have had to do with mail and censorship. The prisoner's right to receive mail and publications is balanced against the prison's right to protect safety and security. For instance, a prisoner has no right to a publication that describes, in detail, how to make a bomb out of kitchen ingredients, nor does he or she have a right to receive a letter detailing an escape attempt. Prisons also have a right to address "order" concerns, so that they are usually free to restrict the number of pieces of outgoing and incoming mail to manage it. Issues that are raised concerning the First Amendment and prison regulations include the following:

- Communication with the news media: generally, courts have upheld the right of prisoners to contact the media through letters, although they have rejected the media's right to interview or visit inmates;
- Communication with public officials: this type of mail is generally considered legal and deserving of legal mail privileges;
- Communication with inmates in other prisons: prison officials have the right to ban this communication;
- Receipt of inflammatory or pornographic material: prisons have the right to ban this material;
- Use of mail lists that restrict inmates to "approved" individuals: these are upheld but there must be a valid reason for denying a request;
- Receipt of books and packages: prisons may prohibit certain items and may have a rule that limits books only to those sent directly from publishers or bookstores; for some classifications of prisoners, all items are withheld.[17]

Media representatives and prisoners have argued that the First Amendment creates the media's right to access prisons to interview certain inmates and tell their story to the world; however, members of the media enjoy no special rights of access over and above the general public to any venue, including prisons. Freedom of the press refers to the freedom to publish, not freedom of access. Courts have made it clear that the governmental objective of preventing the creation of celebrity inmates is a good enough reason to deny reporters access to prisons and noted that there are alternative ways an inmate could reach the public, including writing letters and having visits with a family member who, in turn, could be interviewed by the media. The media can also participate in public tours and speak to inmates during these tours.[18]

Prisoners also have limited rights of association with others. For instance, states cannot punish inmates for joining a prisoner union, but they can prohibit solicitation and meetings.[19] Prisons can also restrict or prohibit visitation without due process.[20] However, the Supreme Court has ruled that prisons cannot unilaterally ban prisoners from marrying each other and must show a security interest for the denial.[21]

Unreasonable Search and Seizure

The Fourth Amendment states that "the right of the people to be secure in their persons, houses, papers, and effects, against unreasonable searches and seizures, shall not be violated, and no warrants shall issue, but upon probable cause, supported by oath or affirmation, and particularly describing the places to be searched, and the persons or things to be seized." Prisoners obviously do not have the same rights under the Fourth Amendment as free people. There is simply no such thing as an unreasonable search of a prisoner, up to and including full body cavity searches. Prisoners have no right to be present during cell searches, which can be done for any reason at any time. States do not need probable cause for any search, even a body cavity search.[22]

Surprisingly, even jail inmates who are pretrial detainees and have not been convicted can be strip searched without probable cause or even reasonable suspicion. In *Florence v. Board of Chosen Freeholders* (2012), the Supreme Court agreed that jail staff had the authority to strip search all those coming into a jail, even before a conviction, and even if there is no evidence that the person may have drugs or weapons. Florence was arrested under a simple traffic warrant, yet he was strip searched twice by jail personnel. He argued that individuals arrested for minor offenses and who posed no risk should not be strip searched, but the Supreme Court did not agree and held that individuals who were arrested and booked into any jail had no Fourth Amendment right to avoid strip searches if that was the practice of the jail admission process.[23]

Some lower courts have recognized some privacy rights of prisoners being strip searched by opposite-sex guards, but these cases are decided under privacy, a Fourteenth Amendment right, and holdings are in conflict across the federal circuit courts.[24]

Cruel and Unusual Punishment

The Eighth Amendment states that "excessive bail shall not be required, nor excessive fines imposed, nor cruel and unusual punishments inflicted." Since *Jackson v. Bishop* (1968), in which whipping was defined as cruel and unusual punishment, any corporal punishment—beatings, whippings, and so on—would be ruled unconstitutional.[25] More recent prisoners' rights cases concern the use of physical force by correctional officials during cell extractions, physical altercations, or incidents of collective violence.

In *Whitley v. Albers* (1986), an inmate alleged that being shot in the leg by correctional authorities during a hostage-taking incident was cruel and unusual punishment. The Supreme Court indicated that state officials had great latitude in determining the use of force necessary to respond to collective violence situations, offering four factors to consider in a balancing test to determine if state actions are malicious and sadistic:

1. the need to apply force;
2. the relationship between that need and the amount of force actually used;
3. the threat to staff and other inmates' safety as reasonably perceived by prison officials; and
4. efforts made to temper the severity of officials' forceful response.[26]

However, the Supreme Court also made it clear that unnecessary force, no matter how minor, was not allowed. In *Hudson v. McMillian* (1992), a prisoner had been hit in the face after being handcuffed and shackled.[27] Because the inmate was already subdued, the injury was deemed wanton and in violation of the Eighth Amendment. Periodically, cases reinforce the view that needless pain or cruelty will not be tolerated. For instance, when an Alabama prisoner was handcuffed to a hitching post for seven hours in the sun with no water or bathroom breaks, the court ruled that any reasonable person should have known that it was a violation of the Eighth Amendment.[28]

Other practices can also inflict gratuitous and unnecessary pain, such as a lack of medical care. The Eighth Amendment also prohibits inadequate medical care when it results in pain and suffering. In *Estelle v. Gamble* (1976), the Supreme Court held that to be deliberately indifferent to the medical needs of an inmate would cause needless pain, unrelated to the goals of incarceration.[29] As such, it would constitute cruel and unusual punishment and violate the individual's constitutional rights. The **deliberate indifference standard** is harder to prove than simple or even gross negligence, although prisoners have won cases when they can prove that the state was indifferent to the medical needs of prisoners.[30]

Mental health treatment is akin to medical treatment; thus, the absence of any psychiatric or psychological treatment for those who are diagnosed with mental illness has been ruled unconstitutional by a federal appellate court.[31] In *Ruiz v. Estelle* (1980), a federal district judge enumerated the minimal necessary elements for a mental health system in prison:

- a systematic screening procedure;
- treatment that entails more than segregation and supervision;
- treatment that involves a sufficient number of mental health professionals to adequately provide services to all prisoners suffering from serious mental disorders;
- maintenance of adequate and confidential clinical records;
- a program for identifying and treating suicidal inmates; and
- a ban on prescribing potentially dangerous medications without adequate monitoring.[32]

In *Helling v. McKinney* (1993), the Supreme Court held that exposing inmates to cigarette smoking by cellmates or correctional officers endangered their health, and that authorities were deliberately indifferent if they did not accommodate requests to be housed away from cigarette smoke.[33] This decision eventually led to states banning tobacco entirely from prisons.

If prison officials are deliberately indifferent to the risk of injury by other inmates, this negligence could result in a finding of cruel and unusual punishment as well. In *Farmer v. Brennan* (1994) a transgender inmate, who was transitioning from being a man to a woman, was placed in general population despite the obvious risk of rape. She was beaten and raped repeatedly and acquired HIV through the sexual assaults. The Supreme Court held that correctional officers were deliberately indifferent to the risk of sexual assault and violated the Eighth Amendment by not placing this inmate in protective housing.[34]

The Eighth Amendment has also been used to challenge being required to participate in treatment programs and/or be subjected to involuntary injection of psychotropic drugs. In *Knecht v. Gillman* (1973), it was decided that prisoners could not be forced to stay in a behavior modification program that was defined as experimental.[35] However, in *Washington v. Harper* (1990), the Supreme Court held that prisoners could be injected with antipsychotic drugs against their will if prison and medical staff felt the inmate posed a continuing danger to himself or others.[36]

Although prisoners have the right to medical attention for injuries or illnesses and mental health treatment for serious mental illness, there is no right to rehabilitative programming (such as education, drug treatment, or vocational training), except perhaps as part of a **totality of the circumstances** case. The Focus box describes one offender who seems to have needed some type of treatment; however, did he need rehabilitative treatment (which he has no right to receive, according to some courts) or psychological treatment (the absence of which can be analyzed as a deprivation of medical care)?

Totality of circumstances cases define cruel and unusual punishment as a combination of living conditions; for example, high levels of violence, lack of staffing, sanitation deficiencies, and lack of rehabilitative programs. Plaintiffs argue that the combination of these factors should be found to constitute cruel

FOCUS ON THE OFFENDER

TRYING TO SURVIVE

Nick began struggling in elementary school when his parents' marriage fell apart. At eight years old, he was disruptive and angry and later was diagnosed with attention deficit disorder (ADD); at 14, he was diagnosed with bipolar disorder. He began smoking marijuana instead of taking prescribed medications and was expelled from school for selling weed at 16. At 18, he was arrested for armed robbery and assault with intent to murder after pointing a gun at three men and robbing them of $100. He was sentenced to six to eight years in prison, where he experienced crippling anxiety and paralyzing depression, yet received little help; as such, his anxiety was channeled into rage, causing frequent fights with other inmates. After being involved in a brutal fight that left another man in the hospital, Nick was so disgusted with himself that he tried to hang himself.

Upon his release from prison, he had been given several weeks' supply of an antidepressant and an antianxiety medication that helped him control his mental health issues; however, the community mental health clinic he attended did not renew the prescriptions. Once they ran out, his anxiety increased, and he returned to using marijuana and alcohol to calm himself. After a violent drug deal, he was arrested and charged with attempted murder. The charges were dropped, but because he had violated his parole, he was sent to a drug treatment facility that disallowed any form of drugs, including antianxiety and antidepressant medication. Nick continued to experience problems: five months after treatment, he failed a drug test; upon learning that his best friend had committed suicide after being sent back to prison for using drugs, Nick overdosed and was revived with Narcan. Then, Nick was involved in a late-night barroom brawl that led to two people being seriously injured. Nick received three to four years for aggravated assault with a dangerous weapon and assault causing bodily injury. He tried to explain in a letter to his father that the drugs he took on the street helped him "fix" his brain; that he needed them like "water" to live. In prison, he wasn't given the same medication as before, so he opted to go without medication and ended up in segregation. When he gets out of prison again, he will be in his thirties.

Questions for Discussion

1. Should Nick have a constitutional right to comprehensive mental health care?

2. Do you think Nick's drug crimes were due to his mental health issues?

Source: M. Cramer and J. Russell, "The Desperate and the Dead," Boston Globe, November 25, 2016, http://apps.bostonglobe.com/spotlight/the-desperate-and-the-dead/series/prisons/?p1=Spotlight_MI_Overview_Read.

and unusual punishment, thus violating the Eighth Amendment. The remedy in many of these cases has been to appoint prison monitors to track the progress of prison systems in meeting court-ordered conditions; sometimes monitors oversee prison systems for years.

One of the first and most notorious cases of this type was *Holt v. Sarver* (1971).[37] In this case, the use of inmates to guard other inmates, extreme levels of violence in open barracks with no guard supervision, overcrowded and unsanitary cells, lack of rehabilitative programming, and lack of medical care at an Arkansas prison constituted cruel and unusual punishment according to the courts. Another totality case was *Ruiz v. Estelle* (1980), in which a federal court found Texas prison conditions, including the use of **building tenders** (inmate guards), the lack of medical care, and the level of violence to be unconstitutional.[38] The case led to court oversight of the prison system for over 20 years until a federal judge finally released Texas from mandatory monitoring in 2002.[39]

In *Wilson v. Seiter* (1991), the Supreme Court made it more difficult for inmates to win a totality of the circumstances case by requiring proof that prison officials were *deliberately* indifferent, not just a clear pattern of deficits.[40] Thus, inmates had to prove that the prison administration knew and deliberately disregarded all the elements that constituted the claim of unconstitutional conditions. This requirement was met in the case of *Madrid v. Gomez* (1995). Inmates at Pelican Island, California's supermax facility, alleged constitutional violations in the lack of medical care, excessive use of force, and the presence of mentally ill inmates in the supermax prison with no access to treatment. The inmates won, and the consent decree, overseen by a special monitor, continues to this day.

In *Brown v. Plata* (2011), the Supreme Court decided another California case concerning prison medical care.[41] Since the mid-1990s, in several class action suits, courts had found deficiencies, including inadequate medical screening of incoming prisoners; delays in or failure to provide access to medical care; untimely responses to medical emergencies; the interference of custodial staff with the provision of medical care; the failure to recruit and retain sufficient numbers of competent medical staff; disorganized and incomplete medical records; a lack of quality control procedures; and a lack of protocols to deal with chronic illnesses, including diabetes, heart disease, hepatitis, and HIV. After giving the state years to address these problems and with no progress made, the Ninth Circuit Court ordered the release of 40,000 prisoners. The state appealed the decision to the Supreme Court, which upheld the lower court's decision, finding that the overcrowded conditions of California prisons created conditions that violated the Eighth Amendment. This led to a drastic reduction of the state's prisoner population and major improvements in medical services.

Due Process

The Fourteenth Amendment states that "No state shall make or enforce any law which shall abridge the privileges or immunities of citizens of the United States; nor shall any state deprive any person of life, liberty, or property, without due process of law; nor deny to any person within its jurisdiction the equal protection of the law." Known as the due process and equal protection clauses, both have been utilized in prisoners' rights suits. The due process clause dictates that every individual facing a possible deprivation of a "liberty interest" by a governmental entity be entitled to certain due process procedures designed to prevent or minimize error in the decision. For instance, when the government seeks to take away one's life, liberty, or property, or any other liberty interest, it must first allow certain fact-finding procedures: notice, a neutral hearing, the right to be present and present evidence, the right to cross-examine, the right to counsel, and the right of appeal. Not all elements are deemed necessary for all deprivations. Generally, the greater the deprivation, the more extensive the due process elements. Note that the due process clause does not protect individuals against these deprivations by the state; the purpose is only to prevent error and arbitrary and capricious state action or deprivations.

The Fourteenth Amendment protects access to courts, which is important because this right protects all other rights. If prisoners have no access to courts, then recognized rights are worthless because there is no way to protect them when they are denied. Even during the hands-off era, the Supreme Court made it clear that state officials could not interfere with access to courts by confiscating legal documents or requiring that prisoners seek permission from prison authorities before filing lawsuits.[42] The Fourteenth Amendment also covers issues such as what due process is necessary before prison transfers (including for mental health reasons), prison discipline, parole and probation revocation hearings, and protections for visitation, a healthy environment, treatment, and so on.

The sequence of access cases clearly illustrates the Supreme Court's shift from the activist era to the due deference era. In *Johnson v. Avery* (1969), the Supreme Court held that a state could not punish a **jailhouse lawyer** (an inmate with expertise in writing legal briefs) for helping inmates with their cases if the state provided no alternative means for inmates to receive legal assistance.[43] Other cases followed requiring prison officials to provide access to law libraries, postage and photocopying, and visits with paralegals or attorney representatives. However, in the next decade, the Supreme Court was not concerned when access required a great deal of inconvenience for the inmate. In *Bounds v. Smith* (1977), the Supreme Court decided that having the prisoner travel to a law library at another prison, giving up his cell and program slot, was not unduly burdensome and satisfied the access-to-court requirement.[44] By 1996, in *Lewis v. Casey*, the Supreme Court made it almost impossible for a prisoner to win an access-to-court case at all when it held that a prisoner must demonstrate that alleged shortcomings of a prison's access to legal assistance (law library and/or some legal representation) caused actual injury and hindered the prisoner's ability to win his or her case.[45] Because it would be difficult, if not impossible, to prove that the lack of legal materials or assistance was the reason why the inmate's petition was denied or case was lost, this case seemed to signal the end of the Supreme Court's interest in making sure that inmates had sufficient access to the courts.

As we discussed, due process is required whenever a protected liberty interest is at stake. It is obviously a liberty interest when the state seeks to incarcerate someone accused of a crime, which is why the most extensive due process exists before someone is sentenced to prison. What if, however, a prisoner is transferred from a minimum-security prison to a maximum-security prison with fewer privileges and harsher living conditions? Whether inmates deserve some type of due process hearing before such a move was the question in *Meachum v. Fano* (1976).[46] The Supreme Court held that a prisoner had *no* due process rights before being transferred to a harsher prison. In their words, the

Prisoners deserve some legal assistance, but the Supreme Court has determined that having access to a prison law library is sufficient.

prison administration could transfer for "good" reasons, "bad" reasons, or "no" reasons. In *Wilkinson v. Austin* (2005), the Supreme Court surprisingly held that there was a liberty interest in transfer to a supermax prison, specifically, because the supermax constituted an appreciably harsher and more punitive environment.[47] However, according to the Supreme Court, due process requirements were met by simply having a classification committee make the decision to transfer, and having the decision reviewed by the warden and a central classification bureau.

The *Meachum* analysis that prisoners had no rights regarding transfer was applied to a challenge of a state prisoner being transferred to a federal prison in *Howe v. Smith* (1981) and to a state prisoner being transferred to another state prison in *Olim v. Wakinekona* (1983).[48] Evidently, prisoners have no due process protections, even when such transfers involve great hardship to the prisoner and/or his or her family because he or she is transferred to another state, making visitation virtually impossible.

The Supreme Court has found that transfer to a mental hospital from a prison does trigger due process requirements. In *Vitek v. Jones* (1980), the Court ruled that involuntary transfer from a prison to a mental hospital setting necessitated a due process hearing.[49] This was because a mental hospital was qualitatively different from a prison, residents had greater limitations on their freedom, there is stigma attached to a stay in a mental hospital (evidently worse than or at least different from a prison sentence), and there was a mandatory behavior modification program in operation. These elements created a "major change in the conditions of confinement" amounting to a "grievous loss." The same due process protections that are required before any of us can be committed to a mental hospital must be in place, which include a presentation of evidence, an opportunity to object and present opposing evidence as to the need for involuntary hospitalization, and a judicial decision. Specifically, in order to transfer someone from a prison to a mental hospital, there must be written notice, a hearing, disclosure of evidence relied upon, an opportunity to be heard in person and present documentary evidence, an opportunity to present testimony and to confront and cross-examine witnesses (except upon a finding, not arbitrarily made, of good cause for not permitting such presentation, confrontation, or cross-examination), an independent decision maker, a written statement by a factfinder as to evidence relied upon and reasons for transferring the inmate, legal counsel (furnished by the state if the inmate is indigent), and effective and timely notice of all foregoing rights.

Prison officials punish inmates by transferring them to other prisons, taking away **good time** (time off the end of their sentence for good behavior), placing them in solitary confinement, putting the inmate in day-lock (confinement in their cell), and/or depriving them of other privileges such as visitation. All involve some form of deprivation and, therefore, the question becomes whether the deprivation is severe enough to deserve due process. *Wolff v. McDonnell* (1974) was one of the first prison disciplinary cases heard by the Supreme Court.[50] In this case, the Court held that a prison must provide some due process before taking away good time or putting an inmate in solitary confinement. Even though there is no right to good time inherent in the due process clause, such a right had been created by the state (by statutory language) and, therefore, required due process protections. The Court held that at a minimum, the procedural protections necessary included

- a disciplinary proceeding by an impartial body,
- 24 hours' advance written notice of the claimed violation,

- a written statement from the fact-finders as to the evidence relied upon and the reasons for the disciplinary action, and
- an opportunity for the inmate to call witnesses and to present documentary evidence (provided this is not hazardous to institutional safety or correctional goals).

Prisoners were not awarded the right to counsel. The Court grouped loss of good time and solitary confinement together because both affected the length and nature of confinement. Solitary confinement, or punitive segregation, was described as a major change, and the Court considered the possibility that a sanction of punitive segregation could later ruin a prisoner's chance for an early parole.

After *Wolff*, most states adopted a two-tier procedure whereby minor infractions that might be punished by less severe sanctions were separated from major infractions that could end in loss of good time and/or segregation. Only the latter charges were processed through disciplinary hearing procedures. Disciplinary hearings are often conducted by adjustment committees, with both classification and treatment staff members represented along with custody staff members. Some states employ outside hearing officers. These hearings do not bear much resemblance to our vision of trials, however, since all participants tend to be prison officials and the level of proof necessary to determine guilt in a prison disciplinary case is merely "some evidence."[51]

Later cases restricted the reach of the *Wolff* decision to only require substantive due process when the deprivation of good time is at stake, not requiring the same level of due process before imposing solitary confinement. First, in *Hewitt v. Helms* (1983), the Supreme Court held that those sent to **administrative segregation** required some due process only because the state created the right with administrative language. The majority held that the transfer of an inmate to more restrictive quarters for non-punitive reasons was within the terms of confinement ordinarily contemplated by a prison sentence and not atypical, therefore not constituting a protected liberty interest and, thereby, not requiring due process protections. Administrative segregation is used for those awaiting transfer, newly transferred prisoners, those seeking protective custody, and those waiting for disciplinary proceedings. It operates the same way as punitive segregation: prisoners are locked in their cells for 23 hours a day, they have no access to programs or yard recreation, they have isolated visitation schedules, and have other restrictions.

Then, in *Sandin v. Conner* (1995), the Supreme Court held that even punitive segregation did not require due process because it was not an "atypical, significant deprivation," and thus it did not trigger due process requirements.[52] Although the Court argued that it was merely reverting back to the analysis first proposed in *Wolff*, this decision effectively overturned *Wolff* because in that earlier case the majority did believe that being locked in one's cell for 23 hours a day and having no opportunity to take part in any programs or education was atypical and implicated a significant liberty interest. In the aftermath of *Sandin*, the only type of liberty interest deserving of due process protection is any deprivation that fundamentally alters the length of the original prison sentence, such as taking away good time. In practice, many states kept the disciplinary procedures in place that had been created in response to *Wolff*.

More recently, cases regarding due process as it pertains to solitary confinement have garnered attention. In *Williams v. Pennsylvania Secretary of Corrections* (2017), the Third Circuit issued a holding that prohibited correctional officials from holding some inmates in solitary confinement indefinitely.[53] The case consolidated challenges from two inmates, Craig Williams and Shawn Walker, with somewhat unique circumstances. Both had been on death row, but had their sentences vacated and were awaiting resentencing. During that time, both continued to be held in solitary confinement, which involved living in a windowless cell measuring 7 by 12 feet. A news story about Walker described how he could leave his cell five times a week to spend two-hour intervals in an exercise area known as the "dog cage," but not before having to endure a body cavity search. Walker spent 20 years under these conditions and developed insomnia, acute emotional distress, and uncontrollable body tremors. The first 14 years he was kept in solitary confinement because he was on death row; however, after his capital sentence was vacated, the state kept him in solitary confinement until a court mandated that he be placed in general population. Walker alleged the last six years he spent in solitary confinement were a violation of due process. The Third Circuit agreed and held that under the Fourteenth Amendment, inmates have a liberty interest in not being subjected to solitary confinement "absent procedural protections that ensured the confinement was appropriate" and "required for penological purposes." The ruling appears to apply to all inmates in solitary confinement.[54]

There seems to be a growing consensus among federal courts that solitary confinement is used too frequently, for too long, and without adequate provisions for due process. The language of the Third Circuit's opinion also brings into question whether solitary confinement is cruel and unusual because of the psychological damage that it inflicts upon inmates, especially those who spend long periods of time there. The Third Circuit cited with approval other court rulings that limited the time inmates could be kept in solitary confinement, with 30 days seeming to be a benchmark for some type of due process hearing to determine if continued solitary confinement was warranted.[55]

Today, under the Supreme Court's current due deference approach, prison administrators have been given broad latitude to run their prisons the way they see fit. Although prisoners still possess certain fundamental rights (of minimal medical care, sanitation, and safety), there are few other recognized rights.

Solitary confinement has been ruled cruel and unusual by some courts if it extends beyond 30 days.

Rights During Community Supervision

Most of this chapter has discussed the rights of prisoners, but those under correctional supervision in the community are also under a restricted liberty status. This means that they do not have the same rights as people not under correctional supervision.

Probation

Recall from Chapter 4 that a state is not required to have probation as a sentencing option; however, once it is given to an offender, it is considered a protected interest and there must be due process before it is taken away. In *Mempa v. Rhay*, in 1967, the Supreme Court ruled that if sentencing was deferred, meaning that the length of the prison term was *not* decided, the revocation hearing became a type of sentencing hearing. Because it was more like a sentencing hearing and considered a critical stage in the proceeding, the probationer had a Sixth Amendment right to an attorney.[56] If an offender's sentence was suspended, meaning that the length of prison term was decided, then the revocation hearing was more like an administrative hearing, not a sentencing hearing, but due process still applied. The right to an attorney in these cases is conditional and is required when there would be a threat to due process if denied. In the *Gagnon v. Scarpelli* (1973) case, the Supreme Court held that if a probationer was facing revocation, he must receive

- the notice of alleged violations of probation and evidence,
- an opportunity to appear and to present evidence and witnesses,
- the right to confront adverse witnesses,
- a neutral decision maker,
- a written report, and
- a *conditional* right to counsel when there is a question of guilt or innocence or the individual is not likely to understand the proceedings.[57]

While the Fourth Amendment protects against unreasonable searches or seizures by governmental actors, generally defined as requiring probable cause, probationers (and parolees) have diminished liberty interests. Courts have upheld the right of the probation officer to search without a warrant even when the search also intrudes upon the privacy of other people living in the house.[58] The reasoning is that the probationer is under a restricted liberty status, and the special need to protect the public justifies the lack of a warrant requirement. The Supreme Court found in *Griffin v. Wisconsin* that it was acceptable for the state to replace the probable cause for a search requirement with a reasonable grounds standard as the test for justifying the search. This is not a reasonable suspicion standard, and, in fact, may be met by the state's regulation requiring probationers to submit to such searches as part of the conditions of probation.[59] Generally, as part of the probation order, probationers have given the probation officer the right to search their person or home without a search warrant.

In *United States v. Knights* in 2001, the Supreme Court upheld a conviction of conspiracy to commit arson, among other related crimes, against a California man who had challenged a search of his home by probation and police officers. The search resulted in the finding of explosives, while he was on probation for drug possession.[60] The search was done because he was suspected of damaging government property. The probationer's challenge made a distinction between searches to ensure conditions are met on the current probation sentence versus law enforcement investigatory searches regarding new crimes, but the Supreme Court declined to make that type of search distinction when done by probation officers. Probationers in California are required to submit to searches with or without warrants or even reasonable cause by any probation officer or law enforcement officer. The Supreme Court stated that the legitimate interests of the state in preventing further crime by convicted probationers greatly outweighed the privacy interests of the probationer because of his/her diminished liberty status.

Recall that a state may recognize greater rights than the Supreme Court through the state constitution. While some states allow warrantless searches of probationers and parolees by police officers, other states limit the scope of the searches, require some standard of proof, or require a police officer to conduct the search with a probation or parole officer.[61] One legal review indicated that 13 states allowed warrantless searches by police officers, although some of these states required reasonable suspicion. North Carolina allows warrantless searches of the person or vehicle, but not the residence. Louisiana permits police to search only convicted sex offenders, with reasonable suspicion. Alaska, Florida, Indiana, Massachusetts, Michigan, Mississippi, Montana, New Hampshire, New York, and Oregon require police officers to be with probation or parole officers who conduct the search. About half of the states do not have enabling statutes or caselaw that allow warrantless searches by police officers, but these states do require the probationer or parolee to agree to a probation or parole condition whereby the person must give permission for any search by a probation or parole officer.[62]

Parole

In *Greenholtz v. Inmates of the Nebraska Penal and Correctional Complex* (1979), the Supreme Court held that no prisoner had a right to parole.[63] States could create a parole system, or they could abolish parole. They could also determine the level of due process in the decision to grant parole. Although prisoners do not have a right to parole, once they have been granted parole, there are some rights recognized by the Supreme Court as belonging to parolees regarding their supervision status.

Parolees, who are considered to have a conditional liberty status, do not have the same Fourth Amendment rights against unreasonable search and seizure as do those who are not on parole. In one case where a parolee challenged a search by police officers, the Supreme Court decided that a clause in a state's penal code that stated parolees must "agree in writing to be subject to search or seizure by a parole officer or other peace officer . . . with or without a search warrant and with or without cause" did not violate the Fourth Amendment's prohibition against unreasonable search or seizure.[64] Current law indicates that warrantless searches of parolees can be conducted if there is an express condition, regulation, or statute that gives the supervision officer or peace officer the authority to conduct such searches, or if the parolee consents, as long as the search isn't for the purpose of harassment.[65]

In *Morrissey v. Brewer*,[66] the Supreme Court held that, if the state wished to revoke parole and send the individual back to prison, a parolee should receive a preliminary hearing at the location where he lives to determine if there is enough evidence to justify a full hearing. Then, if it is determined that there is enough evidence to continue to hold the individual in custody, a full hearing should occur. The parolee has fewer rights at this hearing than he or she did at the criminal trial and fewer rights than a probationer facing revocation because it is presumed that the deprivation of parole is not as serious as the deprivation of probation. The rights recognized included the following:

- notice of the charges and evidence,
- neutral hearing body,
- a right to be present,
- to present evidence,
- a qualified right to present and cross-examine witnesses (the right can be overcome by a showing of unreasonableness),
- right to a statement of the decision and facts relied upon,
- right to appeal, and
- no right to a lawyer unless there is a serious question of competence.

Later court cases indicated that the bifurcated hearing was not necessary if the full hearing took place in a reasonable amount of time after the parolee had been notified of the potential revocation. Many states ask parolees to waive the preliminary hearing even if they still have the formal process in place; thus, in most cases, there is just one revocation hearing. The standard of proof in both the probation and parole revocation hearings is "preponderance," which is a lesser standard that the "beyond a reasonable doubt" standard of a criminal trial. Courts have also ruled that the exclusionary rule does not apply, so evidence obtained illegally can be used in a revocation hearing even though it would not be admissible in a criminal trial.[67]

In sum, parole is considered a conditional liberty status and, therefore, parolees have fewer rights than free people in terms of search and seizure. They do have, however, some due process rights before parole can be revoked and they are sent back to prison.

Collateral Consequences

There has been growing recognition that ex-offenders are subjected to a range of civil sanctions that limit their ability to fully participate in the communities to which they return; these are called **collateral consequences** of punishment. For instance, in most states, ex-felons cannot vote; this is called **disenfranchisement**. In some states, their right to vote is permanently taken away, while, in others, they must wait a long time before they can petition to have their voting right reinstated. The origins of disenfranchisement lie in the concept of "civil death," an idea that goes back to the Greeks and existed through medieval times. For some crimes, if an individual was not executed, he experienced the deprivation of all rights: land and property were taken away, titles were stripped, and he had no recourse under the law to protect any right. This extreme punishment also was brought to the American colonies, but for only a few crimes.

It is estimated that there are around 6 million people that cannot vote because of disenfranchisement due to a criminal conviction. Today, Vermont and Maine are the only states that allow prisoners to vote while they are incarcerated. In 16 states and the District of Columbia, felons lose their voting rights only while incarcerated, and can register to vote upon release. In 21 states, felons lose their voting rights during incarceration and while on parole and/or probation. Former felons may also have to pay any outstanding fines, fees or restitution before their rights are restored as well. In 11 states, felons lose their voting rights indefinitely for some crimes, require a governor's pardon in order for

Type of disenfranchisment	None	Automatic restoration after prison release	Automatic restoration after completion of sentence	Post-sentence waiting or discretionary decision to restore
	ME, VT	CO, HI, IL, IN, MD, MA, MI, MT, NV, NH, ND, OH, OR, PA, RI, UT	AK, AR, CA, CT, GA, ID KS, LA, MN, MI, NJ, NM, NY, NC, OK	AL, AZ, DE, FL, IA, KT, MS, NE, TN, VA, WY

FIGURE 9.2 Felony Disenfranchisement, 2019. Created by author from https://www.ncsl.org/research/elections-and-campaigns/felon-voting-rights.aspx.

voting rights to be restored, face an additional waiting period after completion of sentence (including parole and probation), or require additional action before voting rights can be restored. In all cases, "automatic restoration" does not mean that voter registration is automatic. Typically, prison officials automatically inform election officials that an individual's rights have been restored. The person is then responsible for re-registering through normal processes. Figure 9.2 shows the status of disenfranchisement in 2019. Because several states are in the process of changing disenfranchisement laws, it will no doubt be inaccurate by now.

In the past several years, states have revised disenfranchisement laws allowing more ex-felons to vote. For instance, Florida has recently revised its disenfranchisement law; however, there is ongoing litigation as to how the legislation is to be interpreted (see the Focus on a State box). In many states, the attempt to pass new legislation to allow parolees the right to vote has not been successful. Interestingly, when Puerto Rico changed its law, their rate of voting by ex-felons was much higher than that of the general population.[68]

In addition to disenfranchisement, there are several other limitations that ex-offenders face in their attempt to re-enter society. Many employment licenses bar ex-felons, federal housing bars drug offenders, and there are federal prohibitions against allowing ex-offenders to utilize other forms of financial assistance. In 2012, the American Bar Association (ABA) launched the *National Inventory of the Collateral Consequences of Conviction*. Among the more common collateral consequences it outlines are those that restrict employment or occupational licensing and those that affect tangible benefits, such as education, housing, public benefits, and property rights. Other consequences in the database include

- ineligibility for government contracts and debarment from program participation,
- exclusion from management and operation of regulated businesses,
- restrictions on family relationships and living arrangements, such as child custody, fostering and adoption,
- bond requirements and other heightened standards for licensure,
- registration, lifetime supervision and residency requirements, and
- publication of an individual's criminal record or mandated notification to the general public or to particular private individuals.[69]

The ABA provides an interactive database of collateral consequences across the nation. Users can search by keyword or via a national map to see what collateral consequences exist in a specific state. The database also includes relief provisions by which collateral consequences may be avoided or mitigated.[70]

FOCUS ON A

STATE FLORIDA

In 2018 Florida's citizens initiated and passed a constitutional amendment to automatically restore the voting rights of felons after completion of their sentences (including parole and probation). Those convicted of murder or a felony sexual offense must still apply to the governor for voting rights restoration on a case-by-case basis. Before the amendment, Florida was one of the most restrictive states as to disenfranchisement of ex-felons. The Executive Clemency Board had to approve restoration of voting rights, and every ex-felon had to wait for five to seven years before even applying. Some felons, because of their crimes, could never apply for rights restoration.

In July 2019, SB 7066 was passed by the legislature and signed by the governor of Florida. It defined "completion of sentence" to include, along with completion of any sentence, the full payment of any ordered fines, fees, or costs. The effect of this legislation would be to drastically reduce the number of ex-felons eligible for restoration of voting rights because most offenders are assessed a range of fines and fees that they may never be able to pay.

Four lawsuits against Senate Bill 7066 were consolidated into one case, *Jones v. DeSantis*. Litigants argued that the voters who passed the constitutional amendment did not mean to withhold voting rights from those who owed court costs or supervision fees, and that withholding voting rights from ex-felons in this way amounts to a "poll tax," which has been declared unconstitutional. On January 16, 2020, the Florida Supreme Court issued its opinion, in which it found that "all terms of sentence" does include the satisfaction of all legal financial obligations. The lawsuit then went to the federal courts. In May 2020, the federal judge ruled that the state could not withhold voting rights solely because of financial debt to the state. The case will probably be appealed to a higher appellate level.

Discussion Questions

1. Do you think ex-felons should automatically be allowed to vote once they complete their sentence? Why or why not?

2. Poll taxes were eliminated in the past because they were discriminatory and seen as a way to disenfranchise Blacks. Do you think SB 7066 acts in a similar way?

Source: L. Mower, "A Game-Changer: Five Takeaways from Sunday's Ruling on Felon Voting," Tampa Bay Times, May 25, 2020, https://www.tampabay.com/florida-politics/buzz/2020/05/25/a-game-changer-five-takeaways-from-yesterdays-ruling-on-felon-voting/. J. Mitchell, "Lawsuit Concerning Voting Rights Restoration in Florida Goes to Trial." Ballotpedia, April 29, 2020, https://news.ballotpedia.org/2020/04/29/lawsuit-concerning-voting-rights-restoration-in-florida-goes-to-trial/.

Ex-felons lose Second Amendment rights. There are federal and state laws prohibiting gun ownership by ex-felons. Under federal law, a felon having been convicted of certain crimes and in possession of a firearm could face a mandatory 5-year sentence, or 15 years under the Armed Career Criminal Act.[71] In 2015, the Supreme Court ruled that one clause of the law was unconstitutionally vague in its description of a "violent felony" with no additional guidance as to what crimes would fall under that designation; however, the Court kept intact the remaining portions of the law that specified certain felonies.[72]

Collateral consequences affect a parolee's ability to obtain employment, housing, and re-unite with family members (if they are in housing that bars felons from residence). They may not be able to regain parental custody and may even be barred from volunteering. Criminal punishment may result in deportation, especially in recent years.[73] A Supreme Court case held that a defendant had a legitimate claim of inadequate counsel when a defense attorney did not inform his or her client of the likely potential for deportation after pleading guilty in a plea bargain arrangement.[74]

One of the most problematic aspects of being an ex-offender is being rejected as a potential job applicant simply because of one's status. Most job applications include the question "Have you ever been convicted of a felony?" Also, about 92 percent of employers perform criminal background checks on at least some job candidates, and 73 percent perform checks on all job candidates. This has spurred the "ban the box" efforts to encourage employers to avoid inquiring about criminal convictions unless it is directly relevant to the job. Ex-offenders have no rights against being discriminated against when applying for jobs, making it extremely difficult to build a productive life after a criminal sentence.[75] There has been a concerted effort across several states to reduce the collateral consequences of imprisonment, but such efforts have stalled due to the massive economic disruptions that occurred in 2020 due to the COVID pandemic.

Summary

- Prisoner rights litigation has gone through three distinct eras: *the hands-off era*, where federal courts refused to hear most cases in which prisoners alleged constitutional violations; *the activist era*, where federal courts established prisoner rights in several different areas; and *the due deference era*, in which federal courts are currently siding with states in most prisoner rights cases, unless there are egregious abuses.

- The First Amendment has been used to establish prisoner rights regarding the practice of religion if it does not interfere with safety or security. Prisoners have limited rights when it comes to corresponding or visiting with outside family or friends.

- The Eighth Amendment has been used to establish prisoner rights to minimal levels of medical care and to live in conditions that are not deliberately indifferent to health and welfare.

- The Fourteenth Amendment has been used to establish minimal due process protections when an inmate is punished by the loss of good time. Other types of punishments, such as administrative segregation, have been ruled as not deserving of the same type of due process protections; recently, however, it was held that prisoners in solitary confinement are entitled to periodic due process hearings to determine if they should remain in solitary confinement.

- Probationers and parolees are considered to have "conditional liberty status," meaning that they do not have as many rights as those not under correctional supervision; for example, reduced Fourth Amendment protections. There is no right to probation or parole, but once given, these are protected liberty interests, and there must be some due process before a revocation can occur.

- Collateral consequences are restrictions of the liberties of those who have been convicted of a crime. They include restrictions on rights such as the right to vote, the right to obtain professional licenses, and other rights.

PROJECTS

1. Construct a legal argument as to why inmates should have a legal right to visitation with their family. Now construct an argument as to why the state should be allowed to restrict or ban any visitation from outside friends and family. Explain which side you think would win in a court challenge where a prison banned all visits.

2. Do some online research on ex-felons' voting rights and determine whether Figure 9.1 is still accurate. How should it be changed?

NOTES

1. *Ruffin v. Commonwealth*, 61 Va. 790 (1871).

2. D. Wallace, "Prisoner Rights: Historical Views," in E. Latessa, A. Holsinger, J. Marquart, and J. Sorenson (eds), *Correctional Contexts: Contemporary and Classical Readings* (Los Angeles, CA: Roxbury Press, 2001), 229–38.

3. *Wolff v. McDonnell*, 418 U.S. 539, 539 (1974).

4. R. Harding, "In the Belly of the Beast: A Comparison of the Evolution and Status of Prisoners' Rights in the United States and Europe," *The Georgia Journal of International and Comparative Law.* 27(1998): 1–56; R. Roots, "Of Prisoners and Plaintiffs' Lawyers: A Tale of Two Litigation Reform Efforts," *Willamette Law Review*, 38, 2 (2002): 210–56.

5. *Turner v. Safley*, 482 U.S. 78 (1987).

6. See, for instance, *Cooper v. Pate*, 378 U.S. 546 (1964).

7. *Cruz v. Beto*, 405 U.S. 319 (1972).

8. *Gittlemacker v. Prasse*, 428 F.2d 1 (3rd Cir. 1970) (State did not have to provide Rabbi to the few Jewish prisoners); *Walker v. Blackwell*, 411 F.2d 23 (5th Cir. 1969) (State did not have to provide special meals to Muslim prisoners); *Kahane v. Carlson*, 527 F.2d 592 (2nd Cir., 1975) (State did not have to provide kosher food to Jewish prisoners).

9. *Theriault v. A Religious Office*, 895 F.2d 104 (2d Cir., 1990).

10. *Theriault v. Silbur*, 547 F.2d 1279 (5th Cir., 1977).

11. *O'Lone v. Estate of Shabazz*, 482 U.S. 342 (1987).

12. Religious Freedom Restoration Act [42 U.S.C. Sec. 2000b(b)(1)].

13. *City of Boerne v. Flores*, 117 S. Ct. 2157 (1997).

14. *Cutter v. Wilkinson*, 544 U.S. 709 (2005).

15. See, for instance, *Griffin v. Coughlin*, 88 N.Y. 2d 674 (1996).

16. See, for instance, *Americans United for Separation of Church and State v. Prison. Fellowship Ministries*, 509 F.3d 406 (8th Cir. 2007).

17. See, for instance, *Procunier v. Martinez*, 416 U.S. 396 (1974); *Turner v. Safley*, 482 U.S. 78 (1987); *Thornburgh v. Abbott*, 490 U.S. 401 (1989); *Beard v. Banks*, 548 U.S. 521 (2006).

18. *Pell v. Procunier*, 417 U.S. 817 (1974); *Saxbe v. Washington Post Co.*, 417 U.S. 843 (1974); *Houchins v. KQED*, 438 U.S. 1 (1978).

19. *Jones v. North Carolina Prisoners' Union*, 433 U.S. 119 (1977).

20. *Kentucky v. Thompson*, 109 S. Ct. 1904 (1989); *Overton v. Bazzetta*, 539 U.S. 126 (2003).

21. *Turner v. Safley*, 482 U.S. 78 (1987).

22. *Bell v. Wolfish*, 441 U.S. 520 (1979); *Hudson v. Palmer*, 468 U.S. 517 (1984).

23. *Florence v. Board of Chosen Freeholders of County of Burlington*, 566 U.S. 318 (2012).

24. *Jordan v. Gardner*, 986 F.2d 1521 (9th Cir., 1993); also, see J. Pollock *Women, Prison and Crime*, 2d ed. (Belmont, CA: Wadsworth, 2002), p. 166–67.

25. *Jackson v. Bishop*, 404 F.2d 571 (8th Cir. 1968).

26. *Whitley v. Albers*, 475 U.S. 312 (1986).

27. *Hudson v. McMillian*, 503 U.S. 1 (1992).

28. *Hope v. Pelzer*, 536 U.S. 730 (2002).

29. *Estelle v. Gamble*, 429 U.S. 97 (1976).

30. *Madrid v. Gomez*, 889 F. Supp. 1146 (N.D. Cal. 1995).

31. *Bowring v. Godwin*, 551 F2d 44 (4th Cir 1977).

32. 503 F. Supp. 1265 (S.D. Tex. 1980).

33. *Helling v. McKinney*, 509 U.S. 25 (1993).

34. *Farmer v. Brennan*, 511 U.S. 825 (1994).

35. *Knecht v. Gillman*, 448 F.2d 1136 (8th Cir., 1973).

36. *Washington v. Harper*, 494 U.S. 210 (1990).

37. *Holt v. Sarver*, 442 F.2d 304 (1971).

38. *Ruiz v. Estelle*, 688 F.2d 266 (5th Cir. 1982).

39. Austin American Statesman. 2002, "Protect Prison Reforms Along with Inmates," *Austin American Statesman*, June 19, 2002, A12.

40. *Wilson v. Seiter*, 501 U.S. 294 (1991).

41. *Brown v. Plata*, 131 S. Ct. 1910 (2011).

42. Ex parte Hull, 312 U.S. 546 (1941).

43. *Johnson v. Avery*, 393 U.S. 483 (1969).

44. *Bounds v. Smith*, 430 U.S. 817 (1977).

45. *Lewis v. Casey*, 518 U.S. 343 (1996).

46. *Meachum v. Fano*, 427 U.S. 215 (1976).

47. *Wilkinson v. Austin*, 545 U.S. 209 (2005).

48. *Howe v. Smith*, 452 U.S. 473 (1981); *Olim v. Wakinekona*, 103 S. Ct. 1741 (1983).

49. *Vitek v. Jones*, 445 U.S. 480 (1980).

50. *Wolff v. McDonnell*, 418 U.S. 539 (1974).

51. *Superintendent v. Hill*, 105 S. Ct. 2768 (1985).

52. *Sandin v. Conner*, 115 S. Ct. 2293 (1995).

53. *Williams v. Pennsylvania*, No. 15–1390, (3rd Cir, 2017).

54. *Williams v. Pennsylvania*, No. 15–1390, (3rd Cir, 2017).

55. M. Stern, "A New Court Ruling Takes Important Steps to Rein in Inhumane Incarceration. Will the Supreme Court Be Next?" *Slate Magazine*, February 10, 2017, http://www.slate.com/ articles/news_and_politics/ jurisprudence/2017/02/ the_time_is_right_for_the_ supreme_court_to_rein_in_ solitary_confinement.html.

56. *Mempa v. Rhay*, 389 U.S. 128 (1967).

57. *Gagnon v. Scarpelli*, 411 U.S. 778 (1973).

58. *Griffin v. Wisconsin*, 483 U.S. 868 (1987).

59. *Griffin v. Wisconsin*, 483 U.S. 868 (1987).

60. *United States v. Knights*, 534 U.S. 112 (2001).

61. P. Lyons and T. Jermstad, *Civil Liabilities and Other Legal Issues for Probation/Parole Officers and Supervisors* (Washington, DC: National Institute of Corrections, 2013).

62. A. Matz, J. Turner, and C. Hemmens, "Where and When Police Officers Can Conduct Warrantless Searches of Probationers/Parolees: A Legal Review," *Perspectives* (Winter, 2015), accessed December 27, 2018, http://www.appa-net. org/Perspectives/Perspectives_ V39_N1_P42.pdf.

63. *Greenholtz v. Inmates of the Nebraska Penal and Correctional Complex*, 442 U.S. 1 (1979).

64. *Samson v. California*, 547 U.S. 843 (2006).

65. *Pennsylvania Board of Probation and Parole v. Scott*, 524 U.S. 357 (1998).

66. *Morrissey v. Brewer*, 408 U.S. 471 (1972).

67. *Pennsylvania Board of Probation and Parole v. Scott*, 524 U.S. 357 (1998).

68. J. Manza and C. Uggen. *Locked Out: Felon Disenfranchisement and American Democracy* (Oxford University Press, 2006); V. Newkirk, "Polls for Prisons," *The Atlantic*, March 9, 2016, http://www. theatlantic.com/politics/ archive/2016/03/inmates- voting-primary/473016/.

69. M. Love, J. Roberts, and C. Klingele, *Collateral Consequences of Criminal Convictions: Law,* *Policy and Practice* (Eagan, Minn.: NACDL Press and Thomson Reuters Westlaw, 2013), 521 (section 9:10).

70. To use the database, go to the users' guide with hyperlinks: https://www.nij. gov/topics/courts/documents/ abacollateralconsequences- userguide.pdf.

71. *U.S. v. Bates*, 77 F.3d 1101 (8th Cir. 1996).

72. *Johnson v. United States*, 576 U.S. 591 (2015).

73. *Collateral Damage: America's Failure to Forgive or Forget in the War on Crime* (Washington, DC: National Criminal Defense Attorneys Association, 2014). This publication is available online at www.nacdl.org/ restoration/roadmapreport.

74. *Padilla v. Kentucky*, 130 S. Ct. 1473 (2010).

75. M. Vuolo, S. Lageson, and C. Uggen, "Criminal Record Questions in the Era of 'Ban the Box'," *Criminology and Public Policy* 16, 1 (2017): 139–65; also see *Collateral Damage: America's Failure to Forgive or Forget in the War on Crime* (Washington, DC: National Criminal Defense Attorneys Association, 2014). This publication is available online at www.nacdl.org/ restoration/roadmapreport.

Chapter 10

Female Prisoners

LEARNING OBJECTIVES

1. Outline the history of women's prisons and how they developed differently from prisons for men.

2. Summarize the findings of pathways research regarding the differences between female and male offenders.

3. Compare and contrast the similarities and differences between female and male prisoner subcultures.

4. Discuss the management issues associated with women's prisons.

5. Describe the unique issues that women face when they are released from prison.

CHAPTER OUTLINE

- **Women in Prison** 262

- **Gendered Pathways** 264

- **Female Prisoner Subculture** 271

- **Meeting the Specific Needs of Women** 276

- **Reentry** 284

- **SUMMARY** 285

Women comprise about 7 percent of the total prisoner population.

KEY TERMS

Cottage system
Custodial model
Dyads
Externalizing disorders

Gender-responsive
  programming
Intermediate standard
Internalizing disorders
Pathways approach

Pseudo-families
Rabbits
Reformatory model
Relational model of therapy
Severe functional impairment

Women in Prison

As we discussed in prior chapters, women comprise about 7 percent of the total prisoner population. The incarceration rate for women, like men, began increasing dramatically in the 1980s, and since then, the women's rate of increase has been higher than men's. Between 1980 and 2019, the number of incarcerated women in state and federal prisons increased from a total of 26,378 in 1980 to 107,955 in 2019. However, women's rates of imprisonment are still dramatically lower than men's. In 2019, the rate of imprisonment for all women was 61 per 100,000 compared to 789 for men. In 2019, the imprisonment rate for Black women (84 per 100,000) was twice the rate of imprisonment for white women (48 per 100,000) and Hispanic's rate was 63 per 100,000. The states with the highest rates of female imprisonment are Idaho (138 per 100,000) and Oklahoma (129 per 100,000); the states with the lowest rates are Rhode Island (11 per 100,000) and Massachusetts (10 per 100,000).[1] The increase has occurred in jails as well: between 1970 and 2014, the number of women in jail nationwide increased 14-fold—from under 8,000 to 109,000.[2] In 2016, there were 102,300 women in jail.[3]

Management issues in women's prisons revolve around women's past victimization, substance abuse, mental health problems, and supervision challenges.[4] In this chapter, we will cover the history of women's prisons, pathways to incarceration, the female prisoner subculture, and other aspects of life in women's prisons, from the specific needs of female prisoners to the obstacles women face upon reentry to society.

The History of Women's Prisons

In early gaols, male and female prisoners were housed together in large rooms where the strong preyed upon the weak and prisoners begged, bartered, or stole from each other to survive. Women were sexually exploited by prisoners and guards alike. After male and female prisoners were separated in the 1700s, women's experiences were only marginally better.[5] Because there were so few female offenders sentenced to prison, they were haphazardly housed in cellars or attics, usually crowded together in one room. For instance, at Auburn Prison in 1825, female prisoners were housed in an attic and visited only once a day when a steward came to deliver food and remove waste.[6] In 1825, Baltimore built the first separate prison quarters for women, and in 1835, officials at Ossining State Penitentiary (Sing Sing) built a separate unit for women.[7] Women, some with their children, were housed in an 18-square-foot room where the "hot, crowded, and unsanitary conditions during the summer led to the death of one baby." In

1873, the first separate institution for women was established: the Indiana Reformatory Institute for Women and Girls.[8]

In the 1800s, prison reform advocates pushed for not only separate institutions for women, but also for female staff members to guard female prisoners. Elizabeth Fry, a British prison reformer, advocated for work, training, religion, routine, and matrons to guard and teach manners to female prisoners.[9] Primarily through her efforts, a separate system for female inmates, with female matrons, developed in England. Reformers in the U.S. also believed that female offenders should be supervised by female matrons, partly to avoid sexual exploitation (women were often subject to forced prostitution by male guards).[10] In 1822, Maryland became the first state to hire a female jail keeper. In 1827, Connecticut hired a woman to oversee the unit of the state prison housing female prisoners.[11]

As separate prisons for women were built in northeastern states, the early administrators of these institutions were often the same reformers who had struggled so hard to create them. These women believed they had a moral duty to improve the lives of their female charges.[12]

The Reformatory and Custodial Models

Early prisons for women often followed what is now called the **reformatory model**, or House of Refuge model. The term refers to an institution that utilizes the cottage system of architecture, and pursues the mission of reform rather than punishment. Institutions like the Hudson House of Refuge, which opened in New York in 1887, were built on the **cottage system**, staffed almost entirely by women, and followed a domestic routine. The cottage system refers to building facilities with smaller housing units to give inmates a feeling of domesticity. Housing units may or may not have been physically separate buildings, and there may have been on-site kitchen and laundry facilities. Female staff members, called matrons, taught women sewing and other skills believed to be necessary for young women; however, women also did manual labor, such as gardening, slaughtering pigs, draining swamps, laying floors, and painting cottages.[13] Matrons filled both educational and custodial roles, serving as farm supervisors as well as guards.[14] Prisoners in these institutions were not only felons, but also young women guilty only of misdemeanors, or victims of difficult circumstances. Most were under the age of 25, white, and native born. Two-thirds had been married at some time, but were widowed, divorced, or separated. Most had no prior convictions, and their crimes were minor: more than half had been incarcerated for drunkenness and prostitution.[15]

In addition to reformatories, some states also had institutions for women that followed a **custodial model**. These institutions were more like prisons for men; in fact, custodial placements for women were usually on the grounds of men's prisons. They were not built using the cottage system and may have been simply a housing unit or separate building in the men's prisons, following the same architectural style used with men; for example, tiers of cells or dormitories with no mission of reform. The women sent to custodial institutions were likely to be felons rather than misdemeanants. They were more often older women, women of color, and hardened criminals. The custodial model was followed most often in newly constructed institutions after 1930 as the reformatory era was phased out.[16]

Contemporary Institutions

It wasn't until the 1980s that every state had a separate prison for women. Many states still have only one or two institutions for women. Rhode Island uses a combined jail/prison institution, and some states contract with other states or the Federal Bureau of Prisons to house their female offenders. This means that, whether housed in smaller building units, a Gothic castle, or a dormitory in a portable-style building, all custody grades and all variety of offenders are often housed together in the same state prison. Security is set at medium and maximum levels, even though most women do not need that level of custody. It also means that there may be fewer rehabilitative programs available, and women may be further away from their families.

As the prison population increased in the 1980s, the trend was to build facilities that housed men and women interchangeably. Therefore, more male staff members were assigned to women's prisons, and staff members transferred back and forth between facilities for men and women. Staff training, administrative policies, and unisex architecture all combined to minimize and de-emphasize any differences between the two prisoner population groups.[17]

 # Gendered Pathways

Female prisoners tend to be in their thirties, single, economically disadvantaged, and disproportionately minority. They are likely to be mothers. Women are sentenced to prison most often for drug offenses and/or property crimes—usually larceny. While female prisoners share many characteristics with male prisoners, there are differences worth noting. Women do not have as extensive criminal histories as men, they are less likely to have been employed before incarceration, and they are more likely to have come from dysfunctional families (with histories of sexual and physical abuse), suffer from mental health issues, and report more drug use, whereas men report more alcohol use.[18]

Research shows that women follow different paths to criminality than men; in criminology, this is referred to as the **pathways approach**. This research has identified four major differences between female and male offenders. Female offenders are much more likely to have experienced

1. prior victimization,
2. substance abuse,
3. criminogenic familial and intimate relationships, and
4. economic marginalization.

The pathways approach argues that women have different motivations for committing crimes and correctional programming should address those differences. Pathways research has resulted in a typology of female offenders, some of whom are quite different from male offenders:

- street women: these women fled abusive homes, became addicts, and engaged in survival crimes such as prostitution and drug dealing while living on the street;
- drug-connected women: their crimes include using, manufacturing, or distributing drugs in the context of intimate partner or family relationships;
- harmed and harming women: these women's early lives were marked by turbulence, abuse, and neglect; they have developed a tough, bully-like demeanor with accompanying violent behavior;
- battered women: their violence was confined to relationships with violent intimate partners;
- others: women who did not fit into the above categories, including those who committed crimes from greed or economic necessity.[19]

These differences in female and male offenders translate to differences in female and male prisoners: women are more likely to be caregivers of dependent children, less likely to be convicted of violent crimes (about 37 percent of female prisoners are incarcerated for a violent crime, compared to 57 percent of male prisoners), have no stable work history, have experienced more psychosocial problems, and are more likely to suffer from serious health problems.[20] In the sections that follow, we will examine the issues that have been associated with women's criminality and entry into prison.

Prior Victimization

Research shows that female prisoners are more likely than male prisoners to have experienced both physical and sexual abuse during childhood and adulthood. One-third to over one-half of female prisoners have experienced physical abuse and about 30 to 40 percent have experienced sexual abuse at some point in their lives, with about a quarter having reported such abuse before age 18. Some studies have found even higher percentages.[21] In one study, about 41 percent of female probationers, 48 percent of female jail inmates, and 57 percent of female prisoners reported having been the victim of either sexual or physical abuse.[22] Another study found that 86 percent of female jail detainees experienced some type of sexual victimization, either from a partner, a caregiver (as a child), or both.[23] Women have described experiences of being molested by their mother's boyfriends, raped by strangers and acquaintances, and beaten by fathers, boyfriends, and husbands.

For victims of sexual abuse, the effects can be severe and long lasting. Childhood sexual victimization has been linked to personality disorders, depression, suicidal and self-destructive behaviors, alienation, poor self-esteem, poor interpersonal functioning, trust issues, substance abuse, distant or dysfunctional family relationships, sexual problems, and high-risk sexual behavior.[24] Childhood sexual abuse can lead to post-traumatic stress disorder (PTSD) symptoms, including "over-remembering" (reacting with violence inappropriately), "under-remembering" (disassociation leading to reacting with passivity to

In one study, about 41 percent of female probationers, 48 percent of female jail inmates, and 57 percent of female prisoners reported having been the victim of either sexual or physical abuse.

threats), and cyclical relationships marked by instability, anger, and violence.[25] While there seems to be a correlation between childhood abuse and violent crime with men, the same pattern does not hold for female offenders, except for juveniles.[26]

Childhood victimization often leads to drug use, and drug use has consistently been associated with sex work and high-risk sexual practices.[27] Although this path has been described as typical for female offenders, it is not the only path to criminality. Some female offenders begin using drugs before sexual victimization occurs.[28]

Drug Dependency

Female prisoners are more likely to be drug dependent than male prisoners, with 60 percent being identified as drug dependent in one national study.[29] In another study, 59 percent reported drug use before age 18, and 15 percent began at ages 12 or 13.[30] A consistent finding is that drug use was often introduced to these women by family members.[31] Women who commit drug crimes typically play minor roles in drug distribution systems, such as "mules" (carriers of drugs for sellers) or low-level sellers. Drug use by women has been associated with prostitution, small-scale drug sales, and larceny/theft.[32] In one national study, it was found that female and male drug-abusing offenders were different in that women

- started at an earlier age,
- had greater physical and mental health problems,
- were more likely to be unemployed or under employed,
- had fewer skills or less education,
- had more psychosocial problems (prior victimization),
- were more likely to come from families with histories of addiction, mental illness and/or suicide,
- were more likely to be single parents, without supportive family or social networks, and
- were more likely to have family members in the criminal justice system.[33]

The use of drugs or alcohol to self-medicate is a pervasive theme in research on female prisoners.[34] Researchers have found a strong association between reported heavy drug use and childhood sexual victimization.[35] Drugs and alcohol provide temporary relief, allowing victimized women to cope with grief and anger from childhood abuse, as well as depression and anxiety.[36] Studies show that drug abusers are more likely to have come from dysfunctional families with parents or caregivers suffering from alcoholism or drug addiction and/or mental health issues, report feeling unloved, have been abandoned by at least one parent, and have experienced homelessness or hunger while growing up. The pattern of physical and sexual victimization from childhood carries over into drug-abusing women's adult lives: significantly more drug abusers than non–drug abusers have experienced sexual and physical victimization and homelessness as adults.[37]

Family Dysfunction and Intimate Partner Abuse

One of the most consistent findings in research on female prisoners is that they tend to come from dysfunctional families, marked not only by alcoholism or drug addiction, but also absent parents, instability, parental mental illness, and childhood abuse. The important thing to note is that women in prison are

Female prisoners are more likely to be drug dependent than male prisoners, with 60 percent being identified as drug dependent in one national study.

more likely than men in prison to have experienced dysfunctional childhoods. Earlier research showed that women were twice as likely as men in prison to have grown up in single-parent households, and one-third of women (compared to one-fourth of men) reported that their guardians had abused drugs. Women are also more likely than male offenders to have relatives who are or have been incarcerated.[38]

Female offenders have often lost relatives to sickness, fatal violence, or abandonment. Many recite sad childhoods of constantly trying to gain the affection of a physically or emotionally absent parent.[39] This lack of bonding in childhood has been associated with their willingness to enter into abusive intimate relationships as adults.

Female prisoners are three to four times more likely than male prisoners to have histories of abuse.[40] They are also more likely than women outside of prison to have been victims of intimate partner violence. In one prison study, 75 percent of female prisoner respondents reported having been the victim of severe partner abuse.[41] Another study reported that up to 88 percent of female prisoners report having been the victim of intimate partner abuse. The lifetime prevalence rates for women outside of prison for any type of physical assault is about 52 percent. Female prisoners often exhibit cyclical patterns of abusive relationships outside of prison and may enter into abusive partnerships in prison as well.[42]

Being a victim of severe partner abuse may result in the woman killing her abuser and being convicted and sentenced for it. More often, however, such abuse contributes to life events that create the potential for crime. Battering may force women into poverty and homelessness if they leave their abuser. Lost jobs and lack of welfare benefits, housing, and educational opportunities may force women into other illegal ways to earn money, including prostitution and drug dealing. Arrests of women for domestic violence assaults increased when mandatory and pro-arrest laws and policies were implemented in the 1980s and 1990s, and these arrests hurt women's chances to obtain some jobs and become economically self-sufficient.[43]

Mental Health

As we have discussed, female prison inmates are reported to have much higher rates of mental health problems than male inmates (73 percent compared to 55 percent). In looking more closely at these women, those diagnosed with mental health issues are more likely to come from dysfunctional backgrounds and have difficulty in prison (see Figure 10.1).

Women in jail are also more likely than male inmates to have mental health issues. One study found that 53 percent of female jail prisoners met the criteria for PTSD (compared to only 9.7 percent of the general U.S. population), and 45 percent had **severe functional impairment**, which is defined as when a mental health issue results in "serious interference in their ability to work, manage their homes, and maintain relationships."[44] Studies generally show that incarcerated women suffer from depression and bipolar disorder disproportionately more than the general U.S. population (accounting for both men and women), women in the general U.S. population, and incarcerated men.[45] There is a nexus between mental health and the other characteristics of female prisoners; for example, prior victimization and drug use. In one study, it was found that childhood victimization was correlated with later mental health issues and drug abuse, and these, in turn, affected the level or likelihood of criminality.[46]

In a study of drug offenders in a large jail, it was found that female detainees averaged six types of trauma in their lifetimes, higher than the general U.S. population average of about 3.2.[47] The instrument used to conduct the study recorded 25 types of traumas (e.g., major disaster, very serious accident or fire, being physically assaulted or raped, seeing another person killed, dead, or badly hurt,

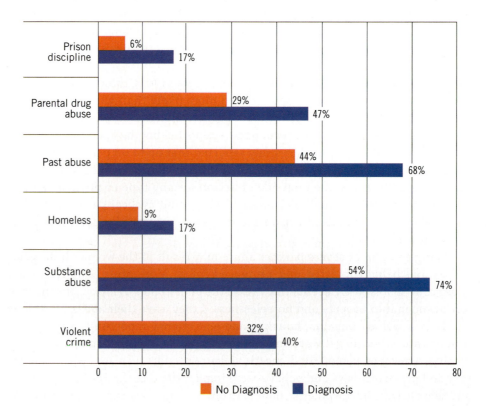

FIGURE 10.1 Female prisoners and mental health. Created by author from D. James and L. Glaze, *Mental Health Problems of Prison and Jail Inmates* (Washington, DC: Bureau of Justice Statistics, U.S. Dept. of Justice, 2006), 1, 10.

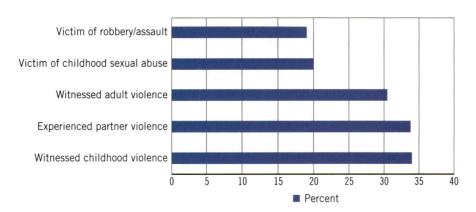

FIGURE 10.2 Percentage of female jail prisoners experiencing trauma. Created by author from S. Lynch, D. DeHart, J. Belknap, B. Green, P. Dass-Brailsford, K. Johnson, and M. Wong, "An Examination of the Associations Among Victimization, Mental Health, and Offending in Women," *Criminal Justice and Behavior* 44, 6 (2017): 796–814.

or hearing about a horrible incident that has happened to a loved one). About 68 percent in the sample reported experiencing such events. Greater trauma exposure was associated with higher rates of past-year symptoms of post-traumatic stress disorder as well as other internalizing, externalizing, and substance use disorders. **Internalizing disorders** are characterized by maladaptive control of an individual's internal emotional and cognitive state, but the disorder is largely internal; that is, there may be no observable behaviors. These disorders include anxiety, PTSD, depression, and suicidal ideation. **Externalizing disorders** are those that can be observed through abnormal behavior patterns, and include attention-deficit/hyperactivity, conduct disorders, and pathological gambling. For example, the percentage of female detainees who reported symptoms of any past-year internalizing disorder increased from 3 percent with zero to one trauma exposures, to 30 percent with two to four exposures, to 47 percent with five to six exposures, and to 69 percent with seven to 25 exposures.[48] Figure 10.2 presents the findings from a sample of female jail inmates, showing much higher percentages of trauma exposure than what the general public experiences in terms of childhood and adult trauma.

Self-injury, mutilation, and suicide or suicide attempts are manifestations of mental health problems. In studies of both self-mutilation and suicide risk in incarcerated women's populations, it has been clear that risk increases with depression, low self-esteem, and social isolation.[49] A study on prison suicide found that male prisoners are less likely to commit suicide than men in the general U.S. population, but female prisoners are more likely to commit suicide than women in the general U.S. population.[50]

Medical Needs

Female prisoners require relatively more medical services than men due to gynecological and obstetric needs. Furthermore, their lifestyle choices prior to prison (including drug use, risky sex practices, poor nutrition, and lack of preventive care) result in a host of health problems.[51] Women show higher rates of AIDS, tuberculosis, depression, and anxiety disorders than do men in prison. The most common medical problems of female prisoners include asthma, diabetes, HIV/AIDS, tuberculosis, hypertension, unintended/interrupted/lost pregnancy, dysmenorrhea, chlamydia, human papillomavirus (HPV), herpes simplex II, cystic and myomatic conditions, chronic pelvic inflammatory disease, anxiety neurosis, and depression. Women in prison are reported to have greater risk than the general female population for cervical cancer, substance abuse, suicide, sexually transmitted diseases, HIV, and gynecological problems.[52] The reason female prisoners have more serious medical issues is not clear, but certainly any history of sex work and drug use contributes to some of these medical issues.

Generally, healthcare is merely adequate in prisons, and sometimes it does not even reach that level. Women are not routinely screened upon arrival for health problems such as hepatitis, most states do not give annual Pap smears to test for cervical cancer, and chronic health problems, such as asthma or diabetes, sometimes goes untreated unless there is a medical emergency. There is an increasing trend in prisons to have prisoners pay for their healthcare, which is problematic because if prisoners cannot afford to receive treatment, contagious diseases can spread: tuberculosis and sexually transmitted diseases (such as hepatitis B and C) may eventually pose even bigger problems than AIDS, with some studies indicating that half of incoming female prisoners tested positive for hepatitis C.[53]

There have been lawsuits in several states that allege and show evidence of lack of adequate medical care. Reports indicate that women are not seen by a doctor when they report heavy bleeding or infection. Even pregnant women may not be seen promptly when reporting physical symptoms that should cause concern.[54] The Eighth Amendment, which bars cruel and unusual punishment, has been used to challenge the lack of medical care when it appears to be deliberate and malicious.[55] Women have alleged and proven in at least one lawsuit that they received little or no prenatal care.[56] Because many prisons do not have the necessary health facilities, many prisoners are transported to local hospitals to give birth. Unfortunately, the lack of immediate care has proved to be a problem, especially when staff members do not call for transportation to take a woman out of the facility when she begins labor. Other lawsuits have been filed concerning the practice of shackling women during labor and vaginal searches after delivery upon return to prison.

About five to 10 percent of women in prison or jail on any given day are pregnant.[57] These pregnancies are often high risk since women in prison may have been drug users, have avoided or neglected medical treatment, and/or have had difficult previous pregnancies. One report indicated that 77 percent of imprisoned women had exposed their fetuses to drugs.[58] There is a higher-than-average rate of pregnancy complications for women in prison. Part of the reason for this is attributed to the fact that women must be transported to outside hospitals for delivery and for medical emergencies.

Some states still shackle women who are transported to an outside hospital to give birth, despite condemnation from international human rights groups.[59] Shackling is commonly used when prisoners are taken out of the prison as a precaution; however, advocates and medical personnel say it is unnecessary and dangerous for women who are about to give birth. Women immobilized by leg chains have difficulty moving to facilitate fetal heart monitors and epidurals, or simply changing positions to help ease labor pains. In *Nelson v. Correctional Medical Services* (2009), an Arkansas female prisoner sued the state for having been shackled by the legs during labor and immediately after giving birth. The inability to move during contractions caused her great pain and evidence showed that she suffered lifelong hip injuries because of the shackling; medical professionals testified this position contributed to injuries she experienced during labor. In this case, the Eighth Circuit ruled that the practice of shackling was cruel and unusual and a violation of the Eighth Amendment because the inmate posed no security risk and it was against medical advice. The holding does not apply to states outside the Eighth Circuit.[60] Even though some states have passed legislation that prohibits shackling, about half of all states still allow it at the discretion of correctional authorities.[61]

Female Prisoner Subculture

Women prisoners' social interactions and subcultural norms are somewhat different from male prisoner subcultures.[62] One main difference is that while men in prison are likely to form or join gang structures, women typically do not. Instead, they tend to form small cliques and **dyads** (friendship pairs). If they do organize in larger groups, communication patterns tend to be less political and more familial. Women also tend to form **pseudo-families**, sometimes called play families.[63] These social structures involve several or many women who take on familial roles. While observations may suggest that these roles are played as stereotypes, they seem to provide needed relationships for some women.[64] Today, play families are less organized or prevalent than in years past.[65]

Women express adherence to some portions of the male inmate code; for instance, the tenet "no snitching" is a well-known admonition in both women's and men's prisons. However, observers note that when the norm is broken, punishment isn't as severe as in facilities for men. Norms of the female inmate code include stay out of "the mix" (homosexuality, gambling, and drug use), don't tell others your business, don't get involved in the wrong group, avoid "messy" women (women who gossip), don't let anyone see you cry, don't talk about your case, don't have an attitude, stand your ground, learn how to say no, and be clean.[66]

In the following sections, we will examine other aspects of the subculture in women's prisons, including the prevalence of violence and its causes, as well as intimate relationships and sexual victimization.

Violence

Some recent reports indicate that female prisoners are more violent than earlier researchers believed.[67] However, women's violence does tend to result in less serious injury than the violence that occurs in men's prisons. Women are less likely to use weapons and more likely to initiate violence spontaneously, which makes it easier for staff to stop it. Fighting is usually caused by interpersonal conflicts, whereas racial violence, black-market disputes, or territory fights over drug dealing are typical causes in men's prisons.[68]

Women report more victimization than men in prison. In one study, about 48 percent of women, but only 24 percent of men, reported being a victim of theft. The rate of physical violence, however, was roughly the same (about 206 per 1,000 inmates), although men were three times as likely to report being victimized with a weapon.[69] About 15 percent of women said they had been slapped, hit, kicked, or bitten (compared to 10 percent of men). Less than 5 percent of women reported physical victimization from staff members, compared to 12 percent of men, and about 10 percent of women said correctional staff members had stolen something from them, compared to 29 percent of men. A more recent study reported roughly similar results.[70]

In one study of a women's prison, half of the conflicts involved disputes over a material interest, such as drugs, personal possessions, games, food, tobacco, and phone cards. Non-material interests, such as self-respect, honor, fairness, loyalty, personal safety, or privacy, were contributing factors in all incidents.[71] Another study found that violence or the threat of violence occurred mostly because of intimate partnerships, debts, and perceived disrespect.[72]

Intimate partners fight with each other primarily because of jealousy stemming from a real or perceived betrayal; for example, when one party begins a relationship with another inmate.[73] Intimate partnerships in prison can sometimes replicate abusive relationships outside of prison. Ironically, a woman who has been the victim of an abusive male partner outside of prison can be the abuser of a female partner in prison. Sometimes, in successive relationships, a woman can be the victim in one relationship and the abuser in another. Other relationships involve mutual violence.

In women's prisons, debts are incurred over any number of items, from drugs to shampoo, candy, and other goods or services. Women buy products at the prison commissary and, in some cases, share their material possessions with new inmates who have nothing or women who have no outside financial support. However, in most cases, product exchanges occur and can lead to debts, and unpaid debts can result in violence. Women, like men, say they must react to willful non-payment with violence; otherwise, they will be perceived as weak and be taken advantage of.[74]

Disrespect has long been a construct associated with male violence.[75] In prison and on the street, cultural norms indicate that men will fight when they feel disrespected, lest they be perceived as less of a man and be victimized. This norm is even stronger in prison, where greater adherence to street culture is associated with a greater willingness to fight when one feels disrespected.[76] Researchers have also found that both juvenile and adult female prisoners place a high value on respect.[77] Researchers hypothesize that the reason both male and female prisoners place such high importance on respect is socioeconomic deprivation: one's identity is not established through material goods, so self-respect is earned via one's reputation and is fiercely guarded.

Women, unlike men, do not generally describe disrespect in the context of someone questioning their strength or courage. Rather, the challenges are to one's reputation or identity as someone who won't "take shit" from anyone.[78] In one study, women were asked about the causes of violence, and disrespect was noted as an important factor. A respectful cellmate abided by the inmate code, was not dirty (kept the cell clean, did not put clothes or towels on the other person's bed), was not loud when the other person was trying to sleep, and did not gossip. Being disrespectful encompassed interpersonal behaviors that threatened the status, reputation, sense of self, personal space, or rights of another. Gossiping or spreading rumors were two of the major reasons for fighting and were considered signs of disrespect as well. Women also described being disrespected by those who interfered with their romantic relationships or did not pay back debts. Like men, women felt that disrespect must be addressed, otherwise, they would be seen as victims.

Female prisoners known as "**rabbits**" are victims of violence because their personal characteristics and demeanor make them targets for extortion and bullying. Women who are young, seemingly frail, and timid in social exchanges are the most likely targets. Other women are predators who are comfortable in the prison world and seek victims from whom they can extort commissary money, services, and sometimes sex through threats and intimidation.[79]

Researchers have found that substance abuse, mental health, self-concept, and relationship issues better predict prison misconduct than criminal history alone.[80] The following factors are significantly correlated with the likelihood that women will commit prison violence:

- age (younger),
- race/ethnicity (minority),
- marriage (not being married),
- having committed past violent crime,
- prior incarceration,
- having been physically or sexually abused,
- having had at least one overnight mental health stay, and
- having been prescribed medication for mental health issues.

Women are less likely to engage in violence if they have children or have been incarcerated for a drug offense.[81]

A study that utilized self-reported violence and victimization in a sample of 334 prisoners found that 18 percent admitted to engaging in violent behavior, 14 percent admitted to engaging in some form of sexual misconduct (excluding rape), only 5 percent reported any kind of drug/alcohol misbehavior, and 15 percent admitted to engaging in some kind of property misconduct. Researchers found both prior violence and aggression were positively correlated with violent misconduct. Prior employment had a negative effect upon violent misbehavior. Consistent with prior research, age was negatively associated with all forms of misconduct except violence (older inmates were less likely to engage) As for victims, one study found that older female inmates and those who received more visits were less likely to be victims of prison violence, but those who had higher education and those who exhibited violence were more likely to be victimized.[82]

In another study, 13 percent of about 650 inmates in one state had committed a violent infraction (assault of either an inmate or CO). In comparison, about a third of the sample had committed a prison infraction that was nonviolent. Researchers found that younger women, Black women, those who identified as lesbian, gay, or bisexual, women who had been abused as children, more impulsive women, those with more antisocial attitudes, women incarcerated for a nonviolent offense, and those designated medium/maximum risk were at higher risk for committing violent infractions. More specifically, women abused during childhood had a 100 percent higher rate of violent offending relative to those who were not abused as children, and women classified into medium/maximum custody status had a 110 percent higher rate of violent offending compared to those designated low risk. A woman's history of abuse during adulthood, mental health problems, substance abuse problems, marital status, education, and reading level did not affect the prevalence or incidence of violent infractions.[83] These studies must be considered cautiously, however, because of single state samples, sample size, and self-reporting.

Some prisons have addressed prison violence through programming. In one 20-week program, 29 inmates were selected to be peer educators. Most were homicide offenders sentenced to life without parole or long-term offenders serving more than 20 years. These peer educators were trained for two days on how to be facilitators for a workbook curriculum on understanding and controlling emotions. Then, 62 general-population inmates who had been convicted of a violent crime or who had committed violent acts in prison, and who had volunteered to go through the program, were chosen. Both peer educators (55 percent) and participants (71 percent) met the criteria for post-traumatic stress disorder.

Findings indicated that mean scores for anxiety and other serious mental illness decreased significantly. Mean scores for expressive anger significantly decreased. PTSD levels also significantly declined. All indicators of aggression/hostility, except verbal aggression, showed significant decreases from pre- to post-assessment, as can be seen in Table 10.1. Even though this was not a random sample, evaluators were optimistic that this gender-responsive, trauma-informed program, led by peer educators, could be successful in addressing the elements that are associated with violence by some women in prison.[84]

Sexual Relationships and Sexual Victimization

As we have discussed, much of the violence committed in prison stems from intimate partnerships. Sexual relationships in men's and women's prisons include consensual sex within or outside of long-term relationships, as well as a continuum of coerced sexual behavior ranging from implied threat to physical rape. One study describes a continuum of coercion in women's prisons, including

- sexual comments and touching,
- sexual intimidation and pressure,
- stalking,
- sexual aggressors,
- sexual violence within relationships, and
- sexual assault.[85]

Consensual sexual relationships take place between women who had a same-sex orientation before prison, as well as those who did not. Heterosexual women enter such relationships because of the need for companionship and sexual release.

TABLE 10.1   Participant Pre- and Post-Intervention Change on Outcome Measures

MEASURE	PRE-TEST MEAN	POST-TEST MEAN	T, DF
Expressive anger	24.3	23.4	.78
PTSD	7.3	4.0	3.12**
Aggression/hostility	78.1	68.1	2.97**
Physical aggression	18.2	15.1	2.96**
Verbal aggression	12.2	11.1	1.83*
Anger	16.1	14.1	2.39**
Hostility	18.2	16.0	2.25**
Indirect aggression	13.4	11.8	2.21*

*$p < 0.05$.

**$p < 0.01$.

Source: N. Messina, J. Braithwaite, S. Calhoun, and S. Kubiak, "Examination of a Violence Prevention Program for Female Offenders," Violence and Gender 3, 3 (2016): 143–49.

As one female inmate explained, sexual relationships are a way to cope with prison life:

> ...Those of us who have long sentences, there's three ways to deal with it: become involved with an officer, turn to homosexuality, or become a Christian. Nine out of ten, you fall into homosexuality. Some try all three. I've tried all three and I am most comfortable in a relationship.[86]

As noted in Chapter 8, women report more sexual victimization from other female inmates than do males from other male inmates.[87] One study found that six-month prevalence rates for any sexual victimization were nearly five times higher for women than for men (212 per 1,000 female inmates compared to 43 per 1,000 male inmates). Most of the victimization was classified as touching, not rape. Female and male inmates reported roughly similar rates for sexual victimization by staff, about 1.7 percent of women and 1.9 percent of men, with touching more likely than nonconsensual sex.[88]

The Bureau of Justice Statistics study done under the requirements of the PREA (discussed in Chapter 8) showed that about 6.9 percent of women, compared to 1.7 percent of men, reported some form of sexual victimization by fellow inmates, with the most common victimization being unwanted touching. For female inmates, age had a negative effect on sexual victimization, whereas race, aggression level, and prior education all had a positive effect on experiencing sexual victimization.[89] About equal numbers of women and men in prison reported staff sexual misconduct of any type (2.3 percent of women compared to 2.4 percent of men). Recall, however, that the surveys showed large differences between institutions, with some institutions showing double-digit percentages and others reporting no sexual victimization at all (an unlikely occurrence).[90]

From the late 1800s until the 1980s, it was standard practice for only female correctional officers to supervise female prisoners. Today, male correctional officers comprise close to half of all correctional officers in women's prisons, a dramatic shift from past practice.[91] Sexual victimization by staff members in women's prisons has been the subject of numerous exposés, investigations, and reports by such organizations as the American Civil Liberties Union (ACLU) and Amnesty International. Some state corrections systems, including New York's and Pennsylvania's, have been sued because of a pattern of sexual abuse and exploitation.[92] Periodically, new stories detail scandals. In 2014, the Justice Department issued a report after investigating sexual abuse allegations in Alabama's prison for women. The report detailed pervasive sexual abuse, with at least 99 COs having had voluntary or coerced sex with inmates. In 2021, dozens of COs at New Jersey's only women's prison were placed on leave following allegations of sexual abuse and beatings of female inmates. Some reports indicate that sexual abuse was pervasive within the facility.[93]

Procedures in prisons such as strip searches, restraints, and isolation can traumatize women who have histories of abuse.[94] The policy of utilizing male officers to supervise, pat down, and even sometimes strip search female inmates puts the United States in conflict with international treaties and the United Nations Standards for the Treatment of Prisoners, both of which mandate that only same-sex guards do such searches in women's prisons.[95]

More pervasive than sexual assault is widespread sexual harassment, or a "sexually charged" atmosphere in some prisons and jails. Observers and advocates have published accounts of instances where officers show off erections, make inappropriate sexual comments, needlessly touch and grope female inmates, and remark on their appearances. These abuses are not restricted to correctional officers; medical professionals, groundskeepers, vocational and educational teachers, chaplains, and other civilian staff members have also been exposed as perpetrators.

In one study, a continuum of sexual misconduct by correctional officers was constructed that included

- love and seduction (both parties at least facially consenting),
- inappropriate comments and conversation,
- sexual requests (with no obvious coercion),
- flashing, voyeurism, and touching,
- abuse of search authority,
- sexual exchange (some form of quid pro quo, often for soda or food),
- sexual intimidation (prisoner consents only because of fear of what an officer might do),
- sex without physical violence (prisoner does not resist, perhaps because of PTSD), and
- sex with physical violence.[96]

Some women in prison actively seek a sexual relationship with a staff member.[97] Women in prison have normal sexual drives, and the presence of men in women's prisons, just like the presence of female correctional officers in men's prisons, will inevitably lead some to ignore the rules against such relationships. Same-sex consensual relationships also develop between staff members and inmates. Regardless of sexual orientation, however, the inherent power differential between officers and inmates makes such relationships unsafe, ill-advised, and illegal. All states have legislation that criminalizes sexual abuse and/or any sexual contact with prisoners.[98] The reason that even consensual sex between staff members and inmates is at least a misdemeanor, and a felony in many states, is that the inmate is presumed incapable of giving consent for such a relationship because of the power differential between the two parties.

Meeting the Specific Needs of Women

The pathways research described previously identified risk factors that are especially criminogenic for women. Substance abuse problems, sexual and physical victimization, mental health (especially depression and co-occurring disorders), unhealthy relationships, and family unification difficulties are some of the issues that affect women in prison. Programs that address these needs have the potential to reduce institutional misconduct. Further, programs that address substance abuse, mental health problems, trauma, unhealthy relationships, parental stress, employment, safe housing, childcare, financial assistance, and education arguably can reduce recidivism in community settings.[99]

Historically, there have been fewer rehabilitative and training programs in prisons for women as compared to men's prisons. Both the equal protection clause of the Fourteenth Amendment and the Civil Rights Act of 1964 call for equal treatment of similarly situated groups and have been used to challenge different treatment of men and women in prison. The Supreme Court has established a test for sex-based differential treatment, which is referred to as the **intermediate standard**, whereby the state can justify different treatment on such grounds as women having different needs or that the state has a legitimate reason for doing so. Prisoners have sued prison officials, arguing that the few programs available for women were not equal to the opportunities afforded men. Some of these early cases were successful. In *Glover v. Johnson* (1979), a Michigan court ordered that more educational courses, an apprenticeship program, a work-release program, and an expanded legal training program be offered for women.[100] In later cases, however, courts were sometimes persuaded by state arguments that the cost of such programs was prohibitive. Because women's prisons are generally smaller than men's prisons, programs have a higher cost per inmate, thereby making them more expensive.

Today, most women's prisons offer some type of drug treatment program, life skills training, and parenting education.[101] However, women's programming in prisons has been criticized as not meeting the needs of female offenders.[102] For example, many state prisons do not screen for such things as childhood abuse or domestic violence victimization. Some states do not even collect information on whether incoming female inmates have children.[103] Pathways research and the experiences of criminal justice practitioners recognize that female offenders are different in substantive ways from male offenders. This recognition has led to efforts to create programming for female offenders that responds to their specific issues and needs.

The United States Commission on Civil Rights published an extensive report detailing their investigation, findings, and recommendations regarding the treatment of women in prison.[104] Most of their findings are well known to researchers in the field and have been or will be described in this chapter. Below are the highlighted findings and recommendations from this report.

- Notwithstanding federal statutory legal protections such as the Civil Rights of Institutionalized Persons Act (CRIPA) and the Prison Rape Elimination Act (PREA), aimed at protecting incarcerated people, many incarcerated women continue to experience physical and psychological safety harms while incarcerated, along with insufficient satisfaction of their constitutional rights.

- Classification systems that are not calibrated for gender-specific characteristics have been shown to classify incarcerated women at higher security requirement levels than necessary for the safety and security of prisons. This classification results in some women serving time in more restrictive environments than is necessary and appropriate.

- Incarcerated parents permanently lose parental rights at higher rates than parents whom courts find to have neglected or abused their children but are not incarcerated.

- Incarcerated women generally have biological healthcare needs distinct from incarcerated men. They have a constitutional right to have these healthcare needs met.

- Sexual abuse and rape remain prevalent against women in prison. This continuing prevalence has led to significant litigation involving several different institutions, at tremendous cost to taxpayers, and provides strong evidence of the need for reform at the institutional level, even following passage of the Prison Rape Elimination Act (PREA) in 2003. Reports include abuse of incarcerated women by staff and other incarcerated women that is prevalent and pervasive.

- Studies have shown that incarcerated women are often given disproportionately harsh punishments for minor offenses while incarcerated compared to incarcerated men. This disproportionality results in such outcomes as placing women in segregation for minor violations of prison regulations, which denies them good time credits and programming privileges, among other restrictions. Reports indicate women are disproportionately punished harshly for offenses such as "being disorderly," whereas men tend more often to be punished for violence.

- Prison officials, supervisors, and correctional officers are inconsistently trained on the prevalence of disproportionate punishment of incarcerated women and evidence-based disciplinary practices.

Recommendations included the following:

- Prison officials should adopt validated assessment tools, currently available, to avoid inaccurately classifying incarcerated women to a higher security level than appropriate.

- Prison officials should enforce policies that support parental rights and familial contact except where inconsistent with safety concerns. Such policies include keeping incarcerated parents apprised of family court proceedings, providing transportation to those proceedings, and assisting in locating counsel. Institutions should implement visitation policies with the goal of maintaining familial relationships.

- Prison officials should implement policies to address women's specific healthcare needs, including gynecological and prenatal care, as is constitutionally required.

- All prisons should prohibit shackling pregnant women and placing them in solitary confinement, as these practices represent serious physical and psychological health risks. The Department of Justice should rigorously enforce the PREA standards, including training and certifying auditors and investigating whether facilities are in fact in compliance. Congress should provide more funds for investigations and audits.

- Prisons should implement evidence-based, trauma-informed discipline policies to avoid harsh punishments for minor infractions, recognizing that significant harms can result from placement in restrictive housing. Prisons should ensure restrictive housing is not used against people of color, LGBT people, and people with mental health challenges in a discriminatory manner based on these characteristics.

- Prison officials should implement staff training to address the high rates of trauma among incarcerated women and adjust prison policies accordingly, including training on evidence-based discipline practices.

Gender-Responsive Programming

The idea that women in prison need different programming from men seems obvious. Historically, women's prisons did have gender-responsive programs, but they were based on sex stereotypes and not helpful in meeting the range of needs of female prisoners. Women learned to cook, clean, sew, and behave like "ladies." No effort was made to provide them with job skills because women were not expected to work. In the 1960s and 1970s, programs were usually secretarial, food service, or domestic programs.[105]

In the 1980s, efforts were made across the nation to improve prison programming for women. Part of the impetus was that there were more female prisoners, so vocational programs could be justified. There was also an attempt to move away from sex-stereotyped programs, such as cosmetology and food

Historically, female prisoners were provided with rudimentary education and sex-stereotyped job training.

service, to computer repair and other neutral or nontraditional skills, such as heavy machinery operation and automotive repair. However, rehabilitative programs and drug programming especially tended to be "men's programs with pink covers." Little attempt was made to adapt programming to female prisoners in terms of their backgrounds, mental health status, and education levels. Even nontraditional vocational programs came under criticism by female prisoners who accused the prison system of simply transferring men's programs into women's prisons, not realizing that the programs were designed to help them achieve higher wages than they could ever make doing "women's work." Unfortunately, women who entered such programs sometimes did so unwillingly and reported that they planned to ignore their training and get a job as a beautician or nurse's assistant upon release.[106]

In the 1990s, gendered pathways research led to **gender-responsive programming** efforts. This approach involves designing programming that considers the special needs of women. For instance, gender-responsive programming includes programs that address incest and childhood sexual abuse. The National Institute of Corrections has promoted guiding principles for gender-responsive strategies:

- Acknowledge gender makes a difference.
- Create an environment based on safety, respect, and dignity.
- Promote healthy relationships with children, family, significant others, and the community.
- Address substance abuse, trauma, and mental health issues.
- Provide women with opportunities to improve their socioeconomic status.
- Establish a system of community supervision and reentry with comprehensive, collaborative services.[107]

OFFENDER · A LIFE WELL-LIVED

Shawna Lynn Jones grew up wanting to be a K9 police officer, but her life didn't turn out that way. She dropped out of high school to work and was first arrested when she was caught sitting in a car next to a boyfriend and a large quantity of crystal methamphetamine. He persuaded Jones to take responsibility for the drugs because of his long criminal record. Jones was convicted of possession with attempt to distribute methamphetamine and marijuana possession. She was sentenced to three years' probation. She made a living by working in the bar her mother managed, selling merchandise and hustling pool games, but did not stay out of trouble. There were several incidents of shoplifting, selling marijuana, and missed court dates; her probation was revoked a year after her first arrest. She began her three-year prison sentence in 2015.

While Jones was waiting to be transported to prison, she heard about a forestry program where California inmates—both male and female—work in fire camps. About 4,000 inmates, including 250 women, train to fight fires and work along with forestry firefighters. Six months after arriving in prison, at her request, she was transferred to one of the prison forestry camps for women. She was elated by the training and told her mother in weekly phone calls about what she was learning, her exhaustion, and the weekend hikes in the mountains that the inmates were allowed. She learned to take apart a chain saw and put it back together, fix the machine, sharpen the chain, and clean the clutch cover; it became like an extension of her body. Her mother believed that, finally, Shawna was on the right track, and had found her purpose in life.

Six weeks before her release, Jones was working a fire near Malibu helping to create a containment trench on a hillside. She was working with a chain saw when a large stone fell suddenly and struck her head, knocking her out. She was transported, unresponsive, to the hospital. Her mother arrived to find her daughter with a swollen face, her eyes taped shut so that they wouldn't dry out, and her head shaved because the doctors had tried to drain a blood clot. She died from her injuries. When Jones' body was driven from the coroner's department to the funeral home, a fire company crew was on every overpass, saluting in full uniform. At her funeral, rows of sheriffs and deputies stood at attention, right hands at their brows. Two fire trucks were parked at the entrance with their ladders raised, crossed in tribute to her. She was 22 years old.

Questions for Discussion

1. Do you think a firefighting program like the one Jones was involved in can change offenders for the better? Is it worth the risk of injury or death?

2. Discuss how such a program can change offenders who participate.

Source: J. Lowe, "The Incarcerated Women Who Fight California's Wildfires," New York Times, August 31, 2017, https://www.nytimes.com/2017/08/31/magazine/the-incarcerated-women-who-fight-californias-wildfires.html?emc=edit_th_20170903&nl=todaysheadlines&nlid=66242298

Gender-responsive programming is likely to be based on a **relational model of therapy**. The relational theory is premised on the concept that women's connections and relationships with others are powerful influencers of behavior. These can be strengths or weaknesses: women may become involved in crime because of relationships, they may turn to drugs to blunt the pain of harmful relationships, but their relationships with children or positive role models can also be strong motivations to change. Women's need for relational support must be validated for them to grow and achieve independence.[108]

Another essential element in gender-responsive programming is recognition of how trauma affects behavior. Trauma and violence, if chronic, may have significant effects on cognitive functioning; for instance, hypervigilance, lack of trust, and aggression may be due to past experiences. Women's involvement in violent relationships may be partially due to unresolved trauma.[109] Institutions that commit to trauma-informed treatment train staff to recognize trauma symptoms and implement practices and procedures that are conducive to creating a safe and secure setting for female prisoners to deal with past trauma. Staff are trained to minimize situations that act as triggers (for instance, male staff members conducting pat-down searches), and utilize de-escalation techniques of supervision that do not trigger past trauma. At a minimum, trauma assessments are conducted, and when there are searches or other prison events that might act as triggers, women are told what is happening and what they can expect in order to reduce stress.

Evaluations of correctional programs have usually either ignored programs for women or included them in general findings where they have been eclipsed by the much larger numbers of programs for men. There has been virtually no research that uses gender as an independent variable when evaluating the effectiveness of correctional programming. It may be that certain characteristics of female offenders make them especially amenable to some programs and not so amenable to others. There does seem to be some evidence, however, that gender-responsive programming is more effective. In one meta-analysis, it was found that gender-responsive and gender-neutral interventions were equally effective with female offenders in reducing recidivism, although recidivism rates varied tremendously across the different programs evaluated. An average of 28 percent of program participants across all evaluations recidivated compared to 34 percent in control groups. When the researchers limited their analysis to only those studies of higher methodological quality, gender-responsive interventions were significantly more likely to be associated with reductions in recidivism.[110]

Parenting Programs

Programs that help build and strengthen bonds with children and other family members are essential to the rehabilitative success of incarcerated mothers and the well-being of their children. Estimates of the number of women prisoners who have children under 18 range from 60 percent to about 85 percent.[111] Many of these women report being the primary caregivers of their children before their imprisonment. While 88 percent of fathers said that their children were being cared for by their mothers while they were in prison, only 37 percent of female prisoners reported that their children were being cared for by the other parent. The most common placement for children of incarcerated women is with a grandparent (44 percent), usually the maternal grandmother; about 10 percent enter foster care. Between 1991 and 2007, the number of children with an incarcerated father grew by 77 percent, whereas the number of children with an incarcerated mother grew by 131 percent.[112]

There is a growing body of research on the effects of parental incarceration on children, much of which concerns male prisoners' children, but there are also studies that measure the effects of maternal incarceration. Findings are mixed. Most researchers find that there are negative effects when a parent is incarcerated; for example, on school performance, behavioral issues, aggression, depression, and anxiety. Some research indicates that maternal incarceration is more likely to result in negative effects than paternal incarceration, with children of incarcerated mothers two and one-half times more likely than children of incarcerated fathers to be incarcerated as adults, and more likely to be arrested as juveniles.[113] Other research has found that criminality and criminal justice system involvement are more likely when the parent is the same sex as the child, and girls are more likely to be affected by a mother's incarceration than boys are by a father's incarceration.[114]

Some women in prison never see their children.[115] Visits are difficult given the long distances between prisons and where children live, not to mention the expense of traveling. There also may be hesitancy on the part of caregivers to take children to prison and/or anger at the mother for her actions that led to the situation. Social workers may feel it is traumatic for a child to see their mother in prison and therefore do not accommodate such visits. Mothers may feel guilty or ashamed and not want their children to see them in a prison setting or subject them to the search and admission procedures required for visitation. Furthermore, visits necessarily include saying goodbye—an experience that is so painful to both mothers and children that many women in prison prefer to avoid it.

Some women may give birth during their imprisonment. Usually, babies are taken away from the mother hours after birth; however, nurseries exist in about eight prisons across the country. At Bedford Hills, New York, a prison nursery has existed since the early 1900s (see Focus on a State: New York's Bedford Hills Nursery Program for more information). In these nurseries, female inmates who meet strict guidelines can live with their newborn if their release date is within a short time (usually no more than 18 months from the birth). There is little research on the effects of prison nurseries on the baby or the mother. However, one study examined long-term outcomes of children who spent their first one to 18 months in a U.S. prison nursery. Researchers measured behavioral development in 47 preschool children who lived in a prison nursery and compared findings to 64 children from a large national dataset who were separated from their mothers because of incarceration. Separation was associated with significantly worse anxious/depressed scores, even after controlling for risks in the caregiving environment. Findings suggest that prison nurseries, if they possess staff who provide developmental support, lead to some resilience in children who experience early maternal incarceration.[116]

In addition to the few prison nurseries across the country, most women's prisons have some type of parenting program, including classes, enhanced visitation, and overnight family visits. Parenting classes provide the inmate-mother with information about child development and advice regarding discipline. Enhanced visitation offers a child-friendly visitation experience, which might include toys and cartoon murals on the wall in a special room away from the general visiting area. This type of visitation might be offered only to those inmates who attend parenting classes or belong to a parenting group that meets weekly (like group therapy), or to those who are nearing release; alternatively, they may be available to anyone who has young children. Some prisons also have programs that allow inmate-mothers to spend the weekend with their children in a trailer or separate living facility inside the walls of the prison. Again, this privilege may be available only to certain inmates. Women who are in prison for child injury or violent crimes are barred from such programs.[117]

In the few published studies that evaluated parenting programs in women's prisons, a reduction of recidivism is rarely stated as a goal or objective; rather, the goal is to increase the bond between mother and child. However, there is some evidence to indicate that family ties and frequent visitation are correlated with a reduction in recidivism.[118] Other studies show that visitation programs assist in reunification of the family after release. Women who were with their children after release were less likely to commit new crimes and more likely to stay drug free.[119] There is a need for more studies on how parenting programs help both the offender and her children.[120]

NEW YORK'S BEDFORD HILLS NURSERY PROGRAM

Bedford Hills, a women's prison in New York, has the longest continuously running prison nursery program in the country, having opened in 1901. Women who meet stringent guidelines can bring their newborns back with them to prison instead of handing the baby to relatives or the state one or two days after birth. According to proponents, allowing women and babies to bond is good for both the baby and the mother. Critics argue that it is unconstitutional to deprive the babies of liberty without due process and that it puts correctional workers into the role of daycare workers.

There are only eight prison nurseries in the United States, but the prison nursery at Bedford Hills is the only one that has never closed. Nurseries were more common before the Second World War, when the cultural expectations of motherhood supported the notion that women and babies should not be separated. In the 1950s, however, many of the programs were closed, partly because of cost, but also because of a belief that babies did not belong in prison. Beginning in the 1990s, the concept of prison nurseries experienced a slight surge of interest, and several states opened new programs, but the actual number of programs and the number of female inmates who can take advantage of them remains extremely small.

The Bedford Hills nursery has space for up to 26 mothers. Women and babies are housed in a special wing of the prison and each inmate-mother has a separate cell with a crib. About 40 women each year qualify for the program and keep their babies with them until release. Only women convicted of nonviolent crimes, with no history with a child welfare agency, and within 18 months of release or who are willing to let their baby go to other caretakers at 18 months until release are eligible. The program offers parenting classes, which are available before and after birth. While mothers are at work or school, babies are cared for by trained prisoners in an on-site daycare. The women receive support services, such as lactation consultation and access to social workers, but they must abide by many rules and show that they can care for their babies.

Evaluation studies are limited, but one five-year study showed that babies in prison nurseries showed similar rates of secure attachments to their mothers to those of a control sample on the outside. Another study found that the three-year recidivism rate for all women released from prison was 26 percent, compared with 13 percent for nursery program participants.

The nonprofit agency Hour Children, whose mission is to help incarcerated women and former inmates (and their children) successfully rejoin society, runs the nursery program at Bedford Hills and runs an optional reentry program in Queens, New York. There, mothers who have been released from prison receive jobs, daycare services, and housing; these are subsidized primarily by donations, with some funding from the state's housing and mental health agencies. If the women are using Hour Children's services, they are allowed to stay as long as they like.

Questions for Discussion

1. What are the advantages and disadvantages of allowing an inmate-mother to keep her baby with her in prison?

2. How might being involved in a prison nursery program affect an inmate's likelihood of recidivism?

Source: E. Chuck, "Raised in Prison: How Incarcerated Mothers Parent their Babies Behind Bars," NBC News, August 4, 2018, https://www.nbcnews.com/news/us-news/prison-nurseries-give-incarcerated-mothers-chance-raise-their-babies-behind-n894171.

Drug Treatment

As we have discussed, women may have different motivations for drug use and varying incentives for change. Women have been found to have higher scores on the Addiction Severity Index than male inmates and experience depression and anxiety more acutely.[121] Thus, drug treatment programs designed for men do not necessarily work as well for women. Like men, women are likely to have co-occurring disorders; for example, drug addiction and depression, or drug addiction and personality disorder, which treatment programs must address simultaneously.[122] Many of the elements of successful drug treatment for women (individualized treatment plans, continuity of care, and sufficient length of stay) are the same as those in programs for men; however, some research indicates that gender-responsive programs are more effective.[123] Women respond better to nurturance; their motivation to change is largely found within their guilt toward their children and others, and their vulnerabilities toward recidivating tend to be found in their low self-worth and inability to cope with stress. These issues must be addressed in any effective drug treatment program.

A survey of the needs of drug-abusing women offenders, as well as a nationwide survey of community-based treatment programs, concluded that there were widespread inadequacies in drug treatment delivery and that women-only programs offered more gender-responsive services. Most programs offered case management, relapse prevention, HIV/AIDS education, counseling, and 12-step meetings. Few residential programs allow children to live with the mother or even have enhanced/extended visitation, although women-only programs were more likely to meet women's special needs. Findings indicated that programs did not generally respond to the multiple needs of female offenders (e.g., poor handling of a dual diagnosis, such as mental illness and drug addiction). It was also noted that treatment programs were often too short to be effective and did not provide continuity in service after release.[124]

The most effective treatment interventions for drug-abusing women take a skill-building approach that focuses on women's roles as caregivers, since that is often a source of stress that drives relapses and a source of particular pain for addicts who feel they are failures as mothers; successful programs also address motivators for drug use (e.g., childhood abuse).[125] Treatment should be delivered in women-only environments because co-ed groups distract women from recovery. Evaluations of gender-responsive drug programs compared to gender-mixed programs have found that gender-responsive programs are more successful in reducing arrests and drug use for women. These programs also reduced symptoms of PTSD. Even though both types of treatment programs show success in increasing psychological well-being and reduced drug use and arrests, the gender-responsive programs provided greater benefits because they respond directly to the needs of women; for example, providing nurturance and childcare advice.[126]

 # Reentry

Women have historically shown lower recidivism rates than male inmates, although that seems to be changing more recently. Recidivism rates of women and men will be discussed in Chapter 12. In this chapter, we will briefly discuss the different issues of reentry for women. While they face many of the same obstacles to reentry as men, they also have some unique issues. Like men, substance abuse treatment in the community is necessary for many offenders, who often go back to the same friends, family, and neighborhoods that were instrumental in their drug use before prison. Also, like men, women face challenges when it comes to finding jobs, obtaining housing, and developing supportive contacts who don't have criminal lifestyles. For women, depression, anxiety, anger, psychosis, and other emotional problems often complicate matters further. Women who leave prison sometimes go back to violent and psychologically abusive relationships, especially if they are financially dependent on the abuser.

Parenting responsibilities weigh heavily on women as well. They may want to regain custody of their children, but often are not in a financial situation to do so. Caregivers may be impatient to hand off childcare to the mother whether she is ready to take on such responsibility or not; conversely, the parolee herself may be anxious to take back a parental role for her children, but the caregiver who has been responsible for them (sometimes for years) is not willing to let go.

When it comes to healthcare, women may not know where to turn for help. Healthcare services are difficult to access on the outside because they may involve confusing health insurance coverage rules, transportation difficulties, making appointments, and long waits, rather than simply filing a request to go to the infirmary or standing in the pill line in prison. While prison healthcare may not be optimal, it is sometimes better than what a woman can access for herself on the outside.[127]

As we have discussed, gender-responsive programming addresses common issues between men and women, but also those that are particularly relevant to women. Gender-responsive programs that offer "wrap-around" services help ease the transition to reentry. Recall that "wrap-around" services refer to programs where the assistance or counseling that began in the prison is available and continues on the outside. The relationship between a parole officer and female parolee is important as well. Some research indicates that women respond to punitive, nonsupportive supervisors with anxiety, which is associated with recidivism.[128] Female parolees whose supervisors encourage, counsel, and advocate on their behalf are more likely to see success in terms of acclimating to life after prison.

Summary

- Women comprise about 7 percent of the national prison population.
- Historically, male and female prisoners were housed together, which resulted in sexual exploitation. Beginning in the late 1800s and continuing until the 1980s, women were housed in separate institutions and guarded by women. Today, male correctional officers are more common, comprising half of all staff in women's prisons.
- The pathways approach identifies four major differences between female and male offenders: women are more likely to have experienced prior victimization, substance abuse, criminogenic familial and intimate relationships, and economic marginalization.
- Female prisoner subculture is less likely to involve gangs and more likely to consist of dyads, cliques, and pseudo-families. In women's prisons, there is a lower risk of serious violence; however, women are typically involved in less serious incidents more often than men.
- Most violence in women's prisons occurs because of intimate partnerships, debts, and disrespect. Younger women with violent histories are more likely to be aggressors.
- Women inmates are more likely to be sexually victimized by each other than by staff members; sexual victimization is usually sexual harassment or unwanted touching.
- Gender-responsive programming acknowledges differences between men and women prisoners and aims to create a safe place for women based on respect and dignity; to promote healthy relationships (especially with children); to address

substance abuse, trauma, intimate partner violence, and mental health issues; and to provide the means for women to improve their socioeconomic status.

- Female prisoners are more likely to be primary caregivers of young children. Prison parenting programs can include classes on child development and discipline, enhanced visitation, or a prison nursery. Research shows that parenting programs are associated with reduced recidivism and better outcomes for children.

- Successful drug treatment programs for female inmates include individualized treatment plans, continuity of care, and sufficient length of stay, and should focus on skill building, women's roles as caregivers, and specific motivators for drug use unique to women.

- Historically, women have had lower recidivism rates than men. Their reentry is complicated by greater stigma attached to being a female ex-con, reunification issues with family and children, and job prospects.

PROJECTS

1. Develop a correctional program that addresses the following risk factors.

   - Risk factors for recidivism for a probation sample: criminal history, substance abuse, financial problems, education, employment, homelessness, current symptoms of mental illness, parental stress, self-esteem, and self-efficacy.

   - Risk factors for parolees: substance abuse, economic, educational, and financial variables, current mental health status, anger/hostility, family support, and current adult domestic violence victimization.

2. Find an example of a female offender in the news. With as much information as you can obtain, determine whether the woman exhibits background traits consistent with the pathways approach.

NOTES

1. E. Carson, *Prisoners in 2019* (Washington, DC: Bureau of Justice Statistics, 2020).

2. E. Swavola, K. Riley, and R. Subramanian, *Overlooked: Women and Jails in an Era of Reform* (New York: Vera Institute, 2016).

3. Z. Zeng, *Jail Inmates in 2016* (Washington, DC: Bureau of Justice Statistics, OJP, 2018).

4. "Not Part of My Sentence": Violations of the Human Rights of Women in Custody (London, England: Amnesty International, March 1999); *All Too Familiar: Sexual Abuse in U.S. State Prisons* (New York: Human Rights Watch, 1996).

5. E. Freedman, "Their Sister's Keepers: A Historical Perspective of Female Correctional Institutions in the U.S.," *Feminist Studies* 2 (1974): 77–95.

6. N. Rafter, *Partial Justice: State Prisons and Their Inmates, 1800–1935* (Boston: Northeastern Press, 1985). Republished as *Partial Justice: Women, Prisons, and Social Control* (New Brunswick, NJ: Transaction Books, 1990).

7. K. Strickland, *Correctional Institutions for Women in the U.S.* (Lexington, MA: Lexington Books, 1976), 40.

8. N. Rafter, *Partial Justice: State Prisons and Their Inmates, 1800–1935* (Boston: Northeastern Press, 1985), 80.

9. E. Fry, *Observations on the Siting, Superintendence and Government of Female Prisoners*, 1825. Available for free download from https://www.forgottenbooks.com/en/books/Observations_on_the_Visiting_Superintendence_and_Government_of_1000133587.

10. C. Feinman, "An Historical Overview of The Treatment of Incarcerated Women: Myths and Realities of Rehabilitation," *The Prison Journal* 63, no. 2 (1983), 15.

11. E. Freedman, "Their Sister's Keepers: A Historical Perspective of Female Correctional Institutions in the U.S.," Feminist Studies 2 (1974): 77–95.

12. N. Rafter, *Partial Justice: State Prisons and Their Inmates, 1800–1935* (Boston: Northeastern Press, 1985/1990).

13. E. Freedman, *Their Sister's Keepers: Women's Prison Reforms in America, 1830–1930* (Ann Arbor, Michigan: University of Michigan Press, 1981); K. Strickland, *Correctional Institutions for Women in the U.S.* (Lexington, MA: Lexington Books,1976).

14. N. Rafter, *Partial Justice: State Prisons and Their Inmates, 1800–1935* (Boston: Northeastern Press, 1985/1990). Republished as *Partial Justice: Women, Prisons, and Social Control* (New Brunswick, NJ: Transaction Books, 1985/1990).

15. E. Freedman, *Their Sister's Keepers: Women's Prison Reforms in America, 1830–1930* (Ann Arbor, Michigan: University of Michigan Press, 1981).

16. N. Rafter, *Partial Justice: State Prisons and Their Inmates, 1800–1935* (Boston: Northeastern Press, 1985/1990). Republished as *Partial Justice: Women, Prisons, and Social Control* (New Brunswick, NJ: Transaction Books, 1985/1990).

17. J. Pollock, *Women, Prison and Crime* (Belmont, CA: Wadsworth, 2002); K. Carbone-Lopez, K. and C. Kruttschnitt, "Assessing the Racial Climate in Women's Institutions in The Context of Penal Reform," *Women and Criminal Justice* 15, 1 (2003): 55–79.

18. J. Pollock, *Women's Crimes, Criminology, and Corrections* (Prospect Heights, IL: Waveland, 2014).

19. K. Daly, "Women's Pathways to Felony Court: Feminist Theories of Lawbreaking and Problems of Representation," *Southern California Review of Law and Women's Studies* 2(1992): 11–52; K. Daly, *Gender, Crime, and Punishment* (New Haven, CT: Yale University Press, 1994).

20. E.A. Carson, E.A. Prisoners in 2016 (Washington, DC: Bureau of Justice Statistics; The Sentencing Project, 2018); *Fact Sheet: Incarcerated Women and Girls, 1980–2016* (Washington, DC: The Sentencing Project); B. Owen, J. Wells, J. Pollock, B. Muscat, and S. Torres, *Gendered Violence and Safety: A Contextual Approach to Improving Security in Women's Facilities* (Washington, DC: National Institute of Justice, 2008).

21. B. Owen and B. Bloom, "Profiling Women Prisoners: Findings from National Surveys and a California Sample," *The Prison Journal* 75, 2 (1995): 165–85; B. Fletcher, L. Shaver, and D. Moon, *Women Prisoners: A Forgotten Population* (Westport, CT: Praeger, 1993); J. Pollock, *Counseling Women in Prison* (Beverly Hills CA: SAGE, 1998); C. Harlow, *Selected Findings: Prior Abuse Reported by Inmates and Probationers* (Washington, DC: Bureau of Justice Statistics, U.S. Dept. of Justice, 1999).

22. L Greenfield and T. Snell, *Women Offenders* (Washington, DC: U.S. Dept. of Justice, 1999).

23. S.M. Lynch, *Women's Pathways to Jail: The Roles and Intersections of Serious Mental Illness and Trauma* (Washington, DC: U.S. Department of Justice, Office of Justice Programs, Bureau of Justice Assistance, 2012), 32.

24. K. Breitenbecher, "Sexual Revictimization Among Women: A Review of the Literature Focusing on Empirical Investigations," *Aggression and Violent Behavior,* 6 (2001): 415–32; T. Messman-Moore and P. Long, "Child Sexual Abuse and Revictimization in the Form of Adult Sexual Abuse: Adult Physical Abuse and Adult Psychological Maltreatment," *Journal of Interpersonal Violence* 15 (2000): 489–502.

25. M. Maeve, "Speaking Unavoidable Truths: Understanding Early Childhood Sexual and Physical Violence among Women in Prison," *Issues in Mental Health Nursing* 21 (2000): 473–98; T. Messman-Moore and P. Long, "Child Sexual Abuse and Revictimization in the Form of Adult Sexual Abuse, Adult Physical Abuse and Adult Psychological Maltreatment," *Journal of Interpersonal Violence* 15 (2000): 489–502.

26. C. Widom, "Childhood Sexual Abuse and Criminal Consequences," *Society* 33, 4 (1996): 47–53; J. Pollock, J. Mullings, J. and B. Crouch, " Violent Women: Findings from the Texas Women Inmates' Study," *Journal of Interpersonal Violence* 21, 4 (2006): 485–502; K. Holsinger, and A. Holsinger, "Differential Pathways To Violence and Self-Injurious Behavior: African American and White Girls In The Juvenile Justice System," *Journal of Research in Crime and Delinquency*, 42, 2 (2005): 211–42.

27. J. Mullings, J. Marquart, and V. Brewer, "Assessing the Relationship between Child Sexual Abuse and Marginal Living Conditions on HIV/AIDS-Related Risk Behavior Among Women Prisoners," *Child Abuse and Neglect* 24, 5 (2000): 677–88; J. Mullings, J. Marquart, and D. Hartley, "Exploring the Effects of Childhood Sexual Abuse

and its Impact on HIV/AIDS Risk-taking Behavior Among Women Prisoners," *The Prison Journal* 83, 4 (2003): 442–63; J. Mullings, J. Pollock, and B. Crouch, "Drugs and Criminality: Results from the Texas Women Inmates Study," *Women and Criminal Justice* 13, 4 (2002): 69–97.

28. Vivian C. Smith, "Substance-Abusing Female Offenders as Victims: Chronological Sequencing of Pathways into the Criminal Justice System, *Victims and Offenders* 12, 1 (2015):113-137.

29. C. Mumola, and J. Karberg, *Drug Use and Dependence, State and Federal Prisoners, 2004* (Washington, DC: Bureau of Justice Statistics, U.S. Dept. of Justice, 2006).

30. B. Owen and B. Bloom, "Profiling Women Prisoners: Findings from National Surveys and a California Sample," *The Prison Journal* 75, 2 (1995): 165–85.

31. J. Mullings, J. Pollock, and B. Crouch, "Drugs and Criminality: Results from the Texas Women Inmates Study," *Women and Criminal Justice* 13, 4 (2002): 69–97; B. Owen and B. Bloom, "Profiling Women Prisoners: Findings from National Surveys and a California Sample," *The Prison Journal* 75, 2 (1995): 165–85.

32. J. Mullings, J. Pollock, and B. Crouch, "Drugs and Criminality: Results from the Texas Women Inmates Study," *Women and Criminal Justice* 13,4 (2002): 69–97; V. Webb, C. Katz, and T. Klosky, "Drug Use Among Traditional Versus Non-Traditional Female Offenders: Findings from the National DUF Project" (paper presented at the American Society of Criminology Meeting, Boston, 1995).

33. J. Wellisch, M. Prendergast, and D. Anglin, D., "Needs Assessment and Services for Drug-Abusing Women Offenders: Results from A National Survey of Community-Based Treatment Programs," *Women and Criminal Justice* 8, 1 (1996): 27–60.

34. C. Battle, C. Zlotnick, L. Najavits, M. Guttierez, and C. Winsor, "Post-traumatic Stress Disorder and Substance Use Disorder Among Incarcerated Women," in P. Ouimette and P. Brown (eds.), *Trauma and Substance Abuse: Causes, Consequences, and Treatment of Co-Morbid Disorders* (Washington, DC: American Psychological Association, 2003), 209–25.

35. D. McClellan, D. Farabee, and B. Crouch, "Early Victimization, Drug Use, and Criminality; A Comparison of Male and Female Prisoners," *Criminal Justice and Behavior* 24, 4 (1997): 455–76.

36. S. Batchelor, "'Prove Me the Bam!': Victimization and Agency in the Lives of Young Women Who Commit Violent Offenses," *The Journal of Community and Criminal Justice* 52, 4 (2005): 358–75; B. Reed, "Developing Women-Sensitive Drug Dependence Treatment Services: Why So Difficult?" *Journal of Psychoactive Drugs* 19, 2 (1987): 151–64.

37. D. McClellan, D. Farabee, and B. Crouch, "Early Victimization, Drug Use, and Criminality; A Comparison of Male and Female Prisoners," *Criminal Justice and Behavior* 24, 4 (1997): 455–76; J. Mullings, J. Pollock, and B. Crouch, "Drugs and Criminality: Results from the Texas Women Inmates Study,"

Women and Criminal Justice 13, 4 (2002): 69–97.

38. J. Pollock, *Women's Crimes, Criminology, and Corrections* (Prospect Heights, IL: Waveland, 2014); B. Owen and B. Bloom, "Profiling Women Prisoners: Findings from National Surveys and a California Sample," *The Prison Journal* 75, no. 2 (1995): 165–85; B. Fletcher, L. Shaver, and D. Moon, *Women Prisoners: A Forgotten Population* (Westport, CT: Praeger, 1993); J. Pollock, *Counseling Women in Prison* (Beverly Hills CA: SAGE, 1998).

39. B. Owen and B. Bloom, "Profiling Women Prisoners: Findings from National Surveys and a California Sample," *The Prison Journal* 75, no. 2 (1995): 165–85; B. Fletcher, L. Shaver, and D. Moon, *Women Prisoners: A Forgotten Population* (Westport, CT: Praeger, 1993; J. Pollock, *Counseling Women in Prison* (Beverly Hills, CA: Sage, 1998).

40. B. Bloom, B. Owen, and S. Covington, *Gender-Responsive Strategies: Research, Practice, and Guiding Principles for Women Offenders* (Washington DC: National Institute of Corrections, 2003); B. Carlson, "The Most Important Things Learned About Violence and Trauma in the Past 20 Years," *Journal of Interpersonal Violence* 20, 1 (2005): 119–26.

41. A. Browne, *When Battered Women Kill* (New York: Free Press, 1997); A. Browne, B. Miller, and E. Maguin, "Prevalence and Severity of Lifetime Physical and Sexual Victimization Among Incarcerated Women," *International Journal of Law and Psychiatry* 22 (1999): 301–22.

42. S. Covington, "Creating Gender-Responsive Programs: The Next Step for Women's Services," *Corrections Today* 61 (2001): 85–7; B. Bloom, B. Owen, and S. Covington, *Gender-Responsive Strategies: Research, Practice, and Guiding Principles for Women Offenders* (Washington DC: National Institute of Corrections, 2003);. B. Owen, J. Wells, J. Pollock, B. Muscat, and S. Torres, *Gendered Violence and Safety: A Contextual Approach to Improving Security in Women's Facilities* (Washington, DC: National Institute of Justice, 2008), 15.

43. M. Gilfus, "Women's Experiences of Abuse as a Risk Factor for Incarceration," National Electronic Network on Violence Against Women, 2002, retrieved March 15, 2019 from https://vawnet. org/sites/default/files/ assets/files/2017–08/AR_ Incarceration.pdf.

44. S.M. Lynch, D.D. DeHart, J.E. Belknap, B.L. Green, P. Dass-Brailsford, K.A. Johnson, and E. Whalley, "A Multisite Study of the Prevalence of Serious Mental Illness, PTSD, and Substance Use Disorders of Women in Jail," *Psychiatric Services* 65,5 (2014), 670–74. 2.

45. M.E. McPhail, D.R. Falvo, and E.J. Burker, "Psychiatric Disorders in Incarcerated Women: Treatment and Rehabilitation Needs for Successful Community Reentry," *Journal of Applied Rehabilitation Counseling* 43, 1 (2012): 19–26.

46. S. Lynch, D. DeHart, J. Belknap, B. Green, P. Dass-Brailsford, K. Johnson, and M. Wong, "An Examination of the Associations Among Victimization, Mental Health, and Offending in Women," *Criminal Justice and Behavior,* 44, 6 (2017): 796–814.

47. R. Kessler, S. Aguilar-Gaxiola, J. Alonso, C. Benjet, E. Bromet, and G. Cardoso, "Trauma and PTSD in the WHO World Mental Health Surveys," *European Journal of Psychotraumatology* 8 (2017), https://doi.org/10.1080/2000 8198.2017.1353383.

48. C. Scott, A. Lurigio, M. Dennis, and R. Funk, "Trauma and Morbidities Among Female Detainees in a Large Urban Jail," *The Prison Journal* 96, 1 (2016): 102–25.

49. N. Scott, T. Hannum, and S. Gilchrist, "Assessment of Depression Among Incarcerated Females," *Journal of Personality Assessment* 46 (1982): 372–79.

50. M. Dye, "The Gender Paradox in Prison Suicide Rates," *Women and Criminal Justice* 21 (2011): 290–307.

51. S. Springer, "Improving Healthcare for Incarcerated Women," *Journal of Women's Health* 19, 1 (2010): 13–15; P. Ross and J. Lawrence, "Health Care for Women Offenders," *Corrections Today* 60, no. 7 (1998): 122–29.

52. P. Ross and J. Lawrence, "Health Care for Women Offenders," *Corrections Today* 60, 7 (1998): 122–29. V. Brewer, J. Marquart, J. Mullings, and B. Crouch,: "AIDS-Related Risk Behavior Among Female Prisoners with Histories of Mental Impairment," *Prison Journal* 78 (1998): 101–19.

53. L. Acoca, "Defusing the Time Bomb: Understanding and Meeting the Growing Health Care Needs of Incarcerated Women in America," *Crime and Delinquency* 44, no. 1 (1998): 49–69.

54. E. Barry, "Women Prisoners and Health Care," in K. Moss (ed.) *Man-Made Medicine* (Durham, NC: Duke University Press, 1996), 250–72.

55. *Estelle v. Gamble,* 429 U.S. 97 (1976).

56. *Morales v. Turman,* 383 F. Supp. 53 (E.D. Tex. 1974).

57. J. Pollock, *Women's Crimes, Criminology, and Corrections* (Prospect Heights, IL: Waveland, 2014).

58. K. Gabel and D. Johnston, *Children of Incarcerated Parents* (New York: Lexington Books, 1995).

59. *"Not Part of My Sentence": Violations of the Human Rights of Women in Custody* (London, England: Amnesty International, 1999).

60. *Nelson v. Correctional Medical Services,* 583 F.3d 522 (2009).

61. L. Grubb and R. del Carmen, "An Analysis of Court Decisions, Statutes, and Administrative Regulations Related to Pregnant Inmates," *The Prison Journal* 96, 3 (2016): 355–91.

62. J. Pollock, *Women, Prison and Crime* (Belmont, CA: Wadsworth, 2002); S. Sharp, *The Incarcerated Woman* (Upper Saddle River, NJ: Prentice-Hall, 2003).

63. C. Kruttschnitt and R. Gartner, *Marking Time in the Golden State: Women's Imprisonment in California* (Cambridge: Cambridge University Press, 2005).

64. J. Pollock, *Women, Prison and Crime* (Belmont, CA: Wadsworth, 2002).

65. B. Owen, *"In the Mix": Struggle and Survival in a Women's Prison* (Albany, NY: State University of Albany Press, 1998); L. Girshick, *No Safe Haven: Stories of Women in*

Prison (Boston: Northeastern University Press, 1999); K. Greer, "The Changing Nature of Interpersonal Relationships in a Women's Prison," *The Prison Journal* 80, 4 (2000): 442–68.

66. B. Owen, J. Wells, J. Pollock, B. Muscat, and S. Torres, *Gendered Violence and Safety: A Contextual Approach to Improving Security in Women's Facilities* (Washington, DC: National Institute of Justice, 2008).

67. L. Girshick, *No Safe Haven: Stories of Women in Prison* (Boston: Northeastern University Press, 1999); K. Greer, "The Changing Nature of Interpersonal Relationships in a Women's Prison," *The Prison Journal* 80, 4 (2000): 442–68; B. Owen, J. Wells, J. Pollock, B. Muscat, and S. Torres, *Gendered Violence and Safety: A Contextual Approach to Improving Security in Women's Facilities* (Washington, DC: National Institute of Justice, 2008).

68. J. Pollock, *Women, Prison and Crime* (Belmont, CA: Wadsworth, 2002).

69. N. Wolff, C. Blitz, J. Shi, J. Siegel, and R. Bachman, "Physical Violence Inside Prisons: Rates of Victimization," *Criminal Justice and Behavior* 34, 5 (2007): 588–99; N. Wolff, N. and J. Shi. 2009, "Type, Source, and Patterns of Physical Victimization: A Comparison of Male and Female Inmates," *The Prison Journal* 89, 2: 172–91.

70. N. Wolff and J. Shi. 2009, "Type, Source, and Patterns of Physical Victimization: A Comparison of Male and Female Inmates," *The Prison Journal* 89, 2: 172–91; J. Wooldredge and B. Steiner,

"Assessing the Need for Gender-Specific Explanations of Prisoner Victimization," *Justice Quarterly* 33, 2 (2014): 209-238.

71. K. Edgar, I. O'Donnell, and C. Martin, *Prison Violence: The Dynamics of Conflict, Fear and Power* (London, England: Routledge, 2003).

72. B. Owen, J. Wells, J. Pollock, B. Muscat, and S. Torres, *Gendered Violence and Safety: A Contextual Approach to Improving Security in Women's Facilities* (Washington, DC: National Institute of Justice, 2008).

73. B. Owen, J. Wells, J. Pollock, B. Muscat, and S. Torres, *Gendered Violence and Safety: A Contextual Approach to Improving Security in Women's Facilities* (Washington, DC: National Institute of Justice, 2008); R. Trammell, T. Wulf-Ludden, and D. Mowder, "Partner Violence in Women's Prison: The Social Consequences of Girlfriend Fights," *Women and Criminal Justice* 25, 4 (2015): 256–72.

74. B. Owen, J. Wells, J. Pollock, B. Muscat, and S. Torres, *Gendered Violence and Safety: A Contextual Approach to Improving Security in Women's Facilities* (Washington, DC: National Institute of Justice, 2008).

75. D. Wilkinson, "Violence Events and Social Identity: Specifying the Relationships Between Respect and Masculinity in Inner-City Violent Youth," *Sociological Studies of Children and Youth* 8 (2001): 235–69.

76. M. Butler, "'What Are You Looking At?' Prisoner Confrontation and the Search for Respect," *British Journal of Criminology* 48 (2008): 856–73; D. Mears, E. Stewart, S. Siennick, and R. Simons, "The

Code of The Street and Inmate Violence: Investigating the Salience of Imported Belief Systems," *Criminology* 51 (2013): 695–728.

77. Batchelor, S., "'Prove Me the Bam!': Victimization and Agency in the Lives of Young Women Who Commit Violent Offenses," *The Journal of Community and Criminal Justice* 52, 4 (2005): 358–75; K. Irwin and C. Adler, "Fighting for Her Honor: Girls' Violence In Distressed Communities," *Feminist Criminology* 7 (2012): 350–80; R. Trammell, *Enforcing the Convict Code: Violence and Prison Culture* (Boulder, CO: Lynne Rienner Press, 2012). C. Kruttschnitt, and K. Carbone-Lopez, "Moving Beyond Stereotypes: Women's Subjective Accounts of Their Violent Crime," *Criminology* 44 (2006): 321–51.

78. B. Owen, J. Wells, J. Pollock, B. Muscat, and S. Torres, *Gendered Violence and Safety: A Contextual Approach to Improving Security in Women's Facilities* (Washington, DC: National Institute of Justice, 2008).

79. B. Owen, J. Wells, and J. Pollock, *In Search of Safety: Confronting Inequality in Women's Imprisonment* (Oakland, CA: University of Calif Press, 2017).

80. E. Wright, E. Salisbury, and P. Van Voorhis, "Predicting the Prison Misconducts of Women Offenders," *Journal of Contemporary Criminal Justice* 23, 4 (2007): 310–40.

81. B. Steiner and J. Wooldredge, "Individual and Environmental Effects on Assaults and Nonviolent Rule Breaking by Women in Prison," *Journal of Research in Crime and Delinquency* 46 (2009): 437–467.

82. K. Lahm, "Violent and Nonviolent Misconduct Among Female Inmates: An Exploration of Competing Theories," *Victims and Offenders* 12, 2 (2015): 175-204.

83. B. Steiner, E. Wright and S. Toto, "The Sources of Violent and Nonviolent Offending among Women in Prison," *Justice Quarterly* 37, 4 (2019): 644-66.

84. N. Messina, J. Braithwaite, S. Calhoun, and S. Kubiak, "Examination of a Violence Prevention Program for Female Offenders," *Violence and Gender* 3, 3 (2016): 143–49.

85. B. Owen, J. Wells, J. Pollock, B. Muscat, and S. Torres, *Gendered Violence and Safety: A Contextual Approach to Improving Security in Women's Facilities* (Washington, DC: National Institute of Justice, 2008).

86. B. Owen, J. Wells, J. Pollock, B. Muscat, and S. Torres, *Gendered Violence and Safety: A Contextual Approach to Improving Security in Women's Facilities* (Washington, DC: National Institute of Justice, 2008), 24.

87. C. Struckman-Johnson, L. Rucker, K. Bumby and S. Donaldson., "Sexual Coercion Reported by Men and Women in Prison," *Journal of Sex Research* 33, 1(1996): 67–76; C. Struckman-Johnson and D. Struckman-Johnson, "A Comparison of Sexual Coercion Experiences Reported by Men and Women in Prison," *Journal of Interpersonal Violence* 21, 12 (2006): 1591–1615; A. Blackburn, J. Mullings, and J. Marquart, "Sexual Assault in Prison and Beyond," *The Prison Journal* 88, 3 (2008): 351–77.

88. N. Wolff, C. Blitz, J. Shi, J. Siegel, and R. Bachman, "Sexual Violence Inside Prisons: Rates of Victimization," *Journal of Urban Health: Bulletin of the New York Academy of Medicine* 83, 5 (2006): 835–48; N. Wolff, C. Blitz, J. Shi, J. Siegel., "Understanding Sexual Victimization Inside Prisons: Factors that Predict Victimization," *Criminology and Public Policy* 6, 3 (2007): 535–64.

89. K. Lahm, "Predictors of Violent and Nonviolent Victimization Behind Bars: An Exploration of Women Inmates," *Women and Criminal Justice* 25, 4 (2015): 273–91.

90. R. Rantala, J. Rexroat, A. Beck, *Sexual Victimization Reported by Adult Correctional Authorities, 2009–11* (NCJ 243904) (Washington, DC: Bureau of Justice Statistics, 2014).

91. J. Wooldredge and B. Steiner, "Assessing the Need for Gender-Specific Explanations of Prisoner Victimization," *Justice Quarterly* 33, 2 (2014): 209-38.

92. N. Siegel, "Stopping Abuse in Prison," in T. Gray (ed.), *Exploring Corrections* (Boston: Allyn and Bacon, 2002), 135–39; F. Flesher, "Cross Gender Supervision in Prisons and the Constitutional Right of Prisoners to Remain Free from Rape," *William and Mary Journal of Women and the Law* (Spring 2007): 841–67.

93. J. Coherty, J. Levine, and P. Thomas, "Alabama Prison Was House of Horrors for Female Inmates, Feds Say," ABCNews.com, January 22, 2014, retrieved from http://abcnews.go.com/US/women-universally-fear-safety-alabama-prison-feds/story?id=21627510; "NJ Officers Suspended Over Alleged Attack at Women's Prison," Associated Press, January 28, 2021, accessed Jan. 29, 2021 from https://apnews.com/article/us-news-new-jersey-prisons-506f89e2d701528e73e58a42cbc0b2af.

94. M. Maeve, "Speaking Unavoidable Truths: Understanding Early Childhood Sexual and Physical Violence among Women in Prison," *Issues in Mental Health Nursing* 21 (2000): 473–98.

95. F. Flesher, "Cross Gender Supervision in Prisons and the Constitutional Right of Prisoners to Remain Free from Rape," *William and Mary Journal of Women and the Law* (Spring 2007): 841–67.

96. B. Owen, J. Wells, J. Pollock, B. Muscat, and S. Torres, *Gendered Violence and Safety: A Contextual Approach to Improving Security in Women's Facilities* (Washington, DC: National Institute of Justice, 2008).

97. R. Trammell, "Relational Violence in Women's Prison: How Women Describe Interpersonal Violence and Gender," *Women and Criminal Justice* 19 (2009): 267–85.

98. L. Teplin, K. Abrams, and G. McClelland, "Prevalence of Psychiatric Disorders Among Incarcerated Women," *Archives of General Psychiatry* 53, 2 (1996): 505–12.

99. E. Wright, P. Van Voorhis, E. Salisbury, and A. Bauman, "Gender-Responsive Lessons Learned and Policy Implications for Women in Prison: A Review," *Criminal Justice and Behavior*, 39 (2012): 1612–32.

100. *Glover v. Johnson*, 478 F. Supp. 1075 (E.D. Mich. 1979).

101. M. Morash and T. Bynum, *Findings from the National Study of Innovative and Promising Programs for Women Offenders* (Washington DC: U.S. Dept. of Justice, 1995).

102. M. Morash and T. Bynum, *Findings from the National Study of Innovative and Promising Programs for Women Offenders* (Washington DC: U.S. Dept. of Justice, 1995).

103. J. Pollock, *Women, Prison and Crime* (Belmont, CA: Wadsworth, 2002).

104. "Women in Prison: Seeking Justice Behind Bars," U.S. Commission on Civil Rights, February 2020, https://www.usccr.gov/pubs/2020/02-26-Women-in-Prison.pdf.

105. J. Pollock, *Women, Prison and Crime* (Belmont, CA: Wadsworth, 2002); D. Young and R. Mattuci, "Enhancing the Vocational Skills of Incarcerated Women Through a Plumbing Maintenance Program," *The Journal of Correctional Education* 57, 2 (2006): 126–40.

106. J. Pollock, *Counseling Women in Prison* (Beverly Hills CA: SAGE, 1998).

107. B. Bloom, B. Owen, and S. Covington, *Gender-Responsive Strategies: Research, Practice, and Guiding Principles for Women Offenders* (Washington DC: National Institute of Corrections, 2003).

108. S. Covington and J. Surrey, "The Relational Model of Women's Psychological Development: Implications for Substance Abuse," in S. and R. Wilsnack (eds.), *Gender and Alcohol: Individual and Social Perspectives* (New Brunswick, NJ; Rutgers Center of Alcohol Studies, 1997), 335–51; B. Bloom and S. Covington, "Effective Gender-Responsive Interventions in Juvenile Justice: Addressing the Lives of Delinquent Girls," Center for Gender and Justice, 2001, https://www.stephaniecovington.com/site/assets/files/1538/7.pdf.

109. E. Wright, P. Van Voorhis, E. Salisbury, and A. Bauman, "Gender-Responsive Lessons Learned and Policy Implications for Women in Prison: A Review," *Criminal Justice and Behavior*, 39 (2012): 1612–32.

110. R. Gobeil, K. Blanchette, L. Stewart, "A Meta-Analytic Review of Correctional Interventions for Women Offenders Gender-Neutral Versus Gender-Informed Approaches," *Criminal Justice and Behavior* 43, 3 (2016): 301–22.

111. C. Mumola, *Incarcerated Children and Their Parents* (Washington, DC: Bureau of Justice Statistics, U.S. Dept. of Justice, 2000); S. Enos, Mothering from the Inside (Albany, NY: SUNY Press, 2001); J. Pollock, *Women's Crimes, Criminology, and Corrections* (Prospect Heights, IL: Waveland, 2014).

112. L. Glaze and L. Maruschak, *Parents in Prison and Their Minor Children* (Washington, DC: Bureau of Justice Statistics, U.S. Dept. of Justice, 2008); C. Mumola, *Incarcerated Children and Their Parents* (Washington, DC: Bureau of Justice Statistics, U.S. Dept. of Justice, 2000).

113. D.H. Dallaire, "Incarcerated Mothers and Fathers: A Comparison of Risks for Children and Families," *Family Relations* 56 (2007): 440–53; M. Tasca, N. Rodriguez, and M.S. Zatz, "Family and Residential Instability in the Context of Paternal and Maternal Incarceration," *Criminal Justice and Behavior* 38 (2011): 231–47; L.R. Muftic, L.A. Bouffard, and G.S. Armstrong, "Impact of Maternal Incarceration On The Criminal Justice Involvement of Adult Offspring," *Journal of Research in Crime and Delinquency* 53 (2016): 93–111.

114. A. Burgess-Proctor, B. Huebner, and J. Durso, "Comparing the Effects of Maternal and Paternal Incarceration on Adult Daughters' and Sons' Criminal Justice System Involvement: A Gendered Pathways Analysis," *Criminal Justice and Behavior* 43, 8 (2016): 1034–55; see also *Policy Report: A Shared Sentence: The Devastating Toll of Parental Incarceration on Kids, Families, and Communities*, Annie E. Casey Foundation, 2016, available at https://www.aecf.org/m/resourcedoc/aecf-asharedsentence-2016.pdf.

115. B. Bloom and D. Steinhart, *Why Punish the Children? A Reappraisal of the Children of Incarcerated Mothers in America* (San Francisco: National Council on Crime and Delinquency, 1993).

116. L. Goshin, M. Byrne, B. Blanchard-Lewis, "Preschool Outcomes of Children Who Lived as Infants in a Prison Nursery," *The Prison Journal*, 94, 2(2014): 139–58.

117. C.K. Villanueva, "Mothers, Infants and Imprisonment: A National Look at Prison Nurseries and Community-Based Alternatives," Women's Prison Association Institute on Women and Criminal Justice, 2009, https://www.prisonlegalnews.org/media/publications/womens_prison_assoc_report_on_prison_

nurseries_and_community_alternatives_2009.pdf.

118. J. Cobbina, "Reintegration Success and Failure: Factors Impacting Reintegration Among Incarcerated and Formerly Incarcerated Women," *Journal of Offender Rehabilitation*.

49 (2010): 210–32; K. Block and M. Potthast, "Living Apart and Getting Together: Inmate Mothers and Enhanced Visitation through Girl Scouts" (paper presented at Academy of Criminal Justice Sciences, March 1997).

119. M. Martin, "Connected Mothers: A Follow-Up Study of Incarcerated Women and Their Children," *Women and Criminal Justice* 8, 4 (1997):1–23.

120. J.L. Sandifer, "Evaluating the Efficacy of a Parenting Program for Incarcerated Mothers," *The Prison Journal* 88, 3 (2008): 423–45.

121. R. Peters and M. Steinberg, "Substance Abuse Treatment in U.S. Prisons," in D. Shewan and J. Davies (eds.), *Drugs and Prison* (London, UK: Harwood Academic Press, 2000), 89–116.

122. M. Morash and P. Schram, *The Prison Experience: Special Issues of Women in Prison* (Prospect Heights, IL: Waveland, 2002).

123. B. Reed, "Developing Women-Sensitive Drug Dependence Treatment Services: Why So Difficult?" *Journal of Psychoactive Drugs* 19, no. 2 (1987): 151–64.

124. J. Wellisch, M. Prendergast, and D. Anglin, D., "Needs Assessment and Services for Drug-Abusing Women Offenders: Results From A National Survey of Community-Based Treatment Programs," *Women and Criminal Justice* 8, 1 (1996): 27–60.

125. T. Ryan, Adult Female Offenders and Institutional Programs: A State-of-the-Art Analysis (Washington, DC: National Institute of Corrections, 1984).

126. N. Messina, S. Calhoun, S. and U. Warda, "Gender Responsive Drug Court Treatment: A Randomized Control Trial," *Criminal Justice and Behavior* 39 (2012): 1539–58.

127. E. Wright, P. Van Voorhis, E. Salisbury, and A. Bauman, "Gender-Responsive Lessons Learned and Policy Implications for Women in Prison: A Review," *Criminal Justice and Behavior*, 39 (2012): 1612–32.

128. M. Morash, D. Kashy, S. Smith and J. Cobbina, "The Connection of Probation/Parole Officer Actions to Women Offenders' Recidivism," *Criminal Justice and Behavior* 43, 4 (2016): 506–24.

Chapter 11

Rehabilitative Programming

LEARNING OBJECTIVES

1. Describe the rehabilitative era of American corrections and why it ended.

2. Outline the different types of programs available in prison and to what degree they are effective in reducing recidivism.

3. Compare and contrast the effectiveness of vocational training and education in reducing recidivism.

4. Describe the four generations of prediction/assessment, the LSI-R, and how prediction and treatment are related in fourth-generation assessment.

5. Outline the issues associated with the methodology of correctional evaluations and findings from recidivism studies.

CHAPTER OUTLINE

- The Mission of Corrections **296**

- Prison Programs **298**

- Prediction and Assessment **308**

- Level of Service Inventory-Revised (LSI-R) and Risk/Need/Responsivity (R/N/R) **310**

- Evaluating Prison Programs **315**

- SUMMARY **321**

Correctional programs are designed to help change prisoners' behavior.

KEY TERMS

Actuarial approach
Ashurst-Sumners Act
Attrition
Clinical approach
Cognitive behavioral programs
Cognitive behavioral therapy (CBT)
Cognitive restructuring
Cognitive skills programs
Contingency contracting
Contract system
Correctional assessment
Correctional Offender Management Profiling

for Alternative Sanctions (COMPAS)
Correctional Program Assessment Inventory (CPAI)
Correctional treatment
Federal Prison Industries Enhancement Act (PIE)
Hawes-Cooper Act
Leased labor system
Level of Service Inventory-Revised (LSI-R)
Medical model
Meta-analysis

Piece-price system
Program fidelity
Rehabilitative era
Risk/Need/Responsivity (R/N/R)
Security classification
Selection bias
Static factors
Therapeutic community (TC)
Treatment ethic

 # The Mission of Corrections

All state and federal corrections systems have as part of their mission to reform and rehabilitate offenders. Correctional programs are created based upon beliefs about why people commit crime in the first place and what intervention is most likely to change their behavior. As you will recall from Chapter 2, criminological theories each have implications for crime prevention programs and rehabilitative aspects of corrections. In the following paragraphs, the major criminological theories from Chapter 3 are summarized with treatment implications.

Biological theories of crime point to genetic and/or postnatal influences that predispose some individuals to criminal choices. Such theories support "healthy start" programs that identify high-risk pregnant women and connect them with nurses for prenatal and postnatal medical assistance and parenting training. Such theories also maintain the importance of early intervention in schools for children who exhibit learning disabilities, lunch programs that provide nutritious meals for children, and comprehensive healthcare to address childhood disease and medical conditions that might predispose individuals to addiction. Correctional programs for adults address physical and mental health issues and learning disabilities that affect earning potential, and help individuals learn how to control their emotions through cognitive behavioral programs.

Psychological theories of crime propose that developmental issues can lead to psychological problems that, in turn, can predispose and individual to commit criminal acts. These theories would promote early diagnosis and intervention for antisocial personality disorder. Other programs are founded on learning theories, such as Big Brother and Big Sister programs (modeling theory) and rewards programs like "stay in school" awards (operational conditioning). Foster parent or adoption programs help high-risk children secure stable and loving homes. Correctional programs for adults based on psychological theories of crime might include group therapy, cognitive behavioral programs, and individual therapy, along with, if necessary, pharmacological treatment to control depression, anxiety disorders, or other mental health issues.

Sociological theories of crime identify both social and individual factors in crime causation. These theories support poverty programs that help with employment and housing, "target hardening" programs that reduce criminal opportunity, or saturation patrols that aim to deter criminality because of pervasive police presence, and initiatives to reduce the influence of gangs in communities. Other programs include those designed to increase the social efficacy of neighborhoods by providing resources like parks, community centers, and neighborhood associations to strengthen social bonds, as well as programs that encourage stronger ties to school, such as interest-based after-school groups, tutoring, or truancy programs), as well as programs that help parents teach children self-control. Correctional programs for adults include education and vocational training, job placement programs, housing assistance, and parenting programs to help individuals meet their responsibilities as parents and citizens.

In this chapter, we will examine how correctional goals regarding rehabilitation have evolved, describing the so-called "rehabilitative era" when the goal of rehabilitation was primary in American corrections. The chapter reviews the major types of programming in prison; for example, education, vocational, and drug treatment. The methodological complexity of evaluating such programs is also discussed, along with a review of research that has attempted to assess the effectiveness of contemporary rehabilitative efforts.

The Rehabilitative Era

Originally, penitentiaries were designed to create a religious transformation in offenders. Later, in the reformatory era of corrections, secular views of change supplanted religion: Constant monitoring, a strong dose of discipline, and education or vocational skills were believed to be the best ways to reform young, amenable offenders. The mission seemed to shift to simple punishment and deterrence in the first part of the 1900s. Then, rehabilitation emerged as the primary mission during a brief period in the 1970s.

From the late 1960s to the late 1970s, the U.S. experienced what is known as the **rehabilitative era** of corrections, a time when the vision of the penitentiary as a correctional institution was at its strongest. Correctional practitioners embraced the so-called **medical model** or **treatment ethic** that espoused that crime was the result of an underlying pathology that could be treated. Although the commitment to rehabilitation varied across the country, many prison systems had diagnostic or classification centers for incoming prisoners that determined which correctional programs were best suited to the prisoners' needs. At the height of the rehabilitative era, a variety of treatment programs existed, including group therapy, behavior modification, transcendental meditation, and even psychodrama therapy in some prisons.

The rehabilitative era ended, arguably, because of the rise of crime in the late 1970s and early 1980s and the emergence of increasingly conservative social policies. Its end was said to be hastened by a widely publicized report commissioned by the state of New York that reviewed the effectiveness of correctional programming. The infamous finding that "nothing works," by sociologist Robert Martinson and his colleagues, contributed to the loss of confidence policymakers expressed toward the goal of reforming offenders. The study was a **meta-analysis**, which reviewed the evaluations of 231 offender rehabilitation programs from the prior 30 years. A meta-analysis is an evaluation that collapses many studies into one data set. The researchers could find no statistically significant improvement in recidivism figures for those who participated in rehabilitation programs, but their larger (ignored) message was that the major problem was that the program evaluations were poorly designed and used poor measures.[1] A later examination of the findings, including some studies that had, at first, been excluded, found "pockets of success," meaning that some programs worked for some offenders.[2] Despite the success of some programs, by the early 1980s proponents of determinative sentencing had convinced legislators to abandon rehabilitation-focused sentencing structures, and programming became subject to budget cuts as prison administrators struggled to accommodate ever-increasing numbers of incoming prisoners.

Today, we are still in an era where punishment and deterrence are prioritized over rehabilitative goals in most states. Correctional administrators continue to face the challenge of feeding, housing, and managing large numbers, a goal that must take precedence over providing rehabilitative programming. More recently, the challenge of protecting inmates and staff from being infected with COVID-19 has eclipsed other priorities. However, there has been progress in developing prediction instruments for recidivism that help to target programming for those who need it most. All prisons now have basic programs, including education and some vocational training options, and evaluations have shown some programs can effectively reduce recidivism.

Prison Programs

We will discuss several specific prison programs in the sections that follow, however, an expansive definition of **correctional treatment** can encompass everything that is not purely custodial; for example, visitation, religion, and medical treatment. Treatment staff includes teachers, counselors, vocational instructors, psychologists, and others who are not involved in custody roles. A more restricted definition of treatment would only include programs designed to reduce recidivism.

Virtually every prison offers some type of basic education and at least a few vocational programs. Prisoners also work at prison jobs. Generally, the goal is to have all inmates engaged in productive activity; however, in many prisons, there are more prisoners than program slots and available services. For instance, although most prison administrators will profess that their prisoners all have work assignments, many of these assignments are rote maintenance tasks, such as sweeping hallways. Many prisoners are idle, not because they choose to be, but because there are not enough program slots or work assignments for everyone. The same is true for treatment slots; many inmates wait months or even years to get into a program. Treatment programs may include psychotherapy, behavior modification, group therapy, family therapy, therapeutic communities, meditation, Alcoholics Anonymous (AA), and a wide range of eclectic programs that are either developed in-house or contracted out to for-profit entities. Some prisons have many different programs; others have very few. These differences are affected by the state, the geographic location of the prison, and the types of inmates housed there.

Recreation Programs

Perhaps no issue of prison life receives more negative publicity than recreation programs. Critics argue that allowing prisoners leisure time to lift weights or play ball make prisons seem like hotels, not punishment facilities. Yet, prison officials are sometimes the biggest supporters of such programs because recreation

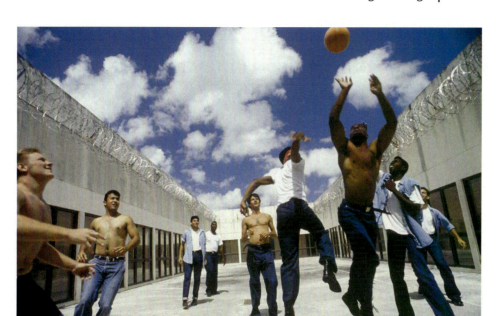

Prison recreation is considered a proactive use of time, and it tends to direct energy away from more deviant pursuits.

is usually a proactive use of time, and it tends to direct energy away from more deviant pursuits. To be sure, at times recreation programs can be the impetus for violence. Fights will break out on the basketball court or on the softball field. Betting takes place over games that can then lead to violence when losers must pay.

Other avenues for recreation exist in hobbies. Most prisons have arts and crafts opportunities for inmates, although they must pay for their own supplies. Prisoners may create beautiful artwork that is sold to the public by the prison administration or given to friends or relatives as gifts. Prisoners also participate in charitable works, such as narrating books on tape for the blind, transcribing print material into braille, or sewing stuffed animals and making toys to be distributed by charitable programs on the outside. The Focus box describes a type of program where inmates socialize and train service dogs or rescues who need to be socialized before adoption. One meta-analysis of 10 studies covering 310 dog-training program participants found significant positive effects on inmates. These studies typically measured attitudinal changes, not recidivism.[3] When asked why they participate, inmates answer much as anyone would—usually some version of wanting to help others or giving back to the community.

While there is no evidence that recreation or volunteer programs in prison have any effect on recidivism, it may be that they at least have the potential to improve behavior in prison. Any type of sport is a healthy addition to an individual's life and may help inmates avoid the temptation to use drugs or engage in less positive pursuits. Other types of recreation keep inmates busy, if nothing else. Volunteer activities also keep inmates busy and help them feel more positive about themselves and their contributions to the community.

Religious Programs

Some rehabilitative prison programs have a religious base, such as Prison Fellowship. According to their website, they are the nation's largest nonprofit organization for current and former prisoners and their families. It was begun

FOCUS ON A
STATE

WASHINGTON'S PRISON PET PARTNERSHIP

Dog-training programs in prison are becoming increasingly popular. Such programs allow inmates to care for and train dogs to be placed as family pets, emotional support animals, or assistance animals for veterans or other groups. One such program is the Prison Pet Partnership (PPP), at the Washington Corrections Center for Women in Gig Harbor, Washington. It began in 1982 as part of Tacoma Community College's inmate education program. The program became an independent Washington nonprofit corporation on May 30, 1990. Since its inception, the program has placed over 700 dogs as service, seizure, or therapy dogs, and as family pets.

The day-to-day operations are the responsibility of an executive director, a training coordinator, and a vocational education coordinator, with support provided by a program assistant, all non-prison employees who work at the prison with inmate workers and trainers. The program consists of a boarding kennel, grooming service, and service dog training. Inmates learn valuable vocational skills and are required to spend a minimum of two years with the program.

Inmates are rigidly screened: no one with a history of abuse toward children or animals can participate. Inmates must have already served one year in the prison before they can be considered for the program and have at least two years left on their sentence. They must be free of major disciplinary infractions for one year, and free of minor infractions for 90 days.

Inmates are required to take classes and pass a test to receive the American Boarding Kennel Association Pet Technician Level One certificate. Then, they may be hired and receive wages as a kennel worker for the boarding and grooming component of the program for the first 90 days, after which they may become dog trainers. The women keep the dogs with them in addition to conducting training sessions in the program area.

The dogs are from rescue organizations or from other service dog organizations. They are trained and placed as service and therapy dogs. Service dogs are placed with individuals who experience seizures or have other disabilities; their role is to assist the person and give them increased independence. It takes approximately two years for trainers to prepare the dogs for their role as support animals. Such training in the private sector would cost approximately $20,000. Those dogs who are not successful as service dogs are trained in basic obedience and placed as family pets.

The program's funding support is through a contract with the Department of Corrections, private foundation, animal welfare organizations, and individual donors, and the proceeds from the boarding and grooming service component of the program. Approximately 30 volunteers assist by taking the dogs out into the community for important socialization training, including such things as learning about elevators, and becoming comfortable in restaurants, doctor's offices, grocery stores, and other public facilities.

Source: Prison Pet Partnership website, http://www.prisonpetpartnership.org/index.html);
J. Werb, "The Prison Pet Partnership Program: Innovative Corrections Programs Give
Hope to Prisoners and Pooches Alike," Modern Dog, n.d., https://moderndogmagazine.
com/articles/prison-pet-partnership-program/273.

by Charles Colson, former Special Counsel to President Richard Nixon, who was imprisoned for his role in Watergate. One criticism of such programs is that the Establishment Clause in the First Amendment of the U.S. Constitution prohibits the government from favoring any specific religion: "Congress shall make no law respecting an establishment of religion, or prohibiting the free exercise thereof…" If participants in a religious prison program receive special treatment or are promised consideration for early release, it could be perceived as an attempt to coerce inmates to adopt that religion. Evaluations have been difficult because there is usually no random assignment or control group. Even if participants do show lower recidivism rates than non-participants do, it could be because of self-selection; that is, the individuals who join such programs would have had low recidivism rates even without participating in the programs (this is also known as **selection bias** which is a type of statistical bias that occurs when there is not random assignment of participants into the treatment group and control group).

In the evaluations that do exist, prisoners self-report better adjustment to prison culture. Some qualitative studies report that religious programs have psychological and emotional benefits that follow offenders through release and reintegration into the community. There also seems to be a reduction in prisoner misconduct among program participants, especially those who take part in programs that employ a mentorship component. Components that are associated with more success include more formal (rather than informal) programming, precise targeting of change, and a structured curriculum. Quantitative studies of recidivism, however, have shown no differences between participants in religious programs and non-participants.[4]

Education

Educational programming in prison is dominated by Adult Basic Education (ABE), which is primarily literacy training or programs of study that lead to either a General Educational Development (GED) degree or a high school diploma. Some state prison systems offer a range of educational programs from basic literacy to college classes, while others offer only ABE, although prisoners can access online college courses if they pay for them.

In a national study of prisoners published in 2003, 40 percent had not received either a high school diploma or a GED; this compares to only 18 percent of the general U.S. population who do not have a diploma or a GED. Only about 11 percent of state prisoners and 24 percent of federal prisoners had some college education (compared to 48 percent of the general U.S. population). Over half of the sample reported that they participated in educational programs in prison.[5] A study done about 10 years later found that only about a quarter of state and federal inmates reported participating in an educational program.[6] Other studies indicate that female prisoners are more likely than male prisoners to have graduated from high school and to have some college. Prisoners of all races and ethnicities are, on average, less educated than their counterparts in the general U.S. population.[7]

As with all types of prison programs, educational programs vary greatly across institutions. Some are vibrant, with committed teachers and prisoners who are invested in bettering themselves, while others are education in name only, with uninterested teachers and inmates who spend classroom time engaged in other pursuits.[8] Just because there is an education program on paper does not necessarily mean that it is helpful in meeting the needs of offenders. Deficient resources, lethargic teachers, and hostile or unaccommodating security staff can sabotage a program.

Federal Pell Grants, which provide money for college tuition and books, had been available to prisoners until an amendment to the Violent Crime Control and Law Enforcement Act of 1994 (also known as the 1994 Crime Bill) barred prisoners from applying for the grants. Some states now use alternative funding for prison college programs, such as private or state grants. Federal Spector Grants (otherwise known as Youthful Offender Grants) are available for inmates under age 25 who have been convicted of a nonviolent crime and have less than five years remaining on their sentence until release. Under the Obama administration, the Department of Education began a program that provided Pell Grants to prisoners in a limited number of prisons, but the program ended after the election of President Trump. It is also important to note that few inmates qualify for prison college programs because most need adult basic education.

Studies from the 1990s showed that inmates who received a college education in prison experienced reduced recidivism after release.[9] Younger property criminals were 37 percent less likely to recidivate if they learned to read while in prison. While some studies show that education has a greater impact on younger inmates than on older inmates, other studies have found the opposite, with older inmates showing greater reductions in recidivism.[10]

A major meta-analysis of prison education evaluations by the RAND Corporation, a nonprofit, nonpartisan research organization, concluded that inmates who participated in correctional education programs (basic and college combined) had 43 percent lower odds of recidivating than inmates who did not (using a three-years-after-release follow-up period). Inmates who had participated in high school/GED programs had 30 percent lower odds of recidivating than those who had not. The odds of obtaining employment post-release among inmates who participated in correctional education programs (either academic or vocational) was 13 percent higher than the odds for those who had not participated. The analysis also found that vocational training programs resulted in better outcomes for employment: participants' odds of employment were 28 percent higher than non-participants' odds; academic programs participants' odds of employment were only 8 percent higher than those of non-participants.[11]

The RAND study estimated that the three-year reincarceration costs for a hypothetical pool of 100 inmates who did not receive correctional education would be between $2.94 million and $3.25 million. In comparison, for those who did receive correctional education, the three-year reincarceration costs would be between $2.07 million and $2.28 million, a savings of $870,000 to $970,000. The costs of providing education to these 100 inmates would range from $140,000 to $174,400. It was estimated that for a correctional education program to be cost effective, it would need to reduce the three-year reincarceration rate by between 1.9 and 2.6 percentage points to break even; but some studies show up to a 13-percentage-point reduction of recidivism over a three-year release period. Ultimately, the study concluded that educational programs are cost effective.[12]

Other studies have reported similar findings, specifically that vocational programs generally result in higher employment and higher incomes upon release, and that both vocational and educational programs are associated with moderate decreases in recidivism, although a few single-state studies did not find significant decreases in recidivism.[13] One study in Ohio examined the in-prison and recidivism effects of education as well as vocational program participation. It found that participation in either basic GED or college-level education or vocational training reduced recidivism for those who completed the programs. Further, completion of an education program was associated with a reduced number of violent infractions in prison, although this was not true for vocational program participation.[14]

Vocational Training

Vocational training grew in importance in reformatories and penitentiaries in the late 1800s and early 1900s, with the idea that institutions should prepare prisoners for release by teaching them a trade. In the 1960s and 1970s, prisons were able to access federal money from several sources to provide vocational

Prison vocational programs and prison labor may involve various types of industries. Issues include whether prisoners have the skill set necessary and the security risks inherent when tools can also be weapons.

training programs, such as typewriter repair, auto mechanics, data processing, electricians' apprentice programs, and commercial cleaning, among many others. By the 1980s, overcrowding and budget shortfalls contributed to the closure of many vocational programs. By the early 2000s, only about half of all prisons had some form of vocational apprenticeship program.[15]

The best vocational model is one that combines prison labor with job training. In this way, a product is produced that can offset the cost of the training. Several researchers have combined educational and vocational training programs to find that they do increase the likelihood of post-prison employment and reduce recidivism.[16] Meta-analyses report a recidivism rate of 50 percent for those who did not participate in any vocational training compared to 39 percent for participants.[17] Other studies, however, have found no effect.[18] It may be that what happens to the offender after release is the most important factor. For those who participated in educational or vocational training in prison but could not find a job upon release, the likelihood of recidivism is no different than for those who did not receive any education or training.[19]

One of the problems with evaluating educational and vocational training is **selection bias**. As stated earlier, if program staff choose certain inmates or the inmates themselves self-select into the program, there may be differences between these inmates and others who are used as a control group. Inmates who seek out such programs may be motivated and committed to changing their lives, and would have succeeded on their own, even without the program. Only comparing program participants to a control group of the same type of inmates would indicate the true impact of the program; this is usually done by random assignment.

Prison Labor

Other work in prison occurs outside of vocational training. In the early 2000s, one study found that only about a quarter of state and federal inmates were considered idle (without a work assignment); 7 percent were employed in prison

The California Department of Corrections runs programs for both female and male prisoners who work with the state forestry department to prevent and fight forest fires.

industries, 5 percent worked on prison farms, 9 percent were employed in prison vocational training or education, and the remainder were employed in maintenance jobs in the institution.[20] A later study reported that about half of all state and federal prisoners had some form of work assignment.[21]

Labor has been associated with confinement facilities since their inception. The belief was that prisoners should be punished by forcing them to perform physical labor, even if it was meaningless (e.g., the infamous rock pile). Gradually, the concept of labor as punishment was abandoned; however, inmates are still employed in a variety of capacities and provide essential labor. It is not an overstatement to say that prisons could not operate without inmate labor.

Prisoners cook food, do laundry, grow crops, and clean the institution. They work in the administration building as file clerks, and some are on work crews as plumbers and electricians. Tens of thousands of agricultural fields are under the control of prisons with inmate field workers employed in cultivating the land while guarded by armed correctional officers. Huge industrial laundries exist in some prisons that process tons of clothing and bedding for that prison as well as other prisons in the state system. Some of these jobs are defined as vocational training because inmates are learning a skill. For instance, inmates who work in the kitchen may learn culinary skills, and cleaning crews may be trained as commercial cleaners. While most of these maintenance tasks do not purport to be vocational training, there is some argument that such work helps inmates learn good work habits and that the skills acquired may translate to outside jobs. Ultimately, however, many maintenance jobs do not result in skill acquisition or lead to outside employment, but inmates earn some money for their work.

Another form of prison labor occurs in prison industries. These are employment opportunities that occur when a prison enters a partnership with an outside entity to produce merchandise of some sort or provide a service undertaken by inmates hired by the entity and paid a wage. The work may take place in the prison, or an outside location where correctional officers supervise the prisoners while they work.

It may come as a surprise to know that many goods are produced in prisons. This may be done as part of an agreement between a prison and a private company, or the prison itself may run the business to produce goods or provide a service using inmate labor. The history of private employers using prisoner labor dates to the advent of the penitentiary in the United States. There are several kinds of private employer–prison agreements. Historically, under the **contract system**, prison officials solicited bids from private employers to hire inmate labor services, and the state received a fixed fee per prisoner, per day. Under the **leased labor system**, private employers took prisoners off-site, often to plantations to work the fields after the Civil War. Under the **piece-price system**, private employers paid the state by the amount of an item, or piece, produced by prisoners.

During the Great Depression, several federal laws were passed that restricted prison-made goods from competing with non-prison labor, including the 1929 **Hawes-Cooper Act**, which made it illegal to sell prison-made goods in another state that did not allow such sales. In 1935, the **Ashurst-Sumners Act** made it illegal to knowingly transport prison-made goods across state lines. "State-use" laws protected civilian workers by limiting prison-made goods for use by governmental entities in that state only—for example, license plates, school desks, and furniture for government offices. The result was that it was not economically feasible for private companies to use inmate labor.

Then, in 1979, the **Federal Prison Industries Enhancement Act (PIE)** was passed by Congress. This legislation allowed prison-made goods to be sold on the open market with certain restrictions. The prison must certify that the prison industry pays the same as outside wages, consults with representatives of private industry, does not displace civilian workers, collects funds for a victim assistance program, provides inmates with benefits in the event of injury, ensures that inmate participation is voluntary, and provides a substantial role for the private sector. The inmate is allowed to keep up to 20 percent of his or her wages, but the rest can be taken to meet legal judgments, or pay restitution, child support, and room and board. If all these conditions are met, then the goods can compete on the open market. In 2011, there were only 4,700 inmates involved in PIE-certified prison industries.[22] Despite the small numbers, companies as diverse as Walmart and Boeing have had prison industry programs.

Critics of private enterprise partnerships with prisons argue that companies circumvent the restrictions of the PIE and do not pay prevailing wages, do not have adequate work environments, or do not consult with outside labor before beginning a prison industry. Some programs have been accused of avoiding paying prevailing wages by extending training periods, during which inmates are paid less, to several years in length. Other programs have been accused of deducting more from the prisoners' wages than allowed by law; for instance, for program operating costs. PIE-certified prison industry programs are not supposed to displace civilian job holders, yet there have been instances of layoffs when a prison program opens.[23]

The Federal Prison Industries (FPI) program, known by its trade name as UNICOR, is the prison industry program of the Federal Bureau of Prisons.[24] Established in 1934 by President Franklin D. Roosevelt, the goal of FPI is to prepare inmates with job training and work skills for reentry to society. The various divisions of FPI include the following groups: clothing and textiles, electronics business, fleet solutions, industrial products, office furniture, recycling business, and services business. Federal prisoners make over 150 different products, from safety goggles to road signs. In 2005, UNICOR employed about 18 percent of all work-eligible federal prisoners (about 19,720 prisoners).[25] Reported earnings for 2017 was $453,762,717.[26] Federal prisoners are obligated to save and/or send home some portion of their earnings to meet financial obligations such as court-ordered fines, child support, and/or victim restitution.

One study, conducted by the federal prison system, found that while incarcerated, UNICOR participants were less likely to incur misconduct reprimands. Following release, they were more likely to find and keep full-time, better-paying jobs, were less likely to commit crimes, and were 24 percent less likely to return to prison than inmates who did not take advantage of UNICOR work/study programs.[27]

Only a small percentage of all inmates, whether in state or federal prisons, are employed in any prison industry.[28] Why do outside industries avoid prison partnerships? One reason is that certification under the PIE act is difficult; it is hard to show how civilian labor is not displaced if there is any amount of unemployment in the surrounding area of the prison. Second, prisons are simply not built with the needs of private industry in mind. There is a lack of space and, often, an inability to accommodate the requirements of a private industry. Third, stringent prison rules and regulations clearly show that custody concerns will always eclipse profit concerns. Fourth, the prison labor force is largely unskilled and uneducated. Even apprentice programs require at least a high school reading level, and many prisoners do not have such skills. Fifth, prison laborers, while they may be there on time, are not necessarily the most committed and energetic group of employees. Finally, some employers are afraid of negative publicity over the use of convict labor.

Drug and Alcohol Treatment

As noted in Chapter 7, up to two-thirds of prisoners may have a substance abuse disorder.[29] This includes alcohol, as well as other forms of drugs. More prisoners have a substance abuse problem than there are treatment program openings available. In fact, some reports indicate that the number of treatment program openings has declined in the last couple of decades.[30] The United States Office of National Drug Control Policy reports that up to 85 percent of prisoners could use drug treatment but only about 13 percent ever receive it.[31]

Competing approaches exist regarding the causation of drug and alcohol addiction and/or dependency. For some, addiction is seen as a disease, perhaps inherited, with those who suffer from it needing both medical and behavioral intervention to live a substance-free life. Like the disease model of alcoholism, this approach holds that no one is cured, they are just "in remission." On the other end of the spectrum are those who see addiction/abuse solely as a reflection of a weak will. In this view, those who abuse chemical substances could stop if they wanted to; they just don't want to. In the middle are a range of positions and approaches. For instance, a psychological predisposition to chemical addiction: a poor self-image, a dependent personality, or an addictive personality, all have been offered as explanations for addiction. Given these different explanations, it is no wonder that drug and alcohol treatment programs have a wide range of approaches also. Modalities include drug education, shock group therapy, behavioral modification, and "talk" therapy, among others.

Some drug and alcohol treatment programs employ medication to help treat substance abuse. Disulfiram is used to treat alcoholism by preventing the body from processing alcohol, thereby inducing unpleasant side effects when a person drinks alcohol. Although effective, one of the problems with its use is that clients may not take it when ordered to by the courts. Naltrexone and acamprosate are two other drugs that stop alcohol cravings but do not induce unpleasant side effects. These pharmacological aids have been shown to be effective in reducing alcohol and drug use when combined with behavioral counseling.[32]

Another type of medication-assisted treatment specifically for opioid addiction is the synthetic narcotic methadone, which has been in use since its introduction in 1964 to prevent withdrawal symptoms. Buprenorphine, a more recent alternative medication for treating addiction to opioids, also prevents cravings and sickness from withdrawal. Though used to treat addiction, these two drugs pose a high risk for dependence themselves and therefore are not used in many jails or prisons for treating addicts because of their abuse potential. Methadone is available in only 22 jails and even fewer prisons. Vivitrol, a long-acting, injectable form of naltrexone, is used in about 200 jails as an alternative to methadone. Only Rhode Island offers all three medications to all inmates in its prisons and jails.[33]

When it comes to reducing drug dependency and related crime, medication-assisted treatment is typically not enough on its own. Some studies have found that drug courts, methadone treatment for opioid abuse, and drug testing without any additional treatment component show no significant effects on recidivism.[34] Programs that combine cognitive-behavioral components and life skill training (such as vocational training or education) seem to be the most successful treatment modality.[35] Successful relapse prevention must involve behavioral counseling that helps individuals recognize situations that trigger substance misuse, and teaches clients alternative responses to high-risk situations. Meta-analyses of drug treatment programs have found success for drug, smoking, and alcohol addiction; however, treatment programs have not been as effective for cocaine or polysubstance abuse, the abuse of multiple illicit drugs or prescription medications. It has also been found that mandatory or coerced treatment is not as effective as voluntary treatment.[36]

Many evaluations and reviews of correctional drug treatment programs indicate that such programs are more likely to be successful if they are intensive, long term, structured, backed by penalties for nonparticipation, and multi-modal (meaning, for instance, a group-therapy component and a curriculum-based program, or individual counseling along with a therapeutic community approach), and include aftercare services.[37] The National Institute on Drug Abuse has published some principles of effective treatment, which include the following:

- Recognize drug addiction as a brain disease.
- Recovery requires treatment and management.
- Treatment must last long enough to produce stable change.
- Assessment is the first step.
- Tailoring services to the individual is important.
- Continuity of care (into the community) is important.[38]

Therapeutic Communities

A common type of program found in prison that has shown some success in reducing recidivism among drug offenders is called the **therapeutic community (TC)**.[39] These self-contained communities allow treatment staff to isolate (to some extent) participants from negative influences present in the general population of the prison and to reduce the temptation and opportunity for acquiring drugs. Therapeutic communities may be housed in an isolated building or separate tier from the general population of the prison and typically employ some type of graduated structure whereby new participants must earn privileges by demonstrating good behavior. Daily group meetings discuss the participants' behavior in the attempt to improve personal responsibility and increase self-esteem. For instance, individuals who refuse to perform their share of chores or engage in altercations with co-workers will be called out and dealt with during the group meeting.[40] Treatment is eclectic, utilizing a variety of methods and techniques. For instance, participants may read biographies, construct "life charts" showing their own development, engage in drama therapy, or participate in trust-building exercises.

Important elements of a successful therapeutic community program are as follows:

- As much as possible, inmates receiving treatment should be isolated from the negative subcultural elements of the general population.
- A healthy partnership between custodial and treatment staff is essential to the success of such a program. Custodial staff are an integral part of a therapeutic community.
- Also needed is a referral system that recruits appropriate inmates, along with a careful screening and selection process.
- A program director who can work well within the correctional environment, mediate staff conflicts, and is sensitive to burnout is necessary.
- Substance abuse counselors must be committed and consistent, and have good decision-making skills. They should be diverse and reflect the population of clients.
- The presence of recovering addicts and/or successful ex-inmates is helpful for inspiring and encouraging client participation.
- Clients should be motivated, have time to complete the program, and not have mental health problems.
- An atmosphere where clients are free to trust, to take risks, and feel free to challenge themselves and others is essential.[41]

Therapeutic communities, combined with cognitive behavioral approaches (discussed in a later section) and practical skill acquisition (i.e., education or vocational training), seem to offer the highest probability for success in prison programming, meaning a reduction in recidivism for program participants. If nothing else, therapeutic communities tend to counteract some of the negativity of the prison experience. In one small study of correctional officers, those associated with a therapeutic community program demonstrated a positive change in supportive attitudes toward prisoners and rehabilitation. Inmates in the program showed an increase in positive attitudes toward officers as well.[42]

 Prediction and Assessment

Prediction is important to determine what to do with an offender. For instance, a security classification is a prediction about what level of custody is necessary for an inmate; for example, a prisoner who has a high risk of escape or violence against COs or other inmates should be in maximum custody. Parole decisions are partially predictions of recidivism; for example, a prisoner may not receive an early release decision because hearing examiners look at his record and decide he will commit additional crimes. **Correctional assessment** is the process of determining the level of recidivism risk by identifying what criminogenic factors are relevant to an offender. This also indicates what correctional interventions may address these criminogenic factors. All too often, the programs that are offered or available to inmates are not necessarily matched to their need.

One of the most prevalent trends in correctional programming today (for both prison and community correctional programs) is more carefully linking assessment with correctional programming. Measurement instruments that predict an offender's risk and amenability to programming are constantly being improved, and these are also linked to program evaluations for a feedback loop. Current efforts are much more sophisticated than earlier generations of prediction.

Four Generations of Prediction/Assessment

The so-called first generation of prediction, or assessment, was the **clinical approach**. This approach refers to correctional professionals who use interviews, social histories, and psychological tests to make predictions about the offender's future behavior. This type of prediction has been shown to have an accuracy rate no better than chance when it comes to the ability to predict.

The second generation of prediction is the **actuarial approach**. This method, begun as early as the 1950s, uses statistics to predict risk (like insurance companies who predict that young men are more likely to have automobile accidents based on accident statistics). Actuarial approaches were found to be better predictors of recidivism than clinical assessments.[43] For instance, one study that compared the two approaches' ability to predict recidivism among sex offenders showed that the actuarial approach outperformed clinical assessments by a wide margin.[44] Actuarial approaches use only what are called **static factors.** These factors cannot change; for example, age at first arrest. Other static factors that are correlated with reoffending include higher number of prior arrests, higher number of prior convictions, having parents with criminal justice involvement, and younger age at first use of drugs.

Third-generation prediction, developed over the 1980s and 1990s, combines the clinical and actuarial approaches. Static factors that do not change (e.g., demographic, file, and historical information) are used along with dynamic, changeable items that are determined with interviews or individual surveys. Dynamic factors that change over time, like employment or educational achievement, have been associated with recidivism. For instance, in one study of 2,850 probationers, the best predictors of success were found to be stability of employment, marital status, and number of past convictions.[45] The number of past convictions is a static factor, whereas the other two are dynamic factors. Similarly, another study of 266 felony probationers found that the best predictors of recidivism were gender, employment, and prior record.[46] Of these factors, two are static (gender and prior record) and one is dynamic (employment).

Third-generation assessment instruments collect information on a range of dynamic factors relevant to offenders to predict risk, including but not limited to the following: vocational and financial information, educational background, family and social relationships (including involvement with criminal peers), living arrangements (with a focus on residence and neighborhood), leisure activities, alcohol and drug use, mental health, and attitudes toward criminality.

Third-generation assessment instruments are designed to be administered to offenders periodically to track changes in an offender's risk for recidivism. Education, mental health, attitude, and drug use may change over time, thus affecting the offender's risk level, or likelihood of reoffending. These assessment instruments are correctional tools because they offer guidance as to what types of programs would be most beneficial. There are several risk instruments that are considered third generation, including the **Correctional Offender Management Profiling for Alternative Sanctions (COMPAS)**.[47]

COMPAS was developed in 1989 by a statistician and correctional professional and distributed by their company, formerly known as Northpointe. COMPAS assesses not just risk but also nearly two dozen criminogenic needs that relate to the major theories of criminality, including criminal personality, social isolation, substance abuse and residence/stability. Defendants are ranked as low, medium, or high risk in each category. COMPAS assesses these risks based on 137 questions that are either answered by defendants or pulled from criminal records. Such questions include the following:

- "Was one of your parents ever sent to jail or prison?"
- "How many of your friends/acquaintances are taking drugs illegally?"
- "How often did you get in fights while at school?"

Criminal personality is measured by the level of agreement with such statements as "A hungry person has a right to steal" and "If people make me angry or lose my temper, I can be dangerous." In a validation study, the instrument was found to have an accuracy rate of 68 percent in a sample of 2,328 people, although it was slightly less predictive for Black men than white men—67 percent versus 69 percent.[48]

There is also growing discussion among researchers and correctional professionals of a fourth-generation approach to risk assessment, which uses third-generation tools while integrating treatment-matching and case management. Treatment-matching means that risk factors are used to identify appropriate services, such as treatment for drug addiction or anger management. Programs are selected based on the risks or needs identified by the assessment tool in use, and the offender is then monitored to determine the effectiveness of the program(s). Programs are also assessed to determine their efficacy generally (e.g., how closely they adhere to correctional treatment principles), as well as specifically when it comes to offender types. Fourth-generation assessment is tied most closely to the LSI-R risk prediction instrument and the related Risk/Need/Responsivity (R/N/R) approach of assessment and treatment.[49]

 # Level of Service Inventory-Revised (LSI-R) and Risk/Need/Responsivity (R/N/R)

The **Level of Service Inventory-Revised or LSI-R** is a 54-item assessment/risk instrument that captures both static and dynamic factors. It is also the instrument that has been most frequently developed into a fourth-generation instrument, meaning that it is used to predict not only risk of violence or recidivism, but also amenability to treatment. The LSI-R instrument includes 10 unique subscales:

1. criminal history (10 items)
2. emotional and personal (5 items)
3. attitude and orientation (4 items)

4. companions (5 items)

5. family and marital (4 items)

6. education and employment (10 items)

7. leisure and recreation (2 items)

8. alcohol and drugs (9 items)

9. financial (2 items)

10. accommodations (3 items)

Total scores range from zero to 54, with higher scores indicating a higher risk level. Correctional psychologists and academics Don Andrews, James Bonta, Paul Gendreau, and others developed these subscales and have provided the theoretical background for the LSI-R.[50] The approach focuses on those factors that are statistically correlated with future offending. Some factors are static, such as whether an offender's parents have been incarcerated, but some are changeable, such as criminal thinking patterns; these are the factors that should be the target of intervention, according to researchers. The LSI-R's "big four" constructs are those that have shown the strongest correlation with future criminality in research over the last several decades:

1. *A history of antisocial behavior (criminal history)*: Scoring looks at the number of prior arrests and incarcerations, the age at first arrest, and the variety of different kinds of arrests.

2. *Antisocial personality pattern (emotional and personal)*: Scoring uses questions to determine the traits most associated with criminality (impulsivity, adventurousness, pleasure seeking, aggressiveness, callous disregard for others). Criminal personality is said to be described as, in addition to the traits above, showing disregard for social norms, rules, or obligations; having an incapacity to maintain enduring relationships; exhibiting frustration; using aggression or violence; having an incapacity to experience guilt or to profit from experience; and blaming others.

3. *Antisocial cognition (attitude and orientation, or criminal thinking)*: Scoring is based on measures of criminal attitudes, values, beliefs, rationalization, and a personal identity that is favorable to crime. The importance of criminal thinking is related to several theories of criminology, including subcultural theory and social learning theory.

4. *Antisocial associates (companions)*: Scoring is based on the number of criminal friends and acquaintances an offender has.

The next four measures are moderately correlated with future offending:

1. *Family and marital circumstances*: Scoring is based on the quality of interpersonal relationships, and on whether family relationships and friendships involve mutual caring and respect. Strong, prosocial family ties have been associated with reduced recidivism.

2. *Quality of education and employment*: Scoring is based on levels of performance and involvement (e.g., grades and attendance for school-age offenders and work history for adults).

3. *Leisure and recreation*: Scoring is based on level of involvement and satisfaction in prosocial (rather than criminal) leisure pursuits.

4. *Substance abuse (alcohol and drugs)*: Scoring is based on age at first use and frequency of use of alcohol and drugs, and negative effects of usage patterns on other aspects of life.[51]

In later work, researchers added the last two measures, which capture a person's financial resources and housing situation, as these have also been shown to correlate with recidivism. The LSI-R has been used in numerous states and with tens of thousands of offenders.[52] Researchers have found the instrument to successfully predict risk across corrections settings, such as probation, parole, and prisons and jails, and across offender populations, including individuals of diverse age, race and ethnicity, and gender.[53]

The **Risk/Need/Responsivity (R/N/R)** approach to assessment and correctional treatment emphasizes that the level of risk posed by an offender, coupled with his or her needs, should influence the type of treatment used to manage underlying criminogenic factors. This treatment approach targets two of the four most important criminogenic factors identified by the LSI-R: antisocial personality and antisocial cognitions. Antisocial personalities demonstrate impulsivity, adventurousness, pleasure seeking, aggressiveness, callous disregard for others and for social norms, rules, or obligations, and lack of guilt. Antisocial cognitions are characterized by criminal attitudes, values, beliefs, rationalization of such a mindset, and a personal identity that is favorable to crime.[54]

Research in this area suggests that correctional treatment should target offenders with the highest LSI-R scores in criminogenic factors/needs; otherwise, treatment is less effective at reducing recidivism. In fact, research has shown that low-risk offenders may be *more* likely to recidivate if subjected to correctional treatment programs.[55] Other needs that are not associated with recidivism should not be the target of correctional programming; specifically, personal distress, poor self-esteem, alienation, history of victimization, and anxiety, which are not considered criminogenic needs. Principles of the R/N/R approach include the following:

- Respect the person, including their personal autonomy.
- Base the program on empirically solid psychological theory.
- Match intensity of service with risk level.
- Avoid mixing low-risk and high-risk offenders.
- Target only criminogenic needs.
- Follow "specific responsivity," which means to adapt the style of service to the setting and characteristics of individuals (strengths, preferences, age, gender, and ethnicity).
- Use a structured assessment of strengths and risk-/need-specific responsivity factors.
- Employ staff with high-quality relationship skills and high-quality structuring skills (those who are respectful, caring, enthusiastic, and collaborative, and who value personal autonomy) to increase program effectiveness.
- Assess staff and programs by introducing monitoring, feedback, and adjustment systems.
- Use manuals, monitor service process, and involve researchers in the design and delivery of service to improve service delivery.[56]

The primary treatment modality in the R/N/R approach is cognitive behavioral counseling. **Cognitive behavioral programs** include **cognitive restructuring,** which focuses on changing the content of what offenders believe, specifically their pro-criminal attitudes and rationalization for crime, while **cognitive skills programs** attempt to change an offender's reasoning ability—for instance, how to control anger or impulses. Some of the more common "errors in thinking" that offenders engage in include self-justification, perceptions of dominance and victimization, misinterpretation of social cues, and failures in moral reasoning. Cognitive behavioral programs focus on behavioral change through adjusting the cues and triggers for criminal behavior rather than exploring the meaning behind them or factors that may have contributed to such behavior, such as childhood or trauma-related experiences. For behavioral change, participants are instructed to identify external cues or rewards for the behavior that they wish to change. For instance, if a person uses drugs only with certain friends, then those friendships must end. Cognitive restructuring seeks to change the cognitive antecedents and reinforcements for negative behavior. For instance, the thought that it is cool to use drugs is identified and critiqued, or the thought that "I deserve to have material goods even if I have to steal them," is analyzed to show why such thinking is wrong.

In cognitive restructuring, participants are sensitized to thinking errors and learn to identify and reject them because they lead to criminal choices. Obviously, participants must be willing to take part in this effort and agree that such thoughts are wrong. Then, cognitive behavioral counseling teaches participants how to replace negative cognitions with positive ones. For instance, the new thought might be something like "I won't go out with these friends because they are going to use drugs; instead, I will go to the gym and work out." Participants gradually build their skills through structured learning. In these programs, participants model the behavior they are taught and practice the new skills via role play in group formats; successful behavior is reinforced, and negative behavior is corrected.[57] Some examples of cognitive behavioral therapy (CBT) programs include Reasoning and Rehabilitation, Moral Reconation Therapy, Aggression Replacement Training, Choosing to Think, Thinking to Choose, and Thinking for a Change.[58]

Evaluating CBT Programs

In one study using random assignment of a program that used probation officer–led classes for probationers, it was found that participants initially had higher violations, but were significantly less likely to be charged with a new offense in a one-year period after release.[59] Another recent study of a single CBT program reported no significant difference in recidivism between participants and non-participants.[60] Because many evaluations of programs do not use random assignment, it is possible that reductions in recidivism are due to **selection bias**. One evaluation study used propensity score matching (matching program participants with non-participants who were similar across relevant factors, such as criminal history and other correlates of recidivism). The analysis demonstrated that the measurable reductions found among program participants as compared to other offenders disappeared when comparing the group matched by propensity scores.[61]

However, many evaluations of CBT programs do show that they result in significant reductions in recidivism. One meta-analysis reported the average reduction in recidivism for program participants was 27 percent. Effect sizes vary across programs with demonstration projects (which are part of a large federally funded national study of a particular modality) showing larger reductions (an average of 49 percent reduction) than practitioner-led programs (an average of

11 percent reduction).[62] This difference across programs that were supposedly using CBT raises the issue of how well the program itself implements the CBT modality.

The **Correctional Program Assessment Inventory (CPAI)** was created to measure the extent to which programs adhere to the R/N/R approach and evidence-based correctional best practices.[63] Studies have shown that higher scores on the CPAI are associated with better success rates for offenders who participate in the programs.[64] The CPAI has been used to evaluate more than 700 individual correctional programs in the United States, and is also employed in Canada, Australia, and New Zealand. The instrument measures the content of the program and whether it conforms to R/N/R principles and other variables that have been associated with program success, such as management and staff characteristics and evaluation policies.

Studies have shown that higher scores on the CPAI are associated with lower recidivism rates; however, evaluators have found that approximately 60 percent of programs have failed to achieve even a passing grade on the instrument because of weaknesses in most of the areas described.[65] Studies have found that programs with higher adherence to R/N/R principles achieve 26 percent reductions in recidivism; those that follow some of the principles achieve an 18 percent decrease; however, those programs that score poorly on adherence to R/N/R principles have shown a 2 percent *increase* in recidivism.[66]

Criticism of Risk/Need/Responsivity and Cognitive Behavioral Therapy

The Risk/Need/Responsivity (R/N/R) approach and cognitive behavioral therapy (CBT) may be the most effective evidence-based approach to rehabilitation for criminal offenders today. However, there is some criticism that this approach and similar risk assessment approaches ignore some important factors, such as poverty and lack of economic opportunities. Criticism of the assessment instruments, including the LSI-R, include the following:

1. The instruments either intentionally or unintentionally include unfair (and perhaps illegal) factors in their algorithms to determine risk, such as race, sex, or socioeconomic status. Many of the factors used have strong correlations to race; for example, prior history, jail confinements, and so on. Socioeconomic status also is correlated with several of the measures identified in the LSI-R and other instruments, such as family structure, education, and employment. [67]

2. The instruments are needlessly complex and do no better in prediction than second-generation assessments that use simple static factors. In fact, one study found that using just two factors, age and total number of previous convictions, resulted in the same level of accuracy as the 137 factors used in COMPAS (which is not the LSI-R, but rather a similar third-generation risk instrument).[68]

3. The instruments are less accurate in prediction for certain groups. Critical evaluations of instruments have shown that Blacks are more likely than whites to have been inaccurately predicted to commit crime. One study found, for instance, that 23 percent of Blacks in the study were predicted to reoffend but did not, compared to 17 percent of Hispanics and 10 percent of whites.[69] That fact that Blacks are more than twice as likely to be the subject of this type of error is problematic considering these instruments are used for sentencing. Other studies have shown that they are less accurate for women than for men. A gender-specific addendum was

developed for the LSI-R, which used measures of self-efficacy, self-esteem, parenting, relationships, and abuse. After evaluating the predictive ability of the LSI-R alone and with the trailer, researchers concluded that gender-neutral models do predict recidivism for women, but the addition of gender-specific factors creates more accurate prediction tools. Some of the items in the LSI-R, such as criminal thinking, were found to be weak predictors for women. More important factors for predicting recidivism of women were substance abuse, economic and educational background, and mental health.[70]

4. The instruments are opaque, and companies closely guard their algorithms as proprietary. The problem is that if there are errors in the instruments, they are not detectable by those who have an interest in determining their accuracy, namely, defendants who may be sentenced at least partially on a risk level determined by the risk scoring of the instruments in question.

5. The instruments are being used inappropriately as sentencing tools rather than as guidance for treatment options. The assessment instruments described in this chapter, such as the LSI-R and COMPAS, were developed for correctional decision-making, such as what level of supervision a probationer should be placed in or what type of program an offender could benefit from. What has happened, however, is that risk assessments are increasingly being used by judges in sentencing decisions.

Evaluating Prison Programs

There is a huge body of literature on correctional program evaluation. Unfortunately, even though the process of evaluation has improved, there are still problems with program evaluations, making correctional decision-making problematic.

Methodological Issues

Evaluations of prison programming have become more sophisticated, but methodological problems exist that threaten the accuracy of findings. In the following sections, eight issues are presented.

1. *Recidivism is defined differently by different researchers.* Recidivism may mean rearrest, reconviction, or reincarceration, or it can mean simply being ejected from a program. Evaluations are not consistent in their measurement of recidivism; therefore, findings are hard to compare. Furthermore, even a reconviction may not be because of program failure; it could be because of legal retainers from prior offenses, such as holds placed on the offender for arrests or convictions from offenses committed prior to the current incarceration that arguably have nothing to do with the potential success of the rehabilitative program.

2. *Another methodological problem with evaluating prison programs is attrition.* Attrition refers to the number of individuals who drop out of or are ejected from a program. Some programs have an attrition rate as high as 60 percent. Even if the remaining participants show a reduced rate of recidivism, the value of the program is questionable; obviously, if few participants remain with the program until completion, it is unlikely to reach many offenders.[71]

3. *Evaluations differ in terms of the length of time studied.* Some evaluations follow offenders only for short periods of time after release to determine the success of a program. The minimum time period to evaluate whether participants of a program are less likely to recidivate than non-participants is one year. A three-year follow-up period is preferable, but few evaluations track offenders after release for this length of time.

4. *There may be no program fidelity, meaning programs may not follow the policies and procedures of the program model.* Programs that have the same name should be the same, but in reality, they may be quite different in practice across different institutions, making comparison of similar types of programs impossible. Another evaluation of the same prison program in several different locations demonstrated that locations with "high fidelity," meaning the program adhered to the principles and components of the original program model, showed success in reducing recidivism, and those with "low fidelity" showed no difference between program participants and a control group.[72]

5. *An important element to consider in terms of program effectiveness is the quality of staff.* Programs are heavily dependent on staff characteristics; thus, a program led by fully participating, enthusiastic staff is likely going to show more success than one run by bored or burned-out staff, regardless of the modality in which they operate.[73] To be effective, correctional program workers should establish high-quality relationships and model anti-criminal thinking patterns. In one study of 54 community correctional facilities, a type of treatment modality in some locations achieved reductions in recidivism of between 24 and 38 percent; however, in places where staff were rated as "not competent," the reductions were only between 10 and 17 percent. Staff training, communication skills, social relationship skills, problem-solving skills, and effective use of authority were all associated with reductions in recidivism. Findings indicated that staff characteristics explained 28 percent of the variation in program effect sizes across the 54 community corrections facilities. Prior experience and educational qualifications were the strongest correlates with program effectiveness.[74] This illustrates that even when a program is called the same thing in different locations, there is still difficulty in measuring the effect of that program because of staff differences.

6. *Meta-analyses are helpful but may be problematic in how they are constructed.* Meta-analyses are important instruments in assessing the effectiveness of prison programs because they combine different studies into one evaluative exercise; however, there are issues that create the need to exercise caution when interpreting the results of meta-analyses. First, there may be a mixing of apples and oranges; in other words, different measures for different things may be collapsed into one meaning. Second, poor-quality research may be included. Third, meta-analyses depend on published research and thus do not include other evaluations that do not get published in academic journals. Fourth, because researchers sometimes count different published evaluations from one data set, multiple results may not be independent of each other.[75]

7. *Researchers cannot control all variables.* In a laboratory setting, one can fully control the environment to determine the effect of an intervention. In the real world, it is impossible to control for all factors that may affect the decision to commit crime. Even if two offenders participate in the same prison rehabilitative program, there are different factors that affect them, both in terms of their pre-prison lives and their current prison experience. Measuring the effect of a program is complicated by all the varying

influences in the participants' lives in prison. Once an offender is released, situational elements vary tremendously as well. For example, one individual may be able to find work and start a new life with assistance from helpful family or friends, but another may not be able to find work, have no choice but to live with drug-using family members, and be inexorably drawn back into a life of crime due to desperation. Such factors cannot be controlled for; therefore, measuring the success or failure of a program is complicated by the inability to measure these other factors.

8. *Selection bias must be addressed.* Selection bias is a kind of statistical bias that occurs when there is not random assignment of participants into the treatment group and control group. In this context, it refers to the idea that a program may be successful only because highly motivated offenders who want to change are attracted to it and would have changed even without the program. To avoid the effects of selection bias, there should be random assignment between a treatment group and a control group; however, very few evaluations are so structured.

Program Evaluations

As discussed earlier, the meta-analysis conducted by sociologist Robert Martinson in the late 1970s supposedly found that "nothing worked" in terms of correctional programming; however, the study also reported that some programs worked for some offenders. A later meta-analysis also found that some programs are effective at reducing recidivism for some people.[76] Researchers have consistently found that some prison treatment programs moderately reduce recidivism.[77] For instance, one study of 33 different evaluations of educational, vocational, or other rehabilitative programs in prison indicated that modest improvements in recidivism existed across all program types.[78] A large study of 40 meta-analyses of correctional interventions found that the majority of studies showed moderate percent reductions in recidivism, and the range was from no effect to a 50 percent reduction in recidivism.[79] A more recent study also found that rehabilitative programs have modest to strong effects on recidivism, ranging between 10 to 30 percent reductions. Table 11.1 illustrates the effectiveness of different programs in terms of percent reduction in recidivism.

Some programs have shown little or no success in reducing recidivism. Boot camps, for example, are militaristic approaches whereby young offenders experience schedules of rigorous physical fitness tasks, harassment, and belittling treatment from drill instructor–like correctional staff. Evaluations consistently show no effect on recidivism, except for programs that also had intensive educational and rehabilitative programming. "Scared Straight" programs, which involve bringing young offenders to prison and having older inmates yell at them about what life is like in prison, also show no effect on recidivism. Drama therapy, acupuncture, and confrontational therapy also have shown no effect on recidivism.[80]

A meta-analysis of 69 research studies on prison programming between 1968 and 1999 included evaluations of behavioral programs that used token economies and other forms of behavior modification. These can be considered cognitive behavioral programs in that behavior change is the goal; this is achieved through restructuring of the thought processes involved in behavioral decisions. Token economies and other forms of behavior modification induce behavior through the promise of rewards. **Contingency contracting** programs involve inmates entering contracts for desirable behaviors to earn rewards. Other cognitive behavioral programs emphasize thought and emotional processes; for instance, identifying

TABLE 11.1	Program Effectiveness in Reducing Recidivism

PROGRAM	PERCENT REDUCTION IN RECIDIVISM
CBT for anger management	51
Therapeutic community (hard drugs)	45
Moral reconation therapy	35
Intensive supervision program	33
Postsecondary correctional education	27
Cognitive behavioral therapy	25
Vocational	22
General vocation/education	21
Counseling (general)	20
Correctional industries	19
Academic/educational	18
Intensive supervision probation with treatment	17.9
Sex offender treatment	16–37
General Domestic Violence treatment (police report)	16–32
Therapeutic community	16–27
Reasoning and rehabilitation	14
Restorative justice	14
General drug treatment	12–22
Boot camp	5
Ex-offender employment	3
Electronic monitoring	2
General Domestic Violence treatment (partner report)	0–10

Selected programs; deleted footnotes.

Source: M. Caudy, L. Tang, S. Ainsworth, J. Lerch, and F. Taxman, "Reducing Recidivism Through Correctional Programming: Using Meta-Analysis to Inform the RNR Simulation Tool," in F. Taxman and A. Pattavina (eds) *Simulation Strategies to Reduce Recidivism: Risk Need Responsivity (RNR) Modeling for the Criminal Justice System*, ((Springer: New York, 2013): 167-202, 170-171. 170–171, 167–202.

so-called criminal thinking or other thinking errors that lead people to make poor decisions. Social skills training, role play, problem solving, rational emotive therapy, and cognitive skills programs were other types of programs categorized under the cognitive behavioral label in these meta-analyses. Findings indicated that cognitive behavioral treatment approaches did reduce recidivism by significant amounts, but the categories that showed the greatest effect were those that employed cognitive skills training and social skills development training, not the token economies or the standard behavior modification programs.[81]

In recent years, there has also been growing consensus regarding what makes for a successful program:

- The program's organizational culture has well-defined goals, ethical principles, staff cohesion, and uses self-evaluation.
- The program is based on empirically defined needs, with professionally trained staff, and uses risk assessment.
- The program targets the criminogenic needs of high-risk offenders using empirically valid behavioral and social learning, or cognitive behavioral therapies.
- The program uses therapeutic practices, including anti-criminal modeling, reinforcement and disapproval, problem-solving techniques, structured learning, cognitive self-change, and relationship practices.
- The program uses referrals and incorporates continuation of services once offenders reenter the community.
- The program incorporates evaluation practices.[82]

The National Institute of Justice and the Bureau of Justice Assistance have a website that lists and describes correctional programs and grades them as effective, promising, or showing no effects (www.crimesolutions.gov/). The national reviewers who evaluate these programs require an evaluation that uses either an experimental or quasi-experimental approach (meaning the use of random assignment and control samples). A promising program can reach effective status if subsequent rigorous evaluations show increasingly significant results.

In 2011, the Washington State Institute for Public Policy conducted a cost-benefit analysis of 57 correctional prevention and intervention programs, resulting in a list of programs and policies that were successful and cost efficient. Each program's cost to taxpayers was calculated, along with the projected cost-benefit of the program. Almost all rehabilitative programs showed a net benefit to taxpayers.[83] More recently, in 2018, they updated the analysis of correctional programming and it is now an inventory of 57 correctional interventions. For each program, the report indicates whether each program is evidence based (meaning that success has been replicated with multiple evaluations), research based (there has been one evaluation showing success), promising (the program is based on sound theory and can be replicated, but no adequate evaluation yet exists), demonstrates poor outcomes, or is null (the program showed no effect on recidivism). Among other findings, this analysis indicates that prison industry programs are evidence based, while halfway houses show poor outcomes on recidivism. Employment counseling and job training in the community are research based, and life skills education has no effect on recidivism.[84] The search for the most effective correctional program model continues, employing increasingly sophisticated research techniques to discover "what works." To conclude this discussion, the Focus box describes one offender for whom predictive instruments clearly were not effective.

FOCUS ON THE
OFFENDER
PREDICTING RISK

A young man in Utah was stopped by a police officer for driving suspiciously and speeding. While searching the man's vehicle, the officer found handcuffs, duct tape, a ski mask, a second mask fashioned from pantyhose, a crowbar, trash bags, a coil of rope, an ice pick, and other items assumed to be burglary tools. He was arrested and later charged with kidnapping and assault when he was identified by a young female victim whom, days earlier, he had tried to handcuff and drag into a van; she managed to get away.

What was known about the man at the time of his conviction was that he was born Theodore Robert Cowell in a home for unwed mothers. His maternal grandparents pretended that he was their son to avoid the stigma of his birth; he learned the truth about his parentage much later, though he never knew who his father was. When he was four, he and his biological mother moved from Philadelphia to Tacoma, Washington, where the man she married adopted him.

As a juvenile, he was arrested several times for burglary and auto theft, but those records were sealed. He graduated from high school and college, earning a degree in psychology. He volunteered for a suicide hotline, was assistant director of the Seattle Crime Prevention Advisory Commission, and worked on political campaigns. Excellent recommendations led to his acceptance into law school. He was handsome, articulate, and intelligent. He began law school in Washington state but quit, and was attending the University of Utah Law School at the time of his first arrest as an adult. He was released on bail before his trial but was convicted in a non-jury trial of kidnapping and sentenced to one to 15 years in prison. Around that same time, he was a suspect in a series of murders in Washington, but police had no evidence against him other than vague descriptions of what could have been him and his car.

This man was Ted Bundy, a notorious serial killer. By the time he was arrested in Utah in 1974, he had already murdered at least eight women in Washington, four in Utah, and four in Colorado. There are strong suspicions that he carried out his first murders when he was as young as 14, although he never admitted to several unsolved murders that investigators believed he committed. While he was in prison for kidnapping, authorities charged him with the murder of a Colorado woman, and Washington and Utah police were gathering evidence for the multiple murders he was suspected of committing. He escaped twice: the first time, he was recaptured after six days, but the second time, he escaped to Florida. There, Bundy seriously assaulted three women and murdered three more before being caught, convicted, and sentenced to death. He is known to have killed at least 30 women, but probably killed more.

By all accounts, Bundy was a psychopath who had no remorse for his acts or empathy toward his victims. He described their murders as a means of ensuring that he possessed them. He often revisited their corpses. In his early murders, he entered the victims' homes and bludgeoned the women to death and then had sex with their bodies. Later, he kidnapped his victims off the street, sometimes by pretending to have his arm or leg in a cast and asking for their help. He would overpower them, take them to a secluded location, sometimes rape them, strangle them to death, and then abuse their bodies. He was executed in 1989 when he was 42 years old.

Questions for Discussion

1. If you were responsible for determining Bundy's level of risk at the point of his first arrest and conviction for kidnapping, how would you have assessed his potential for future crime? How would one of the third-generation instruments have evaluated Bundy based on what was known about him at the time?

2. Do you think it is possible to recognize whether someone is a serial killer or likely to commit further acts of violence simply by interviewing them?

Source: S. Michaud and H. Aynesworth, *Ted Bundy: Conversations with a Killer* (Irving, TX: Authorlink Press, 2000).

Summary

- During the rehabilitative era of the 1970s, there was a strong focus on diagnosing offenders' reasons for committing crimes and providing numerous types of rehabilitative programming. Currently, we are in an era of retribution, where the focus is largely on punishment and identifying which offenders are most likely to recidivate.

- Treatment in prison consists of religious programs, education, labor, vocational training, drug and alcohol treatment programs, and cognitive behavioral programs.

- Education and vocational programs show moderate success in reducing recidivism. Vocational programs are associated with a greater likelihood of obtaining employment after release.

- First-generation risk assessment instruments began with clinical (subjective) predictions, then moved to actuarial tools using factors that were shown to correlate with recidivism, also known as second-generation prediction instruments. Third-generation instruments combine static (actuarial) and dynamic factors (risk and needs, such as criminal personality or criminal attitudes). Blacks and women are more likely to be the subjects of false positive errors in which the prediction of risk is inaccurate.

- Fourth-generation assessment instruments connect assessment to treatment through the R/N/R approach for an integrated approach to correctional intervention.

- The hallmarks of effective correctional programming include well-defined goals and ethical principles, a focus on high-risk offenders, targeting empirically defined needs that are associated with recidivism; the use of cognitive behavioral therapy; high-fidelity, high-quality staff; continuity in services through release; and self-evaluation.

- Evaluating the effectiveness of prison programs can be problematic due to variations in defining what constitutes recidivism; attrition rates; the duration of the follow-up period; variations in program fidelity; differences in quality of staff; and research discrepancies inherent in using the meta-analysis approach.

PROJECTS

1. Pick an offender highlighted in one of the Focus on an Offender features throughout the book and construct a treatment plan for him or her.

2. Develop an evaluation methodology for a prison treatment program, considering all the methodological issues reviewed in this chapter.

NOTES

1. R. Martinson, "What Works? Questions and Answers About Prison Reform," *Public Interest* (Spring 1974): 22–54.

2. D. Farrabee, "Reexamining Martinson's Critique: A Cautionary Note for Evaluators," *Crime and Delinquency* 48, 1 (2002): 189–92.

3. B. Cooke and D. Farrington, "The Effectiveness of Dog-Training Programs in Prison: A Systematic Review and Meta-Analysis of the Literature," *The Prison Journal*, 96, 6 (2016): 854–76.

4. L. Schaefer, T. Sams, and J. Lux, "Saved, Salvaged, or Sunk: A Meta-Analysis of the Effects of Faith-Based Interventions on Inmate Adjustment," *The Prison Journal* 96, 4 (2016): 600–622.

5. C. Harlow, C., *Education and Correctional Populations* (Washington, DC: Bureau of Justice Statistics, U.S. Dept. of Justice, 2003).

6. Reported in F. Cullen and C. Jonson, "Rehabilitation and Treatment Programs," in J. Wilson and J. Petersilia (eds), *Crime and Public Policy* (New York, NY: Oxford University Press, 2011), 293–344.

7. C. Harlow, *Education and Correctional Populations* (Washington, DC: Bureau of Justice Statistics, U.S. Dept. of Justice, 2003).

8. A. Lin, *Reform in the Making: The Implementation of Social Policy in Prison* (Princeton, NJ: Princeton University Press, 2000).

9. M. Welsh, "The Effects of the Elimination of Pell Grant Eligibility for State Prison Inmates," *Journal of Correctional*

Education 53, 4 (2002): 154–58; J. Messemer, "College Programs for Inmates: The Post-Pell Grant Era," *Journal of Correctional Education* 54, 1 (2003): 32–9.

10. G. Susswein, "Report: Reading Class Aids Inmates," *Austin American Statesman*, August 30, 2000, B1, B6; C. Uggen, "Work as a Turning Point in the Life Course of Criminals: A Duration Model of Age, Employment, and Recidivism," *American Sociological Review* 65 (2000): 529–46.

11. L. Davis, R. Bozick, J. Steele, J. Saunders, and J. Miles, *Evaluating the Effectiveness of Correctional Education: A Meta-Analysis of Programs That Provide Education to Incarcerated Adults* (Santa Monica, CA: Rand Corporation, 2013).

12. L. Davis, R. Bozick, J. Steele, J. Saunders, and J. Miles, *Evaluating the Effectiveness of Correctional Education: A Meta-Analysis of Programs That Provide Education to Incarcerated Adults* (Santa Monica, CA: Rand Corporation, 2013).

13. S. Aos, M. Miller, M., and E. Drake, *Evidence-Based Adult Corrections Programs: What Works and What Does Not* (Olympia: Washington State Institute for Public Policy, 2006); R.M. Cho and J.H. Tyler, "Does Prison-Based Adult Basic Education Improve Postrelease Outcomes for Male Prisoners in Florida?" *Crime & Delinquency* 59,(2010): 975–1005; G. Duwe and V. Clark, "The Effects of Prison-Based Educational Programming on Recidivism and Employment," *The Prison Journal* 94, 4 (2014) 454–78.

14. A. Pompoco, J. Wooldredge, M. Lugo, C. Sullivan, and E. Latessa, "Reducing Inmate Misconduct and Prison Returns with Facility Education

Programs," *Criminology & Public Policy* 16, 2 (2017): 515–47.

15. Reported in F. Cullen and C. Jonson. 2011, "Rehabilitation and Treatment Programs," in. J. Wilson and J. Petersilia, *Crime & Public Policy* (New York, NY: Oxford University Press), 293–344.

16. J. Gerber and E. Fritsch, "Adult Academic and Vocational Correctional Education Programs: A Review of Recent Research," *Journal of Offender Rehabilitation* 22, 2 (1995): 119–42; S. Lawrence, D. Mears, G. Dubin, and J. Travis, *The Practice and Promise of Prison Programming* (Washington, DC: Urban Institute, 2002).

17. J. Andrews and D. Bonta, *The Psychology of Criminal Conduct*, 5th Ed. (Cincinnati, OH: Anderson Publishing, 2010), 275.

18. D. Brewster, D. and S. Sharp, "Educational Programs and Recidivism in Oklahoma: Another Look," *The Prison Journal* 82, 3 (2002): 314–34.

19. G. Susswein, G., "Report: Reading Class Aids Inmates," *Austin American Statesman*, August 30, 2000, B1, B6.

20. J. Austin and J. Irwin, *It's About Time: America's Imprisonment Binge* (Belmont, CA: Wadsworth, 2001).

21. Reported in F. Cullen and C. Jonson. 2011, "Rehabilitation and Treatment Programs," in. J. Wilson and J. Petersilia, *Crime & Public Policy* (New York, NY: Oxford University Press), 293–344.

22. B. Sloan, B., "The Prison Industries Enhancement Certification Program: Why Everyone Should Be Concerned," *Prison Legal News*, October 4, 2011. Retrieved 10/4/2011 from https://www.prisonlegalnews.or g/(S(ecx1bqfnc5bdvwud

rukj3zip))/displayArticle. aspx?articleid=22,190&.

23. B. Sloan, B, "The Prison Industries Enhancement Certification Program: Why Everyone Should Be Concerned," *Prison Legal News*, October 4, 2011, retrieved October 4, 2011 from https://www.prisonlegalnews.or g/(S(ecx1bqfnc5bdvwud rukj3zip))/displayArticle. aspx?articleid=22,190&.

24. See https://www.unicor.gov/ index.aspx.

25. UNICOR. *Factories with Fences: 75 Years of Changing Lives* (Washington, DC: US Bureau of Prisons, n.d.).

26. UNICOR. *Sales Report* Washington, DC: Federal Bureau of Prisons, 2017, retrieved from https://www.unicor.gov/ publications/reports/ FY17AnnualSalesReport.pdf.

27. UNICOR. *Factories with Fences: 75 Years of Changing Lives* (Washington, DC: US Bureau of Prisons, n.d.).

28. C. Parenti, *Lockdown America: Police and Prisons in the Age of Crisis* (New York City: Verso New Left Books, 1999).

29. *Behind Bars II: Substance Abuse and America's Prison Population* (New York, NY: National Center on Addiction and Substance Abuse – Columbia University, 2010). Available at http://www.casacolumbia. org/articlefiles/575-report2010behind bars2.pdf.

30. E. Lock, J. Timberlake, and K. Rasinki, "Battle Fatigue: Is Public Support Waning for War-Centered Drug Control Strategies?" *Crime and Delinquency* 48, 3 (2002): 380–98.

31. R. King and M. Mauer, "Distorted Priorities: Drug Offenders in State Prisons," 2002, retrieved Sept. 21,

2002 from http://www.SentencingProject.org.

32. J. Andrews and D. Bonta, *The Psychology of Criminal Conduct*, 5th Ed. (Cincinnati, OH: Anderson Publishing, 2010).

33. C. Vestal, C., "New Momentum for Addiction Treatment Behind Bars," *Stateline*, April 3, 2018, retrieved from http://www.pewtrusts.org/en/research-and-analysis/blogs/stateline/2018/04/04/new-momentum-for-addiction-treatment-behind-bars.

34. J. Andrews and D. Bonta, *The Psychology of Criminal Conduct*, 5th Ed. (Cincinnati, OH: Anderson Publishing, 2010), 287.

35. H. Sung, "Rehabilitating Felony Drug Offenders Through Job Development," *Prison Journal* 81, 2 (2001): 271–86; J. Andrews and D. Bonta, *The Psychology of Criminal Conduct*, 5th Ed. (Cincinnati, OH: Anderson Publishing, 2010).

36. J. Andrews and D. Bonta, *The Psychology of Criminal Conduct*, 5th Ed. (Cincinnati, OH: Anderson Publishing, 2010), 291.

37. Reported in F. Cullen and C. Jonson. 2011, "Rehabilitation and Treatment Programs," in. J. Wilson and J. Petersilia, *Crime & Public Policy* (New York, NY: Oxford University Press), 293–344.

38. B. Fletcher and R. Chandler, *Principles of Drug Abuse Treatment for Criminal Justice Populations* (Washington, DC: National Institute on Drug Abuse, U.S. Dept. of Health and Human Services, 2007).

39. J. Andrews and D. Bonta, *The Psychology of Criminal Conduct*, 5th Ed. (Cincinnati, OH: Anderson Publishing, 2010), 287.

40. H. Toch, *Therapeutic Communities in Corrections* (New York: Praeger, 1980).

41. S. Singer, "Essential Element of the Effective Therapeutic Community in the Correctional Institution," in K. Early (ed.), *Drug Treatment Behind Bars: Prison Based Strategies for Change*, (Chicago: Praeger Publishing, 1996), 75–88.

42. M. Talpade, C. Talpade, and E. Marshall-Story, "Impact of Therapeutic Community Training on Knowledge and Attitudes of Correctional Officers," *International Journal of Psychosocial Rehabilitation*, 17,1 (2012): 6–17.

43. S. Gottfredson and L. Moriarty, "Statistical Risk Assessment: Old Problems and New Applications," *Crime & Delinquency* 52, 1 (2006): 178–200.

44. R. Hanson and M. Bussiere, "Predicting Relapse: A Meta Analysis of Sexual Offender Recidivism Studies," *Journal of Consulting & Clinical Psychology* 66, 3 (1998): 348–62.

45. R. Sims and M. Jones, "Predicting Success or Failure on Probation: Factors Associated with Felony Probation Outcomes," *Crime and Delinquency* 43, 3 (1997): 314–27.

46. K. Morgan, "Factors Associated with Probation Outcome," *Journal of Criminal Justice* 22, 4 (1994): 341–53.

47. F. Taxman and M. Thanner, "Risk, Need, and Responsivity (R/N/R): It All Depends," *Crime & Delinquency* 52, 1 (2006): 28–51.

48. Reported in J. Angwin, J. Larson, S. Mattu and L. Kirchner, "Machine Bias," *ProPublica*, 23 May 2016, accessed December 28, 2018, https://www.propublica.org/article/machine-bias-risk-assessments-in-criminal-sentencing.

49. D. Andrews, J. Bonta, and J. Wormith, "The Recent Past and Near Future of Risk and/or Need Assessment," *Crime & Delinquency* 52, 1(2006): 7–27.

50. D. Andrews and J. Bonta, *The Psychology of Criminal Conduct* (New Providence, NJ: Matthew Bender, 2010).

51. D. Andrews and J. Bonta, *The Psychology of Criminal Conduct*(New Providence, NJ: Matthew Bender, 2010), 55–60; P. Smith, F. Cullen, and E. Latessa, "Can 14,737 be Wrong? A Meta-Analysis of the LSI-R and Recidivism for Female Offenders," *Criminology & Public Policy* 8 (2009): 183–208; also see F. Taxman, A. Pattavina, M. Caudy, J. Byrne, and J. Durso, "The Empirical Basis for the RNR Model with an Updated RNR Conceptual Framework," in F. Taxman and A. Pattavina (eds) *Simulation Strategies to Reduce Recidivism: Risk Need Responsivity (RNR) Modeling for the Criminal Justice System* (Springer: New York, 2013), 73–111.

52. P. Smith, F. Cullen, and E. Latessa, "Can 14,737 be Wrong? A Meta-analysis of the LSI-R and Recidivism for Female Offenders" *Criminology & Public Policy* 8 (2009): 183–208.

53. D. Andrews, J. Bonta, and R. Hoge, "Classification for Effective Rehabilitation: Rediscovering Psychology," *Criminal Justice and Behavior* 17, 1 (1990): 19–52; D. Andrews, "The Risk-Need-Responsivity (RNR) Model of Correctional Assessment and Treatment," in J. Dvoskin, J. Skeem, R. Novaco and K. Douglas (eds) *Using Social Science to Reduce Offending* (New York, NY: Oxford University Press, 2012).

54. J. Andrews and D. Bonta, *The Psychology of Criminal Conduct*, 5th Ed. (Cincinnati, OH: Anderson Publishing, 2010).

55. C. Lowenkamp and E. Latessa, "Increasing the Effectiveness of Correctional Programming

Through The Risk Principle: Identifying Offenders For Residential Placement," *Criminology & Public Policy* 4, 2 (2005): 263–90; D. Andrews, J. Bonta, J. Wormith, "The Recent Past And Near Future Of Risk and/or Need Assessment," *Crime & Delinquency* 52, 1 (2006): 7–27; C. Lowenkamp, E. Latessa, and A. Holsinger, "The Risk Principle In Action: What Have We Learned From 13,676 Offenders And 97 Correctional Programs," *Crime & Delinquency* 52 1 (2006): 77–93; J. Andrews and D. Bonta, *The Psychology of Criminal Conduct*, 5th Ed. (Cincinnati, OH: Anderson Publishing, 2010), 314; D. Andrews, "The Risk-Need-Responsivity (RNR) Model of Correctional Assessment and Treatment," in J. Dvoskin, J. Skeem, R. Novaco and K. Douglas (eds) *Using Social Science to Reduce Offending* (New York, NY: Oxford University Press, 2012).

56. J. Andrews and D. Bonta, *The Psychology of Criminal Conduct*, 5th Ed. (Cincinnati, OH: Anderson Publishing, 2010), 520.

57. J. Andrews and D. Bonta, *The Psychology of Criminal Conduct*, 5th Ed. (Cincinnati, OH: Anderson Publishing, 2010).

58. G. Barnes, J. Hyatt, and L. Sherman, "An Implementation and Experimental Evaluation of Cognitive-Behavioral Therapy for High-Risk Probationers," *Criminal Justice and Behavior*, 44, 4 (2017): 611–30.

59. G. Barnes, J. Hyatt, and L. Sherman, "An Implementation and Experimental Evaluation of Cognitive-Behavioral Therapy for High-Risk Probationers," *Criminal Justice and Behavior*, 44, 4 (2017): 611–30.

60. S. Verweij, B. Wartna, N. Tollenaar, and M. Beerthuizan, "The Effectiveness of a Cognitive Skills Training Program for Adult Offenders," *Criminal Justice & Behavior* 44, 12 (2017): 1559–79

61. B. Strah, N. Frost, J. Stowell and S. Taheri, "Cognitive-Behavioral Programming and the Value of Failed Interventions: A Propensity Score Evaluation," *Journal of Offender Rehabilitation* 57 (2018): 1, 22–46.

62. M.W. Lipsey, G.L. Chapman, and N.A. Landenberger, "Cognitive-Behavioral Programs for Offenders," *Annals of the American Academy of Political and Social Science* 578 (2001): 144–57; M.W. Lipsey, N.A. Landenberger, and S.J. Wilson, *Effects of Cognitive-Behavioral Programs for Criminal Offenders* (Oslo, Norway: Campbell Systematic Reviews, 2007).

63. P. Smith and M. Schweitzer, "The Therapeutic Prison," *Journal of Contemporary Criminal Justice* 28, 1 (2012): 7–22.

64. D. Andrews, J. Bonta, and J. Wormith, "The Recent Past and Near Future of Risk and/or Need Assessment," *Crime and Delinquency* 52, 1 (2006): 7–27.

65. P. Smith and M. Schweitzer, "The Therapeutic Prison," *Journal of Contemporary Criminal Justice* 28, 1 (2012): 7–22.

66. J. Andrews and D. Bonta, *The Psychology of Criminal Conduct*, 5th Ed. (Cincinnati, OH: Anderson Publishing, 2010), 73.

67. J. Angwin, J. Larson, S. Mattu, and L. Kirchner, "Machine Bias" *ProPublica*, 23 May 2016, accessed December 28, 2018, https://www.propublica.org/article/machine-bias-risk-assessments-in-criminal-sentencing.; M. Stevenson, "Is Crime Predictable?" *The Crime Report*, August 8, 2017,

accessed December 28, 2018, https://thecrimereport.org/2017/08/31/does-risk-assessment-work-theres-no-single-answer/; J. Dressel and H. Farid, "The Accuracy, Fairness, and Limits of Predicting Recidivism," *Science Advances* 4 (2018), accessed December 28, 2018, advances.sciencemag.org/content/4/1/eaao5580; J. Skeem and C. Lowenkamp, "Risk, Race, and Recidivism: Predictive Bias and Disparate Impact," SSRN, June 14, 2016, https://ssrn.com/abstract=2687339 or http://dx.doi.org/10.2139/ssrn.2687339.

68. S. Desmarais, K. Johnson, and J. Singh, "Performance of Recidivism Risk Assessment Instruments in U.S. Correctional Settings," *Psychological Services* 13, 3 (2016): 206–22; F. Taxman, A. Pattavina, M. Caudy, J. Byrne and J. Durso, "The Empirical Basis for the RNR Model with an Updated RNR Conceptual Framework," in F. Taxman and A. Pattavina (eds) *Simulation Strategies to Reduce Recidivism: Risk Need Responsivity (RNR) Modeling for the Criminal Justice System* (Springer: New York, 2013), 73–111.

69. S. Picard, M. Watkins, M. Rempel, and A. Kerodal, *Beyond the Algorithm: Pretrial Reform, Risk Assessment, and Racial Fairness* (New York: Center for Court Innovation, 2019).

70. P. Van Voorhis and L. Presser, *Classification of Women Offenders: A National Assessment of Current Practices* (Washington, DC: National Institute of Corrections, 2001); P. Van Voorhis, "Classification of Women Offenders: Gender-Responsive Approaches to Risk/Needs Assessment," *Community Corrections Report* 122 (2005): 19–20; G. Coulson, G. Ilacqua, V.

Nutbrown, D. Giulekas and F. Cudjoe, "Predictive Utility of the LSI for Incarcerated Female Offenders," *Criminal Justice and Behavior* 23 (1996): 427–39; C. Lowenkamp, A. Holsinger, and E. Latessa, "Risk/Need Assessment, Offender Classification, and the Role of Childhood Abuse," *Criminal Justice and Behavior* 28, 5 (2001): 543–63; K. Holtfreter, M. Reisig, and M. Morash, "Poverty, State Capital, and Recidivism Among Women Offenders," *Criminology & Public Policy* 3, 2 (2004): 185–208; L. Van der Knaap, D. Alberda, P. Oosterveld, and M. Born, "The Predictive Validity of Criminogenic Needs for Male and Female Offenders: Comparing the Relative Impact of Needs in Predicting Recidivism," *Law and Human Behavior* 36 5: 413–22; N. Pusch and K. Holtfreter, "Gender and Risk Assessment in Juvenile Offenders: A Meta-analysis," *Criminal Justice and Behavior* 45, 1 (2018): 56–81; M. Ostermann and L. Salerno, "The Validity of the Level of Service Inventory–Revised at the Intersection of Race and Gender," *The Prison Journal* 96, 4 (2016): 554–75.

71. S. Maruna and T.P. LeBel, "The Desistance Paradigm in Correctional Practice: From Programmes to Lives," in F. McNeill, P. Raynor, and C. Trotter (eds.), *Offender Supervision: New Directions in Theory, Research and Practice* (Cullompton, UK: Willan, 2010), 65–88.

72. G. Duwe and V. Clark, "Importance of Program

Integrity: Outcome Evaluation of a Gender-Responsive, Cognitive-Behavioral Program for Female Offenders," *Criminology and Public Policy* 14, 2 (2015): 301–28.

73. A. Lin, *Reform in the Making: The Implementation of Social Policy in Prison* (Princeton, NJ: Princeton University Press, 2000).

74. M. Makarios, L. Lovins, E. Latessa, and P. Smith, "Staff Quality and Treatment Effectiveness: An Examination of the Relationship Between Staff Factors and the Effectiveness of Correctional Programs," *Justice Quarterly* 33, 2 (2016): 348–67.

75. I. Crow, *The Treatment and Rehabilitation of Offenders* (Thousand Oaks, CA: SAGE Publishing, 2001).

76. F. Pearson, F. and D. Lipton, "A Meta-Analytic Review of the Effectiveness of Corrections-Based Treatments for Drug Abuse," *The Prison Journal* 79, 4 (1999): 384–410.

77. P. Gendreau, P. and R. Ross, *Effective Correctional Treatment* (Toronto: Butterworth Publishing, 1980); T. Palmer, *A Profile of Correctional Effectiveness and New Directions for Research* (Albany, NY: SUNY Press, 1994); A. Harland, *Choosing Correctional Interventions that Work* (Beverly Hills, CA: Sage, 1996).

78. P. Wilson, C. Gallagher, M. Coggeshall, and D. MacKenzie, "A Quantitative Review and Description of Corrections Based Educational, Vocational, and Work Programs,"

Corrections Management Quarterly 3, 4 (1999): 8–18.

79. M. Lipsey and F. Cullen, "The Effectiveness of Correctional Rehabilitation: A Review of Systematic Reviews," *Annual Review of Law and Social Science* 3 (2007): 297–320.

80. E. Latessa, F. Cullen, and P. Gendreau, "Beyond Correctional Quakery-Professionalism and the Possibility of Effective Treatment," Federal Probation 66, 2 (2002): 43–49.

81. F. Pearson, D. Lipton, C. Cleland, and D. Yee, "The Effects of Behavioral and Cognitive-Behavioral Programs on Recidivism," *Crime and Delinquency* 48, 3 (2002): 476–96.

82. E. Latessa, F. Cullen, and P. Gendreau, "Beyond Correctional Quakery-Professionalism and the Possibility of Effective Treatment," *Federal Probation* 66, 2 (2002): 43–49.

83. "Return on Investment: Evidence Based Options to Improve State-wide Outcomes," Washington State Institute for Public Policy, 2011, http://www.wsipp.wa.gov/rptfiles/11-07-1201.pdf.

84. "Inventory of Evidence-Based, Research-Based, and Promising Programs for Adult Corrections," Washington State Institute of Public Policy, 2018, http://www.wsipp.wa.gov/ReportFile/1681/Wsipp_Inventory-of-Evidence-Based-Research-Based-and-Promising-Programs-for-Adult-Corrections_Report.pdf.

Chapter 12

Parole and Looking Toward the Future

LEARNING OBJECTIVES

1. Describe the challenges newly released prisoners face.

2. Describe how many people are on parole and their demographic profile.

3. Understand problems in the administration of halfway houses.

4. List and describe the factors that are correlated with recidivism. Compare these to the factors associated with success.

5. Explain the crucial issues for corrections looking toward the future.

CHAPTER OUTLINE

- Reentry 328
- Parole 331
- Halfway Houses 338
- Recidivism and Successful Offenders 339
- Future Directions in Corrections 344
- SUMMARY 353

Most prisoners are released and return to their communities.

KEY TERMS

Absconding

Amnesty

Clemency

Commutation

Desistance

Discretionary
    parole

Due process

Graduated sanctions

Mandatory supervision

Mark system

"Maxed out"

Motivational interviewing

Pardon

Public duty doctrine

Recidivism

Social impact bonds

Technical violation

Ticket of leave

Transportation

 # Reentry

Most prisoners are released and return to their communities. There are two types of post-prison supervision: in some states everyone released from prison receives **mandatory supervision** for a short time, during which the individual may be returned to prison if they violate any of the conditions (rules) of parole. In other states, some inmates receive **discretionary parole**, upon a decision to release by a paroling authority after an inmate becomes statutorily eligible. Even though some inmates are eligible based on statute, they may never be paroled because the decision to release is discretionary. The third method of release comes with no supervision and is known as "maxing out." When an inmate is **"maxed out,"** it means that they have served their full term of imprisonment and are unconditionally released with no supervision at all. Even states that have abolished discretionary parole may still have parole caseloads because of mandatory supervision or because, legally, they must continue to make decisions regarding parole for those individuals who were sentenced before parole was abolished in that state. As the years go by, however, inmates will be released or die, and eventually, those states with no statutory discretionary parole will not have any inmates to release. Indiana, Kansas, and Maine, for instance, reported no discretionary parole releases in 2016.[1]

Challenges

Upon any kind of release, most prisoners face difficult challenges in re-entering society. Most return to the community with limited education, few marketable job skills, no stable housing, chronic health issues, substance abuse needs, and limited family and friend support networks. In recent years, offenders who were sentenced to long 25- or 35-year sentences during the height of the mandatory minimum sentencing era are being released. These individuals went to prison before the arrival of laptops, cellphones, smartphones, Google, Facebook, and other things most of us take for granted. After being in prison for a long time, individuals feel that they do not know how to talk to "straight" people. They may overreact when bumped in public; they may not be comfortable in crowded spaces; and they have difficulty navigating the simplest acts of free society like buying groceries or figuring out what bus to use.

The National Reentry Council has identified the following challenges facing those who are released from prison:

- Three out of four have a substance abuse problem, but only 10 percent have received formal treatment.
- Fifty-five percent have children under 18 to support.
- Forty percent lack a high school diploma or GED.
- Only about 1 in 3 has received vocational training in prison.
- About 1 in 3 has some type of physical or mental disability.
- In most states, needs outweigh available resources.[2]

These challenges affect the releasees' likelihood of recidivating. Relevant needs include housing, job opportunities and employment training, drug treatment, mental health services, and family counseling.

All prior research on parolees and recidivism has found that housing and employment are huge challenges to ex-offenders. Housing is obviously problematic and, often, the releasee either has no family left or has been rejected by family members because of their criminality. In some cases, family members live in federal housing and cannot allow the releasee to live with them. Releasees are often forced to stay temporarily with family, friends, or acquaintances in the same neighborhoods where they were arrested, which are rife with temptation. Employment is obviously extremely important to releasees, yet ex-offenders are routinely rejected solely because of their criminal history. Some sources indicate that unemployment among ex-offenders is as high as 40 percent.[3] Employment provides an income to live on, as well as a routine, access to prosocial individuals, and self-respect.

Despite their importance, these challenges may be underestimated by officials. In one study of reentry of jail inmates, releasees reported structural factors such as employment, lack of housing, and inability to pay fines as the most challenging barriers to success, but correctional officials reported that personal issues (e.g., lack of motivation, temptation to reoffend) were the most problematic, indicating a disconnect between releasees and correctional professionals.[4] In Table 12.1, the challenges identified by officials are compared to those identified by releasees. If practitioners and offenders cannot agree on what needs are

TABLE 12.1   **Challenges Ranked (Top 5)**

CORRECTIONS OFFICIALS	OFFENDERS
Drug or alcohol abuse	Limited employment opportunities
Return to substance abuse	Inability to pay fines or court fees
Associating with the wrong people/peer pressure	Low wages
Temptation/opportunities to reoffend	Return to substance abuse
Developing positive associations	Associating with the wrong people/peer pressure

Source: K. Ward and A. Merlo, "Rural Jail Reentry and Mental Health: Identifying Challenges for Offenders and Professionals," The Prison Journal 96, 1 (2016): 27–52.

important, there may be little success in developing the resources necessary to meet releasees' needs.

In 2008, *The Second Chance Act: Community Safety Through Recidivism Prevention* was passed by Congress with the goal of increasing reentry programming for offenders released from state prisons and local jails. In research funded by *The Second Chance Act* that surveyed service providers, the following needs were identified as especially critical for ex-offenders returning to the community:

- Affordable housing, transitional housing, housing options for sex offenders, housing for ex-drug offenders or former gang members, housing for those with special needs due to disabilities or health issues.

- Employment for participants, especially those with limited academic/educational proficiencies, little work experience, and criminal histories. Better coordination between training in prison and employment opportunities in the community.

- Mental health assessments, individual counseling services, family counseling, staff training in mental health, substance abuse treatment and aftercare services, and services that address family addiction and mental health issues.

- Assistance obtaining identification, including addressing conflicting state procedures.

- Health care, medical insurance, securing medications for participants who are released from the facility with only a one-week supply.

- Family services, services that help participants deal with family members or relationship issues.

- Transportation to get needed services or obtain employment.

- Assistance with fees or fines owed.

- Cognitive behavioral programming.

Other service gaps identified in this research included the following: more culturally specific programs; longer-term work with women; and service delivery strategies that facilitate self-sufficiency among participants rather than dependency on case managers.[5]

In one study, 122 prison releasees were followed for a year after release. Researchers found that releasees sometimes ended up in homeless shelters and/or cycled through psychiatric hospitals. For some, release was a downward spiral from joblessness to homelessness, then drugs, violence, and a return to prison. In this study, 54 percent had reported problems with drugs or alcohol. Two-thirds had a history of mental illness, addiction, or both. One-third reported a medical disability.[6] Personal issues made it difficult to get and keep jobs, and without jobs, use of drugs and homelessness followed. What this research shows is that prison releasees have many needs, yet often have no resources to deal with the challenges of drug addiction, mental illness, joblessness, and homelessness. Violations of parole and/or new crimes are often the result, leading to reincarceration.[7]

Female releasees have, to some extent, special reentry challenges that are specific to their roles as wives and mothers. As noted in Chapter 10, female offenders often have histories of sexual and physical abuse. In fact, some say prison is safer for them than living on the outside. When they are released, there may be pressure to go back to an abusive domestic partner, especially if there is co-parenting involved. Another potential problem is when the abuser is a parent (e.g., father or stepfather) and the releasee must return to their parents' home as the only recourse for housing. Often, female releasees have issues of child custody and care.

They feel great pressure to regain custody of their children even though they may not be ready financially or emotionally. Alternatively, they may be in conflict with family services personnel or other family members when they want to reestablish their maternal role and the caregivers who have stepped in to take care of their children during the woman's imprisonment are not ready to give up custody. As noted in prior chapters, women also are more likely than male releasees to suffer from a range of mental health issues, primarily PTSD and depression.[8]

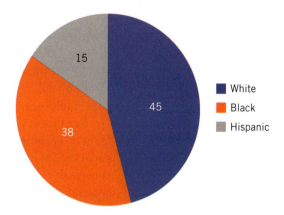

FIGURE 12.1 Parolees' race/ethnicity (percent). Created by author from D. Kaeble, "Probation and Parole in the United States, 2016" (Washington, DC: Bureau of Justice Statistics, OJP, 2018).

Parole

As noted, most offenders are released under either mandatory or discretionary parole. There were approximately 878,900 people on federal and state parole at the end of 2019, an increase of over 6 percent from 2009.[9] As you might expect, the parolee population reflects those who enter prison. Like prison populations, only a small percentage of parolees are women (12 percent). Figure 12.1 shows that the percentage of African Americans is very disproportionate to their percentage of the general population, and the Hispanic parolee population is slightly higher than their percentage of the general population. Figure 12.2 shows that violent offenders represent about a third of parolees.

History

Parole can be traced back to the punishment of **transportation**. In the 1700s, England sent prisoners to the colonies. Once they arrived, prisoners worked as indentured servants for landowners who paid the cost of the transport. They could earn their freedom eventually by paying back the cost of their transportation, generally this took about seven years. After the American Revolution, English prisoners were sent to Australia. In Australia, their labor was leased to the landowner and their liberty was controlled by the Crown. Transportation to Australia as punishment continued through the 1860s.[10]

Parole is usually traced back to Alexander Maconochie's (1787–1860) **mark system** on Norfolk Island, a prison colony 1000 miles off the coast of Australia. Maconochie devised a system of discipline at the prison whereby inmates could earn increasing responsibility through good behavior and meeting work production quotas. Eventually, the offender could live almost independently on the island. Another forerunner of our modern parole was Sir Walter Crofton's (1815–1897) Irish **ticket of leave**, implemented around 1853. Offenders were released early from prison as a final stage of responsibility earned through good behavior. The prisoner received his "ticket to leave" prison, returned to his community, and reported to police, who were supposed to help the offender find a job and monitor his progress. Maconochie's mark system was endorsed by the 1870 Prison Congress in the United States and included in the "Declaration of Principles" that emerged from that national conference on corrections.[11]

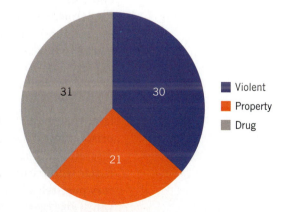

FIGURE 12.2 Parolees' crime of conviction (percent). Created by author from D. Kaeble, "Probation and Parole in the United States, 2016" (Washington, DC: Bureau of Justice Statistics, OJP, 2018).

Zebulon Brockway (1827–1920), who knew of Maconochie's ideas, implemented a type of mark system and an early form of parole at Elmira Reformatory in New York in 1877. Reformatory inmates, who were young men age 16 to 30, could earn their way to "first grade" and then be released to six months of supervision by volunteer guardians. Eventually, this type of supervision was done by paid employees.[12]

Gradually, throughout the late 1800s and early 1900s, states adopted some form of early release or parole, but these either did not include any concept of supervision, or supervision was provided haphazardly or by volunteers. In 1907, New York became the first state to implement parole that included paid employees and a mechanism to return ex-offenders to prison if they violated the law or terms of their parole. The federal system of parole was fully implemented by 1932. By 1942, all states had a parole system, although some continued to use volunteer parole officers.[13]

Today parole is usually a division under a state's department of corrections, but it can also be a separate agency or a variation of these two models.[14] In a few states, felony probation and parole are combined in one agency. In some states, the parole board is separate from the department of corrections, but parole officers and other employees are part of the corrections department. Parole board membership is usually by political appointment. Board members may have backgrounds in law enforcement, education, or counseling, or they may have no relevant background in corrections at all. Parole boards are usually composed of no more than 10 members. The appointment is typically a term lasting from three to six years; however, in some states, the appointment is indefinite. In addition to the power to grant parole, a parole board may, depending on the state, set parole decision dates, revoke parole, issue warrants and subpoenas, set conditions, restore offenders' civil rights, and grant final discharges. In some states, the parole board also makes recommendations to the governor about commutations and pardons. In some larger states, parole boards delegate some of their powers; for instance, hearing examiners rather than parole board members may conduct revocation hearings.

The Decision to Parole

Prisoners do not have a right to parole unless the state creates a right to it. Under state sentencing statutes, in those states that have parole, the inmate becomes eligible after serving some portion of their sentence; typically, when one-half or two-thirds of the sentence has been served, he or she is eligible to be considered for parole. Just because an inmate is eligible for parole does not mean that he or she will receive it. The parole board or paroling authority decides if an eligible inmate will be released.

In the 1970s, most inmates were released on parole. However, the use of parole declined dramatically in the 1980s and 1990s. The Violent Crime Control and Law Enforcement Act of 1994 pressured states to enact truth-in-sentencing laws that required that inmates spend larger percentages of their sentence in prison. Several states either instituted determinate sentencing and abolished discretionary parole entirely or dramatically reduced the number of eligible inmates who received it. Federal parole was abolished and replaced with mandatory post-release supervision under the *Comprehensive Crime Control Act of 1984*, which also created the U.S. Sentencing Commission.

Maine was the first state to abolish discretionary parole in 1976.[15] By 2002, 14 states had abolished discretionary parole (Arizona, Delaware, Illinois, Indiana, Kansas, Maine, Minnesota, Mississippi, New Mexico, North Carolina,

Parole officers check to see that parole conditions have been followed.

Ohio, Oregon, Virginia, Washington), and just 15 states still had full discretionary parole (Alabama, Colorado, Idaho, Kentucky, Montana, Nevada, New Jersey, North Dakota, Oklahoma, Pennsylvania, Rhode Island, South Carolina, Utah, Vermont, Wyoming).[16] The remaining 21 states allowed parole for only some types of prisoners. Most states that abolished parole have a form of mandatory supervision after release that is based on a percentage of time served and good time awarded. The offender is subject to revocation and return to prison until the full expiration of the original sentence.[17]

In *Greenholtz v. Nebraska,*[18] the U.S. Supreme Court held that inmates had no inherent liberty interest in parole; therefore, there was no due process required unless the state created such a right. States can create a right to parole by using language such as "an inmate *shall* be eligible for parole or receive parole," instead of "*may* be eligible or receive parole."[19] Because parole is only a statutory right, a state may eliminate parole by simply revising the law; and, as noted above, many states have done so eliminating discretionary parole. If, however, the state creates the right to parole through the language of a statute, then there must be due process in the decision procedure to award or not award parole. Recall from Chapter 9 that **due process** refers to procedural protections to eliminate bias or error in governmental decision-making when it involves a protected interest. For parole decisions, due process is satisfied by some type of hearing; generally, a panel of parole board members or parole examiners who evaluate file information. There may also be in-person hearings with the prisoners who are eligible for parole (although not all states have in-person hearings). Parole hearings have been criticized as too short and arbitrary, lasting an average of 12 to 15 minutes, but the requirements of due process are met if there is a fair decision-making process by a neutral entity. Court cases have also established that the state must also publicize clear release criteria and make it easily available to inmates. States must also advise inmates if there is any information in their institutional files that may lead to a denial of parole and allow them the opportunity to rebut such evidence.[20]

The board considers a variety of factors in their release decision, including the seriousness of the offense and the amount of time served, as well as

FIGURE 12.3 Percent of prison releases with no supervision. Created by author from J. Petersilia, "Meeting the Challenges of Prisoner Reentry," in *What Works and Why: Effective Approaches to Reentry* (Lanham, MD: American Correctional Association, 2005), 179; W. Sabol, H. West, and M. Cooper, *Prisoners in 2008* (Washington, DC: Bureau of Justice Statistics, 2009), 34; E. Carson, *Prisoners in 2014* (Washington DC: Bureau of Justice Statistics), 20; E. Carson, *Prisoners in 2016* (Washington DC: Bureau of Justice Statistics), 11.

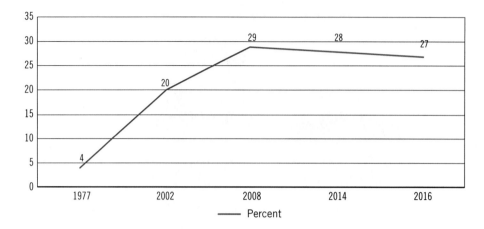

the offender's age, juvenile history, criminal history, number of prison infractions, other arrests, participation in programs, and letters of support or protest. Studies show that board members pay most attention to the severity of the crime in making the release decision, not what the offender has done in prison. Other factors that weigh in the decision include attitude toward family responsibilities, attitude toward authority, and attitude toward the victim.[21] Many states allow victim impact statements and letters from the district attorney to be read at the parole hearing. Research has found that when victims attend the hearing or send letters, offenders are less likely to receive parole.[22] Findings are mixed as to whether race or ethnicity affects the parole decision. An Alabama study found that race did not seem to affect the parole decision. However, a study in a different state found that Blacks spent a longer time in prison before being paroled than whites even when controlling for other factors that might have affected the decision. This study also found that Hispanics served a shorter time in prison than whites before being paroled, controlling for other factors.[23]

Figure 12.3 shows that the percentage of released prisoners who served their full term and were released unconditionally (with no parole) increased dramatically in the 1980s and 1990s. As noted above, in the 1970s, almost all prisoners were released under parole supervision; today, only about a third of prisoners serve their full term. The rate of parole (the ratio of offenders who receive parole to those who are eligible) fluctuates widely between states and sometimes within a state over different time periods or different regions.

Pardons and Commutations

The power to parole is different from the power to pardon convicted offenders. A pardon is basically a release and forgiveness of criminal culpability. This power rests in the executive power of the president and governors. Section 2 of the U.S. Constitution gives the president pardon power over federal crimes. Similar provisions exist in state constitutions for governors to pardon state crimes. In some states, the parole board is called the board of pardons and paroles because the board makes recommendations to the governor on pardons. It is important to note the differences between **clemency** (a temporary postponement of a punishment), **pardon** (deleting any culpability as well as any punishment that has been imposed), **amnesty** (immunity from prosecution), and **commutation** (reducing the punishment imposed). While a pardon is basically forgiveness and removes the conviction, a commutation or clemency is simply a reduction of sentence.

Recall from an earlier chapter that President Obama issued more commutations than any president in history. Most of the commutations were for drug offenders who were sentenced under harsh mandatory minimum sentencing laws. Over 24,000 offenders petitioned for clemency under the 2014 Clemency Initiative. Stated criteria for consideration included the following:

1. currently serving a federal sentence that likely would have received a substantially lower sentence if convicted of the same offense(s) today,

2. non-violent, low-level offenders without significant ties to large scale criminal organizations, gangs or cartels,

3. served at least 10 years of their prison sentence,

4. no significant criminal history,

5. demonstrated good conduct in prison, and

6. no history of violence prior to or during their current term of imprisonment.

Thousands of volunteer lawyers reviewed over 24,000 petitions and referred 2,600 applications to the DOJ and, ultimately, the president. The president commuted the sentences of 1,696 of those offenders. On average, inmates had their sentences reduced by about 40 percent, or 11 years. Men accounted for 94.0 percent of all clemency recipients. About 71 percent were Black, 19 percent were white, and about 9 percent were Hispanic. Most offenders were convicted of crack cocaine trafficking (61 percent). Crimes involving methamphetamine (17 percent), powder cocaine (15 percent), and marijuana trafficking (4 percent) were less common. Original sentences were, on average, over 28 years. About one-third of the commutations required that the prisoner enroll and attend drug treatment in the prison before release.[24] This commutation program was eliminated by the Trump administration. There are some indications that the Biden administration will enact a new commutation program for federal prisoners.

Issues in Parole Supervision

Probation and parole are often confused because they are so similar. Both involve supervision in the community. Both probationers and parolees must agree to abide by a set of rules (conditions) that limit their freedom. **Technical violations** in both probation and parole refer to rule violations not criminal acts; for example, not reporting or associating with a known criminal. Both probationers and parolees have general conditions, such as not to change residences without permission, and specific conditions, such as not opening a checking account (for someone who committed bank fraud) or passing a weekly urinalysis (for someone who has a drug problem). The difference between parole and probation lies in the fact that parolees have been in prison, but probationers are on community supervision instead of serving a prison sentence. In some states, parole officers have greater discretion to arrest and/or carry a weapon because the individuals they supervise are considered more dangerous. While both parole and probation officers have a duty to file violation reports, the decision to revoke parole lies with the parole board (or their appointed hearing examiner), and the decision to revoke probation lies with the sentencing judge.

In some states probation and parole are combined under one state agency; in many states, however, probation is a county agency, while parole is a state agency. Caseloads may be assigned to officers based on geography, classification level, or offender type, or assignment may be random. Parolees are, for the most part, localized in a few zip codes that are also typically marked by high crime, dysfunctional families, and poverty. Most often, parolees are classified according to a risk instrument that predicts the likelihood of recidivism. Those classified as high risk will likely be on an intensive supervision caseload, with parole officers having multiple contacts weekly with the parolee. Medium- and low-risk caseloads have more parolees assigned to each officer; as the risk level decreases, fewer contacts are required.

According to some sources, intensive supervision caseloads should exist at an officer-to-offender ratio of 1:20, moderate- to high-risk caseloads at 1:50, and low-risk caseloads at 1:200.[25] Past research has shown that having fewer parolees on a caseload has not necessarily resulted in better recidivism rates, possibly because increased supervision typically leads to identifying misbehavior and issuing technical violations. When lower caseloads and increased supervision are accompanied by increased rehabilitative programming, recidivism can be reduced. However, it has also been shown that, when evaluating the types of interactions between parole officers and parolees, most parole officers do not employ any evidence-based practices with parolees. Most contact is simply an office visit during which the parole officer checks to see that parole conditions have been followed. Generally, parole officers do not employ **motivational interviewing**, a counseling approach that is directive and goal oriented for eliciting behavior change, or undertake any other type of interaction aside from supervision of conditions.[26]

RELATIONSHIPS BETWEEN PAROLEES AND PAROLE OFFICERS

Research on parole officers has found that they, like probation officers, perform their role based on their personal emphasis of supervision or treatment. Those who have a law enforcement orientation see their role as primarily to supervise and issue violation reports if the parolee violates any of the conditions of parole. Other parole officers have an expanded sense of their role that includes taking on duties related to helping the parolee adapt to freedom. For instance, they may act as an advocate and referral agent to get needed services for parolees. Parole officers also differ in their flexibility about the rules, with some allowing parolees to commit minor violations and others filing violation reports immediately for similar behavior. Officers with an orientation that leans toward authoritarianism are more likely to pursue revocation when parolees violate any conditions.[27] These orientations are also influenced by office norms, with some offices leaning more toward treatment and others emphasizing monitoring parolees and filing violation reports.

There is growing evidence that the relationship between the parole officer and parolee mediates the risk of recidivism. In some research, parolees described how characteristics of trust, respect, flexibility, and understanding on the part of the parole officer led to success on parole.[28] In other research, parole officers who were described as "therapeutic" or "collaborative" received higher ratings from parolees, and parolees who described their parole officers as having these qualities were less likely to violate the terms of their parole. In past studies that measured parolees' perceptions of their parole officers, three elements of the relationship were identified: caring and fairness, trust, and toughness. The caring and fairness measure was negatively correlated with rearrest (meaning that as the parolees' perception of the caring and fairness of their parole officer increased, the likelihood of rearrest went down).[29] These studies are important because if the relationship with the parole officer affects the likelihood of rearrest, then improving parole officer training seems to be a way to improve recidivism. There is a great deal of research to show how a well-trained and empathic professional can influence correctional clients.[30]

LIABILITY OF PAROLE OFFICERS

The extent of civil liability for parole professionals is based on what role they are performing. Parole board members have quasi-judicial immunity, like that held by judges when they make sentencing decisions, or probation officers when they make sentencing recommendations. Thus, if parole board members decide to parole someone, they cannot be sued even if the parolee murders or victimizes others. This is because courts protect those who make discretionary decisions so that they are not afraid to make a mistake.

On the other hand, parole officers who supervise a caseload may be liable if, acting in the course and duty of employment, they violate an offender's constitutional rights. Parole agents do have qualified immunity, meaning that if they perform their duties in good faith that they are acting within the law, they will be protected if their actions are later deemed unconstitutional. Parole officers are sometimes sued under Title 42, United States Code, § 1983. This is a civil action that can be taken against an agent of the government when someone's constitutional rights are violated. It reads as follows:

> Every person who, under color of any statute, ordinance, regulation, custom, or usage, of any State or Territory or the District of Columbia, subjects, or causes to be subjected, any citizen of the United States or other person within the jurisdiction thereof to the deprivation of any rights, privileges, or immunities secured by the Constitution and laws, shall be liable to the party injured in action at law, suit in equity, or other proper proceeding for redress, except that in any action brought against a judicial officer for an act or omission taken in such officer's judicial capacity, injunctive relief shall not be granted unless a declaratory decree was violated or declaratory relief was unavailable.

In *Monroe v. Pape* (1961), the United States Supreme Court ruled that §1983 could be applied to police officers who violated someone's Fourth Amendment rights. Since then, it has been used to challenge many different kinds of violations of constitutional rights by state and local agents of government.[31] Some of the actions of parole officers (and probation officers) that have been subject to court challenges include the following: conspiring with another to wrongfully confine a parolee as a parole violator, arbitrary denial of a furlough or work release, denial of the right to a parole revocation hearing, compelling a probationer to attend faith-based treatment programs for substance abuse, and improper disclosure of a probationer's health status as HIV-positive.[32] It is important to note that parole officers are held liable only if they would reasonably be expected to know that their actions create a violation of constitutional rights. In unsettled areas of law, they would not be presumed to know, and, therefore, would be immune from liability even if the case results in a finding of a constitutional violation.

Generally, there is no liability on the part of parole officers for failing to protect a member of the public if the parolee hurts someone. This protection from liability stems from the "**public duty doctrine**," referring to the idea that government functions are owed to the general public but not to specific individuals. A similar idea protects child welfare workers from liability if a child in their care is injured by a foster parent, unless the childcare worker was grossly negligent. Parole officers who are grossly negligent may be found liable in civil actions if their carelessness or deficient performance in supervision results in loss or injury to a third party. They are not liable if it is found that their actions were in substantial compliance with the directives of superiors and regulatory procedures. In some cases, there is a "special relationship" that creates a duty on the part of the parole officer, and in that case, parole officers may be liable if they do not protect the person. For instance, parole officers have been held liable for failure to warn employers about a parolee's violent background when the parole agent recommended the parolee be hired and there was a subsequent attack.[33]

Liability can also arise when the parole officer carries and uses a firearm. State laws differ on whether they permit or require parole officers to carry weapons. Some states allow the practice solely for self-defense; in other states, parole officers are peace officers with full powers of arrest and can carry a firearm to carry out their duties. In either case, to avoid liability, there should be proper training similar to that of police officers, certification after showing proficiency, and clear policies on use in place.[34]

Halfway Houses

Some prison releasees are housed in halfway houses to ease their transition into the community. There are different models of halfway houses. They can be large institutions, or small ones with only 20 or fewer residents. They can be publicly run, or they can be privately run with contracts to provide housing and services for ex-offenders. They can target a specific group of ex-offenders (e.g., drug abusers), or they can be available for anyone leaving prison. Some states have many halfway house beds, and other states use them infrequently. In all cases, halfway house staff, like probation and parole officers, must balance the rights of offenders against the safety concerns of the community. In some states, pressure to reduce prison populations has resulted in more halfway house beds because prisoners are released sooner with the expectation that they will be more closely supervised in a halfway house than they would have been on regular parole.

While placement in a halfway house can be an important first step in transitioning to the outside, and an important option for those who have nowhere to go, troubling scandals in halfway houses illustrate similar problems to those described regarding private prisons. When there is a financial incentive to provide less-than-adequate services, for-profit companies have been known to cut corners by understaffing and not providing needed programming. In some well publicized scandals, evidence indicated unacceptable levels of drugs, gang activity, violence, and even sexual assault in these facilities. Further, there were virtually no true treatment programs offered. In scandals in New York, New Jersey, and Pennsylvania, the owners and top administrators of the non-profit companies that ran the halfway houses also owned or were employed by the for-profit companies who received contracts for services within the halfway houses (e.g., cleaning or treatment services). These schemes are specifically prohibited by state law because of the potential for fraud.[35] In a related scandal, so-called "sober houses," which purported to be both housing and treatment programs in New York City, were found to be poorly managed, with decrepit and dangerous conditions. Individuals were pressured to stay in treatment as a condition of their residency, and owners received both housing allowances and Medicaid money for each resident that entered treatment. Business was very lucrative, especially if owners put the minimum amount of money into housing and treatment. For prison releasees, however, sometimes these were the only places that they could find to live.[36]

Halfway houses are less expensive to run than prisons; thus, states and the federal government can save money by shortening prison sentences if there are adequate halfway house placements available.[37] There has been some research to indicate that placement in a halfway house contributes to lower recidivism rates, especially if there is a work release/job placement element to the halfway house.[38]

There have been some studies that compare private versus public community correctional residential facilities. About three out of five of these facilities for adults are operated by private companies, and about a third of juvenile residential facilities are private.[39] One study found that the odds of recidivism for an offender housed in a private agency were more than four times that of offenders in a state-run facility. State facilities were found to have better security protocols, more professional and rehabilitation-oriented managers, and better overall conditions than the private community corrections facilities. The authors also reported that the costs of the state and private community correctional facilities were comparable.[40] Clearly, states that do not monitor the quality of private facilities run the risk of scandal and misuse of funds. One of the changes that has taken place is that states may now require a baseline recidivism rate of releasees from halfway houses.[41] However, just as there is a profit motive in keeping someone under supervision if there is a per diem to be earned, there will be a perverse incentive to not find violations if there is a financial incentive to report low rates.

Recidivism and Successful Offenders

As we discussed in Chapter 1, **recidivism** is measured in different ways, including rearrest, reconviction, or any violation of conditions of probation or parole. It should be noted that none of these can be counted at all if misconduct or criminal acts are not detected by officials. The most cited statistics on recidivism come from the Bureau of Justice Statistics (BJS), a part of the Office of Justice Programs in the United States Department of Justice. In a large national study of prisoners released in 1994 and followed for three years, it was reported that 68 percent were rearrested sometime during that three-year period, and about half were sent back to prison.[42] Other studies have also shown that over two-thirds of released inmates recidivate (67.8 percent) within three years, and over three-quarters (76.6%) recidivate within five years. Property offenders are more likely to recidivate than violent offenders, and younger offenders are more likely to recidivate than older offenders.[43] In one study, researchers investigated the recidivism of released prisoners for nine years (2005–2014). They found that 83 percent of state prisoners released in 2005 across 30 states were arrested at least once in the 9 years following their release. It is important to remember that an arrest does not necessarily mean a conviction or even that the individual is guilty of any crime and parolees are more likely to fall under suspicion than those without a criminal record. About 44 percent of prisoners were arrested at least once during their first year of release. Consistent with prior research, the first post-release arrests occurred most frequently during the first three years after release.[44]

One study found that almost half of federal prisoner releasees were rearrested for a new crime or violation of conditions during the eight years after release. About a third were convicted of a new crime, and a quarter were reincarcerated. Most recidivated within two years of release. The most frequent new charge was assault. While about 30 percent of those without a prior criminal history were rearrested, over 80 percent of those with the longest criminal histories were rearrested. Those who were younger than 21 at the time of release had the highest rearrest rate (67.6 percent), while offenders over 60 years old at the time of release had a recidivism rate of 16 percent.[45]

Taken altogether, recidivism studies' findings show a range of 50 to 80 percent within the first three to eight years after release, depending on the demographic group. Younger offenders, those with long criminal histories, those with prior probation violations, those with higher numbers of prison disciplinary infractions, and males had higher rates of recidivism in these studies.[46] A study of reentry programs found that across a broad range of program modalities, the average reduction of recidivism for all programs was only 6 percent. That is, only about 6 percent fewer inmates recidivated after completing a reentry program than those who were in a control group.[47]

In most recidivism studies, researchers gather information about a cohort of prisoners released from prison in a certain year, and then follow this group to see how many commit new crimes. One study approached recidivism in a different way. These researchers examined prisoners in an admission-to-prison sample cohort and tracked them for 15 years. Using national corrections data over a 13-year period covering 17 states, these researchers found that two out of three offenders in their admission cohort never returned to prison and only 11 percent came back multiple times. Why are these numbers so much lower than the recidivism numbers described from earlier studies? The answer lies in the way the data is collected. The most common methodology in recidivism studies is to examine a specific sample cohort *released* from prison in any given year. By using this cross-sectional approach, one is likely to include recidivistic offenders who keep coming back to prison, thus increasing the rate of recidivism. By examining a sample of prisoners who are *admitted* to prison and tracking them over their prison term and release, the problem of chronic offenders who are most likely to recidivate, biasing the sample, is eliminated. To get a true picture of the correctional population, you need to consider a cohort of prison admissions and follow them from their entry into prison until years after release to see how many recidivate. These recidivism rates are much lower.[48]

Prisoners are revoked and return to prison for new crimes, but also sometimes for technical violations that are not criminal acts. Parole revocations have always made up some portion of new admissions to prison. In 1980, about 20 percent of admissions to prison were parolees who had their parole revoked; but, in 2001, about 40 percent of all prison admissions were individuals returning to prison after parole revocations. Then the pattern shifted again and began to decline; in 2008, about 33 percent of prison admissions were parole revocations, and in 2017, that figure dropped to about 27 percent.[49] This is still a large number, however, and it is important to remember that these parolees may not have committed a new crime but rather a rule violation. The cost to incarcerate these people is more than nine billion dollars a year![50]

Completion rates (the number of parolees who complete their term of parole and regain full liberty) vary between states. In Massachusetts about 78 percent of parolees exit through successful completion of parole, but in New Hampshire only 46 percent of exits are successful discharges; the rest are revocations, exits through **absconding** (the parolee doesn't report and cannot be located), or other unsuccessful exits.[51] Figure 12.4 shows the number of exits from parole and the number of exits that were successful completions.

Technical violations or even minor new crimes do not necessarily have to result in revocation and

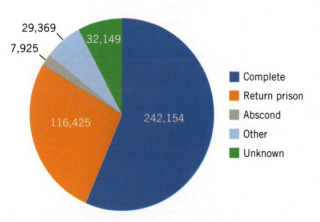

29,369
7,925
32,149
116,425
242,154

- ■ Complete
- ■ Return prison
- ■ Abscond
- ■ Other
- ■ Unknown

FIGURE 12.4 Exits from parole, 2016. Created by author from D. Kaeble, "Probation and Parole in the United States, 2016" (Washington, DC: Bureau of Justice Statistics, OJP, 2018).

return to prison. One practice that can reduce the number of parolees who are returned to prison is the use of **graduated sanctions**. These are sanctions for violating the conditions of parole other than a return to prison. For example, a response to failing a urinalysis might be placing the parolee in a residential drug program; technical violations might result in a curfew and more frequent check-ins with the parole officer; and failing to report might result in the parolee having to pay for electronic monitoring for some period. The idea is that using a more targeted and graduated sanction can help the parolee stay in the community but still protect public safety.

Recidivism Factors

Decades of research on recidivism have consistently found that those with longer criminal histories are more likely to recidivate than first-time offenders, younger offenders are more likely to recidivate than older offenders, property offenders are more likely to recidivate than violent offenders, men are more likely to recidivate than women, and minorities are more likely to recidivate than whites. However, more recently, some of those findings are being called into question.

Both prior and recent research indicates that those who were imprisoned for property offenses are more likely to recidivate than those who were imprisoned for violent offenses. Violent offenders spend more time in prison, so their lower rates of recidivism could be a function of the fact that they are older when they are released.[52] Research has consistently shown that older releasees are less likely to recidivate than younger releasees.[53] In the most recent BJS study, those who were older at the time of their crime of conviction were less likely to recidivate. While 90 percent of those who were 24 or younger when they were sentenced to prison were arrested at some point in the 9 years following release, 77 percent of those who were 40 or older were rearrested.[54]

Older research had indicated that males were more likely than females to recidivate, but newer research seems to show smaller differences in the likelihood of recidivism. In the BJS study of recidivism that followed releasees for nine years, 84 percent of male prisoners were arrested, and 77 percent of female prisoners were arrested.[55]

In the BJS study, a smaller percentage of white prisoners than Black or Hispanic prisoners recidivated during the first year after release: 40 percent of white prisoners, compared to 47 percent of Hispanic and 46 percent of Black prisoners, were arrested. Differences between the racial/ethnic groups declined, however, after the first year. During the nine-year follow-up period, 87 percent of Black prisoners and 81 percent of white and Hispanic prisoners were arrested.[56]

Other factors associated with recidivism include drug use, family situation, and participation in programming. One study, for instance, found that female parolees who participated in employment and drug treatment programming were significantly less likely to recidivate. Those who were least likely to recidivate included older women, minorities, those with few or no children, and those who had committed a personal offense with a low number of prior arrests.[57]

A slightly different question from whether a prison sentence deters future criminal behavior is whether longer sentences deter more effectively than shorter sentences. The evidence is mixed. One study of federal prisoners who were sentenced under federal guidelines found that lengthening a prison term within a guideline range that amounted to about seven months reduced the likelihood of recidivism by a very small amount (about 1 percent).[58] Another study found that short sentences (under a year) were likely to result in increased recidivism, sentences of one to two years decreased recidivism, and longer sentences had no measurable effect on recidivism.[59]

FOCUS ON A

STATE OHIO

According to state sources, there were 49,512 Ohio prison inmates in January 2018, more than triple the number from 1980. Only 13 states have a higher incarceration rate. The share of admissions who are sent to prison after a revocation of probation or parole has increased. Like many states, Ohio's Department of Rehabilitation and Correction (DRC) uses a recidivism risk prediction instrument: the Ohio Risk Assessment System (ORAS). In addition to predicting risk, ORAS can be used to generate case plans that prioritize needs and suggest treatment goals. ORAS scores offenders into recidivism risk groups; identifies dynamic risk factors that can be addressed through programming; and identifies potential barriers to treatment such as intelligence, reading ability, transportation issues, treatment motivation, and language barriers. Five assessment instruments were created that corresponded to the decision points in the justice system: the Pretrial Assessment Tool (PAT), the Community Supervision Tool (CST), the Community Supervision Screening Tool (CSST), the Prison Intake Tool (PIT), and the Reentry Tool (RT). Each tool scores differently for risk, and male and female offenders have different risk cut-off scores for each risk level of high, medium, and low.

Correctional practitioners use a combination of structured interviews, official records, an interview guide, an offender self-report questionnaire, and collateral sources (e.g., police records to verify the self-report responses) to complete the ORAS assessment tools. The benefits of the ORAS system are that it

- provides reliable assessment instruments with consistent meaning;
- reduces duplication and enhances communication and sharing of information;
- gathers information regarding potential barriers to treatment;
- creates a system that expands as the offender moves through different processing stages;
- involves fully automated tools with potential for auto-population to other IT systems;
- provides thorough and useful information to aid in informed decision-making;
- allows for professional discretion and overrides;
- assists in more efficient allocation of supervision and treatment resources;
- generates case plans that identify and prioritize individual offender needs and specific treatment domains; and
- predicts likelihood of rearrest and recidivism at different points in the criminal justice system.

Ohio is not the only state that uses its own risk prediction instrument developed specifically for the state. At least 17 privately developed instruments and over 40 state-specific instruments exist. The unique aspect of ORAS is the comprehensiveness of the system across all levels of corrections in Ohio.

Discussion Questions

1. **What are some problems with using prediction tools when evaluating the decision to release inmates?**

2. **Is there an advantage in having an integrated system that follows an inmate through**

various stages of corrections—for example, probation, prison, and parole? Are there disadvantages?

Sources: S. Desmarais and J. Singh, Risk Assessment Instruments Validated and Implemented in Correctional Settings in the United States *(New York: Council of State Governments Justice Center, 27 March 27, 2013), , retrieved August 29, 2021, https://csgjusticecenter.org/publications/risk-assessment-instruments-validated-and-implemented-in-correctional-settings-in-the-united-states/.*

D. Hutcherson and A. Hanauer, "Issue 1: Reducing Incarceration, Improving Communities," Policy Matters Ohio, https://www.policymattersohio.org/research-policy/quality-ohio/corrections/issue-1-reducing-incarceration-improving-communities.

E. Latessa, L. Lovins, and P. Smith, "Final Report: Follow-up Evaluation of Ohio's Community Based Correctional Facility and Halfway House Programs—Outcome Study (University of Cincinnati, February 2010), https://www.uc.edu/content/dam/uc/ccjr/docs/reports/project_reports/2010%20HWH%20Executive%20Summary.pdf.

E. Latessa, R. Lemke, M. Makarios, P. Smith, and C. Lowenkamp, "The Creation and Validation of the Ohio Risk Assessment System (ORAS)," Federal Probation 74, 1 (2010): 1–10. Ohio Department of Rehabilitation and Corrections, https://drc.ohio.gov/oras.

The challenge of predicting who will recidivate has led to the risk assessment instruments discussed in Chapter 11. Some states have their own risk assessment instruments designed to predict who is most likely to fail on release. The Focus on a State box describes Ohio's instrument.

Reducing Recidivism

Some states have reported reductions in their recidivism rates of as much as 19 percent.[60] Explanations for these reductions include greater use of risk prediction instruments, evidence-based programming, and greater community resources for parolees. The reductions may also indicate that states are less likely to revoke parole and return parolees to prison, and that they are more likely to use graduated sanctions or work with the parolee in the community to address problems.

Desistance is the term used to indicate when a person does not commit further criminal acts and exhibits signs of a prosocial lifestyle. What are the elements of a correctional success? One study reported on the importance of family support. The extent of self-reported illegal activities was significantly different for those who perceived family support versus those who did not (16 versus 23 percent). Interestingly, emotional support was significantly related to success, but instrumental support was not. Instrumental support included such things as providing a place to live or transportation, while emotional support was measured by positive agreement to such statements as "I feel close to my family" and "I have someone in my family who understands my problems." Researchers noted that the findings are supported by criminological theories that point to family bonds as informal social control.[61] Family support for prison releasees can promote desistance; however, family conflict can spur re-offending. It has also been found that female releasees are less likely to benefit from marriage than male releasees, and that women who have drug-using romantic partners are more likely to reoffend.[62]

Research has shown that, in addition to family emotional support, desistance seems to be related to entry into the military, employment, relocation, and community engagement. The key seems to be the development of a prosocial identity to replace the criminal identity that inevitably leads to criminal choices.[63] Consider whether this can be done with offenders as described in the Focus on the Offender box.

Another study of post-release offenders over 10 years found that desistance was associated with pragmatic factors (housing, employment, finances, and alcohol/drug addiction). It was also associated with subjective factors, such as perceived stigma, perceived prejudice, hope, and identity as a good partner/parent.[64]

Based on what we know about recidivism and correctional intervention, some of the approaches that could assist in increasing the number of successful releasees are as follows:

- Use risk prediction instruments to establish risk classifications and supervision levels.
- Use graduated sanctions rather than revocation whenever possible.
- Address challenges and needs as identified by the ex-offenders as problematic; for example, housing and employment.
- Encourage the use of early release from parole to reduce the strain of unrealistic conditions and the financial burden of supervision fees.
- Focus programming on moderate- and high-risk offenders in their first year or two of release because that is when failure is likely to occur.
- Increase programming that supports family integration and supportive relationships.

OFFENDER

MARTIN PANG: WAS JUSTICE SERVED?

Martin Pang, 62, was due to be released from prison in September of 2018 after serving 23 years for manslaughter. Back in 1995, he set fire to his parents' frozen food warehouse in a scheme to get the insurance money for himself. The fire resulted in the deaths of four Seattle firefighters—Lt. Walter Kilgore, 45; Lt. Gregory Shoemaker, 43; Randall Terlicker, 35; and James Brown, 25. Pang fled to Brazil, which would not extradite him to the United States. Finally, after three years of legal wrangling, the prosecutor made a deal with Pang to voluntarily return in exchange for being charged with manslaughter instead of felony murder. In 1998, he was convicted of four counts of manslaughter and received a 35-year sentence, but Washington's sentencing statute in place at the time allowed for early release based on prison "good time" (time off the sentence for good behavior).

The Department of Corrections stated that he had had no prison infractions since 2013. In that year, he was found to have engineered an identity-fraud scheme using the birth dates and Social Security numbers of fire and police personnel who had testified at his trial. He had obtained these using personal information from training records that were included in discovery materials as part of his manslaughter case. He lost his "good time" and was transferred to a more secure prison after his scheme was foiled.

At the time of his initial crime, Pang was described as a violent, spoiled young man who chafed at not getting enough money from his wealthy adoptive parents. He was an aspiring actor and a failed businessman. Ex-wives and girlfriends described how he used threats of arson to intimidate people and had threatened to burn down the warehouse before actually doing so.

He owes nearly $3 million in restitution, other legal costs, and interest; however, by all accounts, he is broke and will leave prison with just $40 and his personal possessions. Because he "maxed out," he will not be supervised by parole officers.[65]

Questions for Discussion

1. Do you think Pang's sentence was just, considering he didn't mean to kill, but acted without regard for the risk to firefighters?
2. Do you think he will be arrested again? Why or why not?
3. Pang is an unusual offender in that he was upper middle class; however, given how he was described by those who knew him, do you think he could have benefited from prison programs? Explain.
4. What elements would be necessary for Pang to be successful on parole?

Future Directions in Corrections

In this last section, we first identify potential challenges and important trends in the future of corrections. Then, we will incorporate international sources to identify some of the innovative approaches taken elsewhere. We will also provide an international perspective on the fundamental rights of all prisoners.

Trends and Challenges

Since the mid-1990s, patterns of imprisonment have not reflected the dramatic decrease in crime rates. The continued challenge of providing correctional services to ever-increasing numbers of people affects everything that happens in corrections. Only in the last several years have those numbers plateaued or decreased in some states. The challenges and changes taking place in corrections are briefly discussed below.

1. Population and Costs. Even though the prisoner population has plateaued, the 6.3 million people under correctional supervision in this country still absorb an enormous portion of limited governmental resources. The cost of housing and/or supervising these individuals eclipses the amount spent on treatment, and the cost of corrections continues to rise. It is estimated that corrections consume one dollar of every 15 dollars of state funds; however, it is difficult to determine the true costs of corrections.[66] Prison costs vary tremendously from state to state, and even within a state, maximum-security institutions cost more than minimum-security, and special-needs offenders cost more to house and care for than regular inmates. Intensive probation or parole costs much more than regular supervision, and probation and parole supervision that includes electronic monitoring and/or GPS tracking is also more expensive. Cost estimates range widely in accuracy, and it is difficult to find consistency among sources.

The Bureau of Justice Statistics reported that the total costs for all justice expenditures (not just corrections) between 1986 and 2006 increased by 301 percent from $54 billion to $214 billion. These increases are after the costs were adjusted for inflation.[67] According to another source, over the past 20 years, state spending on corrections alone has skyrocketed—from $12 billion in 1988 to more than $52 billion in 2011.[68]

In a 2010 study by the Vera Institute involving 40 states, the total taxpayer cost ranged from a low of $76 million in Maine to a high of well over $3 billion in New York and Texas. The total cost to taxpayers for these 40 states in 2010 was $39 billion, $5.4 billion more than the $33.5 billion reflected in corrections budgets alone.[69] A more recent source estimates that in 2017, total operational costs for state and federal corrections was around $81 billion.[70] Even if the total cost is in dispute, there is no doubt that it is crippling state budgets and removing the ability of states to respond to needs in other areas such as education.

2. Older prisoners. Because of the mandatory minimum sentencing and habitual felon laws, an increasing percentage of the prisoner population can be characterized as geriatric, with all the attendant problems of that population. Medical costs are expected to soar. The architecture and practices of some prisons do not easily accommodate the mobility problems and cognitive issues typical of an older population. Prison systems, especially those with larger prisoner populations, will need to respond to this challenge by building and remodeling or revising sentencing patterns to allow release. This challenge was exacerbated in 2020 because of the COVID pandemic. Elderly prisoners were most at risk, and many states undertook drastic measures to reduce prison populations to alleviate the potential of transmission.

3. Poverty penalty and private corrections. The practice, begun in the late 1980s and early 1990s, of transferring some of the costs of corrections onto offenders through supervision fees may have been well intentioned; however, it has created perverse incentives. Now, private companies boast about increased profits for their shareholders because of an expected increase in prisoners, and states have no pressure to reduce jail populations because those in jail are paying for many of the costs. These practices vary widely from state to state, and many states are currently re-examining their practices of charging offenders and their families for supervision costs.

4. Drug treatment and Opiate Epidemic. Clearly, the opiate addiction crisis has shown that drug addiction is not just a problem of the poor, nor does it exist solely within the criminal population. What is important to note, however, is that one's financial resources generally indicate whether medically supervised drug addiction services or a jail or prison cell is the response. Drug treatment works best when it is provided early, is comprehensive and residential, and includes aftercare. There are not enough drug treatment beds in the community, and some individuals must become offenders before they are able to access treatment.

5. Gender-specific programs. It is important to consider the problems of both male and female offenders, but female offenders have gained special attention because they have been neglected and their needs are somewhat different from those of male offenders. Even though they still represent a small percentage of offenders (roughly 7 percent of prison populations), their numbers are increasing and may continue to increase unless programming responds to their needs.

International Solutions

Considering the above challenges and other future issues, it is important to be open to new ideas; thus, turning our focus to international correctional innovations is helpful. For instance, in New Zealand, a new high-security facility in Auckland is run by a private correctional company, but the difference from the U.S. system is that they have a financial incentive to make sure people do not return to prison. As has been discussed previously, it is generally not in the interest of private corrections firms to reduce the prisoner population. This creates a perverse incentive to encourage lawmakers to put more people in prison and keep them there longer. The Auckland South Correctional Facility, known as Wiri, is the largest privately run prison in New Zealand. The contract is set up as a payment-by-results, which links payments to outcomes. Expected outcomes include a 10 percent reduction in the rate of recidivism. If Wiri outperforms state facilities, the private entity will receive incentive payments. Incidents such as riots, inmate deaths, or escapes results in a financial penalty. The government of New Zealand estimates that this payment structure will save NZD $170 million (about USD $123 million) over the 25-year life of the contract.

A somewhat similar concept is exemplified by **social impact bonds**, which have been used in the United States. These pay investors in a correctional enterprise only if the desired social outcomes are achieved. This financial model of correctional intervention has investors paying for the initial cost of a new correctional program. If it meets outcome goals, then the city or state pays incentive rewards on the money invested. This encourages innovation but puts the risk on private investors rather than taxpayers. The best-known example of correctional programming by social impact bonds was a Rikers Island, New York, program for incarcerated youth, known as the New York City Adolescent Behavioral Learning Experience (ABLE) Project for Incarcerated Youth. Unfortunately, ABLE did not meet initial targets for outcomes, and no outcomes-based payment were paid to investors. Even though this particular program did not show the outcomes desired, the financial model of investors being involved in designing and managing correctional innovations has some promise.[71] Currently, however, there is nothing in the United States that rivals the ambitiousness of the Wiri model. As of 2019, there were three private prisons in Australia that had financial incentives based on recidivism rates built into the contract; however, in all cases, the potential value of the incentives was small compared to the total revenue of the prison contract[72]

German prisons have been showcased as a better model than those in the United States. Prison is reserved for murderers, rapists, and career criminals; low-level offenders get fines or probation. Prisons are small, and over 75 percent of prisoners are paroled within 20 years or less. Prisoners can earn weekend leave with good behavior. German prisons have little violence, and prisoners have keys to their rooms (not cells), private bathrooms, and good food. Germans call it "normalization," which refers to the idea that prisons should be as similar to outside life as possible. Correctional officers are well paid and highly trained—they spend two years learning psychology, communication skills, and conflict management. They take a very low-key approach to supervision, and the result is that prisoners think highly of them, calling them "calm down" experts. Psychologists assess new inmates and create personalized prison plans, including recommendations for counseling, classes, vocational training, and work. Inmates who follow the plan earn greater freedoms and early release. German crime rates are lower, and recidivism rates are half those of the United States. Study groups of politicians and correctional leaders have toured German prisons and come away with confidence that, even though the two countries are different, some of the elements of the vastly different German approach to corrections could be successful in the United States.[73]

Scandinavian prisons have long been touted as more humane and effective than prisons in the United States. Periodically, U.S. professionals visit Norway, Sweden, and other countries and make comparisons. The main difference in those countries is that prisons are used very seldom, usually only for violent or habitual criminals. Prisoners have more autonomy, correctional workers are given more training, and there is a committed goal of the offender being prepared for release. Recidivism is also lower upon release. It is important to identify whether any of the components of these international prison systems could be adapted to prisons in the United States.[74] Indeed, the question of how to build and run a humane and effective justice and corrections system is shared by many countries around the globe, and various international committees have provided blueprints or guidance in this matter, such as the International Red Cross.[75]

International Human Rights and Prisoners

Prisons around the world are quite different from those in the United States. Some can be considered better and more effective; some are decidedly worse. The United Nations has promulgated guidelines for all countries regarding how prisoners should be treated based on fundamental human rights. The United Nations Commission on Crime Prevention and Criminal Justice drafted revisions to 60-year-old international standards on treatment of prisoners in May 2015. They were adopted and published by the UN General Assembly and called the Mandela Rules in honor of Nelson Mandela, who spent 27 years in a South African prison for his role in challenging apartheid. These 144 rules cover all aspects of imprisonment including due process, accommodations, programming, visitation, and discipline. They also distinguish between prisoners who have been convicted versus those who have not or who are being held for debt.

There are aspects of U.S. imprisonment that are in violation of the Mandela Rules. For instance, the rules call for keeping people who have not been convicted of a crime separate from those who have been convicted, but U.S. jails routinely house these groups together. The Rules call for at least one hour of suitable exercise in the open air daily, but in some supermax prisons, inmates may not receive this. Other rules call for free healthcare services and judicial review of disciplinary sanctions, yet some states charge prisoners for healthcare and, as Chapter 9 explains, disciplinary procedures are conducted by prison staff. The Rules also call for an end to prolonged solitary confinement, which still exists in the United States. Several problematic rules relate to the treatment of female prisoners, stating that a prison for women should be run by a woman and its staff should be women, but as described in Chapter 10, close to half of the staff in some women's prisons are men. Further, searches are supposed to be conducted by same-sex guards, but pat-downs are routinely conducted by opposite-sex guards. Headings and excerpts of the Mandela Rules are presented in the following.

Excerpts and Headings of the UN Standard Minimum Rules for the Treatment of Prisoners
(Nelson Mandela Rules)

BASIC PRINCIPLES

All prisoners shall be treated with the respect due to their inherent dignity and value as human beings.

No prisoner shall be subjected to, and all prisoners shall be protected from, torture and other cruel, inhuman or degrading treatment or punishment.

The present rules shall be applied impartially [with] no discrimination.

[T]he period of imprisonment is used to ensure, so far as possible, the reintegration of such persons into society upon release so that they can lead a law-abiding and self-supporting life.

[P]rison administrations and other competent authorities should offer education, vocational training and work, as well as other forms of assistance that are appropriate and available, including those of a remedial, moral, spiritual, social and health- and sports-based nature.

[P]risoners with physical, mental or other disabilities have full and effective access to prison life on an equitable basis.

Prisoner file management

There shall be a standardized [confidential] prisoner file management system in every place where persons are imprisoned, [including his or her history, legal processing decisions, disciplinary record, medical history, and other information].

Men and women shall so far as possible be detained in separate institutions; . . . Untried prisoners shall be kept separate from convicted prisoners; . . . Persons imprisoned for debt and other civil prisoners shall be kept separate from persons imprisoned by reason of a criminal offence; . . . Young prisoners shall be kept separate from adults.

Accommodation

Where sleeping accommodation is in individual cells or rooms, each prisoner shall occupy by night a cell or room by himself or herself. . . . Where dormitories are used, they shall be occupied by prisoners carefully selected as being suitable to associate with one another in those conditions. There shall be regular supervision by night, in keeping with the nature of the prison.

All accommodation provided for the use of prisoners and in particular all sleeping accommodation shall meet all requirements of health, due regard being paid to climatic conditions and particularly to cubic content of air, minimum floor space, lighting, heating and ventilation.

[Various specific rules related to windows, lighting, heating, minimum floor space, etc.]

Personal hygiene

Prisoners shall be required to keep their persons clean, and to this end they shall be provided with water and with such toilet articles as are necessary for health and cleanliness.

Clothing and bedding

Every prisoner who is not allowed to wear his or her own clothing shall be provided with an outfit of clothing suitable for the climate and adequate to keep him or her in good health. Such clothing shall in no manner be degrading or humiliating.

Food

Every prisoner shall be provided by the prison administration at the usual hours with food of nutritional value adequate for health and strength, of wholesome quality and well prepared and served.

Exercise and sport

Every prisoner who is not employed in outdoor work shall have at least one hour of suitable exercise in the open air daily if the weather permits.

Health-care services

Prisoners should enjoy the same standards of health care that are available in the community, and should have access to necessary health-care services free of charge without discrimination on the grounds of their legal status.

The health-care service shall prepare and maintain accurate, up-to-date and confidential individual medical files on all prisoners, and all prisoners should be granted access to their files upon request. A prisoner may appoint a third party to access his or her medical file.

Clinical decisions may only be taken by the responsible health-care professionals and may not be overruled or ignored by non-medical prison staff.

In women's prisons, there shall be special accommodation for all necessary prenatal and postnatal care and treatment. Arrangements shall be made wherever practicable for children to be born in a hospital outside the prison. If a child is born in prison, this fact shall not be mentioned in the birth certificate.

An absolute prohibition on engaging, actively or passively, in acts that may constitute torture or other cruel, inhuman or degrading treatment or punishment, including medical or scientific experimentation that may be detrimental to a prisoner's health, such as the removal of a prisoner's cells, body tissues or organs.

Restrictions, discipline and sanctions

No prisoner shall be sanctioned except in accordance with the terms of the law or regulation . . . and the principles of fairness and due process. . . . Prison administrations shall not sanction any conduct of a prisoner that is considered to be the direct result of his or her mental illness or intellectual disability.

Prisoners shall be informed, without delay and in a language that they understand, of the nature of the accusations against them and shall be given adequate time and facilities for the preparation of their defense.

Prisoners shall have an opportunity to seek judicial review of disciplinary sanctions imposed against them.

In no circumstances may restrictions or disciplinary sanctions amount to torture or other cruel, inhuman or degrading treatment or punishment. The following practices, in particular, shall be prohibited:

(a) Indefinite solitary confinement;
(b) Prolonged solitary confinement [22 hours a day/excess of 15 days];
(c) Placement of a prisoner in a dark or constantly lit cell;
(d) Corporal punishment or the reduction of a prisoner's diet or drinking water;
(e) Collective punishment.

Disciplinary sanctions or restrictive measures shall not include the prohibition of family contact.

Health-care personnel shall not have any role in the imposition of disciplinary sanctions or other restrictive measures. . .

Instruments of restraint

The use of chains, irons or other instruments of restraint which are inherently degrading or painful shall be prohibited.

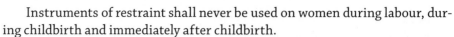
Instruments of restraint shall never be used on women during labour, during childbirth and immediately after childbirth.

Searches shall not be used to harass, intimidate or unnecessarily intrude upon a prisoner's privacy.

Intrusive searches shall be conducted in private and by trained staff of the same sex as the prisoner.

Body cavity searches shall be conducted only by qualified health-care professionals other than those primarily responsible for the care of the prisoner or, at a minimum, by staff appropriately trained by a medical professional in standards of hygiene, health and safety.

Prisoners shall have access to, or be allowed to keep in their possession without access by the prison administration, documents relating to their legal proceedings.

INFORMATION TO AND COMPLAINTS BY PRISONERS

Safeguards shall be in place to ensure that prisoners can make requests or complaints safely and, if so requested by the complainant, in a confidential manner. A prisoner or other person mentioned in paragraph 4 of rule 56 must not be exposed to any risk of retaliation, intimidation or other negative consequences as a result of having submitted a request or complaint.

CONTACT WITH THE OUTSIDE WORLD

Prisoners shall be allowed, under necessary supervision, to communicate with their family and friends at regular intervals:

Prisoners shall be allocated, to the extent possible, to prisons close to their homes or their places of social rehabilitation.

Prisoners should have access to effective legal aid.

Every prison shall have a library for the use of all categories of prisoners, adequately stocked with both recreational and instructional books, and prisoners shall be encouraged to make full use of it.

RELIGION

If the prison contains a sufficient number of prisoners of the same religion, a qualified representative of that religion shall be appointed or approved.

So far as practicable, every prisoner shall be allowed to satisfy the needs of his or her religious life by attending the services provided in the prison and having in his or her possession the books of religious observance and instruction of his or her denomination.

RETENTION OF PRISONERS' PROPERTY

NOTIFICATIONS

INVESTIGATIONS

Notwithstanding the initiation of an internal investigation, the prison director shall report, without delay, any custodial death, disappearance or serious injury to a judicial or other competent authority that is independent of the prison administration and mandated to conduct prompt, impartial and effective investigations into the circumstances and causes of such cases. The prison administration shall fully cooperate with that authority and ensure that all evidence is preserved.

REMOVAL OF PRISONERS

When prisoners are being removed to or from an institution, they shall be exposed to public view as little as possible, and proper safeguards shall be adopted to protect them from insult, curiosity and publicity in any form.

INSTITUTIONAL PERSONNEL

The prison administration shall provide for the careful selection of every grade of the personnel, since it is on their integrity, humanity, professional capacity and personal suitability for the work that the proper administration of prisons depends.

The prison administration shall ensure the continuous provision of in-service training courses . . . [on relevant law, rights and duties, security and safety, first aid, and mental health issues . . .].

So far as possible, prison staff shall include a sufficient number of specialists such as psychiatrists, psychologists, social workers, teachers and trade instructors.

In a prison for both men and women, the part of the prison set aside for women shall be under the authority of a responsible woman staff member who shall have the custody of the keys of all that part of the prison.

No male staff member shall enter the part of the prison set aside for women unless accompanied by a woman staff member.

Women prisoners shall be attended and supervised only by women staff members. This does not, however, preclude male staff members, particularly doctors and teachers, from carrying out their professional duties in prisons or parts of prisons set aside for women.

Prison staff shall not, in their relations with the prisoners, use force except in self-defence or in cases of attempted escape, or active or passive physical resistance to an order based on law or regulations.

INTERNAL AND EXTERNAL INSPECTIONS

II. Rules applicable to special categories

A. PRISONERS UNDER SENTENCE

Guiding principles

Before the completion of the sentence, it is desirable that the necessary steps be taken to ensure for the prisoner a gradual return to life in society.

Treatment
Classification and individualization

So far as possible, separate prisons or separate sections of a prison shall be used for the treatment of different classes of prisoners.

As soon as possible after admission and after a study of the personality of each prisoner with a sentence of suitable length, a programme of treatment shall be prepared for him or her in the light of the knowledge obtained about his or her individual needs, capacities and dispositions.

Privileges

Systems of privileges appropriate for the different classes of prisoners and the different methods of treatment shall be established at every prison, in order to encourage good conduct, develop a sense of responsibility and secure the interest and cooperation of prisoners in their treatment.

Work

Sentenced prisoners shall have the opportunity to work and/or to actively participate in their rehabilitation, subject to a determination of physical and mental fitness by a physician or other qualified health-care professionals.

Prisoners shall not be held in slavery or servitude.

The precautions laid down to protect the safety and health of free workers shall be equally observed in prisons.

There shall be a system of equitable remuneration of the work of prisoners.

Education and recreation

Provision shall be made for the further education of all prisoners capable of profiting thereby, including religious instruction in the countries where this is possible. The education of illiterate prisoners and of young prisoners shall be compulsory and special attention shall be paid to it by the prison administration.

Social relations and aftercare

Special attention shall be paid to the maintenance and improvement of such relations between a prisoner and his or her family as are desirable in the best interests of both.

B. PRISONERS WITH MENTAL DISABILITIES AND/OR HEALTH CONDITIONS

Persons who are found to be not criminally responsible, or who are later diagnosed with severe mental disabilities and/or health conditions, for whom staying in prison would mean an exacerbation of their condition, shall not be detained in prisons, and arrangements shall be made to transfer them to mental health facilities as soon as possible.

C. PRISONERS UNDER ARREST OR AWAITING TRIAL

Unconvicted prisoners are presumed to be innocent and shall be treated as such.

Untried prisoners shall be kept separate from convicted prisoners.

Young untried prisoners shall be kept separate from adults and shall in principle be detained in separate institutions.

An untried prisoner shall be allowed to wear his or her own clothing if it is clean and suitable. If he or she wears prison dress, it shall be different from that supplied to convicted prisoners.

An untried prisoner shall always be offered the opportunity to work, but shall not be required to work. If he or she chooses to work, he or she shall be paid for it.

An untried prisoner shall be allowed to be visited and treated by his or her own doctor or dentist if there are reasonable grounds for the application and he or she is able to pay any expenses incurred.

D. CIVIL PRISONERS

E. PERSONS ARRESTED OR DETAINED WITHOUT CHARGE

Source: United Nations. United Nations Standard Minimum Rules for the Treatment of Prisoners (the Nelson Mandela Rules). January 2016. https://undocs.org/A/RES/70/175

Principles for a Humane and Effective Corrections System

There are many groups and associations that have presented a variety of agendas, principles, or advice to guide correctional decision-making and use of resources. For instance, the Vera Institute of Justice, in their report "Reimagining Prison," presented a list of principles to guide changes that should take place in correctional systems, including the following:

1. Respect the intrinsic worth of each human being.
2. Elevate and support personal relationships.
3. Respect a person's capacity to grow and change.
4. People in prison must be provided with reasonable access to justice.[76]

More generally, in order to have a humane and effective corrections system, the entire system— from sentencing to restoration of rights for ex-offenders— should be addressed. A consideration of international human rights should be included as well. With these provisions, some basic principles may be as follows:

- Increase options for prosecution and punishment by allowing prosecutors to use diversion practices combined with treatment.

- Streamline and reconsider duplicative and trivial laws that entrap people in the justice system.

- Reconsider practices that create the "poverty penalty," which entrap the poor in a cycle of non-payment and further entrenchment in the correctional system, including such things as bail, probation supervision fees, charging for electronic monitoring and urinalysis, and so on.

- Reserve prison for those convicted of the most serious crimes by re-evaluating habitual felon laws and mandatory minimum sentencing laws.

- Make effective community drug treatment accessible to all, particularly those who may begin a life of crime through drug addiction.

- Undertake rigorous research to determine if states that have legalized marijuana have experienced any public safety consequences.

- Promote a culture of safety and rehabilitation in all institutions.

- Utilize the best risk-predictive programming and evidence-based programming at all stages of the correctional process.

- Reinvest savings from reducing prison populations to support community supervision and treatment.

- Use private correctional providers with caution in both community supervision and residential settings; reset incentives to encourage reductions in recidivism rather than just paying per capita for inmates or clients.

- Consider expanding discretionary parole to provide needed transitioning to the outside world.

- Reduce the collateral consequences that do not serve public safety and make it more difficult for parolees to adopt a prosocial identity.[77]

Summary

- Prisoners face daunting challenges when released, including housing, employment, mental health and addiction treatment, health care, family reunification, and other transitional services.

- There were 878,900 people on federal and state parole at the end of 2019, under either a mandatory or discretionary type of parole.

- This history of parole can be traced to Alexander Maconochie's mark system and the Irish ticket of leave. Almost all inmates were paroled in the 1970s, but many states restricted or eliminated parole in the 1980s and 1990s. About 27 percent leave prison with no parole supervision at all.

- Prison inmates have no constitutional right to parole, but if a state creates a statutory right, then they must receive some type of due process in the decision to grant parole. They must also receive more due process protections in decisions about whether to revoke parole and return the individual to prison.

- While most recidivism studies estimate that as many as two-thirds of releasees recidivate, other studies that have used a different statistical approach estimate that two out of three inmates never return to prison.

- The factors of recidivism include age, type of crime, sex, employment, and drug addiction,

among others. Desistance has been associated with family support and developing a prosocial identity.

- International bodies such as the United Nations have promulgated various statements of rights of prisoners that should be aspirational for any country. Correctional practices in the United States are problematic in that they violate various provisions of these international guidelines.

PROJECTS

1. Review the Mandela Rules and determine which of its other rules might be violated by practices in U.S. prisons besides those mentioned in this chapter.

2. Take one of the challenges identified for the future and investigate it, then provide your own recommendations on how to address that challenge.

NOTES

1. D. Kaeble, *Probation and Parole in the United States, 2016* (Washington, DC: Bureau of Justice Statistics, OJP, 2018).

2. Reentry Council, *Report of the Re-entry Policy Council* (New York, NY: Council of State Governments, 2004).

3. E. Gunnison and J. Helfgott, *Offender Reentry: Beyond Crime and Punishment* (Boulder, CO: Lynne Rienner Publishers, 2013), 47.

4. K. Ward and A. Merlo, "Rural Jail Reentry and Mental Health: Identifying Challenges for Offenders and Professionals," *The Prison Journal* 96, 1 (2016): 27–52.

5. C. Lindquist, J. Willison, S. Rossman, J. Walters, and P. Lattimore, *Second Chance Act Adult Offender Reentry Demonstration Programs: Implementation Challenges and Lessons Learned.* (Washington, DC: RTI International and Urban Institute, 2015).

6. B. Western, "Boston Reentry Project," https://scholar.

harvard.edu/brucewestern/research-briefs.

7. E. Gunnison and J. Helfgott, *Offender Reentry* (Boulder, CO: Lynne Rienner Publishers, 2013).

8. E. Gunnison and J. Helfgott, *Offender Reentry* (Boulder, CO: Lynne Rienner Publishers, 2013).

9. T. Minton, L. Beatty and Z. Zeng, "Correctional Populations in the United States, 2019-Statistical Tables" (Washington, DC: Bureau of Justice Statistics, USDOJ, 2021).

10. R. Hughes, *The Fatal Shore* (New York: Vintage Books, 1986).

11. H. Barnes and N. Teeters, *New Horizons on Criminology*, Third ed. (Englewood Cliffs, NJ: Prentice Hall, 1959); J. Petersilia, *Reforming Probation and Parole* (Lanham, MD: American Correctional Association, 2002), 130.

12. D. Rothman, *Conscience and Convenience* (Boston, MA: Little, Brown & Co, 1980).

13. J. Petersilia, *Reforming Probation and Parole* (Lanham,

MD: American Correctional Association, 2002).

14. T. Bonczar, "Characteristics of State Parole Supervising Agencies, 2006" (Washington, DC: Bureau of Justice Statistics, 2008).

15. E. Gunnison and J. Helfgott, *Offender Reentry* (Boulder, CO: Lynne Rienner Publishers, 2013), 14.

16. J. Petersilia, *Reforming Probation and Parole* (Lanham, MD: American Correctional Association, 2002), 131.

17. For more information on parole, go to the National Parole Resource Center at http://nationalparoleresourcecenter.org/ and the Association of Paroling Authorities International at http://www.apaintl.org/.

18. 442 U.S. 1 (1979).

19. *Board of Pardons et al. v. Allen et al.*, 482 U.S. 369 (1987) stated that the use of the word "shall" in the enabling statute created a parole right that was then deemed to be a protected liberty interest.

20. *Williams v. Missouri Bd. of Probation and Parole*, 661 F.2d 697 (8th Cir. 1981).

21. R. Burns, P. Kinkade, M. Leone, and S. Phillips, "Perspectives on Parole: The Board Members' Viewpoint," *Federal Probation Journal* 63,1 (1999): 16–22.

22. K. Morgan and B. Smith, "Victims, Punishment and Parole: The Effect of Victim Participation on Parole Hearings, *Criminology & Public Policy* 4,2 (2005): 333–60.

23. K. Morgan and B. Smith, "The Impact of Race on Parole Decision-Making," *Justice Quarterly* 25, 2 (2008): 411–35; B. Huebner and T. Bynum, "The Role of Race and Ethnicity in Parole Decisions," *Criminology* 46, 4 (2008): 907–37.

24. G. Schmitt, T. Drisko, and C. Stewart, *An Analysis of the Implementation of the 2014 Clemency Initiative* (Washington, DC: United States Sentencing Commission, 2017).

25. A. Matz, T. Conley, and N. Johanneson, "What Do Supervision Officers Do? Adult Probation/Parole Officer Workloads in a Rural Western State," *Journal of Crime and Justice*, 41, 3(2018): 294–309.

26. Research reviewed in A. Matz, T. Conley, and N. Johanneson, "What Do Supervision Officers Do? Adult Probation/Parole Officer Workloads in a Rural Western State," *Journal of Crime and Justice*, 41, 3(2018): 294–309.

27. Riane M. Bolin and Brandon K. Applegate, "Supervising Juveniles and Adults: Organizational Context, Professional Orientations, and Probation and Parole Officer Behaviors," *Journal of Crime and Justice*, 41, 4(2018): 410–426. See also B. Steiner, L.F. Travis, M.D. Makarios, and T. Brickley, "The Influence of Parole Officers' Attitudes on Supervision Practices," *Justice Quarterly* 28,6 (2011): 903–27.

28. E. Gunnison and J. Helfgott, *Offender Reentry: Beyond Crime and Punishment* (Boulder, CO: Lynne Rienner Publishers, 2013), 129–32.

29. B. Blasko, P. Friedmann, A. Rhodes, and F. Taxman, "The Parolee–Parole Officer Relationship as a Mediator of Criminal Justice Outcomes," *Criminal Justice and Behavior* 42, 7 (2015): 722–40.

30. J. Pollock, N. Hogan, E. Lambert, J. Ross, and J. Sundt, "A Utopian Prison: Contradiction in Terms?" *Journal of Contemporary Criminal Justice* 28, 1: 60–76.

31. *Monroe v. Pape*, 365 U.S. 167 (1961).

32. P. Lyons and T. Jermstad, *Civil Liabilities and Other Legal Issues for Probation/Parole Officers and Supervisors* (Washington, DC: National Institute of Corrections, 2013).

33. *Georgen v. State*, 196 N.Y.S.2d 455 (1959); *Rieser v. District of Columbia*, 563 F. 2d 462 (D. C. Cir. 1977). Also see P. Lyons and T. Jermstad, *Civil Liabilities and Other Legal Issues for Probation/Parole Officers and Supervisors* (Washington, DC: National Institute of Corrections, 2013).

34. P. Lyons and T. Jermstad, *Civil Liabilities and Other Legal Issues for Probation/Parole Officers and Supervisors* (Washington, DC: National Institute of Corrections, 2013).

35. Lubrano, A., "'Pimping Out' Drug Addicts for Cash," Philly. com, http://www.philly.com/ philly/health/addiction/ Philadelphia_exploited_ heroin_addicts_recovery_ houses_treatment_centers_ kickbacks_Medicaid.html; L. Sevilleand G. Kates, "The Narco Freedom Case: Who's Watching the Caregivers?" *The Crime Report*, January 5, 2015, www. thecrimereport.org/news/ inside-criminal-justice/2015-01-the-narco-freedom-case-whos-watching-the-caregivers; S. Dolnick, "Poorly Staffed: A Halfway House in New Jersey Is Mired in Chaos," *New York Times*, June 18, 2012, A1; S. Dolnick, "Executive at Company Tied to New Jersey's Halfway Houses Is Leaving," *New York Times,* November 9, 2012, A23; S. Dolnick, "Halfway Houses Prove Lucrative to Those at Top," *New York Times*, December 30, 2012, A1.

36. K. Barker, "City Task Force to Investigate 'Sober' Homes," *New York Times*, June 1, 2015, A14; K. Barker, "Bills Passed to Help Tenants of New York 'Three-Quarter Homes'," *New York Times*, February 1, 2017, https://www.nytimes. com/2017/02/01/nyregion/ bills-tenants-protection-three-quarter-homes-new-york.html.

37. J. Albanes, "Demystifying Risk Assessment: Giving Prisoners a Second Chance at Individualized Community Confinement Under the Second Chance Act," *Administrative Law Review* 937, 943 (2012), 64.

38. D. Routh and Z. Hamilton, "Work Release as a Transition: Positioning Success Via the Halfway House." *Journal of Offender Rehabilitation*, 54(2015): 239–255.

39. E. Latessa and L. Lovins, "Privatization of Community Corrections," *Criminology & Public Policy* 18 (2019): 323–41.

40. T. Alladin and D. Hummer, "The Relationship Between Individual Characteristics, Quality of Confinement and Recidivism by Offenders Released From Privately and

Publicly Managed Residential Community Corrections Facilities," *The Prison Journal* 98, 5 (2018): 560–579.

41. E. Latessa and L. Lovins, "Privatization of Community Corrections," *Criminology & Public Policy* 18 (2019): 323–41.

42. Langan, P. and Levin, D. 2002, "Recidivism of Inmates Released in 1994: (Washington, DC: Bureau of Justice Statistics, U.S. Dept. of Justice).

43. M. Durose, A. Cooper and H. Snyder, "Recidivism of Prisoners Released in 30 States in 2005: Patterns from 2005 to 2010" (Washington, DC: Bureau of Justice Statistics, OJP, 2014).

44. M. Alper, M. Durose, J. Markman, "Update on Prisoner Recidivism: A 9-Year Follow-up Period (2005–2014)" (Washington DC: BJS, May 2018).

45. United States Sentencing Commission, "Recidivism Among Federal Offenders: A Comprehensive Overview" (Washington, DC: United States Sentencing Commission, 2016).

46. K. Zgoba and L. Salerno, "A Three-Year Recidivism Analysis of State Correctional Releases," *Criminal Justice Studies* 30, 4 (2017): 331–45.

47. M. Ndrecka, "The Impact of Reentry Programs on Recidivism: A Meta-Analysis" (Unpublished doctoral dissertation, University of Cincinnati, 2014). Cited in C. Pettus-Davis, T. Renn, C.. Veeh, and J. Eikenberry, "Intervention Development Study of the Five-Key Model for Reentry: An Evidence-Driven Prisoner Reentry Intervention," *Journal of Offender Rehabilitation*, 58, 1 (2019): 1–30.

48. W. Rhodes, G. Gaes, and J. Luallen, "Following Incarceration, Most Released Offenders Never Return to Prison," *Crime & Delinquency* 62, 8 (2014): 1003-1025. L. Neyfakh, "Why Do So Many Ex-cons End Up Back in Prison? Maybe They Don't," *Slate*, October 29, 2015,http://www.slate.com/articles/news_and_politics/crime/2015/10/why_do_so_many_prisoners_end_up_back_in_prison_a_new_study_says_maybe_they.single.html.

49. P. Burke, M. Tonry, *Successful Transition and Reentry for Safer Communities: A Call to Action for Parole* (Silver Spring, MD: Center for Effective Public Policy, 2006), 22; E. Carson, *Prisoners in 2016* (Washington, DC: Bureau of Justice Statistics, OJP), 11.

50. "Confined and Costly: How Supervision Violations Are Filling Prisons and Burdening Budgets," Council on State Governments, 2019, https://csgjusticecenter.org/confinedandcostly/.

51. D. Kaeble, "Probation and Parole in the United States, 2016" (Washington, DC: Bureau of Justice Statistics. USDOJ), Appendix Table 7.

52. M. Alper, M. Durose, J. Markman, "Update on Prisoner Recidivism: A 9-Year Follow-up Period (2005–2014)" (Washington DC: BJS, May 2018).

53. S. Maruna and H. Toch, *Making Good: How Ex-Convicts Reform and Rebuild Their Lives* (Washington, DC: American Psychological Association, 2001).

54. M. Alper, M. Durose, J. Markman, "Update on Prisoner Recidivism: A 9-Year Follow-up Period (2005–2014)" (Washington DC: BJS, May 2018).

55. M. Alper, M. Durose, J. Markman, "Update on Prisoner Recidivism: A 9-Year Follow-up Period (2005–2014)" (Washington DC: BJS, May 2018).

56. M. Alper, M. Durose, J. Markman, "Update on Prisoner Recidivism: A 9-Year Follow-up Period (2005–2014)" (Washington DC: BJS, May 2018).

57. N. Pearl, "Use of Community-Based Social Services to Reduce Recidivism in Female Parolees," *Women & Criminal Justice* 10 1 (1998): 27–52.

58. W. Rhodes, G. Gaes, R. Kling, and C. Cutler, "Relationship Between Prison Length of Stay and Recidivism: A Study Using Regression Discontinuity and Instrumental Variables with Multiple Break Points," *Criminology & Public Policy*, 17 (2018): 731–69.

59. D. Mears, J. Cochran, W. Bales, and A. Bhatithe, "Recidivism and Time Served in Prison," *Journal of Criminal Law and Criminology* 106, 1(2016): 81–122.

60. "Reducing Recidivism: States Deliver on Results" (Washington, DC: Council on State Governments / National Reentry Resource Center, 2014).

61. C. Taylor, "The Family's Role in the Reintegration of Formerly Incarcerated Individuals: The Direct Effects of Emotional Support," *The Prison Journal*, 96, 3(2016): 331–54.

62. E. Gunnison and J. Helfgott, *Offender Reentry: Beyond Crime and Punishment* (Boulder, CO: Lynne Rienner Publishers, 2013); C. Taylor, "The Family's Role in the Reintegration of Formerly Incarcerated Individuals: The Direct Effects of Emotional Support," *The Prison Journal*, 96, 3(2016): 331–54.

63. S. Maruna, S. and H. Toch, *Making Good: How Ex-Convicts Reform and Rebuild Their Lives* (Washington, DC: American Psychological Association, 2001). E. Gunnison and J. Helfgott, *Offender Reentry: Beyond Crime and Punishment* (Boulder, CO: Lynne Rienner Publishers, 2013).

65. Reported in B. Bersani and E. Dohert, "Desistance from Offending in the 21st Century," *Annual Review of Criminology* 1 (2018): 311–34.

64. C. Clarridge, "Martin Pang, Who Set Fire That Led to Deaths Of 4 Seattle Firefighters, to Leave Prison as Early as September," *Seattle Times*, May 25, 2018, https:// www.seattletimes.com/ seattle-news/crime/seattle-arsonist-martin-pang-to-be-released-from-prison-sept-27/.

66. S. Listwan, C. Jonson, F. Cullen, E. Latessa, "Cracks in the Penal Harm Movement: Evidence from the Field," *Criminology & Public Policy* 7, 5 (2008): 423–65.

67. "Bureau of Justice Statistics, Expenditures and Employment Extracts, 2010," http:// bjs.ojp.usdoj.gov/index. cfm?ty=tp&tid=5.

68. "Lessons from the States: Reducing Recidivism and Curbing Corrections Costs Through Justice Reinvestment" (Washington, DC: Council of State Governments Justice Center, 2013), 1.

69. C. Henrichson and R. Delaney, "The Price of Prisons: What Incarceration Costs Taxpayers" (New York: Vera Institute, Center on Sentencing and Corrections, January 2012), https://shnny.org/research/ the-price-of-prisons-what-incarceration-costs-taxpayers/.

70. P. Wagner and B. Rabuy, "Following the Money of Mass Incarceration" (New York: Prison Policy Institute, January 25, 2017), https:// www.prisonpolicy.org/reports/ money.html.

71. For more information, see Vera Institute of Justice, "Impact Evaluation of the Adolescent Behavioral Learning Experience (ABLE) Program at Rikers Island," (July 2015), https://www.vera. org/publications/ impact-evaluation-of-the-adolescent-behavioral-learning-experience-able-program-at-rikers-island; (July 2015); and MDRC, "MDRC Statement on the Vera Institute's Study of the Adolescent Behavioral Learning Experience (ABLE) Program at Rikers Island," (July 2015), https://www.mdrc. org/news/announcement/ mdrc-statement-vera-institute-s-study-adolescent-behavioral-learning-experience.

72. R. Rani, "New Zealand Tries a Different Kind of Private Prison," Citylab.com, August 31, 2017, https://www.citylab. com/equity/2017/08/new-zealand-tries-a-different-kind-of-private-prison/538506/. A. Bushnell. *Cutting costs and Reducing Reoffending: Redesigning Private Prison Contracts for Better Results* (Sydney, Australia: Institute of Public Affairs) retrieved August 29, 2021, https://ipa.org.au/ wp-content/uploads/2019/10/ IPA-Cutting-costs-and-reducing-reoffending-Redesigning-private-prison-contracts-for-better-results.pdf.

73. "Privacy, Weekend Leaves, Keys . . . This is Prison?" *60 Minutes*. Transcript available at https:// www.cbsnews.com/news/60-minutes-germany-prisons-crime-and-punishment/.

74. Doran Larson, "Why Scandinavian Prisons Are Superior," *The Atlantic*, September 24, 2013, https://www.theatlantic. com/international/ archive/2013/09/why-scandinavianprisons-are-superior/279949/; Nicholas Turner and Jeremy Travis, "What We Learned from German Prisons," *The New York Times*, op. ed., August 6, 2015, https://www.nytimes. com/2015/08/07/opinion/ what-welearned-from-german-prisons.html.

75. "Towards Humane Prisons" (Geneva, Switzerland: International Committee of the Red Cross, June 2020), https://www.icrc.org/en/ publication/4286-towards-humane-prisons. https://www. icrc.org/en/publication/4286-towardshumane-prisons.

76. "Reimaging Prison" (New York: Vera Institute for Justice, 2018).

77. "Transforming Prisons, Restoring Lives: Final Recommendations of the Charles Colson Task Force" (Washington, DC: Urban Institute, January 2016); H. Schoenfeld, "A Research Agenda on Reform: Penal Policy and Politics Across the States," *Annals of American Academy of Political Science*, 664 (March 2016): 155–74; "State Advances in Criminal Justice Reform, 2016" (Washington, DC: The Sentencing Project); "Law Enforcement Leaders to Reduce Crime and Incarceration Organization: Statement of Principles, 2017," www. lawenforcementleaders.org.; L. Eisen and I. Chettiar, *Criminal Justice: An Election Agenda for Candidates, Activists, and Legislators* (New York: Brennan Center for Justice, 2018).

GLOSSARY

A

Absconding: not reporting to probation or parole officer and whereabouts are unknown

Activist era: the period in the1960s and 1970s when Earl Warren was Chief Justice of the Supreme Court and the Court decided in favor of prisoners in cases challenging prison conditions and practices

Actuarial approach: risk assessment using static factors such as number of prior arrests

Administrative segregation: similar to punitive segregation in practice, but used for individuals before transfer or before being classified

Age segregation: housing the elderly and vulnerable inmates separately from the general population

Americans with Disabilities Act of 1990 (ADA): legislation that requires governmental agencies to make accommodations for illness or disability

Amnesty: immunity from prosecution

Anomie: normlessness

Appearance bond: the amount a person must submit in order to be released before adjudication

Ashurst-Sumners Act: legislation that made it a federal offense to take prison-made goods across state lines

Attrition: dropout rate

B

Bail: the amount of money that is assessed by the judge to release a defendant before adjudication; if the defendant fails to appear or violates the conditions of the release, he or she might forfeit the total amount of bail

Benefit of clergy: a way of escaping a death sentence, originally used for clergymen who were exempt from civil punishments because they would be punished by church. Reciting Psalm 54 was the way to prove one was a member of the clergy, but others memorized it and could also use the method.

"Big house" prisons: prisons that existed from the early 1900s to the rehabilitative era in the 1960s and 70s

Bond: the amount provided on a defendant's behalf, usually by a bail bond company, to secure his or her release

Booking: the process of being admitted into jail

Building tenders: inmates who were given power to control other inmates

Burnout: when workers are not invested in their job; includes emotional exhaustion, a perception that they have not accomplished personal and professional goals, and depersonalization

C

Casework model: the professional (the probation officer) interacts with each client (the probationer) individually, serving as the primary, and sometimes only, service provider

Chicago school of criminology: 1930s sociologists who observed that crime occurred in interstitial areas of the city

Chivalry hypothesis: the theory that women were less likely than men to be arrested or convicted, and were sentenced to less punishment than men who had committed similar crimes

Citation: ticket in lieu of arrest

Civil Rights of Institutionalized Persons Act (CRIPA): federal law that provides rights of basic health care to people in prison or otherwise institutionalized

Classical school of criminology: Bentham and Beccaria believed that people could be deterred from crime by adjusting the legal system; they assumed crime was a rational decision.

Clemency: a temporary postponement of a punishment

Clinical approach: risk assessment using interviews and professionals' judgment

"Code of silence": correctional officer subculture norm to not testify or report other COs even when they are doing something illegal or wrong

Cognitive behavioral programs: programs that emphasize behavioral change through adjusting the cues and triggers for criminal behavior rather than exploring the meaning behind them

Cognitive behavioral therapy (CBT): focuses on thinking and behavioral patterns that lead to criminality; helps offenders change maladapted and antisocial thought patterns by teaching them to observe and manage such thoughts

Cognitive restructuring: focuses on changing the content of what offenders believe, specifically their pro-criminal attitudes and rationalization for crime

Cognitive skills programs: target an offender's reasoning ability; for instance, how to control anger or impulses

Collateral consequences: voting disenfranchisement and other restrictions that occur with a felony conviction

Common Law: collected court decisions over hundreds of years in England

Commutation: reducing the punishment imposed

Compassionate release: releasing inmates before the end of their sentence because of terminal illness or disability

Comprehensive Crime Control Act: federal law passed in 1984 that included the Sentencing Reform Act, which abolished federal parole and created a Sentencing Commission that, in turn, created the Sentencing Guidelines for federal crimes

CompStat: developed by the NYPD, utilized up-to-date crime statistics to inform division commanders and encourage accountability

Conditions: rules of probation

Congregate care system (Auburn system): a type of prison in which inmates slept in separate cells but worked, ate, and exercised together

Contingency contracting: behavioral change through targeted "contracts" to help an individual change behavior through rewards; for example, an individual will learn to walk away from an argument rather than engage and, as a reward, will be able to have extra free time

Contract system: an arrangement whereby private employers hired inmates and the state received a fixed fee per prisoner, per day

Co-occurring disorders: having more than one diagnosable health issue, e.g., addiction and schizophrenia

Corporal punishment: punishment administered to the body

Correctional assessment: prediction and classification for security and treatment

Correctional Offender Management Profiling for Alternative Sanctions (COMPAS): third-generation assessment/prediction tool

Correctional Program Assessment Inventory (CPAI): an assessment tool to measure the extent to which programs adhere to the R/N/R approach and to evidence-based correctional best practices

Correctional treatment: encompasses everything that may assist in behavioral change of offenders

Correctional supervision rate: the rate per 100,000 of individuals under any form of correctional supervision

Corrections: Everything done after sentencing to encourage the desistance of criminality, e.g., probation, prison, drug treatment, etc.

Correlates: factors that are statistically associated with another factor

Cottage system: architectural style of early women's prisons and institutions for juveniles, smaller buildings set up in a "family" style

Criminology: study of crime and criminals

Cultural deviance theory: the premise that crime is normal in some communities

Custodial model: model of prisons for women similar to men's penitentiaries

Crime correlate: factor that is statistically associated with crime

D

Dark figure of crime: incidents of crime that are unreported to police

Day fines: fines set by income

Decarceration: the trend to reduce the number of people in prison

Deferred adjudication: diversion program whereby offender completes required conditions and charges are dismissed

Deferred sentencing: when the decision regarding length of sentence is put off while giving an offender a chance to succeed on probation

Deliberate indifference standard: a situation where prison staff are aware of a need for treatment in order to prevent or alleviate pain or injury yet deliberately refuse or neglect to provide such treatment; it is the test used to determine whether an Eighth Amendment violation has occurred

Deprivation theory: the notion that elements of prisoner subculture develop because of the deprivations of prison

Desistance: lack of recidivism

Determinate sentencing: when length of sentence is set instead of provided as a range

Deterrence theory: the premise that people will not commit crime if the perceived punishment is greater than the perceived reward

Differential association theory: the premise that delinquents receive more messages supportive of delinquency through associations with delinquent/criminal family and friends

Differential opportunity theory: the premise that some groups of boys had access to legitimate opportunities, some to illegitimate opportunities, and some to neither leading to uncontrolled delinquency

Discretionary parole: the decision to release on parole supervision (as opposed to mandatory supervision)

Disenfranchisement: inability to vote

Due deference approach: the era after the activist era when the Supreme Court deferred to prison officials' expertise in most cases challenging conditions or practices of the prison

Due process: steps taken to prevent error in the governmental deprivation of life, liberty, or property

Dyads: friendship pairs

E

Effective Practices in Community Supervision (EPICS): a type of cognitive behavioral therapy, taught by trained probation officers, that helps offenders learn self-control

Externalizing disorders: mental health issues that can be observed in abnormal behavior patterns, including attention-deficit/hyperactivity, conduct disorders, and pathological gambling (see also *internalizing disorders*)

F

Fair Sentencing Act of 2010: chaned the ratio of federal sentence length for crack cocaine compared to powder cocaine from 100 to 1 down to 18 to 1.

Federal Prison Industries Enhancement Act (PIE): legislation that enabled prisons to use inmate labor to manufacture and sell goods on the open market

Fee system: early system of funding jails whereby offenders had to pay for their room and board while being held there

G

Gaol: early English word for *jail*

Gender dysphoria: discomfort or distress due to a mismatch between biological sex and gender identity

Gender-responsive programming: programming that addresses the specific issues of female offenders

General deterrence: what is done to an offender to deter others from committing crime

General strain theory: the premise that individuals who are subject to strains (economic and person) and do not have coping skills, will experience anger and frustration that will lead to delinquency/criminality

General theory of crime: the premise that crime results from low self-control

Good time: time off the end of a sentence for good behavior

Graduated release: an early term for *parole*

Graduated sanctions: more targeted and intermediate punishment for technical violations on probation or parole; used instead of revocation

H

Habitual felon laws: sentencing laws that punish a second or third felony with a much longer prison term; for example, "three-strikes" laws

Hands-off era: time period up to the 1960s during which federal courts rarely heard cases challenging prison conditions

Harrison Act of 1914: early drug control law that required documentation of prescriptions and taxation of drugs

Hawes-Cooper Act: legislation that allowed a state to bar prison-made goods from being transported across state lines to compete with private businesses

Hedonistic calculus: Bentham's idea that the individual weighs the potential punishment against the potential pleasure or profit from a criminal act and decides accordingly

Houses of correction: early correctional institution that housed minor offenders

Hulks: floating ships used as prisons in England

I

Importation theory: the notion that elements of the prisoner subculture develop as they are imported from street subcultures

Imprisonment rate: the number of people in prison per 100,000, constructed by dividing the number of people in prison by the population, multiplied by 100,000

Incapacitation: making someone incapable of performing a crime

Incarceration rate: the number of people in prison or jail per 100,000, constructed by dividing the number of people in prison or jail by the population, multiplied by 100,000

Indeterminate sentencing: a sentence range as punishment, e.g., 5–10 years, the actual time served is determined by good time and parole

Indigency: without funds, defined as when a person can't afford a lawyer and still pay their monthly bills

Inmate code: the dos and don'ts of living in prison

Intellectually disabled: having an IQ of 70 or below with significant limitations in intellectual functioning (reasoning, learning, and problem solving) and adaptive behavior (a range of social and practical skills)

Intensive supervision probation: model of probation with smaller caseloads, more frequent contacts, and tighter supervision

Intermediate sanctions: responses to violations of conditions less than revocation, e.g., weekend jail or earlier curfews

Intermediate standard: a Supreme Court test to determine whether different treatment violates the equal protection clause of the 14th Amendment; the state can justify different treatment on such grounds as women having different needs or simply that the state has a legitimate reason for doing so

Internalizing disorders: mental health issues that may not have external behavioral indices, e.g., anxiety, PTSD, or suicidal ideation (see also *externalizing disorders*)

Interstate Compact for Adult Offender Supervision (ICAOS): contract among states to supervise each other's probationers when they move into any state

J

Jailhouse lawyer: an inmate who helps other inmates with their legal issues

Justice Reinvestment Initiative (JRI): federal program that helped jurisdictions reduce their prison population and invest savings into community programs

L

Labeling theory: the premise that we all commit primary deviance, but only those who are stigmatized and change their master identity go on to commit secondary deviance

Leased labor system: the practice of leasing inmates for farm labor in the South after the Civil War and into the 1940s

Legal financial obligations (LFOs): fines, fees, restitution, court charges

Level of Service Inventory-Revised (LSI-R): third-generation assessment/prediction tool

Lockstep: a method of moving large groups of prisoners; each inmate had to place his hand on the opposite shoulder of the man in front of him

Longitudinal research: following a cohort for a long period of time

M

Mandatory minimum laws: sentencing laws that mandate a certain type or length of sentence for certain crimes

Mandatory supervision: same supervision as discretionary parole but used for all offenders who are released

Mark system: the historical practice of graduated release practiced at Norfolk Island prison colony where prisoners could earn liberties through good behavior

Martinson Report: a 1974 report on correctional programs that was widely summarized as "nothing works"

Maturation effect: the observation that crime declines dramatically after the age of 35

"Maxed out": completing the full term of one's prison sentence

Medical model: the concept that crime is a symptom of an underlying pathology

Mental disorder: a syndrome characterized by a clinically significant disturbance in an individual's cognition, emotion regulation, or behavior that reflects a dysfunction in the psychological, biological, or developmental processes underlying mental functioning

Meta-analysis: evaluation by combining many different evaluations into one data set and analyzing the results

Motivational interviewing: approach that is directive and goal oriented for eliciting behavior change

N

National Crime Victimization Survey (NCVS): survey that goes to households to collect information about crime victimization

Net-widening: process by which a diversionary program gets used for offenders who would have received a less intrusive correctional sentence

O

Organizational commitment: workers' commitment to the workplace, associated with higher work performance and satisfaction

Organizational justice: measure of whether workers' feel that organization treats them fairly, distinct subthemes are: voice, fairness, respect, and trustworthiness

P

Pardon: deleting any culpability as well as punishment that has been imposed

Parole: early release from prison combined with supervision in the community

Partially secured bond: when the defendant has to offer only a portion of the total bail amount in the form of money or property

Pathways approach: research that showed women begin to commit crime through different pathways than men, often through abuse, living on the street, and drug use

Penal harm era: a period from the 1980s onward where rehabilitation was less emphasized as a correctional goal

Piece-price system: type of labor program whereby private employers paid the state by the number of items produced by prisoners

Plantation prisons: prisons in the South after the U.S. Civil War; prisoners were used for labor

Plea bargaining: an agreement to plead guilty in return for a certain sentence promised by the prosecutor

Pluralistic ignorance: when members of a group believe fellow members think differently than they do; specifically, when correctional officers (COs) are actually more in favor of rehabilitation than fellow COs think they are

Positivist school of criminology: school of thought from the 1800s that perceived criminals as different (biologically) from law-abiding citizens; can also be used to describe any scientific approach that looks for causes

Poverty penalty: refers to the idea that many correctional punishments now require payment; therefore, poor offenders have different opportunities and experience punishment differently

Powder keg theory: theory of prison riots that say elements contribute to a situation where violence only needs a trigger

Power vacuum theory: the notion that violence occurs because of a lack of powerful authority

Pre-sentence investigation: the investigation done by the probation officer to help a judge decide sentencing

Pre-sentence report (PSR): the report submitted to the judge by a probation officer after a pre-sentence investigation

Pretrial diversion programs: see deferred adjudication

Preventive detention hearing: a hearing to determine if the defendant is too dangerous to release prior to trial or adjudication

Prison argot: language of the prisoner subculture

Prison Rape Elimination Act (PREA): legislation that mandated survey of prisons to determine level of sexual violence

Prisoner Litigation Reform Act (PLRA): legislation that made it difficult for prisoners to litigate cases challenging prison conditions

Prisonization: socialization to prisoner subculture

Probation: supervision in the community in lieu of being incarcerated in jail or prison

Probation subsidies: payments to the county for keeping offenders supervised in the community rather than being sent to a state prison

Program fidelity: the level to which a program follows the fundamental principles and implementation guidance of the original

Pseudo-families: a group of inmates who have organized themselves loosely into a family structure; also known as *play families*

Public duty doctrine: the idea that government functions are owed to the general public but not to specific individuals

R

Rabbits: victims in a women's prison

Rational relationship test: a test to determine if prison practice or condition is unconstitutional; basically allows any practice that is rationally related to a legitimate state objective

Realignment: California sentencing law that dramatically reduced the prison population

Recidivism: Measure of correctional failure, by rearrest, reconviction, revocation or return to prison

Reciprocity: when COs depend on inmates to help them complete tasks

Reformatory: a correctional institution for younger offenders or minor offenders amenable to treatment

Reformatory model: model of early women's prisons that encouraged female offenders to learn "womanly skills" through the role model of matrons

Rehabilitation: a change in an inmate's attitude from lawbreaking to law-abiding

Rehabilitative era: the late 1960s and 1970s when rehabilitation was foremost as a correctional goal

Relational model of therapy: using the human need for connection to encourage change

Rational choice theory: the premise that committing crime is a rational decision, criminals weigh whether they can escape punishment and decide accordingly

Relative deprivation/rising expectation theory: the notion that when conditions improve, but don't improve fast enough, there is a higher likelihood of a disturbance

Release on recognizance (ROR): a defendant is released without bail and simply with a promise to return for adjudication

Religious Freedom Restoration Act (RFRA): a law that required strict scrutiny in testing whether state practice or law infringed upon religious freedoms

Religious Land Use and Institutionalized Persons Act (RLUIPA): passed by Congress after the Supreme Court had ruled some parts of the RFRA were unconstitutional; it basically reiterated religious liberties and specifically extended them to prisoners

Restitution: payment by the offender to the victim to compensate for harm or injury

Retribution: Deserved punishment, i.e., an eye for an eye

Revocation: failure on probation or parole, either by new crime or technical violation

Risk/Needs/Responsivity (R/N/R) model: model of risk classification and intervention that looks at the objective and dynamic factors to determine the offender's risk and amenability to reform

S

Scarlet letter conditions: shaming conditions of probation; for example, a sign on one's door notifying the public that a sex offender lives there, or a DUI designation on one's car

Section 1983 suit: strips officials of immunity when they violate a constitutional right while acting within their official role

Secured bond: when the total bail amount must be promised by cash or property as collateral

Security classification: prediction of risk of escape or violence to determine custody level

Selection bias: a kind of statistical bias that occurs when there is no random assignment between the treatment group and the control group, either because participants self-select or the researcher decides who is going to be in the treatment group

Serious mental illness (SMI): defined as major depressive disorder; depressive disorder not otherwise specified; bipolar disorder I, II, and not otherwise specified; schizophrenia spectrum disorder; schizoaffective disorder; schizophreniform disorder; brief psychotic disorder; delusional disorder; and psychotic disorder not otherwise specified

Serious psychological distress (SPD): a score of 13 or higher on the Kessler 6 (K6) Nonspecific Psychological Distress Scale, a six-question tool developed to screen for serious mental illness among adults age 18 or older

Split sentencing (shock probation): a short term in jail followed by probation

Static factors: factors that do not change, e.g., age at first arrest

Strict scrutiny test: allows a state practice or law only if it can be shown to be the only way to accomplish a legitimate state interest and if it is the least burdensome way to do so

Surety bond: when someone else can put up the bond for an offender to be released

Suspended sentencing: when the length of sentence is determined by held in abeyance, giving the offender a chance to succeed on probation

Sentencing disparity: the difference in sentence length between two similar offenders or crimes

Sentencing Guidelines: the federal government and some states have guidelines that assign the length of imprisonment based on seriousness of the crime and offender risk score, judges have very little discretion when mandatory sentencing guidelines are used

Sentencing Reform Act of 1984: Part of the Comprehensive Crime Control Act, this legislation created federal sentencing guidelines and mandated that all federal prisoners had to serve 85 percent of their sentences before becoming eligible for release

Separate system (Philadelphia or Pennsylvania system): the practice whereby inmates spent their entire sentence isolated in a single cell

Severe functional impairment: a mental health issue that results in serious interference in a person's ability to work, manage their home, and maintain relationships

Silent system: a discipline system used in the Auburn prison and other congregate systems that punished inmates from talking to each other

Social control theory: the premise that people don't commit crime because of bonds to society, e.g., attachment, commitment, involvement and belief; if these are weak, delinquency results

Social disorganization theory: the premise that areas in a community that have no elements of social organization (church, home ownership, community clubs, etc.) and show signs of neglect (overgrown lots, abandoned buildings) also have more delinquency/criminality

Social impact bonds: method of funding correctional programs, investors get return on money only if program successfully reduces recidivism

Social support theory: the premise that when there are church, social groups, strong families, these provide support and reduce delinquency/criminality

Specific deterrence: what is done to an offender to convince him or her not to commit future crime

Strain-opportunity theory: the premise that crime results when there are no legitimate means to success; if they don't have legitimate access: innovation, retreatism, rebellion, ritualism or conformance results

Structured conflict: the inherent conflict between inmates and COs because of their respective roles

Supermax prison: a prison that keeps most inmates locked in their cells most of the day with limited programming

Symbolic interactionism: the idea that our self-concept is shaped by what we perceive others to believe

T

Technical violations: breaking the rules of probation or parole

Therapeutic community (TC): a correctional program where participants live together and everyday living elements are used to help encourage change

Three-strikes law: habitual felon/offender law; a third felony may result in a life sentence

Ticket of leave: historical Irish early release system

Tokenism: when individuals are scrutinized more closely when they are members of a disproportionately small group

Totality of the circumstances: a type of Eighth Amendment case where a variety of conditions and practices are combined to show that the prison has cruel and unusual conditions

Transportation: the practice of transporting prisoners to the American colonies and then Australia

Treatment ethic: similar to the medical model, the concept that crime is a symptom of an underlying pathology that can be treated

Truth-in-sentencing laws: part of the 1994 Violent Crime Control bill that required states to eliminate or sharply reduce good time and make sure offenders served the length of sentence they received

U

Uniform Crime Reports (UCR): FBI collects reports of crime and produces this report titled "Crime in the United States" yearly

Unsecured bond: when bail does not need to be secured by cash or collateral

V

Violent Crime Control Law Enforcement Act: passed in 1994, this law provided money to states to build new prisons if they would institute "truth in sentencing" laws that required offenders to serve the sentence they were given rather than have it shortened through good time or parole

W

Walnut Street Jail: early jail in Philadelphia, where the practice of classification was first implemented

Warehouse prisons: prisons in the 1980s and later that have been criticized as making little attempt to rehabilitate inmates

CREDITS

Chapter 1
[photo 1.1] © Skyward Kick Productions / Shutterstock
[photo 1.2] © vshal / shutterstock
[photo 1.3] © Denis Paquin/AP/Shutterstock
[photo 1.4] © Robert Schwemmer / Shutterstock

Chapter 2
[photo 2.1] © Gorodenkoff / Shutterstock
[photo 2.2] © Natata / Shutterstock
[photo 2.3] © AYA Images / Shutterststock
[photo 2.4] © Sukjai Photo / Shutterstock
[figure 2.6] © Sharon Davis Sr. Executive Assistant

Chapter 3
[photo 3.1] © wavebreakmedia / shutterstock
[photo 3.2] © Jon Weller / Shutterstock
[photo 3.3] © Mark Reinstein / Shutterstock
[photo 3.4] © Everett Collection / Shutterstock

Chapter 4
[photo 4.1] © lev radin / shutterstock
[photo 4.2] © The Corgi / Shutterstock
[photo 4.3] © Wikipedia
[photo 4.4] © a katz / shutterstock
[figure 4.1] © Prison Policy Initiative

Chapter 5
[photo 5.1] © TonelsonProductions / Shutterstock
[photo 5.2] © MikeDotta / Shutterstock
[photo 5.3] © Ragma Images / Shutterstock
[photo 5.4] © Stock City / Shutterstock

Chapter 6
[photo 6.1] © Anon Wangkheeree / shutterstock
[photo 6.2] © Mike Ver Sprill / Shutterstock
[photo 6.3] © Everett Collection / Shutterstock
[photo 6.4] © meunierd / shutterstock

Chapter 7
[photo 7.1] © Joseph Sohm / Shutterstock
[photo 7.2] © Lynn Yeh/Shutterstock
[photo 7.3] © Lou Oates / Shutterstock
[photo 7.4] © Alvaro German Vilela / Shutterstock
[figure 7.4] © Carson, 2020, op. cit.
[figure 7.8] © March 2015. Urban Institute.

Chapter 8
[photo 8.1] © Joseph Sohm / Shutterstock
[photo 8.2] © ES James / Shutterstock
[photo 8.3] © Motortion Films / Shutterstock
[photo 8.4] © Ann Kosolapova / Shutterstock

Chapter 9
[photo 9.1] © Tapui / Shutterstock
[photo 9.2] © Tolga Sezgin / Shutterstock
[photo 9.3] © Luca Rei / Shutterstock
[photo 9.4] © Oscity / Shutterstock

Chapter 10
[photo 10.1] © Kittirat roekburi / Shutterstock
[photo 10.2] © Ermolaev Alexander / Shutterstock
[photo 10.3] © nokkaew / Shutterstock
[photo 10.4] © Everett Collection / Shutterstock

Chapter 11
[photo 11.1] © Rebekah Zemansky / Shutterstock
[photo 11.2] © Joseph Sohm / Shutterstock
[photo 11.3] © Edward R / Shutterstock
[photo 11.4] © Melissamn / Shutterstock

Chapter 12
[photo 12.1] © Volodymyr Herasymshuck / Shutterstock
[photo 12.2] © Elnur / Shutterstock

INDEX

Page numbers followed by *f* and *t* refer to figures and tables, respectively.

A

AA. *See* Alcoholics Anonymous
ABA (American Bar Association), 255
ABE (Adult Basic Education), 301
ABLE Project for Incarcerated Youth, 346
abortion, legalization of, 36
absconding, 340
acamprosate, 307
ACLU (American Civil Liberties Union), 155, 275
activist era, 238
actuarial approach, 309
acupuncture, 317
ADA (Americans with Disabilities Act of 1990), 190, 200
Adams, John Quincy, 147
addiction, 306–7
Addiction Severity Index, 283
administrative segregation, 153, 250, 277–78
Adolescent Learning Experience (ABLE) Project for Incarcerated Youth, 346
adoption programs, 296
Adult Basic Education (ABE), 301
affirmative action, 10
age
    and capital punishment, 64
    as correlate of prison misconduct, 221
    as crime correlate, 37, 38*f*
    imprisonment rates by, 69
    and medical costs, 187
    and minimum sentencing, 345
    prisoners by, 181, 181*f*
    probation failure by, 127
    and recidivism, 339
age segregation, 190
aggravated assault, in cities, 35
aging population, 36
Agnew, Robert, 47
agreeableness (personality trait), 43
AIDS, 184, 269, 270
Alabama, 9, 18, 19, 160, 185, 244, 275, 333, 334
Alabama v. Shelton, 109
Alaska, 10, 12, 19, 80, 125, 253
Alcatraz prison (California), 153, 153*f*, 184*f*
alcohol consumption, decreased, 36
Alcoholics Anonymous (AA), 120, 242, 298
alcoholism and alcohol abuse, 306–7

and mental illness, 194
    stress-related, 161, 162
    treatment for, 306–7
alcohol-related offenses, 13
almshouses, 61
American Bar Association (ABA), 255
American Civil Liberties Union (ACLU), 155, 275
American Correctional Association, 102
American Probation and Parole Association, 128
American Psychiatric Association, 192
American Psychological Association, 154
American Revolution, 331
Americans with Disabilities Act of 1990 (ADA), 190, 200
amnesty, 334
Amnesty International, 275
Amsterdam, Holland, 146
Andrews, Don, 311
anomie, 46
Anti-Drug Abuse Act (1986), 11–12
Anti-Drug Abuse Act (1988), 12, 71
anti-psychotic drugs, 196
antisocial associates, 311
antisocial behavior, 44, 311
antisocial cognition, 311, 312
antisocial personality disorder, 43, 194, 312
antisocial personality pattern, 311
anxiety neurosis, 269
appearance bond, 90–91
appellate courts, 241–42
Argersinger v. Hamlin, 108
argot, prison, 215–16
Arizona, 185, 332
Arkansas, 10, 246, 270
Armed Career Criminal Act, 256
arrests
    custodial, 88–89
    drug, 33–34, 34*f*
    as measure of crime, 30, 31
    statistics on, 37, 38*t*
    trends in, 32*t*, 33
    by type of crime, 33–34, 33*f*
arrest warrants, 88–89
arts and crafts, 299
Aryan Brotherhood, 216
Ashurst-Sumners Act, 155, 305
assessment(s), 308–15
    Cognitive Program Assessment Inventory (CPAI), 314
    Level of Service Inventory-Revised (LSI-R), 310–12
    Risk/Need/Responsivity (R/N/R), 312–14
associates, antisocial, 311

association, freedom of, 243
asthma, 270
Atkins v. Virginia, 64
attentive parenting, 43
Attica Correctional Facility (New York State), 152
Attica prison riot (1971), 152, 218, 226
attorneys
    court-appointed, 89
    "jailhouse lawyers," 248
attrition, 315
Auburn model, 146–48
Auburn Prison (New York State), 147–48, 262
Auckland South Correctional Facility (New Zealand), 346
Augustus, John, 118
Australia, 314, 331
"automatic restoration" of voting rights, 255

B

background checks, criminal, 257
bad checks, writing, 12–13
bail, 90–91
    Blacks and, 13, 78
    definition of, 89
    excessive, 90
    for felony vs. misdemeanor cases, 90
    and growth in jail population, 91–93
bail-bond industry, 94
bail bonds offices, 90
Baltimore, Md., 35, 262
Barr, William, 18
battered women (in pathways approach), 264
Baze v. Rees, 64
Bearden v. Georgia, 109
Beaumont, Gustave de, 148
Beccaria, Cesare, 40
Bedford Hills (New York State), 41, 282, 283
behavioral explanation of criminology, 44
Bell v. Wolfish, 99–100
"benefit of clergy," 60
"beyond a reasonable doubt" standard of proof, 254
Biden, Joe, 18, 74, 158, 335
Big Brother/Big Sister programs, 46, 296
"Big Five" personality traits, 43
"big house" prisons, 150
Bill of Rights, 62, 238, 239, 240
binding out, 60
biological theories of crime, 42–43, 50, 296
bipolar disorder, 192, 194, 268

BJS. *See* Bureau of Justice Statistics
Black Guerrilla Family, 216
black markets, prison, 212, 214–17, 228, 271
Black Muslims, 241
Black Panthers, 218
Black Power, 216, 218
Blacks and Black prisoners
    as correctional officers, 166
    criminal arrests of, 37
    disparate sentencing of, 11, 77–79
    inaccurate prediction of criminal behavior in, 314
    incarceration rate for, 13
    in jails, 101
    and mass incarceration, 13
    mental health disorders in, 192
    migration of, to northern cities, 11
    as parents in prison, 186
    as parolees, 331, 334
    as percentage of prison population, 180–81
    in "plantation prisons," 150*f*, 150
    prison experience of, 229
    and prison violence, 218–19
    as probation officers, 129
    proportion of, in state populations, and imprisonment rates, 69
    recidivism of, 341
Black women
    imprisonment rate for, 262
    and violence/victimization, 273
Blakely v. Washington, 72
Bland, Sandra, 102, 103*f*
body cavity searches, 243
Boeing, 305
bond
    appearance, 90–91
    partially secured, 91
    secured, 91
    surety, 90–91
    unsecured, 91
bond theory, 48, 89
Bonta, James, 311
booking, 89
boot camps, 317
BOP. *See* Bureau of Prisons
borderline personality disorder, 194
"born criminals," 41, 44
Bounds v. Smith, 248
bounty hunters, 90
Boys Clubs, 46
brain chemistry, 42
branding, 60
brank ("gossip's bridle"), 60
Brennan Center for Justice, 16, 35, 36, 106
Bridewell Palace, 61, 146
brief psychotic disorder, 192
Brockway, Zebulon, 67, 149, 332
Brooklyn, N.Y., 75
Browder, Kalief, 93
Brown v. Plata, 20, 247
Buddhism, 241
building tenders, 246
"building tenders," 151
Bundy, Ted, 320
buprenorphine, 307

Bureau of Justice Assistance, 19, 319
Bureau of Justice Statistics (BJS), 8, 9, 34, 70, 117, 181, 183, 192–93, 197, 219, 220, 223, 224, 275, 339, 341, 345
Bureau of Prisons (BOP), 16–17, 17*f*, 146, 153, 158, 189, 263
Burger, Warren, 238
Burger Court, 238
burning, 196
burnout, 129, 161
Bush, George H. W., 71
Butner, N.C., 145
C
California
    Alcatraz prison, 153, 153*f*, 184*f*
    correctional facilities in, 146
    correctional officer overtime in, 159
    correctional officer suicide in, 161–62
    decarceration in, 18, 36
    fire camps in, 280
    indeterminate sentencing in, 67
    Justice Realignment in, 19–21
    Pelican Bay State Prison, 155, 247
    prison gangs in, 216
    probationers in, 124, 252–53
    Proposition 36 in, 68, 80
    Proposition 47 in, 20–21, 80
    Proposition 57 in, 80
    San Quentin prison, 185, 218, 229
    searches in, 252–53
    street gangs in, 217
    three-strikes law in, 68, 80
    transgender inmates in, 201
Canada, 314
capital punishment (death penalty), 61–64
    and crime rate, 36
    as cruel and unusual punishment, 62–63
    federal death penalty, 12
    and life without possibility of parole, 69
    for participation in "continuing criminal enterprises," 71
    by state, 63*f*
cardiac problems, stress-related, 161
"cars," 145
Carter, Jimmy, 71
caseloads, special offender, 132
casework model, 122, 124–25
castration, chemical, 14
CBT. *See* cognitive behavioral therapy
CCA (Corrections Corporation of America), 156
cellphones, 167
Center on Addiction and Substance Abuse (Columbia University), 80
Centers for Medicare and Medicaid Services (CMS), 190, 191
cervical cancer, 270
Charlotte, N.C., 35
chemical castration, 14
Chicago, Ill., 35, 96, 121
Chicago School of criminology, 44–46
childbirth, in prison, 270, 282
childhood abuse (childhood sexual abuse), 186, 265–66

childrearing, effect of, 43
children
    and attentive parenting, 43
    effects of parental incarceration on, 281–82
    identifying of "difficult," 51
    impact of neighborhood groups and non-profits on, 36
chivalry hypothesis, 76
chlamydia, 269
"Choosing to Think, Thinking to Choose" program, 135
Christianity, 240, 241
chronic offenders, incarceration of, 35–36
chronic pelvic inflammatory disease, 269
"Church of the New Song" (CONS), 241
cigarette smoke, exposure to, 245
citations, 88
cities
    crime rates in, 35
    decline of industry-related jobs in northern, 10–11
    "interstitial zones" of, 44–46
    migration of southern Blacks to northern, 11
citizenship (sentencing guideline), 15
City College of New York, 152
City of Boerne v. Flores, 242
civil asset forfeiture, 11
civil debt, 110
Civil Rights Act (1964), 276
Civil Rights Code, 119
civil rights demonstrations, 152
civil rights movement, 10
Civil Rights Movement, 218
Civil Rights of Institutionalized Persons Act (CRIPA), 102–3, 277
Clackamas County, Ore., 133
class, and delinquency, 46
classical school of criminology, 40–42
classification centers, 152
clemency, 17, 73–74, 334
Clemency Initiative, 335
Clemency Project, 73
clinical approach, 309
Clinton, Bill, 12, 12*f*
cliques, 145, 271
close custody, 221
Cloward, Richard, 46
CMS (Centers for Medicare and Medicaid Services), 190, 191
COs. *See* correctional officers
cocaine, 12, 70, 194, 335
code of silence, 164
coercive power, 166, 167
cognition, antisocial, 311, 312
cognitive behavioral programs, 47, 312–13, 317, 319
cognitive behavioral therapy (CBT), 134, 308, 313–14
Cognitive Program Assessment Inventory (CPAI), 314
cognitive restructuring, 312–13
cognitive skills programs, 313
Cohen, Albert, 46
Coker v. Georgia, 63

collateral consequences, 254–57
Colonial America, 59, 96
Colorado, 18, 92, 217, 333
Colson, Charles, 300
Columbia University, 80
Common Law, 59
community-based corrections, 130
community-based mental health services, 193
community centers, 297
community gardens, 44*f*
community policing, 12
community service, 121–22, 122*f*
community supervision, rights during,
   252–54
commutations, 73–74, 334–35
COMPAS. *See* Correctional Offender
   Management Profiling for
   Alternative Sanctions
compassionate release, 188
Comprehensive Crime Control Act
   (1984), 11, 71, 332
CompStat, 36
Concerned Citizens of South Central Los
   Angeles, 37
conditioning, operational, 296
conditions of probation, 120–22
confidence rape, 223
confidentiality, of presentence reports,
   119
conflicts, between female prisoners,
   271–72
conformity (as form of adaptation), 46
confrontational therapy, 317
congregate care facilities, 61
congregate care system, 148
Connecticut, 10, 19, 188, 190,
   191, 263
CONS ("Church of the New Song"), 241
conscientiousness (personality
   trait), 43
consensual sexual relationships, between women, 274–76
conspiracy laws, 17
constitutional amendments. *See individual amendments*
contempt citations, 88
contingency contracting, 317
"continuing criminal enterprises," 71
contraband, 100, 158, 167, 168, 216
contract system, 305
control theory, 48
co-occurring disorders, 194
Cook County, Ill., 96
CoreCivic, 156, 158
corporal punishment, 58, 61, 151, 244
correctional assessment, 309. *See also
   assessment(s)*
correctional institutions, first, 151
Correctional Offender Management
   Profiling for Alternative Sanctions
   (COMPAS), 310, 314, 315
correctional officers (COs), 159–68
   assessment/screening by, 190
   code of silence among, 164
   cross-sex supervision by, 159–61
   exposure of, to disease, 185
   female, 159–61, 163, 166–67

health and social problems faced by,
   161–62
and job satisfaction, 162–63
minority, 161, 163, 166
organizational commitment of, 167
and organizational justice, 167–68
salaries of, 157
sexual misconduct by, 224
and structured conflict, 159
subculture of, 163–66
in supermax prisons, 154
support of, for rehabilitation, 163
turnover of, 161
types of power exerted by, 166–67
correctional personnel (corrections professionals), 5–6, 105
correctional supervision
   number of individuals under, 5
   by type, 116, 117*f*
correctional supervision rate, 74–75, 75*f*
correctional treatment, 298
corrections
   definition of, 4
   future directions in, 343–47
   as industry, 6, 156
   and international human rights,
      347–52
   international innovations in, 346–47
   mission of, 296
   principles for humane and effective
      system of, 352–53
   purposes of, 14
   scope of, 4
   in United States, 5
Corrections Corporation of America
   (CCA), 156
correlates, 221–22
costs
   of corrections, 344–45
   of educational programming, 302
   medical, 187, 189–90
   of private prisons, 157
   and support for decarceration, 16
cottage system, 263
Council for State Governments (CSG), 19
court-appointed attorneys, 89
COVID-19 pandemic, 102, 185, 257, 298,
   345
CPAI (Cognitive Program Assessment
   Inventory), 314
crack cocaine, 12, 71, 78, 194, 335
crime(s), 30–39
   biological theories of, 42–43, 50, 296
   cultural deviance theory of, 45–46
   dark figure of, 31
   downgrading of, by police, 31
   general agreement of relative serious-
      ness of various, 14
   index, 30–31
   labeling theory of, 49
   measures of, 30–34
   prisoner convictions by, 182, 182*f*,
      183*f*
   psychological theories of, 43–44
   public order, 90
   reported, 31, 31*f*
   social control theories of, 48–49
   sociological theories of, 297

strain-opportunity theory of, 46–48
theories of (table), 50*t*
unreported, 31
Crime Bill (1994). *See* Violent Crime
   Control and Law Enforcement Act
crime correlates, 37–39
crime rate(s)
   in California, 20, 21
   in cities, 35
   drop in, 14, 35–37
   incarceration patterns and, 36
   incarceration rate and, 14, 58
   and mass incarceration, 10
   and state imprisonment rates, 69
crime reports, as measure of crime, 30
criminal background checks, 257
criminal contempt, 109
criminal history, 311
criminal justice process, 4, 4*f*
criminals, types of, 49–51
criminal thinking, 311, 319
criminology, 40–51
   behavioral explanation of, 44
   Chicago School of, 44–46
   classical school of, 40–42
   positivist school of, 41, 42
CRIPA (Civil Rights of Institutionalized
   Persons Act), 102–3, 277
Crofton, Walter, 331
cross-sex supervision, 159–61
cruel and unusual punishment, 121,
   155, 244–47. *See also* Eighth
   Amendment
Cruz v. Beto, 241
CSG (Council for State Governments), 19
cuddling, 43
cultural deviance theory, 45–46
custodial arrests, 88–89
custodial model, 263
Cutter v. Wilkinson, 242
cutting, 196
cystic conditions, 269
D
dark figure of crime, 31
Darwinian theories, 41, 42
date rape, 223
Davis, Katharine, 41
"dawgs," 215
day fines, 106
day reporting centers, 132
Dearborn County (Indiana), 75
death penalty. *See* capital punishment
Death Penalty Information Center, 64
debts, 61, 96
   civil, 110
   imprisonment for failure to
      pay, 105
   in women's prisons, 272
decarceration, 15–21
   arguments against, 16
   definition of, 15
   growing support for, 16–18
   state initiatives in, 18–21
deferred adjudication, 94
deferred sentencing, 126
Delaware, 9, 18, 227, 332
deliberate indifference standard, 198,
   245

delinquency, 45
  class-based theory of, 46
  and gender, 51
delinquency programs, 49
delusional disorder, 192
Democratic Party, 10
demonstration field experiments (DFEs), 133
depression (depressive disorders), 162, 192–94, 196, 265, 268, 269
deprivation theory, 212
desegregation, court-imposed, 218–19
desistance, 343
determinate sentencing, 64, 65, 67–69
deterrence
  capital punishment and, 61
  as purpose of corrections, 14
  as purpose of sentencing, 58
deterrence theory, 40–42
Detroit, Mich., 35
DFEs (demonstration field experiments), 133
diabetes, 270
Diagnostic and Statistical Manual of Mental Disorders (DSM-V), 185–86
Dickens, Charles, 147
diet, and religion, 240
differential association, 45
differential opportunity theory, 46
dignity, treating prisoners with, 135
discretionary parole, 328
disenfranchisement, 254–56
disputes, between female prisoners, 271–72
disrespect, 272
district attorneys, 13
District of Columbia, 254
disulfiram, 306–7
diversion, pretrial, 88, 94–95
dopamine, 42
Dothard v. Rawlinson, 160
drama therapy, 317
drug and alcohol treatment, 306–7
drug arrests, 33–34, 34*f*
drug-connected women (in pathways approach), 264
drug courts, 12
drug crimes, 11
  arrests for, 33
  commutations of sentences for, 335
drug czar, 12
drug dependency and abuse, 6
  and childhood victimization, 266
  and economic strain, 52
  in female prisoners, 266
  and mental illness, 194
  in prisoners, 185–86
  and prison violence, 218
  and risk of victimization, 222
drug laws, and sentencing, 69
drug offenders, 5
  clemency for, 17–18, 74
  in federal vs. state prisons, 183
  sentencing of, 13, 17, 70–73
  women as, 76
drug rape, 223
drug smuggling, into prisons, 167

drug treatment (drug treatment programs)
  as condition of probation, 120
  effectiveness of, 345
  for female prisoners, 283–84
Drug Treatment Alternative to Prison (DTAP) program, 80
drug treatment programs, residential, 14
DSM-V (*Diagnostic and Statistical Manual of Mental Disorders*), 185–86
DTAP (Drug Treatment Alternative to Prison) program, 80
ducking stool, 60
due deference approach, 238, 248, 251
due process, 63, 99, 100, 119, 153–54, 163, 247–51, 333
DUI, 13, 106, 121
DWI, 120, 121
dyads, 271
dysmenorrhea, 269
E
early interventions, 296
early release, 67, 190, 332. *See also* parole
Eastern State Penitentiary (Philadelphia), 96, 97, 147, 147*f*, 148
"ecology of cruelty," 154
economic opportunity, 46–48, 52
economy, during 1970s, 10–11
education
  as correlate of future offending, 311
  prisoners' level of, 183–84
  probation failure by, 127
educational programing, 301–2
education requirements, as condition of probation, 120
Edward III, 146
Edward VIII, 147
Effective Practices in Community Supervision (EPICS), 135
Eighth Amendment, 62–64, 90, 103, 109, 154–55, 239, 244–47, 270
elderly prisoners, 187–91
  financial implications of, 189–90
  vulnerabilities of, 189
electronic monitoring, 108, 131–32, 131*f*
Elmira Reformatory (New York State), 67, 149, 332
embezzlement, 33, 76
employment
  as correlate of future offending, 311
  and criminal background checks, 257
  effect of increased, 36
  for parolees, 330
  and probation failure, 127
employment programs, 46–47
England, 263
environmental factors, 50
EPICS (Effective Practices in Community Supervision), 135
equal protection (Equal Protection Clause), 99, 106, 109, 158
Essex County, Mass., 133
Establishment Clause, 300
Estelle v. Gamble, 198, 244–45
ethnicity. *See* race/ethnicity

eugenics, 41
excessive bail, 90
executions, number of, 61–62, 62*f*
expert power, 166, 167
externalizing disorders, 269
extortion, in prisons, 219–20
extortion rape, 223
extraversion (personality trait), 43
F
failure to appear, 88
failure to pay, 108–10
fairness, and organizational commitment, 167
Fair Sentencing Act (2010), 12, 17, 72
families, pseudo-, 271
Families Against Mandatory Minimums, 81
family abuse, prisoners' experience of, 186
family circumstances, 311
family dysfunction, and female prisoners, 266–67
family visits, 243
Farmer v. Brennan, 202, 245
Federal Bureau of Investigation (FBI), 30, 31, 305–6
federal crimes, 11, 12
federal death penalty, 12
Federal Guidelines Sentencing Commission, 68
federal highway monies, withholding of, 12
Federal Prison Industries Enhancement Act (PIE), 305–6
federal prisons, number of, 5
federal prosecutors, 18
Federal Rules of Criminal Procedure, 119
fees, 107–10
fee system, 96
felons, disenfranchisement of, 254–56
felony cases
  bail amounts in, 90
  fines in, 107
felony charges, 13, 18
female prisoners, 262–86
  at Bedford Hills, 41
  consensual sexual relationships between, 274–76
  drug dependency in, 266
  drug treatment for, 283–84
  in early penitentiaries, 150
  family dysfunction and intimate partner abuse in backgrounds of, 266–67
  and gender bias, 42
  gender-responsive programming with, 278–81
  healthcare costs for, 184
  inaccurate prediction of criminal behavior in, 314–15
  medical needs of, 269–71, 277
  mental health of, 192–93, 268–69, 268*f*
  parenting programs for, 281–83
  as parolees, 331
  and pathways approach, 264–71
  in penal harm era, 153

as percentage of inmates, 101–2
prior victimization of, 265–66
prison experience of, 229
reentry by, 284–85
rehabilitative programs for, 151
sexual minority, 201, 202
and sexual relationships/victimization, 274–76
specific needs of, 276–84
subculture of, 271–76
trauma in, 268–69, 269f, 280–81
and violence, 271–74
in women's prisons, 262–64
Ferguson, Mo., 108
fidelity, program, 316
Fifth Amendment, 126
fighting, among female prisoners, 271–72
fines, 58, 60, 61, 88, 106–7, 109–10
fingerprinting, 89
Finley, James, 148
First Amendment, 239, 241f, 242–43, 300
"fish," 215, 223, 226
"fishcops," 216, 223
Florence v. Board of Chosen Freeholders, 244
Florence v. County of Burlington, 100
Florida, 19, 121, 125, 154, 253, 255, 256
Focus on a State
  California, 20–21
  Connecticut, 191
  Florida, 256
  New York, 136, 283
  Ohio, 342
  Texas, 65–66
  Washington, 300
Focus on History
  Early Jails, 97–98
  Positivism at Bedford Hills, 41
Focus on the Offender
  Camp Fluffy, 145
  The Cycle of Crime, 6
  Drugs and Economic Strain, 52
  George Luna, 229
  A Juvenile in Jail, 93
  A Life Ruined, 73
  A Life Well-Lived, 280
  The Long Arm of the Law, 199
  Martin Pang, 344
  A Slap on the Wrist?, 123
  Trying to Survive, 246
FOIA (Freedom of Information Act), 158
force, unnecessary, 244
Ford, Gerald, 71
Ford v. Wainwright, 64
forestry camps, 144
for-profit companies, 185
  electronic monitoring programs run by, 132
  fees charged by, 108
  and halfway houses, 338
foster care, 186, 296
Fourteenth Amendment, 99, 109, 238, 239, 244, 247–48, 251, 276. *See also* equal protection (Equal Protection Clause)
Fourth Amendment, 124, 243–44, 252, 253, 337

Franklin, Benjamin, 97
freedom of association, 243
Freedom of Information Act (FOIA), 158
freedom of the press, 243
free speech, 242–43
Fry, Elizabeth, 263
"full sleeves," 216
Furman v. Georgia, 63
G
Gagnon v. Scarpelli, 252
gallows, 60
Gallup Organization, 61, 81
Gall v. United States, 72
gang intervention, 45–46
gangs, 46, 214
  in communities, 297
  prison, 216–18, 216f
gaols, 59, 61, 95, 96, 105, 146, 262
gasoline, lead in, 36
GED. *See* General Education Development
gender
  as crime correlate, 37, 38t–39t
  crimes committed by, 182, 182f
  in-prison physical victimization by, 229t
  jail population by, 101–2
  probation failure by, 127
  and recidivism, 341
  sentencing disparity by, 76–77
  and violent crime, 42
  See also men; women
gender bias, 42
gender dysphoria, 202
gender-responsive programming, 278–81, 285
gender-specific programming, 346
Gendreau, Paul, 311
general deterrence, 14, 58
General Education Development (GED), 183, 301, 302
general strain theory, 47
general theory of crime, 48
genetic theories, 42, 296
geographic disparity, in sentencing, 74–76
GEO Group, Inc., 132, 156, 158
Georgia, 10, 18, 63, 75, 109, 117
Germany, 7, 346–47
Ghent, Belgium, 96, 146
global positioning system (GPS), 131
Glossip et al. v. Gross et al., 64
Glover v. Johnson, 277
good behavior, 67
goods, prison-made, 155
good time, 67, 249–50
"gossip's bridle," 60
Gottfredson, Michael, 48
GPS (global positioning system), 131
graduated liberties, 67
graduated release, 149. *See also* parole
graduated sanctions, 341
Great Depression, 305
Greenholtz v. Inmates of the Nebraska Penal and Correctional Complex, 253
Greenholtz v. Nebraska, 333

Gregg v. Georgia, 63
Griffin v. Wisconsin, 124, 252
GRIP (Guiding Rage into Power), 229
group belongingness, 42–43
group violence, 217
guards. *See* correctional officers (COs)
Guiding Rage into Power (GRIP), 229
gynecological care, 269
H
habitual felon laws, 13, 64, 66. *See also* three-strikes laws
halfway houses, 151, 338–39
Hall v. Florida, 64
hands-off era, 238
Hare's Psychopathy Checklist, 43
harmed and harming women (in pathways approach), 264
Harris County, Tex., 92, 96, 102
Harrison Act (1914), 70
Hawaii, 9, 132–33, 156
Hawaii's Opportunity Probation with Enforcement (HOPE), 132–33
Hawes-Cooper Act, 155, 305
healthcare
  comprehensive, 296
  in jails, 102–4
  preventive, 190
  for released women, 285
  for women prisoners, 269–71
health risks, faced by correctional officers, 161–62
"healthy start" programs, 296
"heartchecks," 216
hedonistic calculus, 40
Helling v. McKinney, 245
hepatitis B and C, 184–85, 270
Heritage Foundation, 16
heroin, 70, 75
herpes simplex II, 269
Hewitt v. Helms, 250
high self-control, 47
Hispanics and Hispanic prisoners
  in California, 21
  and changes in sentencing patterns, 13
  as correctional officers, 166
  criminal arrests of, 37
  disparate sentencing of, 77–79
  imprisonment rate for, 262
  mental health disorders in, 192
  as parents in prison, 186
  as parolees, 331
  paroling of, 334
  as percentage of prison population, 181
  prison experience of, 229
  recidivism of, 341
HIV, 201, 222, 245, 269
hobbies, 299
holding cells, 89
Holt v. Hobbs, 242
Holt v. Sarver, 246
home searches, 124
homicide (murder)
  arrests for, 33
  capital punishment for, 64
  in cities, 33
  in-prison, 219
  "right" level of imprisonment for, 13

HOPE (Hawaii's Opportunity Probation with Enforcement), 132–33
Hospice of San Michele (Rome), 96, 146
hospice programs, prison, 191
hospitals, 61, 148
Hour Children, 283
houses of correction, 61, 146, 148
housing, for parolees, 329, 330
Houston, Tex., 35, 92, 96
Houston Chronicle, 102
Howard, John, 96, 146–47
Howe v. Smith, 249
HPV (human papillomavirus), 269
Hudson House of Refuge (New York State), 263
The Huffington Post, 102
hulks, 146
human papillomavirus (HPV), 269
"hypomania," 194
I
ICAOS (Interstate Compact for Adult Offender Supervision), 125
Idaho, 185, 262, 333
Illinois, 216, 217, 332
Immigration and Customs Enforcement (ICE), 183
immigration detention facilities, 146
importation theory, 212, 214
imprisonment rate
    by country, 7f
    and crime rate, 58
    factors influencing, 7
    incarceration rate vs., 8
    punishment rate vs., 10
    in United States, 8f
impulsivity (personality trait), 44
incapacitation, as purpose of corrections, 14
incarceration
    alternatives to, 80
    and public safety, 15
    See also decarceration
incarceration rate
    for Blacks, 13
    and crime rate, 36
    definition of, 8
    for drug crimes, 11
    imprisonment rate vs., 8
    in United States, 5–10, 9f
income levels, 36, 183–84
indentureship, 60
indeterminate sentencing, 67–68
index crimes, 30–31
Indiana, 75, 109, 125, 253, 328, 332
Indianapolis, Ind., 75
Indiana Reformatory Institute for Women and Girls, 263
indigency, 89
inmate code, 214–15
innovation (as form of adaptation), 46
institutional violence, 217
integrated theories, 49, 51
intellectually disabled, 200
intensive supervision probation, 130–31
intermediate sanctions, 132
intermediate standard, 276–77
internalizing disorders, 269
interpersonal violence, 217

Interstate Compact for Adult Offender Supervision (ICAOS), 125
"interstitial zones," 44–46
interviewing, motivational, 336
intimate partner abuse/violence, and female prisoners, 266–67, 272
intrapersonal violence, 217
Iowa, 19
IQ, 200
Ireland, 331
Islam, 240–42, 241f
J
Jackson, Andrew, 147
Jackson, George, 152, 218
Jackson v. Bishop, 244
jailhouse lawyers, 248
jails, 95–105
    bail and, 91–93
    conditions of, 102–5
    core standards for, 102, 104t
    crimes committed by those serving sentences in, 100, 100f
    historical background, 95–98
    increase in population of, 91–93, 98, 99t
    location of, 98
    pay-to-stay, 108
    population in, by race/ethnicity, 101, 101f
    staffing of, 105
    types of, 96, 98
    unconvicted inmates in, 99–102, 99f
jail uniforms, 89
job satisfaction, 162–63
job stress, 161, 162
job training programs, 46–47
"jockers," 223–24
John D. and Catherine T. MacArthur Foundation, 92–93
Johnson, Lyndon B., 10, 11, 46
Johnson, Robert, 150
Johnson v. Avery, 248
Jones, Shawna Lynn, 280
Jones v. DeSantis, 256
JRI (Justice Reinvestment Initiative), 19
Judaism, 240, 241
judges
    and sentencing, 64, 72
    surety bonds assigned by, 91
juries, and sentencing, 64
Justice Department. *See* U.S. Department of Justice
Justice Reinvestment Initiative (JRI), 19
juvenile offenders
    correctional institutions for, 5
    in jails, 101
    reformatories for, 149, 150
K
K6 (Kessler 6) Nonspecific Psychological Distress Scale, 192
Kansas, 19, 328, 332
Kennedy v. Louisiana, 63
Kentucky, 92, 105, 191, 220, 333
Kessler 6 (K6) Nonspecific Psychological Distress Scale, 192
kickbacks, 168
"kids," 223–24

kiosk reporting, 133–34
"kites," 216
Klaas, Polly, 68
Knecht v. Gillman, 245
L
labeling theory, 49
labor
    meaningless, 150
    prison, 303–6
Laboratory of Social Hygiene, 41
Lafayette, Marquis de, 147
La Nuestra Familia, 216
latent traits, 51
"lawdogs," 215
Law Enforcement Assistance Act of 1965 (LEAA), 11
law libraries, prison, 248
laws, sentencing, 11–13, 64–69
LEAA (Law Enforcement Assistance Act of 1965), 11
leaded gasoline, 36
learning disabilities, 42
leased labor system, 149f, 150, 151, 305
Lee Correctional Institution (South Carolina), 227
legal assistance, access to, 248
legal financial obligations (LFOs), 107
legitimate power, 166, 167
Lerner, Jimmy, 215
lethal drug combinations, for executing offenders, 64
letters, 243
Level of Service Inventory–Revised (LSI–R), 134, 310–12
Lewis v. Casey, 248
LFOs (legal financial obligations), 107
LGBTQ inmates, 200
liberty interest, 247–52
libraries, prison, 248
life charts, 308
life-course theories, 49
life sentences, 187
lifestyles, pre-prison, 184
life without possibility of parole laws, 69
Lipton, Douglas, 152
literacy, 183, 301
lobbying, 158
local jails, number of, 5
lockstep, 148
Lombroso, Cesare, 41f, 41, 42, 44
London, England, 61, 146
longitudinal research, 49–51
Los Angeles, Calif., 37, 108
Los Angeles County, 75, 96
Louisiana, 9, 74, 125, 253
Louisianans for Prison Alternatives, 81
low self-control (personality trait), 44, 47, 48
LSI–R (Level of Service Inventory–Revised), 134, 310–12
Luna, George, 229
lunch programs, 296
M
MacDougall-Walker Correctional Institution (Connecticut), 191
Madoff, Bernie, 145
Madrid v. Gomez, 247

magistrates, 89
Maine, 74, 75, 254, 328, 332, 345
Maison de Force (Ghent), 96, 146
major depressive disorder, 192
mandatory minimum laws, 68, 72
mandatory sentencing guidelines,
    11–13, 18, 77, 78
mandatory supervision, 328
Mandela, Nelson, 347
Mandela Rules, 347–52
Manhattan Bail Project, 91
"mania," 194
marijuana and marijuana laws, 12, 70–
    71, 72, 81, 101, 194, 335
Marijuana Tax Act (1937), 70
marital circumstances, 311
marital status, probation failure by, 127
mark system, 331
Martinson, Robert, 152, 297–98, 317
Martinson Report, 152
Maryland, 134, 263
Massachusetts, 9, 61, 118, 125, 219, 253,
    262, 340–41
mass incarceration, 6–15
    and criminal/sentencing laws,
        11–13
    explanations for, 10–11
    and prison violence, 218
    and racial disparities, 13
    and "right" level of imprisonment,
        13–15
    and variations between states, 8–10
matrons, 263
maturation effect, 37, 51
"maxed out" inmates, 328
maximum-security facilities, 144, 221.
        See also supermax prisons
McCleskey v. Kemp, 63
McKay, Henry D., 45
McNeil Island, Wash., 153
Meachum v. Fano, 248–49
media
    and free speech rights, 243
    opiate crisis in, 72
Medicaid, 190, 191, 198, 199, 338
medical examinations, 152
medical model, 297
medical needs, 244–45
    of female prisoners, 269–71, 277
    of prisoners, 184–85
    See also healthcare
Medicare, 120, 190, 191
meditation, 151
medium-security facilities, 144–45
Mempa v. Rhay, 126, 252
men
    crimes committed by, 182, 182f
    criminal arrests of, 37
    disparate sentencing of, 76
    sexual minority, 201
meningitis, 185
mental disorders, 192
mental health
    of female prisoners, 268–69, 268f
    of parolees, 330
    of supermax prison inmates, 154
mental health disorders (term), 192
mental health treatment, 197–200, 245
mental hospitals, 249

mental illness, 14, 191–200
    in jail inmates, 102, 104–5
    prevalence of, in prisoners, 192–94,
        193f
    and suicide/self-harming behavior,
        195–97
    and supervision, 194–95
    treatment for, 197–200, 245
mental institutions, 61, 148
Mentality of Criminal Women
        (Weidensall), 41
mentally handicapped people, execution
        of, 64
Mentally Ill Offender Treatment and
        Crime Reduction Act, 104–5
mentally ill people, execution of, 64
mentoring programs, 46
Merton, Thomas, 46
meta-analyses, 297, 316
methadone, 307
methamphetamine, 335
Mexican Mafia, 216
Michigan, 36, 125, 162, 191, 253, 277
"midnight basketball" programs, 46
military service, 222
Mill, Meek, 199
minimum-security facilities, 144, 151
Minneci v. Pollard, 158
Minnesota, 130, 332
Minnesota model, 130
minority correctional officers, 161, 163,
        166
Miranda warnings, 126
misdemeanor cases, 88
    bail amounts in, 90
    fines in, 107
Mississippi, 18, 125, 153, 253, 332
Missouri, 110, 188
"the mix," 271
Moconochie, Alexander, 331–32
modeling theory, 296
monitoring
    electronic, 108, 131–32, 131f
    of private institutions, 158
monoamine oxidase, 42
Monroe v. Pape, 337
Montana, 125, 156, 253, 333
Moore, A. T., 157
Moore v. Texas, 64
moral performance, 228
Morrissey v. Brewer, 253–54
motion to revoke probation
        (MRP), 125
motivational interviewing, 336
"mules," 266
murder. *See* homicide
Muslims, 240–42
mutilation, 196, 269
myomatic conditions, 269
N
naltrexone, 307
National Academy of Sciences, 13, 154
National Commission on Correctional
        Health Care (NCCHC), 154
National Conference of Charities and
        Correction, 97
National Crime Victimization Survey
        (NCVS), 34
National Institute of Corrections, 279

National Institute of Justice, 132–33,
        319
National Institute on Drug Abuse, 307
*National Inventory of the Collateral
        Consequences of Conviction,* 255
National Prison Congress (1870), 67,
        149, 331
National Prison Congress (1970), 149
National Prisoner Statistics Program
        (NPS), 181
National Reentry Council, 329
Native Americans, 240
Nazi Lowriders, 216
NCCHC (National Commission on
        Correctional Health Care), 154
NCVS (National Crime Victimization
        Survey), 34
Nebraska, 18, 19, 62
negative emotionality (personality
        trait), 44
neighborhood associations, 297
neighborhood groups, 36
Nelson v. Correctional Medical Services,
        270
neo-Nazis, 216
net-widening, 130
neuroticism (personality trait), 43
neurotransmitters, 42
Nevada, 10, 110, 217, 333
New Hampshire, 110, 117, 125, 253,
        340–41
New Jersey, 10, 18, 19, 36, 58, 92, 275,
        333, 338
New Mexico, 10, 131, 156, 217, 332
New Orleans, La., 110
New York City
    ABLE program in, 346
    bail amounts in, 90
    crime rate in, 80
    kiosk reporting in, 134
    murder rate in, 35
    pretrial custody in, 93
    unsecured/partially-secured bonds
        in, 92
    See also Rikers Island
New York City Criminal Justice Agency, 94
New York City Department of Probation,
        134
New York Police Department (NYPD),
        31, 36
New York State
    Attica Correctional Facility, 152, 218,
        226
    Auburn Prison, 147–48, 262
    bail and release in, 90–91
    Bedford Hills prison, 41, 282, 283
    decarceration in, 18, 19, 36, 80
    Elmira Reformatory, 67, 149, 332
    first house of correction in, 61
    halfway houses in, 338
    Hudson House of Refuge, 263
    "nothing works" finding in, 297
    pre-sentence reports in, 119
    probation in, 118
    punishment rates in, 10
    Rockefeller drug laws in, 12
    searches in, 125, 253
    sexual-victimization lawsuits in, 275
    taxpayer cost of prisons in, 345

New York State Commission on Corrections, 104
New York Times, 104
New Zealand, 314, 346
Nixon, Richard, 300
nonconsensual sex acts, 223
non-profits, effect of, on crime rate, 36
Norfolk Island, 331
normalization, 346
North Carolina, 125, 219, 253, 332
North Dakota, 333
Norway, 347
NPS (National Prisoner Statistics Program), 181
nurseries, prison, 282, 283
NYPD (New York Police Department), 31, 36
O
Obama, Barack, 12, 17–18, 72–74, 72*f*, 301–2, 334–35
obstetric care, 269
Office of Justice Programs, 223, 339
Ohio, 97–98, 106, 109, 135, 153, 185, 220, 227, 242, 302, 333
Ohio Risk Assessment System (ORAS), 342
Ohlin, Lloyd, 46
Oklahoma, 19, 156, 262, 333
"old heads," 216
Olim v. Wakinekona, 249
O'Lone v. Shabazz, 242
openness (personality trait), 43
operational conditioning, 296
opiate crisis, 72, 345
opioids, 307
opportunity theory, 46
ORAS (Ohio Risk Assessment System), 342
Oregon, 12, 18, 19, 125, 188, 253, 333
organizational commitment, 167
organizational culture, 319
organizational justice, 167–68
organized violence, 217. *See also* prison riots
orphanages, 61, 148
Ossining State Penitentiary (Sing Sing), 262
"over-remembering," 265
oxytocin, 42–43
P
PACs (political action committees), 158
Palm Beach, Fla., 131
Pang, Martin, 344
Pap smears, 270
pardons, presidential, 74, 334
parental rights, 277, 278
parenting
attentive, 43
by released women, 285
parenting programs, 49, 186, 281–83
parents, incarcerated, 186, 277
parole, 67, 331–38
completion rates for, 340, 340*f*
decision to grant, 332–34
definition of, 116
discretionary, 328
history of, 331–32
imprisonment for violations of, 183

pardons/commutations vs., 334–35
revocations of, 340
rights under, 253–54
supervision during, 335–38
parolees
by crime of conviction, 334*f*
number of, 5
parole officers
liability of, 337–38
relationship of, with parolees, 336
parsimony (sentencing guideline), 15
partially secured bond, 91
partner abuse, and female prisoners, 266–67
Pasquotank Correctional Institution (North Carolina), 219
pathways approach, 264–71
pay-to-stay jails, 108
PCP, 218
peer educators, 273–74
Pelican Bay State Prison (California), 155, 247
Pell Grants, 301–2
penal harm era, 152–53
"penal punitiveness," 21
penitence, 147
penitentiary, first, 146
Pennsylvania, 10, 61, 78, 153, 275, 333, 338
Pennsylvania Horticultural Society, 36–37
Pennsylvania model, 146–48
Pennsylvania Prison Society, 96, 97
personality traits, 42–44, 311
personal property, surrender of, 89
personal searches, 124, 125
pets, 300
Pew Center for the States, 19
Pew Charitable Trust, 10
Pew Research Center, 61
Philadelphia, Pa., 96, 97, 135, 146–48, 224
Philadelphia Model, 146–48
Philadelphia Society for Alleviating the Miseries of Public Prisons, 96, 97
physical assaults, in prisons, 220
PIE (Federal Prison Industries Enhancement Act), 305–6
piece-price system, 305
pillory, 60
"plantation prisons," 150*f*, 150
play families, 271
plea offers (plea bargaining), 13, 64, 77, 88
PLRA (Prisoner Litigation Reform Act), 238–39
pluralistic ignorance, 105, 164
pneumococcal pneumonia, 185
police and policing, 12, 36. *See also* arrests
political action committees (PACs), 158
politics, 158
poorhouses, 61, 148
Portland, Ore., 35
positivist school of criminology, 41, 42
postnatal influences, 43
post-traumatic stress disorder (PTSD), 162, 187, 198, 222, 265–66, 274

poverty penalty, 105–10, 352
and failure to pay, 108–10
and fees, 107–8
and fines, 106–7
and private companies, 345
and restitution, 107
poverty programs, 297
powder cocaine, 12, 335
powder keg theory, 227
power, exerted by correctional officers, 166–67
power vacuum theory, 227
PPP (Prison Pet Partnership), 300
PREA. *See* Prison Rape Elimination Act
preconviction release, 88–94
prediction, 308–10, 320
pregnant prisoners, 269, 270, 278, 282
"preponderance of the evidence" standard of proof, 254
prerelease programs, 151
pre-sentence investigations, 118–20
pre-sentence report (PSR), 118–19
presidential pardons, 74, 334
President's Commission on Law Enforcement and the Administration of Justice, 130
press, freedom of the, 243
pretrial custody
and bail, 91–93
and severity of sentencing, 94
pretrial diversion (pretrial diversion programs), 88, 94–95
pretrial release, 76, 89–94, 106
pretrial services divisions, 91
preventive detention, 11
preventive detention hearings, 90
preventive healthcare, 190
prison(s), 144–58
"big house," 150
as deterrent, 58
first, 147
history of, 146–55
moral performance of, 228
Philadelphia and Auburn models of, 146–48
"plantation," 150*f*, 150
private, 155–58
rapid building of, 10
in rehabilitative era, 151–52
as "schools of crime," 46
supermax, 144, 153–55, 247, 249
in United States, 144–46
warehouse, 152–53
See also correctional officers (COs)
prison admissions
increase in number of, 72
by type of crime, 70, 70*f*
prison argot, 215–16
Prisoner Litigation Reform Act (PLRA), 238–39
prisoner rights, 238–51
cruel and unusual punishment, protection from, 244–47
due process, 247–51
parental rights, 277, 278
religion, 240–42
unreasonable search/seizure, security against, 243–44

prisoners, 180–203
　by age, 181, 181*f*
　crimes committed by, 182–83, 182*f*,
　　183*f*
　demographics of, 180–81
　drug dependency and addiction in,
　　185–86
　drug offenders as, 5
　education levels of, 183–84
　elderly, 187–91
　income levels of, 183–84
　intellectually disabled, 200
　LGBTQ, 200
　medical needs of, 184–85
　mentally ill, 191–200
　number of, 5
　pre-prison lives of, 183–86
　by race/ethnicity, 180–81, 180*f*
　reentry of, after release, 328–31,
　　329*t*
　"stacking up" of, 182–83
prisoners' rights groups, 154–55
prison farms, 150
Prison Fellowship, 299–300
prison gangs, 216–18, 216*f*
prison guards. *See* correctional officers
　(COs)
prison homicides, 219
prison hospice programs, 191
prison industries, 304–5
prisonization, 228–29
prison labor, 303–6, 304*f*
prison nurseries, 282, 283
Prison Pet Partnership (PPP), 300
Prison Policy Initiative, 16
prison privatization, debate surround-
　ing, 156–58
Prison Rape Elimination Act (PREA),
　223, 224, 277, 278
prison reform, federal efforts at, 16–17
prison riots, 152, 215, 226–27
Prison Social Climate Survey, 161
prison subculture, 212–17
　among female prisoners, 271–76
　definition of, 212
　deprivation theory of, 212
　importation theory of, 212, 214
　and inmate code, 214–15
　and prison argot, 215–16
　and prisoner typologies, 214
prison violence, 217–28
　correlates of, 221–22
　by gender, 220, 220*t*
　prevalence of, 218–20
　recommendations for reducing,
　　227–28
　riots and collective violence, 152,
　　215, 226–27
　sexual victimization, 222–26, 225*t*
　types of, 217
privacy rights, 244, 252
privately-run prisons, 144, 155–58, 345
probation, 116–37
　and casework model, 122, 124–25
　conditions of, 120–22
　definition of, 116
　development of, 59, 61
　discharge of, 126–27, 127*f*

fees for, 108
Hispanics and, 13
history of, 118
intensive supervision, 130–31
number of people on, 116–17, 117*t*
proposals for increasing effectiveness
　of, 135–37
recent innovations in, 133–35
and recidivism, 125–27, 132–34
revocation of, 126–27
rights during, 252–53
shock, 116
state variations in use of, 9
supervision during, 118–25, 130–35
technical violations of, 126
probation officers, 118–20, 128–29
　burnout of, 129
　caseloads of, 132
　and casework model, 122
　and Fifth Amendment rights, 126
　first, 61
　searches by, 124
　types of, 128–29
probation subsidies, 130
program fidelity, 316
programming. *See* rehabilitative
　programming
property, surrender of personal, 89
property crime(s), 10, 18, 35
property crime index, 31
property offenders
　recidivism of, 339, 341
　sentencing of, 13
proportionality (sentencing guideline),
　15
Proposition 36 (California), 68, 80
Proposition 47 (California), 20–21, 80
Proposition 57 (California), 80
prosecution patterns, changes in, 13
prosecutors, federal, 18
prostitution, 31, 264
protest movements, 152
pseudo-families, 271
PSR (presentence report), 118–19
psychiatric care, 104
psychological theories of crime, 43–44
psychopathy, 43, 320
psychotic disorder not otherwise speci-
　fied, 192
psychotropic medications, 196, 198, 245
PTSD. *See* post-traumatic stress disorder
public defenders, 13, 76, 78, 89, 108
public demonstrations, 10
public duty doctrine, 337–38
public housing, 12, 71
public opinion
　about crime rate, 35, 35*f*
　on capital punishment, 61
　and state imprisonment rates, 69
public order offenders, sentencing of, 13
public order offenses, 6, 90, 100*f*
public protest movements, 152
public punishment, 58, 59
public safety, incarceration and, 15
Public Safety Realignment Act
　(California), 20–21
Puerto Rico, 255
punishment(s)

capital, 61–64
　in classical school of criminology,
　　40–42
　in Colonial America, 59–60
　corporal, 58, 61, 151, 244
　in late 1700s, 60–61
　in prison, 151–52
　public, 58, 59
　publicizing of, 41–42
　by transportation, 331
　See also sentencing
"punishment rate," 10
punitive segregation, 153,
　163, 250
"punks," 215, 223
Q
Quakers, 96, 146–47
"queens," 215, 223
R
"rabbits," 272–73
race/ethnicity
　as crime correlate, 37, 39*f*
　jail population by, 101, 101*f*
　mental health disorders by, 192
　parolees by, 331, 331*f*
　prisoners by, 180–81, 180*f*
　probation failure by, 127
　and recidivism, 341
　See also specific groups, e.g.: Blacks and
　　Black prisoners
race problem, perception of crime
　as, 11
race riots, 215
racial disparities
　and capital punishment, 63
　and mass incarceration, 13
　in sentencing, 77–79
RAND Corporation, 302
rape
　death sentence for, 63
　prison, 225, 277
　threat of, 223
Rastafarianism, 240
rational choice theory, 40–42
rational relationship test, 239, 242
"rats," 214
Rawlinson, Diane, 160
Reagan, Ronald, 71, 71*f*
Realignment, 20–21
rebellion (as form of adaptation), 46
recidivism, 58, 339–44
　definition of, 5, 125
　and educational programming, 302
　electronic monitoring and, 131
　factors in, 341, 343
　HOPE model and, 132–33
　measuring, 339–41
　in older inmates, 188, 339
　and parole officer–parolee relations,
　　336
　and prison programming, 315,
　　318*t*
　of private vs. public prison releasees,
　　157
　probation and, 125–27, 132–34
　reducing, 343
　"tough-on-crime" policies and, 152
reciprocal violence, 166

reciprocity, 164–65
recreation programs, 298–99, 299f
reentry, 328–31
    challenges of, 329t
    by female prisoners, 284–85
referent power, 166–67
Reform and Corrections Act (2015), 16
reformatories, 149, 150
reformatory model, 263
rehabilitation, as purpose of corrections, 14
rehabilitative era, 151–52, 297–98
rehabilitative programming, 296–321
    drug and alcohol treatment, 306–7
    drug treatment programs, 283–84
    educational programs, 301–2
    evaluating, 315–20
    gender-responsive, 278–81, 285
    gender-specific, 346
    and mission of corrections, 296–98
    mitigation of prison violence via, 273–74, 274t
    parenting programs, 281–83
    and prediction/assessment, 308–15, 320
    prison labor, 303–6
    recreation programs, 298–99
    religious programs, 299–301
    therapeutic communities, 307–8
    vocational training, 302–3
"Reimagining Prison" (report), 352
relational model of therapy, 280
relative deprivation/rising expectation theory, 227
release
    early, 67, 190, 332
    graduated, 149
    preconviction, 88–94
    pretrial, 76, 89–94, 106
release on recognizance (ROR), 91
Religious Freedom Restoration Act (RFRA), 242
Religious Land Use and Institutionalized Persons Act (RLUIPA), 242
religious programs, 299–301
religious rights, 240–42, 241f
reported crime, 31, 31f
reporting kiosks, 133–34
reporting practices, state variations in, 9
Republican Party, 10, 158
residential drug treatment programs, 14
respect
    and organizational commitment, 167
    treating prisoners with, 135
    in women's prisons, 272
restitution, 107, 121
retreatism (as form of adaptation), 46
retribution
    as purpose of corrections, 14
    as purpose of sentencing, 58
revocation, 20–21, 126–27
reward power, 166
RFRA (Religious Freedom Restoration Act), 242
Rhode Island, 9, 19, 98, 219, 262, 263, 333
Right on Crime, 16
rights

and collateral consequences, 254–57
    during community supervision, 252–54
    See also prisoner rights
right-to-carry laws, 36
Rikers Island (New York City), 93, 104, 346
Ring v. Arizona, 64
riots, prison, 152, 215, 226–27
risk-assessment tools, 92
Risk/Need/Responsivity (R/N/R) model, 134–35, 312–14
ritualism (as form of adaptation), 46
RLUIPA (Religious Land Use and Institutionalized Persons Act), 242
robbery arrests, 33
Rockefeller drug laws, 12
role ambiguity, 162
role conflict, 162
role overload, 162
Rome, Italy, 96, 146
Roosevelt, Franklin D., 305
Roper v. Simmons, 64
ROR (release on recognizance), 91
Rothman, David, 148
Ruffin v. Commonwealth, 238
Ruiz v. Estelle, 198, 245, 246
rural areas, disparate sentencing in, 75–76
S
Saline County, Ark., 133
SAMSA (Substance Abuse and Mental Health Services Administration), 186
sanctions
    graduated, 341
    intermediate, 132
Sandin v. Conner, 250
San Francisco, Calif., 75, 110
San Quentin prison (California), 185, 218, 229
Santa Fe riots (1980), 226
Satanism, 242
Scandinavia, 7, 347
"Scared Straight" programs, 317
Scarlet Letter conditions, 120–21
schizoaffective disorder, 192
schizophrenia, 194
schizophrenia spectrum disorder, 192
Scott v. Illinois, 108
scratching, 196
searches, 124–25
    body cavity, 243
    home, 124
    personal, 124, 125
    strip, 100, 244, 275
    unreasonable searches and seizures, 243–44, 253
    vehicle, 125
    warrantless, 252–53
Second Amendment, 256
The Second Chance Act (2008), 330
Section 1983 suits, 238–39
secured bond, 91
Segal, G. F., 157
segregation
    administrative, 153, 250, 277–78
    punitive, 250

selection bias, 301, 303, 313, 317
self-control, 47–49
self-harming behavior, 195–97
self-injury, 196, 269
self-medication, with drugs and alcohol, 266
sentencing, 58–82
    and aging prison population, 345
    changes in, 13, 79–81
    and clemency/commutation, 73–74
    deferred, 126
    drug, 70–73
    gender bias in, 42
    guidelines for, 11–13, 15, 68, 71
    history of, 59–64
    indeterminate vs. determinate, 67–69
    patterns of, 69–74
    pretrial custody and severity of, 94
    purpose of, 58
    split, 116, 199
    statutes, 64–69
    suspended, 126
sentencing disparity, 11, 14, 68, 74–79
    gender, 76–77
    racial/ethnic, 77–79
    between states, 74–76
sentencing laws, state, 12
Sentencing Project, 16
Sentencing Reform Act (1984), 68, 71
separate system, 147
serial killers, 320
serious mental illness (SMI), 192, 195
serious psychological distress (SPD), 192, 193, 197
serotonin, 42, 43
service officers, 129
Sessions, Jeff, 18, 158
severe functional impairment, 268
sex acts, nonconsensual, 223
sex crimes, 189
sex offenders, 120–21, 123, 309
sexual abuse, of women prisoners, 265–66, 277
sexual assault, 245
    "right" level of imprisonment for, 13
sexual harassment, 275–76
sexually transmitted diseases, 222, 269. See also HIV
sexual minorities, 200
sexual relationships
    between officers and inmates, 160–61
sexual relationships, consensual, between women, 274–76
sexual victimization
    of non-heterosexual inmates, 201
    in prisons for women, 160, 275
    by staff, 275
    by type of incident, 225t
    of women, 262, 265–66
sexual violence, 222–26
shackling, 270, 278
Shaw, Clifford, 45
shock probation, 116
shoplifting, 12–13
"shot-callers," 215, 216

shower baths, 151
silent system, 148
Sing Sing (Ossining State Penitentiary), 262
Sixth Amendment, 64, 89, 93, 108, 126, 252
60 West, 191
skill acquisition, 308
slave labor, 151
SMI (serious mental illness), 192, 195
snitching, 214, 215, 271
sober houses, 338
social bonds (social bond theory), 47*f*, 48
social control theory, 48–49
social disorganization theories, 45
social impact bonds, 346
socialization, 43
social justice (sentencing guideline), 15
social support theories, 45
social unrest, 10
The Society of Captives (Sykes), 150–51
sociological theories of crime, 297
sociopathy, 43
solitary confinement, 154, 249–51
South Carolina, 10, 18, 219, 227, 333
South Dakota, 10
Southern Ohio Correctional Facility, 227
Southern Poverty Law Center, 81
southern states
    incarceration rates of, 8–9
    plantation prisons in, 150*f*, 150
"southern strategy," 10
SPD. *See* serious psychological distress
specific deterrence, 14, 58
Spector Grants, 301
speech, freedom of, 242–43
SPI (Survey of Prison Inmates), 181
split sentencing, 116, 199
stabilizing drugs, 104
"stacking up," 182–83
staff, quality of, 316
standards of proof, 254
Stanford prison experiment, 165–66
Stanford University, 123
Stanford v. Kentucky, 64
starvation, 151
state crimes, 11
state laws, 12–13
"Statement of Principles," 16
state prisons
    decarceration initiatives, 18–21
    elderly in, 187–88
    number of, 5
    See also specific prisons
static factors, 309
statutes, sentencing, 11–13, 64–69
"stay in school" awards, 296
stimulus seeking (personality trait), 44
stocks, 59, 59*f*
strain-opportunity theory, 46–48, 52
street activism, 216
street women (in pathways approach), 264
stress, job, 161, 162
strict scrutiny test, 239
strip searches, 100, 244, 275
structured conflict, 159
subculture
    correctional officer, 163–66

prison *See* (*see* prison subculture)
substance abuse
    as correlate of future offending, 312
    in prisoners, 185–86
    treatment for, 306–7
    See also alcoholism and alcohol abuse;
        drug dependency and abuse
Substance Abuse and Mental Health
    Services Administration (SAMSA),
    186
suicide(s)
    of correctional officers, 161–62
    of female prisoners, 269
    of prisoners, 195–97
    of sexual abuse victims, 265
supermax prisons, 144, 153–55, 247, 249
supervision
    cross-sex, 159–61
    mandatory, 328
    and mental health issues, 194–95
    during probation, 130–35
    rights during community, 252–54
    typologies of, 128–29
Supreme Court
    on bail, 90
    on capital punishment, 63–64
    on collateral consequences, 256–57
    on delegation of imprisonment to
        private actors, 158
    on inmate fines, 106, 108–9
    and intermediate standard, 276–77
    on parole, 252–54, 333, 337
    on pre-sentence reports, 119
    on prison conditions, 20, 103
    on prisoners' rights in general, 238,
        239, 244–51
    on probationers' rights, 126, 252–54
    on punitive segregation, 163
    on religion in prisons, 241, 242
    on right to counsel, 89, 108
    on right to mental health treatment,
        198
    on right to see a magistrate, 89
    on searchers, 124
    on sentencing guidelines, 72, 78
    on states' obligation to protect pris-
        oners from assault, 202
    on states' refusal to allow women to
        work in prisons, 160
    on unconvicted inmates, 99–100
surety bond, 90–91
surveillance officers, 129, 130
Survey of Prison Inmates (SPI), 181
suspended sentencing, 126
Sutherland, Edwin, 45
Sweden, 347
Sykes, Gresham, 150–51, 164
symbolic interactionism, 49
T
target hardening, 41
Tarrant County, Tex., 133
Tate v. Short, 106
TCs (therapeutic communities), 307–8
technical violations, 126, 335, 340–41
Tennessee, 10, 156
testing, 152
testosterone, 42
Texas

capital punishment in, 63
compassionate release in, 188
correctional facilities in, 146
COVID-19 pandemic in, 185
decarceration in, 36
incarceration-related fines/fees in,
    106, 107
Justice Reinvestment Initiative in, 19
local correctional facilities in, 9
penal code sentencing statute in,
    65–66
prison argot in, 215
prison conditions in, 246
prison gangs in, 216
prison homicides in, 219
prison population of, 20, 219
probationers and parolees in, 117
Sandra Bland case in, 102
state jails in, 101
taxpayer cost of prisons in, 345
use of building tenders in, 151
Texas Syndicate, 216
theft, in prisons, 219–20
therapeutic communities (TCs), 307–8
third-generation assessment instru-
    ments, 309–10
"Thorazine shuffle," 197
three-strikes laws, 12, 13, 64, 66, 68
ticket of leave, 331
Tison v. Arizona, 64
"toads," 216
Tocqueville, Alexis de, 148
tokenism, 160
totality of the circumstances, 245–47
"tough-on-crime" platforms, 11, 152
traffic citations, 88
transcendental meditation, 151
transgender people, 200–202, 245
transportation, 331
trauma
    in correctional staff, 162
    drug use/addiction and childhood, 73
    female prisoners' experience of, 268–
        69, 269*f*, 280–81
    and mental health of inmates, 193
    from prison sexual violence, 222
    from solitary confinement, 154
    See also post-traumatic stress
        disorder (PTSD)
treatment ethic, 297
Trenton State Prison, 150–51
Trump, Donald, 18, 74, 158, 302
trust in others, 42–43
trustworthiness, and organizational
    commitment, 167
truth-in-sentencing laws, 12, 68
tuberculosis, 185
Turner, Brock, 123
Turner v. Safley, 239
turnover, among correctional officers, 161
typhus, 96
U
UCR (Uniform Crime Reports), 30–34
*UN Convention Against Torture and
    Other Cruel, Inhuman or Degrading
    Treatment or Punishment,* 154
"under-remembering," 265–66
unemployment, decreased, 36

UNICOR, 305–6
Uniform Crime Reports (UCR), 30–34
uniforms, jail, 89
unions, 155, 157, 164
United Kingdom, 7
United Nations Commission on Crime Prevention and Criminal Justice, 347
United Nations Standards for the Treatment of Prisoners, 275
United States
    incarceration rates in, 5, 7–10, 8f
    prisons in, 144–46
    recidivism in, 5
United States Commission on Civil Rights, 277
United States v. Booker, 72
United States v. Fanfan, 72
United States v. Knights, 124, 252–53
University of Chicago, 41, 44–45
unnecessary force, 244
unreasonable searches and seizures, 243–44, 253
unreported crime, 31
unsecured bond, 91
Urban Institute, 19
urban work release facilities, 144
urinalysis, 335
U.S. Department of Education, 301–2
U.S. Department of Justice, 18, 19, 73, 74, 92, 102, 103, 108, 186, 202, 275, 278, 335, 339
U.S. Sentencing Commission, 11, 17, 71, 74, 332
U.S. territories, 5
Utah, 18, 117, 333
V
vagrants, 61
variables, controlling for, 316–17
vehicle searches, 125
Vera Institute of Justice, 18, 69, 91, 345, 352
Vermont, 9, 10, 19, 254, 333
veterans, 198
victim-centered restitution, 121
victimization
    inmate–inmate, 224
    of older prisoners, 189
    physical, by gender, 229t
    prior, of female prisoners, 265–66
    and prison violence, 220–22, 220t
    rates of, 34, 34f
    of women, 271
    See also sexual victimization
victim surveys, as measure of crime, 30
Vietnam War, 152
violence
    female prisoners and, 271–74, 274t

reciprocal, 166
    See also prison violence
violent crime
    in cities, 35
    gender disparity in, 42
    and history of abuse, 186
    and mass incarceration, 10
    prisoner convictions by, 182, 182f
Violent Crime Control and Law Enforcement Act (1994), 12, 71, 301, 332
violent crime index, 31
violent offenders, sentencing of, 13
Virginia, 10, 62, 188, 333
visits and visitation programs, 19, 48
    with children, 282
    with family members, 243
    and family programs, 186
    female inmates and, 153, 273, 278, 282
    in jails vs. prisons, 98, 249
    video visits, 156
    in women's prisons, 153
Vitek v. Jones, 249
vivitrol, 307
vocational programs, for women, 278–79, 279f
vocational training, 302–3, 303f
voice, 167
voting rights, 254–56
W
Wackenhut, 156
Walker, Shawn, 251
Walmart, 305
Walnut Street Jail (Philadelphia), 96, 97, 146–47, 159
Walpole Prison (Massachusetts), 219
warehouse prisons, 152–53
war on drugs, 8, 70, 71, 79, 218
war on poverty, 11, 46
warrantless searches, 252–53
warrants, 88–89
Warren, Earl, 238
Warren Court, 238
Washington, DC, 72, 92
Washington Corrections Center for Women, 300
Washington State, 72, 107, 153, 188, 199, 300, 333, 344
Washington State Institute for Public Policy, 319
Washington v. Harper, 245
Watergate scandal, 300
Weidensall, Jean, 41
Weller, Mark, 73
West Virginia, 10
whipping post, 60
"white hats," 163

whites
    and drug crimes, 79
    incarceration rates for, 13, 77, 180
    mental health disorders in, 192
    paroling of, 334
    as percentage of prison population, 180
    prison argot for, 215–16
    sentencing guidelines and, 78
Whitley v. Albers, 244
Wiccanism, 242
"wiggers," 216
Wilkinson v. Austin, 249
Wilks, Judith, 152
Williams, Craig, 251
Williams v. Illinois, 109
Williams v. Pennsylvania Secretary of Corrections, 250–51
Wilson v. Seiter, 247
Wiri model, 346
Wisconsin, 10, 19, 188, 191
withdrawal symptoms, in jail inmates, 102
"wobblers," 77
Wolff v. McDonnell, 163, 238, 249–50
"wolves," 223
women
    as correctional officers, 159–61, 163, 166–67
    crimes committed by, 182, 182f
    disparate sentencing of, 76
    as probation officers, 129
    See also female prisoners
women's prisons, 262–64
    contemporary, 263–64
    history of, 262–63
    reformatory vs. custodial models of, 263
    sexual victimization in, 160, 275
"woods," 215
Woodson v. North Carolina, 63
work ethic, 147
workhouses, 61, 148
work release facilities, urban, 144
World Health Organization, 196
Wyoming, 10, 19, 188, 333
Y
"yard tricks," 216
Yates, Sally, 158
yoga, 151
"yoke," 151
York Correctional Institution (Connecticut), 191
Youthful Offender Grants, 301
Z
zero tolerance programs, 49
Zimbardo, Phillip, 165